MASS COMMUNICATION THEORY

Foundations, Ferment, and Future

EIGHTH EDITION

STANLEY J. BARAN, PH.D.
BRYANT UNIVERSITY

DENNIS K. DAVIS, PH.D.
PENNSYLVANIA STATE UNIVERSITY

NEW YORK   OXFORD
OXFORD UNIVERSITY PRESS

Oxford University Press is a department of the University of Oxford.
It furthers the University's objective of excellence in research, scholarship,
and education by publishing worldwide. Oxford is a registered trademark of
Oxford University Press in the UK and certain other countries.

Published in the United States of America by Oxford University Press
198 Madison Avenue, New York, NY 10016, United States of America.

For titles covered by Section 112 of the US Higher Education
Opportunity Act, please visit www.oup.com/us/he for the latest
information about pricing and alternate formats.

Library of Congress Cataloging-in-Publication Data

Names: Baran, Stanley J., author. | Davis, Dennis K., author.
Title: Mass communication theory : foundations, ferment, and future / Stanley
    J. Baran, Ph.D., Bryant University, Dennis K. Davis, Ph.D., Pennsylvania
    State University.
Description: Eighth edition. | New York, NY, United States of America :
    Oxford University Press, [2021] | Includes bibliographical references and
    index.
Identifiers: LCCN 2019021362 (print) | LCCN 2019021808 (ebook) | ISBN
    9780190942786 (Ebook (EPUB)) | ISBN 9780190086879 (Ebook (UPDF)) | ISBN
    9780190942779 (pbk.)
Classification: LCC P90 (ebook) | LCC P90 .B285 2021 (print) | DDC
    302.2301—dc23
LC record available at https://lccn.loc.gov/2019021362

Printing number: 9 8 7 6 5 4 3 2 1
Printed by Sheridan Books, Inc.,
United States of America

To Sidney Kraus

*His words and actions—indeed, how he chose to live
his life and career—in the years since the first edition of this
book have convinced us of the wisdom of our original decision
to honor him—our friend, mentor, and colleague.*

CONTENTS

Preface   xiii

CHAPTER 1   Understanding and Evaluating Mass Communication Theory   1

Learning Objectives   2

Overview   3

Defining and Redefining Mass Communication   3

Science and Human Behavior   8

Defining Theory   13

Postpositivist Theory   14

Cultural Theory   15

Critical Theory   15

Normative Theory   16

Evaluating Theory   18

Flexible Social Science   19

Mass Communication Theory   19

Four Trends in Media Theory   19

The Mass Society and Mass Culture Trend in Mass Communication Theory   20

The Media-Effects Trend in Mass Communication Theory   21

The Critical Cultural Trend in Mass Communication Theory   23

The Meaning-Making Trend in Mass Communication Theory   24

Revitalized Effects Research   25

Review of Learning Objectives   26

Critical Thinking Questions   28

CHAPTER 2   Establishing the Terms of the Debate over Media: The First Trend in Mass Communication Theory— Mass Society and Mass Culture Theories   31

Learning Objectives   33

Overview   33

Mass Society Critics and the Debate over Media   35

Assumptions of Mass Society Theory   35

Early Examples of Mass Society Theory   41

Gemeinschaft and Gesellschaft   41

Mechanical and Organic Solidarity   43

Mass Society Theory in Contemporary Times   44

The Origin of Propaganda   46

Propaganda Comes to the United States   48

Behaviorism   50

Freudianism   51

Harold Lasswell's Propaganda Theory   51

Walter Lippmann's Theory of Public Opinion Formation   53

Reactions against Early Propaganda Theory   55

Modern Propaganda Theory   56

Libertarianism Reborn and Challenged   60

Review of Learning Objectives   60

Critical Thinking Questions   63

CHAPTER 3   Normative Theories of Mass Communication   65

Learning Objectives   67

Overview   67

The Origin of Normative Theories of Media   69

The Origin of Libertarian Thought on Communication   70

The Marketplace of Ideas: A New Form of Radical Libertarianism   73

Government Regulation of Media   77

Professionalization of Journalism   78

Social Responsibility Theory of the Press: A Postwar Compromise   79

Using Social Responsibility Theory to Guide Professional Practice   81

Limitations of Professionalization   82

The Dual Responsibility Model   84

Is There Still a Role for Social Responsibility Theory?   85

The Public Interest in the Internet Era   87

Other Normative Theories   93

Review of Learning Objectives   95

Critical Thinking Questions   96

CHAPTER 4   The Emergence of the Media-Effects Trend
in Mass Communication Theory   99

Learning Objectives   100

Overview   101

The Development of the Postpositivist Effects Trend   101

From Propaganda Research to Attitude-Change Theories   103

Carl Hovland and the Experimental Section   103

The Communication Research Program   105

Do Mass Media Influence the Way People Vote?   107

The Strengths and Limitations of the Effects Trend in Media Research   109

The Selective Processes   110

Review of Learning Objectives   115

Critical Thinking Questions   116

CHAPTER 5   The Consolidation of the Media-Effects Trend   118

Learning Objectives   119

Overview   119

Theories of the Middle Range and the Rise of the Functional
Analysis Approach   122

Information-Flow Theory   126

Personal Influence: The Two-Step Flow Theory   128

Joseph Klapper's Phenomenistic Theory   130

The Entertainment Function of Mass Media   132

Systems Theories of Communication Processes   134

The Rise of Systems Theory   135

Modeling Systems   135

Applying Systems Models to Human Communication   136

Adoption of Systems Models by Mass Communication Theorists   137

Functionalism's Unfulfilled Promise   138

Review of Learning Objectives   139

Critical Thinking Questions   141

CHAPTER 6   The Emergence of the Critical Cultural Trend
in North America   143

Learning Objectives   144

Overview   145

Changing Times   146

The Critical Cultural Theory Trend   148

Macroscopic Versus Microscopic Theories   148

Critical Theory   149

Comparing the Media Theory Trends   151

The Rise of Cultural Theories in Europe   152

Marxist Theory   152

Neo-Marxism   154

Textual Analysis and Literary Criticism   154

The Frankfurt School   155

Development of Neo-Marxist Theory in Britain   156

Political Economy Theory   159

The Debate between Cultural Studies and Political Economy Theorists   160

Cultural Studies: Transmissional Versus Ritual Perspectives   162

Research on Popular Culture in the United States   163

Research on News Production in the United States   165

Critical Feminist Scholarship   167

Marshall McLuhan: The Medium is the Message and the Massage   170

Harold Innis: The Bias of Communication   171

McLuhan: Understanding Media   173

Review of Learning Objectives   175

Critical Thinking Questions   177

CHAPTER 7   **Theories of Media and Social Learning   180**

Learning Objectives   180

Overview   181

Focus on Children and Violence   183

Television Violence Theories   184

Catharsis   185

Social Learning Theory   186

Social Cognition from Mass Media   187

Aggressive Cues   190

The Context of Mediated Violence   192

Active Theory of Television Viewing   193

The Developmental Perspective   194

Video Games Reignite Interest in Media Violence   196

The General Aggression Model   197

Review of Learning Objectives   200

Critical Thinking Questions   201

CHAPTER 8   **Theories of Media and Human Development   204**

Learning Objectives   205

Overview   205

Media and Children's Development   206

Gender Issues   207

Advertising to Children   209

Loss of Childhood   210

Growing Up Connected: New Personal Technologies and
Development   213
Social Media and Well-Being   217

Review of Learning Objectives   219

Critical Thinking Questions   220

CHAPTER 9   Audience Theories: Uses and Reception   222

Learning Objectives   224

Overview   225

Audience Theories: From Source-Dominated to Active-Audience
Perspectives   226
Limitations of Early Audience-Centered Research   227
Confusion of Media Functions and Media Uses   229

Revival of the Uses-and-Gratifications Approach   231
The Active Audience Revisited   233

Entertainment Theory   238

Uses-and-Gratifications and Social Networking   243

Development of Reception Studies: Decoding and Sense Making   244
Feminist Reception Studies   247

Review of Learning Objectives   248

Critical Thinking Questions   250

CHAPTER 10   Theories of Media Cognition and Information
Processing   252

Learning Objectives   253

Overview   253

Information-Processing Theory   255
Processing Television News   258

Schema Theory   260

Hostile Media Effect   264

Elaboration Likelihood Model   266

Narrative Persuasion Theory and the Extended Elaboration
Likelihood Model   269
Health Communication   273

The Delay Hypothesis   274

Affective Intelligence, Motivated Reasoners, and the Backfire
Effect   276

The Neuroscience Perspective   277

Review of Learning Objectives   281

Critical Thinking Questions   283

CHAPTER 11   Theories of the Effect of Media on Knowledge, Information, and Perception of Social Issues   286

Learning Objectives   288

Overview   289

Knowledge Gaps, Digital Divides, and Digital Inequalities   291

Information (Innovation) Diffusion Theory   294

  Social Marketing Theory   297

Agenda-Setting, Priming, and Agenda-Building   300

The Spiral of Silence   304

Review of Learning Objectives   307

Critical Thinking Questions   308

CHAPTER 12   Theories of the Effect of Media on Community and Everyday Culture   310

Learning Objectives   310

Overview   311

Media and Social Capital/Community Research   311

Cultivation Analysis   314

  The Products of Cultivation Analysis   317

Media Literacy   321

  Elements and Assumptions of Media Literacy   323

  Media Literacy Interventions   324

Review of Learning Objectives   327

Critical Thinking Questions   328

CHAPTER 13   Media and Culture Theories: Meaning Making in the Social World   331

Learning Objectives   332

Overview   332

Symbolic Interactionism   333

  Pragmatism and the Chicago School   337

  Current Applications of Symbolic Interactionism   339

Social Constructionism   341

Framing and Frame Analysis   346

The Development of Theories of Frames and Framing   352

  Effects of Frames on News Audiences   354

  Postpositivist vs. Critical Cultural Approaches to Framing   357

Review of Learning Objectives   358

Critical Thinking Questions   359

CHAPTER 14   Media and Culture Theories: Commodification of Culture and Mediatization   362

Learning Objectives   363

Overview   363

Media as Culture Industries: The Commodification of Culture   364

Commodification of Culture in the Age of Social Media   368

Advertising: The Ultimate Cultural Commodity   371

Mediatization Theory   372

Review of Learning Objectives   376

Critical Thinking Questions   377

References   379

Index   417

PREFACE

In this edition we mark a milestone in the development of the American media system. We detail the reasons our media system has entered an important new stage in its development, one that appears likely to bring stability after what has been a tumultuous two decades of rapid change in media technology and, therefore, mass communication theory. In previous editions we noted the many changes to the media system caused by the introduction of the Internet and mobile communication technology that began in the 1990s. Along with other scholars we were challenged by these changes and speculated about the revisions to media theory required to address them. Was mass media theory even useful in this new era? Prominent media scholar Steven Chaffee (Chaffee & Metzger, 2001) asserted, "Many people no longer consider the term *mass communication* to be an accurate descriptor of what it is that some communication scholars study" (p. 365). But if these scholars weren't studying mass communication, what were they studying? Was it going to be necessary to create an entirely new body of theory so we could explain what people were doing with Internet and mobile media–based applications? Among the many predictions made about the future of social media was that virtual communities would develop, centered around shared production and consumption of media content. The more time people spent in these communities, the less time they would spend using legacy media.

Chaffee articulated a perspective on the rise of virtual communities. He explained why new media would bring an end to mass communication. Internet-based media would enable everyone to produce as well as consume media content. People would be active participants in virtual communities rather than passive members of mass audiences. Attractive new mobile devices would permit people to be much more creative and involved in their use of media. Media use would center around personal passions for cooking, classical music, modern dance, politics, country music, romance fiction, anything that stirred the interest of ordinary individuals. Personal passions would be shared—not just by passing along content we liked but by producing our own. We would all become "produsers" (producers and users) of media content. Myriad taste cultures of virtual communities would replace mass culture dominated and promoted by big media corporations. Communities would jointly produse bodies of knowledge that would enhance the collective intelligence of society. Power in society would be effectively redistributed. Elites would be no longer be able to use their control over centralized media technology to promote ideologies that served their interests first. If this change happened on a large scale, we would need to develop new theories to understand it.

If Internet-based media held the potential to free us from the grip of "big media," why does that potential seem to have evaporated after less than two decades? One answer resides in what has happened with the media industries that have rapidly grown up around these new digital technologies—Facebook, Google, Amazon, Twitter, YouTube, Snapchat, Instagram, Netflix, and their kin. For the most part these industries have sought to exploit the easy profits available to them by delivering what mass audiences numbering in the billions want rather than risk trying to cultivate and serve small virtual communities. They worked hard to become large-scale media capable of reaching millions of people on a daily basis. Though they delivered content via new technology, that content served the same purposes as the content delivered by traditional media. Though there was the potential to allow users control over content production, these corporations chose to retain a high level of control and discourage or limit user involvement. Much of the content that was delivered was the very same content distributed by the traditional media. Content that appeared to be innovative was actually produced according to old formulas developed by older media. When truly innovative content was created, it often was problematic, less useful in attracting or holding mass audiences, or likely to ignore standards for truth or aesthetics. The most watched YouTube videos are music videos produced by major studio recording artists, not the expression of communities of music lovers. Many other highly viewed YouTube videos are created by entrepreneurs who earn money based on the number of people who see the ads associated with their videos. We are not completely pessimistic about the long-term outcome of innovative media technology, but we are realistic about what current technology is or isn't doing for most people. Some might wish for the end of *mass* communication, longing for the emancipation from the influence of big media companies once envisioned by the coming of the Internet, but we don't see that happening soon, now that the newer forms of media have fallen under the control of corporations dedicated to profits rather than public service.

There is another reason Internet-based media have failed to deliver the future Chaffee envisioned. As a society we simply haven't found the time, energy, or resources needed to use them to serve innovative purposes. We have allowed large-scale social media corporations to take control of them. Often we welcomed this control when it delivered free services we thought useful in our daily lives. For over a decade, as it grew, Facebook worked quite effectively to maintain a façade as a company that existed mainly to provide services to people while it crushed its competitors and aggressively pursued advertising revenue and income from the sale of its users' data. On the whole, Americans have demonstrated very limited interest in the truly innovative purposes that Internet-based media could serve. To a very great extent we continue to use all forms of media to serve the same purposes served by media in the past. There have been important shifts in where and how we access media content, but for the most part we are accessing content that does what media content has done for much of the last century. We continue to participate in mass audiences rather than virtual communities. We spend most of our time seeking entertainment and information produced and distributed by centralized sources. The only change that has occurred is that large-scale social media have become the new mass media.

Our thinking on these tech giants parallels that of technology scholar Shoshana Zuboff (2019), articulated in *The Age of Surveillance Capitalism*. She argues that older forms of capitalism, where people exchanged goods and services, have been disrupted by these data-gathering giants, giving them massive economic control over just about all aspects of human discourse, if not human life. These "attention merchants . . . generate wealth by putting as many trackers, devices, and screens inside our homes and as close to our bodies as possible," explains law professor Tim Wu (2019). "Accumulated data creates competitive advantage, and money can be made by consolidating everything that is known about an individual" (p. SR3). In a traditional media system operating under traditional capitalism, the economic exchange was media content for audience attention. In surveillance capitalism, however, our very existence, all our experiences, become a free source of raw material to be mined and exploited. In this "new" mass communication system, the exchange is similar to, but different from, the older content/attention exchange. It is no longer enough for media corporations "simply to gather information about what people do," explains tech writer Jacob Silverman (2019). "Eventually, [they] have to influence behavior, beyond the simple suasion practiced by targeted ads. It's not about showing someone the right ad; [they] have to show it at the right place and time, with the language and imagery calibrated for precise effect. [They] have to lead people through the physical world, making them show up at the sponsored pop-up store or vote for the preferred candidate. Armed with a veritable real-time feed of a user's thoughts and feelings, companies are beginning to practice just this kind of coercion" (p. 10). As such, this remains *mass* communication, sufficiently similar to our traditional notions of that process to render existing theories—sometimes "as is," sometimes with refinement or addition—useful, but sufficiently different to demand new understandings.

In our presentation and assessment of these theories, we focus some attention on how they are being adapted to study all forms of mass media, including large-scale social media. We trace how new research methods are being applied to assess large-scale social media. These media are earning large profits by gathering Big Data from their users. But Big Data can also be gathered by researchers, and it can be used to develop theories that explain the social role and effects of social media.

As in previous editions, we place the development of media theory in historical context. We point out that the rise of large-scale social media should have been expected. In our capitalist society, control over new forms of media has always fallen into the hands of bright, aggressive entrepreneurs who recognize their potential to earn profits by delivering mass audiences. As the companies founded by these entrepreneurs grow, they aren't bound by the regulations and ethical standards that have been imposed on and accepted by older media corporations. Debates over regulation of Internet-based media and the need to rein in their unethical actions will likely go on for decades. They will likely mirror similar debates from the 1920s, the 1950s, and the 1970s. Though they will be framed as necessary to better serve the public, the biggest players in these debates will be the media corporations. It will be important that media theory and research play a significant role in this conversation. The debate should be grounded in an understanding of media provided by mass communication theory.

This edition of the textbook follows the basic structure of the last edition. We have made substantial revisions within some of the chapters to recognize the latest research and to explain how specific theories or bodies of theory are developing. Research is changing now that researchers have access to Internet-based tools that allow them to access and analyze media content in ways that were impossible just a few years ago. Big Data has found its uses in academia as well as in industry and politics. It's an exciting time to be involved in media research and in the development of media theories.

A UNIQUE APPROACH

One unique feature of this book is the balanced, comprehensive introduction to the two major bodies of theory currently dominating the field: the social/behavioral theories and the cultural/critical theories. We need to know the strengths and the limitations of these two bodies of thought. We need to know how they developed in the past, how they are developing in the present, and what new conceptions they might produce, because not only do they represent the mass communication theory of today, they also promise to dominate our understanding of mass communication for some time to come. This balanced approach is becoming even more useful as more and more prominent scholars are calling for the integration of these bodies of theory (Potter, 2009; Delli Carpini, 2013; Jensen & Neuman, 2013).

Many American textbooks emphasize social/behavioral theories and either ignore or denigrate cultural/critical theories; European texts do the opposite. As cultural/critical theories have gained popularity in the United States, there have been more textbooks written that explain these theories, but they often ignore or disdain social/behavioral theories. Instructors and students who want to cover all types of media theories are forced to use two or more textbooks and then need to sort out the various criticisms of competing ideas these works offer. To solve this problem (and we hope advance understanding of all mass communication theory), we systematically explain the legitimate differences between these theories and the research based on them. We also consider possibilities for accommodation or collaboration. This edition considers these possibilities in greater depth and detail, especially with the development of large-scale social media. It is becoming increasingly clear how these bodies of theory can complement each other and provide a much broader and more useful basis for thinking about and conducting research on media.

THE USE OF HISTORY

In this book we assume that it is important for those who study mass communication theory to have a strong grounding in its historical development. Therefore, in the pages that follow, we trace the history of theory in a clear, straightforward manner. We include discussions of historical events and people we hope students will find inherently interesting, especially if instructors use widely available DVDs, video downloads and streams, and other materials to illustrate them (such as political propaganda, the *War of the Worlds* broadcast, newsreels from the World War II era and the early days of television, and so on).

Readers familiar with previous editions of this textbook will find that we've made some significant changes in the way we present the unfolding of media theory. For example, one theme of this book ever since its first edition is that theory is inevitably a product of its time. You will see that this edition is replete with examples of media's performance during the recent presidential and congressional elections, the administration of Donald Trump, large-scale social movements, and their own ongoing institutional upheaval, but you will also see that many individual conceptions of mass communication theory themselves have been reinvigorated, challenged, reconsidered, or otherwise altered.

We have made an important change in how we discuss the emergence of the two important bodies of media theory. We no longer refer to specific eras in theory development, and we don't use the term *paradigm* to refer to them. Instead we talk about the development of *trends in media theory*, as we think this approach better represents the way the field has evolved. We identify four trends in theory development. The first—the mass society and mass culture theory trend—was dominant from the 1920s until the 1940s. It gradually gave way to the media effects theory trend—a trend that dominated media research from the 1950s until the 1980s, when it began to be challenged by the critical cultural theory trend. Eventually, the discipline's dominant focus turned to questions of how people make meaning through mass communication.

NEW TO THIS EDITION

As has been the case in each of the past editions, we have updated all statistics and examples. And as in the past, we have made a number of more significant changes. Although we have substantially reduced our discussion of older theories, our condensed consideration of the history of the discipline is still much more extensive and detailed than in other theory textbooks. This paring of history made room for a wide variety of new thinking in mass communication theory. Some of the ideas you'll encounter that are new to this edition are

- a revised definition of mass communication that incorporates new large-scale social media
- mediatization theory
- deep mediatization
- intersectionality in critical research and theory
- Big Data
- the obsolescence of the First Amendment
- the marketplace of attention
- automaticity in media consumption
- the argument that all science is value-laden
- the relationship between hate speech and propaganda
- the renewed interest in and research on propaganda in the Trump era
- undermining propaganda and undermining demagoguery
- challenged norms of journalism in the Trump era and declining respect for journalism
- captured agencies and regulation of media
- disintermediation (loss of gatekeepers)
- social network sites and selective processes
- the specification of ignorance

- the selective perception of African Americans and crime and police shootings
- an increased focus on critical feminist theory
- media and rape culture
- media and theory of mind
- the scope of self model
- recent (further debunking) thinking on catharsis
- scripting theory
- nomophobia
- the brain drain hypothesis
- social comparison theory
- the selective exposure self- and affect-management (SESAM) model
- the temporarily expanding the boundaries of the self perspective
- social media addiction
- Facebook depression
- the affective forecasting error
- the social skills model of problematic social media use
- epistemic spillover and political division
- outrageous political opinion
- the sufficiency principle of information processing
- digital inequalities
- the OMA (opportunities-motivation-ability) model
- municipal broadband
- social capital theory
- news deserts
- intermedia agenda-building
- genre-specific cultivation theory
- parental mediation theory for digital media
- enabling mediation
- news media literacy
- critical media education
- health communication
- health literacy
- agenda-chasing
- ideology-based polarization in news selection
- social media and cross-cutting vs. ideological homophily
- manosphere and Gamergate

THE USE OF TOPICS FOR CRITICAL THINKING

It is important, too, that students realize that researchers develop theories to address important questions about the role of media—enduring questions that will again become important as new media continue to be introduced and as we deal with a world reordered by the ongoing war on terrorism, systemic economic distress, and seemingly intractable political and cultural divides. We must be aware of how the radical changes in media that took place in the past are related to the changes now taking place.

We attempt this engagement with mass communication theory in several ways. Every chapter begins with a list of Learning Objectives designed to guide student thinking. Each chapter also includes a Critical Thinking Questions section. Its aim, as the title suggests, is to encourage students to think critically, even skeptically, about how that chapter's theories have been applied in the past or how they are being applied today. Also designed to encourage critical thinking, Thinking about Theory boxes are placed at appropriate places throughout the text. Some of these discuss how a theorist addressed an issue and tried to resolve it, while others highlight and criticize important, issue-related examples of the application of media theory. Students are asked to relate material in these boxes to contemporary controversies, events, and theories. A few examples are Chapter 4's essay on drug arrests, police shootings, and race; Chapter 14's box on #GamerGate and its attacks on women in video gaming; and Chapter 12's essay on media literacy as the antidote to the fake news plague. We hope that students will find these useful in developing their own thinking about these issues. We believe that mass communication theory, if it is to have any meaning for students, must be used by them.

We have also sprinkled the chapters with Instant Access boxes, presenting the advantages and disadvantages of the major theories we discuss. The advantages are those offered by the theories' proponents; the disadvantages represent the critics' views. These presentations are at best sketchy or partial, and although they should give a pretty good idea of the theories, the picture needs to be completed with a full reading of the chapters and a great deal of reflection on the ideas they present. All chapters also provide glossary definitions of important terms, chapter summaries, and chapter-ending reviews tied specifically to each chapter's learning objectives. Finally, at the end of the text there are a thorough index and complete chapter-based reference lists.

THE BIG PICTURE

This textbook offers a comprehensive, authoritative introduction to mass communication theory. We provide clearly written examples, graphics, and other materials to illustrate key theories. We trace the emergence of four trends in media theory—mass society/mass culture, media effects, critical/cultural, and meaning-making. Then we discuss how each contributes to our understanding of media and human development, the use of media by audiences, the influence of media on cognition, the role of media in society, and finally the links between media and culture. We offer many examples of social/behavioral and critical/cultural theory and an in-depth discussion of their strengths and limitations. We emphasize that media theories are human creations typically intended to address specific problems or issues. We believe that it is easier to learn theories when they are examined with contextual information about the motives of theorists and the problems and issues they addressed.

In the next few years, as mass media industries continue to experience rapid change and our use of media evolves, understanding of media theory will become even more necessary and universal. We've continued to argue in this edition that many of the old questions about the role of media in culture, in society, and in people's lives have resurfaced with renewed relevance. This book traces how researchers and theorists have traditionally addressed these questions, and we provide insights into how they might do so in the future.

THE SUPPORTING PHILOSOPHY OF THIS BOOK

The philosophy of this book is relatively straightforward: Though today's media technologies might be new, their impact on daily life might not be so different from that of past influences. Changes in media have always posed challenges but have also created opportunities. We can use media to improve the quality of our lives, or we can permit our lives to be seriously disrupted. As a society we can use media wisely or foolishly. To make these choices, we need theories—theories explaining the role of media for us as individuals and guiding the development of media industries for our society at large. This book should help us develop our understanding of theory so we can make better use of media and play a bigger role in the development of new media industries.

ADDITIONAL RESOURCES

For Instructors: An **Online Instructor's Manual** is available to assist faculty teaching a mass communication theory or media and society course. The Instructor's Manual offers assignment ideas, suggestions for audiovisual materials and for using many of the text's special features, syllabus preparation tools, and a sample syllabus. A Test Bank features chapter-by-chapter test questions in both multiple-choice and discussion/essay formats. You can download the Instructor's Manual by accessing the text's password-protected Instructor Companion Site, which also provides PowerPoint summations of the chapters.

ACKNOWLEDGMENTS

In preparing this eighth edition we have had the assistance of many people. Most important, we have drawn on the scholarly work of several generations of social and cultural theorists. Their ideas have inspired and guided contemporary work. It's an exciting time to be a communication scholar! We work within a research community that, although it may be in ferment, is also both vibrant and supportive. In these pages we acknowledge and explain the contributions that our many colleagues across the United States and around the world have made to mass communication theory. We regret the inevitable errors and omissions, and we take responsibility for them. We are also grateful to our reviewers:

Beth Bradford
La Salle University

Kim Walsh-Childers
University of Florida

Maggie Cogar
Ashland University

Kami Danaei
Western Wyoming Community College

Traci Gillig
University of Southern California

Megan Hopper
Illinois State University

Melissa Janoske
University of Memphis

Tia Smith
Xavier University of Louisiana

These reviewers helped us avoid some errors and omissions, but they bear no responsibility for those that remain. We also wish to thank our Oxford University Press friends, whose encouragement and advice sustained us. If you're reading this preface, you likely have some familiarity with what is happening in the textbook industry. Much of it isn't pretty. But Oxford, more than any other publisher, remains committed to *the book* and the ideas that venerable medium houses and generates. Their task was made less difficult than it might otherwise have been by our first editor, Becky Hayden, and Chris Clerkin, the editor for the first edition of this text. These accomplished professionals taught us how to avoid many of the sins usually committed by novice authors. The Oxford team, especially Alyssa Quinones, is as sharp as any we have worked with in the past and quite adept at using a gentle hand with what by now are two veteran textbook authors.

We must also thank our families. The Davis children—Jennifer, Kerry, Andy, Mike—are now scattered across the Midwest in Norman, Lincoln, Nashville, and Chicago, so they have been less involved with (or impacted by) the day-to-day development of this edition. Nonetheless, they often assisted with insights drawn from the academic fields in which they themselves have become expert: history, philosophy, Asian studies, marketing, and computer science. The Baran kids—Jordan and Matt Dowd—are scattered as well, but because of Internet and phone access, they were always available when the authors had questions about those "newfangled" technologies. They suffered our questions with charm and love.

It would be impossible to overstate the value of our wives' support. Nancy Davis continues to provide a sympathetic audience for efforts to think through media theory and brainstorm ways to apply it. Susan Baran, an expert in media literacy in her own right, has a remarkable ability to find the practical in the most theoretical. This is why more than a few of the ideas and examples in these pages found their refinement in her sharp mind. She keeps her husband grounded as a thinker and author while she lifts him as a man and father.

Finally, this book is the product of a collaboration that has gone on for nearly 50 years. We started our professional careers at Cleveland State University in 1973 in a communication department headed by Sidney Kraus. Sid inspired us, along with most other junior faculty, to become active, productive researchers. Today a disproportionate number of active communication scholars have direct or indirect links to the Cleveland State program. Sid, who, sadly, passed in 2014, demonstrated the many ways that one individual can have a powerful impact on a discipline. Through his scholarship, his mentorship, and his friendship, he has left a truly indelible mark.

S.J.B. & D.K.D

CHAPTER 1

Understanding and Evaluating Mass Communication Theory

Social media site Facebook debuted on the Internet in 2003. Within 5 years it grew to 100 million users, and in October 2012 the company proudly announced it had one billion members visiting monthly, networking in over 70 languages (Delo, 2012). Six years later technology writer Mathew Ingram (2018) declared Facebook "one of the most powerful forces in media—with more than 2 billion users every month and a growing lock on the ad revenue that used to underpin most of the media industry" (p. 1). But what is Facebook? How can it be earning so much advertising income? Isn't it just a world community of happy teens posting what they had for lunch, gossiping, and uploading party pictures? It is not. Yes, 62% of Americans ages 12 to 34 use the platform, but so do 69% of 35- to 54-year-olds and 53% of people over 55 (McCarthy, 2019). Teens are not the only people on Facebook.

So maybe the typical Facebooker isn't who we usually think of when we consider who's using the site. What else do we want to know about these two billion-plus users? How many friends does a typical Facebooker have? Forty percent have fewer than 200 friends; 38% have 200 to 500; and 21% have more than 500 ("Average Number," 2016). But this raises another question. What exactly is a *friend*? If you can have 500, are they really friends? Of course they are, claim psychologists Ashwini Nadkarni and Stefan Hofmann (2012), who argue that Facebook fosters a sense of belonging and lets people express themselves as they'd like, two obvious functions served by real friends. But in a two-billion-person community there must be a lot of different kinds of people looking for different things from their online friendships. Of course there are. Researchers Laura Buffardi and Keith Campbell (2008) claim that narcissists and people with low self-esteem spend more time on Facebook than do others. But according to other scholars, personality differences may have little to do with *why* people use Facebook. As Samuel D. Gosling and his research team discovered, rather than using the site to compensate for aspects of their offline personalities, users simply carry those everyday characteristics over to their online selves (Gosling, Augustine, Vazire, Holtzman, & Gaddis, 2011).

Clearly Facebook is a useful medium for a lot of people. Many log onto the site several times every day and frequently post updates. The Facebook News Feed, a constantly updated list of news stories tailored to users' needs and interests, provides many users with all the news they care to read or watch. Despite the fact that 57% of Americans expect the news they get from social media to be largely inaccurate, four in 10 get at least some of their news from Facebook (the number increasing to seven in 10 if we count all social media sites; Matsa & Shearer, 2018). How can this be? The answer is that most users don't give much thought to what they are doing and why. If asked, most say they are simply passing time, being entertained, or engaging in casual communication with friends and family. The News Feed helps them keep up on what they care to know. But could Facebook be more important than they realize? What about your own use of Facebook? Is it making an important difference in your life, or is it just another way for you to pass time? How do you view the company that provides you with this service? How much profit do you think it earns from selling your attention and your personal data to advertisers? If you regularly upload a lot of personal information, you are trusting that Facebook will not misuse this information and will provide you with the level of privacy that you want. But should you be so trusting? Facebook aggressively markets what it calls "Audience Insights" to businesses, helping them more precisely target ads aimed at you. Should you care more about what Facebook does with the information you provide? Does it trouble you that 40% of your fellow Facebook users have lost trust in the site to protect their personal information, five times more than those who distrust Twitter and Amazon (Feldman, 2018)?

Your answers to these questions are naturally based on *your* ideas or assumptions about Facebook, its users, and your own experiences. You can take into account what your friends say about Facebook and what you happen to read in the media. You might wonder if what you think is happening for you and your friends is the same for all those "old people" Facebook says are there. Researchers Nadkarni, Hofmann, Buffardi, Campbell, and Gosling and his colleagues had their ideas and assumptions, too, but they moved beyond their immediate personal experience to conduct research. They collected data and systematically assessed the usefulness of their ideas. They engaged in social science. Working together with others in a research community, they sought to develop a formal, systematic set of ideas about Facebook and its role in the social world. They are helping develop a mass communication theory that can be used to better understand large-scale social media use.

LEARNING OBJECTIVES

After studying this chapter you should be able to

- Define *legacy media*, *large-scale social media*, and *mass communication*.
- Explain differences in the operation of the natural and social sciences.
- Describe the relationship between the scientific method and causality.
- Define *theory*.
- Differentiate the four broad categories of mass communication theory—postpositive, cultural, critical, and normative theory—by their ontology, epistemology, and axiology.
- Establish criteria for judging theory.
- Differentiate the four trends in media theory—the mass society and mass culture, media-effects, critical cultural, and meaning-making trends.

OVERVIEW

In this chapter we will define *mass communication* and explain how it has changed since the introduction of social media in the 1990s. We will consider what separates an idea, a belief, or an assumption from a theory. We will examine mass communication theories created by social scientists and humanists. We'll look at some of the difficulties faced by those who attempt to systematically study and understand human behavior. We'll consider the particular problems encountered when the concern involves human behavior *and* the media. We'll see, too, that the definition of *social science* can be quite elusive. We'll define *theory* and offer several classifications of communication theory and mass communication theory. We'll trace the way theories of mass communication have been created and we will examine the purposes they serve. Most important, we will try to convince you that the difficulties that seem to surround the development and study of mass communication theory aren't really difficulties at all; rather, they are challenges that make the study of mass communication theory interesting and exciting.

DEFINING AND REDEFINING MASS COMMUNICATION

In recent decades the number and variety of mass communication theories have steadily increased. Development of media technologies has radically altered how media are used, and that has encouraged revision of existing theories and the development of new ones. Mass communication theory has emerged as a more or less independent body of thought in both the social sciences and the humanities. This book is intended as a guide to this diverse and sometimes contradictory thinking. You will find ideas developed by scholars in communication and in many other social sciences, from history and anthropology to sociology and psychology. Ideas have also been drawn from the humanities, especially from philosophy and literary analysis. The resulting ferment of ideas is both challenging and heuristic. These theories provide the raw materials for constructing even more useful and powerful theoretical perspectives.

If you are looking for a concise, definitive definition of *theory*, you won't find it in this book. We have avoided narrow definitions of theory in favor of an inclusive approach that finds value in most systematic, scholarly efforts to make sense of media and their role in society. We include theories that have sparked controversy and criticism. Some of the theories we review are **grand**; they try to explain entire media systems and their role in society. Others are narrowly focused and provide insight into specific uses or effects of certain types of media. Our selection of theories is based partly on their enduring historical importance, partly on their continuing use by some researchers, and partly on their potential to contribute to future scholarship. This process is necessarily subjective and is based on our own understanding of media and mass communication. Our consideration of contemporary perspectives is focused on those that illustrate enduring or innovative conceptualizations. But before we embark on that examination, we need to offer definitions of a number of important concepts.

First, we need to define and differentiate between two different types of mass media—**legacy media** and **large-scale social media**. *Legacy media* refers to older forms of mass media such as newspapers, magazines, radio, movies, and most importantly television. These media are operated by large, complex organizations directly responsible for producing and distributing content using media technology. Their technology permits large numbers of messages to be cheaply and easily reproduced and distributed to large audiences. These legacy media have developed over the past 200 years.

The newest forms of mass media are large-scale social media. Unlike legacy media, large-scale social media are dependent on Internet technology for distribution of messages. Users must access the Internet using computers or mobile devices. But much like legacy media, large-scale social media are developed and controlled by complex organizations. These organizations seek to attract the attention of large audiences by a variety of strategies. Some strategies resemble those of legacy media, but others are quite different. Social media enable audiences to do many different things. They allow users to routinely access, create, and share messages. They provide access to attractive content from many sources, and they serve a variety of needs for users. Like legacy media much of what they do serves to entertain or inform. Initially some social media, like Facebook and YouTube, relied on individuals to create content, but as they became more successful they turned to other content sources such as computer game makers and independent video producers. Large-scale social media organizations, such as Facebook, YouTube, and Twitter, operate in other ways that resemble legacy media. They are highly dependent on advertising income, and they prioritize policies and strategies that maximize this income even when it reduces the usefulness of the services they provide or disrupts the communities they serve. In the worst cases these services are operated in ways that threaten the welfare of individuals and the public at large. Unlike legacy media, large-scale social media are largely unregulated and are bound by few social or professional norms. Regulations that do exist are often ignored, since regulators are highly dependent on these companies themselves to provide information about their actions or policies. Facebook has been especially reluctant to share information about its activities.

Second, we have adopted a revised definition of mass communication that can be applied to both legacy media and large-scale social media. The old definition of mass communication was fairly simple. **Mass communication** was said to occur when a large organization employed a technology as a medium to communicate with a large, geographically dispersed audience. This definition has been routinely used for over a century, but the rise of social media has necessitated a rethinking. James Potter (2013) proposed a more contemporary definition:

> [In mass communication] the sender is a complex organization that uses standardized practices to disseminate messages while actively promoting itself in order to attract as many audience members as possible, then conditioning those audience members for habitual repeated exposures. Audiences members are widely dispersed geographically, are aware of the public character of what they are seeing or hearing, and encounter messages in a variety of exposure states, but most often in a state of automaticity. Channels of message dissemination are technological devices that can make messages public, extend the availability of messages in time and space, and can reach audiences within a relatively short time. (p. 1)

Some of the concepts used in this definition will be briefly explained here. Longer explanations will come later. Mass communication occurs when large organizations, whether legacy media or social media, use media technology to attract large numbers of people and train or condition them to routinely and frequently use their messages. They do this in order to cultivate large audiences that enable them to earn profits by selling messages directly to users or by selling those users' attention to advertisers. Mass media organizations usually structure messages so they will be used without much thought. They intentionally induce **automaticity**—a state of mind in which audience members automatically take in and respond to message content without critical reflection. When you "zone out" while watching television or YouTube or browsing through Facebook pages, you are experiencing automaticity. We will later review research that has found that automaticity has important consequences. For example, you can be more easily persuaded by messages if you simply take them in and don't think about them.

Let's consider now some questions about what constitutes mass communication. You could achieve some fame and maybe even a bit of income by posting funny cat videos on YouTube that go viral. Does this make you a mass communicator? Are you engaging in mass communication? Potter's definition makes it clear that, in this scenario, *you* are not a mass communicator because you are not a complex organization. YouTube is the mass communicator. By agreeing to YouTube's policies so that you are permitted to post the video, you become a member of that organization and YouTube gives you access to its medium. In contrast to people who work in legacy mass media, you don't have a job title, office, or regular salary. You have to rely on YouTube to promote your work and pay you fairly. Your ability to engage in mass communication is completely dependent on YouTube's policies and protocols, written to maximize YouTube's ability to make money from advertisers who put ads in your cat videos.

When social media were initially developed it was assumed that they would empower individuals and undermine the ability of legacy media to hold people's attention and interest. These new media would provide more useful ways of spending time, unleashing the creativity of individuals and connecting people in innovative and useful ways. Virtual communities would be created in which people could participate meaningfully without the barriers of income, social class, nationality, or race. But with the rise of large-scale social media over the past decade, much of this potential has been lost. We have seen the transformation of social media organizations from small groups of technology-minded "geeks" with grand visions into complex organizations spanning the globe, regularly attracting millions of users, and earning staggering profits. In 1995 few people predicted that social media could earn even small profits. How could they make money? Most people didn't have access to the Internet, and those who did had little interest in using it to network with other people. They had telephones and e-mail; what use was there for social media? Social media became successful only after they demonstrated their usefulness as a medium for advertising. Once social media organizations started earning advertising revenue, they changed their policies and practices to earn even more. They incorporated applications (apps) that would attract the time and attention of users. They collected and sold user data to advertisers and to app developers. Above all, they focused on growth, adding more and more users who spent more time on their sites. These changes inevitably "massified" social media— they became less useful for individuals and more useful for social media organizations and their shareholders and investors. Social media technology was harnessed just as newspapers, radio, movies, and television were harnessed to earn profits for powerful media organizations. As social media have changed, their role in society and their effects have become similar to those of legacy media.

James Webster (2017) offers useful insights into the way that large-scale social media operate in what he calls the **marketplace of attention**. In this marketplace social media are competing against each other and against legacy media to gain and hold the attention of people. Users approach social media with the belief that, within these media, they will have the freedom to choose what they want, the freedom to create, and the freedom to share. Webster argues that each of these abilities has been compromised and diminished by social media themselves—the existence of such freedoms is a myth. Instead social media have come to dominate their users. "Today," he observes, "websites instantly recognize a person's presence, auction their attention to an advertiser, and serve them a targeted advertisement—all in a fraction of a second. This can happen anywhere, anytime" (p. 354). Users are unable to make rational choices about media content because there is simply too much content and they have only limited ability to make meaningful choices. Instead they rely on algorithms to steer them toward content that will attract and hold their attention. As a result, social media users engage in mass behaviors that are useful to advertisers but of limited usefulness to themselves. These mass behaviors are much more complex than those of television audiences during the era when three networks dominated the industry. However, the behaviors can be measured and analyzed by the same social media computers that deliver content. These measurements generate gigantic datasets, or **big data**. Big data is yielding powerful insights into user behavior, allowing large-scale social media to gain ever greater control over users. As you'll see in later chapters, big data has become increasingly important to media researchers as well (Neuman, Guggenheim, Mo Jang, & Bae, 2014).

Throughout this textbook we discuss how theories originally developed to understand legacy media remain useful despite the introduction of social media. Most existing theories can be adapted to apply to the range of mass media that includes large-scale social media. The "massified" social media are best studied as another form of mass media, not as a transformative force producing useful, radical changes. But you might ask how this can be true when your use of media is so different from that of your parents. You don't spend as much time on a couch in front of a glowing screen; media must be doing different things for you and to you. But is your use of media really so different? If most of the time you spend communicating involves legacy mass media and large-scale social media, it's unlikely that the purposes it serves or its effects are all that much different. Your choices of media content are being dominated and directed. You are engaging in mass behavior that can be sold to advertisers. This is especially true if your primary use of media is to be passively entertained or informed, whether by television shows, Facebook, Snapchat, or YouTube.

How can you evaluate whether your use of media is different? One beneficial way to do this is to think of **mediated communication** as existing on a continuum that stretches from **interpersonal communication** at one end to mass communication at the other. Where different media fall along this continuum depends on the amount of control and involvement people have in the communication process. The telephone, for example (the phone as traditionally understood—not the smartphone you might own that has Internet access, GPS, and some 500 other "killer apps"), sits at one end. It is obviously a communication technology, but one that is most typical of interpersonal communication. At most a very few people can be involved in communicating at any given time, and they have a great deal of involvement with and control over that communication. The conversation is theirs, and they determine its content. A big-budget Hollywood movie or a network telecast of the Super Bowl sits at the opposite pole. Viewers have limited control over the communication that occurs. Certainly people can apply idiosyncratic interpretations to the content before them, and they can choose to direct however much attention they wish to the screen. They can choose to actively seek meaning from media content, or they can choose to passively decode it. But their control and involvement cannot directly alter the content of the messages being transmitted. Message content is centrally controlled by media organizations, and those organizations are seeking to maximize profits.

When social media were introduced, their various forms and technologies seemed to fit in the middle of the continuum between interpersonal and mass communication. Proponents of these new media argued that some features allowed ordinary people to effectively engage in creative forms of mass communication while others promised to connect people more efficiently and effectively to friends and family. New communication technologies could fill the middle of the continuum between the telephone and television. Suddenly media consumers would have the power to alter message content if they were willing to invest the time and had the necessary skill and resources. People could choose to be more *active* with media, and that could have many useful consequences for themselves, their friends, and their communities.

In earlier editions of this textbook we were optimistic about the way that social media would develop. We saw signs that media users were taking advantage of the control over messages offered by some new media companies. We had hope that the increasingly successful and powerful social media companies—Google, Facebook, Apple—might develop social media so that individuals were empowered. They might facilitate the creation of new communities and strengthen existing ones. But after almost 30 years it's become clear that large-scale social media provide us primarily with another form of mass communication. They're more diverse and seemingly tailored to our personal interests, but we have quite limited control over or involvement in message production. Facebook is a good example of the problematic development of social media. Initially Facebook facilitated creation and sharing of individually created content. It claimed an ability to build and sustain groups or even communities. Now the individually created content on Facebook serves mainly to attract users to the site so that they can be held there by more engaging content while they are exposed to advertising. Facebook has become one of the most successful competitors in the marketplace of attention. It proudly touts to advertisers its ability to attract and hold the attention of users so they are more likely to be influenced by the ads. It sells information about users that enables advertisers to target ads at people who are more likely to be influenced by and act on advertising messages. Large-scale social media offer little that is truly innovative. Social media companies are delivering the same basic content offered by legacy media but are packaging it in new ways and allowing easier access to it. For example, Twitter runs programming from producers like Walt Disney, ESPN, Viacom, and Vice News. Snapchat has an original video channel, Snap, and for payment provides "monetization opportunities" to scores of "influencers" who sell their online fame to sponsors (Sloane, 2018). YouTube has thousands of professional (as opposed to amateur or amateurs-hoping-to-make-some-money) channels. And Facebook alone spends a billion dollars a year on entertainment, news, and sports programming produced by legacy media companies ABC, CNN, Fox, and Univision for its video-on-demand service, Facebook Watch (Spangler, 2018).

SCIENCE AND HUMAN BEHAVIOR

This is a social science textbook. It presents theories that can be used to scientifically explore, describe, and explain mass communication. We can assess the usefulness of these theories, and we can them to make them more useful. To do this we must use scientific methods—methods that have been developed over centuries. You likely have a basic understanding of these methods and are aware of the enormous power over the physical world provided by scientific theories and research. Physical science theorists and researchers like Albert Einstein, Isaac Newton, Charles Darwin, and Louis Pasteur are widely known and respected, and science is one of the fundamental reasons we enjoy our admirable standard of living and have a growing understanding of the world around us. But not all scientists or the science they practice are understood or revered equally. When nations confront difficult problems, there is frustration when science can't provide easy solutions. There is even more frustration when science and the industries it spawns seemingly generate as many problems as they solve.

If there are doubts about the problems associated with the natural sciences, there tends to be even more skepticism about the social sciences. What has social science done for us lately? Is the social world a better place as a result of social science? Do we understand ourselves and others better? Are there stunning achievements that compare to splitting the atom or landing on the moon? Compared to the natural sciences, the social sciences seem much less useful and their theories less practical and more controversial.

Why does our society seem to have greater difficulty accepting the theories and findings of **social scientists**, those who apply logic and observation—that is, science—to the understanding of the social world rather than the physical world? Why do we have more trust in the people who wield telescopes and microscopes to probe the breadth of the universe and the depth of human cells, but skepticism about the tools used by social observers to probe the breadth of the social world or the depth of human experience? You can read more about the levels of respect afforded to scientists of different stripes in the box entitled "All Scientific Inquiry Is Value-Laden."

One important basis for our society's reluctance to accept the findings of the social scientists is the logic of **causality**. We readily understand this logic. You've no doubt had it explained to you during a high school physics or chemistry class, so we'll use a simple example from those classes: boiling water. If we (or our representatives, the scientists) can manipulate an independent variable (heat) and produce the same effect (boiling at 100 °C) under the same conditions (sea level) every time, then a **causal relationship** has been established. Heating water at sea level to 100 °C will cause water to boil. No matter how many times you heat beakers of water at sea level, they will all boil at 100 °C. Lower the heat; the water does not boil. Heat it at the top of Mount Everest; it boils at lower temperatures. Go back to sea level (or alter the atmospheric pressure in a laboratory test); it boils at 100 °C. This is repeated observation under controlled conditions. We even have a name for this—the **scientific method**—and there are many definitions for it. Here is a small sample:

ALL SCIENTIFIC INQUIRY IS VALUE-LADEN

Science writer Shawn Lawrence Otto (2011) would argue that the elevated respect afforded the natural sciences, to the positivists, is not as high as this text's discussion might lead you to believe. "At its core, science is a reliable method for creating knowledge, and thus power," he wrote, "Because science pushes the boundaries of knowledge, it pushes us to constantly refine our ethics and morality, and that is always political. But beyond that, science constantly disrupts hierarchical power structures and vested interests in a long drive to give knowledge, and thus power, to the individual, and that process is also political. . . . Every time a scientist makes a factual assertion—Earth goes around the sun, there is such a thing as evolution, humans are causing climate change—it either supports or challenges somebody's vested interests" (p. 22). In other words, the findings of the natural scientists are increasingly likely to be just as unsatisfying to some as those of the social scientists.

Public reaction to the theory of evolution and the science behind climate change offer two obvious examples. Vincent Cassone, chair of the University of Kentucky's biology department, defends evolution as the central organizing principle of all the natural sciences, "The theory of evolution is the fundamental backbone of all biological research. There is more evidence for evolution than there is for the theory of gravity, than the idea that things are made up of atoms, or Einstein's theory of relativity. It is the finest scientific theory ever devised" (as cited in Blackford, 2012). Yet the legislature of his state moved to strike the teaching of evolution from Kentucky's public schools. Climate scientists do not fare much better. Despite overwhelming evidence that the earth is warming, that human activity contributes to that change, and that the oceans are rising, the Virginia legislature has banned the term "sea-level rise" from a state-commissioned study of the problem because it was a "left-wing term," replacing it with "recurrent flooding" (Pollitt, 2012). In a time of massive wildfires, destructive droughts, murderous famines, giant hurricanes, and record high temperatures across the globe, 40% of Americans refuse to accept the scientific evidence of the existence of man-made global warming (Wise, 2018). Why the resistance to even traditional physical sciences? Otto (2011) answers, "The very essence of the scientific process is to question long-held assumptions about the nature of the universe, to dream up experiments that test those questions, and, based on the observations, to incrementally build knowledge that is independent of our beliefs and assumptions" (p. 24). Still, this doesn't explain why social scientists seem to suffer greater skepticism than their physical science colleagues? Why do you think this is the case?

1. "A means whereby insight into an undiscovered truth is sought by (1) identifying the problem that defines the goal of the quest, (2) gathering data with the hope of resolving the problem, (3) positing a **hypothesis** both as a logical means of locating the data and as an aid to resolving the problem, and (4) empirically testing the hypothesis by processing and interpreting the data to see whether the interpretation of them will resolve the question that initiated the research" (Leedy, 1997, pp. 94–95).

2. "A set of interrelated constructs (concepts), definitions, and propositions that present a systematic view of phenomena by specifying relations among variables, with the purpose of explaining and predicting phenomena" (Kerlinger, 1986, p. 9).

3. "A method . . . by which our beliefs may be determined by nothing human, but by some external permanency—by something upon which our thinking has no effect. . . . The method must be such that the ultimate conclusion of every man [sic] shall be the same. Such is the method of science. Its fundamental hypothesis . . . is this: There are real things whose characters are entirely independent of our opinions about them" (Pierce, 1955, p. 18).

Throughout the last century and into this one, some social researchers have tried to apply the scientific method to the study of human behavior and society. As you'll soon see, an Austrian immigrant to the United States, Paul Lazarsfeld, was an especially important advocate of applying social research methods to the study of mass media. But although the essential logic of the scientific method is quite simple, its application in the social (rather than physical) world is necessarily more complicated. Philosopher Karl Popper, whose 1934 *The Logic of Scientific Discovery* is regarded as the foundation of the scientific method, explained, "Long-term prophecies can be derived from scientific conditional predictions only if they apply to systems which can be described as well-isolated, stationary, and recurrent. These systems are very rare in nature; and modern society is not one of them" (as cited in Stevens, 2012).

Take, for example, the much-discussed issue of press coverage of political campaigns and its impact on voter turnout. Or the issue of how much fake news on social media affected the outcome of the 2016 presidential election. We know that more media attention is paid to elections than ever before. Today television permits continual eyewitness coverage of candidate activity. Mobile vans trail candidates and beam stories off satellites so that local television stations can air their own coverage. The Internet and Web offer instant access to candidates, their ideas, and those of their opponents—Twitter and YouTube let us continually track their every move. Yet despite advances in media technology and innovations in campaign coverage, voter participation in the United States remains low. During the past 30 years, in spite of the ever-growing media coverage, presidential election turnout has averaged below 60%, with some dips into the mid-50s. Even in the 2008 race between Barack Obama and John McCain, considered "the most technologically innovative, entrepreneurially driven campaign in American political history," only 61.6% of the voting-eligible population (VEP) cast ballots (US Election Project, 2018b). Though the contentious 2016 Donald Trump–Hillary Clinton election drew enormous media coverage, featured millions of dollars in political advertising, and exacerbated political divisions, it elicited only 60.1% of the VEP (US Election Project, 2018a). Should we assume that media campaign coverage suppresses potential voter turnout? This is an assertion that some mass communication observers might be quick to make. But would they be right? Perhaps turnout would have been even lower without this flood of media coverage? How could or should we verify which of these assertions is valid?

As we shall see, the pioneers of mass communication research faced a similar situation during the 1930s. There were precious few scientific studies of, but many bold assertions about, the bad effects of mass media. A small number of social scientists began to argue that these claims should not be accepted before making **empirical** observations that could either support them or permit them to be rejected. While these early researchers often shared the widely held view that media were powerful, they believed that the scientific method might be used to harness this power to avoid negative effects like juvenile delinquency. They hoped to produce positive effects such as promoting Americans' trust in their own democratic political system while subverting the appeal of totalitarian propaganda. In this way scientific research would allow media to be a force for good in shaping the social world. If their dreams had been fulfilled, we would be living in a very different sort of social world. Social scientists would be engineering the construction of social institutions in much the same way that natural scientists engineer the construction of skyscrapers or Mars rovers. But that didn't happen. Why?

Researchers faced many problems in applying the scientific method to the study of the social world. When seeking to observe the effects of political news or political ads, how can there be repeated observations? No two audiences, never mind any two individuals, who see news stories are the same. No two elections are the same. News stories vary greatly in terms of content and structure. Even if a scientist repeatedly conducted the same experiment on the same people (showing them, for example, the same excerpts of coverage or ads and then asking them if and how they might vote), these people would now be different each additional time because they would have learned from previous exposure and had a new set of experiences. Most would complain about having to watch the same story or ad over and over. They might say whatever they think the researcher wants to hear in order to get out of the experiment.

How can there be control over conditions that might influence observed effects? Who can control what people watch, read, or listen to, or to whom they talk, not to mention what they have learned about voting and civic responsibility in their school, family, and church? One solution is to put them in a laboratory and limit what they watch and learn. But people don't grow up in laboratories or use social media with the types of strangers they meet in a laboratory experiment. They don't consume media messages hooked to galvanic skin response devices or scanned by machines that track their eye movements. And unlike atoms under study, people can and sometimes do change their behaviors as a result of social scientists' findings, which further confounds claims of causality. And there is another problem. Powerful media effects rarely happen as a result of exposure to a few messages in a short amount of time. Effects take place slowly, over long periods of time. At any moment, nothing may seem to be happening.

As a result, this implementation of the scientific method is difficult for those studying the social world for four reasons:

1. **Most of the significant and interesting forms of human behavior are quite difficult to measure.** We can easily measure the temperature at which water boils. With ingenious and complex technology, we can even measure the weight of an atom or the speed at which the universe is expanding. But how do we measure something like civic duty? Should we count the incidence of voting? Maybe a person's decision not to vote is her personal expression of that duty. Try something a little easier, like measuring aggression in a television violence study. Can aggression be measured by counting how many times a child hits a rubber doll? Is maliciously gossiping about a neighbor an aggressive act? How do we measure an attitude (a predisposition to do something rather than an observable action)? What is 3 kg of tendency to hold conservative political views or 16.7 mm of patriotism?

2. **Human behavior is exceedingly complex.** Human behavior does not easily lend itself to causal description. It is easy to identify a single factor that causes water to boil. But it has proved impossible to isolate single factors that serve as the exclusive cause of important actions of human behavior. Human behavior may simply be too complex to allow scientists to ever fully untangle the different factors that combine to cause observable actions. We can easily control the heat and atmospheric pressure in our boiling experiment. We can control the elements in a chemistry experiment with relative ease. But if we want to develop

a theory of the influence of mediated communication on political campaigns, how do we control which forms of media people choose to use? How do we control the amount of attention they pay to specific types of news? How do we measure how well or poorly they comprehend what they consume? How do we take into account factors that influenced people long before we started our research? For example, how do we measure the type and amount of political socialization fostered by parents, schools, or peers? All these things (and countless others) will influence the relationship between people's use of media and their behavior in an election. How can we be sure what *caused* what? The very same factors that lead one person to vote might lead another to stay home.

3. **Humans have goals and are self-reflexive.** We do not always behave in response to something that has happened; very often we act in response to something we hope or expect will happen. Moreover, we constantly revise our goals and make highly subjective determinations about their potential for success or failure. Water boils *after* the application of heat. It doesn't think about boiling. It doesn't begin to experience boiling and then decide that it doesn't like the experience. We think about our actions and inactions; we reflect on our values, beliefs, and attitudes. Water doesn't develop attitudes against boiling that lead it to misperceive the amount of heat it is experiencing. It stops boiling when the heat is removed. It doesn't think about stopping or have trouble making up its mind. It doesn't have friends who tell it that boiling is fun and should be continued even when there is insufficient heat. But people do think about their actions, and they frequently make these actions contingent on their expectations that something will happen. "Humans are not like billiard balls propelled solely by forces external to them," explained cognitive psychologist Albert Bandura (2008). "Billiard balls cannot change the shape of the table, the size of the pockets, or intervene in the paths they take, or even decide whether to play the game at all. In contrast, humans not only think, but, individually and collectively, shape the form those external forces take and even determine whether or not they come into play. Murray Gell-Mann, the physicist Nobelist, underscored the influential role of the personal determinants when he remarked, 'Imagine how hard physics would be if particles could think'" (pp. 95–96).

4. **The simple notion of causality is sometimes troubling when it is applied to ourselves.** We have no trouble accepting that heat causes water to boil at 100 °C at sea level; we relish such causal statements in the physical world. We want to know how things work, what makes things happen. As much as we might like to be thrilled by horror movies or science fiction films in which physical laws are continually violated, we trust the operation of these laws in our daily lives. But we often resent causal statements when they are applied to ourselves. We can't see the expanding universe or the breakup of the water molecule at the boiling point, so we are willing to accept the next best thing, the word of an objective expert—that is, a scientist. But we can see ourselves watching cable news and not voting and going to a movie and choosing a brand-name pair of jeans and learning about people from lands we've never visited. Why do we need experts telling us about ourselves or explaining to us why we do things? We're not so easily influenced by media, we say. But ironically most of us are convinced that

other people are much more likely to be influenced by media (the **third-person effect**). So although we don't need to be protected from media influence, *others* might; they're not as smart as we are (Grier & Brumbaugh, 2007). We are our own men and women—independent, freethinking individuals. We weren't affected by those McDonald's ads; we simply bought that Big Mac, fries, and a large Coke because, darn it, we deserved a break today. And after all, we did need to eat something, and Mickey D's did happen to be right on the way back to the dorm.

DEFINING THEORY

Scientists, natural or social (however narrowly or broadly defined), deal in **theory**. "Theories are stories about how and why events occur. . . . Scientific theories begin with the assumption that the universe, including the social universe created by acting human beings, reveals certain basic and fundamental properties and processes that explain the ebb and flow of events in specific processes" (Turner, 1998, p. 1). "A good theory clarifies things, aids our understanding," explains Stephen Kearse (2018). "It's prepared for us to scrutinize and audit, testing its explanatory power. The strongest ones have been refined, continually, until the case they make is as resilient as it is persuasive" (p. 9). Theory has numerous other definitions. John Bowers and John Courtright (1984) offered a traditional scientific definition: "Theories . . . are sets of statements asserting relationships among classes of variables" (p. 13). So did Charles Berger (2005): "A theory consists of a set of interrelated propositions that stipulate relationships among theoretical constructs and an account of the mechanism or mechanisms that explain the relationships stipulated in the propositions" (p. 417). Kenneth Bailey's (1982) conception of theory accepts a wider array of ways to understand the social world: "Explanations and predictions of social phenomena . . . relating the subject of interest . . . to some other phenomena" (p. 39).

Our definition, though, will be drawn from a synthesis of two even more generous views of theory. Assuming that there are a number of different ways to understand how communication functions in our complex world, Stephen Littlejohn and Karen Foss (2011) defined theory as "any organized set of concepts, explanations, and principles of some aspect of human experience" (p. 19). Emory Griffin (1994) also takes this broader view, writing that a theory is an idea "that explains an event or behavior. It brings clarity to an otherwise jumbled situation; it draws order out of chaos. . . . [It] synthesizes the data, focuses our attention on what's crucial, and helps us ignore that which makes little difference" (p. 34). These latter two writers are acknowledging an important reality of communication and mass communication theories: There are a lot of them; the questions they produce are testable to varying degrees; they tend to be situationally based; and they sometimes seem contradictory and chaotic. As communication theorist Katherine Miller (2005) explained, "Different schools of thought will define *theory* in different ways depending on the needs of the theorist and on beliefs about the social world and the nature of knowledge" (pp. 22–23). As such, scholars have identified four major categories of communication theory—(1) postpositivism, (2) cultural theory, (3) critical theory, and (4) normative theory—and although they "share a commitment to an increased understanding of social and communicative life and a value for high-quality scholarship" (Miller, 2005, p. 32), they differ in:

- their goals;
- their view of the nature of reality, what is knowable and worth knowing—their **ontology**;
- their view of the methods used to create and expand knowledge—their **epistemology**; and
- their view of the proper role of human values in research and theory building—their **axiology**.

These differences not only define the different types of theory but also help make it obvious why a broader and more flexible definition of *social science* in mass communication theory is useful.

Postpositivist Theory

When researchers in the 1930s wanted to systematically study the role of mass media in social world, some turned to the natural sciences for their model. Those in the natural sciences (physics, chemistry, astronomy, and so on) believed in *positivism*, the idea that knowledge could be gained only through empirical, observable, measurable phenomena examined through the scientific method. But as we saw earlier in this chapter, the social world is very different from the physical world. Causality needs to be understood and applied differently. After a half century of trial and error, social scientists committed to the scientific method developed **postpositivist theory**. This type of theory is based on empirical observation guided by the scientific method, but it recognizes that humans and human behavior are not as constant as elements of the physical world.

The goals of postpositivist theory are the same as those set by physical scientists for their theories: explanation, prediction, and control. For example, researchers who want to explain the operation of political advertising, predict which commercials will be most effective, and control the voting behavior of targeted citizens would, of necessity, rely on postpositivist theory. Its ontology accepts that although the world, even the social world, exists apart from our perceptions of it, human behavior is sufficiently predictable to be studied systematically. Postpositivists recognize that the social world does have more variation than the physical world, hence the *post* of postpositivism. Its epistemology argues that knowledge is advanced through the systematic, logical search for regularities and causal relationships employing the scientific method. Advances come when there is **intersubjective agreement** among scientists studying a given phenomenon. That is, postpositivists find confidence "in the community of social researchers," not "in any individual social scientist" (Schutt, 2009, p. 89). It is this cautious reliance on the scientific method that defines postpositivism's axiology—the objectivity inherent in the application of the scientific method keeps researchers' and theorists' values out of the search for knowledge (as much as is possible). They fear that values could bias the choice and application of methods so that researchers would be more likely to get the results that they want (results that are consistent with their values). Postpositivist communication theory, then, is theory developed through a system of inquiry that resembles as much as possible the rules and practices of what we traditionally understand as science.

Cultural Theory

But many communication theorists do not want to explain, predict, and control social behavior. Their goal is to *understand* how and why that behavior occurs in the social world. This **cultural theory** seeks to understand contemporary cultures by analyzing the structure and content of their communication. Cultural theory finds its origin in **hermeneutic theory**—the study of understanding, especially through the systematic interpretation of actions or texts. Hermeneutics originally began as the study or interpretation of the Bible and other sacred works. As it evolved over the last two centuries, it maintained its commitment to the examination of "objectifications of the mind" (Burrell & Morgan, 1979, p. 236), or what Miller (2005) calls "social creations" (p. 52). Just as the Bible was the "objectification" of early Christian culture, and those who wanted to understand that culture would study that text, most modern applications of hermeneutics are likewise focused on understanding the culture of the users of a specific text.

There are different forms of cultural theory. For example, **social hermeneutics** has as its goal the understanding of how those in an observed social situation interpret their own place in that situation. Ethnographer Michael Moerman (1992) explained how social hermeneutic theory makes sense of "alien" or "unknown" cultures. Social hermeneutic theory tries to understand how events "in the alien world make sense to the aliens, how their way of life coheres and has meaning and value for the people who live it" (p. 23). Another branch of cultural theory looks for hidden or deep meaning in people's interpretation of different symbol systems—for example, in media texts. As you might have guessed from these descriptions, cultural theory is sometimes referred to as *interpretive theory.* It seeks to interpret the meaning of texts for the agents that produce them and the audiences that consume them. Another important idea embedded in these descriptions is that any **text**, any product of social interaction—a movie, the president's State of the Union Address, a series of Twitter tweets, a conversation between a soap opera hero and heroine—can be a source of understanding. Understanding can in turn guide actions.

The ontology of cultural theory says that there is no truly "real," measurable social reality. Instead "people construct an image of reality based on their own preferences and prejudices and their interactions with others, and this is as true of scientists as it is of everyone else in the social world" (Schutt, 2009, p. 92). As such, cultural theory's epistemology, how knowledge is advanced, relies on the subjective interaction between the observer (the researcher or theorist) and his or her community. Put another way, knowledge is local; that is, it is specific to the interaction of the knower and the known. Naturally, then, the axiology of cultural theory embraces, rather than limits, the influence of researcher and theorist values. Personal and professional values, according to Katherine Miller (2005), are a "lens through which social phenomena are observed" (p. 58). A researcher interested in understanding teens' interpretations of social networking websites like Instagram, or one who is curious about meaning making that occurs in the exchange of information among teen fans of an online simulation game, would rely on cultural theory.

Critical Theory

There are still other scholars who do not want explanation, prediction, and control of the social world. Nor do they seek understanding of that world as the ultimate goal for their work. They start from the assumption that some aspects of the social world are deeply flawed and in need of transformation. Their aim is to gain knowledge of that social world so they can change it. This goal is inherently—and intentionally—political because it challenges existing ways of organizing the social world and the people and institutions exercising power in it. **Critical theory** is openly political (therefore its axiology is aggressively value-laden). It assumes that by reorganizing society we can give priority to its most important human values. Critical theorists study inequality and oppression. Their theories do more than observe, describe, or interpret; they criticize. Critical theories view "media as sites of (and weapons in) struggles over social, economic, symbolic, and political power (as well as struggles over control of, and access to, the media themselves)" (Meyrowitz, 2008, p. 642). Critical theory's epistemology argues that knowledge is advanced only when it serves to free people and communities from the influence of those more powerful than themselves. Critical theorists call this emancipatory knowledge. Its ontology, however, is a bit more complex.

According to critical theory, what is real, what is knowable, in the social world is the product of the interaction between **structure** (the social world's rules, norms, and beliefs) and **agency** (how humans behave and interact in that world). Reality, then, is constantly being shaped and reshaped by the **dialectic** (the ongoing struggle or debate) between the two. When elites control the struggle, they define reality (in other words, their control of the structure defines people's realities). When people are emancipated, *they* define reality through their behaviors and interactions (agency). Researchers and theorists interested in the decline (and restoration) of the power of the labor movement in industrialized nations or those interested in limiting the contribution of children's advertising to the nation's growing consumerism would rely on critical theory. Some critical theorists are quite troubled by what they view as the uncontrolled exercise of **capitalist** corporate power around the world. They see media as an essential tool employed by corporate elites to constrain how people view their social world and to limit their agency in it. They worry about the spread of what they see as a global culture of celebrity and consumerism that is fostered by capitalist-dominated media.

Normative Theory

Social theorists see postpositivist and cultural theory as *representational*. That is, they are articulations—word pictures—of some other realities (for postpositivists, those representations are generalizable across similar realities, and for interpretive theorists, these representations are local and specific). Critical theory is *nonrepresentational*. Its goal is to *change* existing realities.

There is another type of theory, however. It may be applied to any type of social institution, but our focus will be on media institutions. Its aim is neither the representation nor the reformation of reality. Instead its goal is to set an ideal standard against which the operation of a given media system can be judged. A **normative media theory** explains how a media system *should* operate in order to conform to or realize a set of ideal social values. As such, its ontology argues that what is known is situational (or like interpretive theory, local). In other words, what is real or knowable about a media system is real or knowable only for the specific social system in which that media system exists. Its epistemology, how knowledge is developed and advanced, is based in *comparative analysis*—we can judge (and therefore understand) the worth of a given media system only in comparison to the ideal espoused by the particular

social system in which it operates. Finally, normative theory's axiology is, by definition, value-laden. Study of a media system or parts of a media system is undertaken in
the explicit belief that there is an ideal mode of operation based in the values of the
larger social system. Theorists interested in the press's role in a democracy would most
likely employ normative theory, as would those examining the operation of the media
in an Islamic republic or an authoritarian state. Problems arise if media systems based
on one normative theory are evaluated according to the norms or ideals of another
normative theory. Chapter 3 is devoted in its entirety to normative theory. You can
more deeply investigate the role of values in the four broad categories of theory we've
discussed when reading the box entitled "True Values: A Deeper Look at Axiology."

THINKING ABOUT THEORY

TRUE VALUES: A DEEPER LOOK AT AXIOLOGY

As we've seen, different communication theorists deal differently with the role of values in the construction of their ideas. Inasmuch as they model their research on that of those who study the physical world, postpositivists would ideally like to eliminate values from their inquiry. But they know they can't, so objectivity becomes their regulatory ideal; that is, they rely on the scientific method to reduce the impact of values on their work as much as possible. They also distinguish between two types of values in their work. Postpositivists cherish **epistemic values**—they value high standards in the conduct of research and development of theory. But they also confront **nonepistemic values**—the place of emotion, morals, and ethics in research and theory development. There is little debate about the former among postpositivists—who wouldn't want high standards of performance? But what about emotions, morals, and ethics? Why, for example, would researchers want to study media violence? Certainly they believe a relationship exists between media consumption and human behavior on some level. But what if an individual theorist strongly believes in the eradication of all violence on children's television because of her own son's problems with bullies at school? How hard should she work to ignore her personal feelings in her research and interpretation of her findings? Should she examine some other aspect of mass communication to ensure greater objectivity? But why should anybody have to study something that he or she has no feeling about?

Interpretive theorists, even though they more readily accept the role of values in their work, also wrestle with the proper application of those values. Accepting the impossibility of separating values from research and theory development, interpretive theorists identify two ends of a continuum. Those who wish to minimize the impact of their personal values on their work **bracket** their values; that is, they recognize them, set them aside by figuratively putting them in brackets, and then do their work. At the other end of the continuum are those who openly celebrate their values and consciously inject them into their work. In truth, most interpretive researchers and theorists fall somewhere in the middle. If you were really thinking about theory, though, you would have asked, "But if an interpretive theorist openly celebrates his or her values and injects them into the research or theory development, hasn't she moved into critical theory?" And you would be correct, because it is hard to conceive of someone willing to inject personal values into social research and theory who did not want, at the very least, to advance those values. And in advancing those values, the status quo would be altered—hence, critical theory.

Critical and normative theorists, in their open embrace of values, face fewer questions about objectivity than do other theorists. But they, like all social researchers and theorists, must employ high epistemic values. Critical theorists advocate change; normative theorists advocate media striving to meet a social system's stated ideals of operation. These open articulations of nonepistemic values, however, do not excuse sloppy data gathering or improper data analysis.

What should be clear is that all involved in the serious study of human life must maintain the highest standards of inquiry within the conventions of their research and theory development communities. Given that, which axiology do you find most compatible with your way of thinking about human behavior? Should you someday become a mass communication researcher or theorist, which set of values do you think would prove most valuable in guiding your efforts?

/ALUATING THEORY

ıch philosopher André Gide wrote, "No theory is good unless it permits, not rest, ʋut the greatest work. No theory is good except on condition that one uses it to go on beyond" (as cited in Andrews, Biggs, & Seidel, 1996, p. 66). In other words, good theory pushes, advances, improves the social world. There are some specific ways, however, to judge the value of the many theories we will study in this book.

When evaluating postpositivist theory, we need to ask these questions:

1. How well does it explain the event, behavior, or relationship of interest?
2. How well does it predict future events, behaviors, or relationships?
3. How testable is it? That is, is it specific enough in its assertions that it can be systematically supported or rejected based on empirical observation?
4. How parsimonious is it? Is it the simplest explanation possible of the phenomenon in question? Some call this *elegance*. Keep in mind that communication theories generally tend to lack parsimony. In fact, one of the reasons many social scientists avoid the study of communication is that communication phenomena are hard to explain parsimoniously.
5. How practical or useful is it? If the goals of postpositivist theory are explanation, prediction, and control, how much assistance toward these ends is provided by the theory?

When evaluating cultural theory, we need to ask these questions:

1. How much new or fresh insight into the event, behavior, or relationship of interest does it offer? How much does it advance our understanding?
2. How well does it clarify the values inherent in the interpretation, not only those embedded in the phenomenon of interest, but those of the researcher or theorist?
3. How much support does it generate among members of the scholarly community also investigating the phenomenon of interest?
4. How much aesthetic appeal does it have? In other words, does it enthuse or inspire its adherents?

When evaluating critical theory, we need to ask the same questions we do of cultural theory, but we must add a fifth:

5. How useful is the critique of the status quo? Does it provide enough understanding of elite power so that power can be effectively challenged? Does the theory enable individuals to oppose elite definitions of the social world?

When evaluating normative theory, we need to ask the following questions:

1. How stable and definitive are the ideal standards of operation against which the media system (or its parts) under study will be measured?
2. What, and how powerful, are the economic, social, cultural, and political realities surrounding the actual operation of a system (or its parts) that must be considered in evaluating that performance?
3. How much support does it generate among members of the scholarly community also investigating a specific media system (or its parts)?

FLEXIBLE SOCIAL SCIENCE

Now that you've been introduced to the four broad categories of social scientific theory, you might have guessed another reason that those who study the social world often don't get the respect accorded their physical science colleagues. Sociologist Kenneth Bailey (1982) wrote, "To this day you will find within social science both those who think of themselves as scientists in the strictest sense of the word and those with a more subjective approach to the study of society, who see themselves more as humanists than as scientists" (p. 5). His point, as you've just seen, is not all who call themselves social scientists adhere to the same standards for conducting research or accepting evidence. But complicating matters even more is the fact that social science researchers and theorists often blend (or mix and match) categories as they do their work (Benoit & Holbert, 2008). To some observers, especially committed postpositivists, this seems unsystematic. It also generates disagreement among social scientists, not about the issue under examination, say the influence of video violence on children's behavior, but about the appropriateness of the methods used, the value of the evidence obtained, or the influence of values on the work (that is, debates over ontology, epistemology, and axiology).

MASS COMMUNICATION THEORY

One way to approach the study of media theory is to consider how theories have developed over the past two centuries. Not surprisingly, theories have evolved in part as a reaction to changes in mass media technology and the rise of new mass media organizations that exploited this technology. Proponents for the four types of theories developed different but sometimes related theories. Specific issues or concerns such as the effects of violent content or elite control of media have motivated the development and evolution of theories. Whenever new forms of media have been developed, they have been praised by some and condemned by others. Debates over the usefulness of new forms of media have spawned numerous theories.

FOUR TRENDS IN MEDIA THEORY

For some time, those who study the shifting history of mass communication theory have pointed to large-scale paradigm shifts, as once-popular notions in one era gave way to very different views in the next. Critics have challenged this way of looking at media theory, arguing that these overarching perspectives were not as well integrated or as dominant as they might appear to have been in retrospect (for example, Neuman & Guggenheim, 2011). These shifts were rarely as clear-cut as often assumed, and the retelling of the interaction between proponents of different types of theory tended to dwell on conflict between their advocates rather than on the potential for collaboration or corroboration. Here, instead of distinct *eras* of mass communication theory, we identify *trends* in theory development. To some extent these trends are similar to eras in that they trace the development of relatively stable perspectives on mass communication, and over time there has been a shift from one trend to another. At given points in time, however, trends overlap and to some extent influence each other.

The Mass Society and Mass Culture Trend
in Mass Communication Theory

Our description of the eras of mass communication theory begins with a review of some of the earliest thinking about media. These ideas were initially developed in the latter half of the 19th century, at a time when rapid development of large factories in urban areas was drawing more and more people from rural areas to cities. At the same time, ever more powerful printing presses allowed the creation of newspapers that could be sold at declining prices to rapidly growing populations of readers. Although some theorists were optimistic about the future that would be created by industrialization, urban expansion, and the rise of print media, many were extremely pessimistic (Brantlinger, 1983). They blamed industrialization for disrupting peaceful, rural communities and forcing people to live in urban areas, merely to serve as a convenient workforce in large factories, mines, or bureaucracies. These theorists were fearful of cities because of their crime, cultural diversity, and unstable political systems. For these social thinkers mass media symbolized everything that was wrong with 19th-century urban life. They singled out media for virulent criticism and accused them of pandering to lower-class tastes, fomenting political unrest, and subverting important cultural norms. Most of these theorists were educated **elites** who feared what they couldn't understand. The old social order was crumbling, and so were its culture and politics. Were media responsible for this, or did they simply accelerate or aggravate these changes? These types of concerns about the role of media are still prevalent today. As we'll see in Chapter 14, there is a new European theory of media, mediatization theory, that also considers the power of media to subvert and transform social institutions.

The dominant perspective on media and society that emerged during this period has come to be referred to as **mass society theory**. It is an inherently contradictory theory that is often rooted in nostalgia for a "golden age" that never existed, and it anticipates a nightmare future in which social order is broken down, ruthless elites seize power, and individual freedom is lost. Some version of mass society theory seems to recur in every generation as we try to reassess where we are and where we are going as individuals and as a nation wedded to technology as the means of improving the quality of our lives. Each new version of mass society theory has its criticisms of contemporary media. It is useful to recognize that this trend in media theory is still found today even though many earlier forms of mass society theory have been discarded.

Mass society theory can be regarded as a collection of conflicting notions developed to make sense of what is happening whenever there is large-scale and/or disruptive social change. Mass society notions can come from both ends of the political spectrum. Some are developed by people who want to maintain the existing political order, and others are created by revolutionaries who want to impose radical changes. But these ideological foes often share at least one assumption—mass media are troublesome if not downright dangerous. In general, mass society ideas hold strong appeal for any social elite whose power is threatened by change. Media industries, such as the **penny press** in the 1830s, **yellow journalism** in the 1890s, movies in the 1920s, radio in the 1930s, and TV in the 1950s, were easy targets for elites' criticisms. They catered to audiences in middle and lower social classes using simple, often sensational content. Content mostly entertained rather than informed or educated people. These industries were easily attacked as symptomatic of a sick society—a society needing to either return to traditional, fundamental values or be forced to adopt a set of totally new values fostered by media. Many intense political conflicts strongly affected thinking about the mass media, and these conflicts shaped the development of various forms of mass society theory.

An essential argument of mass society theory is that media subvert and disrupt the existing social order. But media are also seen as a potential solution to the chaos they engender. They can serve as a powerful tool that can be used to either restore the old order or institute a new one. But who should be trusted to use this tool? Should established authorities be trusted to control media—to produce or censor media content? Should media be freely operated by private entrepreneurs whose primary goal is to make money? Should radical, revolutionary groups be given control over media so they can pursue their dreams of creating an ideal social order? At the end of the 19th century and the beginning of the 20th, fierce debate erupted over these questions. This conflict often pitted traditional elites, whose power was based on an agrarian society, against urban elites, whose power was increasingly based on industrialization and urbanization.

Today the fallacies of both the critics and advocates of older forms of media technology are readily apparent. Early mass society notions greatly exaggerated the ability of media to quickly undermine social order, just as media advocates exaggerated their ability to create an ideal social order. These ideas failed to consider that media's power ultimately resides in the freely chosen uses that audiences make of it. Most mass society thinkers were unduly paternalistic and elitist in their views of average people and media's ability to have powerful effects on them. Those who feared media exaggerated their power to manipulate the masses and the likelihood they would bring inevitable social and cultural ruin. Technology advocates were also misguided and failed to acknowledge the many unnecessary, damaging consequences that resulted from applying technology without adequately anticipating its impact.

The Media-Effects Trend in Mass Communication Theory

In the late 1930s and early 1940s mass society notions began to be empirically investigated by Paul Lazarsfeld, who would eventually overturn some of its basic assumptions. Trained in psychological measurement, Lazarsfeld fled the Nazis in Austria and came to the United States on a Ford Foundation fellowship (Lazarsfeld, 1969). For the emerging field of mass communication research, he proved to be a seminal thinker and researcher. Like many of his academic colleagues, Lazarsfeld was interested in exploring the potential of newly developed social science methods, such as surveys and field experiments, to understand and solve social problems. He combined academic training with a high level of entrepreneurial skill. Within a few years after arriving in the United States, he had established a very active and successful social research center, the Bureau for Applied Social Research at Columbia University.

Lazarsfeld provides a classic example of a transitional figure in theory development—someone well grounded in past theory but also innovative enough to consider other concepts and methods for evaluating new ideas. Though quite familiar with and very sympathetic to mass society notions (Lazarsfeld, 1941), Lazarsfeld was committed to the use of empirical social research methods in order to establish the validity of theory. He was a strong advocate of postpositivism as a basis for doing so. He argued that it wasn't enough to merely speculate about the influence of media on society. Instead he advocated the conduct of carefully designed, elaborate surveys and even field experiments in which he would be able to observe media influence and measure its magnitude. It was not enough to assume that political propaganda is powerful—hard evidence was needed to prove the existence of its effects (Lazarsfeld, Berelson, & Gaudet, 1944). Lazarsfeld's most famous research efforts, the "American Voter Studies," actually began as an attempt to document the media's power during election campaigns, yet they eventually raised more questions about the influence of media than they answered.

By the mid-1950s Lazarsfeld's work and that of other empirical media researchers had generated an enormous amount of data (by precomputer standards). Interpretation of these data led Lazarsfeld and his colleagues to conclude that media were not nearly as powerful as had been feared or hoped. Instead these researchers found that people had numerous ways of resisting media influence, and their attitudes were shaped by many competing factors, such as family, friends, and religious communities. Rather than serving as a disruptive social force, media more often seemed to reinforce existing social trends and strengthen rather than threaten the status quo. They found little evidence to support the worst fears of mass society theorists. Though Lazarsfeld and others never labeled this theory, it came to be referred to as **limited-effects theory**.

Throughout the 1950s limited-effects notions about media continued to gain acceptance within academia. These ideas dominated the new field of mass communication research as it was developing in the 1950s and 1960s. Several important clashes occurred between their adherents and those who supported mass society ideas (Bauer & Bauer, 1960). This is hardly surprising since the rise of communism across Eastern Europe seemed to provide ample evidence that media could be used as powerful tools to meld increasingly large masses of individuals into an ever more powerful totalitarian state. How could the United States expect to win the Cold War unless it could somehow find a way to use mass media to confront and overcome the Soviets?

In 1960 several classic studies of media effects (Campbell, Converse, Miller, & Stokes, 1960; Deutschmann & Danielson, 1960; Klapper, 1960) provided apparently definitive support for the limited-effects view. Limited-effects notions about mass communication theory were now supported by a decade of postpositivist research. By contrast, advocates of mass society notions came under increasing attack as "unscientific" or "irrational" because they questioned "hard scientific findings." Mass society notions were further discredited within academia because they became associated with the anticommunist **Red Scare** promoted by Senator Joseph McCarthy in the early 1950s. McCarthy and his allies focused considerable attention on ridding alleged communists from the media. They justified these purges using mass society arguments—average people needed to be protected from media manipulation. Limited-effects theorists produced research showing that average people were well protected from media influence by opinion leaders who filtered out communist propaganda before it reached their followers.

By the mid-1960s the debate between mass society and limited-effects advocates appeared to be over—at least within the postpositivist research community. The body of empirical research findings continued to grow, and almost all were consistent with the latter view. Little or no empirical research supported mass society thinking. Most postpositivist researchers stopped looking for powerful media effects and concentrated instead on documenting minimal, limited effects. Some of the original media researchers had become convinced that media research would never produce any important new findings and returned to work in political science or sociology. In a controversial essay, Bernard Berelson (1959), who worked closely with Paul Lazarsfeld, declared the field of communication research to be "worn out," its "great ideas" exhausted (p. 6). There simply was nothing left to study when it came to the mass media.

Ironically, Berelson's essay was published just before the field of mass communication research underwent explosive growth. As postpositivist researchers in sociology and psychology abandoned media research, they were quickly replaced by the increasing numbers of faculty members working in rapidly growing programs dedicated to the study of media and communication. As these programs grew, so did the volume of postpositivist research on media. Initially this research largely replicated work done by sociologists and psychologists, but by the 1970s media researchers began to make important new contributions to our understanding of media.

The Critical Cultural Trend in Mass Communication Theory

While postpositivist media research flourished in the 1970s and 1980s, it came under increasing criticism from European researchers. In Europe both left-wing and right-wing scholars had concerns about the power of media deeply rooted in World War II experiences with propaganda and government control over media. Europeans were also skeptical about the power of postpositivist, quantitative social research methods to verify and develop social theory (they saw this approach to research as reductionist—reducing complex communication processes and social phenomena to little more than narrow propositions generated from small-scale investigations). They viewed this **reductionism** as a distinctly American fetish, and some European academics were resentful of the influence enjoyed by American social researchers after World War II. They argued that American empiricism was both simplistic and intellectually sterile. Although some European academics welcomed and championed American notions about media effects, others strongly resisted them and argued for maintaining approaches considered less constrained or more traditionally European.

One group of European social theorists who vehemently resisted postwar US influence were the **neo-Marxists** (Hall, 1982). Consistent with communist theory, first formulated by Karl Marx, these left-wing social theorists argued that media enable dominant social elites to consolidate and maintain their economic power. Neo-Marxist theory is a form of critical theory. It argues that media provide elites with a convenient, subtle, yet highly effective means of promoting worldviews favorable to their interests. Mass media can be understood, they contended, as a public arena in which cultural battles are fought and a dominant, or hegemonic, culture is forged and promoted. Elites dominate these struggles because they start with important advantages. Opposition is marginalized, and the status quo is presented as the only logical, rational way of structuring society. Values favored by elites are subtlety woven into and promoted by the narratives of popular programs—for example, even in children's cartoons. Within neo-Marxist theory, efforts to examine media institutions and interpret media content came to have high priority. Such theories differ from older forms of Marxism because they assume that culture is an important arena for political struggle. Elites can be challenged in the media as well as in the streets.

During the 1960s some neo-Marxists in Britain developed a school of social theory widely referred to as **British cultural studies**. It focused heavily on mass media and their role in promoting a hegemonic worldview and a dominant culture within society at large. British cultural studies drew on both critical theory and cultural theory to create **critical cultural theory**. Researchers studied how members of various subgroups used media and assessed how this use might serve group interests (cultural theory) or might lead people to develop ideas that supported dominant elites (critical theory). This research eventually produced an important breakthrough. As they conducted audience research, social scientists at Birmingham University discovered that people often resisted the hegemonic ideas and propagated new, alternative interpretations of the social world (Mosco & Herman, 1981). Although British cultural studies began with **deterministic assumptions** about the influence of media (that is, the media have powerful, direct effects), their work came to focus on audience reception studies that revived important questions about the potential power of media in certain types of situations and the ability of audience members to actively resist media influence—questions that 1960s postpositivist media scholars ignored because they were skeptical about the power of media and assumed that audiences were passive.

During the 1970s questions about the possibility of powerful media effects were again raised in American universities. Initially these questions were advanced by scholars in the humanities who were unaware of the limited-effects perspective, skeptical about postpositivism, and well trained in cultural theory. Their arguments were routinely ignored and marginalized by social scientists because they were unsupported by "scientific evidence." Some of these scholars were attracted to European-style critical cultural theory (Newcomb, 1974). Others attempted to create an "authentic" American school of cultural studies—though they drew heavily on Canadian scholars like Harold Innis and Marshall McLuhan (Carey, 1977). This **cultural criticism**, although initially greeted with considerable skepticism by "mainstream" effects researchers, gradually established itself as a credible and valuable alternative to limited-effects notions.

The Meaning-Making Trend in Mass Communication Theory

During the 1970s and 1980s there was increasing competition between postpositivist and critical cultural scholars in both the United States and Europe. During much of this period postpositivist researchers were at a disadvantage because limited-effects theories failed to address how media might be playing a role in the social movements that were obviously transforming society—the civil rights, anti-war, and feminist social movements. Additionally, they could not address the possible consequences of small but cumulative effects of exposure to popular media content (such as televised violence) or to advertising. Gradually, limited-effects notions were altered, partially because of pressures from critical cultural studies, but also because of the emergence of new communication technologies that forced a rethinking of traditional assumptions about how people use (and are used by) media. During the past three decades researchers have been challenged by the rise of powerful new media that clearly are altering how most of us live our lives and relate to others. Children are growing up in a world dominated by screens. To address this challenge postpositivists have developed new research strategies and methods (as explained in later chapters) that provide them with better measures of media influence and that have already identified a number of contexts in which media can have powerful effects (for example, Scheufele, 2000; Holbert, Garrett, & Gleason, 2010; Gurevitch, Coleman, & Blumler, 2010; Knobloch-Westerwick, 2015).

At the same time that postpositivist researchers moved toward a focus on use of media rather than media effects, critical cultural scholars advanced a similar but slightly different focus. Their research traced the way that cultural groups rather than individuals use media to serve group purposes. They studied how groups used various forms of media content, from music to news. They found that group members often band together to criticize and resist ideas being promoted by media (Alasuutari, 1999).

At the heart of the meaning-making trend in theory is a focus on a more or less active audience that uses media content to create meaningful experiences. Theorists recognize that important media effects often occur over longer time periods and these effects can be intended by users. People, as individuals or as groups, can make media serve certain purposes, such as using media to learn information, manage moods, promote group identity, or seek excitement. When audiences use media in these ways, they are intentionally working to induce meaningful experiences. The various meaning-making perspectives assert that when people use media to make meaning—when they are able to intentionally induce desired experiences—there often are significant results, some intended and others unintended. So when young adults stream billions of songs from the Net in order to alter or sustain a mood, there will be consequences. Or have you ever sought thrills from a horror movie and then been troubled afterward by disturbing visual images? Some consequences of media use are intended, but sometimes the results are unanticipated and unwanted. Factors that intrude into and disrupt meaning making can have unpredictable consequences. The trend in meaning-making theory implies that future research will focus on people's successes or failures in their efforts to make meaning using media, and on intended and unintended consequences. These consequences should be considered both from the point of view of individuals and from the point of view of groups or society.

REVITALIZED EFFECTS RESEARCH

The popularity of critical cultural studies, new postpositivist research methods, and the rise of meaning-making theory have intensified and renewed research on many different types of media effects. Postpositivist and critical cultural scholars are addressing a variety of important research questions involving these effects. Here are just a few that we will consider in later chapters. What are the short-term and long-term consequences of routine exposure to violent images and sexual behavior in video games? Are these effects similar to those found for televised violence, or are there important differences? How much do television commercials for fast food and blockbuster movie tie-ins for junk food contribute to our country's epidemic of obesity? Does media coverage of important issues such as war, elections, or the economy contribute to or diminish public understanding and democratic discourse? Have social media aided or subverted democratic discourse? To what extent are media responsible for political polarization and political incivility? How susceptible are we as a nation to Internet-based foreign propaganda such as the Russian propaganda transmitted during the 2016 election campaign? Is there a relationship between some kids' social media or video game use and poor school performance? Do sexy television shows or Internet-based pornography contribute to rising rates of teen pregnancy? Does political corruption grow and social conflict increase when local newspapers are forced to cut staff or close altogether? How much responsibility must teen and fashion magazines or YouTube videos take for young girls' dissatisfaction with their bodies? How much freedom of the press is too much—and who gets to decide? Are social media responsible for the rise of bullying? Have they increased social isolation or lowered adolescent self-esteem?

Even though these and a thousand similar questions serve to stimulate increased research and the development of better theories, they are also generating renewed controversy about the role of media. Critics use research findings to sometimes unfairly critique media, while defenders find ways to explain away problematic findings. Large-scale social media are being criticized for many of the same reasons that television was attacked in the 1960s. They're a plug-in drug without the plug. We must better understand why it has been so hard to come to a clear understanding of media influence and why it has been so easy to promote fallacious ideas about media. Media are powerful tools that can be used to generate profits and serve public interests. We need theory and research to use these tools wisely.

REVIEW OF LEARNING OBJECTIVES

• Define *legacy media*, *large-scale social media*, and *mass communication*.

Legacy media are older forms of mass media such as newspapers, magazines, radio, movies, and television. They are operated by large, complex organizations directly responsible for producing and distributing content using media technology. Like legacy media, large-scale social media are developed and controlled by complex organizations, but unlike legacy media, they are dependent on Internet technology for distribution of messages. In mass communication, senders—both legacy media and large-scale social media—are complex organizations that use standardized practices to distribute messages, actively promote themselves in order to attract as many audience members as possible, and strive to produce habitual, repeated exposure. They compete in a marketplace of attention. Big data is used to understand and dominate audience behavior. Audience members are geographically dispersed, aware that many others are consuming the messages, and exposed to content in a variety of ways but most often in a state of automaticity. Media users have limited or no control over media content production and distribution.

• Explain differences in the operation of the natural and social sciences.

Social science is sometimes controversial because it suggests causal relationships between things in the social world and people's attitudes, values, and behaviors. In the natural sciences, causal relationships are often easily visible and measurable. In the study of human behavior, however, they rarely are. Human behavior is quite difficult to quantify, often very complex, and often goal-oriented. Social science and human behavior make a problematic fit. The situation is even further complicated because social science itself is somewhat variable—it has many forms and can serve very different purposes.

- Describe the relationship between the scientific method and causality.

A causal relationship occurs when a given factor influences another, even by way of an intervening variable. The best, some scientists say, the only way to demonstrate causality is through the application of the scientific method, traditionally understood as identifying a problem, gathering data in hope of resolving the problem, offering a hypothesis, and testing that hypothesis.

- Define *theory*.

Because there are a number of ways to understand how communication functions in our complex world, theory is an organized set of concepts, explanations, and principles of some aspect of social life that explains a human event or behavior. Media theories are developed to understand the effects that media have on individuals and the role mass communication plays in their lives and in the world around them.

- Differentiate the four broad categories of mass communication theory—postpositive, cultural, critical, and normative theory—by their ontology, epistemology, and axiology.

Postpositivist theory is traditionally social scientific. Its ontology accepts that the world is knowable and measurable; its epistemology argues that knowledge is advanced through the systematic, logical search for regularities and causal relationships; its axiology is objective. Cultural theory is based on interpretation of texts. Its ontology says that there is no truly "real," measurable social reality; its epistemology relies on the subjective interaction between the observer and his or her community; and its axiology embraces the influence of researcher and theorist values. Critical theory, in seeking to challenge the status quo, studies the struggle—the dialectic—between society's structure and its agency. The product of that struggle is its ontology; its epistemology is emancipatory knowledge; its axiology is political and value-laden. Normative theory is designed to judge the operation of a given media system against a specific social system's norms or ideals so these values can be achieved. Its ontology argues that what is known is situational; its epistemology is based on comparative analysis; and its axiology is value-laden.

- Establish criteria for judging theory.

When evaluating postpositivist theory, ask how well does it explain the event, behavior, or relationship of interest? How well does it predict future events, behaviors, or relationships? How testable is it? How parsimonious is it? How practical or useful is it? When evaluating cultural theory, ask how much new or fresh insight into the event, behavior, or relationship of interest does it offer? How well does it clarify the values inherent in the interpretation? How much support does it generate among members of the scholarly community investigating the phenomenon of interest? How much aesthetic appeal does it have? When evaluating critical theory, ask the same questions as of cultural theory, but add how useful is the critique of the status quo? When evaluating normative theory, ask how stable and definitive are the ideal standards of operation against which the media system under study will be measured? What, and how powerful, are the economic, social, cultural, and political realities surrounding the actual operation of a system that must be considered in evaluating that performance? How much support does it generate among members of the scholarly community investigating a specific media system?

• Differentiate the four trends in media theory—the mass society and mass culture, media-effects, critical cultural, and meaning-making trends.

The mass society and mass culture trend emerged in mass communication's earliest years. Often rooted in nostalgia for a "golden age" that never existed, it anticipated a nightmare future in which social order is broken down, ruthless elites seize power, and individual freedom is lost. In the late 1930s and 1940s the media-effects theory trend emerged. It viewed media as having little power to directly influence people; media's dominant effect was to reinforce existing social trends and strengthen the status quo. The critical cultural trend, in which researchers studied how members of various subgroups used media and assessed how this use might serve group interests (cultural theory) or might lead people to develop ideas that supported dominant elites (critical theory), emerged in the 1970s and 1980s. The current meaning-making trend focuses on a more or less active audience that uses media content to create meaningful experiences and recognizes that important media effects often occur over longer time periods and these effects can be intended by users.

CRITICAL THINKING QUESTIONS

1. Can you think of any social science findings on media that you reject? What are they? On what grounds do you base your skepticism? Can you separate your personal experience with the issue from your judgment of the scientific evidence?

2. How do you interact with and use large-scale social media and legacy media? Can you identify effects that have occurred because of that use? Do you encounter fake news on social media, and how do you deal with it? Have you checked other news sources or warned your friends about it? Can you offer any possible negative effects to balance any positive effects that might have occurred from any of your media use?

3. How skilled are you at making meaning from media content? How media literate do you think you are? Do you often make meaning from content that is markedly different from that of your friends, or do you share their experience and interpretations of media? If so, why do you suppose this happens?

KEY TERMS

grand theory	interpersonal communication
legacy media	social scientists
large-scale social media	causality
mass communication	causal relationship
automaticity	scientific method
marketplace of attention	hypothesis
big data	empirical
mediated communication	third-person effect

theory
ontology
epistemology
axiology
postpositivist theory
cultural theory
hermeneutic theory
intersubjective agreement
social hermeneutics
text
epistemic values
nonepistemic values
bracket
cultural theory
critical theory
structure

agency
dialectic
capitalists
normative media theory
elites
mass society theory
penny press
yellow journalism
limited-effects theory
Red Scare
reductionism
neo-Marxists
British cultural studies
critical cultural theory
deterministic assumptions
cultural criticism

GLOSSARY

grand theory: Theory designed to describe and explain all aspects of a given phenomenon

legacy media: Mass media such as newspapers, radio, movies, and television that use older forms of technology to routinely attract large audiences by providing specific services

large-scale social media: Media that use Internet technology to routinely attract large audiences by providing many services while collecting information about users

mass communication: A large-scale organization's use of a communications technology and active promotion of itself to attract as many audience members as possible for habitual repeated exposures

automaticity: A state of media exposure in which media content is processed with little or no critical awareness or reflection

marketplace of attention: Audience attention is attracted and held by media so they can sell this attention to advertisers

big data: In media research, massive datasets created by measuring social media users' online behavior

mediated communication: Communication between a few or many people that employs a technology as a medium

interpersonal communication: Communication between two or a few people, typically face to face

social scientists: Scientists who examine relationships among phenomena in the human or social world

causality: When a given factor influences another, even by way of an intervening variable

causal relationship: When the alterations in a particular variable under specific conditions always produce the same effect in another variable

scientific method: A search for truth through accurate observation and interpretation of fact

hypothesis: A testable prediction about some event

empirical: Capable of being verified or disproved by observation

third-person effect: The idea that "media affect others, but not me"

theory: Any organized set of concepts, explanations, and principles of some aspect of human experience

ontology: The nature of reality, what is knowable

epistemology: How knowledge is created and expanded

axiology: The proper role of values in research and theory building

postpositivist theory: Theory based on empirical observation guided by the scientific method

intersubjective agreement: When members of a research community independently arrive at similar conclusions about a given social phenomenon

cultural theory: Theory seeking to understand contemporary cultures by analyzing the structure and content of their communication

hermeneutic theory: The study of understanding, especially by interpreting action and text

text: Any product of social interaction that serves as a source of understanding or meaning

social hermeneutics: Theory seeking to understand how those in an observed social situation interpret their own lot in that situation

critical theory: Theory seeking transformation of a dominant social order in order to achieve desired values

structure: In critical theory, the social world's rules, norms, and beliefs

agency: In critical theory, how humans behave and interact within the structure

dialectic: In critical theory, the ongoing struggle between agency and structure

capitalists: Economic elites whose power is based on the profits they generate and then reinvest

cultural theory: A form of hermeneutic theory that focuses on how communication shapes and is shaped by social groups

normative media theory: Theory explaining how a media system should be structured and operate in order to conform to or realize a set of ideal social values

epistemic values: High standards in the conduct of research and theory development

nonepistemic values: The place of emotion, morals, and ethics in research and theory development

bracket: In interpretive theory, setting values aside

elites: People occupying elevated or privileged positions in a social system

mass society theory: Perspective on Western, industrial society that attributes an influential but often negative role to media

penny press: Newspapers that sold for one penny and earned profits through newsstand sales and advertising

yellow journalism: Newspaper reporting catering to working and other lower social class audiences using simple, often sensational content

limited-effects theory: View of media as having little ability to directly influence people. The dominant effect of media is to reinforce existing social trends and strengthen the status quo

Red Scare: Period in US history, late 1950s to early 1960s, in which basic freedoms were threatened by searches for "Reds," or communists, in media and government

reductionism: Reducing complex communication processes and social phenomena to little more than narrow propositions generated from small-scale investigations

neo-Marxism: Social theory asserting that media enable dominant social elites to maintain their power

British cultural studies: Perspective focusing on mass media and their role in cultural groups and in promoting a public forum in which definitions of the social world are negotiated

critical cultural theory: An integration of critical theory and cultural theory first attempted by British cultural studies scholars

deterministic assumptions: Assumptions that media have powerful, direct effects

cultural criticism: Collection of perspectives concerned with the cultural disputes and the ways communication perpetuates domination of one group over another

Establishing the Terms of the Debate over Media: The First Trend in Mass Communication Theory—Mass Society and Mass Culture Theories

In India, mobs beat to death and lynched dozens of people—men, women, and toddlers—convinced, by fake and photoshopped posts on Facebook-owned WhatsApp, that their children were in danger of being stolen. In Brazil, false WhatsApp messages warned that the government-mandated yellow-fever vaccine was dangerous, leading people to avoid the life-saving treatment (Dwoskin & Gowen, 2018). Other phony social media posts, primarily from agents of the Russian government, were implicated in spreading chaos and racial and social discord in the United States during the 2016 presidential election in hope of securing the election of Russia's preferred candidate, Donald Trump (Apuzzo & LaFraniere, 2018), efforts that continued through the 2018 mid-term elections and into 2019 and were expanded in an effort to disrupt elections in other countries as well (Frenkel, Conger, & Roose, 2019).

These were not the only controversies swirling around social media at this time. Chamath Palihapitiya, one-time Facebook vice president, and Sean Parker, Facebook's founding president, independently admitted that the site was created expressly to foster addiction. Mr. Parker admitted that he and "other early Facebookers built the platform to consume as much of your time and conscious attention as possible," employing a "system of users posting content and receiving likes as 'a social-validation feedback loop'" (as cited in Kircher, 2017). Mr. Palihapitiya described the site's "short-term, dopamine-driven feedback loops" as "destroying how society works" (as cited in Gelles, 2018, p. B1). The American Psychiatric Association had several years before added "Internet addiction disorder" to the American *Diagnostic and Statistical Manual of Mental Disorders*, its authoritative list of recognized mental illnesses. Online video games, too, came under scrutiny; in 2018 the World Health Organization added "Internet gaming disorder" to its manual of psychiatric diagnoses (Carey, 2018).

Technology-driven hate, political intrigue, and addiction are not the only media controversies of our times. Arguing that their State Constitution requires "government to protect the virtue and purity of the home," legislators on the Idaho House State Affairs Committee passed a 2013 resolution asking the federal government to prohibit conversations about and the portrayal, even implied, of premarital sex on television dramas, comedies, reality and talk shows, and commercials in order to, in the words of Representative Darrell Bolz, "stand up for the morality of what is best for the citizens of Idaho" (as cited in KBOI, 2013). Elsewhere, researchers at the National Institutes of Health discovered that 50 minutes of cellphone use could alter normal brain function (Parker-Pope, 2011); the scientific journal *Pediatrics* published a report tying teens' consumption of online and other media violence to subsequent "seriously violent behavior" (Ybarra et al., 2008) and another report linking exposure to sexual content on television to teen pregnancy (Chandra et al., 2008); the journal *Archives of Pediatrics & Adolescent Medicine* presented evidence of lagging language development in children as a result of infant television viewing (Bryner, 2009); and *Circulation: Journal of the American Heart Association* published research demonstrating that every daily hour spent watching television is linked to an 18% greater risk of dying from heart disease, an 11% greater risk of all causes of death, and a 9% greater risk of death from cancer (Dunstan et al., 2010). There is also evidence that consuming Disney movies, television shows, and marketing increases the likelihood that young boys and girls approve of girls adhering to traditionally feminine, subservient behaviors (Maldonado, 2017); that with the release of the Netflix hit *13 Reasons Why* (about teen suicide) "the overall suicide rate among 10- to 17-year-olds increased significantly" (Bridge et al., 2019); and watching the cable channel HGTV made the hanging of barn doors inside the home an acceptable interior design option (Buckman, 2018).

On the more optimistic side, research shows that women who watched the television show *The X-Files* were more likely to pursue careers in science, technology, engineering, and math (Ifeanyi, 2018); that when members of majority groups "meet" members of minority groups in the media, they demonstrate lower levels of real-world prejudice (Schiappa, Gregg, & Hewes, 2005); that fictional television narratives can improve viewers' health-related knowledge, attitudes, and behaviors (Murphy, Frank, Chatterjee, & Baezconde-Garbanati, 2013); and that well-designed prosocial video games can be used to reduce people's propensity for reckless and risky driving (Greitemeyer, 2013).

Fake social media accounts lead to murder, increased incidence of disease, and disrupted elections? Social media and video games are addictive? Watching TV and movies can influence career choices, foster sexist notions, and increase interest in suicide? Media can reduce prejudice, improve people's health, short-circuit reckless driving, and change the inside of people's homes? Cellphones mess with our brains? Watching television and going online creates violent kids, gets teens pregnant, stunts language acquisition, and increases the risk of death? Some say yes; some say no.

For more than a century now, society has debated the role of media. Conservatives lament the decline of values sped by a "liberal media elite." Liberals fear the power of a media system more in tune with the conservative values of its corporate owners than of its audiences. School boards and city councils debate installing filtering software on school and library computers, pitting advocates of free expression against proponents of child protection. Controversial rappers are celebrated on television while their music is banned on scores of radio stations because it is considered racist and misogynistic. Online storing of our every computer keystroke robs us of our privacy, and our cell-phones become tracking devices for use by companies and government alike.

Media industries promise their sponsors significant impact for their advertising dollars but claim their fare has little or no influence when challenged on issues of violence, gender stereotyping, and drugs; nonetheless, the advertising and marketing industries annually take in more than $1.3 trillion in revenues globally (40% of that total in the United States; Mandese, 2018). Why would anyone bother to spend such huge sums of money on media if they have little or no impact? Why would the **First Amendment** to our Constitution, our "First Freedom," protect the expression of media industries if they have no influence? Why do we grant media outlets and their person-nel special protection if their contributions to our society are so insignificant?

LEARNING OBJECTIVES

After studying this chapter you should be able to

- Explain the social, cultural, and political conditions that led to the development of mass society theory and propaganda theory.
- Place the role of the mass media in scholars' conceptions of those theories.
- Understand mass society and propaganda theorists' perceptions of the audience and its ability to interact with mass media.
- Explain why and in what form contemporary articulations of mass society theory and propaganda theory exist.
- List mass society theory's assumptions about media and audiences.
- Detail some early examples of mass society theory.
- Explain the details of behaviorism, Freudianism, and the propaganda theories of Harold Lasswell and Walter Lippmann, as well as those of John Dewey's alternative perspective.

OVERVIEW

Clearly a lot is at stake when we debate the role of media and develop and test theory to guide that conversation. Controversy over media influence can have far-reaching consequences for society and for media institutions. In this chapter we trace the rise of mass society theory, a perspective on society that emerged at the end of the 19th cen-tury and was especially influential through the first half of the 20th century. It is an all-encompassing perspective on Western industrial society that attributes an influential and largely negative role to media. It views media as having the power to profoundly shape our perceptions of the social world and to manipulate our actions, often without our conscious awareness. This theory argues that media influence must be controlled. The strategies for control, however, are as varied as the theorists who offer them.

This chapter's second major section will consider the **propaganda** theories that were developed after World War I and that share many of mass society theory's concerns and assumptions. Both are examples of what we have labeled the mass society/mass culture trend in media theory. We will discuss how political propaganda was initially used to manipulate mass audiences and then consider some of the theories developed to understand and control it. With the normative theories discussed in the next chapter, these were the first true mass communication theories. Mass society theory saw media as only one of many disruptive forces. In propaganda theories, however, media became the focus of attention. Propaganda theorists specifically analyzed media content and speculated about its ability to influence people's thoughts and actions. They wanted to understand and explain the ability of messages to persuade and convert thousands or even millions of individuals to extreme viewpoints and engage in seemingly irrational actions.

Propaganda commanded the attention of early media theorists because it threatened to undermine the very foundation of the US political system and of democratic governments everywhere. By the late 1930s many, if not most, American leaders were convinced that democracy wouldn't survive if extremist political propaganda was allowed to be freely distributed. But censorship of propaganda meant imposing significant limitations on that essential principle of Western democracy, communication freedom. This posed a terrible dilemma. Strict censorship might undermine democracy just as corrosively as would propaganda.

Even though the threat of propaganda was great, some propaganda theorists believed there could be a silver lining to this cloud. If we could find a way to harness the power of propaganda to promote good and just ideals, then we would not only survive its threat but have a tool to help build a better social order. This was the promise of what came to be called **white propaganda**—a top-down communication strategy that used propaganda techniques to fight "bad" propaganda and promote those objectives elites considered good. After World War II these white propaganda techniques provided a basis for the development of strategic (promotional) communication methods that are widely used today in advertising, political communication, and public relations. In fact, propaganda theory is experiencing a resurgence of interest in part because many contemporary observers argue that the techniques used in modern promotional efforts appear to be even more effective in our contemporary world of near-universal Internet access and corporate media ownership (Bajomi-Lázár, & Horváth, 2013; Laitinen & Rakos, 1997). Critics also argue that the rise of modern forms of populism seems linked to propaganda and the new forms of media that distribute it (Mudde & Kaltwasser, 2017; Moffitt, 2016).

The social world in which propaganda was originally widely practiced and in which propaganda theory evolved was especially turbulent. Industrialization and urbanization were reshaping both Europe and the United States. Important books of the time had titles like Ortega y Gasset's 1930 *The Revolt of the Masses*, Elton Mayo's 1933 *Human Problems of an Industrial Civilization*, and Erich Fromm's 1941 *Escape from Freedom*. During this era many new forms of technology were developed and quickly disseminated. Electricity became available in cities and later in rural areas, and that opened the way for the spread of thousands of electrical appliances. This technological change, however, occurred with little consideration for its environmental, social, or psychological impact. Social change could be rationalized as progress, but a high price was paid—workers were brutalized, vast urban slums were created, and huge tracts of wilderness were ravaged.

Media were among the many technologies that shaped and were shaped by this modern era. An industrial social order had great need for the fast and efficient distribution of information. There was need to command and control factories and vast corporate enterprises that spread across the continent. The advantages of new media like the telegraph and telephone were soon recognized, and each new communication technology was quickly adopted—first by businesses and then by the public.

In the mid and late 19th century, large urban populations' growing demand for cheap media content drove the development of several new media: the penny press, the nickel magazine, and the dime novel. High-speed printing presses and Linotype machines made it practical to mass produce the printed word at very low cost. Urban newspapers boomed all along the East Coast and in major trading centers across the United States. Newspaper circulation wars broke out in many large cities and led to the development of sensationalistic journalism that seriously challenged the norms and values of most readers. But substitute today's Internet, social media, virtual reality, and highly partisan news outlets for those traditional media, and replace the brutalization of workers and the spread of slums with the contemporary loss of reliable manufacturing jobs (Guilford, 2018), the decline of the middle class (Krause & Sawhill, 2018), severe income disparity between societies' haves and have-nots (Galbraith, 2019), and constant war and political turmoil and its resulting displacement of millions of people (Lind, 2018), and you'll have the second reason propaganda theory is again of interest to social science researchers.

MASS SOCIETY CRITICS AND THE DEBATE OVER MEDIA

Changes in media industries often increase the pressure on other social institutions to change. Instability in the way we routinely communicate can have unsettling consequences for all other institutions. Some leaders of these institutions resent external pressures and are reluctant to alter their way of doing things. Consider how the widespread use of the Internet and smartphones has forced alterations in the way we do many routine and important things. The changes associated with new media in the first half of the last century were far more disruptive because people were less experienced at dealing with communication changes. Not surprisingly, conservative critics interpreted the rise of the media industries as threatening to subvert all other social institutions, including politics, religion, business, education, and the military. Social critics even accused media of profoundly altering families—the most basic social institution of all. Many of these worrisome views are consistent with mass society theory. This venerable theory has a long and checkered history. Mass society theory is actually many different theories sharing some common assumptions about the role of media and society. You can judge for yourself the worthiness of the criticism that accompanied the arrival of some of the media we now enjoy by reading the box entitled "Fearful Reactions to New Media."

Assumptions of Mass Society Theory

Mass society theory first appeared late in the 19th century as traditional social elites struggled to make sense of the disruptive consequences of modernization. Some (for example, the landed aristocracy, small-town shopkeepers, schoolteachers, the clergy, and upper-class politicians) lost power or were overwhelmed in their efforts to deal with social problems. For them the mass media were symbolic of all that was wrong with modern society. They viewed the mass newspapers of the yellow journalism era as gigantic, monopolistic enterprises employing unethical practices to pander to semiliterate

THINKING ABOUT THEORY

FEARFUL REACTIONS TO NEW MEDIA

The introduction of each new mass medium of the 20th century was greeted with derision, skepticism, fear, and sometimes silliness. Here is a collection of the thinking of the times that welcomed movies, talkies, radio, and television (all from Davis, 1976). Can you find examples of mass society theory's most obvious characteristics—the conceit that the elite way is the right way and condescension toward others?

Once you have read through these examples, go online and find similar dire predictions about the Internet and the Web. No doubt you've already read or heard concerns about Internet addiction, loss of parental authority, child pornography, online gambling, sexting, the loss of community, reduced attention spans, violent and offensive online gaming, privacy invasion, and identity theft. Can you identify other concerns associated with the coming of the new digital communication technologies?

Movies and Talkies

When you first reflect that in New York City alone, on a Sunday, 500,000 people go to moving picture shows, a majority of them perhaps children, and that in the poorer quarters of town every teacher testifies that the children now save their pennies for picture shows instead of candy, you cannot dismiss canned drama with a shrug of contempt. It is a big factor in the lives of the masses, to be reckoned with, if possible to be made better, if used for good ends. Eighty percent of present-day theatrical audiences in this country are canned drama audiences. Ten million people attended professional baseball games in America in 1908. Four million people attend moving pictures theaters, it is said, every day. $50,000,000 are invested in the industry. Chicago has over 300 theaters, New York 300, St. Louis 205, Philadelphia 186, even conservative Boston boasts more than 30. Almost 190 miles of film are unrolled on the screens of America's canned drama theaters every day in the year. Here is an industry to be controlled, an influence to be reckoned with.

Source: *American Magazine,*
September, 1909, p. 498.

And if the speech recorded in the dialogue (of talking pictures) is vulgar or ugly, its potentialities for lowering the speech standard of the country are almost incalculable. The fact that it is likely to be heard by the less discriminating portion of the public operates to increase its evil effects; for among the regular attendants at moving picture theaters there are to be found large groups from among our foreign-born population, to whom it is really vitally important that they hear only the best speech.

Source: *Commonweal,*
April 10, 1929, p. 653.

Radio

In general, one criterion must be kept in mind: the radio should do what the teacher cannot do; it ought not to do what the teacher can do better. However radio may develop, I cannot conceive of the time when a good teacher will not continue to be the most important object in any classroom.

Source: *Education,* December 1936, p. 217.

Is radio to become a chief arm of education? Will the classroom be abolished, and the child of the future stuffed with facts as he sits at home or even as he walks about the streets with his portable receiving set in his pocket?

Source: *Century,* June 1924, p. 149.

Television

Seeing constant brutality, viciousness and unsocial acts results in hardness, intense selfishness, even in mercilessness, proportionate to the amount of exposure and its play on the native temperament of the child. Some cease to show resentment to insults, to indignities, and even cruelty toward helpless old people, to women, and other children.

Source: *New Republic,*
November 1, 1954, p. 12.

Here, in concept at least, was the most magnificent of all forms of communication. Here was the supreme triumph of invention, the dream of the ages—something that could bring directly into

(Continued)

THINKING ABOUT THEORY (Continued)

the home a moving image fused with sound-reproducing action, language, and thought without the loss of measurable time. Here was the magic eye that could bring the wonders of entertainment, information, and education into the living room. Here was a tool for the making of a more enlightened democracy than the world had ever seen. Yet out of the wizardry of the television tube has come such an assault against the human mind, such a mobilized attack on the imagination, such an invasion against good taste as no other communications medium has known, not excepting the motion picture or radio itself.

Source: *Saturday Review,*
December 24, 1949, p. 20.

mass audiences. Leaders in education and religion resented media's power to attract readers using content they considered highly objectionable, vulgar, even sinful (Brantlinger, 1983). "A new situation has arisen throughout the world," wrote the editors of *Public Opinion Quarterly* in 1937, "created by the spread of literacy among the people and the miraculous improvement of the means of communication. Always the opinion of relatively small publics have been a prime force in political life, but now, for the first time in history, we are confronted nearly everywhere by *mass* opinion as the final determinant of political, and economic action" (as cited in Beniger, 1987, pp. S46–S47).

Envy, discontent, and outright fear were often at the roots of mass society notions. Note the use of the words "we are confronted." Mass society theory critic Edward Shils (1962) mocked the thinking of the threatened elites. In their view, he wrote, "Power is concentrated in this society, and much of the power takes the form of manipulation of the mass through the media of mass communication. Civic spirit is poor, local loyalties are few, primordial solidarity is virtually non-existent. There is no individuality, only a restless and frustrated egoism" (p. 46). Despite Shils's disdain, this understanding of the modern world undergirded the development of a theory that is both radically conservative and potentially revolutionary. It fears the emergence of a new type of social order—a mass society—that would fundamentally and tragically transform the social world. To prevent this, technological change generally and changes in media specifically must be controlled or even reversed. A conservative effort must be made to restore an idealized, older social order, or revolutionary action must be taken so that technology and media are brought under elite control and used to forge a new and better social order.

The mass society theories that were developed in the last century make several basic assumptions about individuals, the role of media, and the nature of social change. As you read about these assumptions, think about whether you have recently heard any similar arguments. They may have been altered to fit contemporary society, but they exist. Here we list the assumptions and then discuss each in some detail:

1. The media are a powerful societal force that can subvert essential norms and values and thus undermine the social order. To deal with this threat media must be brought under elite control.
2. Media are able to directly influence the minds of average people, transforming their views of the social world.
3. Once people's thinking is transformed by media, all sorts of bad long-term consequences are likely to result—not only bringing ruin to individual lives but also creating social problems on a vast scale.

4. Average people are vulnerable to media because in mass society they are cut off and isolated from traditional social institutions that previously protected them from manipulation.
5. The social chaos initiated by media will likely be resolved by establishment of a totalitarian social order.
6. Mass media inevitably debase higher forms of culture, bringing about a general decline in civilization.

The first assumption is that the media subvert essential norms and values and threaten the social order. Thus, elite control of media is necessary. Opponents of the newly emerging media consistently proposed turning their control over to elites who would preserve or transform the social order. In Europe this argument won out during the 1920s, and broadcast media were placed under the control of government agencies. These efforts may have produced laudatory results in some countries—for example, in the establishment of the much-admired British Broadcasting Corporation—but it had disastrous consequences elsewhere—for example, when Hitler narrowly won election in Germany. His Nazi Party gradually turned radio and movies into effective propaganda tools that helped consolidate his power. In the United States many schemes were proposed in the 1920s that would have turned control of broadcasting over to churches, schools, or government agencies. Ultimately a compromise was reached, and a free-enterprise broadcasting industry was created under the more or less watchful eye of a government agency—the Federal Radio Commission, which later evolved into the Federal Communications Commission.

But why were the media so dangerous to society? What made them threatening? How were they able to subvert traditional norms and values? A second assumption is that media have the power to reach out and directly influence the minds of average people so that their thinking is transformed (Davis, 1976). Media can act independently of all the other things influencing people in their daily lives. This is known as the **direct-effects assumption**, and it has been hotly debated since the 1940s. Sociologist James Carey (1996) offered this accurate articulation of mass society theory's view of the influence of mass communication: "The media collectively, but in particularly the newer, illiterate media of radio and film, possessed extraordinary power to shape the beliefs and conduct of ordinary men and women" (p. 22). Although each version of mass society theory has its own notion about the type of direct influence different media may have, all versions stress how dangerous this influence can be and the extreme vulnerability of average people to immediate media-induced changes.

The third assumption is that once media transform people's thinking, all sorts of bad long-term consequences result—not only bringing ruin to individual lives but also creating social problems on a vast scale (Marcuse, 1941). Over the years virtually every major social problem the United States has confronted has been linked in some way to media—from prostitution and delinquency to urban violence and drug usage to the reemergence of open White supremacy in the United States and ultra-nationalism and xenophobia in Europe. Teenage delinquents have seen too many gangster movies. Disaffected housewives watch too many soap operas; teenage girls hate their bodies because of beauty magazines; and drug addicts have taken too seriously the underlying message in most advertising: The good life is achieved through consumption of a product, not by hard work.

Mass society theory's fourth assumption is that average people are vulnerable to media because they have been cut off and isolated from traditional social institutions that previously protected them from manipulation. As Dwight Macdonald wrote in 1953, "The mass man is a solitary atom, uniform with and undifferentiated from thousands and millions of other atoms who go to make up 'the lonely crowd,' as David Riesman well calls American society" (p. 14).

Mass society theorists tended to idealize the past and hold romantic visions of what life must have been like in medieval villages in Europe or in small rural towns on the American frontier. They assumed that these older social orders nurtured and protected people within communities whose culture gave meaning to their lives. Although these views have some validity (most social orders have some redeeming qualities), they fail to consider the severe limitations of traditional social orders. Most premodern social orders limited individual development and creativity for most community members. People were routinely compelled to do the jobs their parents and grandparents had done. People learned specific social roles based on the accident of being born in a certain place at a certain time. The freedom to develop in ways that people find meaningful was unknown.

Yet despite evidence that the public was not nearly as isolated and atomized as mass society theorists believed (Lang & Lang, 2009), these claims about the vulnerability to manipulation of isolated individuals are compelling. These arguments have been restated in endless variations with every revolution in media technology. They assert that when people are stripped of the protective cocoon provided by a traditional community, they necessarily turn to media for the guidance and reassurance previously provided by their communities. Thus, when people left sheltered rural communities and entered big cities, media could suddenly provide communication that replaces messages from social institutions that have been left behind. Media can become the trusted and valued sources of messages about politics, entertainment, religion, education, and on and on. Under these conditions people tend to learn new information and develop different ideas. But were people removed from rural communities actually so vulnerable to media? As you will see in Chapter 4, young men drafted into the military when the US entered WWII were resistant to propaganda that tried to counter their well-developed beliefs.

The fifth assumption is that the social chaos initiated by media will be resolved by establishment of a totalitarian social order (Davis, 1976). This assumption was developed during the 1930s and flourished at the time of the war against fascism, reaching its peak of popularity in the United States during the witch hunt for communists in government and media of the 1950s. Mass society is envisioned as an inherently chaotic, highly unstable form of social order that will inevitably collapse and then be replaced by totalitarianism. Mass society, with its teeming hordes of isolated individuals, must give way to an even worse form of society—highly regimented, centrally controlled, totalitarian society. Thus, to the extent that media promote the rise of mass society, they pave the way for totalitarianism.

Throughout the 20th century, fear of the spread of totalitarianism grew in most democracies. For many it symbolized everything that was loathsome and evil, but others saw it as the "wave of the future." Fascist and communist advocates of totalitarianism dismissed democracy as well-meaning but impractical because average people could never effectively govern themselves—they were too apathetic and ignorant to do that. Even people with a desire to be politically active simply don't have the time and energy to be involved on a day-to-day basis. The masses must be led by a totalitarian leader who can weld them into a powerful force to achieve great things. Cultivation of individuality leads to inefficiency, jealousy, and conflict. Democracies were perceived as inherently weak, unable to resist the inevitable rise of charismatic, strong, determined leaders. Across Europe, in Latin America, and in Asia, fledgling democracies faltered and collapsed as the economic Great Depression deepened. Fascism in Germany and communism in Russia provided examples of what could be accomplished by totalitarian rule. The people could be led to rise from the pit of lost wars and economic depressions to forge seemingly prosperous and highly productive social orders. The United States was not immune to totalitarian appeals. Radical political movements arose, and their influence spread rapidly. In several states right-wing extremists were elected to political office. Pro-fascist groups held gigantic public rallies to demonstrate their support for Hitler. The supremacist and anti-Semitic writings of automaker Henry Ford were translated and published in Nazi Germany. Radio propagandists like Father Charles Coughlin achieved notoriety and acceptance. Radicals fought for control of labor unions. The thousand-year Reich envisioned by Hitler seemed a more realistic outcome than the survival of democracy in modern nation-states.

Why was totalitarianism so successful? Why was it sweeping the world just as the new mass media of radio and movies were becoming increasingly prominent? Was there a connection? Were radio and movies to blame? Many mass society theorists believed they were. Without these media, they thought, dictators wouldn't have gained popularity or consolidated their power. They argued that radio and later television were ideally suited for reaching out into homes and directly persuading average people so that vast numbers of them could be molded into a regimented, cohesive society. Movies were able to communicate powerful images that instilled the positive and negative associations those dictators desired.

What these critics failed to note is that when the Nazis or communists were most successful, average people had strong reasons for *wanting* to believe the promises about jobs and personal security made by extremists. Personal freedom has little value when people are starving and a wheelbarrow full of money won't buy a loaf of bread. The success of Nazi or communist propaganda was also dependent on silencing critics and shutting down media that provided competing viewpoints. Hitler didn't gain popularity quickly. He methodically suppressed competing individuals and groups over a period of years, not days. He effectively used radio and movies, but he had at his disposal all the other weapons of suppression typically available to a ruthless demagogue. But viewing Hitler from across the Atlantic, American elites saw only what they most feared—a demagogue relying mostly on media to achieve and hold power.

Totalitarianism was the biggest fear aroused by mass society theorists, but they also focused attention on a subtler form of societal corruption—mass culture. The sixth and final assumption of mass society theory, then, is that mass media inevitably debase higher forms of culture, bringing about a general decline in civilization. Mass culture is "a spreading ooze . . . a parasitic, a cancerous growth on High Culture. . . . It threatens High Culture by its sheer pervasiveness, its brutal, overwhelming *quantity*" (all from Macdonald, 1953). To understand this criticism you must understand the perspective held by Western cultural and educational elites during the previous two centuries. In the decades following the **Enlightenment** (an 18th-century European social and philosophical movement stressing rational thought and progress through science), these elites saw themselves as responsible for nurturing and promulgating a superior form of culture, high culture, not only within their own societies but also around the world. For example, British and other colonial elites believed they were carrying the light of civilization to the people they conquered in much the same way American elites viewed their "enlightenment" of Native Americans.

In retrospect the high culture perspective suffers from some serious limitations. The literary canon, one of the tools used to promote high culture, consisted mostly of works written by White, male, Western, Anglo-Saxon, and Protestant authors. Symphony music, ballet, and opera don't communicate effectively outside of the urban, higher class culture in which they developed. And as for those colonialized peoples, they had no say in the replacement of their local cultures by those of their conquerors. For defenders of high culture, mass media represented an insidious, corrosive force in society—one that threatened their influence by popularizing ideas and activities they considered trivial or demeaning. Rather than glorify gangsters (as movies did in the 1930s), why not praise great educators or religious leaders? Why pander to popular taste—why not seek to raise it to higher levels? Give audiences Shakespeare, not Charlie Chaplin. Why give people what they want instead of giving them what they need? Why trivialize great art by turning it into cartoons (as Disney did in the 1930s)? Mass society theorists raised these questions—and had long and overly abstract answers for them.

EARLY EXAMPLES OF MASS SOCIETY THEORY

Now we'll summarize a few of the early examples of mass society theory. This set of theories is by no means complete. The ideas we describe and discuss were influential at the time they were written and provided important reference points for later theorists. It is important to remember, too, that even where not specifically mentioned, the emerging mass media were clearly implicated in most examples.

In the latter chapters of this book we will consider important new theories that articulate innovative thinking about popular culture—including ideas about the influence of US-style mass entertainment in other nations. These inevitably draw on older notions about mass society and mass culture, but most reject the simplistic assumptions and criticisms of earlier eras. These newer theories no longer accept elite high culture as the standard against which all others must be measured. Current criticism tends to focus on the inherent biases of media when it comes to developing new forms of culture. Media are no longer necessarily seen as corrupting and degrading high culture. Rather, they are viewed as limiting or disrupting cultural development. They promote forms of culture that attract attention so that attention can be sold to advertisers. Media don't subvert culture, but they do play a major and sometimes counterproductive role in cultural change. Critics of Facebook usually don't argue that it degrades culture, but they do present important evidence of its ability to be disruptive.

Gemeinschaft and Gesellschaft

Among the originators of mass society notions was a German sociologist, Ferdinand Tönnies. He sought to explain the critical difference between earlier forms of social organization and European society as it existed in the late 19th century. In an 1887 book, *Gemeinschaft und Gesellschaft*, he proposed a simple dichotomy—***gemeinschaft***, or folk community, and ***gesellschaft***, or modern industrial society. In folk communities people were bound together by strong ties of family, by tradition, and by rigid social roles—basic social institutions were very powerful. *Gemeinschaft* "consisted of a dense network of personal relationships based heavily on kinship and the direct, face-to-face contact that occurs in a small, closed village. Norms were largely unwritten, and individuals were bound to one another in a web of mutual interdependence that touched all aspects of life" (Fukuyama, 1999, p. 57). In addition "a collective has the character of a *gemeinschaft* insofar as its members think of the group as a gift of nature created by a supernatural will" (Martindale, 1960, p. 83). Although folk communities had important strengths as well as serious limitations, Tönnies emphasized the former. He argued that most people yearn for the order and meaning provided by folk communities. They often find life in modern societies troublesome and meaningless. *Gesellschaft*, Tönnies (1887/1922) wrote, exists as "a circle of people who, as a community, live and reside peacefully near one another but are not quintessentially connected but substantially detached and, while on the one hand they remain connected despite their detachment, they remain, on the other, detached despite their connectedness" (p. 39).

Gesellschaft represents "the framework of laws and other formal regulations that characterized large, urban industrial societies. Social relationships were more formalized and impersonal; individuals did not depend on one another for support . . . and were therefore much less morally obligated to one another" (Fukuyama, 1999, pp. 57–58). As such, people were bound together by relatively weak social institutions based on rational choices rather than tradition. Naturally it was the established elites (the traditional wielders of power and the most vocal champions of mass society theory) who stood to lose the most influence in the move from *gemeinschaft* to *gesellschaft*, as "average" people came to depend less on their influence and more on formalized and more objectively applied rules and laws. For example, when you take a job, you sign a formal contract based on your personal decision. You don't sign it because you are bound by family tradition to work for a certain employer. You make a more or less rational choice.

Over the years media have been continually accused of breaking down folk communities (*gemeinschaft*) and encouraging the development of amoral, weak social institutions (*gesellschaft*). The late Reverend Jerry Falwell, founder of the Moral Majority, and fellow televangelist Pat Robertson reflected this view in 2001 when they charged that the September 11 terrorist attacks on the World Trade Center and the Pentagon were the products not of Islamic radicalism but of the "American cultural elite's" systematic subversion of traditional family and social values (Adbusters, 2002); the 2016 mass murder of 50 people in the Orlando, Florida, Pulse nightclub was the result not of easy access to guns and scant societal attention to mental illness but of America's embrace of homosexuality, according to Tennessee pastor Jesse Price (Howard, 2016); and according to Ohio State Representative Candice Keller, the El Paso and Dayton mass shootings within 13 hours of one another in August 2019, killing 31 people, were not products of White supremacy or easy access to guns, they were the result of the acceptance of "drag queen advocates," the "breakdown of the traditional American family," and "acceptance of recreational marijuana" (Vaglanos, 2019, para. 4). We are all familiar with popular television shows that prominently feature unwed couples living together, same-sex unions, and unwed mothers bearing children. Do these programs merely reflect social changes, or are they somehow responsible for them? As we'll see throughout this text, there is no simple answer to this question.

Mechanical and Organic Solidarity

In his 1893 *Division of Labor in Society*, translated into English in 1933, French sociologist Émile Durkheim offered a theory with the same dichotomy as that of Tönnies, but with a fundamentally different interpretation of modern social orders. Durkheim compared folk communities to machines in which people were little more than cogs. These machines were very ordered and durable, but people were forced by a collective consensus to perform traditional social roles. Think for a moment about all the family names used today that are derived from professions: Farmer, Taylor, Hunter, Goldsmith, Forester, Toepfer, and Shumacher (German for Potter and Shoemaker). Your name was, literally, what you were: John the Smith. Or consider the many family names that end in "son" or "sen." People were identified by their father's name: Peterson is Peter's son. People were bound by this consensus to one another like the parts of a great engine, by **mechanical solidarity**.

Durkheim compared modern social orders to animals rather than to machines. As they grow, animals undergo profound changes in their physical form. They begin life as babies and progress through several developmental stages on their way to adulthood and old age. The bodies of animals are made up of many different kinds of cells—skin, bone, blood—and these cells serve very different purposes. Similarly, modern social orders can undergo profound changes, and therefore the people in them can grow and change along with the society at large. In Durkheim's theory, people are like the specialized cells of a body rather than like the cogs of a machine. People perform specialized tasks and depend on the overall health of the body for their personal survival. Unlike machines, animals are subject to diseases and physical threats. But they are capable of using mental processes to anticipate threats and cope with them. Durkheim used the term **organic solidarity** to refer to the social ties that bind together modern social orders. Specialization, division of labor, and interdependence characterize social orders bound by organic solidarity (Martindale, 1960, p. 87). Be warned, though, it is easy to confuse Durkheim's labeling of mechanical and organic solidarity, because we naturally associate machines with modernity. Remember that he uses the metaphor of the machine to refer to folk cultures—not modern society.

You can see worries about and hopes for traditional and modern society in the writings of two important mass society thinkers, Dwight Macdonald and Edward Shils, men holding markedly different perspectives on modernity. We can see hints of Tönnies disdain for modern, mass society (*gesellschaft*) in this quote from Macdonald's 1953 essay, *A Theory of Mass Culture*:

> Being in so far as people are organised (more strictly disorganised) as masses, they lose their human identity and quality. For the masses are in historical time what a crowd is in space: a large quantity of people unable to express themselves as human beings because they are related to one another neither as individuals nor as members of communities—indeed they are not related to each other at all but only to something distant, abstract, non-human. (p. 14)

MASS SOCIETY THEORY

Strengths

1. Speculates about important effects
2. Highlights important structural changes and conflicts in modern cultures
3. Draws attention to issues of media ownership and ethics
4. Draws attention to macroscopic media effects on the social order

Weaknesses

1. Is unscientific
2. Is unsystematic
3. Is promulgated by elites interested in preserving power
4. Underestimates intelligence and competence of "average people"
5. Underestimates personal, societal, and cultural barriers to direct media influence

And we see hints of Durkheim's optimism for the benefits of organic solidarity (modern, mass society) in this quote from Shils's 1962 essay, *The Theory of Mass Society*:

> Despite all internal conflicts . . . there are, within the mass society, more of a sense of attachment to the society as a whole, more sense of affinity with one's fellows, more openness to understanding, and more reaching out of understanding among men than in any earlier society. . . . The mass society is not the most peaceful or "orderly" society that ever existed; but it is the most consensual. . . . Mass society has witnessed a reinterpretation of the value of a human being. Simply by virtue of his quality or membership in the society he acquires minimal dignity. (pp. 53, 62)

Mass Society Theory in Contemporary Times

Although mass society theory has little support among contemporary mass communication researchers and theorists, its basic assumptions of a corrupting media and helpless audiences have never completely disappeared. Attacks on the pervasive dysfunctional power of media have persisted and will persist as long as dominant elites find their power challenged by media and as long as privately owned media find it profitable to produce and distribute content that challenges widely practiced social norms and values. Vestiges of mass society resonate today on three fronts, in the laments of high culture proponents, in critics' warnings of media concentration, and in social science circles where there is concern over the relationship between powerful new forms of mass media and the rapid rise of populist social movements.

The high culture canon's most influential contemporary champion is British social critic, philosopher, and intellectual Roger Scruton. In *An Intelligent Person's Guide to Modern Culture* (2000), he wrote, "Something new seems to be at work in the contemporary world—a process that is eating away the very heart of social life, not merely by putting salesmanship in place of moral virtue, but by putting everything—virtue included—on sale" (p. 55). This work also makes clear mass society's elitism and support of elite culture:

> This book presents a theory of modern culture, and a defense of culture in its higher and more critical form. It is impossible to give a convincing defense of high culture to a person who has none. I shall therefore assume that you, the reader, are both intelligent

and cultivated. You don't have to be familiar with the entire canon of Western literature, the full range of musical and artistic masterpieces or the critical reflections which
all these things have prompted. Who is? But it would be useful to have read *Les fleurs
du mal* by Baudelaire and T. S. Eliot's *Waste Land*. I shall also presume some familiarity with Mozart, Wagner, Manet, Poussin, Tennyson, Schoenberg, George Herbert,
Goethe, Marx, and Nietzsche. (p. x)

The second factor in contemporary rearticulations of mass society theory involves
concentration of ownership of different media companies in fewer and fewer hands.
Journalist and media critic Ben Bagdikian (2004) reported that from 1992 to 2004 the
number of corporations controlling most of the country's newspapers, magazines, radio
and television stations, book publishers, and movie studios—those with "dominant
power in society"—had shrunk from 50 to 10. Today four companies—Comcast (owned
by AT&T, the world's largest media and entertainment company), News Corp., Disney,
and movie theater and mass media holding company National Amusements (owner of
Viacom and CBS)—control 90% of the media content consumed by Americans (Molla &
Kafka, 2018; Corcoran, 2016).

Bagdikian (1992) has this to say about the concentration of ownership of media
industries:

> Left to their own devices, a small number of the most powerful firms have taken con-
> trol of most of their countries' printed and broadcast news and entertainment. They
> have their own style of control, not by official edict or state terror but by uniform eco-
> nomic and political goals. They have their own way of narrowing political and cultural
> diversity, not by promulgating official dogma but by quietly emphasizing ideas and
> information congenial to their profits and political preferences. Although they are not
> their countries' official political authorities, they have a disproportionate private influ-
> ence over the political authorities and over public policy. (pp. 239–240)

Bagdikian, a strong proponent of media freedom, is no mass society theorist. But his
concern is shared by many who hold to traditional notions of an involved public able
to avail itself of a wide array of entertainment, news, and opinion. Concentration, they
argue, gives people merely the illusion of choice.

Finally, it is the media's promotion of populist politicians and their anti-elite rhetoric
that has contemporary social researchers suggesting a reconsideration of some of mass society
theory's themes. Benjamin Moffitt (2016), for one, linked populism to changes in the media:

> In this global environment, idealised views of populism as an unmediated or direct
> phenomenon that exists between the leader and "the people" must be abandoned, and
> its intensely mediated nature needs to be addressed and explored. We are no longer
> dealing with the romantic notion of the populist speaking directly to "the people"
> from the soapbox, but witness a new breed of savvy populist leaders who know how to
> utilise new media technologies to their advantage. How has the increased mediatisa-
> tion of the political helped populism? How do populist actors relate to, or use, different
> aspects of the media to reach "the people"? And how has the rise of the Internet and
> social networking changed contemporary populism? (p. 3)

James Beniger (1987) points to a number of well-respected modern theories of
media influence that envision the potential for large-scale or mass control wielded

by various elites. We'll look at these theories in detail later, but for now ideas such as *agenda-setting theory* (media may not tell us what to think, but they do tell us what to think about), *spiral of silence* (alternative points of view are spiraled into silence in the face of overwhelming expression of a dominant view in the media), *cultivation analysis* (a false "reality" is cultivated among heavy television viewers by the repetitive, industrially created stories that dominate the medium), and *framing* (news conventions present a dominant interpretive background for making sense of events and public policy) argue for a powerful, public discourse–shaping mass media. Concerns about the role of media in the rise of populism and effects theories such as these have given new life to another early conception of all-powerful media, propaganda theory.

THE ORIGIN OF PROPAGANDA

Throughout the first half of the 20th century, social elites debated the meaning of propaganda. In fact, propaganda "was the foundation upon which the communication field was built" (Curnalia, 2005, p. 237), and the questions they were asking and attempting to answer were of serious import to Western democracies. Was propaganda necessarily bad, or was it a good form of communication that could be corrupted? Many forms of communication seek to persuade people—were all of them propaganda? Gradually, the term *propaganda* came to refer to a certain type of communication strategy involving the no-holds-barred use of communication to propagate specific beliefs and expectations. The ultimate goal of propagandists is to change the way people act and to leave them believing that those actions are voluntary—that is, that the newly adopted behaviors, and the opinions underlying them, are their own (Pratkanis & Aronson, 1992, p. 9). To accomplish this, though, propagandists must first change the way people conceive of themselves and their social world. They use a variety of communication techniques to guide and transform those beliefs. During the 1930s the new media of radio and movies provided authoritarian propagandists with powerful new tools.

Fritz Hippler, head of Nazi Germany's film propaganda division, said that the secret to effective propaganda is to (a) simplify a complex issue and (b) repeat that simplification over and over again ("World War II," 1984). J. Michael Sproule (1994) argues that effective propaganda is covert: It "persuades people without seeming to do so" (p. 3), features "the massive orchestration of communication" (p. 4), and emphasizes "tricky language designed to discourage reflective thought" (p. 5). The propagandist believes that the ends justify the means. Therefore, it is not only right but necessary that half-truths and even outright lies be used to convince people to abandon ideas that are "wrong" and to adopt those favored by the propagandist. Propagandists also rely on **disinformation** to discredit their opposition. They spread false information about opposition groups and their objectives. Often the source of this false information is concealed so that it can't be traced to the propagandist. Today's disinformation has taken on a new form—**fake news**, intentionally false news stories posted and spread on the Internet.

As US theorists studied propaganda, they came to differentiate black, white, and gray propaganda, but definitions of these types of propaganda varied (Snowball, 1999; Becker, 1949). Today we find the attribution of labels like "black" and "white" to the concepts of bad and good propaganda offensive. But remember one of this book's constant themes: These ideas are products of their times. Nonetheless, white propaganda, as we have seen, involves intentional suppression of contradictory information and ideas, combined with deliberate promotion of highly consistent information or ideas that support the objectives of the propagandist. Sometimes white propaganda is used to draw attention away from problematic events or to provide interpretations of events that are useful for the propagandist. Becker asserts that to be white propaganda, it must be openly identified as coming from an "outside" source—one that doesn't have a close relationship to the target of the propaganda. **Gray propaganda** involves transmission of information or ideas that might or might not be false. Propagandists simply make no effort to determine their validity and actually avoid doing so—especially if dissemination of the questionable content would serve their interest. Becker argues that the truth or falsity of propaganda is often hard to establish, so it isn't practical to use veracity as a criterion for differentiating types of propaganda. Fake news typically falls into the gray propaganda category. It's a tool that the current generation of populist leaders use to advance their interests.

Black propaganda involves the deliberate and strategic transmission of lies—its use is well illustrated by the Nazis, Soviets, and other authoritarian regimes throughout history. This is what we today typically think of when considering propaganda, and its goal is far more insidious that the mere spreading of falsehoods—it is the erasure of objective truth altogether. In his study of tyranny in the 20th century, historian Timothy Snyder (2017) wrote that the first step toward totalitarian control of truth is "the open hostility to verifiable reality, which takes the form of presenting inventions and lies as if they were facts" (p. 66). In this he echoed philosopher and political theorist Hannah Arendt (1951), who witnessed Nazi propaganda firsthand as a young scholar in Germany:

> In an ever-changing, incomprehensible world the masses had reached the point where they would, at the same time, believe everything and nothing, think that everything was possible and nothing was true. . . . The totalitarian mass leaders based their propaganda on the correct psychological assumption that, under such conditions, one could make people believe the most fantastic statements one day, and trust that if the next day they were given irrefutable proof of their falsehood, they would take refuge in cynicism; instead of deserting the leaders who had lied to them, they would protest that they had known all along that the statement was a lie and would admire the leaders for their superior tactical cleverness. (p. 382)

Contemporary propaganda theory, particularly in the writing of philosopher Jason Stanley, expands the idea of black propaganda to acknowledge not only its eradication of objective truth, but its erosion—undermining—of the ideals that truth purports to uphold. Black propaganda, Stanley (2015) argues, can be better understood as **undermining propaganda**, "a contribution to public discourse that is presented as an embodiment of certain ideals, yet is of a kind that tends to erode those very ideals" (p. 53). And undermining propaganda is best served by **undermining demagoguery**, "a contribution to public discourse that is presented as an embodiment of a worthy political, economic, or rational ideal, but is in the service of a goal that tends to undermine that very ideal" (p. 69). So the demagogue's message is that to remain free we must accept limits on our freedom; to secure the sanctity of the vote we accept restrictions on voting; to have peace we must accept constant war.

This undermining of important ideals is acceptable as propagandists, then and now, live in an either/or, good/evil world. American propagandists in the 1930s had two clear alternatives. On one side were truth, justice, and freedom—in short, the American way—and on the other side were falsehood, evil, and slavery—totalitarianism. Of course, communist and Nazi propagandists had their own versions of truth, justice, and freedom. For them the American vision of Utopia was at best naive and at worst likely to lead to racial pollution and cultural degradation.

Thus, for the authoritarian propagandist, mass media were a very practical means of mass manipulation—an effective mechanism for controlling large populations. If people came to share the views of the propagandist (because all other information was suspect), they were said to be converted: They abandoned old views and took on those promoted by propaganda. Once consensus was created, elites could then take the actions that it permitted or dictated. They could carry out the "will of the people," who have become, in the words of journalism and social critic Todd Gitlin (1991), "cognoscenti of their own bamboozlement."

Propagandists typically held elitist and paternalistic views about their audiences. They believed that people needed to be converted for their "own good"—not just to serve the interest of the propagandist. Propagandists often blamed the people for the necessity of engaging in lies and manipulation. They thought people so irrational, so illiterate, or so inattentive that it was necessary to coerce, seduce, or trick them into learning bits of misinformation. The propagandists' argument was simple: If only people were more rational or intelligent, we could just sit down and explain things to them, person to person. But most aren't—especially the ones who need the most help. Most people are children when it comes to important affairs like politics. How can we expect them to listen to reason? It's just not possible.

In the post–World War I United States, when propaganda theory was originally developed, the beneficial use of propaganda became known as the **engineering of consent**, a term coined by "the father of modern public relations," Edward L. Bernays. Social historian Andrew Marshall (2013) quotes Bernays's kind words about propaganda: "The conscious and intelligent manipulation of the organized habits and opinions of the masses is an important element in democratic society. Those who manipulate this unseen mechanism of society constitute an invisible government which is the true ruling power of our country." As a result, Bernays believed that traditional democratic notions of freedom of press and speech should be expanded to include the government's "freedom to persuade. . . . Only by mastering the techniques of communication can leadership be exercised fruitfully in the vast complex that is modern democracy." Why did Bernays see propaganda and democracy as a good fit? Because in a democracy, results "do not just happen" (Sproule, 1997, p. 213). The propagandist also uses similar reasoning for suppressing opposition messages: Average people are just too gullible. They will be taken in by the lies and tricks of others. If opponents are allowed to freely communicate their messages, a standoff will result in which no one wins. Propagandists are convinced of the validity of their cause, so they must stop opponents from blocking their actions.

Propaganda Comes to the United States

Americans first began to give serious consideration to the power of propaganda in the years following World War I. The war had demonstrated that modern propaganda techniques could be used with startling effectiveness to assemble massive armies and to maintain civilian morale through long years of warfare. Never before had so many people been mobilized to fight a war. Never before had so many died with so little to show for it over such a long period of time and under such harsh conditions. Earlier wars had been quickly settled by decisive battles. But in the Great War, massive armies confronted each other along a front that extended for hundreds of miles. From their trenches they bombarded each other and launched occasional attacks that ended in futility.

Harold Lasswell, a political scientist who developed several early theories of media, expressed considerable respect for the propaganda efforts marshaled in the cause of the First World War. He wrote:

> When all allowances have been made and all extravagant estimates pared to the bone, the fact remains that propaganda is one of the most powerful instrumentalities in the modern world. . . . In the Great Society [modern industrial society] it is no longer possible to fuse the waywardness of individuals in the furnace of the war dance; a newer and subtler instrument must weld thousands and even millions of human beings into one amalgamated mass of hate and will and hope. A new flame must burn out the canker of dissent and temper the steel of bellicose enthusiasm. The name of this new hammer and anvil of social solidarity is propaganda. (1927a, pp. 220–221)

Many social researchers in the 1920s and 1930s shared these views. Propaganda was an essential tool that had to be used to effectively manage modern social orders, especially when they are in deadly competition with other nations that rely on propaganda to mobilize their masses. After World War I the propaganda battle continued, and inevitably it traveled beyond Europe, as nations sought to spread their influence and new political movements attracted members. During the 1920s radio and movies provided powerful new media for propaganda messages. Hitler's rise to power in Germany was accompanied by consolidation of his control over all forms of media—beginning with radio and the film industry, extending to newspapers. In the United States the battle lines in the propaganda war were quickly drawn. On one side were the elites dominating major social institutions and organizations, including the major political parties, businesses, schools, and universities. On the other side was a broad range of social movements and small extremist political groups. Many were local variants of fascist, socialist, or communist groups that in Europe were much larger and more significant. From the point of view of the old-line elites, these groups were highly suspect. Foreign subversion was a growing fear. The elites believed the influence of these movements and groups had to be curbed before they ruined our way of life.

Extremist propagandists, whether foreign-based or domestically grown, found it increasingly easy to reach and persuade audiences during the 1930s. Only a part of this success, however, can be directly attributed to the rise of the powerful new media. In the United States large newspapers, movies, and radio were controlled mainly by the existing elites. Extremists were often forced to rely on older media like pamphlets, handbills, and political rallies. When the social conditions were right and people were receptive to propaganda messages, however, even older, smaller media could be quite effective. And conditions were right (remember our discussion of *gemeinschaft* and *gesellschaft* from earlier in this chapter). Mass society theorists and the elites they supported believed that "average people" were particularly open to demagogic propaganda because those "unfortunates" lived in a rapidly industrializing world characterized by psychological and cultural isolation and the loss of the security once sustained by traditional, binding, and informal social rules and obligations. As the economic depression deepened in the 1930s, many people no longer had jobs to provide an income to support their families and their relationships with others.

American elites therefore watched with increasing horror as extremist political groups consolidated their power in Europe and proceeded to establish authoritarian governments wielding enormous control over vast populations. How could they remain complacent when madmen like Hitler's propaganda chief, Joseph Goebbels, could openly espouse such antidemocratic ideas as, "It would not be impossible to prove with sufficient repetition and psychological understanding of the people concerned that a square is in fact a circle. What after all are a square and a circle? They are mere words and words can be molded until they clothe ideas in disguise" (as cited in Thomson, 1977, p. 111).

We will review the propaganda theories of three of the most prolific, imaginative, and complex thinkers of their time: Harold Lasswell, Walter Lippmann, and John Dewey. Given the number of books these men wrote, it is impossible to provide a complete presentation of their work. Instead we will highlight some of their most influential and widely publicized ideas. In nearly every case, these men later refined or even rejected some of these ideas.

Most of the propaganda theories that developed during the 1930s were strongly influenced by two theories: behaviorism and Freudianism. Some combined both. Before presenting the ideas of the major propaganda theorists, we will first look at the two theories that often guided their thinking.

Behaviorism

John B. Watson, an animal experimentalist who argued that all human action is merely a conditioned response to external environmental stimuli, first popularized stimulus-response psychology. Watson's theory became known as **behaviorism** in recognition of its narrow focus on isolated human behaviors. Behaviorists rejected psychology's widely held assumption that higher mental processes (that is, conscious thought or reflection) ordinarily control human action. In contrast to such "mentalist" views, behaviorists argued that the only purpose served by consciousness was to rationalize behaviors *after* they are triggered by external stimuli. Behaviorists attempted to purge all mentalist terms from their theories and to deal strictly with observable variables—environmental stimuli on the one hand and behaviors on the other. By studying the associations that existed between specific stimuli and specific behaviors, behaviorists hoped to discover previously unknown causes for action. One of the central notions in behaviorism was the idea of conditioning. Behaviorists argued that most human behavior is the result of conditioning by the external environment. We are conditioned to act in certain ways by positive and negative stimuli—we act to gain rewards or avoid punishments.

Early mass communication theorists, who saw the media as providing external stimuli that triggered immediate responses, frequently used behaviorist notions. For example, these ideas could be applied to the analysis of Fritz Hippler's notorious Nazi propaganda film, *The Eternal Jew*. Its powerful, grotesque presentations of Jews, equating them to disease-bearing rats, were expected to trigger negative responses in their German audiences. Repeated exposure to these images would condition them to have a negative response whenever they see or think about people of the Jewish faith.

Freudianism

Freudianism, on the other hand, was very different from behaviorism, though Sigmund Freud shared Watson's skepticism concerning people's ability to exercise effective conscious or rational control over their actions. Freud spent considerable time counseling middle-class women who suffered from what he called hysteria. During hysterical fits, seemingly ordinary women would suddenly "break down" and display uncontrolled and highly emotional behavior. It was not uncommon for quiet and passive women to "break down" in public places. They would scream, have fits of crying, or become violent. Often these outbursts occurred at times when the likelihood of embarrassment and trouble for themselves and others was at its highest. What could be causing this irrational behavior?

To explain hysteria (a sexist term—*hystera* is Greek for uterus—no longer in medical use), Freud reasoned that the self that guides action must be fragmented into conflicting parts. Normally one part, the rational mind, or **ego**, is in control, but sometimes other parts become dominant. Freud speculated that human action is often the product of another, darker side of the self—the **id**. This is the egocentric pleasure-seeking part of ourselves that the ego must struggle to keep under control. The ego relies on an internalized set of cultural rules (the **superego**) for guidance. Caught between the primitive id and the overly restrictive superego, the ego fights a losing battle. When the ego loses control to the id, hysteria or worse results. When the superego becomes dominant and the id is completely suppressed, people turn into unemotional, depressed social automatons who simply do what others demand.

Contemporary researchers now deem Freud's analysis a "useful metaphor" rather than a description of the actual workings of the mind (Menand, 2017, p. 79). Nonetheless, propaganda theorists of the time used Freudian notions to develop very pessimistic interpretations of media influence. For example, propaganda would be most effective if it could appeal directly to the id and short-circuit or bypass the ego. Alternatively, if through effective propaganda efforts the cultural rules (the superego) moved the self in the direction of the id, people's darker impulses would become normal—a strategy that some propaganda theorists believed was skillfully used by the Nazis.

Behaviorism and Freudianism were combined to create propaganda theories that viewed the average individual as incapable of rational self-control. These theories saw people as highly vulnerable to media manipulation using propaganda; media stimuli and the id could trigger actions that the ego and the superego were powerless to stop. Afterward the ego merely rationalizes actions that it couldn't control and experiences guilt about them. According to these notions, media could have instantaneous society-wide influence on even the most educated, thoughtful people.

Harold Lasswell's Propaganda Theory

Lasswell's theory of propaganda blended ideas borrowed from behaviorism and Freudianism into a particularly pessimistic vision of media and their role in structuring modern social orders. Lasswell was one of the first political scientists to recognize the usefulness of various psychological theories and to demonstrate how they could be applied to understanding and dominating politics. The power of propaganda was not so much the result of the substance or appeal of specific messages but, rather, the result of the vulnerable state of mind of average people. Lasswell argued that economic depression and escalating political conflict had induced widespread psychosis, and this made most people susceptible to even crude forms of propaganda. When average people are confronted daily by powerful threats to their personal lives, they turn to propaganda for reassurance and a way to overcome the threat. When people are jobless and their homes are in foreclosure, propaganda appeals find a ready audience. Similar arguments have been made about the link between the Great Recession of 2008 and the rise of populism around the world (Moffitt, 2016).

In Lasswell's view, democracy has a fatal flaw. It seeks to locate truth and make decisions through openly conducted debates about issues. But if these debates escalate into verbal or even physical conflict between advocates for different ideas, widespread psychosis will result and spectators to these conflicts will be traumatized. Lasswell concluded that even relatively benign forms of political conflict were inherently pathological. When conflict escalates to the level it did in Germany during the Depression, an entire nation could become psychologically unbalanced and vulnerable to manipulation. Lasswell argued that the solution was for social researchers to find ways to "obviate conflict." This necessitates controlling those forms of political communication likely to lead to conflict. In Lasswell's view, even routine forms of political debate could escalate into conflicts threatening the social order. Lasswell critic Floyd Matson (1964) wrote, "In short, according to Lasswell's psychopathology of politics, the presumption in any individual case must be that political action is maladjustive, political participation is irrational, and political expression is irrelevant" (p. 91). But how do you maintain a democratic social order if all forms of political debate or demonstration are problematic? Lasswell had an answer to this question: replace public discourse with democratic propaganda.

Lasswell rejected simplistic behaviorist notions about propaganda effects. Here is how he described the task of the propagandist in a 1927 article:

> The strategy of propaganda, which has been phrased in cultural terms, can readily be described in the language of stimulus-response. Translated into this vocabulary, which is especially intelligible to some, the propagandist may be said to be concerned with the multiplication of those stimuli which are best calculated to evoke the desired responses, and with the nullification of those stimuli which are likely to instigate the undesired responses. Putting the same thing into terms of social suggestion, the problem of the propagandist is to multiply all the suggestions favorable to the attitudes which he wishes to produce and strengthen, and to restrict all suggestions which are unfavorable to them. (1927b, p. 620)

In other words, a few well-targeted messages wouldn't bring down a democratic social order. He argued that propaganda was more than merely using media to lie to people in order to gain temporary control over them. People need to be slowly prepared to accept radically different ideas and actions. Communicators need a well-developed, long-term campaign strategy ("multiplication of those stimuli") in which new ideas and images are carefully introduced and then cultivated. Symbols must be created, and people must be gradually taught to associate specific emotions such as love or hate with these symbols. If these cultivation strategies are successful, they create what Lasswell referred to as **master (or collective) symbols** (Lasswell, 1934). Master symbols are associated with strong emotions and possess the power to stimulate beneficial large-scale mass action if they are used wisely. In contrast to behaviorist notions, Lasswell's theory envisioned a long and quite sophisticated conditioning process. Exposure to one or two extremist messages would not likely have significant effects. And propaganda messages can be delivered through many different media, not just radio or newspapers. Lasswell wrote, "The form in which the significant symbols are embodied to reach the public may be spoken, written, pictorial, or musical, and the number of stimulus carriers is infinite. . . . Consider, for a moment, the people who ride the street cars. They may be reached by placards posted inside the car, by posters on the billboards along the track, by newspapers which they read, by conversations which they overhear, by leaflets which are openly or surreptitiously slipped into their hands, by street demonstrations at halting places, and no doubt by other means. Of these possible occasions there are no end" (1927b, p. 631).

Lasswell argued that successful social movements gain power by propagating master symbols over a period of months and years using a variety of media. For example, the emotions we experience when we see the American flag or hear the national anthem are not the result of a single previous exposure. Rather, we have observed the flag and heard the anthem in countless past situations in which a limited range of emotions was induced and experienced. The flag and the anthem have acquired emotional meaning because of all these previous experiences. When we see the flag on television with the anthem in the background, some of these emotions may be aroused and reinforced. Once established, such master symbols can be used in many different types of propaganda. The flag is used continually during political campaigns as a means of suggesting that political candidates are patriotic and can be trusted to defend the nation.

Lasswell believed that past propagation of most master symbols had been more or less haphazard. For every successful propagandist, there were hundreds who failed. Although he respected the cunning way that the Nazis used propaganda, he was not convinced that they really understood what they were doing. Hitler was an evil artist but not a scientist. Lasswell proposed combating Hitler with a new science of propaganda. Power to control delivery of propaganda through the mass media would be placed in the hands of a new elite, a **scientific technocracy** who would pledge to use its knowledge for good rather than evil—to save democracy rather than destroy it. Lasswell and his colleagues developed a term to refer to this strategy for using propaganda. They called it the "science of democracy" (Smith, 1941). But could a democratic social order be saved by propaganda? Wouldn't essential principles of democracy be sacrificed? Is democracy possible without free and open public discourse? These questions have taken on renewed importance with the rise of populism, fake news, and the actions taken by the Russians to deliberately undermine Western politics (Jamieson, 2018; Nyhan, 2019).

In a world where rational political debate is impossible because average people are prisoners of their own conditioning and psychoses (remember behaviorism and Freudianism) and therefore subject to manipulation by propagandists, Lasswell argued, the only hope for us as a nation rested with social scientists who could harness the power of propaganda for Good rather than Evil. It is not surprising, then, that many of the early media researchers took their task very seriously. They believed that nothing less than the fate of the world lay in their hands.

Walter Lippmann's Theory of Public Opinion Formation

Throughout the 1930s many other members of the social elite, especially those at major universities, shared Lasswell's vision of a benevolent, social science–led technocracy. They believed that together physical and social science held the keys to fighting totalitarianism and preserving democracy. As such, Lasswell's work commanded the attention of leading academics and opinion leaders, including one of the most powerful opinion makers of the time—Walter Lippmann, a nationally syndicated columnist for the *New York Times*.

Lippmann shared Lasswell's skepticism about the ability of average people to make sense of their social world and to make rational decisions about their actions. In *Public Opinion* (1922), he pointed out the discrepancies that necessarily exist between "the world outside and the pictures in our heads." Because these discrepancies were inevitable, Lippmann doubted that average people could govern themselves as classic democratic theory assumed. The world of the 1930s was an especially complex place, and the political forces were very dangerous. People simply couldn't learn enough from media to help them understand it all. He described citizens in his 1925 book, *The Phantom Public*, as a "bewildered herd" of "ignorant and meddlesome outsiders" who should be sidelined as "interested spectators of action" and no more (as cited in Marshall, 2013). Even if journalists took their responsibility seriously, they couldn't overcome the psychological and social barriers that prevented average people from developing useful pictures in their heads. Political essayist Eric Alterman (2008) quoted and summarized Lippmann's position, arguing that the famous columnist saw the average American as "a deaf spectator sitting in the back row. He does not know what is happening, why it is happening, what ought to happen. 'He lives in a world he cannot see, does not understand and is unable to direct.'" Journalism, with its inclination toward sensationalism, "made things worse. Governance was better left to a 'specialized class of men' with inside information. No one expects a steel-worker to understand physics, so why should he be expected to understand politics" (p. 10)?

These ideas raised serious questions about the viability of democracy and the role of a free press. What do you do in a democracy if you can't trust the people to cast informed votes? What good is a free press if it is impossible to effectively transmit enough of the most vital forms of information to the public? What can you do if people are so traumatized by dealing with everyday problems that they have no time to think about and develop a deeper understanding of global issues? The fact that Lippmann made his living working as a newspaper columnist lent credibility to his pessimism. In advancing these arguments, he directly contradicted the libertarian assumptions (free speech and free press; see Chapter 3) that were the intellectual foundation of the American media system.

Like Lasswell, Lippmann believed that propaganda posed such a severe challenge that drastic changes in our political system were required. The public was vulnerable to propaganda, so some mechanism or agency was needed to protect them from it. A benign but enormously potent form of media control was necessary. Media self-censorship most likely wouldn't be sufficient. Lippmann shared Lasswell's conclusion that the best solution to these problems was to place control of information gathering and distribution in the hands of a benevolent technocracy—a scientific elite—who could be trusted to use scientific methods to sort fact from fiction and make good decisions about who should receive various messages. To accomplish this, Lippmann proposed the establishment of a quasi-governmental intelligence bureau that would carefully evaluate information and supply it to other elites for decision-making. This bureau could also determine which information should be transmitted through the mass media and which information people were better off not knowing. He believed that these social engineers and social scientists, by enforcing "intelligence and information control," would be able to "provide the modern state with a foundation upon which a new stability might be realized" (as cited in Marshall, 2013). Though this agency was never created, the notion that government should act as a gatekeeper for problematic information did gain broad acceptance among American elites during WWII and the Cold War, continuing through the Vietnam War and into many contemporary military actions (Mathis-Lilly, 2018; Nordland, Ngu, & Abed, 2018). An obvious example is the way that the federal government carefully controlled information about atomic weapons and atomic energy so that adverse public reactions were minimized throughout the Cold War (Davies, 1997).

Reactions against Early Propaganda Theory

Lasswell and Lippmann's propaganda theories seemed to carry the weight of real-world proof—the globe had been engulfed by a devastating world war—The War to End All Wars, in fact—and global turmoil continued to rage. These conflicts were infused with sophisticated and apparently successful propaganda. Yet there was opposition. One prominent critic of propaganda theory was philosopher John Dewey. In a series of lectures (Dewey, 1927), he outlined his objections to Lippmann's views. Throughout his long career, Dewey was a tireless and prolific defender of public education as the most effective means of defending democracy against totalitarianism. He refused to accept the need for a technocracy that would use scientific methods to protect people from themselves. Rather, he argued that people could learn to defend themselves if they were only taught the correct defenses. He asserted that even rudimentary public education could enable people to resist propaganda methods. Dewey "took violent issue" with Lippmann's "trust in the beneficence of elites," wrote Alterman (2008). "'A class of experts,' Dewey argued, 'is inevitably too removed from common interests as to become a class of private interests and private knowledge.' . . . He saw democracy as less about information than conversation. The media's job, in Dewey's conception, was 'to interest the public in the public interest'" (p. 10).

Dewey's critics saw him as an idealist who talked a lot about reforming education without actually doing much himself to implement concrete reforms (Altschull, 1990, p. 230). Dewey did no better when it came to reforming the media. He argued that newspapers needed to do more than simply serve as bulletin boards for information about current happenings. He issued a challenge to journalists to do more to stimulate public interest in politics and world affairs—to motivate people to actively seek out information and then talk about it with others. Newspapers should serve as vehicles for public education and debate. They should focus more on ideas and philosophy and less on descriptions of isolated actions. They should teach critical thinking skills and structure public discussion of important issues. His efforts to found such a publication never got very far, however. Nonetheless, this philosophy of a mutually beneficial audience/journalism relationship (e.g., Blatchford, 2018; Rosenstiel & Elizabeth, 2018) has found recent articulation in the wake of precipitous declines in respect and trust in media (Friedman, 2018). Some sympathetic critics of the press have argued that it could restore public trust by serving communities more explicitly and effectively.

Dewey based his arguments on **pragmatism**, a school of philosophical theory emphasizing the practical function of knowledge as an instrument for adapting to reality and controlling it. We'll take a closer look at this theory in Chapter 13. James Carey (1989)

INSTANT ACCESS

PROPAGANDA THEORY

Strengths

1. Is first systematic theory of mass communication
2. Focuses attention on why media might have powerful effects
3. Identifies personal, social, and cultural factors that can enhance media's power to have effects
4. Focuses attention on the use of campaigns to cultivate symbols

Weaknesses

1. Underestimates abilities of average people to evaluate messages
2. Ignores personal, social, and cultural factors that limit media effects
3. Overestimates the speed and range of media effects

contends that Dewey's ideas have continuing value. He argues that Dewey anticipated many of the concerns now being raised by cultural studies theories. And as you'll also read in Chapter 9, Dewey's belief that educating people to think critically about media content and how they use it is at the heart of the media literacy movement and contemporary concerns about public education and public discourse (for example, Wineburg, McGrew, Breakstone, & Ortega, 2016; Hobbs & McGee, 2014). He believed that communities, not isolated individuals, use communication (and the mass media) to create and maintain the culture that bonds and sustains them. When media assume the role of external agents and work to manipulate the "pictures in people's heads," they lose their power to serve as credible facilitators and guardians of public debate; they become just another competitor for our attention. The potentially productive interdependence between the community and media is disrupted, and the public forum itself is likely to be destroyed.

MODERN PROPAGANDA THEORY

Consider the Hippler and Sproule characterizations of propaganda from earlier in this chapter: Simplify a complex issue, and repeat that simplification; use covert, massively orchestrated communication; and use tricky language to discourage reflective thought. Remember, too, Lasswell's contention that tough economic times and political discord leave people susceptible to propaganda's sway. Finally, recall, too, undermining propaganda's ultimate goal, to render "truth" meaningless. Doing so, you'll understand why contemporary critical theorists argue that propaganda today is alive and well and that it is practiced with a stealth, sophistication, and effectiveness unparalleled in history. They point to a number of "natural beliefs" that have been so well propagandized that meaningful public discourse about them has become difficult if not impossible—we must always honor the troops; the invisible hand of the market will solve all social problems; the United States is the freest nation on Earth. When alternatives to those natural beliefs *are* considered, those who raise them are viewed as radicals, out of the mainstream, or peculiar. Additionally, this failure to consider alternatives benefits those same economic elites most responsible for limiting that consideration and reflection. As such, political discourse and advertising are frequent areas of modern propaganda study, and the central argument of this modern propaganda theory is that powerful elites so thoroughly control the mass media and their content that they have little trouble imposing their truth on the culture. Sproule has written thoughtfully and persuasively on advertising as propaganda in *Channels of Propaganda* (1994) and *Propaganda and Democracy: The American Experience of Media and Mass Persuasion* (1997). Philosopher Jason Stanley (2015) has also tackled advertising, classifying it as propaganda precisely because it undermines that which it purports to extoll: "A contribution to public discourse that is presented as an embodiment of certain ideals, but in service of a goal that is irrelevant to those very ideals" (p. 56). Advertisers, whose goal is the maximization of profit, transform important cultural values to meet their ends. Freedom becomes choosing between different flavors of soda; love becomes buying children the latest toy or our partners the newest car; happiness becomes acquiring more stuff.

This narrowing of public discourse and debate is also examined in works such as historian Herb Schiller's *Culture, Inc.: The Corporate Takeover of Public Expression* (1989); communication theorist Robert McChesney's *Corporate Media and the Threat to Democracy* (1997), *The Problem of the Media* (2004), and *Dollarocracy: How the Money-and-Media-Election Complex Is Destroying America* (2013); mass communication researchers Kathleen Hall Jamieson and Paul Waldman's *The Press Effect* (2003); and linguist Noam Chomsky's *American Power and the New Mandarins* (1969), *Deterring Democracy* (1991), and with Edward S. Herman, *Manufacturing Consent* (Herman & Chomsky, 1988). All offer a common perspective. In Jamieson and Waldman's words, "'Facts' can be difficult to discern and relate to the public, particularly in a context in which the news is driven by politicians and other interested parties who selectively offer some pieces of information while suppressing others" (p. xiii).

This current reconsideration of propaganda theory comes primarily from critical theorists, and as a result, its orientation tends to be from the political left. Behaviorists Richard Laitinen and Richard Rakos (1997) offer a typical critical view of contemporary propaganda. They argue that modern propaganda—in their definition, "the control of behavior by media manipulation" (p. 237)—is facilitated by three factors: an audience "that is enmeshed and engulfed in a harried lifestyle, less well-informed, and less politically involved, . . . the use of sophisticated polling and survey procedures, whose results are used by the propagandists to increase their influence, . . . [and] the incorporation of media companies into megaconglomerates" (pp. 238–239). These factors combine to put untold influence in the hands of powerful business and governmental elites without the public's awareness. In contemporary democracies, wrote Laitinen and Rakos (1997), "the absence of oppressive government control of information is typically considered a fundamental characteristic of a 'free society.' However, the lack of aversive control does not mean that information is 'free' of controlling functions. On the contrary, current mechanisms of influence, through direct economic and indirect political contingencies, pose an even greater threat to behavioral diversity than do historically tyrannical forms. Information today is more systematic, continuous, consistent, unobtrusive, and ultimately powerful" (p. 237).

There is also renewed interest in propaganda theory from the political right. This conservative interest in propaganda takes the form of a critique of liberal media bias (see, for example, Coulter, 2006; Goldberg, 2003, 2009; Morris & McGann, 2008; Shapiro, 2011).

Other than an occasional survey indicating that among journalists, Democrats outnumber Republicans (the majority identify as Independent; Gold, 2014), there is little serious scholarship behind this assertion. First, as media critic Eric Alterman (2017) argues, "a journalist's party identification tells us precisely nothing about the actual content of the news," but what research there is tends to negate the liberal media bias thesis, as the large majority of media outlet managers and owners tend to vote Republican; the majority of the country's syndicated newspaper columnists write with a conservative bent; and the majority of 'newsmakers' on network and cable public affairs talk shows are politically right of center. On the basis of audience size, conservative Fox News is the top-rated cable news network, with an audience more than double that of liberal MSNBC; the 10 highest–rated cable news shows are all on conservative Fox; five of the top six social media news sites slant right; and all five of the top-rated talk-radio opinion news shows are extremely conservative ("The Right," 2017). Robert McChesney (1997) raises the added dimension of media ownership: "The fundamental error in the conservative notion of the 'liberal' media [is] it posits that editors and journalists have almost complete control over what goes into news. . . . In conservative 'analysis,' the institutional factors of corporate ownership, profit-motivation, and advertising support have no effect on media content. . . . The notion that journalism can regularly produce a product that violates the fundamental interests of media owners and advertisers and do so with impunity simply has no evidence behind it" (p. 60). Media law expert Charles Tillinghast (2000) concurs, noting, "One need not be a devotee of conspiracy theories to understand that journalists, like other human beings, can judge where their interests lie, and what risks are and are not prudent, given the desire to continue to eat and feed the family. . . . It takes no great brain to understand one does not bite the hand that feeds—or that one incurs great risk by doing so" (pp. 145–146). For example, Sinclair Broadcasting, the largest owner of local television stations in the country, with 173 stations in 81 broadcast markets across America, produces "conservative-tinged" editorials and requires local anchors to read them verbatim in their on-air newscasts and to represent them as their own (Rosenberg, 2018).

Finally, as we saw in the case of contemporary interest in mass society theory, some postpositivist researchers are rethinking propaganda theory in light of effects theories such as agenda-setting, framing, and spiral of silence. For example, arguing that today's "process and effects of propaganda conforms to the definitions offered by propaganda analysts and empirical studies of media effects," Rebecca Curnalia (2005) wrote, "Propaganda involves using (a) rhetorical devices to frame an attitude object, (b) disseminating the message widely enough to influence the public agenda, making the issue (c) more accessible and, therefore, more salient to individuals, thereby (d) influencing perceptions of the issue as broadly supported. This process affects people as they (e) perceive the majority opinion to be more in favor of the attitude object and experience normative pressure to conform or be silent" (p. 253).

To support their contention that elites continue to utilize propaganda for their own ends, contemporary propaganda theorists point to the engineering of consent that sent the United States into an invasion of Iraq on what is now acknowledged as false premises (Suskind, 2004) and the media's complicity in hiding the economic conditions and practices that would eventually disable the world economy and bring on the Great Recession in 2008 (Mitchell, 2009). Even more recently, at a time of significant economic worry and historically high levels of political division (Jones, 2019), the presidency of Donald Trump has revived the interest of American scholars in undermining propaganda, long thought an exclusively "foreign" contemporary phenomenon. Before the first two years of his presidency had come to pass, Mr. Trump made 7,645 verifiably false or misleading claims, or more than 10 a day (Bunch, 2019). Official Counselor to the President Kellyanne Conway explained that these were not false or misleading claims, they were simply "alternative facts" (*Meet the Press*, 2017). In a later *Meet the Press* interview, presidential lawyer Rudy Giuliani argued that when it comes to the events surrounding possible criminal conspiracy between the Russian government and Mr. Trump during the previous election, "truth is not truth" (Gomez, 2018). And President Trump himself, who consistently referred to the press as "dishonest," "scum," "the enemy of the people," and "fake news" (Williams, 2017), told a gathering in Kansas City, Missouri, that "what you're seeing and what you're reading [in the news] is not what's happening" (Wise, 2018). *Washington Post* editor Marty Baron channeled propaganda theory to explain the intent of these events, arguing that the president "wants to disqualify the press as an independent arbiter of fact. He does not want there to be an independent arbiter of fact. He certainly doesn't want the press to be that arbiter, he doesn't want scientists to be that arbiter, he doesn't want the courts to be that arbiter, he doesn't want the intelligence agencies to be the arbiter—he wants himself, and his White House, to be the arbiter of fact" (Institute of Politics & David Axelrod, 2018). Here he was reiterating Mr. Trump's own words to *60 Minutes* reporter Lesley Stahl: "You know why I do it? I do it to discredit you all and demean you all so that when you write negative stories about me, no one will believe you" (as cited in Boboltz, 2018). Pulitzer Prize–winning investigative journalist James Risen (2018) warned that the president "is seeking nothing less than the destruction of the legitimacy of the American press" (para. 13). This "dismemberment of a public discourse centered on objective truth," in the words of conservative writer and social critic Andrew Sullivan (2018), "is fomented by unceasing dissemination of outright lies from the very top, metabolized by tribal social media, ever more extreme talk radio, and what is essentially a state propaganda channel, Fox News" (p. 1). Analyses by fact-checking organization Politifact determined that only 10% of "statements made on air by Fox, Fox News and Fox Business personalities and their pundit guests" were fully true ("FOX's File," 2018).

Research at the time seems to have confirmed the effectiveness of this "firehose of falsehood," in the words of investigative journalist Monika Bauerlein (2017). A 2018 survey by the well-respected Voter Study Group discovered that four in 10 Americans say they are dissatisfied with how democracy is working in the Unites States, and nearly a quarter say that a strong leader who doesn't have to bother with Congress or elections would be "fairly good" or "very good." Nearly one quarter support either a "strong leader" or "army rule" (Drutman, Diamond, & Goldman, 2018). Another survey found that 43% of President Trump's supporters thought that he should have the "authority to close down" news outlets he thought were engaging in "bad behavior." Just under half believed that "the news media is the enemy of the people" (Stein, 2018). But how can that be? Don't people know better? They may, but research in cognitive psychology has demonstrated that repeated misstatements are easier to process and are therefore subsequently perceived to be more truthful than that which people already know to be the truth (Fazio, Brashier, Payne, & Marsh, 2015).

Libertarianism Reborn and Challenged

By the end of the 1930s, pessimism about the future of democracy was widespread. Most members of the old-line elites were convinced that totalitarianism couldn't be stopped. They pointed to theories like those of Lasswell and Lippmann as proof that average people could not be trusted. Hope for the future resided solely with technocracy and science. Today the rebirth in interest in undermining propaganda has given new life to these concerns and possible solutions.

In the chapter on normative theories (Chapter 3), we trace the development of ideas that arose in opposition to these technocratic views. Advocates of these emerging theories didn't base their views of media on social science; rather, they wanted to revive older notions of democracy and media. If modern democracy was being threatened, maybe the threat was the result of having strayed too far from old values and ideals. Perhaps these could be restored, and modern social institutions could somehow be purified and renewed. Theorists sought to make the **libertarianism** of the Founding Fathers once again relevant to democracy. In doing so, they created views of media that are still widely held.

Mass society theory, propaganda theory, and the ideas discussed in the normative theories chapter, taken together, shaped the early research and initial development of mass communication theory, rightly or wrongly, for the first decades of the discipline's history (Sproule, 1987; Jowett & O'Donnell, 1999). The mass society/mass culture trend in media theory is still important. As you've read, some contemporary scholars argue that its influence persists. Moreover, these early conceptions of media influence established the terms of the debate: Media do or do not have significant influence; people are or are not capable of resisting media influence; and, as you'll read, the media do or do not have an obligation to operate in a way that limits their negative influence while serving the interests of the larger society.

REVIEW OF LEARNING OBJECTIVES

- Explain the social, cultural, and political conditions that led to the development of mass society theory and propaganda theory.

The social world in which mass society and propaganda theory originally developed was quite turbulent. Industrialization and urbanization were reshaping both Europe and the United States. This technological change, however, occurred with little consideration for its larger social and cultural impact. Social change could be rationalized as progress, but a high price was paid, especially by everyday people. Media were among the many technologies that shaped and were shaped by this modern era. An industrial social order had great need for the fast and efficient distribution of information. In the mid and late 19th century, large urban populations' growing demand for cheap media content drove the development of several new media. High-speed printing presses and Linotype machines made it practical to mass produce the printed word at very low cost. Urban newspapers boomed all along the East Coast and in major trading centers across the United States. Newspaper circulation wars broke out in many large cities and led to the development of sensationalistic journalism that seriously challenged the norms and values of most readers. Across the globe, totalitarian leaders seemed to be taking advantage of the turmoil of the time and the new technologies to move people to their authoritarian points of view.

- Place the role of the mass media in scholars' conceptions of those theories.

Changes in media industries often increase the pressure on other social institutions to change. Instability in the way we routinely communicate can have unsettling consequences for all other institutions. Leaders of these institutions resent external pressures and are reluctant to alter their way of doing things. The changes associated with new media in the first half of the last century were highly disruptive because people were inexperienced at dealing with developments in mass media. Conservative critics interpreted the rise of the media industries as threatening to subvert every other social institution, including the family, political, religious, business, military, and educational institutions.

- Understand mass society and propaganda theorists' perceptions of the audience and its ability to interact with mass media.

Mass society theorists saw people as alone, atomized, distanced from the traditional institutions that long protected them. Many propaganda theorists typically held elitist and paternalistic views about the public. They believed that people needed to be converted for their "own good." They blamed the people for the necessity of engaging in lies and manipulation. They thought people so irrational, so illiterate, or so inattentive that it was necessary to coerce, seduce, or trick them into learning bits of misinformation. Some theorists, however, held a more optimistic view of people, thinking if educated properly, they would be able to engage in public discourse that would render propaganda ineffective.

- Explain why and in what form contemporary articulations of mass society theory and propaganda theory exist.

Mass society theory's basic assumptions of a corrupting media and helpless audiences have never completely disappeared. Attacks on the pervasive dysfunctional power of media will persist as long as dominant elites find their power challenged by media and as long as privately owned media find it profitable to produce and distribute content that challenges widely practiced social norms and values. Vestiges of mass society resonate today on three fronts: high culture proponents, opponents of media concentration, and in social science circles where researchers see the operation of a powerful mass media facilitating the rise of populism and fake news. Contemporary propaganda theory centers on political discourse and advertising, and its central argument is that powerful elites so thoroughly control the media and their content that they have little trouble imposing their truth on the culture.

- List mass society theory's assumptions about media and audiences.

The media are a powerful force within society that can subvert essential norms and values and thus undermine the social order. As such, they must be brought under elite control. Media are able to directly influence the minds of average people, transforming their views of the social world. Once people's thinking is transformed by media, all sorts of bad long-term consequences are likely to result—not only bringing ruin to individual lives but also creating social problems on a vast scale. Average people are vulnerable to media because in modern mass society they are cut off and isolated from traditional social institutions that previously protected them from manipulation. The social chaos initiated by media will likely be resolved by establishment of a totalitarian social order. Mass media inevitably debase higher forms of culture, bringing about a general decline in civilization.

- Detail some early examples of mass society theory.

Ferdinand Tönnies proposed a dichotomy—*gemeinschaft*, or folk community, and *gesellschaft*, or modern industrial society—to explain the difference between earlier forms of social organization and European society as it existed in the late 19th century. In folk communities, people were bound together by strong ties of family, by tradition, and by rigid social roles—basic social institutions were very powerful. In *gesellschaft*, social relationships were more formalized and impersonal; individuals did not depend on one another for support and were therefore much less morally obligated to one another. People were bound together by relatively weak social institutions based on rational choices rather than tradition. Émile Durkheim offered the same dichotomy but with a fundamentally different interpretation. He compared folk communities to machines in which people were little more than cogs. These machines were very ordered and durable, but people were forced by a collective consensus to perform traditional social roles. People were bound by this consensus to one another like the parts of a great engine—mechanical solidarity. He compared modern social orders to animals rather than to machines. As they grow, animals undergo profound changes in their physical form. Similarly, modern social orders can undergo profound changes, and therefore the people in them can grow and change along with the society at large. People perform specialized tasks and depend on the overall health of the body for their personal survival. Durkheim used the term organic solidarity to refer to the social ties that bind together modern social orders.

- Explain the details of behaviorism, Freudianism, and the propaganda theories of Harold Lasswell and Walter Lippmann, as well as those of John Dewey's alternative perspective.

Behaviorism is the idea that all human action is a conditioned response to external environmental stimuli, and Freudianism argued that human behavior is the product of the conflict between an individual's id, ego, and superego. Propaganda could easily take advantage of these human "frailties." Harold Lasswell held that propaganda typically influenced people in slow and subtle ways. It created new master symbols that could be used to induce new forms of thought and action. His theories assumed that media could operate as external agents and be used as tools to manipulate essentially passive mass audiences. Also believing in the propaganda power of mass media was columnist Walter Lippmann, whose skepticism at the public's self-governance abilities and distrust of lazy media professionals brought him to the conclusion that the inevitably incomplete and inaccurate "pictures in people's heads" posed a threat to democracy. John Dewey's solution to propaganda's threat relied on traditional notions of democracy. Because people were in fact good and rational, the counter to propaganda was not control of media by a technocratic elite, but more education of the public.

CRITICAL THINKING QUESTIONS

1. Roger Scruton wants to tell us what it means to be an intelligent person. He assumes that he can do this only if we already have a basic understanding of the great works. "It would be useful to have read *Les fleurs du mal* by Baudelaire and T. S. Eliot's *Waste Land*," he wrote. "I shall also presume some familiarity with Mozart, Wagner, Manet, Poussin, Tennyson, Schoenberg, George Herbert, Goethe, Marx, and Nietzsche." How many of these masters and masterworks are you familiar with? If you don't know many of them, does that make you an unintelligent person? Can you make an argument for different definitions of intelligence? What would you say to Scruton about his definition of an intelligent person should you run in to him on campus?

2. National Founder Benjamin Franklin said that Americans who would exchange a bit of freedom in order to secure a bit of security deserve neither freedom nor security. What does he mean by this? Can you relate this sentiment to the debate over the role of propaganda in a democracy? Where would Franklin have stood on the issue?

3. Can the traditional news media ever be truly "liberal," given their corporate ownership and their reliance on advertising for their survival? In the face of evidence that there are many very successful openly conservative media outlets, do complaints that the media are too liberal in actuality apply only to those outlets critics might dislike? Should profit-making news media be replaced by nonprofit public service-oriented news media?

KEY TERMS

First Amendment
propaganda
white propaganda
direct-effects assumption
Enlightenment
gemeinschaft
gesellschaft
mechanical solidarity
organic solidarity
concentration
disinformation
fake news
gray propaganda

black propaganda
undermining propaganda
undermining demagoguery
engineering of consent
behaviorism
Freudianism
ego
id
superego
master (or collective) symbols
scientific technocracy
pragmatism
libertarianism

GLOSSARY

First Amendment: Amendment to the US Constitution that guarantees freedom of speech, press, assembly, and religion

propaganda: No-holds-barred use of communication to propagate specific beliefs and expectations

white propaganda: Intentional suppression of potentially harmful information and ideas, combined with deliberate promotion of positive information or ideas to distract attention from problematic events

direct-effects assumption: Assumption that the media, in and of themselves, can produce direct effects

Enlightenment: Eighteenth-century European social and philosophical movement stressing rational thought and progress through science

gemeinschaft: In Tönnies's conception, traditional folk cultures

gesellschaft: In Tönnies's conception, modern industrial society

mechanical solidarity: In Durkheim's conception, folk cultures bound by consensus and traditional social roles

organic solidarity: In Durkheim's conception, modern social orders bound by culturally negotiated social ties

concentration: Ownership of different and numerous media companies concentrated in fewer and fewer hands

disinformation: False information spread about the opposition to discredit it

fake news: Intentionally false news reports posted and spread via the Internet

gray propaganda: Transmission of information or ideas that might or might not be false. No effort is made to determine their validity

black propaganda: Deliberate and strategic transmission of lies

undermining propaganda: A contribution to public discourse presented as an embodiment of certain ideals, yet that tends to erode those very ideals

undermining demagoguery: A contribution to public discourse presented as an embodiment of a worthy political, economic, or rational ideal, but that is in the service of a goal that tends to undermine that very ideal

engineering of consent: Official use of communication campaigns to reach "good" ends

behaviorism: The notion that all human action is a conditioned response to external environmental stimuli

Freudianism: Freud's notion that human behavior is the product of the conflict between an individual's id, ego, and superego

ego: In Freudianism, the rational mind

id: In Freudianism, the egocentric pleasure-seeking part of the mind

superego: In Freudianism, the internalized set of cultural rules

master (or collective) symbols: Symbols that are associated with strong emotions and possess the power to stimulate large-scale mass action

scientific technocracy: An educated social science–based elite charged with protecting vulnerable average people from harmful propaganda

pragmatism: School of philosophical theory emphasizing the practical function of knowledge as an instrument for adapting to reality and controlling it

libertarianism: A normative theory that sees people as good and rational and able to judge good ideas from bad

CHAPTER 3

Normative Theories of Mass Communication

On August 16, 2018, nearly 350 American news outlets—big and small; rural, urban, and suburban; print and online; Republican-leaning, Democratic-leaning, and Independent; East Coast, West Coast, and in between—published editorials in their own words and from their individual perspectives decrying President Donald Trump's attacks on the press and defending freedom of speech. *The Boston Globe* had issued the invitation in response to what it called the president's "dirty war against the free press." The paper was referring to events of the first 18 months of his time in office, during which Mr. Trump had called journalists "absolute scum," "fake news," "the enemy of the American people," "disgusting," and "totally dishonest." He advocated "opening up our libel laws" to chasten critical reporting, and repeatedly sought to have journalists he considered unfriendly banned from press events. He warned rally-goers that what they were reading and seeing in the news "is not what's happening" (Durkin, 2018; Landler, 2018; Coppins, 2017). At a Michigan rally he offered his opinion of journalists: "I hate some of these people, but I would never kill them" (Yilek, 2015). Many observers saw the constant anti-journalism rhetoric leading not only to a decline in respect for democracy-sustaining freedom of press, but as the prime factor in the growing number of verbal and physical attacks on working journalists themselves (Magra, 2019; Landler, 2018). These attacks on journalism by a sitting president were so unprecedented that the United States Senate felt compelled to unanimously pass a resolution reaffirming that the press is *not* the enemy of the people (Frei, 2018) and the House of Representatives to take up the Journalist Protection Act, making it a federal crime to intentionally cause bodily injury at a journalist (Concha, 2019).

Indeed, despite some evidence that the public had been regaining trust in the press *because* of its performance during the first year of Mr. Trump's presidency (54% of Americans reported "a great deal" or "a fair amount" of trust and confidence in the media in 2018, a five-percentage-point improvement over that time; Friedman, 2018), among the president's conservative followers, mistrust was the rule: 86%—nearly 9 out of 10—of Republicans (Mr. Trump's political party) believe the national news media intentionally publish false reports for political purposes (Fishburne, 2019), and one loyalist, Robert Chain, specifically citing their role as enemies of the people, threatened to shoot reporters in the head. He was quickly arrested, but not before newsrooms across America had routinely begun to post security outside their facilities (Raymond, 2018). Clearly President Trump's words were having an effect. Columbia University president Lee Bollinger (2018), when hosting the 2018 Pulitzer Prize luncheon, stated, "I think it is clear that the nation is facing the most serious internal attacks on the fundamental values and institutional structures that define a democracy since the Pulitzers were introduced a century ago" (para. 2). But how could this be in the very nation that had enshrined freedom of the press as its "first freedom"?

Perhaps the answer to this question is simple—the media may not warrant the trust we have long granted them. Perhaps the media, in an era of fragmenting audiences and contracting resources, simply are not worthy of our trust as they turn increasingly toward entertainment, scandal, and opinion and away from serious reporting to hold on to what audiences they may still have. For example, long before Mr. Trump assumed office, Arthur Brisbane (2012), public editor of the *New York Times*, wondered aloud online if reporters should be "truth vigilantes," calling out the lies of politicians and other powerful people. "How can telling the truth ever take a back seat in the serious business of reporting the news?" replied media critic Jay Rosen (2012). "That's like saying medical doctors no longer put 'saving lives' or 'the health of the patient' ahead of securing payment from insurance companies. It puts the lie to the entire contraption. It *devastates* journalism as a public service and honorable profession" (para. 13).

The operation of our modern media system is rife with challenges such as this. For example, journalists undertook years of self-examination after they "failed spectacularly" (Benton, 2016) in their reporting of the 2016 presidential election: Coverage focused too heavily on the horse race and not the issues; personality received significantly more media attention than policy; coverage of candidate Hillary Clinton was sexist and of candidate Trump superficial; journalists were out of touch with the lives of most Americans and failed to sense the true mood of the country; journalists provided extensive coverage of the Democrat e-mails stolen by the Russians and released by Wikileaks; traditional media gave life to Internet-spawned rumor (Chait, 2016). Journalists also failed in their election coverage in their elevation of "scandal" over policy. Using the nation's "paper of record" as its laboratory, researchers Duncan Watts and David Rothschild (2017) discovered that "only five out of 150 front-page articles that the *New York Times* ran over the last, most critical months of the election, attempted to compare the candidate's policies, while only 10 described the policies of either candidate in any detail." Elsewhere, as more than 43 million Americans live in poverty, meaningful reporting on poverty makes up less than 1% of major media news coverage (Jones, 2018); journalists serving as moderators did not ask a single question about climate change of any candidate in either the 2012 or 2016 presidential debates (Alterman, 2017); and in 2018, despite murderous heat waves, massive wildfires and droughts across the globe, global temperatures exceeding all-time highs, and landmark climate reports published by both the United Nations and the American government, the four major broadcast television news operations, ABC, CBS, FOX, and NBC, devoted a mere 142 minutes combined to coverage of climate change, one third of which came from a single December episode of *Meet the Press* (MacDonald & Hymas, 2019).

These media and journalistic troubles are not easily overcome. The American media system is in a state of massive upheaval and overhaul. For example, the number of people working as journalists in US newsrooms fell by 25% in the 10 years between 2008 and 2018, with the greatest decline at newspapers (Grieco, 2019). "We are, for the first time in modern history, facing the prospect of how societies would exist without reliable news," warns Alan Rusbridger, long-time editor-in-chief of the *Guardian* newspaper. "There are not that many places left that do quality news well or even aim to do it at all" (as cited in Lepore, 2019, p. 19). Yet more optimistic observers argue that the media are simply undergoing *disruptive transition*—that is, change is inevitable, especially in light of the explosive growth of the Internet, and it will produce a new, better media and a new, more powerful journalism. After all, there is evidence that despite widespread distrust of the media and the press, Americans, especially young Americans, are relying on their computers, smartphones, and tablets to access more news than ever before (Anderson & Jiang, 2018; Watson, 2019) and that enrollments in college journalism programs have actually increased in "the age of 'enemy of the people' rhetoric" (Orso, 2019).

What will the American media system look like in the immediate future and in a future that we might have difficulty envisioning, given the remarkable speed with which our communication technology is being transformed and new relationships between "the people formerly known as the audience" (Gilmor, 2004) and the mass media are developed? What will guide that development, and how will we know if what it produces is good or bad, serves us or harms us, fosters or weakens our democracy? The answers reside in normative theory.

LEARNING OBJECTIVES

After studying this chapter you should be able to

- Explain the origins of normative media theories.
- Evaluate libertarianism as a guiding principle for the operation of mass media.
- Recognize the strengths and limitations of the marketplace-of-ideas approach to media freedom.
- Judge the worthiness and continued utility of social responsibility theory, especially in the Internet era.

OVERVIEW

During the era of yellow journalism most media professionals cared very little for the niceties of accuracy, objectivity, and public sensitivities. But in the first decades of the 20th century, some media industry people and various social elites began a crusade to clean up the media and make them more respectable and credible. The watchword of this crusade was *professionalism*, and its goal was elimination of shoddy and irresponsible content.

Some sort of theory was needed to guide this task of media reform. The goal of this theory would be to answer questions such as

- Should media do something more than merely distribute whatever content will earn them the greatest profits in the shortest time?

- Are there some essential public services that media should provide even if no immediate income can be earned?
- Should media become involved in identifying and solving social problems?
- Is it necessary or advisable that media serve as watchdogs and protect consumers against business fraud and corrupt bureaucrats?
- What should we expect media to do for us in times of crisis?

These broad questions about the role of media are linked to issues concerning their day-to-day operation. How should media management and production jobs be structured? What moral and ethical standards should guide media professionals? Do they have any obligation beyond personal and professional self-interest? Exactly what constitutes being a journalist? Are there any circumstances when it is appropriate or even necessary to invade people's privacy or risk ruining their reputations? If someone threatens to commit suicide in front of a television camera, what should a reporter do—get it on video or try to stop it? Should a newspaper print a story about unethical business practices even if the company involved is one of its biggest advertisers? Should television networks broadcast a highly rated program even if it routinely contains high levels of violence?

Answers to questions like these are found in normative theory—a type of theory that describes an ideal way for a media system to be structured and operated. Normative theories are different from most of the theories we study in this book. They don't describe things as they are, nor do they provide scientific explanations or predictions. Instead they describe the way things *should be* if some ideal values or principles are to be realized. Normative theories come from many sources. Sometimes media practitioners themselves develop them; sometimes social critics or academics do. Most normative theories develop over time and contain elements drawn from previous theories. This is especially true of the normative theory that currently guides mass media in the United States; it is a synthesis of ideas developed over the past three centuries.

This chapter examines a variety of normative media theories, including some that are questionable or even objectionable. We proceed from earlier forms of normative theory to more recent examples. Our attention is on the normative theory that is predominantly used to guide and legitimize most legacy media operation in the United States: **social responsibility theory.** For a long time, debates about normative theory were muted in the United States. Social responsibility theory seemingly provided such an ideal standard that further debate was simply unnecessary. But the past 50 years have seen unprecedented growth and consolidation of control in the media industries, and as a result, gigantic conglomerates—conceivably more committed to the bottom line than to social responsibility—dominate the production and distribution of media content. In addition, the Internet has greatly expanded the number and variety of "media outlets," all with varying commitments to traditional standards of social responsibility. As Michael Hirsh, national editor of news site *Politico* explains, today's journalism is "in some ways [at] the tail end of a long arc of history. We started with a few authorized outlets that really spoke authoritatively; and that's largely gone with the wind. The *Times* and the *Post* are still around, but there's a question of how much they really dictate the agenda in the way that they used to. And in the meantime 10,000 weeds have bloomed on the Internet, sites where like-minded people gather, where they get a lot of their information, much of it just garbage. There's no real anchor" (as cited in in Chait, 2016).

In this chapter we will assess why social responsibility theory has had enduring appeal for American media practitioners. We will speculate about its future, as its assumptions are now regularly challenged by an ever-evolving media landscape featuring new relationships between content creators and providers and their audiences. We will also contrast it with theories popular in other parts of the world. As Internet-based media come to dominate news distribution (Newman, 2019), will social responsibility theory serve to guide them or will alternatives develop? Social responsibility theory is suited to a particular era of national development and to specific types of media. As the media industries change, this guiding theory might very well have to be substantially revised or replaced.

THE ORIGIN OF NORMATIVE THEORIES OF MEDIA

Since the beginning of the last century, the role of mass media in American society, as we've already seen, has been hotly argued. At one extreme of the debate are people who argue for **radical libertarian** ideals. They believe that there should be no laws governing media operations. They are **First Amendment absolutists** who take the notion of "free press" quite literally to mean that all forms of media must be totally unregulated. These people accept as gospel that the First Amendment dictate—"Congress shall make no law . . . abridging the freedom of speech or of the press"—means exactly what it says. As Supreme Court Justice Hugo Black succinctly stated, "No law means no law" (*New York Times Co. v. United States*, 1971).

At the other extreme are people who believe in direct regulation of media, most often by a government agency or commission. These include advocates of **technocratic control**, people like Harold Lasswell and Walter Lippmann. They argue that media practitioners can't be trusted to communicate responsibly or to effectively use media to serve vital public needs—especially during times of crisis or social upheaval. Some sort of oversight or control is necessary to ensure that media satisfy important public needs.

As we saw in Chapter 2, advocates of this control based their arguments on propaganda theories. The threat posed by propaganda was so great that they believed information gathering and transmission had to be placed under the control of wise people—technocrats who could be trusted to act in the public interest. These technocrats would be highly trained and have professional values and skills that guaranteed that media content would serve socially valuable purposes—for example, stopping the spread of terrorism or informing people about natural disasters or warning the public of a coming pandemic. Other proponents of regulation based their views on mass society theory. They were troubled by the power of media content to undermine high culture with trivial forms of entertainment. Their complaints often centered on media's presentation of sex and violence. These regulation proponents also objected to the trivialization of what they considered important moral values.

Thus, both propaganda and mass society theories can be used to lobby for media regulation. Both perspectives view media as powerful, subversive forces that must be brought under the control of wise people, those who can be trusted to act in the public interest. But who should be trusted to censor media? Social scientists? Religious leaders?

The military? The police? Congress? The Federal Communications Commission (FCC)? Although many powerful people believed in the necessity of controlling media, they couldn't reach consensus about who should do it. Media practitioners were able to negotiate compromises by pointing out the dangers of regulation and by offering to engage in self-regulation—to become more socially responsible.

Eventually social responsibility theory emerged from this debate. It represents a compromise between views favoring government control of media and those favoring total press freedom. This didn't satisfy everyone, but it did have broad appeal, especially within the media industries. Even today most mainstream media practitioners use some variant of social responsibility theory to justify their actions. To fully understand social responsibility theory, we must review the ideas and events that led to its development.

The Origin of Libertarian Thought on Communication

Modern libertarian thinking about communication can be traced back to 16th-century Europe—a time when feudal aristocracies exercised arbitrary power over the lives of most people. This era was also rocked by major social upheaval. International trade and urbanization undermined the power of these rural aristocracies, and several social and political movements sprang up, most notably the Protestant Reformation, which demanded greater freedom for individuals over their own lives and thoughts (Altschull, 1990).

Libertarian communication theory arose in opposition to **authoritarian theory**—an idea that placed all forms of communication under the control of a governing elite or authorities (Siebert, Peterson, & Schramm, 1956). Authorities justified their power as a means of protecting and preserving a divinely ordained social order. In most countries this control rested in the hands of a king, who in turn granted royal charters or licenses to media practitioners. These publishers could be jailed for violating their charters, and charters or licenses could be revoked. Censorship of all types, therefore, was easily possible. Authoritarian control tended to be exercised in arbitrary, erratic ways. Sometimes considerable freedom might exist to publicize minority viewpoints and culture, as long as authorities didn't perceive a direct threat to their power. Unlike totalitarianism, authoritarian theory doesn't prioritize cultivation of a homogeneous national culture. It only requires acquiescence to the governing elite.

In rebelling against authoritarian theory, early libertarians argued that if individuals could be freed from the arbitrary limits on communication imposed by church and state, they would "naturally" follow the dictates of their conscience, seek truth, engage in public debate, and ultimately create a better life for themselves and others (McQuail, 1987; Siebert, Peterson, & Schramm, 1956). Libertarians blamed authorities for preserving unnatural, arbitrary social orders. They believed strongly in the power of unrestricted public debate and discussion to create more natural ways of structuring society. Many early libertarians were Protestants rebelling against Catholic Church restrictions on their freedom to communicate. They believed that without these restrictions, individuals could follow their conscience, communicate accordingly, and ultimately come to a knowledge of the truth.

In *Areopagitica*, a powerful libertarian tract on communication freedom published in 1644, John Milton asserted that in a fair debate, good and truthful arguments will always win out over lies and deceit. It followed that if this were true, a new and better social order could be forged through public discourse. This idea came to be referred to as Milton's **self-righting principle**, and it continues to be widely cited by contemporary media professionals as a rationale for preserving media freedom (Altschull, 1990). It is a fundamental principle within social responsibility theory. Unfortunately most early libertarians had a rather unrealistic view of how long it would take to find the "truth" and establish an ideal social order. This ideal order was not necessarily a democracy, and it might not always permit communication freedom. Milton, for example, came to argue that Oliver Cromwell had found "truth." After all, the Puritan leader's battlefield victories had been guided by God. Because he was convinced that the resulting social order was ideal, Milton was willing to serve as the chief censor in Cromwell's regime. He expressed few regrets about limiting what Catholic leaders could communicate (Altschull, 1990). As far as Milton was concerned, Catholic ideas had been demonstrated to be false on the battlefield and therefore should be censored so right-thinking people wouldn't be confused by them.

When it became clear during the 18th century that definitive forms of "truth" couldn't be quickly or easily established, some libertarians became discouraged. Occasionally they drifted back and forth between libertarian and authoritarian views. Even Thomas Jefferson, author of the Declaration of Independence, wavered in his commitment to press freedom and his faith in the self-righting principle. Jefferson, who famously affirmed Milton's self-righting principle in a letter to a friend—"Were it left to me to decide whether we should have a government without newspapers or newspapers without government, I should not hesitate to prefer the latter" (as cited in Altschull, 1990, p. 117)—voiced deep frustration with scurrilous newspaper criticism during the second term of his presidency. Nevertheless, he placed libertarian ideals at the heart of the United States' long-term experiment with democratic self-government. The revolution of the American Colonies against Britain was legitimized by those ideals. As Jefferson himself wrote in 1779, "That truth is great and will prevail if left to herself, that she is the proper and sufficient antagonist to error, and has nothing to fear from the conflict, unless by human interposition disarmed of her natural weapons, free argument and debate" (as cited in Packer, 2006, p. 59).

John Keane (1991) identified three fundamental concepts underpinning the Founders' belief in press freedom:

1. *Theology*: Media should serve as a forum allowing people to deduce between good and evil.
2. *Individual rights*: Press freedom is the strongest, if not the only, guarantee of liberty from political elites.
3. *Attainment of truth*: Falsehoods must be countered; ideas must be challenged and tested or they will become dogma.

As such, the newly formed United States was one of the first nations to explicitly adopt libertarian principles, as it did in the Declaration of Independence and the **Bill of Rights**. The latter, articulated in the first 10 Amendments to the Constitution, asserts that all individuals have natural rights that no government, community, or group can unduly infringe upon or take away. Various forms of communication freedom—speech, press, and assembly—are among the most important of these rights. The ability to express dissent, to band together with others to resist laws that people consider wrong, to print or broadcast ideas, opinions, and beliefs—these rights are proclaimed as central to democratic self-government. You can test your own commitment to freedom of expression in the box entitled "A Stirring Defense of Free Expression."

Despite the priority given to communication freedom, however, it is important to recognize that many restrictions on communication—accepted by media practitioners and media consumers alike—do indeed exist. Libel laws protect against the publication of information that will damage reputations. Judges can issue gag orders to stop the publication of information they think will interfere with a defendant's right to a

THINKING ABOUT THEORY

A STIRRING DEFENSE OF FREE EXPRESSION

Concurring with the majority in the 1927 Supreme Court decision in *Whitney v. California*, Justice Louis Brandeis penned this stunning defense for freedom of expression:

> Those who won our independence believed that the final end of the State was to make men free to develop their faculties; and that in its government the deliberative forces should prevail over the arbitrary. They valued liberty both as an end and as a means. They believed liberty to be the secret of happiness and courage to be the secret of liberty. They believed that freedom to think as you will and speak as you think are means indispensable to the discovery and spread of political truth; that without free speech and assembly discussion would be futile; that with them, discussion affords ordinarily adequate protection against the dissemination of noxious doctrine; that the greatest menace to freedom is an inert people; that public discussion is a political duty; and that this should be a fundamental principle of the American government. They recognized the risks to which all human institutions are subject. But they knew that order cannot be secured merely through fear of punishment for its infraction; that it is hazardous to discourage thought, hope, and imagination; that fear breeds repression; that repression breeds hate; that hate menaces stable government; that the path of safety lies in the opportunity to discuss freely supposed grievances and proposed remedies; and that the fitting remedy for evil counsels is good ones. Believing in the power of reason as applied through public discussion, they eschewed silence coerced by law—the argument of force

in its worst form. Recognizing the occasional tyrannies of governing majorities, they amended the Constitution so that free speech and assembly should be guaranteed. (as cited in Gillmor & Barron, 1974, pp. 21–22)

Of course you see and support the wisdom of Justice Brandeis's powerful enunciation of our First Freedom. But the world was a much different place in 1927. In 2007 American helicopter troops in Iraq shot and killed several people they took to be enemy combatants, but among those victims were two Reuters News reporters. The United States government classified the video footage of the exchange "Top Secret" and denied its existence when the news organization asked to review it. Three years later, Army intelligence analyst Bradley (now Chelsea) Manning, believing his government was hiding a war crime, made the video available to investigative Internet news site Wikileaks, which released it under the title "Collateral Murder." Treason, cried those critical of the soon-to-be court marshalled and imprisoned soldier; free speech hero, countered his supporters (Selk, 2017). In 2017 a group of White supremacists and Nazis descended on Charlottesville, Virginia, proudly shouting their slogans in front of hundreds of cameras. Among them was Californian Cole White, who was identified by name on the Twitter account "Yes, You're Racist." The restaurant where he worked promptly fired him (Perez, 2017). Both Manning and White were engaging in free expression—Manning to protest a potential war crime and White to protest what he viewed as a threat to his racial superiority. Given his impassioned defense of free expression, how do you think Justice Brandeis would have felt about Manning's imprisoning and White's firing?

fair trial. Other laws and regulations protect against false advertising, child pornography, and offensive language. The limits to communication freedom are constantly renegotiated.

In some eras the balance shifts toward expanding communication freedom, but at other times, most notably in times of war or violent social unrest, freedom is curtailed. In the wake of the September 11, 2001, terrorist attacks on New York City and Washington, DC, for example, Congress passed legislation known as the Patriot Act that imposed a variety of restrictions on Americans' communication freedom. And whenever new media technologies are invented, it becomes necessary to decide how they should be regulated. The debate over communication freedom never ends, as we see today in the ongoing and heated debates over censoring, controlling, or otherwise mitigating the influence of fake news, offensive media content, press access to military activities in times of armed conflict, and the right of domestic Islamic groups to engage in activities that others worry may threaten national security.

Why is it necessary to place limits on communication freedom? The most common reason for curtailing communication freedom is a conflict over basic rights. The Bill of Rights guarantees citizens many different rights in addition to communication freedom. But where do the rights guaranteed to you end and those of another person begin? Do you have the right to shout "Fire!" in a crowded movie theater if there is no fire? The US Supreme Court has ruled you don't. If you did, many people would be hurt—don't they have a right to be protected against your irresponsible behavior? Similar questions arise when groups attempt to stir up hatred and resentment against racial or ethnic minorities. In 2018, angering Internet freedom and free speech groups alike, virtually all the major American social network sites banned conspiracy-monger Alex Jones from their platforms for "abusive behavior"—for example, threatening critics and encouraging his followers to harass them (Grothaus, 2018b). Who has the moral high ground here? Should YouTube take down videos blamed for causing violence, anorexia, or suicide? Should Nazi social media posts denying the Holocaust be censored? Does a fundamentalist religious group have the right to raise giant billboards accusing a pro-choice politician of being the anti-Christ and exhorting citizens to pray for his or her descent into hellfire? Shouldn't such irresponsible forms of communication be controlled? Over the years, the US Congress, state legislatures, and even many municipalities have addressed questions like this. They have written laws to restrict communication freedom so that other, seemingly equally important rights might be guaranteed. Courts have upheld many of these laws, and others have been struck down because they deemed communication freedom more important.

The Marketplace of Ideas: A New Form of Radical Libertarianism

Though libertarian thought in the United States dates from the country's founding, it has undergone many transformations. An important variant emerged in the 1800s during the penny press and yellow journalism eras. Throughout this period, public confidence in both business and government was shaken by recurring economic depressions, widespread corruption, and injustice. As we noted in Chapter 2, large companies led by robber barons—most notably in the oil, railroad, and steel industries—created nationwide monopolies to charge unfair prices and reap enormous profits. Workers were paid low salaries and forced to labor under difficult or hazardous conditions.

Public respect for newspapers also ebbed as publishers pursued profits and created "news" to boost circulation. They ignored or suppressed actual news about the abuses of the robber barons. Several social movements, especially the progressive (liberal) and populist (champion of average folks) movements sprang up to call for new laws and greater government regulation (Altschull, 1990). They were effective, as Congress eventually enacted antitrust legislation to break up the big monopolies.

But libertarians feared that these laws and regulations would go too far. Wanting to rekindle public support for libertarian ideals, media practitioners developed a cogent response to progressive and populist criticisms. They argued that media should be regarded as a *self-regulating* **marketplace of ideas**. This theory is a variation of a fundamental principle of capitalism—the notion of a self-regulating market. In classical capitalist theory, as formulated by Adam Smith, there is little need for the government to regulate markets. An open and competitive marketplace should regulate itself. If a product is in high demand, prices will "naturally" rise as consumers compete to buy it. This encourages other manufacturers to produce the product. Once demand is met by increased manufacturing, the price falls. If one manufacturer charges too much for a product, competitors will cut their prices to attract buyers. No government interference is necessary to protect consumers or to force manufacturers to meet consumer needs. Another term used to refer to these ideas is the **laissez-faire doctrine**.

According to the marketplace-of-ideas theory, the laissez-faire doctrine should be applied to mass media; that is, if ideas are "traded" freely among people, the correct or best ideas should prevail. The *ideas* compete, and the best will be "bought." They will earn profits that will encourage others to compete and market similar good ideas. Bad ideas will have no buyers, and thus there will be no incentive to produce and market them. But there are some difficulties in applying this logic to our large contemporary media. Media content is far less tangible than other consumer products. The meaning of individual messages can vary tremendously from one person to the next. Just what is being traded when news stories or television dramas are "bought" and "sold"? When we buy a magazine, we don't buy individual stories; we buy packages of them bundled with features like advertisements and crossword puzzles. We can choose to ignore anything in the package that we find offensive. And there is no direct connection between our purchase of the magazine and the fact that we may or may not find some useful ideas in it. When we watch commercial television, we don't pay a fee to the networks. Yet buying and selling are clearly involved. Advertisers buy time on these shows and then use them as vehicles for their messages. When they buy time, they buy access to the audience for the show; they do not necessarily buy the rightness or correctness of the program's ideas. Sponsors pay more to advertise on programs with large or demographically attractive audiences, not for programs with better ideas in them. If violent or misogynistic content attracts more people, so be it. What about large-scale social media—how could marketplace-of-ideas notions apply? The Facebook News Feed supplies users with news articles picked from a variety of sources and uses a computer algorithm that Facebook says tailors the choices to fit user interests. But that algorithm also seeks to maximize user time spent on Facebook. Facebook pays very little for these articles and earns advertising income when users spend time reading them. We don't know much about the algorithm, so it could be ignoring hard news in favor of sensational or entertaining news. There is little evidence that Facebook seeks to maximize public service. Clearly the media marketplace is a bit more complicated than the

WHICH MODEL OF THE MARKETPLACE?

The marketplace-of-ideas theory sees the operation of the mass media system as analogous to that of the self-regulating product market. Take this example and judge for yourself the goodness of fit.

What do these models imply about the quality of candy in the United States? What do they say about the quality of television?

Product	Producer	Consumer
Model 1 A product producer	produces a product as efficiently and inexpensively as possible	for its consumers, who wield the ultimate power: to buy or not to buy.
Model 2 Hershey's	produces candy efficiently and inexpensively on a production line	for people like us. If we buy the candy, Hershey's continues to make similar candy in a similar way.
Model 3 NBC	produces people using programs (its production line)	for advertisers. If they buy NBC's product, NBC continues to produce similar audiences in similar ways.

marketplace for refrigerators or toothpaste, as you can investigate in the box entitled "Which Model of the Marketplace?"

In the American media system, the marketplace of ideas was supposed to work like this: Someone comes up with a good idea and then transmits it through some form of mass medium. If other people like it, they buy the message. When people buy the message, they pay for its production and distribution costs. Once these costs are covered, the message producer earns a profit. If people don't like the message, they don't buy it, and the producer goes broke trying to produce and distribute it. If people are wise message consumers, the producers of the best and most useful messages will become rich and develop large media enterprises, and the producers of bad messages will fail. Useless media will go out of business. If the purveyors of good ideas succeed, these ideas should become more easily available at lower cost. Producers will compete to supply them. Similarly, the cost of bad ideas should rise and access to them should diminish. Eventually truth should win out in the marketplace of ideas, just as it should triumph in the public forum envisioned by the early libertarians. According to marketplace-of-ideas theory, the self-righting principle should apply to mass media content as well as to public debate. But what if advertiser support permits bad messages to be distributed for free? What if advertisers support the use of social media algorithms that undermine the public interest by prioritizing fake news? Will people be less discriminating if they don't have to pay directly to receive these messages, as with Internet sites like YouTube, where cat videos, people hurting themselves, and conspiracy theorists win much larger audiences than serious discussion of problems of the day? What if the bad messages are distributed as part of a large bundle of messages (e.g., a newspaper or television news program, a package of cable television channels, or a social media newsfeed)? If you want the good messages, you also directly or indirectly pay to subsidize the bad messages. What is bad for you might be good for someone else. You might not like horoscopes or soap operas, but you have friends who do.

MARKETPLACE-OF-IDEAS THEORY

Strengths

1. Limits government control
2. Allows "natural" fluctuations in tastes, ideals, and discourse
3. Puts trust in the audience
4. Assumes "good" content will ultimately prevail

Weaknesses

1. Mistakenly equates media content with more tangible consumer products
2. Puts too much trust in profit-motivated media operators
3. Ignores the fact that content that is intentionally "bought" is often accompanied by other, sometimes unwanted or problematic content
4. Has an overly optimistic view of audiences' media consumption skills
5. Mistakenly assumes audience—not advertiser—is consumer
6. Definition of "good" is not universal (for example, what is "good" for the majority might be bad for a minority)

Just how useful is the marketplace-of-ideas theory? After all, government regulation of the consumer marketplace is now generally accepted as necessary. Few people question the need for consumer protection laws or rules regulating unfair business practices. The consumer marketplace benefited from regulation, so why not regulate the marketplace of ideas? Since 1930 media critics have asked this question more and more frequently, and the recent rampant concentration of media companies, the sudden domination of large-scale social media by a few companies, and rapid diffusion of mobile technologies have added new urgency to the call for government intervention.

Even so, marketplace-of-ideas theory enjoys significant support within the media industries. That support resides in the "duality" inherent in the marketplace-of-ideas philosophy, one that "has allowed widely divergent interpretations of the metaphor to develop" (Napoli, 1999, p. 151). Media policy researcher Philip Napoli (1999) identified two interpretations of the marketplace of ideas. "Economic theory–based interpretations of the marketplace of ideas emphasize efficiency, consumer satisfaction, and competition," he wrote. "Whereas democratic theory–based interpretations emphasize citizen knowledge, informed decision making, and effective self-government" (pp. 151–152). Economic theory–based interpretations, he argued, are used in support of arguments against government regulation, and democratic theory–based interpretations are typically used to support calls for regulation.

Media practitioners are satisfied with this distinction because, as numerous researchers have demonstrated (e.g., Lavey, 1993; Simon, Atwater, & Alexander, 1988), government—especially through agencies such as the FCC and the Federal Trade Commission, which regulates advertising—"historically has devoted much greater empirical attention to the economic effects of its policies than to the social and political effects" (Napoli, 1999, p. 165). Media critics, however, are less satisfied as they regard these regulatory bodies as *captured agencies*; they are controlled by the industries they are supposed to regulate (Alster, 2015). For example, they point to the 2017 FCC vote to do away with **net neutrality**, the regulatory principle established during the Barack Obama administration that all Internet data, sites, and services should be treated equally. Under those rules users were able to access any site or service they wished without an Internet provider blocking them or otherwise impeding them—for example, slowing download rates or charging more for different levels of access; nor could those providers promote their own sites and services to the detriment of others. The FCC move to end net neutrality clearly benefitted Internet service providers and cable TV owners. It went into effect without the usual public comment period, and despite the fact that 83% of Americans, including 75% of Republicans, 89% of Democrats, and 86% of Independents, favored maintaining net neutrality as it stood (Neidig, 2017).

GOVERNMENT REGULATION OF MEDIA

During the 1920s and 1930s a new normative theory of mass communication began to emerge that rejected radical libertarianism, technocratic control, and marketplace-of-ideas notions. One of its sources was congressional hearings over government regulation of radio. In 1927 these hearings led to the establishment of the Federal Radio Commission (FRC), which was the forerunner of the FCC. As the debates raged, some people—especially progressive and populist politicians—argued that the excesses of yellow journalism proved that self-regulation wasn't enough. Overdramatized and fictitious news was so profitable that publishers and broadcasters couldn't resist producing and distributing it. Without some sort of regulation, radio was not likely to serve the public interest as well as it should. Even so, progressives were cautious about turning control of radio over to government technocrats. A compromise solution was needed.

By the 1920s the American public had come to accept government regulation of public utilities as a means of ending wasteful competition while preserving private enterprise. Before government regulation of power and telephone companies, cities were blanketed with competing networks of wires. Anyone who wanted to talk to people on other networks had to buy phones from all the competing companies. The cost of building entirely independent networks increased the cost of phone service and electricity. The solution to these problems was to allow one company to have a monopoly on supplying these needed services. In return for the grant of that monopoly, the company accepted government regulation of prices and services. In this way public utilities were created, with government commissions to oversee their operation. Could a government commission be used to regulate radio as a public utility? The answer was yes. In fact, Secretary of Commerce (later President) Herbert Hoover himself was moved to remark that this was one of the few instances in history where the country—industry and public alike—was unanimous in its desire for more regulation (Barnouw, 1966).

In the debate over the establishment of the FRC, Secretary Hoover championed one especially important philosophy—the airwaves belong to the people. If airwaves are public property like other national resources (national forests, for example), privately operated stations can never own them. Instead they must be licensed from the people and used in the public interest. If license holders violate the public trust, their licenses can be revoked. The FRC was created to act on behalf of the public. But some historians claim that the "compromise solution" between populist demands for freedom and technocrats' calls for control produced a somewhat limited definition of the "public interest." In fact, they argue, the intent of the legislation creating the FRC, the Radio Act of 1927, was *not* to encourage an open forum for public debate because such a freewheeling discussion was considered a threat to the very "public interest, convenience, and necessity" that Congress wanted broadcasters to serve. Congress specifically designed the 1927 act to "deny the public access to the ideas of their enemies, such as unions, socialists, communists, evolutionists, improper thinkers, non-Christians, and immigrants. . . . Broadcasters could have free speech as long as they served the public interest by denying access to speakers who did not serve the public interest as they [Congress] defined it" (Goodman, 2001).

Nonetheless the relative success of the FRC encouraged efforts to regulate other media industries. Government censorship of movies was widely advocated, especially by religious groups. Over time the movie industry adopted various forms of self-censorship in an effort to avoid government regulation. As the threat of propaganda grew, even regulation of newspapers was seriously considered. In 1942, for example, the Hutchins Commission on Freedom of the Press was established to weigh the merits of and necessity for newspaper regulation (we'll say more about this later).

Professionalization of Journalism

As pressure for government regulation of media mounted in the 1920s, industry leaders responded with efforts to professionalize. Leaders in the newspaper industry lobbied for and occasionally subsidized the establishment of professional schools to train media practitioners. Rather than cede control of media to a government agency, media managers went on record with pledges to serve public needs. In 1923 the American Society of Newspaper Editors (ASNE) adopted a set of professional standards entitled *The Canons of Journalism* (which were replaced in 1975 by the *ASNE Statement of Principles*). Since then virtually every association of media practitioners has adopted similar standards. In doing so these associations are emulating professionals in fields like law and medicine. These standards typically commit media practitioners to serving the public as effectively as possible.

Industry codes of ethics began to formalize another important conception about the role of media—that of a watchdog guarding the welfare of the public. Media should continually scan the social world and alert the public to problems. This gave rise around the turn of the 20th century to **muckrakers,** crusading journalists who typically challenged the powerful on behalf of those less so. Their investigations of corruption proved so popular that newspapers specializing in them came to dominate the markets in some large cities. The Scripps Howard newspaper chain adopted the lighthouse as its symbol and chose the phrase "Give light and the people will find their own way" as its motto. The current slogan of the *Washington Post* is "Democracy dies in darkness." Gradually the watchdog role was widely accepted as a necessary and appropriate one for news media.

Some ambitious formulations of this role envision the media as independent watchdogs, a social institution, the **Fourth Estate** of government, charged with making certain that all other institutions—the three branches of government, business, religion, education, and family—serve the public. In the words of social critic and veteran journalist Bill Moyers (2001), properly functioning media are needed "to keep our leaders honest and to arm the powerless with the information they need to protect themselves against the tyranny of the powerful, whether that tyranny is political or commercial" (p. 13). This perspective assumes that once people are informed about wrongdoing, incompetence, inequality, or inefficiency, they will take action against it. But there has always been concern that the watchdog might be subverted by the powerful, becoming a lapdog. Or the watchdog could become irresponsible, exaggerating its criticism of government or business to build and grow audiences. What type of watchdog coverage should we expect from media when most are owned by the very corporations they are expected to police? And how likely is it that these media will criticize governments having the power to make decisions that affect their profits? Is it still reasonable to expect our profit-oriented press to comfort the afflicted and afflict the comfortable? After all, there are critical scholars who believe that journalism's troubles reside in the fundamental incompatibility of democracy itself and capitalism (Jensen, 2010; Stoll & McManus, 2005). As timely as these questions may be today, eight decades ago they were at the heart of the search for a theory to guide the operation of a growing American mass media system and its interactions with its growing audiences. Social responsibility theory was the result.

SOCIAL RESPONSIBILITY THEORY OF THE PRESS: A POSTWAR COMPROMISE

Despite moves toward professionalization and self-regulation, pressure for greater government regulation of media mounted throughout World War II and continued during the anti-communist agitation that followed. In response, Henry Luce, CEO of Time Inc., provided funding for an independent commission to make recommendations concerning the role of the press. The Hutchins Commission on Freedom of the Press was established in 1942 and released a major report of its findings in 1947 (Davis, 1990; McIntyre, 1987). Its members consisted of leaders from many areas of society, including academics, politicians, and heads of social groups.

Commission members were divided between those who held strongly libertarian views and those who thought some form of press regulation was necessary. Those who favored regulation were fearful that the marketplace of ideas was much too vulnerable to subversion by antidemocratic forces. Several of these regulation proponents were guided by a philosophy of public communication developed by social researchers at the University of Chicago. The **Chicago School** envisioned modern cities to be "Great Communities" composed of hundreds of small social groups—everything from neighborhood social organizations to citywide associations. For these Great Communities to develop, all constituent groups had to work together and contribute. These were referred to as **pluralistic groups** in recognition of their cultural and racial diversity (Davis, 1990).

The Chicago School opposed marketplace-of-ideas notions and argued that unregulated mass media inevitably served the interests and tastes of large or socially dominant groups. In their view, *protecting* the right of expression was not equivalent to *providing* for it. They wanted a *positive* role for government regulation, "an interventionary role—to provide enabling structures for a healthy public sphere" (Pickard, 2010, p. 394). Their concern, reinforced by what they regularly saw in the media of their day, was that small or powerless pluralistic groups would be either neglected or denigrated.

They also worried that ruthless elites could use media as a means of gaining personal political power. These demagogues could manipulate media to transmit propaganda to fuel hatred and fear among a majority and unite them against minorities. Hitler's use of media to arouse hatred of the Jews served as a prime example.

To prevent this tyranny by the majority and to mandate support for pluralistic groups, some commission members favored creation of a public agency—a press council—made up of people much like themselves and having the power to prevent publication of hate propaganda. In the view of these Hutchins Commission members, this "new and independent agency [would] appraise and report annually upon the performance of the press." It would base that appraisal on its comparison of "the accomplishments of the press with the aspirations which the people have for it" (as cited in Bates, 1995, p. 72). A press council might, for example, require that newspapers and radio stations devote a certain portion of their coverage to minority groups. Or it might require that these groups be given regular columns or programs in which they could express whatever they wanted. Commission members recognized that such regulations might impose additional costs on media outlets. If this happened, government subsidies might cover these expenses. By serving pluralistic groups, media would strengthen them and enable them to contribute to the Great Community. This fostering of pluralism and restraint on propaganda were seen as essential to preventing the spread of totalitarianism in the United States.

Although the majority of the Hutchins Commission members had some sympathy for Chicago School ideas, they opposed any direct form of press regulation (Davis 1990; McIntyre, 1987). This meant they faced a serious dilemma. On the one hand, they recognized that the marketplace of ideas was not self-regulating and that the media were doing less than they could to provide services to society's smaller voices. But on the other hand, they feared that any form of press regulation would open the door to official control of media—the very thing they were trying to prevent. Ultimately the Hutchins Commission members decided to place their faith in media practitioners, calling on them to redouble their efforts to serve the public:

> [They] endorsed professional responsibility . . . [as] a way of reconciling market flaws with the traditional conception of the democratic role of the media. [The Hutchins Commission's report] asserted journalists' commitment to higher goals—neutrality, detachment, a commitment to truth. It involved the adoption of certain procedures for verifying facts, drawing on different sources, presenting rival interpretations. In this way, the pluralism of opinion and information, once secured through the clash of adversaries in the free market, could be recreated through the "internal pluralism" of monopolistic media. Market pressures to sensationalize and trivialize the presentation of news could be offset by a commitment to inform. (Curran, 1991, p. 98)

The synthesis of ideas put forward in the Hutchins Commission report has become known as the *Social Responsibility Theory of the Press* (Siebert, Peterson, & Schramm, 1956). It emphasized the need for an independent press that scrutinizes other social institutions and provides objective, accurate news reports. The most innovative feature of social responsibility was its call for media to be responsible for fostering productive and creative Great Communities. It said that media should do this by prioritizing cultural pluralism—by becoming the voice of all the people—not just elite groups or groups that had dominated national, regional, or local cultures.

In some respects social responsibility theory is a radical statement. Instead of demanding that media be free to print or transmit whatever their owners want, social responsibility theory imposes a burden on media practitioners. As the commission argued, "The press is not free if those who operate it behave as though their position conferred on them the privilege of being deaf to ideas which the processes of free speech have brought to public attention" (Commission on Freedom of the Press, 1947, p. 9).

Social responsibility theory appealed to the idealism and professionalism of many media practitioners and tried to unite them in the service of cultural pluralism—even when this might reduce their profits or antagonize existing social elites. The theory challenged media professionals' ingenuity to develop new ways of serving their communities. It encouraged them to see themselves as front-line participants in the battle to preserve democracy in a world drifting inexorably toward totalitarianism. By helping pluralistic groups, media were building a wall to protect democracy from external and internal foes. Denis McQuail (2010, p. 171) summarized the basic propositions of social responsibility theory as follows:

- The media have obligations to society, and media ownership is a public trust.
- News media should be truthful, accurate, fair, objective, and relevant.
- The media should be free, but self-regulated.
- The media should follow agreed codes of ethics and professional conduct.
- Under some circumstances, government may need to intervene to safeguard the public interest.

Using Social Responsibility Theory to Guide Professional Practice

The ideals of social responsibility theory have proved quite durable, even if their full implications are rarely understood by working media professionals. In fact, many scholars argue "social responsibility doctrine has always been relegated to the fringes of journalism education and the newsroom. More than 60 years after the Hutchins Commission report, news personnel generally remain hostile to its focus on the public good and on broad-based reporting about significant events of the day" (Christians, Ferre, & Fackler, 1993, p. 38). Furthermore, in the competing "ethos of news as business [and] that of news as socially responsible institution," social responsibility often comes in second (Lind & Rockier, 2001, p. 119). In our current era of large media corporations, "Friends of the 'liberty of the press' must recognize that *communication markets restrict freedom of communication* by generating barriers to entry, monopoly and restrictions upon choice, and by shifting the prevailing definition of information from that of a public good to that of a privately appropriated commodity" (Keane, 1991, pp. 88–89).

So if social responsibility theory is to remain a viable normative theory, greater effort might be needed to implement it, particularly when large-scale social media play an ever-growing role in the distribution of news. Compared with the vast amount of research conducted on media effects, relatively little work has examined whether existing news production practices, as intended, actually serve societal goals. For example, one primary journalistic goal is communicating accurate information about important events to the public. Research findings on this goal are mixed. Evidence indicates that people don't learn much from news reports, and what they do learn is quickly forgotten (Graber, 1987). People become easily confused by TV news stories that are poorly structured or use dramatic but irrelevant pictures. This research has had little or no impact on the practice of journalism. Its findings have been largely ignored or misinterpreted by media practitioners (Davis & Robinson, 1989).

In the 1970s and 1980s researchers published a series of studies that raised important questions about the value of routine news production practices (Bennett, 1988; Epstein, 1973; Fishman, 1980; Gans, 1979; Glasgow University Media Group, 1976, 1980; Tuchman, 1978). Journalists have consistently ignored most of this work as biased, irrelevant, and misguided. It deserves a more careful reading. Gaye Tuchman, for example, presents a well-developed argument concerning the role played by media in the discovery and cultivation of social movements. She sees news production as bound by "strategic rituals" and believes that these practices appear to satisfy the requirements imposed by social responsibility norms but fall far short of achieving their purpose. For example, journalists ritualistically construct "balanced" stories in which they contrast opposing views. However, these conventions might actually undermine rather than advance pluralism. She maintains that "balanced stories" about minority groups frequently contain statements from social or political leaders that subtly or blatantly denigrate groups and their ideas. The emotionally charged opinions of little-known group leaders are contrasted with reasoned pronouncements from well-known credible officials. Researchers in Scotland raised similar concerns about TV news reporting (Glasgow University Media Group, 1976, 1980). Reporters make little effort to create a context for new groups' broader goals or culture. Instead their reports tend to focus on dramatic events staged by isolated group members. There's much more to be said about the impact of routine news production practices in Chapter 6 and Chapter 13.

Limitations of Professionalization

Those practicing contemporary journalism in a manner consistent with social responsibility theory's norms of professionalism face additional difficulties. In their move toward professionalization, media practitioners, like doctors and lawyers before them, pledge to uphold standards of professional practice. They promise to weed out irresponsible people and give recognition to those who excel. Those who violate standards should be censured. In extreme cases, they could be barred from professional practice. And as an alternative to direct government regulation, media professionalization has worked relatively well. Certain limitations, however, especially in our time of dramatic technological and economic change in the media industries, lead to recurring problems:

1. **Professionals in every field, including journalism, are been reluctant to identify and censure colleagues who violate professional standards.** To do so is often seen as admitting that problems exist. Public trust in all media professionals might be shaken if too many people are barred from practice. Professional societies tend to operate as closed groups in which members are protected against outside threats and criticism. Attacks from outsiders are routinely dismissed as unwarranted, even when evidence against a practitioner mounts. For years, a major German news magazine, *Der Spiegel*, ignored credible complaints that one of their reporters was fabricating news (Noack & Beck, 2018).

Often, as was true for *Der Spiegel*, action is taken only in extreme instances, when it cannot be avoided. Even then, news media either avoid covering the case or provide brief and superficial coverage. Do you remember hearing about the *Der Spiegel* case or the name of the award-winning reporter, Claas Relotius? It wasn't widely covered in the US even though many of his fabricated stories were about Americans and fostered problematic stereotypes of those people.

2. **Professional standards can be overly abstract and ambiguous.** They can be difficult to implement and enforce. Mission statements and broad codes of ethics are notoriously vague. The Radio Television Digital News Association's Code of Ethics and Professional Conduct (2015), for example, instructs its members that their "obligation is to pursue the truth and report, not withhold it." But news directors must make choices concerning allocation of resources. What if an independent journalistic investigation leads a large advertiser to cancel its account? Why risk producing stories that might prove embarrassing to someone or some organization? In the news business, telling the truth can sometimes be difficult and expensive. Professional standards are vague, so nothing forces journalists to endanger relationships with friendly sources or the company's profit margins. In fact, in the case of television, research indicates that "power pressures" (influence from owners and top-level executives) and "pocketbook concerns" (economic pressures) not only significantly shape the news but often lead to **agenda cutting**, editorial decisions keeping specific coverage out of the news or out of the main news agenda (Colistra, 2018). International news is one of the first topics to be limited when agendas are cut. Evidence exists that this process is at play across all news media (Stoll & McManus, 2005). It's likely that the computer algorithms used by social media to create their newsfeeds have a very limited agenda that excludes or marginalizes news on a range of topics considered less interesting or relevant to users and therefore less likely to keep them on those sites.

3. **In contrast with medicine and law, media professionalization doesn't include standards for professional training and licensing.** Other professions mandate that practitioners receive long and closely monitored professional training. For example, doctors and lawyers undergo from four to 10 years of specialized training in addition to completing four years of college. But media practitioners are unwilling to set requirements for professional training and have strongly resisted efforts to license journalists. They argue that these requirements would inevitably be used by government to control the press. If the press is to remain free from control, it must be free to hire anyone—no matter how untrained or unqualified. Anyone should be able to claim the title of journalist, start a news operation, and exercise his or her rights to free press. No government agency should be able to step in and shut down a news organization just because some of its reporters or editors are unlicensed. But, as veteran reporter David Marsh (2012) asks,

> What makes someone a journalist? As recently as 10 years ago, the answer would have been straightforward: journalists made their living by producing editorial material (written or otherwise) which was then published or broadcast to an

audience of readers, listeners, or viewers. In the new digital age of the web and social media, things are more complicated. If I tweet from a major news event—the Arab Spring, say—is that journalism? If I start my own political blog, does that make me a journalist? If I'm a teacher, say, but contribute stories to a newspaper, does that make me a "citizen journalist"? Does it make any difference whether people are paid, or not, for such work? Should **bloggers** [writers who maintain blogs, regularly updated online journals of news and opinion], tweeters and "citizen journalists" be held to, and judged by, the same standards as people working in more traditional journalistic roles? (paras. 1–2)

4. **In contrast with other professions, media practitioners tend to have less independent control over their work.** Media practitioners don't work as autonomous practitioners and therefore have difficulty assuming personal responsibility for their work. They tend to work in big, hierarchically structured bureaucracies. Individual reporters, editors, producers, and directors have only a limited ability to control what they do. Reporters are given assignments by editors, advertising designers work for account executives, and television anchors and camera operators follow the instructions of news directors. Editors, account managers, and directors are all responsible to higher management. In these large bureaucracies, it is difficult to assign responsibility. Those at lower levels can claim that they are only "following orders," whereas people at higher levels can simply disavow any knowledge of what was going on below them.

5. **In the media industries, violation of professional standards rarely has immediate, directly observable consequences.** Thus, it is hard for critics to cite violations or to identify the harm that has been done. When doctors fail, people die. When lawyers fail, people go to jail unnecessarily. The results of unethical or incompetent media practice are harder to see.

The Dual Responsibility Model

Communication researchers Terry Adams-Bloom and Johanna Cleary (2009), acknowledging these pressures on journalists' professionalism, proposed an update of social responsibility theory that "upholds the high ideals and First Amendment considerations of social responsibility theory while recognizing the economic realities of today's mega-corporate environment" (p. 2). Their revision, the **dual responsibility theory**, "acknowledges the reality of bottom-line considerations . . . [and] delineates a place for fiscal, as well as social, responsibility in news decision making in a 24-hour news cycle world. . . . This orientation does not, in and of itself, necessarily produce poor quality content. However, it does represent a shift in prioritizing content that may be the more relevant question when looking at today's news media" (p. 6). You can visually examine the shift they propose in Figure 3.1.

Adams-Bloom and Cleary base their revision on **stakeholder theory**, the idea that companies should operate in the best interests of *all* those who depend on them—their stakeholders—not simply those who benefit financially. Maximizing profit, in and of itself, should not be companies' primary goal. They suggest that this orientation "allows a wide berth for ethical business practices and good corporate citizenship and lessens the importance of pure capitalism" (p. 3).

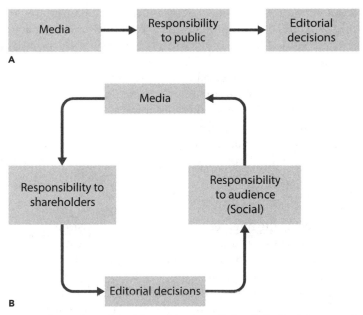

FIGURE 3.1   A. Traditional Model of Social Responsibility & **B.** Dual Responsibility Model

Critics of social responsibility theory (e.g., Altschull, 1995; McQuail, 2005; Pickard, 2010) would argue that most media organizations, even without license from the dual responsibility model to grant even more consideration to profit, have long favored profit over responsibility. Maybe contemporary media companies are simply more obvious about it in what Adams-Bloom and Cleary (2009) call today's "mega-corporate environment," emboldened by "an atmosphere of deregulation and sweeping policy change" (p. 2). Nonetheless, these researchers have undertaken one of the few serious reexaminations of the normative theory that has ostensibly guided American media practices for more than half a century.

IS THERE STILL A ROLE FOR SOCIAL RESPONSIBILITY THEORY?

Although US media have developed many professional practices in an effort to conform to the ideals of social responsibility theory, the long-term objective—the creation of Great Communities—has never seemed more elusive. Our cities have undergone decades of urban renewal, yet slums remain, and in some cities they continue to spread. Social inequality has reached levels not seen for over a century (Galbraith, 2019). There have been national "wars" to combat poverty, crime, pollution, disease, and drugs, but the quality of life for many Americans has not improved. Many suffered losses during 2008's Great Recession and still have not recovered. The opioid epidemic has ravaged communities across the country (Misra, 2019). Non-dominant ethnic and racial cultures are still widely misunderstood. Minority group members continue to be discriminated against and harassed. There are millions of undocumented immigrants in the United States whose work is critical to the economy but whom many Americans distrust and would deport if possible. There is evidence that hate groups are increasing in number and size and that their propaganda is effectively reaching a growing audience (Heim, 2018). Politicians still find it far too easy to win elections by stirring up public fear of "others."

Does this mean that social responsibility theory is wrong? Has it been poorly implemented? What responsibility can or should media practitioners assume on behalf of the Great Communities they serve? More important, how should this responsibility be exercised? With news helicopters circling over riot scenes? With inflammatory coverage of hate groups? With boring coverage of the routine work of neighborhood associations? With sensational coverage of political candidates when they demean and stereotype minorities? Was there merit in the Chicago School arguments concerning coverage of pluralistic groups? If so, what forms might that coverage take? Should group members be allowed some direct control over what is printed about them in newspapers, circulated on the Internet, or broadcast on television?

Our society's experience with local access channels on cable television suggests that it is not easy to use media to support pluralistic groups. In 1972 the FCC for the first time required local cable companies to provide local access channels in an effort to serve pluralistic groups, and although these **local origination (or mandatory access) rules** have been altered, suspended, and otherwise tinkered with during the last 60 years, they have generally failed to serve their intended purpose. Very few people watch the access channels, and few groups use them. When social media began two decades ago, there were high hopes that it would build communities. Facebook CEO Mark Zuckerberg (2017) has asserted that Facebook, now quite profitable, has turned its attention to building a global community. Have you seen evidence that large-scale social media have done much in this area?

Many observers believe that social responsibility theory will be given new strength by emerging technologies that allow communities greater power to disseminate information. The FCC licenses **low-power FM radio (LPFM)** stations, community-based, noncommercial stations broadcasting over small areas, typically 5 to 10 km. The nearly 2,500 stations currently operating in all 50 states are maintained by community groups, labor unions, churches, and other nonprofit groups usually absent from the airwaves (Johnson, 2018). Cable television, though never approaching the

INSTANT ACCESS

LIBERTARIANISM

Strengths	Weaknesses
1. Values media freedom	1. Is overly optimistic about media's willingness to meet responsibilities
2. Is consistent with US media traditions	2. Is overly optimistic about individuals' ethics and rationality
3. Values individuals	3. Ignores need for reasonable control of media
4. Precludes government control of media	4. Ignores dilemmas posed by conflicting freedoms (for example, free press versus personal privacy)

INSTANT ACCESS

SOCIAL RESPONSIBILITY THEORY

Strengths

1. Values media responsibility
2. Values audience responsibility
3. Limits government intrusion in media operation
4. Allows reasonable government control of media
5. Values diversity and pluralism
6. Aids the "powerless"
7. Appeals to the best instincts of media practitioners and audiences
8. Is consistent with US legal tradition

Weaknesses

1. Is overly optimistic about media's willingness to meet responsibility
2. Is overly optimistic about individual responsibility
3. Underestimates power of profit motivation and competition
4. Legitimizes status quo
5. Rarely leads to proactive efforts to aid pluralism or the "powerless"

reempowering-the-public revolution predicted for it in the 1960s, has at least made literally hundreds of channels available, many of which are dedicated to ethnic and specific-interest communities. Now, with the near-total diffusion of the Internet, audience size and ability to make a profit have become relatively unimportant concerns for literally millions of "voices." The website for a tribe of Native Americans, for example, sits electronically side by side with those of the most powerful media organizations. What many theorists fear, however, is that this wealth of voices—each speaking to its own community—will **Balkanize** the larger US culture. That is, rather than all Americans reading and viewing conscientiously produced content about all the Great Communities that make the United States as wonderfully diverse and pluralistic as it is, communities will talk only to people residing within their cultural borders. The values, wants, needs, and ideas of others will be ignored. Journalist Bree Nordenson (2008), for example, argues that "shared public knowledge is receding, as is the likelihood that we come in contact with beliefs that contradict our own. Personalized home pages, newsfeeds created by algorithms, and e-mail alerts, as well as special-interest publications lead us to create what sociologist Todd Gitlin disparagingly referred to as 'my news, my world.' Serendipitous news—accidently encountered information—is far less frequent in a world of TiVo and online customization tools" (p. 37). William Gibson, author of *Neuromancer* and guru to the cybergeneration, predicts that there will indeed be Great Communities, but they will be communities built around brands—Planet Nike and the World of Pepsi—rather than around common values and aspirations (Trench, 1990).

THE PUBLIC INTEREST IN THE INTERNET ERA

In the Internet era, "my news, my world" is typically discussed in terms of the **filter bubble**, the idea that online personalization tools and computer algorithms such as those utilized by Facebook and Google render people more partisan and less open to different or opposing points of view by exposing them to only the news and information with which they already agree or enjoy. And at a time of massive disruption of the traditional media landscape in which 2,100 local newspapers have gone out of business in the last 15 years ("Sizing Up," 2019) and the audiences for every major legacy medium of news other than radio continue to fall (Barthel, 2018), the Internet era is clearly upon us. More than 327 million North Americans, 89% of the population, use the Internet; globally, 4.3 billion people go online, 56% of the world's people and a 1,104% increase since 2000 ("Internet Users," 2019). Of the 11 hours and 6 minutes the average American adult spends with media each day, 4 hours and 23 minutes of that time is online (Katsingris, 2018). One quarter of Americans say they are "almost constantly" online (Perrin & Jiang, 2018), a proportion that rises to nearly half when considering only teenagers (Anderson & Jiang, 2018). This audience makes heavy use of the Internet for their news. Forty-three percent of American adults report "often" getting the news online, just 7 percentage points below the 50% who often get news on television (Gottfried & Shearer, 2017); two thirds report getting their news "at least occasionally" from social media sites such as Facebook and Twitter (Shearer & Matsa, 2018).

News also lives elsewhere on the Net. Many people get their news from **podcasts**, digital Internet audio files downloaded or streamed to a computer or mobile device, usually sent automatically to subscribers. Many are popular culture–based and fan-oriented, but a large proportion of the hundreds of thousands of active shows (Apple Podcasts alone lists more than 550,000; Quah, 2018) feature news and information. Seventy-three million Americans listen to a podcast at least once a month (Bromwich, 2018). Finally, as we've seen, people frequently access the news on blogs, of which more than 31 million are active in the United States ("Number of Blogs," 2019). While some are no doubt personal diaries, family gathering sites, and other idiosyncratic outlets, many others are "citizen publishers," "stand-alone journalists," and "networks of dedicated amateurs" who do meaningful journalism (Stepp, 2006, p. 62). "Freedom of the press now belongs not just to those who own printing presses," wrote journalism scholar Ann Cooper (2008), "but also to those who use cell phones, video cameras, blogging software, and other technology to deliver news and views to the world" (p. 45). In addition, blogging itself has become professionalized. Scores of trained, paid journalists ply their trade on highly sophisticated, advertising-supported blogs. *Politico*, *Huffington Post*, and *Talking Points Memo* are only three examples. Moreover, virtually every mainstream news outlet, from local newspapers to national television networks, requires its journalists to regularly blog on the company's website as well as maintain a presence on Twitter and Facebook. The *New York Times*, for example, offers more than 50 news and opinion blogs on its website. As such, the Internet has assumed a growing news-gathering and dissemination function in our society as well as a central role in our democracy's public discourse.

Bloggers, for example, are routinely granted official access to major news events such as presidential press conferences and Supreme Court hearings; they have a professional association, the Online News Association (at https://journalists.org), and a code of ethics; online journalists are eligible for Pulitzer Prizes; and in 2009, in order to include online journalists among their members, both the Radio and Television News Directors Association (RTNDA) and the American Society of Newspaper Editors (ASNE) changed names. The RTNDA became the RTDNA—the Radio Television Digital News Association—and the ASNE dropped "paper" from its name to become the American Society of News Editors (in 2019 it merged with the Associated Press Media Editors to form the News Leaders Association).

The Internet as a source for news, then, is forcing a major reconsideration not only of the practice of journalism but of social responsibility and the public interest. For example, there was once guarded optimism for the Internet's ability to make room in public discourse for a wider variety of information and opinion (e.g., Goode, 2009; Papacharissi, 2002). Long-time journalist and retired dean of the Columbia School of Journalism Nicholas Lemann surveyed the digital media environment and proclaimed, "As a consumer of news, this is the best time there has ever been" (as cited in Moynihan, 2012). But sociologist and historian Paul Starr (2012) foresaw an "unexpected crisis" in the media's ability to serve social responsibility in an era of digital technology. "The digital revolution has been good for freedom of expression because it has increased the diversity of voices in the public sphere," he wrote. "It has been good for freedom of information because it has made government documents and data directly accessible to more people and has fostered a culture that demands transparency from powerful institutions. But the digital revolution has had mixed effects on freedom of the press. Yes, it has allowed new entrants into the media and generated promising innovations in journalism. But by undermining the economic basis of professional reporting and by fragmenting the public, it has weakened the ability of the press to act as an effective agent of public accountability" (p. 234).

New-journalism theorist Jay Rosen (2009) acknowledges that the traditional media's social responsibility role has indeed been weakened, but offers an alternative, more optimistic view of what that means. His position is that the Internet can give more voice to more people, creating "great communities" built around information and ideas. "In the age of mass media," he wrote, "the press was able to define the sphere of legitimate debate with relative ease because the people on the receiving end were atomized—meaning they were connected 'up' to Big Media but not across to each other. But today one of the biggest factors changing our world is the falling cost for like-minded people to locate each other, share information, trade impressions, and realize their number" (para. 18). He argued that "big media" limit public discourse by "deciding what does and does not legitimately belong within the national debate." He slightly modified political scientist Daniel Hallin's (1986) sphere-of-influence model to explain how this self-serving selection diminishes public discussion of important issues (see Figure 3.2).

According to Rosen (2009, citing Hallin, 1986), democratic public discourse consists of three spheres that are strictly policed by traditional, mainstream media journalists:

1. *Sphere of legitimate debate*—journalists recognize this "as real, normal, everyday terrain. They think of their work as taking place almost exclusively within this space. . . . Hallin: 'This is the region of electoral contests and legislative debates, of issues recognized as such by the major established actors of the American political process'" (para. 3)
2. *Sphere of consensus*—"the 'motherhood and apple pie' of politics, the things on which everyone is thought to agree. Propositions that are seen as uncontroversial to the point of boring, true to the point of self-evidence, or so widely held that they almost universally lie within this sphere. Here, Hallin writes, 'Journalists do not feel compelled either to present opposing views or to remain disinterested observers'" (para. 5)

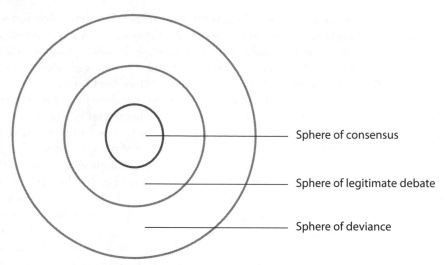

Sphere of consensus

Sphere of legitimate debate

Sphere of deviance

FIGURE 3.2   Spheres of Consensus, Legitimate Debate, and Deviance (adapted from Hallin, 1986)

3. *Sphere of deviance*—here "we find 'political actors and views which journalists and the political mainstream of society reject as unworthy of being heard.' . . . [J]ournalists maintain order by either keeping the deviant out of the news entirely or identifying it within the news frame as unacceptable, radical, or just plain impossible. The press 'plays the role of exposing, condemning, or excluding from the public agenda' the deviant view, says Hallin. It 'marks out and defends the limits of acceptable political conduct.'" (para. 7)

Legitimate debate appears on the front and home pages of American newspapers, in their opinion sections, and on the Sunday morning television news roundtables. Objectivity and balance are the dominant norms. *Consensus* is "the American creed." Capitalism is good and the market serves all Americans well; America's global motives are always right and just. *Deviance* is disagreement with America's two major political parties, disbelief that what benefits Wall Street benefits Main Street, views that are never reflected in the news. "It's not that there's a one-sided debate," wrote Rosen (2009), "there's no debate . . . The established media . . . are not passive agents here. They have an overt bias for consensus and against 'deviancy', which means they want the doughnut hole [what is not subject to debate] to be as big as possible and they want to exclude as much 'deviancy' as possible from admission to the sphere of 'legitimate' debate . . . [A]lternative—or even worse, radical—points of view, which might enliven the sphere of 'legitimate' debate are consistently excluded" (para. 8–32).

Rosen's point about the new online journalism is not only that there are more voices, which is certainly the case, but that because of the Internet people are connected into issue or idea communities; they are no longer atomized. The Internet, he told investigative reporter Glenn Greenwald (2009), "connects us to other people who feel the same way when they're watching the news, who have said to themselves: 'Wait, that's not the range of debate. Oh, wait a minute, that doesn't sound such a deviant idea to me, I know you're portraying it that way.'" And once the mainstream media's authority to define the sphere of legitimate debate is weakened, a greater number and variety of issues will enter public discourse and they will be debated from a greater number of perspectives. This will enrich democracy, which, in the words of journalism scholars Stephan Coleman and Jay Blumler (2009), suffers from a "deficit of deliberation." "The most exciting and innovative participatory exercises," they wrote, "have in common an aspiration to promote and utilise public discussion as a means of engendering the collective production of policy decisions worthy of public consent" (p. 15). In other words, the Internet furthers social responsibility theory's goal of giving voice to all and fostering community. The question facing blogs, podcasts, social media newsfeeds, and other Internet news outlets, then, is no longer whether they practice journalism; it is whether they can serve the larger journalistic goals envisioned for social responsibility theory or if their many voices, Michael Hirsh's "10,000 weeds," will kill that promise.

This question is rooted in the theory's assumption of the professionalism of media practitioners. Reporters, editors, and other news gatherers and disseminators traditionally plied their trade as part of large institutions—a newspaper, magazine, or television network, for example—and that membership brought with it certain journalistic obligations. As we've seen, there are limits to professionalism's influence, but that influence did indeed exist. In the Internet era, when anyone can write, post, and disseminate anything, there is no limiting authority, no institution-owed fealty, no organizational reputation (or profit) to protect. The Internet boasts—and suffers from—**disintermediation**, the elimination of gatekeepers between content (in this case, news) producers and their audiences. Yes, there are more voices—the latitude of deviance has greatly expanded, but at what cost to journalism and its democratic role? What if those voices intentionally lie; what if they belong to bad actors intent on damaging democracy? As we saw in Chapter 2, agents of the Russian government used social media posts to intentionally spread chaos and racial and social discord in the United States during the 2016 presidential election in hopes of compromising American democracy and securing the election of Russia's preferred candidate (Apuzzo & LaFraniere, 2018; Wu, 2017). Social media sites, podcasts, YouTube videos, and streamed audio and video offer "news" including stories of a child sex ring run out of a Washington, DC–area pizza parlor; claims that the 20 six- and seven-year-old children murdered at the Sandy Hook Elementary School in Newtown, Connecticut, never existed; reports that the 17 teens and staff members murdered in the Marjory Stoneman Douglas High School in Parkland, Florida, were actors; and speculation that North Korean Supreme Leader Kim Jong-un is a puppet ruler installed by the Central Intelligence Agency, among other items. Compounding the problem, stories such as these are shared on social media sites hundreds of thousands of times, often by humans (who are far more likely to spread a false story than a true one; Vosoughi, Roy, & Aral, 2018), and often by **bots**, automated social media accounts used for posting content or interacting with other users without direct human involvement. In just two months, May and June of 2018, Twitter alone suspended more than 70 million bots or otherwise fake accounts (Timberg & Dwoskin, 2018), and an analysis by the Pew Research Center found that 66% of responses to news and current events posts on Twitter are from bots (Wojcik, Messing, Smith, Rainie, & Hitlin, 2018). This development renders public discourse unintelligible, if not useless. Media critic Eric Alterman (2018) wrote, "The problem of intellectual integrity in our public life is now almost beyond repair," citing research indicating that "most Americans believe it is now harder to be well-informed and to determine which news is accurate. They increasingly perceive the media as biased and struggle to identify objective news sources. They believe the media continue to have a critical role in our democracy but are not very positive about how the media are fulfilling that role" (para. 4).

The expansion of voices on the Internet raises an additional challenge to social responsibility theory inasmuch as its influence also presumes a media system that enjoys the protection of the First Amendment. But what if the First Amendment itself is obsolete? This question, posed by legal scholar Tim Wu (2017), is based on the fact that it is no longer speech that is scarce. What is scarce is the *attention* of listeners. The First Amendment, he wrote,

> presupposes an information-poor world, and it focuses exclusively on the protection of speakers from government, as if they were rare and delicate butterflies threatened by one terrible monster. But today, speakers are more like moths—their supply is apparently endless. The massive decline in barriers to publishing makes information abundant, especially when speakers congregate on brightly lit matters of public controversy. The low costs of speaking have, paradoxically, made it easier to weaponize speech as a tool of speech control. The unfortunate truth is that cheap speech may be used to attack, harass, and silence as much as it is used to illuminate or debate. (pp. 2–3)

Rather than expanding public discourse, Wu argues that the Internet actually suppresses speech. He cites what he calls *troll armies*, "abusive online mobs who seek to wear down targeted speakers and have them think twice about writing critical content, thus making political journalism less attractive. Whether directly employed by, loosely associated with, or merely aligned with the goals of the government or particular politicians, the technique relies on the low cost of speech to punish speakers" (p. 11). These are, in the words of Melissa Tidwell, general counsel of social network site Reddit, the "thousands of people screaming, '$&%@ you, light yourself on fire, I know where you live'" (as cited in Marantz, 2018, p. 66). Wu (2017) also points to *reverse censorship* or *flooding*, "counter-programming with a sufficient volume of information to drown out disfavored speech, or at least distort the information environment. Politically motivated reverse censorship often involves the dissemination of fake news (or atrocity propaganda) in order to distract and discredit" and bots "harnessed *en masse* to help spread fake news before and after important events" (pp. 15–16).

Recognizing that the First Amendment forbids the censoring of most content, Wu proposed a number of remedies, including regulating Internet sites that carry discourse-diminishing speech. Platforms such as Google, Facebook, and Twitter have long argued that they are simply service providers like a telephone company, not publishers like newspapers or television stations. No one would sue the phone company for threatening remarks made in a phone call, they say. But these sites do indeed curate or otherwise choose what content reaches their audiences, just as those decisions are made at traditional media outlets. On the Net, editorial decisions are sometimes made by people (monitors), sometimes by algorithms, but they are editorial decisions nonetheless. A second corrective rests in examining what the First Amendment *permits*. There are already federal cyberstalking laws that protect people from egregious trolling and harassment, and he recommends "that the First Amendment must be interpreted to give wide latitude for new measures to advance listener interests, including measures that protect some speakers from others" (p. 23). He and other critics of the Internet's unprecedented influence in contemporary public discourse point to an often-unrecognized aspect of First Amendment thinking, the government's duty to promote and protect the environment for free speech. Governments, argued First Amendment scholar Alexander Meiklejohn (1960) more than half a century ago, are "not forbidden to engage in that positive enterprise of cultivating the general intelligence upon which the success of self-government so obviously depends. On the contrary, in that positive field the Congress of the United States has a heavy and basic responsibility to promote the freedom of speech" (pp. 19–20).

Clearly Internet-based media will be at the center of debates over social responsibility of media and communication freedom for years to come. While it is possible that a new normative theory will be created, it is far more likely that existing notions will be repurposed. If you read statements from large-scale social media executives defending their control over media, you'll find many acknowledgments of the need for social responsibility along with assertions about communication freedom. They admit they have made mistakes, but they are doing what they can to serve the public interest. Increasingly politicians and government agencies are growing impatient about these promises. This rising concern was voiced in a United Kingdom House of Commons Committee report on disinformation and fake news. "In our Interim Report," the committee wrote, "we stated that the dominance of a handful of powerful tech companies has resulted in their behaving as if they were monopolies in their specific area, and that there are considerations around the data on which those services are based. Facebook, in particular, is unwilling to be accountable to regulators around the world. The Government should consider the impact of such monopolies on the political world and on democracy" (House of Commons Digital, Culture, Media, and Sport Committee, 2019, p. 91).

OTHER NORMATIVE THEORIES

As they are based on the social, political, and economic realities in which a given media system must operate, there are, of course, normative theories other than social responsibility theory. William Hachten (1992) provided the now-classic perspective on normative theories guiding the media systems of different countries and political systems. He identified five "concepts": (1) Western, (2) development, (3) revolutionary, (4) authoritarian, and (5) communism. The **Western concept**, exemplified by the United States, Great Britain, and most other well-developed industrial nations, combines aspects of libertarianism and social responsibility theory. It recognizes that there are no completely free media systems and that even in the most profit-oriented systems there exists not only a public expectation of service and responsibility, but an official expectation as well, one backed by "significant communication related activities of government"—in other words, regulation (Stevenson, 1994, p. 109).

The **development concept** describes systems in which government and media work in concert to ensure that media aid the planned, beneficial development of a given nation. This concept is exemplified by the media systems of most developing nations in Africa, Asia, the former Eastern bloc of Europe, and Latin America. Media and government officials work together to produce content that meets specific cultural and societal needs—for example, disease eradication and the dissemination of new farming techniques. There is more government involvement in the operation of the media than there is in the Western concept, but little overt official censorship and control.

The **revolutionary concept** describes a system in which media are used in the service of revolution. No country officially embraces this concept, but that doesn't mean that the people and media professionals cannot use a nation's communication technologies to challenge the government. The goals of media in the revolutionary concept are to end government monopoly over information, building an opposition to the existing government, destroying the legitimacy of an existing government, and bringing down that government (Stevenson, 1994). The revolutionary concept was in clear evidence in the Polish democracy movement—Solidarity—and its adroit manipulation of that country's media system in its 1989 overthrow of its communist regime. More recently the rise, success, and defeat of democracy movements in several Middle Eastern and African countries—the Arab Spring—demonstrate how the Internet has forced a reconsideration of the revolutionary concept just as it has led to new thinking on social responsibility theory. The tools of revolutionary media had long been pamphlets and newspapers, loudspeaker trucks, clandestine radio and television broadcasts from inside and outside a country's borders, and even guerilla takeover of government-controlled media. These methods are usually thwarted by arrests, military crackdowns, and electronic blocking of broadcast signals. The Internet, especially social media, has changed that. "The Arab Spring had many causes," wrote communication researcher Philip Howard and his colleagues. "One of these sources was social media and its power to put a human face on political oppression. [Tunisian vegetable merchant Mohammed] Bouazizi's self-immolation [in protest of government corruption] was one of several stories told and retold on Facebook, Twitter, and YouTube in ways that inspired dissidents to organize protests, criticize their governments, and spread ideas about democracy" to several countries in the region, including not only Tunisia, but Egypt, Libya, Algeria, Morocco, Syria, and Yemen (Howard et al., 2011). Unfortunately, and just as Tim Wu would have predicted, challenged authorities quickly learned how to turn those very same revolutionary technologies against the freedom movements they helped spawn. They spread false information to discredit movement leaders, unleashed troll armies on commentators, shut down social networking sites, and jailed and tortured users and site administrators alike. As Egyptian strongman president Abdel Fattah el-Sisi boasted, "With the assistance of two web brigades, I can shut down the pages, take them over, and make them my own" (Grothaus, 2018a).

Because there are now only three remaining communist countries (North Korea, China, and Cuba), the **authoritarian** and **communism concepts** are typically discussed as one. Both advocate the complete domination of media by the government for the purpose of forcing those media to serve, in the case of the authoritarian system, the government's desires and, in the case of the communism concept, the Communist Party's.

Recently, however, some scholars have been arguing for a less category-based, more flexible approach to normative theory. Chengju Huang (2003), for example, argued for a **transitional media approach** to evaluating specific media systems, because "the post-Cold War era in the information age is witnessing an accelerated social and media transition across the world." As such, media researchers "confront more mixed social and media systems than the standard ones described by various normative models" (p. 456). This approach would be *nonnormative*, making media system "change and adaptation its primary orientation." It would accept change and adaptation as "a historical process occurring through both revolution and evolution." And it would be culturally open-minded, maintaining "that media transition in various societies may take different paths in different political, cultural, and socioeconomic contexts, and therefore may lead to different and often complex media systems" (pp. 455–456). Naturally it is the changing global political environment, advances in communication technologies (especially "borderless" technologies such as satellite and the Internet), and rapid globalization encouraging this call for a more flexible approach to evaluating a given media system against that society's hypothetical ideal (the basis for normative theory).

REVIEW OF LEARNING OBJECTIVES

- Explain the origins of normative media theories.

Normative theories describe the ideal way for a media system to be structured and operated. They don't describe things as they are, nor do they provide scientific explanations or predictions. Instead they describe the way things *should be* if some ideal values or principles are to be realized. Those who would reign in what they see as media's negative influence and those who favor a free and open media system call for varying levels of government control. Normative theory is designed to provide a basis for their differing viewpoints.

- Evaluate libertarianism as a guiding principle for the operation of mass media.

Modern libertarian thinking about communication can be traced back to 16th-century Europe—a time when feudal aristocracies exercised arbitrary power over the lives of most people. Its basic premise is that in a fair debate, good and truthful arguments will always win out over lies and deceit. It followed that if this were true, a new and better social order could be forged using public debate. This is the self-righting principle, and it continues to be widely cited by contemporary media professionals as a rationale for preserving media freedom. Yet modern societies recognize that it is sometimes necessary to place limits on communication freedom, especially when there is conflict over basic rights or communication freedom threatens other important rights such as the right to privacy or to a fair trial.

- Recognize the strengths and limitations of the marketplace-of-ideas approach to media freedom.

A self-regulating marketplace of ideas is a variation of a fundamental principle of capitalism. The theory asserts that there is little need for the government to regulate markets because an open and competitive marketplace should regulate itself. If a product is in high demand, prices will "naturally" rise as consumers compete to buy it. According to the marketplace-of-ideas theory, the laissez-faire doctrine should be applied to mass media; that is, if ideas are "traded" freely among people, the correct or best ideas should prevail. The *ideas* compete, and the best will be "bought." But media content is far less tangible than other consumer products. The meaning of individual messages can vary tremendously from one person to the next. What is being traded when news stories or television dramas are "bought" and "sold"? Sponsors pay more to advertise on content with large or demographically attractive audiences, not for programs with better ideas in them. Advertisers on large-scale social media are mainly concerned with their ability to attract attention so that their ads are exposed to users. They have little concern about the mechanisms used to draw users to social media and hold their attention.

- Judge the worthiness and continued utility of social responsibility theory, especially in the Internet era.

During the 1940s social responsibility theory emerged as the predominant normative theory of media practice in the United States, representing a compromise between radical libertarian views and calls for technocratic control. Social responsibility theory put control of media content in the hands of media practitioners, who were expected to act in the public interest. No means existed, however, to compel them to serve the public. They were free to decide what services were needed and to monitor the effectiveness of those services. Despite little revamping or reexamination, social responsibility theory remains the normative theory guiding most media operation in the United States today. But recent changes in media technology and world politics make it reasonable to reassess social responsibility theory's usefulness. New media such as niche cable channels and low-power FM radio (LPFM) are available at low cost to ethnic or other minority groups, and the Internet has made it possible for even the smallest groups to enter their voices into the marketplace of ideas and shift public discourse toward issues otherwise ignored by traditional media. Others see the Internet expanding the range of public discourse across greater numbers of people, as it connects people otherwise connected "up" to traditional media rather than across to each other. Still others see those new, smaller voices as holding real potential to damage public discourse, as it is not speech that must be protected, but the ability to "hear" it. Large-scale social media have been found to act in many ways that undermine or ignore the public interest. Critics see the necessity for government regulations to force social media to act more responsibly.

CRITICAL THINKING QUESTIONS

1. Libertarianism is based on the self-righting principle—if all the information is available, good ideas will survive and bad ideas will die. But this also assumes that the "debate" between the ideas is fair. Do you think fairness can be achieved in contemporary mass media? Libertarianism also assumes that people are good and rational, that they can tell good ideas from bad ideas. Do you think this highly of your fellow citizens? Why or why not?
2. There can be no debate that the Internet has expanded the number of voices in our public discourse. But where do you come down on the "weeds" versus greater-variety-of-expression debate? Defend your answer.

3. Is there a need for social media to act more responsibly? If so, what specific actions must be changed and how might this be done? Are you optimistic that large-scale social media will engage in useful self-regulation? Why or why not? If they don't do so, what should be done?

KEY TERMS

social responsibility theory
radical libertarian
First Amendment absolutists
technocratic control
authoritarian theory
self-righting principle
Bill of Rights
marketplace of ideas
laissez-faire doctrine
net neutrality
muckrakers
Fourth Estate
Chicago School
pluralistic groups
agenda cutting
bloggers

dual responsibility theory
stakeholder theory
local origination (or mandatory access) rule
low-power FM radio (LPFM)
Balkanize
filter bubble
podcasts
disintermediation
bots
Western concept
development concept
revolutionary concept
authoritarian concept
communism concept
transitional media approach

GLOSSARY

social responsibility theory: A normative theory that substitutes media industry and public responsibility for total media freedom on the one hand and for external control on the other

radical libertarianism: The absolute belief in libertarianism's faith in a good and rational public and totally unregulated media

First Amendment absolutists: Those who believe in the strictest sense that media should be completely unregulated

technocratic control: Direct regulation of media, most often by government agency or commission

authoritarian theory: A normative theory that places all forms of communication under the control of governing elite or authorities

self-righting principle: Milton's idea that in a fair debate, good and truthful arguments will win out over lies and deceit

Bill of Rights: The first 10 amendments to the US Constitution

marketplace of ideas: In libertarianism, the notion that all ideas should be put before the public, and the public will choose the best from that "marketplace"

laissez-faire doctrine: Idea that government shall allow business to operate freely and without official intrusion

net neutrality: Regulatory principle that all Internet data, sites, and services on should be treated equally

muckrakers: Crusading journalists who typically challenged the powerful on behalf of those less so

Fourth Estate: Media as an independent social institution that ensures that other institutions serve the public

Chicago School: Social researchers at the University of Chicago in the 1940s who envisioned modern cities as "Great Communities" made up of hundreds of interrelated small groups

pluralistic groups: In a Great Community, the various segments defined by specific unifying characteristics

agenda cutting: Editorial decisions keeping specific coverage out of the news or out of the main news agenda

bloggers: Writers who maintain blogs, regularly updated online journals of news and opinion

dual responsibility theory: Revision of social responsibility theory delineating a role for fiscal, as well as social, responsibility in news decision-making

stakeholder theory: Idea that companies should operate in the best interests of all those who depend on them—their stakeholders

local origination (or mandatory access) rule: Rule requiring local cable television companies to carry community-based access channels

low-power FM radio (LPFM): Community-based, noncommercial stations broadcasting over small areas, typically three to seven miles

Balkanize: Divide a country, culture, or society into antagonistic subgroups

filter bubble: Online personalization tools render people more partisan and less open to different or opposing points of view by exposing them to only the news and information with which they already agree

podcasts: Internet-streamed digital audio files downloaded to a computer or mobile device, usually sent automatically to subscribers

disintermediation: Elimination of gatekeepers between content producers and their audiences

bots: Automated social media accounts used for posting content or interacting with other users without direct human involvement

Western concept: A normative theory combining aspects of libertarianism and social responsibility theory

development concept: A normative theory describing systems in which government and media work in concert to ensure that the media aid the planned, beneficial development of a given nation

revolutionary concept: A normative theory describing a system in which media are used in the service of revolution

authoritarian concept: A normative theory advocating the complete domination of media by a government for the purpose of forcing those media to serve the government

communism concept: A normative theory advocating the complete domination of media by a communist government for the purpose of forcing those media to serve the Communist Party

transitional media approach: A less category-based, more flexible approach to evaluating media systems than traditional normative theory

CHAPTER 4

The Emergence of the Media-Effects Trend in Mass Communication Theory

In 1928 William Short and W. W. Charters assembled a group of prominent social scientists to conduct research they hoped would provide definitive evidence concerning the effects of movies on children. Short was a Congregational minister, and Charters held a degree in education research from the University of Chicago. Both men firmly believed that postpositivist research on the effects of movies could serve a very practical purpose. They saw film as a danger to society, and they strongly supported government regulation to limit its influence (Jowett, Jarvie, & Fuller, 1996). Unfortunately, in their view, the film industry had developed a very effective strategy for blocking government intervention, putting in place a self-regulation effort led by former postmaster general of the United States Will Hays. How could they counter these strategies and convince policymakers that more rigorous regulation was necessary? They decided that empirical research findings would provide the best evidence. The Payne Fund—an entity financed by Frances Bolton, niece of a wealthy Cleveland industrialist who shared their concerns about the problematic influence of movies— supported their work.

The Payne Fund research was the first well-funded effort to comprehensively study media effects using postpositivist methods (Jowett, Jarvie, & Fuller, 1996). Researchers used content analysis, surveys, and experiments to probe the way children were affected by movies. In 1933 they published 12 books reporting their findings. Though the researchers were reputable and their books provided the most in-depth look ever at the influence of a mass medium, their work was largely ignored even by other researchers and had no influence on efforts to regulate movies. Why? There were a number of reasons. For example, Charters (1933) wrote a summary of the research that focused on evidence of disturbing effects but ignored findings that showed benign or nonexistent influence. He may have been postpositivist in method, but his mass society thinking is clear in his "Conclusion." "A single exposure to a picture may produce a measurable change in attitude," he wrote. "Emotions are measurably stirred as the scenes of a drama unfold and this excitement may be recorded in deviations from the norm in sleep patterns, by visible gross evidences of bodily movement, and by refined internal responses. They constitute patterns of conduct in daydreaming, phantasy, and action. The evidence of their influence is massive and irrefutable" (p. 60).

In addition, many of the Payne Fund social scientists were young and they were using relatively new, crudely developed empirical methods. By the time the research was published, the flaws in their methods had become apparent. The usefulness of postpositivist research methods and the value of its findings had yet to be established. That would take decades to achieve. Finally, the movie industry's plan for self-regulation, the 1930 Motion Picture Production Code, appeared not only reasonable, but successful, tempering even the most extreme criticism leveled at Hollywood's excesses (Jowett, Jarvie, & Fuller, 1996).

By 1960, 30 years after the Payne Fund research, the way many social scientists looked at mass media had been radically altered. Most postpositivist scholars no longer feared media as potential instruments of political oppression and cultural subversion, but instead saw mass communication as a relatively unimportant force with limited potential for harm and some potential for social good. Research methods initially marshaled to document the power of media had instead revealed them to be a benign force. As empirical research was conducted in the 1950s, scholars gradually came to see media's power over the public as limited—so limited that no government regulations were necessary to control bad effects. Social scientists viewed the public itself as resistant to media influence. The belief grew that most people were influenced by other people rather than by the media; opinion leaders in every community and at every level of society were responsible for guiding and stabilizing public views. Only a very small minority of people had psychological traits that made them vulnerable to direct manipulation by media. Media were conceptualized as relatively powerless in shaping public opinion in the face of more potent intervening variables like people's individual differences and their group memberships. This new view of media was grounded in an ever-increasing array of empirical research findings and persisted even after the new medium of television transformed and dominated everyday life in American households. The postpositivist media-effects trend had become well established.

LEARNING OBJECTIVES
After studying this chapter you should be able to
- Chart the development of the postpositivist effects trend in mass communication theory.
- Appreciate the contributions of Paul Lazarsfeld and Carl Hovland to advances in social science in general, and mass communication theory in particular.
- Provide a description of the limited- or minimal-effects perspective.
- Explain the relationship between the selective processes, cognitive consistency, and attitude change.

OVERVIEW

In this chapter we trace the rise of a new way of conceptualizing and studying media—the **media-effects trend**, an approach to media theory and research that came to dominate how many US researchers studied and thought about media in the last half of the 20th century. When research on media first began in the 1920s, scholars in many different fields used a broad array of research methods. Qualitative methods were widely used even in the social sciences. The disciplines of psychology, social psychology, and sociology were still relatively new, and the potential of empirical research methods was still unclear. Scholars in the more established humanities tended to dominate research on media. Media, especially newspapers, movies, and radio, were widely viewed as important forces in society, but there was considerable disagreement over the best ways to study and understand them. Fifty years later, empirical research on media effects had become so well accepted that it was widely regarded (and criticized) as a "dominant paradigm"—the best if not the only way to scientifically study media (Gitlin, 1978; Tuchman & Farberman, 1980).

To understand how this type of effects research became so dominant, we consider the central roles played by two people in the development of postpositivist media research—Paul Lazarsfeld and Carl Hovland. Lazarsfeld was a pioneer in the use of survey research to measure media influence on how people thought and acted. In the 1940s his surveys provided increasing evidence that media rarely had powerful direct influence on individuals. Effects that did occur were quite limited in scope—affecting only a few people or influencing less important thoughts or actions. Other factors such as political party membership, religion, and social status were more important.

Hovland was also a methodological innovator. He demonstrated how experimental methods could be used to evaluate media influence. He, too, found that media lacked the power to instantly convert average people away from strongly held beliefs. Even in laboratory situations where the potential for media influence was exaggerated, he could find only modest media influence. Effects varied depending on many factors, including message structure and content, preexisting, knowledge or attitudes, and the source of messages.

THE DEVELOPMENT OF THE POSTPOSITIVIST EFFECTS TREND

The people who developed media-effects theory and research during the 1940s and 1950s were primarily methodologists—not theorists. In this chapter we focus attention on two such men, Paul Lazarsfeld and Carl Hovland. Both social scientists were convinced that we could best assess the influence of media by employing objective empirical methods. They argued that new research methods such as experiments and surveys made possible observations that would allow them to draw objective conclusions about the effects of media. These conclusions would guide the construction of more useful theory grounded in systematic observation, not wild speculation.

Both Lazarsfeld and Hovland were trained in the empirical research methods that had been developed in psychology. In addition, Lazarsfeld spent time as a social statistician in Austria and was trained in survey methods. Working independently, they demonstrated how their research techniques could be adapted to the study of media effects. Unlike the Payne Fund researchers, both were gradually successful in convincing others of the usefulness and validity of their approach. With ongoing backing from the Rockefeller Foundation, Lazarsfeld secured government and private funding that enabled him, at Columbia University, to undertake expensive large-scale studies of media influence. After conducting propaganda experiments on soldiers for the Office of War Information during World War II, Hovland established a research center at Yale, where he and a team of assistants conducted hundreds of persuasion experiments for more than a decade. Both Columbia and Yale became very influential research centers, attracting and educating some of the most prominent social researchers of the time. These social scientists spread across the United States and established similar research centers at major universities.

Neither Lazarsfeld nor Hovland set out to overturn the way mass communication was understood. They had broader objectives. During the war years, they, along with many other postpositivist scholars, were drawn into the study of mass media as part of the larger effort to understand the power of propaganda—the threats it posed as well as the opportunities it offered, as you read in Chapter 2. Government agencies looked to them for advice on how to control Nazi propaganda and to mobilize a population of isolationist and pacifist Americans to fight the Axis powers. Unlike many colleagues who automatically assumed that media were quite powerful, Lazarsfeld and Hovland were determined to conduct empirical research that might reveal how media influence worked. They hoped that if media's power could be better understood, it might be controlled and used toward positive ends.

Lazarsfeld and Hovland were part of a new generation of empirical social researchers who argued that scientific methods provided the essential means to understand the social world and to control media's power in society. These researchers sought to remake their academic disciplines: to convert sociology, psychology, political science, and even history into what they regarded as true social sciences grounded in empirical research. They cited the tremendous accomplishments made in the physical sciences. Fields like physics and chemistry vividly demonstrated the ability of science to understand and control the physical world. Some of the most striking examples could be found in new military technology: amazing aircraft, highly destructive bombs, and unstoppable tanks. These weapons could be used for either good or evil, to defend democracy or bolster totalitarianism. Like Harold Lasswell, these aspiring social scientists believed that if democracy were to survive, it would have to produce the best scientists, and these people would have to do a better job of harnessing technology to advance their political ideology.

As the new social scientists conducted their research, they found that media were not as powerful as mass society or propaganda theory had suggested. Media influence over public opinion or attitudes often proved hard to locate. Typically it was less powerful than that of factors such as social status or education. Those media effects that researchers did find seemed to be isolated and sometimes contradictory. Despite the weak findings—study after study provided growing insight into the limited power of media—funding for additional research was easy to secure. Much of this support was provided by a government anxious to maintain control in a fearful nation under siege by communist ideology and nuclear weapons, perceived dangers that by comparison render pale today's threats from stateless Islamic radicals or Russian trolls pedaling fake Internet news (Pooley, 2008).

FROM PROPAGANDA RESEARCH TO ATTITUDE-CHANGE THEORIES

Although persuasion and attitude change have been speculated about almost since the beginning of recorded history, systematic study of these phenomena began only in the 20th century, and World War II provided the "laboratory" for the development of a cohesive body of thought on attitude change and, by obvious extension, media and attitude change. As we saw in Chapter 2, the United States entered that conflict convinced it was as much a propaganda battle as it was a shooting war. The Nazis had demonstrated the power of the Big Lie. America needed to be able to mount an effective counteroffensive. Before the United States could confront the Japanese and the Germans on the battlefield, however, it had to change people's opinions on the home front. During the 1930s there were powerful isolationist and pacifist sentiments in the country. These movements were so strong that in the election of 1940, eventually successful candidate Franklin D. Roosevelt promised to keep the United States out of the war, even though the Nazis were quickly conquering much of Western Europe and the Japanese were in the process of taking over parts of Asia. Aid to Britain was conducted secretly. Until the bombing of Pearl Harbor, American and Japanese diplomats were engaged in peace negotiations.

Thus, the war provided three important motivations for people interested in what would come to be known as attitude-change research. First, the success of the Nazi propaganda efforts in Europe challenged the democratic and very American notion of the people's ability to make wise, informed decisions based on media content. It seemed quite likely that powerful bad ideas could overwhelm inadequately defended good ideas. Strategies were needed to counter Nazi propaganda and defend American values. Second, after the declaration of war in 1941 large numbers of men and women from all parts of the country and from all sorts of backgrounds were rapidly recruited, trained, and tossed together in the armed forces. The military needed to determine what these soldiers were thinking and to find a way to intellectually and emotionally bind them—Yankee and Southerner, Easterner and Westerner, city boy and country girl—to a common cause, winning the war.

The third motivation was simple convenience: Whereas the military saw soldiers in training, psychologists saw research subjects—well-tracked research subjects. The availability of many people about whom large amounts of background information had already been collected proved significant because it helped define the research direction of what we now call attitude-change theory.

Carl Hovland and the Experimental Section

The army's Information and Education Division had a research branch, inside which was the Experimental Section, headed by psychologist Hovland. Its primary mission "was to make experimental evaluations of the effectiveness of various programs of the Information and Education Division" (Hovland, Lumsdaine, & Sheffield, 1949, p. v).

At first, the Experimental Section focused on documentary films and the war department's orientation movie series, *Why We Fight*, produced by Hollywood director Frank Capra. But because of the military's increasing use of media, the Experimental Section also studied "other media . . . quite diverse in character" (p. vi). As the researchers themselves wrote, "The diversity of topics covered by the research of the Experimental Section made it unfeasible to publish a single cohesive account of all the studies. However, it did appear possible to integrate the group of studies on the effects of motion pictures, film strips, and radio programs into a systematic treatment concerning the effectiveness of mass communication media" (p. vii). The researchers called their account *Experiments in Mass Communication*, and it bore the mark of group leader Hovland.

With his background in behaviorism and learning theory, Hovland's strength was in identifying elements in the mass communication process that might influence attitudes and devising straightforward experiments employing **controlled variation** to assess the strength of its different elements. Hovland took some piece of stimulus material (a film, lecture, or pamphlet, for example) and systematically isolated and varied its potentially important elements (for example, exposure vs. no exposure; immediate vs. later reaction; one-sided vs. two-sided argument) independently and in combination to assess their effects on audience members undergoing similar variation (for example, high vs. low motivation; high vs. low intelligence; initially in favor vs. initially opposed).

To meet the military's immediate needs, the Experimental Section began with evaluation research, simply testing whether the *Why We Fight* film series met its indoctrination goals. Prevailing notions about the power of propaganda implied that the researchers would find dramatic shifts in attitude as a result of viewing the films. According to mass society or propaganda theory, every soldier, no matter his or her background or personality, should have been easily manipulated by the messages in the films. Military training should have induced an ideal form of mass society experience. Individual soldiers were torn from their families, jobs, and social groups. They were isolated individuals, supposedly highly vulnerable to propaganda.

Nevertheless, Hovland's group found that the military's propaganda wasn't as powerful as had been assumed. They discovered that although the movies were successful in increasing knowledge about the films' subjects, they were not highly effective in influencing attitudes and motivations (their intended function). Even the most effective films primarily strengthened (reinforced) existing attitudes. Conversions were rare. Typically only the attitudes specifically targeted by the films showed any change, and those changes were relatively small. More global attitudes, such as optimism or pessimism about the war, were resistant to change.

The fact that the films produced little attitude change and that what change did occur was influenced by people's individual differences directly contradicted mass society theory assumptions that media could radically change even strongly held beliefs and attitudes. If isolated soldiers being hurriedly prepared for battle were resistant to the most sophisticated propaganda available, were average people likely to be any more susceptible? These empirical facts contradicted the prevailing theoretical notions and implied that it would be necessary to radically rethink them.

A second outcome of the initial evaluation work was important in determining the direction of future attitude-change theory. In examining one of the three films in the series, the 50-minute *The Battle of Britain*, Hovland and his colleagues found that, although initially more effective in imparting factual information than in changing attitudes about the British, as time passed factual knowledge decreased but attitudes toward the British actually became more positive. Time, the researchers discovered, was a key variable in attitude change. Possibly propaganda effects were not as instantaneous as mass society theory or behaviorist notions suggested. Hovland's group formulated various explanations for these slow shifts in attitude. But with no ready way to scientifically answer the question of why the passage of time produced increased attitude change in the direction of the original media stimulus, Hovland and his research team developed a new type of research design—controlled variation experiments—"to obtain findings having a greater degree of generalizability. The method used is that of systematically varying certain specified factors while other factors are controlled. This makes it possible to determine the effectiveness of the particular factors varied" (Hovland, Lumsdame, & Sheffield, 1949, p. 179).

One of the most important variables the researchers examined was the presentation of one or two sides of a persuasive argument. Using two versions of a radio program, they presented a one-sided argument (that the war would be a long one) and a two-sided argument (the war would be long, but the alternative view that the war would be short was also addressed). Of course, those who heard either version showed more attitude change than those who had heard no broadcast, but there was no difference in attitude change between the groups who had listened to the two versions. Hovland had anticipated this. Accordingly, he had assessed the participants' initial points of view, and here he did find attitude change. What he demonstrated was that one-sided messages were more effective with people already in favor of the message; two-sided presentations were more effective with those holding divergent perspectives. In addition, Hovland looked at educational level and discovered that the two-sided presentation was more effective with those people who had more schooling.

Thus, this group of psychologists determined that attitude change was a very complex phenomenon and that attributes of the messages themselves can and often did interact with attributes of the people receiving them. An enormous number of significant research questions suddenly opened up. What happens, for example, when two-sided presentations are directed toward people who are initially predisposed against a position but have low levels of education? Such questions fueled several decades of persuasion research and challenged two generations of researchers.

The Communication Research Program

The concept of attitude change was so complex that Hovland proposed and conducted a systematic program of research that occupied him and his colleagues in the postwar years. He established the Communication Research Program at Yale University, funded by the Rockefeller Foundation. Its work centered on many of the variables Hovland considered central to attitude change. He and his colleagues systematically explored the power of both communicator and message attributes to cause changes in attitudes, and they examined how audience attributes mediated these effects (made effects more or less likely). This work produced scores of scientific articles and a number of significant books on attitude and attitude change, but the most seminal was the 1953 *Communication and Persuasion*. Although a close reading of the original work is the best way to grasp the full extent of its findings, a general overview of this important research offers some indication of the complexity of persuasion and attitude change.

Examining the communicator, Hovland and his group studied the power of source credibility, which they divided into trustworthiness and expertness. As you might expect, they found that high-credibility communicators produced increased amounts of attitude change; low-credibility communicators produced less attitude change.

Looking at the content of the communication, Hovland and his group examined two general aspects of content: the nature of the appeal itself and its organization. Focusing specifically on fear-arousing appeals, the Yale group tested the logical assumption that stronger, fear-arousing presentations will lead to greater attitude change. This relationship was found to be true to some extent, but variables such as the vividness of the threat's description and the audience's state of alarm, evaluation of the communicator, and already-held knowledge about the subject either mitigated or heightened attitude change.

The Hovland group's look at the organization of the arguments was a bit more straightforward. Should a communicator explicitly state an argument's conclusions or leave them implicit? In general, the explicit statement of the argument's conclusions is more effective, but not invariably. The trustworthiness of the communicator, the intelligence level of the audience, the nature of the issue at hand and its importance to the audience, and the initial level of agreement between audience and communicator all influence the persuasive power of a message.

Regardless of how well a persuasive message is crafted, not all people are influenced by it to the same degree, so the Yale group assessed how audience attributes could mediate effects. Inquiry centered on the personal importance of the audience's group memberships and individual personality differences among people that might increase or reduce their susceptibility to persuasion.

Testing the power of what they called "counternorm communications," Hovland and his cohorts demonstrated that the more highly people value their membership in a group, the more closely their attitudes will conform to those of the group and therefore the more resistant they will be to changes in those attitudes. If you attend a Big Ten university and closely follow your school's sports teams, it isn't very likely that anyone will be able to persuade you that the Atlantic Coast Conference fields superior athletes. If you attend that same Big Ten university but care little about its sports programs, you might be a more likely target for opinion change, particularly if your team loses to an Atlantic Coast Conference team year after year.

The question of individual differences in susceptibility to persuasion is not about a person's willingness to be persuaded on a given issue. In persuasion research, *individual differences* refers to those personality attributes or factors that render someone generally susceptible to influence. Intelligence is a good example. It is easy to assume that those who are more intelligent would be less susceptible to persuasive arguments, but this isn't the case. Intelligent people are more likely to be persuaded if the message they receive is from a credible source and based on solid logical arguments. Self-esteem, aggressiveness, and social withdrawal were several of the other individual characteristics the Yale group tested. But, as with intelligence, each failed to produce the straightforward, unambiguous relationship that might have seemed warranted based on commonsense expectations. Why? None of a person's personality characteristics operates apart from his or her evaluation of the communicator, judgments of the message, or understanding of the social reward or punishment that might accompany acceptance or rejection of a given attitude. As we'll see, these research findings and the perspective on attitude change they fostered were to color our understanding of media theory and effects for decades.

Do Mass Media Influence the Way People Vote?

Lazarsfeld was not a theorist, yet by promoting empirical research, he did more than any of his peers to transform social theory generally and media theory specifically. Lazarsfeld believed theory must be strongly grounded in empirical facts. He was concerned that macroscopic social theories, including the various mass society and propaganda theories, were too speculative to guide decision-making in government or industry. He preferred a highly **inductive approach to theory construction**—that is, research should begin with empirical observation of important phenomena, not with armchair speculation. After the facts are gathered, they are sifted, and the most important pieces of information are selected. Researchers use this information to construct empirical generalizations—assertions about the relationships between variables. Then they can gather more data to see whether these generalizations are valid.

This research approach is cautious and inherently conservative. It avoids sweeping generalizations that go beyond empirical observations and demands that theory construction be "disciplined" by data collection and analysis (observation leads to research . . . and more research . . . and more research very gradually leads to theory development). Theory, therefore, is never too far removed from the data on which it is based. The re search process proceeds slowly—building step-by-step on one data-collection effort after another. You'll recognize this from Chapter 1 as the epistemology of postpositivism. Eventually, researchers will find and test a large number of empirical generalizations. These generalizations are "added up" and used to build what Robert Merton (1967) referred to as **middle-range theory** (discussed in more detail in Chapter 5).

FDR

During the presidential election campaign of 1940, pitting incumbent Franklin Delano Roosevelt against Republican Wendell Willkie, Lazarsfeld had his first major opportunity to test the validity of his approach and its ability to assess the power of media. He designed and carried out what was, at the time, the most elaborate mass communication field experiment ever conducted. Lazarsfeld assembled a large research team in May 1940 and sent it to Erie County, Ohio—a relatively remote region surrounding and including the town of Sandusky, west of Cleveland along the shores of Lake Erie. The total population of the county was 43,000, and it was chosen because it was considered an average American locality. Though Sandusky residents tended to vote Democratic, the surrounding rural area was strongly Republican. By the time the research team left in November, members had personally home-interviewed more than 3,000 people. Six hundred were selected to be in a panel that was interviewed seven times—once every month from May until November. The researchers estimated that an interviewer visited one out of every three of the county's households (Lazarsfeld, Berelson, & Gaudet, 1944).

In his data analysis, Lazarsfeld focused attention on changes in voting decisions. As people were interviewed each month, their choice of candidates was compared with the previous month's choice. During the six months, several types of changes were possible. Lazarsfeld created a label for each. *Early deciders* chose a candidate in May and never changed during the entire campaign. *Waverers* chose one candidate, then were undecided or switched to another candidate, but in the end, they voted for their first choice. *Converts* chose one candidate but then voted for that candidate's opponent—they had been converted from one political ideology to another. *Crystallizers* had not chosen a candidate in May but made a choice by November. Their choice was predictable, based on their political party affiliation, their social status, and whether they lived on a farm or in the city. Lazarsfeld reasoned that for these people, mass media simply served as a means of helping them sort out a choice that was to some extent predetermined by their social situation.

Lazarsfeld used a very long and detailed questionnaire dealing extensively with recent exposure to specific mass media content, such as candidate speeches on radio. If media were as powerful as propaganda theories predicted, his research should have allowed him to pinpoint their influence. If these notions were valid, he reasoned that he should have found that most voters were either converts or waverers. He should have observed people switching back and forth between candidates as they consumed the candidates' latest media messages. Those who showed the most change should have been the heaviest users of media since they were most exposed to conflicting messages.

But Lazarsfeld's results directly contradicted the outcome that propaganda theory might have predicted. Fifty-three percent of the voters were early deciders. They chose one candidate in May and never changed. Twenty-eight percent were crystallizers—they eventually made a choice consistent with their position in society and stayed with it. Fifteen percent were waverers, and only 8% were converts. Lazarsfeld could find little evidence that media played an important role in influencing the crystallizers, the waverers, or the converts. Media use by those in the latter two categories was lower than average, and very few of them reported being specifically influenced by media messages. Instead these voters were much more likely to say that they had been influenced by other people. Many were politically apathetic. They failed to make clear-cut voting decisions because they had such low interest. Often they decided to vote as the people closest to them voted—not as radio speeches or newspaper editorials told them to vote.

Lazarsfeld concluded that the most important influence of mass media was to reinforce a vote choice that had already been made. Media simply gave people more reasons for choosing a candidate whom they (and the people around them) already favored. For some voters—the crystallizers, for example—media helped activate existing party loyalties and reminded them how people like themselves were going to vote. Republicans who had never heard of Willkie were able to at least learn his name and a few reasons he would make a good president. On the other hand, Lazarsfeld found very little evidence that media converted people. Instead the converts were often people with divided loyalties; as Lazarsfeld described this situation, they were "cross-pressured." They had group ties or social status that pulled them in opposing directions. Willkie was Catholic, so religion pulled some people toward him and pushed others away. Most Republican voters were rural Protestants; to vote for Willkie they had to ignore his religion. The same was true of urban Catholic Democrats; they had to ignore religion to vote for Protestant Roosevelt.

By 1945 Lazarsfeld seemed convinced that media were unimportant during election campaigns. In a coauthored article summarizing his views on the prediction of political behavior in US elections, he makes no reference to any form of mass communication (Lazarsfeld & Franzen, 1945). Changes in vote decisions are noted as due to social and psychological variables, not exposure to media. But if media weren't directly influencing voting decisions, what was their role? As Lazarsfeld worked with his data, he began to formulate an empirical generalization that ultimately had enormous importance for mass communication theory. He noticed that some of the hard-core early deciders were also the heaviest users of media. They even made a point of seeking out and listening to opposition speeches. On the other hand, the people who made the least use of media were most likely to report that they relied on others for help in making a voting decision. Lazarsfeld reasoned that the "heavy user/early deciders" might be the same people whose advice was being sought by more apathetic voters. These people might be sophisticated media users who held well-developed political views and used media wisely and critically. They might be capable of listening to and evaluating opposition speeches. Rather than be converted themselves, they might actually gain information that would help them advise others so that they would be more resistant to conversion. Thus, these heavy users might act as **gatekeepers**—screening information and passing on only items that would help others share their views. Lazarsfeld chose the term **opinion leaders** for these individuals. He labeled those who turned to opinion leaders for advice **opinion followers**. In Chapter 5 we will look at the research he designed to follow-up on this insight and provide its clear confirmation.

The Strengths and Limitations of the Effects Trend in Media Research

From the 1950s to the 1990s persuasion research provided a predominant framework for conducting inquiry on media. Even after this dominance ended, researchers continued to use its model for effects experiments; for example, many researchers today conduct experiments on social media effects in laboratories where subjects are exposed to carefully structured content under controlled conditions. Persuasion research represented an important shift away from concerns about the role of propaganda in society and toward a focus on what happens when people are exposed to a broad range of media content. Similarly survey research on media focused on the consequences of exposure to various forms of media content, from violent cartoons to political advertising. Following the models provided by the early persuasion studies as well as those of Lazarsfeld's group, empirical media research focused heavily on the study of media effects, and as a result, the media-effects trend had become the dominant force in media research. Sociologist Melvin DeFleur (1970, p. 118) wrote, "The all-consuming question that has dominated research and the development of contemporary theory in the study of the mass media can be summed up in simple terms—namely, 'what has been their effect?' That is, how have the media influenced us as individuals in terms of persuading us?"

The study of media effects was obviously a worthwhile focus for research, but should it have been the dominant focus? In their pursuit of insights into media-effects processes, few researchers were aware that they were ignoring larger questions about the role of media in society. They were focused on administrative rather than critical questions. Some researchers defended this emphasis on effects by arguing that larger questions about the role of media couldn't be answered by empirical research—such inquiry would be too costly or intrusive. Others maintained that they could address these larger questions only after they had a thorough understanding of the basic processes underlying media effects. The pursuit of this understanding has occupied many mass communication researchers over the past ninety years. Effects research articles still fill the pages of most of the major academic journals devoted to mass communication theory and research. The rise of new forms of media has sparked a new round of inquiry to see if these media have effects that are different from those of legacy media. Improvements in experimental and survey methods, along with powerful new data analysis techniques, have produced many new insights. Internet-based media often create enormous datasets of information recording user's online behavior and can be used to assess media effects. We'll examine many of these efforts in several upcoming chapters.

Although the individual findings of effects research were enormously varied and even contradictory, two interrelated sets of empirical generalizations emerged from the early research: (1) The influence of mass media is rarely direct, because it is almost always mediated by *individual differences*; and (2) the influence of mass media is rarely direct, because it is almost always mediated by *group membership or social relationships*. These sets of generalizations emerged out of both survey and experimental research. They identify two factors that normally serve as effective barriers to media influence but which can also increase the likelihood of influence. Both sets of generalizations are consistent with the limited-effects perspective and thus serve to buttress it. Study after study confirmed their existence and expanded our understanding of how they operate. Over time these sets of generalizations allowed construction of a body of middle-range theory that is widely referred to as the **limited-** or **minimal-effects theory** because of its assumption that the media have minimal or limited effects, as those effects are mitigated by a variety of mediating or intervening variables. This body of theory includes the following two specific theories as well as the others described in this chapter:

1. **Individual differences** theory argues that because people vary greatly in their psychological makeup and because they have different perceptions of things, media influence differs from person to person. More specifically, "media messages contain particular stimulus attributes that have differential interaction with personality characteristics of members of the audience" (DeFleur, 1970, p. 122).

2. **Social categories** theory "assumes that there are broad collectives, aggregates, or social categories in urban-industrial societies whose behavior in the face of a given set of stimuli is more or less uniform" (DeFleur, 1970, pp. 122–123). In addition, people with similar backgrounds (e.g., age, gender, income level, religious affiliation) will have similar patterns of media exposure and similar reactions to that exposure.

The Selective Processes

One central tenet of attitude-change theory that was adopted (in one way or another or under one name or another) by most mass communication theorists is the idea of **cognitive consistency**. We noted earlier, for example, that Lazarsfeld found that people seemed to seek out media messages consistent with the values and beliefs of those around them. This finding implied that people tried to preserve their existing views by avoiding messages that challenged them. As persuasion research proceeded, researchers sought more direct evidence. Cognitive consistency is "a tendency (on the part of individuals) to maintain, or to return to, a state of cognitive balance, and . . . this tendency toward equilibrium determines . . . the kind of persuasive communication to which the individual may be receptive" (Rosnow & Robinson, 1967, p. 299). These same authors wrote, "Although the consistency hypothesis is fundamental in numerous theoretical formulations, . . . of all the consistency-type formulations, it is Leon Festinger's theory of **cognitive dissonance** which has been the object of greatest interest and controversy" (pp. 299–300).

Festinger explained that the bedrock premise of dissonance theory is that information that is not consistent with a person's already-held values and beliefs will create a psychological discomfort (dissonance) that must be relieved; people generally work to keep their knowledge of themselves and their knowledge of the world somewhat consistent (Festinger, 1957). Later, and more specifically, Festinger (1962) wrote, "If a person knows various things that are not psychologically consistent with one another, he will, in a variety of ways, try to make them more consistent" (p. 93). Collectively these "ways" have become known as the **selective processes**. Some psychologists consider these to be defense mechanisms we routinely use to protect ourselves (and our egos) from information that would threaten us. Others argue that they are merely routinized procedures for coping with the enormous quantity of sensory information constantly bombarding us. Either way, the selective processes function as complex and highly sophisticated filtering mechanisms screening out useless sensory data while quickly identifying and highlighting the most useful patterns in this data.

Attitude-change researchers studied three forms of selectivity: exposure, retention, and perception. Keep in mind that these notions have since been widely criticized and should be interpreted very carefully. We will point out some of the major limitations as we discuss each. It's important to note that many contemporary media researchers believe that the emergence of new forms of polarized political content in traditional media and on the Internet has given renewed important to the study of selectivity. You can read more about this is the box entitled "Selective Exposure and Social Media."

Selective exposure is people's tendency to attend to (become exposed to) media messages they feel are in accord with their already-held attitudes and interests and the parallel tendency to avoid those that might create dissonance. Democrats will watch their party's national convention on television but go bowling when the GOP gala is aired. Paul Lazarsfeld, Bernard Berelson, and Hazel Gaudet (1944), in their Erie County voter study, discovered that "about two-thirds of the constant partisans (Republicans and Democrats) managed to see and hear more of their own side's propaganda than the opposition's. . . . But—and this is important—the more strongly partisan the person, the more likely he is to insulate himself from contrary points of view" (p. 89).

In retrospect we now realize that during the 1940s people commonly had media-use patterns strongly linked to their social status and group affiliation. Newspapers had definite party connections. Most were Republican. Thus, Republicans read newspapers with a strongly Republican bias, and Democrats either read Democratic newspapers or learned how to systematically screen out pro-Republican content. Radio stations tried to avoid most forms of political content but occasionally carried major political speeches. These weren't hard to avoid if you knew you didn't like the politics of the speaker. Labor unions were very influential during this era and structured the way their members used media.

SELECTIVE EXPOSURE AND SOCIAL MEDIA

Selective exposure to news and information has been a constant source of interest for effects researchers, especially as mass communication has continually evolved since Festinger's time. For example, with the coming of cable TV and the explosion of partisan outlets like Fox News on the political right and MSNBC on the left, Shanto Iyengar and Kyu Hahn (2009) examined ideological selectivity in media use, discovering that "selective exposure based on partisan affinity held not only for news coverage of controversial issues but also for relatively 'soft' subjects such as crime and travel." This tendency was particularly pronounced for more politically engaged partisans, leading the authors to express concern that "the further proliferation of new media and enhanced media choices may contribute to the further polarization of the news audience" (p. 19). This concern animated scholars troubled by the growing anger expressed on those partisan media. Sarah Sobieraj and her colleagues discovered that outrage-based content—for example, much of talk radio and programming like Fox News's now-cancelled show *The O'Reilly Factor*—was selected by partisans, especially on the right, not so much for its attitude-confirming information as for its satisfaction of the social need to find community in safe ideological spaces (Sobieraj, Berry, & Connors, 2013). It is no surprise, then, that the Internet, especially large-scale social media—part news source, part community—would attract scholarly interest.

Early thinking was that the Internet would lead to greater political division as general-interest news and information from traditional sources would be replaced by personalized, self-selected information sources—what early Net theorist Nicholas Negroponte (1995, p. 153) called "the Daily Me"—leading to political polarization and extremism. Maybe that made sense before social networking (Facebook went online in 2004), but with social media, much of the content from which people select comes not from their Daily Me but from two other sources: friends and the social media platform's algorithmically selected stories. Eytan Bakshy and his colleagues discovered that people were more likely to select content for themselves rather than accept the platform's choices (Bakshy, Messing, & Adamic, 2015), and that did indeed produce exposure to a wider array of material than early Internet critics imagined. This is because few

people have purely like-minded others as friends (which would produce *ideological homophily*), and most enjoy a somewhat heterogeneous circle of friends, exposing them to *cross-cutting* (ideologically discordant) content. Also important to selectivity in social media stories, even more so than the presumed partisan bent of the original source, is "social endorsement," that small note under a story's title indicating that "X number of people recommend." "Social media provide readers a choice of stories from different sources that come recommended from politically heterogeneous individuals, in a context that emphasizes social value over partisan affiliation," write Solomon Messing and Sean Westwood (2014). As a result, "stronger social endorsements increase the probability that people select content, [reducing] partisan selective exposure" (p. 1042). What happens when social media users do encounter ideologically discordant stories? Yes, they tend to expose themselves to opinion-reinforcing content to a greater degree than they do to opinion-challenging material, but once "having decided to view a news story, evidence of an aversion to opinion challenges disappears: There is no evidence that individuals abandon news stories that contain information with which they disagree" (Garrett, 2009, p. 265).

Selective exposure to social media news and information may not be as limiting as early Internet critics might have feared, but research demonstrates that it exists. As Robert Faris and his colleagues at Harvard University's Berkman Klein Center for Internet & Society Research wrote after examining social media's impact on the 2016 Presidential election, "What is clear is that the mechanisms in play are complex, involving short-term and long-term effects, selective exposure, and effects that vary across different segments of the population. Even if the effects are isolated to the most engaged and partisan segments of the electorate, there are compelling arguments that they have an outsized influence on politics and electoral outcomes" (Faris et al., 2017, p. 42).

Are you a cross-cutter? That is, how open are you to ideologically discordant online news? Does it make a difference if a potentially counterattitudinal story comes with 2,800 "recommends"? Are you more likely to read a counterattitudinal story if it's "liked" by or sent to you by a friend?

Selective retention is the process by which people tend to remember best and longest information consistent with their preexisting attitudes and interests. Name all the classes in which you've earned the grade of A. Name all the classes in which you've earned a C. Which of these classes maintain your interest and attention? The As have it, no doubt. But often we remember disturbing or threatening information. Name the last class or test you almost failed. Have you managed to forget it and the instructor, or are they etched among the things you wish you could forget? If selective retention always operated to protect us from what we don't want to remember, we would have no difficulty forgetting bad experiences. Although some people seem able to do this with ease, others tend to dwell on disturbing information. Contemporary thinking on selective retention links higher retention to the perceived level of importance—whether good or bad—the recalled phenomenon holds for individuals. If we think something is important we will remember it even if it troubles us.

Keeping in mind that these processes are not discrete (you cannot retain that to which you have not been exposed), **selective perception** is the mental or psychological recasting of a message so that its meaning is in line with a person's beliefs and attitudes. Gordon Allport and Leo Postman's (1945) now-classic study of rumor is among the first and best examples of selective perception research. The two psychologists showed a picture of a fight aboard a train to different groups of people (Figure 4.1). The combatants were a Caucasian male grasping a razor and an unarmed African American male. Those who saw the scene were then asked to describe it to another person who had not seen it, who in turn passed it on and so on. In 1945 America, people of all races and ages who recounted the story of the picture inevitably became confused, saying the blade was in the hands of the Black man, not the White man. Allport and Postman concluded, "What was outer becomes inner; what was objective becomes subjective" (p. 81).

The attitude researchers who documented the operation of selective processes were good scientists. But their findings were based on people's use of a very different set of media and very different forms of media content than those we know today. In the 1940s and 1950s movies were primarily an entertainment medium; radio disseminated significant amounts of news, but typically as brief, highly descriptive reports

FIGURE 4.1 Allport and Postman's Stimulus Drawing

that expressed no partisan opinion; <u>newspapers were the dominant news medium</u>; and television did not exist. Television moved all the media away from dissemination of information and toward the presentation of images and symbols. Many contemporary movies sacrifice storyline and character development for exciting and interesting visuals; your favorite radio station probably presents minimal news, if any; newspaper stories—on paper and online—are getting shorter and shorter and their graphics more colorful and engaging. Social media present us with every type of message and allow us to create and disseminate our own. It's not surprising that we process information very differently today than our grandparents and great-grandparents did in the 1940s.

Let's transport the valuable Allport and Postman (1945) experiment to our times to explain why the selective processes categorized by the attitude researchers and quickly appropriated by mass communication theorists might be less useful now in understanding media influence than they were in the 1940s. If a speaker were to appear on television and present the argument, complete with charts and "facts," that a particular ethnic group or race of people was inherently dangerous, prone to violent crime, and otherwise inferior to most other folks, the selective processes should theoretically kick in. Sure, some racists would tune in and love the show. But most people would not watch. Those who might happen to catch it would no doubt selectively perceive the speaker as stupid, sick, beneath contempt. Three weeks later, this individual would be a vague, if not nonexistent, memory.

But what if television news—because covering violent crime is easier, less expensive, and less threatening to the continued flow of advertising dollars than covering white-collar crime, and because violent crime, especially crimes committed downtown near the studio, provides better pictures than a scandal in the banking industry—were to present inner-city violence to the exclusion of most other crime? What if entertainment programmers, because of time, format, and other pressures (Gerbner, 1990), continually portrayed their villains as, say, dark, mysterious, different? Do the selective processes still kick in? When the ubiquitous legacy media or social media we routinely rely on repeatedly provide homogeneous and biased messages, where will we get the dissonant information that activates our defenses and enables us to hold onto views that are inconsistent with what we are being told? Does this situation exist in the United States today? Do most mainstream media or social media routinely provide inherently biased messages? We will return to these and similar questions in later chapters.

INSTANT ACCESS

ATTITUDE-CHANGE THEORY

Strengths

1. Pays deep attention to process in which messages can and can't have effects
2. Provides insight into influence of individual differences and group affiliations in shaping media influence
3. Attention to selective processes helps clarify how individuals process information

Weaknesses

1. Experimental manipulation of variables overestimates their power and underestimates media's
2. Focuses on information in media messages, not on more contemporary symbolic media
3. Uses attitude change as only measure of effects, ignoring reinforcement and more subtle forms of media influence

THINKING ABOUT THEORY

ALLPORT AND POSTMAN REVISITED

What would happen if Allport and Postman replicated their research today? Would contemporary American culture "put the razor" in the Black man's hands—that is, routinely attribute violence and crime to African Americans? Our judicial system's treatment of African Americans offers real-world evidence that the selective perception that the two psychologists discovered long ago still operates as it did back then.

The number of crimes committed by Americans of all races is roughly equal to their representation in the population. So, if the "razor" remains in the hands of its wielder, the racial composition of American prisons should match that of the population. Yet African Americans, making up 12% of the adult population, constitute 33% of those in prison (Gramlich, 2018). On the roads, African American drivers are more likely to be searched during routine traffic stops than are Whites and Asians, and those searches are conducted on the basis of less evidence, even though those more numerous searches are less likely to uncover illegal drugs or weapons than are those of vehicles with White or Asian drivers (Fletcher, 2018).

But how can this be? Do police, prosecutors, judges, juries, and the police selectively perceive crime and criminal activity, the razor, primarily in Black hands? If so, how might media contribute to this perception? Perhaps it's the ease with which they label rampaging White sports fans "revelers" while identifying African Americans protesting the police shooting of an unarmed Black man "rioters"

(Posner, 2018). Or it may be their practice of demonizing those shooting victims as "thugs" and "brutes," not because their reporters and editors are consciously racist but because, as Calvin Smiley and David Fakunle (2016) note, easy cultural assumptions about race "allow journalists and other media outlets to report on these cases the way they do, without self-reflection of how the words, images, and storylines are disseminated. These narratives play a role in the initial assumption of the victim and can shift the perspective of how these victims are viewed" (p. 363). Maybe it's the movies. Zachary Crockett (2016) examined 160,000 acting credits from 26,000 recent major American movies and compiled a list of every background actor who was identified in the role of "gang member," "gangster," "gangbanger," or "thug." Although federal statistics indicate that 35 % of gang members are Black, on screen 62% of "gang members" were African American, as were 61% of the "gangsters." Sixty percent of "gangbangers" and 66% of the "thugs" were African American. The somewhat loftier "henchmen," however, were 81% White.

Would Allport and Postman be surprised that the "reality" of race and crime that many Americans perceive today is so out of tune with objective reality? Are you? Would they predict that crime, like the razor, is most often wielded by African Americans? Would you? Can you, using the media examples offered above and before you read further into this text, explain media's contribution to this perception?

Today, some 80 years after the Allport and Postman study, would the knife still find its way from the White man's hand into the Black man's? Have the civil rights movement and the scores of television shows and movies offering realistic, rich, and varied representations of African Americans made a difference? Or does routine news coverage of violent crime continue to fuel our apprehensions and therefore our biases? Later chapters that deal with theories that view mass communication as more symbolically, rather than informationally, powerful will address these questions. But for now, you can explore the issue with the help from the box entitled "Allport and Postman Revisited."

REVIEW OF LEARNING OBJECTIVES

- Chart the development of the postpositivist effects trend in mass communication theory.

The 1933 Payne Fund research ushered in the postpositivist media-effects trend, which concentrated research attention on the search for specific effects on individuals cause by exposure to certain forms of content. Later researchers benefited from the refinement of empirical research methods; the failure of the mass society and propaganda thinkers to offer empirical evidence for their views; the commercial nature of the new research methods and their support by government agencies, private foundations, and business; and the spread of these methods to a wide variety of academic disciplines.

- Appreciate the contributions of Paul Lazarsfeld and Carl Hovland to advances in social science in general, and mass communication theory in particular.

Lazarsfeld championed the inductive approach to theory construction and developed the idea of a two-step flow of media influence. This produced important generalizations about media influence: Media rarely have direct effects; media influence travels from media, through opinion leaders, to opinion followers; group commitments protect people from media influence; and when effects do occur, they are modest and isolated. Hovland and other psychologists also provided evidence of limited media influence. Using controlled variation, they demonstrated that numerous individual differences and group affiliations limited media's power to change attitudes.

- Provide a description of the limited- or minimal-effects perspective.

The power of media is limited or minimal because there are so many other important factors that influence what people think, say, or do. Children are primarily socialized by parents, churches, schools, and peer groups. The beliefs and actions of adults are dominated by their workplace, churches, family, and social groups.

- Explain the relationship between the selective processes, cognitive consistency, and attitude change.

People seek cognitive consistency. When they confront information that is inconsistent with already-held values and beliefs, psychological discomfort—that is, dissonance—occurs. Therefore, they work consciously and unconsciously to limit the influence of those messages. This dissonance reduction operates through selectivity in exposure (attention), retention, and perception.

CRITICAL THINKING QUESTIONS

1. If you were a media researcher in the 1940s and 1950s, do you think you would have focused your research on media effects? What reasons would you have given for your focus? What types of media theory and research would you avoid? Why?
2. How do you view Paul Lazarsfeld and Carl Hovland? Both were entrepreneurs who were quite successful in providing leadership for the study of media and empirical research generally. Their work was well-funded by public and private agencies. However, in retrospect they played an important role in narrowing the focus of media research and the development of media theory. Could they have provided different leadership?
3. Contemporary critics of the media effects trend have argued that the trend marginalized the Chicago School perspective on media that we introduced in

Chapter 2. This perspective saw media playing a critical role in Great Communities. Should this perspective been given more attention? How different a nation might the United States have become with more focus on the value of its disparate communities?

KEY TERMS

media-effects trend
controlled variation
inductive approach to theory
   construction
middle-range theory
gatekeepers
opinion leaders
opinion followers
limited- or minimal-effects theory

individual differences
social categories
cognitive consistency
cognitive dissonance
selective processes
selective exposure
selective retention
selective perception

GLOSSARY

media-effects trend: Media effects on individuals, because of their importance, should be the focus of research; postpositivist methods provide the best way to study effects

controlled variation: Systematic isolation and manipulation of elements in an experiment

inductive approach to theory construction: Approach to theory construction that sees research beginning with empirical observation rather than speculation

middle-range theory: Theory composed of generalizations derived from empirical observations

gatekeepers: People who screen media messages and pass on those messages and help others share their views

opinion leaders: Those who pass on information to opinion followers

opinion followers: Those who receive information from opinion leaders

limited- or minimal-effects theory: Theory that media have minimal or limited effects because those effects are mitigated by a variety of mediating or intervening variables; media are only one of many factors that influence individuals

individual differences: Individuals' different psychological makeups that explain why media influence varies from person to person

social categories: Idea that members of given groups or aggregates will respond to media stimuli in more or less uniform ways; provides a basis for targeting persuasive messages

cognitive consistency: Idea that people consciously and unconsciously work to preserve their existing views

cognitive dissonance: Information that is inconsistent with a person's already-held attitudes creates psychological discomfort, or dissonance

selective processes: Exposure (attention), perception, and retention; psychological processes designed to reduce dissonance

selective exposure: Idea that people tend to expose themselves to messages that are consistent with their preexisting attitudes and beliefs and avoid those that are inconsistent

selective retention: Idea that people tend to remember best and longest those that are most meaningful to the these messages that are consiste strongly held beliefs

selective perception: Idea that peo alter the meaning of messages become consistent with preexisti tudes and beliefs

CHAPTER 5

The Consolidation of the Media-Effects Trend

The United States stood triumphant in the years following the Second World War. Its forces had defeated the Axis, saved Europe, secured the Pacific, and were rebuilding defeated foes Germany and Japan. The "boys" came home to high employment, burgeoning suburbs soon to make routine once-rare home ownership, and the material riches of a manufacturing colossus. An expanding system of state colleges and universities offered them a chance to build better lives than those of their parents, paid for by the GI Bill. They quickly accounted for 50 percent of all enrollees (Berman, 2015). The economy was booming, and the president was a benevolent war hero with plenty of time to golf. A modern, safe interstate highway system connected East and West Coasts, northern and southern borders, and everything in between. The country was further united by the new national television networks, carrying the programming of that remarkable new in-home technology, the TV set. When the 1950s opened, 108 stations were broadcasting to 17 million television homes. By decade's end, there were 559 stations, and sets were in nearly 90% of all households. In 10 years, more television sets were sold in the United States (70 million) than there were children born (40.5 million) (Kuralt, 1977).

And what was on those 70 million screens? Images of a stable, strong, well-functioning country: situation comedies like *The Adventures of Ozzie and Harriet, Father Knows Best, Leave It to Beaver, Andy of Mayberry*; marvelous Golden Age live dramas; news from around the corner and around the world; tales of the old American West and the grit and determination of its heroes—*Gunsmoke, The Rifleman, Daniel Boone, Davy Crockett, Bonanza*—and those of a dedicated and fair police and legal system—*Dragnet, Peter Gunn, The Untouchables, Perry Mason*. And all of this programming housed delightful 60-second mini-programs showcasing fast foods, fast cleaners, fast appliances, and even faster cars—their promise of ready comfort and luxury reinforced by the burgeoning newspaper and magazine industries, themselves enriched by that same consumer-product advertising.

Of course, there was another America, one just as real yet out of sight. People of color and the poor and working class, largely invisible on television, were denied the country's full benefits, and young people were impatient with the old ways, as you'll read in the next chapter. But for most Americans, at least on the surface, optimism was high—this was a country that worked, and its media system seemed to be working as well.

LEARNING OBJECTIVES

After studying this chapter you should be able to

- Explain how the media-effects trend was consolidated into a dominant approach to media research.
- Understand the contribution of Robert Merton to the development of middle-range theory and its importance for media-effects research.
- Understand the strengths and weaknesses of several foundational but still important mass communication theories such as information-flow theory, two-step flow theory, phenomenistic theory, and mass entertainment theory.
- See the value and drawbacks of applying theories of the middle range, functionalism, and systems theory to explaining media influence.

OVERVIEW

During the 1950s, 1960s, and into the 1970s the limited-effects perspective came to dominate American mass communication research. As the preceding chapter suggested, new bodies of theory were created by loosely knit research communities with inspiration from key individuals like Paul Lazarsfeld and Carl Hovland. These communities formed at a handful of universities, and their influence gradually spread outward. Their members shared a common perspective acquired through collaboration on research and through graduate education. Fledgling researchers were trained to use specific theories and research methods.

As those research communities evolved, the body of theory on which they were based gradually matured. At a certain point, as a particular community grew in size and produced widely accepted research, it published landmark studies. In this chapter we will consider several of the "classic" studies from these three decades that heralded the growing importance and utility of the limited-effects perspective. These findings demonstrated the power of the perspective and its ability to produce findings that had immediate, practical value. They addressed important questions concerning the role of media. We will place these theories—functional analysis, information-flow theory, information diffusion theory, phenomenistic theory, mass entertainment theory, and systems theory—into historical perspective and gauge their continuing impact on communication research.

In this chapter we look at how data from an impressive array of empirical studies were assembled into reports that still form a canon for some postpositivist researchers (e.g., Bauer & Bauer, 1960; Campbell, Converse, Miller, & Stokes, 1960; Klapper, 1960; DeFleur & Larsen, 1958; Katz & Lazarsfeld, 1955). A careful reading of these studies shows a remarkably consistent and mostly benign view of mass media. Most of these works proposed functionalist theories of media—theories that saw media as one force among many that determine how society functions. In general, problematic functions of media were balanced or offset by positive functions. Media were seen as having very limited power to threaten or undermine the social order.

We consider how **functionalism** became a dominant perspective among postpositivist social scientists. In their view American technological know-how had helped win World War II, and in the 1950s it provided many citizens with a comfortable and independent lifestyle. At the heart of this success were increasingly complex, large-scale social, economic, and technological systems. Surely factors such as new communication technologies, efficient superhighways, universally available home ownership and higher education, the population's migration to the suburbs, an exploding advertising industry, women entering the workforce in ever larger numbers, expanded leisure time, the geographic displacement of millions of GIs as they were ushered out of the military, and the Cold War with its threat of imminent global destruction (to name only a few) worked—or functioned—together to produce the America that offered so much that was good and so much that was potentially troubling.

As such, functionalism "became dominant in American [social] theory in the 1950s and 1960s. The cornerstone of functionalist theory is the metaphor of the living organism, whose parts and organs, grouped and organized into a system, function to keep its essential processes going. Similarly, members of a society can be thought of as cells and its institutions as organs whose functioning . . . preserves the cohesive whole and maintains the system's homeostasis" (Bryant & Miron, 2004, p. 677). Through functionalism, mass communication's obvious influence on the social world could be explained and understood, and at the same time that effect could be seen as "limited" by other parts of the system.

During the 1950s, as the media-effects trend became increasingly dominant, new media research centers modeled after those at Yale and Columbia opened across the United States. One of the early leaders in the field, Wilbur Schramm, was personally responsible for establishing communication research centers at the University of Illinois, Stanford University, and the University of Hawaii. By 1960 many of the "classic studies" of media effects had been published and had become required reading for the first generation of doctoral students in the newly created field of mass communication research.

How did the creators of the media-effects perspective view the power of media? Most of their early research suggested that media influence was minimal except in rare situations. As we discuss the early research, we will illustrate the factors that combined to make development of the media-effects trend possible. We list these factors here, and we will refer to them in later sections.

1. **The refinement and broad acceptance of empirical social research methods was an essential factor in the emergence of the media-effects trend.** Throughout this period empirical research methods were effectively promoted as an ideal means of measuring, describing, and ultimately explaining social phenomena. A generation of empirical social scientists working in several academic disciplines declared them to be the only "scientific" way of dealing with social phenomena. They dismissed other approaches as overly speculative, unsystematic, or too subjective.

2. **Empirical social researchers successfully branded as "unscientific" those who advocated mass society and propaganda notions.** They accused mass

society theory advocates of being fuzzy-minded humanists, religious fanatics, doomsayers, political ideologues, or biased against media. Also, mass society and propaganda notions lost some of their broad appeal as the threat of propaganda seemed to fade in the late 1950s and 1960s.

3. **Social researchers exploited the commercial potential of the new research methods and gained the support of private industry.** One of the first articles Lazarsfeld wrote after arriving in the United States was about the use of survey research methods as a tool for advertisers (Kornhauser & Lazarsfeld, 1935). Researchers promoted surveys and experiments as a means of probing media audiences and interpreting consumer attitudes and behaviors. Lazarsfeld coined the term **administrative research** to refer to these applications. He persuasively argued for the use of empirical research to guide administrative decision-making.

4. **The development of empirical social research was strongly backed by various private and government foundations, most notably the Rockefeller Foundation and the National Science Foundation.** This support was crucial, particularly in the early stages, because large-scale empirical research required much more funding than had previous forms of social research. Without support from the Rockefeller Foundation, Lazarsfeld might never have come to the United States or been able to develop and demonstrate the validity of his approach. Government funding during World War II was critical to Hovland's research. Without the government funding provided during the Cold War, large mass communication research centers might never have been established at major universities.

5. **As empirical research demonstrated its usefulness, media companies began to sponsor and eventually conduct their own research on media.** In time, broadcasting networks CBS, NBC, and ABC formed their own social research departments and employed many outside researchers as consultants. Two of the most influential early media researchers were Frank Stanton and Joseph Klapper; the former collaborated with Lazarsfeld on numerous research projects in the 1940s, and the latter was Lazarsfeld's student. Both Stanton and Klapper rose to become executives at CBS. As media corporations grew larger and earned sizable profits, they could afford to fund empirical research—especially when that research helped justify the status quo and block moves to regulate their operations. Media funding and support were vital to the development of commercial audience ratings services such as Nielsen and Arbitron. These companies pioneered the use of survey research methods to measure the size of audiences and guide administrative decision-making in areas such as advertising, marketing, and programming. Media support was also crucial to the growth of various national polling services, such as Gallup, Harris, and Roper. Media coverage of polls and ratings data helped establish their credibility in the face of widespread commonsense criticism. After all, how could a survey of a few hundred or even a thousand or so individuals provide useful insight into the thinking of an entire population of a city, a state, or the nation?

6. **Empirical social researchers successfully established their approach within the various social research disciplines—political science, history,**

social psychology, sociology, and economics. These disciplines, in turn, shaped the development of communication research. During the 1960s and 1970s several communication areas—for example, advertising, broadcasting, and journalism—rapidly expanded to meet growing college student interest in studying communication and preparing for careers in related industries. As these areas developed, empirical social researchers from the more established social sciences provided leadership. Social science theories and research methods borrowed from the more established disciplines assumed an important—often dominant—role in structuring research conducted in university journalism, advertising, speech communication, and broadcasting departments. Empirical research became widely accepted as the most scientific way to study communication, even though this research rarely provided conclusive evidence of media influence.

THEORIES OF THE MIDDLE RANGE AND THE RISE OF THE FUNCTIONAL ANALYSIS APPROACH

One of the most influential social theorists of the 1940s and 1950s was Robert Merton, a sociologist who, when at Columbia University, collaborated with Paul Lazarsfeld. Merton was trained as a social theorist but was intrigued by Lazarsfeld's empirical research. Lazarsfeld rarely relied on social theory to plan his research. He used his surveys to investigate things that intrigued him, such as his fascination with opinion leaders, and he looked for what he termed *natural field experiments*—situations where important decisions had to be made or social changes implemented. As such, elections were a logical focus for his research. His surveys generated hundreds of findings. But how, he questioned, should these findings be interpreted? Could they be used to construct theory? Was there a strategy that could be used to integrate findings so the social structures underlying them might be revealed?

The questions posed by Lazarsfeld's research were not unique. As funding and respect for empirical research grew, findings increased exponentially. In an era before computers revolutionized data analysis, results were generated in rooms filled with boxes of questionnaires and people punching numbers into tabulation machines. When results from several hundred questionnaires had to be compiled, it could take weeks to produce a set of cross-tabulation tables or to calculate a small set of correlation coefficients. And once the results were obtained, how should they be interpreted? Most empirical research wasn't based on theory. At best, researchers conceptualized attributes that could be measured using questionnaire items. Research could show that some attributes were related to other attributes, but it couldn't explain how or why these relationships existed. What was needed was a way to inductively develop theory based on these findings. Merton offered a solution.

In 1949 he wrote *Social Theory and Social Structure*, a book that established his reputation as a sociologist and earned him the gratitude of the first generation of empirical social scientists. He continued to develop his ideas, and eventually published *On Theoretical Sociology* (1967). For more than two decades, Merton tutored a host of thoughtful and reflective empirical researchers. He gave them a perspective from which to plan and then interpret their work, and he taught them a practical way of combining induction with deduction.

Merton's solution to the dilemma posed by the rising tide of research findings was development of "theories of the middle range." Unlike grand social theories (e.g., mass society theory) that attempt to explain a broad range of social action, middle-range theories were designed to explain only limited domains or ranges of action that had been or could be explored using empirical research. These theories could be created by carefully interpreting empirical findings. According to Merton (1967),

> Some sociologists still write as though they expect, here and now, formulation of the general sociological theory broad enough to encompass the vast ranges of precisely observed details of social behavior, organization, and change and fruitful enough to direct the attention of research workers to a flow of problems for empirical research. This I take to be a premature and apocalyptic belief. We are not ready. Not enough preparatory work has been done (p. 45).

Merton (1967) described middle-range theory as follows:

1. Middle-range theories consist of limited sets of assumptions from which specific hypotheses are logically derived and confirmed by empirical investigation.
2. These theories do not remain separate but are consolidated into wider networks of theory.
3. These theories are sufficiently abstract to deal with differing spheres of social behavior and social structure, so that they transcend sheer description or empirical generalization.
4. This type of theory cuts across the distinction between micro-sociological problems.
5. The middle-range orientation involves the **specification of ignorance**; every answer produces new questions. Rather than pretend to knowledge where it is in fact absent, this approach expressly recognizes what must still be learned to lay the foundation for still more knowledge (p. 68).

Middle-range theory provided a useful rationale for what most empirical researchers, including media scientists, were already doing. Many were determined to ignore what they considered unnecessary theoretical baggage and focus on developing and applying empirical research methods. They believed that the future of social science lay in producing and collating empirical generalizations. Following the examples set by Lazarsfeld and Hovland, researchers conducted endless surveys and experiments, gathering data to support or reject individual generalizations and constantly discovering new research questions requiring yet more empirical research. Merton argued that all this research work would eventually be brought together to first create an array of middle-range theories, and then to construct a comprehensive theory having the power and scope of theories in the physical sciences. Moreover, when it was finally constructed, this theory would be far superior to earlier forms of social theory not empirically grounded.

Thus, middle-range theory provided an ideal rationale and justification for continuing small-scale, limited-effects studies. It implied that eventually all these individual pieces of scientific inquiry would add up, permitting the construction of a broad perspective on the role of media. Yet middle-range theory had important short-comings that were not immediately apparent. Countless empirical generalizations were studied, but the effort to combine them into broader theories proved more dif-ficult than expected. In this and later chapters we will consider numerous interesting and useful middle-range theories, but when broader theories were developed based on these middle-range notions, they had crucial limitations. The first generations of empirical researchers had little success at integrating their empirical generalizations into broader theories. But that may be changing. During the last two decades media researchers have begun a serious effort to integrate findings into broader theories (Potter, 2009). Unfortunately this is a time that also saw unprecedented changes in media, so much of the research on which newer middle-range theories are based may be obsolete.

In *Social Theory and Social Structure* (1949), Merton proposed what he called a "par-adigm for functional analysis" outlining how an inductive strategy centered on the study of social artifacts (such as the use of mass media) could eventually lead to the construction of theories that explained the "functions" of these items. Merton derived his perspective on functional analysis from carefully examining research in anthro-pology and sociology. Functionalism, as we've seen, assumes that a society can be usefully viewed as a "system in balance." That is, the society consists of complex sets of interrelated activities, each of which supports the others. Every form of social activ-ity is assumed to play some part in maintaining the system as a whole. By studying the functions of various parts of such systems, a theory of the larger system might be developed. This would be a middle-range theory, because it would integrate research findings from studies that examined the different parts of the system.

One feature of functional analysis that appealed to Merton and his followers was its apparent *value-neutrality.* Older forms of social theory had characterized various parts of society as either "good" or "evil" in some ultimate sense. For example, mass society theory saw media as essentially disruptive and subversive, a negative force that some-how must be brought under control. Functionalists rejected such thinking and instead argued that empirical research should investigate both the functions and dysfunctions of media. In that way a systematic appraisal could be made of media's overall impact by weighing useful outcomes of media use against negative outcomes. Functionalists argued that social science had no basis and no need for making value judgments about media. Rather, empirical investigation was necessary to determine whether specific media perform certain functions for the society. Merton also distinguished **manifest functions**—those consequences that are intended and readily observed—and **latent functions**—those unintended and less easily observed.

Functional analysis was widely adopted as a rationale for many mass communica-tion studies during the late 1950s and 1960s. Researchers tried to determine whether specific media or forms of media content were functional or dysfunctional; they inves-tigated manifest and latent functions of media. In his classic 1959 book, *Mass Commu-nication: A Sociological Perspective*, Charles Wright identified what have become known as the **classic four functions of the media**. He wrote, "Harold Lasswell, a political scientist who has done pioneering research in mass communications, once noted three activities of communication specialists: (1) surveillance of the environment, (2) cor-relation of the parts of society in responding to the environment, and (3) transmission of the social heritage from one generation to the next" (Wright, 1959, p. 16). To these, he added a fourth: entertainment. Inasmuch as any one of these functions could have positive or negative influence, and because each carried manifest as well as latent functions, it's clear that functional analysis could give rise to very complicated assessments of the role of media.

For example, various forms of media content can be functional or dysfunctional for society as a whole, for specific individuals, for various subgroups in the society, and for the culture. Media advertising for fast-food chains might be functional for their corporations and stockholders, and for the economy as a whole, but dysfunctional for the growing number of obese children enticed by their music and images (Kunkel et al., 2004). As obesity-related health problems increase, insurance costs spiral, a dysfunction for working parents but functional for those selling weight-reduction programs and fitness camps to exasperated parents. Thus, the functions for society can be offset by the dysfunctions for individuals or for specific groups of individuals.

Lance Holbert, Kelly Garrett, and Laurel Gleason (2010) offer a contemporary example. We can judge the self-selected, echo-chamber media consumption facilitated by cable television, talk radio, and social media as a dysfunction because it fosters antagonism toward opposing political parties and the overall political system. This view assumes that "trust and confidence" in the political system are "unqualified goods." But, they argue, "Trust and confidence are *not* unqualified goods; they must be earned or warranted" (p. 29). Loss of trust may be a dysfunction for individuals as they lose confidence in a system designed to support them (a micro-level assessment), but it may ultimately be a beneficial function because it will force the system to improve (a macro-level assessment).

This thinking leads to one of functionalism's primary problems—it rarely permits the drawing of definitive conclusions about the overall functions or dysfunctions of media. For example, one of the first media effects to be studied in some depth using functional analysis was the **narcotizing dysfunction**, the idea that as news about an issue inundates people, they become apathetic to it, substituting knowing about that issue for action on it (Lazarsfeld & Merton, 1948). The narcotizing dysfunction was used to explain why extensive, often dramatic coverage of 1950 congressional hearings concerning organized crime didn't lead to widespread public demands for government action. Although the heavily reported hearings went on for 15 months, were conducted in 14 cities, and featured more than 800 witnesses, researchers found that average

INSTANT ACCESS

FUNCTIONALISM

Strengths

1. Positions media and their influence in larger social system
2. Offers balanced view of media's role in society
3. Is based on and guides empirical research

Weaknesses

1. Is overly accepting and uncritical of status quo
2. Asserts that dysfunctions are "balanced" by functions
3. Asserts that negative latent functions are often "balanced" by positive manifest functions
4. Rarely permits definitive conclusions about media's role in society

Americans thought that nothing could be done to combat organized crime. These findings were disturbing because they suggested that even when media are effective at surveying the environment and calling attention to societal problems (a manifest function), the public may react by doing nothing. Instead of activating people to demand solutions to problems, extensive media coverage might "narcotize" them so they become apathetic and decide they are powerless to do anything (a latent dysfunction). But what would account for this narcotizing effect? Researchers argued that members of the public will be narcotized when they are exposed day after day to dramatic negative news coverage dwelling on the threats posed by a problem and emphasizing the difficulty of dealing with it. This research was one of the first studies to suggest that media can fail to perform an important function even when practitioners do what their profession defines as the socially responsible thing. Is the narcotizing dysfunction still a useful way of understanding media effects? Recent polling suggests that despite extensive news coverage of multiple data breaches and misuse of their personal information, most Americans are relatively apathetic about the way large-scale social media invade privacy and market them to advertisers (Castro & McQuinn, 2018).

INFORMATION-FLOW THEORY

During the 1950s social scientists conducted many surveys and field experiments to assess the flow of information from media to mass audiences. Among them were studies of how quickly people found out about individual news stories (Funkhouser & McCombs, 1971). The overall objective of this work was to measure the effectiveness of media in transmitting information to mass audiences. The research was patterned after persuasion research, but instead of measuring shifts in attitudes, it investigated if information was learned. Survey research rather than controlled experiments was used to gather data. This work drew on methods pioneered by both Lazarsfeld and Hovland. It was based on the empirical generalizations growing out of their work, and it yielded similar empirical generalizations.

Information-flow research addressed questions researchers thought quite important. Many believed that if our democracy was to survive the challenges of the Cold War, it was critical that Americans be well informed about a variety of issues. For example, Americans needed to know what to do in the event of a nuclear attack. They also needed to know what their leaders were doing to deal with threats from abroad. They needed to understand the nature of the threat posed by communism. Classic theories of democracy assume that people must be well informed in order to make good political decisions. As such, the effective flow of information from elites to the public was essential if the United States was to counter the communist threat or deal with the consequences of nuclear war. Some believed that the strength of democracy would likely have to be demonstrated by its ability to enable survival and recovery from seemingly inevitable nuclear attacks.

Persuasion research had identified numerous barriers to persuasion, and information-flow research focused on determining whether similar barriers impeded the flow of news from media to typical audience members. It gathered findings derived from laboratory-based attitude-change research and assessed their usefulness in understanding real-world situations and problems. Some of the barriers investigated included level of education, amount of media use for news, interest in news, and talking about news with others. The researchers differentiated between "hard" and "soft" news. Hard news typically included news about politics, science, world events, and community organizations. Soft news included sports coverage, gossip about popular entertainers, and human-interest stories about average people.

Information-flow research found that most people learned very little about hard news because they were poorly educated, made little use of media for hard news, had low interest in it, and didn't talk to other people about it (Davis, 1990). Except for major news events such as President Eisenhower's heart attack or the assassination of President John F. Kennedy, most people didn't know or care much about national news events. Soft news generally was more likely to be learned than hard news, but even the flow of soft news was not what might have been hoped. The most important factor accelerating or reinforcing the flow of news of any kind was the degree to which people talked about individual news items with others. News of the Kennedy assassination reached most people very rapidly because people interrupted their daily routine to tell others about it (Greenberg & Parker, 1965). Without talk, learning about most hard news events rarely reached more than 10% to 20% of the population and was forgotten by those people within a few days or weeks.

Studies of the flow of civil defense information identified similar barriers. In most cases members of the public were even less interested in mundane civil defense information than they were in politics. In a series of field experiments, researchers Melvin DeFleur and Otto Larsen (1958) dropped hundreds of thousands of leaflets on small, isolated towns in the state of Washington. They used leaflets because Civil Defense officials had decided that in the event of a nuclear attack all radio stations would need to be shut down so Soviet bombers couldn't hone in on their broadcasts. DeFleur and Larsen indicated their view of the importance of their research by titling it "Project Revere"—like the American Revolution's Paul Revere, they were seeking ways to inform the nation about an impending attack. They wanted to determine how effective leaflets would be in warning people about incoming Russian bombers. For example, one set of leaflets announced that a civil defense test was being conducted. Every person who found a leaflet was instructed to tell someone else about it and then drop the leaflet in a mailbox so it could be returned to the researchers.

The researchers were disappointed that relatively few people read or returned the leaflets. Children were the most likely to take them seriously. To get the most useful effect, eight leaflets had to be dropped for every resident in town. Speculating that people were ignoring the leaflets because they only warned of a hypothetical attack, and threatening people with a real attack was considered unethical, the researchers designed another field experiment in which people were supposed to tell their neighbors about a slogan for a new brand of coffee. Survey teams visited homes in a small town and told people that they could earn a free pound of coffee by teaching their neighbors the coffee slogan. The survey team promised to return the following week, and if it found that neighbors knew the slogan, then both families would receive free coffee. Coffee was chosen because it had been severely rationed during the war and was a valued product. The experiment produced mixed results. Yes, almost every neighboring family had heard about the coffee slogan and tried to reproduce it. But unfortunately many could only remember fragments of the slogan, or they gave the wrong

---

INSTANT ACCESS

INFORMATION-FLOW THEORY

Strengths

1. Examines process of mass communication in real world
2. Provides theoretical basis for successful public information campaigns
3. Identifies barriers to information flow
4. Helps the understanding of information flow during crises

Weaknesses

1. Is simplistic, linear, and source-dominated
2. Assumes ignorant, apathetic populace
3. Fails to consider utility or value of information for receivers
4. Is too accepting of status quo

---

slogan—often one they likely heard in a radio ad for a different brand. The research confirmed the importance of motivating people to pass on information, but it suggested that even a free gift was insufficient to guarantee the *accurate* flow of information. If word of mouth was crucial to the flow of information, the possibility of distortion and misunderstanding was high. Even if media deliver accurate information, the news that reaches most people might be wrong after being passed along by word of mouth. These were discouraging findings since they implied that even a very extensive and expensive propaganda campaign was unlikely to prepare most Americans for the consequences of nuclear war. How relevant are these findings today? Do you trust the accuracy of the information passed along by others? How about your own recall of advertising slogans? Do you confuse slogans for competing products? Is your knowledge of slogans fragmentary? What about accuracy of information passed along from other people via Twitter or other social media?

The most important limitation of this **information-flow theory** is that it is a simplistic, linear, **source-dominated theory**. Information originates with authoritative or elite sources (the established media or the government, for example) and then flows outward to "ignorant" individuals. It assumes that barriers to the flow of information can be identified and overcome, but little effort is typically made to consider whether the information has any value or use for average audience members. Audience reactions to messages are ignored unless they form a barrier to that flow. Then those barriers must be studied only so they can be overcome. Like most limited-effects theories, information-flow theory assumes that the status quo is acceptable. Elites and authorities are justified in trying to disseminate certain forms of information, and average people will be better off if they receive and learn it. Barriers are assumed to be bad and, where possible, must be eliminated. Information-flow theory is also an example of a middle-range theory. It serves to summarize a large number of empirical generalizations into a more or less coherent explanation of when and why media information will be attended to and what sorts of learning will result.

PERSONAL INFLUENCE: THE TWO-STEP FLOW THEORY

In Chapter 4 we noted that Lazarsfeld made some useful generalizations about the importance of personal influence based on his 1940 Erie County research. In 1945 he conducted research to directly investigate these empirical generalizations concerning opinion leaders and followers (Katz & Lazarsfeld, 1955). He refused to speculate about the attributes of opinion leaders or their role—he wanted empirical facts (Summers, 2006). To get them, he sent a research team to Decatur, Illinois, to interview more than 800 women about how they made decisions on fashion, product brands, movies, and politics. Why study just women? Why ask about fashion or movies? Funding for the research was provided by MacFadden, a publisher of magazines targeted mainly at lower middle-class women (*True Story, True Confessions, True Romance, True Love, Motion Picture*). The company had no interest in men. It wanted to know whether its customers could be opinion leaders among their peers on topics like fashion or movies—something that was then doubted by most advertisers (everybody knew that elites were the tastemakers). If these women were leaders, MacFadden magazines could be used to target them, and the company would be able to sell more advertising. MacFadden had no interest in whether these women were leaders on politics, but Lazarsfeld did. What proved to be one of the most influential studies in the history of media research had a rather shaky foundation.

Decatur, a city in the heartland of America, was widely viewed as representative of most small- to medium-sized cities. Lazarsfeld's researchers used a "snowball" sampling technique, contacting an initial sample of women. During the interviews they asked these women if they had influenced or been influenced by other people in their thinking about international, national, or community affairs or news events. The researchers then followed up, conducting interviews with those who had been identified as influential. In this way Lazarsfeld tried to empirically locate women who served as opinion leaders. Their nomination by themselves or others was taken as factual evidence of their opinion-leader status.

More than 10 years passed before findings from the Decatur research were published. Part of the reason was that the field director for the research, C. Wright Mills, had a dispute with Lazarsfeld over the interpretation of the findings. When he couldn't write an acceptable summary of the research, Mills left Columbia and later became an influential critical theorist. His book *White Collar* (1951) may have been inspired by his time on the Decatur project, as were his views about postpositivism, which he labeled *abstracted empiricism* (Mills, 1959). Lazarsfeld eventually turned to one of his graduate students, Elihu Katz, and together they used the Decatur data as the basis for their 1955 *Personal Influence*. It formally advanced the **two-step flow theory**—a middle-range theory that influenced communication research for more than three decades.

In their book, Katz and Lazarsfeld (1955) provided a very positive depiction of American society and assigned a restricted and benign role to media. These depictions can be contrasted with the view provided by Mills's *White Collar* (1951) and *The Power Elite* (1956). Katz and Lazarsfeld interpreted their data to show that opinion leaders existed at all levels of society (so advertising shouldn't be targeted only at elites) and that the flow of their influence tended to be horizontal rather than vertical. Opinion leaders influenced people like themselves rather than those above or below them in the social order. Opinion leaders differed from followers in many of their personal attributes—they were more gregarious, used media more, were more socially active—but they often shared the same social status. But what if Lazersfeld had studied men rather than women? In 1945 women had had the right to vote for only 25 years. Would the research have found such clear evidence of a two-step flow? Were men as likely to engage in the sort of conversations that underlie a two-step flow? Would there have been more evidence of a vertical rather than a horizontal flow of influence?

TWO-STEP FLOW THEORY

Strengths

1. Focuses attention on the environment in which effects can and can't occur
2. Stresses importance of opinion leaders in formation of public opinion
3. Is based on inductive rather than deductive reasoning
4. Effectively challenges simplistic notions of direct effects

Weaknesses

1. Is limited to its time (1940s) and media environment (no television)
2. Uses reported behavior (for example, voting) as only test of media effects
3. Downplays reinforcement as an important media effect
4. Uses survey methods that underestimate media impact
5. Later research demonstrates a multistep flow of influence

Jefferson Pooley (2006) argues that *Personal Influence* did more than introduce an innovative way of understanding why the power of media is limited. In its first 15 pages, *Personal Influence* offered a summary of the history of propaganda research that provided boilerplate language that would be used in media theory textbooks and literature reviews written over the next five decades. These few pages dismissed pre–World War II theory and research as naive and overly speculative, erroneously grounded in the myth of media power. They promoted empirical, postpositivist research as providing more accurate findings that encouraged useful skepticism of media's power, further cementing the limited-effects trend as the basis for mass communication theory.

JOSEPH KLAPPER'S PHENOMENISTIC THEORY

In 1960 Joseph Klapper finally published a manuscript originally developed in 1949 as he completed requirements for a PhD at Columbia University and worked as a researcher for CBS. *The Effects of Mass Communication* was a compilation and integration of all significant media-effects findings produced through the mid-1950s and was intended for both scholars and informed members of the public. Klapper was concerned that average people feared the power of media. Though informed academics (i.e., empirical researchers) had rejected mass society theory, too many people still believed that media had tremendous power, and their fears were stoked by demagogic politicians like Joseph McCarthy who argued that Hollywood studios and broadcasting networks were staffed by communists. Klapper wanted to calm these fears by showing how constrained media actually were in their ability to influence people.

Klapper introduced a classic example of a middle-range theory of media that he called **phenomenistic theory** but is typically referred to as **reinforcement theory**. It states that media rarely have any direct effects and are relatively powerless when compared to other social and psychological factors such as social status, group membership, strongly held attitudes, and education. According to Klapper (1960):

1. Mass communication ordinarily does not serve as a necessary and sufficient cause of audience effects but, rather, functions among and through a nexus of mediating factors and influences.

2. These mediating factors are such that they typically render mass communication as a contributory agent, but not the sole cause, in the process of reinforcing existing conditions. (p. 8)

These generalizations about media were not very original, but Klapper expressed them forcefully and cited hundreds of findings to support them. His book came to be viewed as a definitive statement on media effects—especially by postpositivist researchers and those outside the media research community.

Klapper's theory is usually referred to as reinforcement theory because its key assertion is that the primary influence of media is to reinforce (not change) existing attitudes and behaviors. Instead of disrupting society and creating unexpected social change, media generally serve as agents of the status quo, giving people more reasons to go on believing and acting as they already do. Klapper argued that there are too many barriers to media influence for dramatic change to occur except under very unusual circumstances.

Even today, 60 years after its introduction, reinforcement theory is still raised by those unconvinced of media's power. Yet with benefit of hindsight, we can easily see its drawbacks. When published in 1960, Klapper's conclusions relied heavily on studies (from Lazarsfeld, Hovland, and their contemporaries) of a media environment that did not include the mass medium of television and the restructured newspaper, radio, and film industries that arose in response to television. Certainly Klapper's work did not envision a world of the Internet or large-scale social media—YouTube, Facebook, Twitter, and Google. Much of the research he cited examined the selective processes, but with the coming of television, media were becoming more symbolically rather than informationally oriented, producing potentially erroneous conclusions. In addition, the United States that existed after World War II looked little like the nation that existed before. As we'll see in later chapters, Klapper's "nexus of mediating variables"—that is, church, family, work, and school—began to lose their powerful positions in people's socialization (and therefore in limiting media effects) at the very same time that mass media were changing how, where, and when they delivered messages.

INSTANT ACCESS

PHENOMENISTIC THEORY

Strengths

1. Combines impressive amount of research into a convincing theory
2. Highlights role of mediating variables in the mass communication process
3. Persuasively refutes lingering mass society and propaganda notions

Weaknesses

1. Overstates influence of mediating factors
2. Is too accepting of status quo
3. Downplays reinforcement as an important media effect
4. Is too specific to its time (pre-1960s) and media environment (no television)

Finally, Klapper might have erred in equating reinforcement with no effects. Even if it were true that the most media can do is reinforce existing attitudes and beliefs, this is hardly the same as saying they have no effect. You'll see in Chapter 6, as you did in the Chapter 2's discussion of contemporary propaganda theory, that many contemporary critical scholars see this as media's most potentially negative influence.

THE ENTERTAINMENT FUNCTION OF MASS MEDIA

In general, functional analysis tends to produce conclusions that largely legitimize or rationalize the status quo. A classic example is the work of Harold Mendelsohn (1966). He was concerned that people widely misunderstood the influence of television, the powerful new medium of his era. He blamed elite critics of media (mostly mass society theorists) for fostering misconceptions about television's entertainment function, charging them with protecting their own self-interests and ignoring empirical research findings, and he dismissed most criticisms as prejudiced speculation inconsistent with empirical data.

According to Mendelsohn, mass society critics were paternalistic and elitist. They were upset because television entertainment attracted people away from the boring forms of education, politics, or religion they themselves wanted to promote. Mendelsohn argued that people needed the relaxation and harmless escapism that television offered. If this entertainment weren't available, people would find other releases from the tensions of daily life. They would turn to movies, radio dramas, dime-store novels, or comic books. Television simply served these needs more easily, powerfully, and efficiently than alternatives. Instead of condemning television, Mendelsohn argued that critics should acknowledge that it performs its function very well and at extremely low cost. He was concerned that critics had greatly exaggerated the importance and long-term consequences of television entertainment, and he asserted that it had a limited and ultimately quite minor social role. Television entertainment did not disrupt or debase high culture; it merely gave average people a more attractive alternative to high-brow entertainment like operas and symphony concerts. It did not distract people from important activities like religion, politics, or family life; rather, it helped them relax so that they could later engage in these activities with renewed interest and energy.

Mendelsohn cited numerous psychological studies to support his **mass entertainment theory**. He admitted that a small number of people might suffer because they became addicted to television entertainment. These same people, however, would most likely have become addicted to something else if television weren't available. Chronic couch potatoes might otherwise become lounge lizards or fans of romance fiction. Mendelsohn viewed addiction to television as rather benign compared to other alternatives; it didn't hurt other people, and viewing might even be slightly educational. Similar arguments can, and have as you'll see in Chapter 9, easily be made to defend the way social media entertain us.

Functionalist arguments continue to hold sway in many contemporary effects debates. Here, for example, is developmental economist Charles Kenny (2009) wondering

MASS ENTERTAINMENT THEORY

Strengths	Weaknesses
1. Stresses media's prosocial influence	1. Is too accepting of the status quo
2. Provides cogent explanation for why people seek entertainment from media	2. Claims to advocate for the interests of average people, but paints an implicitly negative picture of their use of media

about the impact of the world's more than one billion television households and the average of four hours a day consumed by each individual living in them: "So," he asks, "will the rapid, planetwide proliferation of television sets and digital and satellite channels, to corners of the world where the Internet is yet unheard of, be the cause of global decay [as] critics fear?" His near-perfect, "yes, but" functionalist answer: "A world of couch potatoes in front of digital sets will have its downsides—fewer bowling clubs, more Wii bowling. It may or may not be a world of greater obesity. . . . But it could also be a world more equal for women, healthier, better governed, more united in response to global tragedy, and more likely to vote for local versions of *American Idol* than shoot at people" (p. 68).

Mass entertainment theory and the narcotizing dysfunction provide excellent examples of how functional analysis and its findings can legitimize the status quo. Harmful effects are balanced by a number of positive effects. Who can judge whether the harm being done is great enough to warrant making changes? Congress? The courts? The public? When the evidence is mixed, the best course of action would appear to be inaction, especially in a democratic system that seems to have functioned quite well in the two and a half centuries since the Founders penned the First Amendment, and as the chapter's opening suggests, when things for most people seem to be just fine.

Functionalism allows researchers and theorists to easily avoid drawing controversial conclusions by simply noting that dysfunctions are balanced by functions. After all, we wouldn't want media to avoid publishing news about organized crime or social media abuse of our privacy just because some people will be narcotized. Sure, a few folks may abuse mass entertainment, but the benefits of such wonderful diversions surely outweigh this small problem. There is a conservative logic inherent in these arguments. It says that if the social world isn't literally falling apart with riots in the streets and people jumping off rooftops, things must be "in balance." Dysfunctions of media must certainly be balanced by other functions. If society is in balance, we can deduce that the overall influence of factors such as media must be either positive or only slightly negative. Obviously negative effects are offset by positive effects. If we eliminate the negative effects, we might also eliminate the positive effects balancing them. Are we willing to pay that price?

Functional analysis, middle-range theory, and limited-effects notions made a good fit. If media influence was modest, media couldn't be too dysfunctional, and findings from effects research could be combined to create a middle-range theory. For example, in their classic and influential 1961 book, *Television in the Lives of Our Children*, Wilbur Schramm, Jack Lyle, and Edwin Parker found that although viewing certain forms of violent television content encouraged *some* children to be aggressive, this was more than offset by *most* children, who showed little or no influence. And there were important positive functions. Children who watch TV read fewer violent comic books. Some might even learn how to anticipate and cope with aggressive peers. Thus, Schramm, Lyle, and Parker concluded that as far as the social system as a whole was concerned, violent television content makes little difference despite being dysfunctional for a few children (those "damned" by their "bad" parents to be manipulated by television violence). By contrast, and as you'll see in Chapter 7, at precisely the same time Schramm, Lyle, and Parker were explaining television's impact in such balanced terms, researchers from the field of psychology, bound by neither functionalism nor limited-effects findings, were making significant and persuasive arguments about the harmful effects of mediated violence.

SYSTEMS THEORIES OF COMMUNICATION PROCESSES

Other communication researchers were not so sanguine about media's "balancing" of effects. Systems engineers alerted them to the possibility of developing holistic explanations for societal, or macro-level, effects. Those engineers were concerned with designing and analyzing increasingly complex mechanical and electrical systems. They had achieved great successes during World War II and had laid the basis for many of the spectacular postwar technological breakthroughs in broadcasting and computers. It is no surprise, then, that their approach would be attractive to researchers interested in studying the most complex system of all, society.

A **system** *consists of a set of parts that are interlinked so that changes in one part induce changes in other parts.* System parts can be directly linked through mechanical connections, or they can be indirectly linked by communication technology. Because all parts are linked, the entire system can change as a result of alterations in only one element. Systems can be *goal-directed* if they are designed to accomplish a long-term objective. Some systems are capable of *monitoring the environment and altering their operations in response to environmental changes.*

During World War II electronics engineers began to develop systems that were programmed to pursue goals, monitor the environment, and adjust actions to achieve those goals. One example occurs when a guided missile is able to make midcourse adjustments by monitoring internal and external changes. Engineers were concerned with designing systems in which communication links functioned efficiently and transmitted information accurately. Communication was a means to an end. If a communication link didn't work properly, the solution was obvious: Communication technology had to be improved so the desired levels of effectiveness and accuracy were achieved. Thus, in designing and engineering systems of this type, communication problems could be solved by technological change.

Could communication problems in the society be solved in the same way? Could improving the accuracy, reliability, and range of communication solve societal problems? Would a nation bound together by networks of telephone cables be less troubled by regional disputes? Would a world bound together by satellite-based communication be less troubled by war? During the 1950s and 1960s there was increasing optimism that important societal-level communication problems might also be solved by improving the accuracy of message transmissions.

The Rise of Systems Theory

Observing the successes achieved by systems engineers during World War II, social theorists became intrigued by systems notions as a way of conceptualizing both macroscopic and microscopic phenomena. Some decided that the idea of systems offered a means of constructing useful models of various social processes, including communication. Rather than merely adding more variables, these models clarified how relationships between variables were understood. In developing these models, theorists drew on a variety of sources. But most 1960s social systems theorists acknowledged that the greatest and most recent impetus toward the development of systems theories came from an engineering subfield known as **cybernetics**, the study of regulation and control in complex machines. Cybernetics investigates how communication links between the various parts of a machine enable it to perform very complex tasks and adjust to changes taking place in its external environment.

Cybernetics emerged as an important new field during World War II, partly because of its use for designing sophisticated weapons (Wiener, 1954, 1961). It proved especially useful for communications engineering—the design of powerful new communication systems for military applications, such as radar and guided missiles. Communications engineers had abandoned simple linear models of the communication process by the 1940s. They conceptualized a circular but evolving communication process in which messages come back from receivers to influence sources that in turn alter their messages. They referred to these circular processes as **feedback loops**. In these systems, ongoing mutual adjustment is possible, ultimately leading to the achievement of a long-term objective or function.

Feedback loops enable sources to monitor the influence of their messages on receivers. But just as important, receivers can in turn influence sources. If the effects are not what was expected or desired, a source can keep altering a message until the desired feedback is obtained. As World War II progressed, machines were built that used ever more powerful forms of communication technology, such as radar and television cameras, to monitor the environment. These provided sophisticated means of detecting subtle changes so that a weapons system could achieve its objective. We refer to these as **communication systems** if their function is primarily to facilitate communication. By this definition, a guided missile is not a communication system; it is a weapons system that contains a communication subsystem.

Modeling Systems

Any representation of a system, whether in words or diagrams, is a **model**. The term *system* is used in communication engineering and cybernetics to refer to any set of interrelated parts that can influence and control one another through communication and feedback loops. In systems with many interrelated parts, a change in one part affects the others because all are interconnected through channels. Interdependence and self-regulation are key attributes of such systems. Each part can have a specialized role or function, but all must interrelate in an organized manner for the overall system to operate properly and regulate itself so that goals are achieved. Systems can be relatively simple or quite complex. They can display a high or low level of internal organization. They can operate in a static fashion, or they can evolve and undergo profound change over time. They can operate in isolation or be interconnected with a series of other machines to form an even larger system.

Another key attribute of systems is that they are **goal-oriented**. That is, they constantly seek to serve a specific overall or long-term purpose. We usually associate goals with thinking and planning. But, of course, machines can't think. Their goal-orientation is built in, hardwired, or otherwise programmed. Once a machine is started, it will seek its goal even if the goal is mistaken or can't be achieved. Like the robots in a science fiction movie, machines carry out their mission even if doing so makes no sense.

Although complex systems can be hard to describe and understand, the basic principles of a self-regulating system can be illustrated by looking at the way the furnace in your home operates. That device is part of a self-regulating system that uses a simple feedback loop to adjust to the external environment. The furnace communicates with a thermostat monitoring the environment, signaling it when it needs to turn on or off. As long as the temperature in your home remains within a desired range, the furnace remains inactive. When the thermostat detects a temperature below the desired range, it sends an electronic message telling the furnace to turn on. The furnace communicates with the thermostat by heating the air in your home. The thermostat monitors the air temperature, and when that reaches the desired level, the thermostat sends another message telling the furnace to turn off. In this simple system, the furnace and the thermostat work together to keep the temperature in balance. Communication in the form of a simple feedback loop linking the furnace and the thermostat enables the system to operate effectively.

Applying Systems Models to Human Communication

Even simple systems models can be used to represent some forms of human communication. You and a friend can be seen as forming a system in which your friend plays the role of "thermostat." By maintaining communication with your friend either in person or via social media, you find out whether your actions are appropriate or inappropriate. Are these the right clothes to wear for the interview? Should you go to a dance or join friends for a movie? During your communication you might not be trying to affect your friend but, rather, want your friend to guide you. You want your friend's feedback so you can adjust your actions.

This example also illustrates key limitations of systems models when they are used to represent human communication—the easiest models to create tend to be too simple and too static. Unless you and your friend have a very unusual relationship, you will play many other kinds of roles and communicate with each other across a very broad range of topics using a variety of media. If the only function your friend serves for you is that of a thermostat, you probably need to reexamine your relationship. Assuming that you do have a more complex relationship, you could probably spend weeks trying to map out a systems model to represent the intricacies of your interrelationship. By the time you finished, you would discover that significant changes have occurred and the model is no longer accurate. Unlike mechanical parts linked by simple forms of communication, both you and your friend can easily alter your roles, your communication links, and the content and purposes of your messages. In other words, you regularly and routinely transform the system that links you to others. Social media certainly increase the ease with which such changes can be made. New feedback loops spring up while old ones vanish. New purposes develop, and old purposes are forgotten.

Adoption of Systems Models by Mass Communication Theorists

Like other social scientists in the 1950s and 1960s, mass communication researchers were drawn to systems models. They came to see moderately complex systems models as an ideal means of representing communication processes—a big advance over simplistic linear communication process models common before 1960. Gradually, systems models replaced the **transmissional model** implicit in most of the early effects research. Harold Lasswell (1949) provided a cogent, succinct version of this model when he described the communication process as *who says what to whom through what medium with what effect*. This linear model assumes that a message source dominates the communication process and that its primary outcome is some sort of effect on receivers—usually one intended by the source. Influence moves or flows in a straight line from source to receivers. This model ignores the possibility that the message receivers might also influence the source. It focuses attention on whether a source brings about intended effects and whether unintended negative effects occur. It doesn't consider the possibility of mutual or reciprocal influence.

Communication theorists proposed new models of communication processes with feedback loops in which receivers could influence sources and mutual influence was possible. The potential for modeling mutual influence was especially attractive for theorists who wanted to understand interpersonal communication. Most conversations involve mutual influence. Participants send out messages, obtain feedback, and then adjust their actions. In everyday life, people are constantly adjusting to one another. The overall social environment can be understood as something created and maintained by ongoing negotiation between actors.

The usefulness of systems models for representing mass communication processes involving legacy media was less obvious. With legacy media, there are few if any *direct* communication links from receivers to sources. Message sources can be unaware of the impact of their messages or find out what that impact was only after days or weeks have elapsed. During the 1960s, however, refinement of media ratings systems and improved, more scientific public opinion polls allowed the establishment of indirect communication links between message sources and receivers. Ratings and opinion poll results provided message producers with feedback about audience reaction to their messages. For television ratings this feedback was quite crude—either people watch a program or they don't. If they don't, producers change the message without much understanding of what people want. If ratings are high, they provide more of the same—until people get so tired of the same programming that they ultimately tune to something else. With opinion polls, the feedback can provide a bit more information to message sources, but not much. Politicians, for example, are constantly experimenting with messages in an effort to alter voter opinions and produce favorable evaluations of themselves.

INSTANT ACCESS

SYSTEMS THEORY

Strengths

1. Can be conceptualized as either micro- or macro-level theory
2. Represents communication as a process
3. Can be used to model a limitless variety of communication processes
4. Moves mass communication theory beyond simple linear-effects notions

Weaknesses

1. Has difficulty assessing causal relationships
2. Is often too simplistic to represent complex communication patterns
3. Is perceived by some as overly mechanistic and dehumanizing
4. Focuses attention on observable structures, ignoring the substance of communication
5. Is unparsimonious

Functionalism's Unfulfilled Promise

Although they did indeed help advance mass communication theory beyond a focus on specific limited-effects findings and middle-range theory, functionalism and systems theory suffered much criticism and are rarely considered among the central schools of thought in contemporary thinking about media. However, they have influenced the development of some important theories. These approaches to theory have not been more influential because scholars who construct interpretive and postpositivist theories see them as having serious limitations.

Humanistic scholars who develop interpretive theories tend to reject the mechanistic or biological analogies inherent in functionalism and systems models. They are fundamentally opposed to the use of functional analysis and systems models, perceiving them to be dehumanizing and overly simplistic. They argue that systems models are often nothing more than elaborate metaphors—sets of descriptive analogies. They are dissatisfied with the ability of functional analysis and systems models to adequately represent complex human or societal interrelationships. After all, people aren't parts of machines. The relationships aren't like the mechanism in an old-fashioned pocket watch. Even complex mechanical systems are simple when compared with the human relationships that are found within a family. Humanists are fearful that in applying functional or mechanistic analogies we demean or trivialize human existence and experience.

Social scientists who develop postpositivist theories argue that research must stay focused on development of *causal* explanations and predictions. They reject complicated systems models because they don't permit the assessment of causality. In our earlier heating system model, which is the causal agent and which agent is being affected? Does the furnace cause the thermostat to act? Yes. Does the thermostat cause the furnace to act? Yes. So, which is dominant in this relationship? Which controls the other? In this model neither agent is clearly *causal*. Each causes the other to change. Thus, in even this very simple process involving feedback, causality can be hard to assess. If we measure the furnace and the thermostat at only one point in time, we are likely to get a completely mistaken impression of their relationship. When these processes become more complicated with more agents and more feedback loops, we need a schematic diagram to sort out the flow of influence. The effort to assign causality soon becomes a meaningless exercise. For example, given the complexity of the systems we create when we interact with other people, it becomes literally impossible to sort out causality—except for the simplest and most narrowly defined systems or parts of systems.

Should we be concerned about the difficulty of assigning causality in systems models? Is assignment of causality necessary to have a truly scientific theory? Or should we be satisfied that our theories are useful for other purposes? If we could simulate a set of interrelationships that provides insight into people playing certain roles in a particular situation over a limited time span, is that enough? Do we need to be able to say that the person playing role X has .23 causal dominance over the person playing role Y, whereas the person in role Y has .35 dominance over person X? Just how precise must our understanding of these interrelationships be for the simulation to be of value? Just how precise can we afford to make our simulations, given the time and research effort necessary?

Researchers who assert the importance of assigning causality are concerned that if they lower their concern for causality, they will create and use systems models based on little more than informed speculation. Although sophisticated systems models might allow the construction of fascinating computer simulations, will they serve any practical purpose? How can their utility be evaluated if causality is not used as an explanatory standard? It might appear that a model fits a particular set of relationships and gives insight into interconnections between particular parts, but how can researchers be sure? How can they choose between two competing models that seem to represent a particular set of relationships equally well? These critics are deeply skeptical of the value of constructing models that contain complex interconnections between agents. Critics view systems models as unparsimonious—containing too many unnecessary variables and overly complex interrelationships.

Finally, as already noted, functionalism and systems theory have a third limitation that many find troublesome: They have a bias toward the status quo. Because they tend to concentrate attention on observable structures (e.g., the functioning parts of the organism or machine), functionalism and systems theory often lead to the assumption that the primary function or role of these structures is to maintain and serve the overall system. However, it is likely that complex systems models will become more important for many social science fields including mass communication. Computers give us the ability to create and analyze quite complex models. If we can simulate weather systems and make accurate predictions about weather, what might we do with mass communication?

REVIEW OF LEARNING OBJECTIVES

• Explain how the media-effects trend was consolidated into a dominant approach to media research.

During the 1950s, 1960s, and into the 1970s the limited-effects perspective came to dominate American mass communication research. New bodies of theory were created by research communities with inspiration from key individuals like Lazarsfeld and

Hovland. Their members shared a common perspective acquired through collaboration on research and graduate education. Fledgling researchers were trained to use specific theories and research methods. As those research communities evolved, the body of theory on which they were based gradually matured. At a certain point, as a particular community grew in size and produced widely accepted research, it published landmark studies, demonstrating the power of the limited-effects perspective and its ability to produce findings that had immediate, practical value. These studies showed a consistent view of a benign mass media. They proposed functionalist theories of media—media were only one force among many that determine how society functions. Problematic functions of media were balanced by positive functions. Media, therefore, had limited power to threaten or undermine the social order.

- Understand the contribution of Robert Merton to the development of middle-range theory and its importance for media-effects research.

Unlike grand social theories that attempted to explain a broad range of social action, middle-range theories explain only limited domains or ranges of action that had been or could be explored using empirical research. These theories could be created by carefully interpreting empirical findings. Middle-range theories consist of limited sets of assumptions from which specific hypotheses are logically derived and confirmed by empirical investigation. They do not remain separate but are consolidated into wider networks of theory sufficiently abstract to deal with differing spheres of social behavior and social structure. Middle-range theory cuts across the distinction between micro-sociological problems and involves the specification of ignorance.

- Understand the strengths and weaknesses of several foundational but still important mass communication theories such as information-flow theory, two-step flow theory, phenomenistic theory, and mass entertainment theory.

Information-flow theory serves as the basis for successful information campaigns and identifies barriers to information, but it is a linear, source-dominated view of the communication process that assumes a passive audience. Two-step flow theory focuses attention on the environment in which effects can and cannot occur and stresses the importance of opinion leaders, but it is a product of its time (pre-TV era) and ignores reinforcement as an important media effect. Phenomenistic (sometimes reinforcement) theory highlights the role of mediating variables in the mass communication process, but it overstates the power of those variables, is a product of its time (pre-TV era), and ignores reinforcement as an important media effect. Mass entertainment theory stresses media's prosocial value and helps explain why people seek entertainment from media, but it is too accepting of the status quo and views average people somewhat negatively.

- See the value and drawbacks of applying theories of the middle range, functionalism, and systems theory to explaining media influence.

Middle-range theories made scientific inquiry into the social world manageable, and the hope was that many individual-effects studies would add up, permitting the construction of a broad perspective on the role of media. But the effort to combine these theories of the middle range into broader theories proved more difficult than expected.

Functionalism positioned media and their influence in the larger social system and offered a balanced view of media's role in society, but it is overly accepting of the status quo and assumes that dysfunctions are balanced by functions and that negative latent functions are balanced by positive manifest functions. Systems theory was useful in moving media theory beyond the limited-effects perspective and allowed the consideration of many factors involved in the mass communication process, especially in its application to legacy media, where there are few if any *direct* communication links from receivers to sources. However, its overly mechanistic view of people and its inability to identify causality made it troubling to humanists and postpositivists alike.

CRITICAL THINKING QUESTIONS

1. Are you typically an opinion leader or an opinion follower? Are there specific topics on which you are one or the other? Identify an issue (movies, music, sports, fashion, politics) on which you can identify another whose opinion you usually seek. How well does that person fit the description of opinion leaders embodied in two-step flow? Has membership in a social networking site such as Facebook or Twitter altered your role as an opinion leader or follower or that of any of your friends? How? What types of information typically flow between you and your friends? How accurate is the information?

2. Klapper's phenomenistic theory argues that media's greatest power rests in their ability to reinforce existing attitudes and values. At the time this was evidence that media had limited effects—they were limited to reinforcement. But more contemporary thinking sees reinforcement as anything but a limited effect. Can you explain some of the arguments in support of this view? What about reinforcing some people's tendency toward political apathy? Could that influence a close election outcome?

3. Could you create a systems model that shows your communication links with other people? How complex would this model be? What forms of communication provide links in your model? How important are the links provided by social media? How useful is this model? How could you conduct research to assess its validity?

KEY TERMS

functionalism
administrative research
specification of ignorance
manifest functions
latent functions
classic four functions of the media
narcotizing dysfunction
information-flow theory
source-dominated theory
two-step flow theory

phenomenistic theory
reinforcement theory
mass entertainment theory
system
cybernetics
feedback loops
communication system
model
goal-oriented
transmissional model

GLOSSARY

functionalism: Theoretical approach that conceives of social systems as living organisms whose various parts work, or function, together to maintain essential processes

administrative research: Research that examines audiences to interpret consumer attitudes and behaviors; the use of empirical research to gather data about audiences that can guide practical administrative decisions

specification of ignorance: Idea that in science that every answer produces new questions

manifest functions: Intended and observed consequences of media use; often involve purposes claimed by media agents

latent functions: Unintended and less easily observed consequences of media use; can be negative and offset manifest functions

classic four functions of the media: Surveillance, correlation, transmission of the social heritage, and entertainment

narcotizing dysfunction: Theory that as news about an issue inundates people, they become apathetic to it, substituting knowing about that issue for action on it

information-flow theory: Theory of how information moves from media to audiences to have specific intended effects (now known as information or innovation diffusion theory)

source-dominated theory: Theory that examines the communication process from the point of view of some elite message source

two-step flow theory: Idea that messages pass from the media, through opinion leaders, to opinion followers

phenomenistic theory: Theory that media are rarely the sole cause of effects and are relatively weak when compared with other social factors

reinforcement theory: More common name for phenomenistic theory, stressing the theory's view that media's most common and important effect is reinforcement

mass entertainment theory: Theory asserting that television and other mass media, because they relax or otherwise entertain average people, perform a vital social function

system: Any set of interrelated parts that can influence and control one another through communication and feedback loops

cybernetics: The study of regulation and control in complex systems whether machines, computers, or social systems

feedback loops: Ongoing mutual adjustments in systems

communication systems: Systems that function primarily to facilitate communication

model: Any representation of a system, whether in words or diagrams

goal-oriented: Characteristic of a system that serves a specific overall or long-term purpose

transmissional model: View of mass media as mere senders or transmitters of information; places an emphasis on accurate, efficient transmission of information

CHAPTER 6

The Emergence of the Critical Cultural Trend in North America

Close your eyes, and imagine the 1960s anti-Vietnam war movement. What did the protesters look like? How old were they? How were they dressed? How did they protest? What about the folks on the other side of that debate? What did they look like? How old were they? How were they dressed? Keep your eyes closed, and imagine the women's rights movement of that same time. What did the feminist protesters look like? How old were they? How were they dressed? How did they protest? What about the folks on the other side of that debate? Today, some 50 or 55 years later, the answers are easy. The anti-war protesters were weirdly dressed hippies, mostly young, generally engaged in at best disruptive and at worst violent action. The other side? Good, up-standing Americans, the Silent Majority whose voices were drowned out by the raucous radicals. The feminists? Young hippies burning their bras. The other side? Good, up-standing Americans, the Silent Majority whose voices were drowned out by the raucous radicals. Both images are accurate . . . and inaccurate. Yes, there were weirdly dressed anti-war radicals engaging in violent action, but there were many, many more people inveighing against the war who were nothing of the sort. And feminists may have thrown bras, along with girdles, curlers, popular women's magazines, and pageant brochures, into a Freedom Trash Can to protest the 1968 Atlantic City Miss America contest, but this produced what might be called "bra-smoldering," not "bra-burning" (Campbell, 2011). And there were many, many more people, male and female, fighting for equality for women who neither burned nor smoldered their bras.

So where did our myths of anti-war radicals and bra-burning feminists come from? Myths usually combine elements of both truth and fantasy, and indeed these particular versions of our history were jointly created by the movements themselves and the mass media. "The media needed stories, preferring the dramatic; the movement[s] needed publicity for recruitment, for support, and for political effect. Each could be useful to the other; each had effects, intended and unintended, on the other" (Gitlin, 1980, p. 25). But there was more at work in the coverage of these important social movements than a symbiotic relationship gone awry. There was the operation of presumably objec-tive reporting requirements in which every Viet Cong flag-waving hippy was balanced by "reasonable-sounding, fact-brandishing authorities" (Gitlin, 1980, p. 4). Audience demands—and media acquiescence to those demands—that stories be reported in terms of recognizable narratives were also at work, so feminist protestors "burned bras" just as anti-war protesters burned draft cards (Polo, 2012). And underlying both processes there is the natural and historic tendency of elites, in this case media, political, and social elites, to maintain power. As sociologist Herbert Gans (1972) wrote, "In any modern society in which a number of classes, ethnic and religious groups, age groups, and political interests struggle among each other for control over society's resources, there is also a struggle for the power to determine or influence the society's values, myths, symbols, and information" (p. 373). In agreement, sociologist Todd Gitlin (1980) wrote, "Calm and cautionary tones of voice affirm that all 'disturbance' is or should be under control by rational authority; code words like *disturbance* commend the established normality; camera angles and verbal shibboleths ('and that's the way it is') enforce the integrity and authority of the news anchorman and commend the inevitability of the established order. Hotheads carry on, the message connotes, while wiser heads, officials and reporters both, with superb self-control, watch the unenlightened ones make trouble" (p. 4).

That was then; this is now. Certainly things have changed. But ask yourself why media accounts of sports fans celebrating their team's football championship, as they did in Philadelphia in 2018, are referred to as "revelers" despite rampant vandalism and looting and eight arrests, but those protesting the killing of an unarmed African American young man, as they did in 2015 after the police shooting of Freddie Gray, are labeled "rioters" (Posner, 2018)? Why, in news reports, is the Muslim shooter who murdered 49 people at the Pulse nightclub in Orlando, Florida, in 2016 a "terrorist," but the White man who killed 58 people and wounded more than 400 others from the 32nd floor of the Mandalay Bay Hotel in Las Vegas in 2017 is a "lone wolf," "gunman," or "sniper," (Lalami, 2017)? Why do CNN anchors label as "far-left positions" raising taxes on the wealthy and universal health care when large majorities of Americans (61% and 70%, respectively) favor both these policies (Pleat, 2019)? These questions about the peculiarities of media storytelling can't be answered by the media-effects theory trend, but in this chapter we consider how a different perspective—the critical cultural theory trend—can.

LEARNING OBJECTIVES

After studying this chapter you should be able to

- Describe the critical cultural media trend, contrast it with the media-effects trend, and differentiate the types of research questions that can be answered by each.
- Draw distinctions between macroscopic and microscopic mass communication theory, between critical and cultural theories and those based on empirical research, and between the transmissional and ritual perspectives on mass communication.
- Identify the roots of critical and cultural theory in Marxism, neo-Marxism, the Frankfurt School, textual analysis and literary criticism, political economy theory, and critical feminist scholarship.
- Identify differences and similarities in political economy theory and cultural studies.

OVERVIEW

During the 1950s and 1960s interest in cultural theories of mass communication began to develop and take hold—first in Europe, then in Canada and other British Commonwealth nations, and finally in the United States. As we noted in Chapter 4's discussion of the media-effects trend, that perspective made some questionable assumptions and had important limitations. It focused on whether specific types of media content could have an immediate and direct effect on individuals' specific thoughts and actions. Researchers typically looked for evidence of these effects using traditional postpositivist approaches, primarily highly structured quantitative experiments or surveys. But it eventually became apparent that it was possible to study mass communication in other ways—that is, through cultural studies and critical theory approaches. "The space for these newer models grew," explained researcher Joshua Meyrowitz (2008), "as it became clearer that the stimulus-response concept (even when refined through studies of individual and group differences in response to messages and even when explored in terms of the modulating influence of the opinions of influential peers) did not sufficiently account for the complexity of interactions with media" (p. 642). As a result, writes media scholar Jefferson Pooley (2007), in the 1970s,

> [w]ith more or less force, every social science discipline registered a protest against the confident scientism of the postwar decades—a backlash against natural science envy and blind faith in quantitative methods. In each field, insurgents elevated history and particularity over explanation and the search for timeless laws. To their opponents they affixed pejoratives like "positivist" and "behaviorist." The new, more humanist and interpretive social science drew upon, and contributed to, a much broader recognition across many fields that knowledge and interest are entangled with one another. (p. 469)

Now, instead of focusing on specific, measurable effects on individuals, theory could focus on how media are related to changes in culture, on how shared understandings and social norms change. Instead of trying to locate hundreds of small effects and add them all up, researchers could ask whether the development of mass media has profound implications for the way people create, share, learn, and apply culture.

In this chapter we will trace the emergence of the critical cultural theory trend that addresses questions about the way media might produce profound changes in social life through their subtle influence on the myriad of social practices that form the foundation of everyday life. This perspective argues that media might have the power to intrude into and alter how we make sense of ourselves and our social world. Media could influence how we view ourselves, our relationship to others, even the image that we have of our body. Social institutions, including political, economic, and educational institutions, might be disrupted and transformed as media institutions play an increasingly central role in contemporary societies. In 1941, when the media-effects trend was at the height of its scientific certainty, the "father of American social science," Paul Lazarsfeld, challenged his colleagues to address precisely these larger societal issues:

> Today we live in an environment where skyscrapers shoot up and elevateds [commuter light rail trains] disappear overnight; where news comes like shock every few hours;

where continually new news programs keep us from ever finding out details of previous news; and where nature is something we drive past in our cars, perceiving a few quickly changing flashes which turn the majesty of a mountain range into the impression of a motion picture. Might it not be that we do not build up experiences the way it was possible decades ago? (p. 12)

But the media-effects trend couldn't conduct research or produce theories that could address these issues. A different approach to research and theory construction was needed. The theories developed to address issues like this are quite diverse and offer very different answers to questions about the role of media in social life, but the concept of **culture** is central to all of them. As cultural theorist Jeff Lewis (2008) explains, "Media texts—music, TV, film, print, Internet—meet their audiences in a complex intersection of systems and personal imaginings. To this end, the transformation of the world into a *global media sphere* is the result of a dynamic interaction between macro processes (history, economy, technology, politics and modes of social organization) and the profoundly intimate and intricate microcosms of a person's life—the realm of the individual subject. Culture, in a very profound sense, is formed through these processes: an assemblage of dynamic engagements that reverberate through and within individual subjects and the systems of meaning making of which they are an integral part" (pp. 1–2).

Cultural theories, then, offer a broad range of interesting ideas about how media can affect culture and provide many different views concerning the long-term consequences of the cultural changes affected by media. The theories introduced in this chapter are quite useful for raising questions about the role of media for individuals and for society and they provide intriguing, cogent answers.

CHANGING TIMES

Modern mass media dominate everyday communication. From the time children learn to talk, they are mesmerized by the sounds and moving images of *Sesame Street.* By third grade 70% of kids have a television in their bedrooms (Kelman, 2018). During the teen years media supply vital information on peer group culture and—most important—the opposite sex. In middle age, as people rear families, they turn to video on an expanding number of technologies for convenient entertainment and to magazines and the Internet for tips on raising teenagers. In old age, as physical mobility declines, people turn to television for companionship and advice. As the screens delivering media content multiply and deliver an ever-changing array of content, our overall use of media continues to increase, now making up 70% of our waking time (Mandese, 2018). As screen time rises, it displaces many important everyday activities and disrupts our lives in ways we rarely notice.

Media have become a primary means by which most of us experience or learn about many aspects of the world around us. The importance of media as a source of experience about the social world continues to increase. As we spend more time in front of screens, we have less time to experience things first-hand. Even when we don't learn about these things directly from media, we learn about them from others who get their ideas of the world from media. With the advent of mass media, many forms of folk culture fell into sharp decline. Everyday communication was fundamentally altered. Storytelling, game playing, and music making ceased to be important for extended families. Instead nuclear families gathered in front of an enthralling electronic storyteller, watching others play games and make music. Informal social groups dedicated to cultural enrichment disappeared, as did vaudeville and band concerts. It is no coincidence that our culture's respect for older people and the wisdom they hold has declined in the age of media. If respected theorists like Joshua Meyrowitz (1985), Robert McChesney (2004), and Henry Giroux (2011) are correct, we're losing touch with locally based cultures and moving into a media-based global cultural environment. If new-media researchers like Gwenn Schurgin O'Keeffe and Kathleen Clarke-Pearson (2011) and Scott Caplan (2005) are correct, young adults who have inadequate social skills and difficulty with face-to-face communication will turn to e-mail, texting, and instant messaging as more comfortable ways of developing or maintaining social relations.

Mass society theory, as you read in Chapter 2, greeted similar types of social change with alarm. It viewed mediated culture as inferior to elite culture. As mass culture spread, theorists feared it would undermine the social order and bring chaos. People's lives would be disrupted. The sudden rise of totalitarian social orders in the 1930s seemed to fulfill these prophecies. In fascist and communist nations alike, media were used to propagate new and highly questionable forms of totalitarian culture. But were media ultimately responsible for the creation and promotion of these forms of government? Was the linkage between the new forms of media and their messages so great that the drift into totalitarianism was inevitable? Or could media promote individualism and democracy as easily as they did collectivism and dictatorship? We have struggled with these questions for more than a century of mass communication theory. The theories in this chapter and in Chapter 14 provide different answers—some cautiously optimistic and others quite pessimistic.

During the 1960s and 1970s, as the overt threat of a totalitarian takeover of the United States and the world declined, mass society theory lost its relevancy. By 1960 research in the media-effects trend had concluded that media rarely produce significant, widespread, long-term changes in people's thoughts and actions. Media-effects trend researchers no longer assumed that mediated mass culture was inherently antidemocratic. American media had become highly effective promoters of capitalism, individualism, and free enterprise. Today some critics argue that new media technologies, such as social media, the Internet, and smartphones, are "personal media," inherently biased toward individualism and market economies rather than toward collectivism and state control. So the role of media in culture seems to be settled—doesn't it? After all, the West won the Cold War. Shouldn't we conclude that media are benign? Can't we safely ignore the warnings in books like *1984* and *Brave New World*? In *1984* cameras mounted on television sets allowed Big Brother to constantly monitor people's viewing and spot those who reacted suspiciously to propaganda messages. How far from *1984*'s spying TV sets are Vizio's Internet-connected TVs that secretly collect and sell their owners' viewing information to advertisers (Smith, 2017)? And today's digital media monitor us in ways that are even more subtle. Should we trust Facebook and Google to use the data they collect to serve our interests as well as theirs?

THE CRITICAL CULTURAL THEORY TREND

The various cultural theories of media can be identified in several ways. In this chapter we use a dichotomy widely employed by cultural theorists themselves to differentiate their scholarship (Garnham, 1995). *Microscopic interpretive theories* focus on how individuals and social groups use media to create and foster forms of culture that structure everyday life. As such, they sit at "the borderland between textual and social research" (Jensen, 1991, p. 27). These theories are usually referred to as **cultural studies** theory. *Macroscopic structural theories* focus on how media institutions are structured within capitalist economies. They focus attention on the way social elites operate media to earn profits and exercise influence in society. They assess how different social institutions are affected by the way media are structured and controlled and argue that elites sometimes use media to propagate **hegemonic culture** as a means of maintaining their dominant position in the social order, encouraging "subordinated groups [to] actively consent to and support belief systems and structures of power relations that do not necessarily serve—indeed may work against—those interests" (Mumbry, 1997, p. 344). They also contend that elites use media to create and market seemingly apolitical cultural commodities that serve to earn profits for those elites. This set of theories is called **political economy theory** because it places priority on understanding how economic power provides a basis for ideological and political power. Some researchers speculate about how alternate forms of culture and innovative media uses are systematically suppressed. These theories directly challenge the status quo by exposing elite manipulation of media and criticizing both hegemonic culture and cultural commodities. These concerns over elite domination of media have grown with the rise of large-scale social media. Suppression of competing media and innovative uses by the biggest companies is eroding much of the potential that social media was once believed to hold.

Macroscopic Versus Microscopic Theories

Cultural studies theories are less concerned with the long-term consequences of media for the social order and more concerned with looking at how media affect the lives of groups of people who share a culture. They are micro-level, or *microscopic*, because they deemphasize larger issues about the social order in favor of questions involving the everyday life of groups of average people. Political economy theories, by contrast, are *macroscopic* cultural theories, less concerned with developing detailed explanations of how individuals or groups are influenced by media and more interested with how the social order as a whole is affected. Ideally, these theories ought to be complementary. Individual- or group-level explanations of what media do to people (or what people do with media) should link to societal-level theories. Yet, until recently, macroscopic and microscopic cultural theories developed in relative isolation. Theorists were separated by differences in geography, politics, academic discipline, and research objectives. Some theorists were critical of the approach taken by others. Microscopic theories were criticized as failing to take into account the power of elites to use media to dominate everyday culture, while macroscopic theories were faulted for failing to give adequate credit to the power of individuals to gain insight into media and take important control over everyday culture.

Microscopic cultural studies researchers prefer to interpret what is going on in the world immediately around them. Many find the social world an endlessly fascinating place. They are intrigued by the mundane, the seemingly trivial, the routine. They view our experience of everyday life and of reality itself as an artificial social construction that we somehow maintain with only occasional minor breakdowns. They want to know what happens when mass media are incorporated into the routines of daily life and play an essential role in shaping our experience of the social world—are there serious disruptions, or do media enhance daily experience? Could media be causing problems that are somehow being compensated for or concealed? If so, how does this happen? Will there eventually be a breakdown—are we being systematically desensitized and trained to be aggressive? Or is everyday life being transformed in useful ways—are we somehow becoming kinder and gentler?

Macroscopic researchers are troubled by the narrow focus of microscopic theory. So what if some people experience everyday life in certain ways? Why worry if everyday-life culture is enhanced by media? These researchers demand answers to larger questions. They view media as industries that turn culture into a commodity and sell it for a profit. They want to assess the overall consequences to the social order when these industries become a major part of national economies. In what ways do media affect how politics is conducted, how the national economy operates, how vital social services like education and health care are delivered? Macroscopic researchers want to know if media are intruding into or disrupting important, large-scale social processes. For example, have media disrupted the conduct of national politics and therefore increased the likelihood that inferior politicians will be elected? Have primary school students become so addicted to entertainment and to screens that they can't adjust to routine educational activities in classrooms? Macroscopic researchers believe that such large-scale questions can't be answered if you focus on what individuals are doing with media.

Critical Theory

Some cultural studies and political economy theories are also referred to as **critical theories** because their axiology openly espouses specific values and uses them to evaluate and criticize the status quo. Those who develop critical theories seek social change that will implement their values. Political economy theories are inherently critical, but many cultural studies theories are not. Critical theory raises questions about the way things are and provides alternate ways of interpreting the social role of mass media. For example, some critical theorists argue that media in general sustain the status quo—even, perhaps especially, when it is under stress or breaking down. Critical theory often provides complex explanations for media's tendency to consistently do so. For example, some critical theorists identify constraints on media practitioners that limit their ability to challenge established authority. They charge that few incentives exist to encourage media professionals to overcome those constraints and, even more troubling, that media practitioners consistently fail to even acknowledge them.

Critical theory often analyzes specific social institutions, probing the extent to which valued objectives are sought and achieved. Naturally, then, mass media and the mass culture they promote have become an important focus for critical theory. Critical researchers link mass media and mass culture to a variety of social problems. Even when they do not see media as the source of specific problems, they criticize them for aggravating or preventing problems from being identified or addressed and solved. A theorist might argue that content production practices either cause or perpetuate specific problems. For example, TV drama producers need to identify villains who challenge heroes, but if they consistently choose Italian, Muslim, or Chinese characters, they risk perpetuating problematic stereotypes. A common theme in critical theories of media is that content production is so constrained that it inevitably reinforces the status quo and undermines useful efforts to effect constructive social change.

Consider, for example, the last time you read news reports about members of an American social movement strongly challenging the status quo—Black Lives Matter or the Occupy movement, for example. How were their actions described? How were movement members and their leaders portrayed? These are the questions raised in the chapter's opening paragraphs. Consider veteran journalist Daniel Schorr's (1992) personal recollection of media coverage of the civil rights movement. "I found [in the mid-1960s] that I was more likely to get on the *CBS Evening News* with a black militant talking the language of 'Burn, baby, burn!'" he wrote. So when he covered a 1968 Reverend Martin Luther King, Jr., press conference, he was prepared to "get the most threatening sound bite I could to ensure a place on the evening news lineup." But while waiting for his production crew to pack up, he "noticed that King remained seated behind a table in an almost empty room, looking depressed. Approaching him, I asked why he seemed so morose. 'Because of you,' he said, 'and because of your colleagues in television. You try to provoke me to threaten violence and, if I don't, then you will put on television those who do. And by putting them on television, you will elect them our leaders. And if there is violence, will you think about your part in bringing it about?'" (p. 5C).

Stories about social movements usually imply problems with the status quo. Movements typically arise because they identify social problems that go unaddressed, and they make demands for social change. Media professionals are caught in the middle. Movement leaders demand coverage of their complaints, and they stage demonstrations designed to draw public attention to their concerns. Elites want to minimize coverage or exercise "spin control" so coverage favors their positions. How do journalists handle this? How should they handle it? Existing research indicates that this coverage almost always denigrates movements and supports elites (Duncan-Shippy, Murphy, & Purdy, 2017; Cissel, 2012; Goodman, 2004). Coverage focuses on the deviant actions or appearance of some movement members and ignores the way movements define problems and propose solutions for them.

INSTANT ACCESS

CRITICAL THEORY

Strengths	Weaknesses
1. Is politically based, action-oriented	1. Is too political; call to action is too subjective
2. Uses theory and research to plan change in the real world	2. Typically lacks scientific verification; based on subjective observation
3. Asks big, important questions about media control and ownership	3. When subjected to scientific verification, often employs innovative but controversial research methods

Comparing the Media Theory Trends

It is useful to keep in mind both the strengths and the limitations of the theories introduced in this chapter. Many of the theorists whose ideas we discuss believe that media play a central role in modern social orders or our daily lives. Rather than presenting us with the types of empirical evidence favored by proponents of the media-effects trend, they ask us to accept their view of media influence using logic, argument, and our own powers of observation. Some describe compelling examples to illustrate their arguments. Others offer empirical evidence for their belief in powerful media, but they use innovative research methods, and so their work is challenged and questioned by traditional postpositivist researchers. During the 1970s and 1980s supporters of the media-effects trend were especially troubled by the rise of the critical cultural trend. This new trend directly and aggressively challenged many of the assumptions underlying the media-effects trend. Postpositivists were quick to question the evidence offered by critical cultural theorists. They saw cultural theories as new variations of mass society theory—a theory they felt they had quite effectively debunked in the 1950s and 1960s. Effects researchers believed that cultural theories were too speculative and the empirical research generated from these theories was too loosely structured and inherently biased.

Cultural studies and political economy theorists do employ a broad range of research methods and theory-generation strategies, including some that are unsystematic and selective. As a result, critics believe that personal biases and interests inevitably motivate culture researchers and affect the outcome of their work. But, argue cultural theory's defenders, this is acceptable as long as researchers openly acknowledge those biases or interests. They point out that media-effects research has its own biases, which postpositivists seem unwilling to identify and acknowledge.

In contrast with the quantitative empirical research methods, the techniques used by many critical or cultural researchers are often qualitative methods; that is, they highlight essential differences (distinctive qualities) in phenomena. Epistemologically, knowledge is often created or advanced through discourse (debate and discussion) involving proponents of contrasting or opposing theoretical positions. Theory is advanced through the formation of schools of thought in which there is consensus about the validity of a specific body of theory. Often rival schools of theory emerge to challenge existing theories while developing and defending their own. Proof of a theory's power often rests in its ability to attract adherents and be defended against attacks from opponents.

Not surprisingly, researchers who adopt a postpositivist approach find cultural theories hard to accept. They are skeptical of theories evaluated more through discourse than through empirical research. Postpositivist media researchers place far less importance on theory development or criticism. They don't develop competing schools of theory. Their research methods are used to generate theory and to *test* theory rather than as a means of making qualitative differentiations. They argue that if empirical research is conducted according to prevailing standards, findings can be readily accepted throughout the research community. There is no need for competing schools of theory. If other researchers doubt the validity of specific findings, they can replicate (duplicate) the research and then report conflicting findings. But in truth, these conflicting reports are quite rare and provoke considerable controversy when they are published. Though there is verbal debate between those who espouse conflicting empirically based theories, these disagreements rarely appear in print. When they do, both sides present empirical findings to support their positions. Arguments often center on methodological disputes about the reliability and validity of research findings rather than the strength of the theoretical propositions—researchers disagree about whether appropriate methods were used, question the application of specific methods, or argue that the data were improperly analyzed or interpreted. Much less attention is given to the structure and consistency of theoretical propositions. When theory is developed it takes the form of middle-range theory—theory that summarizes sets of empirical generalizations and often doesn't make strong assertions or assumptions about the role of media in the development of culture or social institutions.

THE RISE OF CULTURAL THEORIES IN EUROPE

Despite its popularity in American social science, the media-effects trend was not widely accepted by most social researchers in Europe. European social research has instead continued to be characterized by what some US observers regard as **grand social theories**—highly ambitious, macroscopic, speculative theories that attempt to understand and predict important trends in culture and society. Mass society theory was a 19th-century example of a European-style grand social theory. It illustrated both the strengths and the limitations of this type of theory. Dissatisfied with these limitations, American social researchers, especially those trained in the Columbia School of empirical social research, chose to construct more modest middle-range theories.

In Europe the development of grand social theory remained a central concern in the social sciences and humanities after World War II. Mass society theory gave way to a succession of alternate schools of thought. Some were limited to specific nations or specific academic disciplines or even certain universities. Others achieved widespread interest and acceptance. Most were not theories of media—they were theories of society offering observations about media and their place in society or the lives of individuals. Some of the most widely accepted were based on the writings of Karl Marx. **Marxist theory** influenced even the theories created in reaction against it. Marx's ideas formed a foundation or touchstone for much post–World War II European social theory, but Cold War politics made them quite controversial in the United States. Theories developed in France or Germany often remained untranslated into English until several years after they became popular in Europe. Even theories developed in Britain were treated with skepticism and suspicion in the United States.

In the 1970s and 1980s, at the very time that Marxism itself was being rejected across Europe as a practical guide for politics and economics, grand social theories based in part on Marxist thought were gaining increasing acceptance in the United States (Grossberg & Nelson, 1988). We briefly summarize key arguments in the Marxist perspective and pay particular attention to ideas about media. Then we present some more recent theories based on these ideas.

Marxist Theory

Karl Marx developed his theory in the latter part of the 19th century, during one of Europe's most volatile periods of social change. In some respects his is yet another version of mass society theory—but with several very important alterations and additions.

Marx was familiar with the grand social theories of his era. He was a student of the most prominent German Idealist philosopher, Georg Wilhelm Friedrich Hegel. Early in his career Marx drew on Hegel's ideas, but later he constructed his own in opposition to them. From Hegel he derived insights into the human construction of the social world and of human reason itself. But while Hegel attributed social change to a metaphysical force, a "World Spirit," Marx eventually adopted a materialist position—human beings shape the world using the technology and physical resources available to them. It is the availability of and control over technology and resources that limit and determine what people can achieve.

Like some mass society theorists, Marx identified the myriad problems associated with industrialization and urbanization as the consequence of actions taken by powerful elites. Industrialization and urbanization were not inherently bad, he reasoned. Problems resulted when unethical capitalists attempted to maximize personal profits by exploiting workers. Using a similar analysis, American conservative mass society theorists demanded restoration of traditional social orders, but Marx was a Utopian, calling for the creation of an entirely new social order in which all social class distinctions would be abolished. The workers should rise against capitalists and demand an end to exploitation. They should band together to seize the means of production (i.e., labor, factories, and land) so they might construct an egalitarian democratic social order—Communism. In Marx's theory, media are one of many modern technologies that must be controlled and used to advance Communism.

Marx argued that the hierarchical class system was at the root of all social problems and must be ended by a revolution of the workers, or proletariat. He believed that elites dominated society primarily through their direct control over the means of production, the **base (or substructure) of society**. But elites also maintained themselves in power through their control over social institutions and technologies that support culture (media, religion, education, and so on) or the **superstructure** of society. Marx saw culture as something elites freely manipulated to mislead average people and encourage them to act against their own interests. He used the term **ideology** to refer to these biased forms of culture. Ideology fostered a "false consciousness" in the minds of average people so they came to support elite interests rather than their own. Marx believed an ideology operated much like a drug. Those who are under its influence fail to see how they are being exploited—it blinds or distracts them. In the worst cases they are so deceived that they actually undermine their own interests and do things that increase the power of elites while making their own lives even worse. Philosopher Jason Stanley (2015) recently expanded on this idea. "Elites in civil society invariably acquire a flawed ideology to explain their possession of an unjust amount of goods of society," he writes. "The purpose of the flawed ideology is to provide an apparently factual (in the best case, apparently scientific) justification for the otherwise manifestly unjust distribution of society's goods." This false consciousness then becomes a powerful mechanism of social control, as "negatively privileged groups acquire the beliefs that justify the very structural features of their society that cause their oppression" (p. 269).

Marx concluded that the only realistic hope for social change was a revolution in which the masses seized control of the base—the means of production. Control over the superstructure—over ideology—would naturally follow. He saw little possibility that reforms in the superstructure could lead to social evolution, or if they could,

---

INSTANT ACCESS

CULTURAL STUDIES THEORY

Strengths

1. Provides focus on how individuals develop their understanding of the social world
2. Asks big, important questions about the role of media for individuals
3. Respects content consumption and sharing by media users

Weaknesses

1. Has little explanatory power at the macroscopic level
2. Focuses too narrowly on individual compared with societal role of media
3. Typically relies on qualitative research; is based on unsystematic subjective observation

---

the resulting transformation would be very slow in coming. These views stemmed in part from his rejection of German Idealist philosophy. Ideologies could be endlessly debated, and existing elites always had ways of making sure their ideas remained dominant. Revolution was the quickest and most certain way to bring about necessary change. Elites would never willingly surrender power; it must be taken from them. Little purpose would be served by making minor changes in ideology without first dominating the means of production. But there proved to be problems when you change the base but neglect the superstructure. Revolution can simply give rise to new elites who manipulate culture to serve their interests.

Neo-Marxism

Many European cultural studies theories are called *neo-Marxist theories* because they deviate from classic Marxist theory in at least one important respect—they focus concern on the superstructure issues of ideology and culture rather than on the base. The importance that neo-Marxists attach to the superstructure has created a fundamental division within Marxist studies. Many neo-Marxists assume that useful change can be achieved through ideological battles—through discourse in the public arena—rather than by violent revolution. Some neo-Marxists have developed critiques of culture that demand radical transformations in the superstructure, whereas others argue that modest reforms can lead to useful changes. Tensions have arisen among Marxist scholars over the value of the work undertaken by the various schools of neo-Marxist theory. Nonetheless, since the end of the Cold War, neo-Marxist positions have achieved great popularity and broad acceptance in the social sciences generally and media studies in particular.

Textual Analysis and Literary Criticism

Modern European cultural studies have a second, very different source—a tradition of humanist criticism of religious and literary texts based in hermeneutics. Humanists have specialized in analyzing written texts since the Renaissance. One common objective was to identify those texts having greatest cultural value and interpreting them so their worth would be appreciated and understood by others. These humanists saw texts as a civilizing force in society (Bloom, 1987), and hermeneutics was seen as a scholarly tool that could enhance this goal. Humanist scholars ranged from religious humanists, who focused on the Bible or the writings of great theologians, to secular humanists working to identify and preserve what came to be known as the "literary canon"—a body of the great literature. The literary canon was part of what theorists referred to as **high culture**, a set of cultural artifacts including music, art, literature, and poetry that humanists judged to have the highest value. By identifying and explaining these important texts, humanists attempted to make them more accessible to more people. Their long-term goal was to preserve and gradually raise the level of culture—to enable even more people to become humane and civilized. In this way it would be possible to advance civilization in Europe and its colonies.

Over the years, hermeneutic theory has given rise to many different methods for analyzing written texts. They are now being applied to many other forms of culture, including media content. They share a common purpose: to criticize old and new cultural practices so those most deserving of attention can be identified and explicated and the less deserving can be dismissed. This task can be compared with that of movie critics who tell us which films are good or bad to assist us in appreciating or avoiding them. But movie critics are typically not committed to promoting higher cultural values; most only want to explain which movies we are likely to find entertaining.

Contemporary critical theory includes both neo-Marxist and hermeneutic approaches. Hybrid theories combine both. Before examining these, we will look at some of the historically important schools of critical theory that have produced still-influential work.

The Frankfurt School

One early prominent school of neo-Marxist theory developed during the 1920s and 1930s at the University of Frankfurt and became known as the **Frankfurt School**. Two of the most prominent individuals associated with the school were Max Horkheimer, its longtime head, and Theodor Adorno, a prolific and cogent theorist. In contrast with some later forms of neo-Marxism, the Frankfurt School combined Marxist critical theory with hermeneutic theory. Most Frankfurt School theorists were trained in humanistic disciplines but adopted Marxist theories as a basis for analyzing culture and society. Frankfurt School writings identified and promoted various forms of high culture such as symphony music, great literature, and art. Like most secular humanists, its members viewed high culture as having its own integrity and inherent value and thought that it should not be used by elites to enhance their personal power. Oskar Negt (1978) has argued that Frankfurt School writing can best be understood from a political position that "takes a stand for people's needs, interests, and strivings toward autonomy and which also conscientiously undertakes practical steps toward making these things a reality today" (p. 62).

The Frankfurt School celebrated high culture while denigrating mass culture (Arato & Gebhardt, 1978). Adorno, for example, likened the 1940s dance, the jitterbug, to "St. Vitus' dance or the reflexes of mutilated animals" (in Ross, 2014, p. 94). In one of their later and most influential books, Adorno and Horkheimer (1972) criticized mass media as **culture industries**—industries that turned high culture and folk culture into commodities sold for profit. The goal of that commodification was "to deceive and mislead . . . [having] only one real function: to reproduce incessantly the values of capitalist culture" (O'Brien & Szeman, 2004, p. 105). They saw the American culture industry as a symptom of a "latent totalitarianism" (Huyssen, 1975, p. 4), offering people a meaningless "freedom to choose what is always the same" (in Ross, 2014, p. 88). Here is how Adorno and Horkheimer (1972) themselves expressed this view:

> Under monopoly all mass culture is identical, and the lines of its artificial framework begin to show through. The people at the top are no longer so interested in concealing monopoly: as its violence becomes more open, so its power grows. Movies and radio need no longer pretend to be art. The truth that they are just business is made into an ideology in order to justify the rubbish they deliberately produce. They call themselves industries; and when their directors' incomes are published, any doubt about the social utility of the finished products is removed. (p. 121)

Many of the specific criticisms of mass culture offered by Frankfurt School theorists were not that different from those of conservative humanistic scholars. But humanist critics tended to focus on specific media content, whereas Horkheimer and Adorno began to raise questions about the larger industries producing the content.

The Frankfurt School had a direct impact on American social research because the rise of the Nazis forced its Jewish members into exile. Horkheimer, for one, took up residency at the New School for Social Research in New York City. Adorno found a job working for Paul Lazarsfeld at Columbia University. During this period of exile Frankfurt School theorists remained productive. They devoted considerable effort, for example, to the critical analysis of Nazi culture and the way it undermined and perverted high culture. In their view Nazism was grounded on a phony, artificially constructed folk culture cynically created and manipulated by Hitler and his propagandists. But they also criticized the way capitalist media promoted problematic forms of mass culture. This led to serious disputes that tended to marginalize Frankfurt School theory in the United States, especially after Cold War politics aroused suspicion of any form of Marxist thought.

Development of Neo-Marxist Theory in Britain

During the 1960s and 1970s two important schools of neo-Marxist theory emerged in Great Britain: British cultural studies and political economy theory. British cultural studies combines neo-Marxist theory with ideas and research methods derived from diverse sources, including literary criticism, linguistics, anthropology, and history (Hall, 1980). It attempted to trace historic elite domination over culture, to criticize the social consequences of this domination, and to demonstrate how it continues to be exercised over specific minority groups and subcultures. British cultural studies criticizes and contrasts elite notions of culture, including high culture, with popular everyday forms practiced by minorities and other out-groups. It challenges the superiority of all forms of elite culture, including high culture, and compares it with useful, meaningful forms of popular culture. Hermeneutic attention is shifted from the study of elite cultural artifacts to the study of minority group "lived culture" and the way that media are used by those groups to enhance their lives.

Graham Murdock (1989b) traced the rise of British cultural studies during the 1950s and 1960s. Most of its important theorists came from the lower social classes. The British cultural studies critique of high culture and ideology was an explicit rejection of what its proponents saw as alien forms of culture imposed on minorities.

They defended indigenous forms of popular culture as legitimate expressions of minority groups. Raymond Williams was a dominant early theorist and a literary scholar who achieved notoriety with his reappraisals of cultural development in England. He pieced together a highly original perspective of how culture develops based on ideas taken from many sources, including literary theories, linguistics, and neo-Marxist writing. He questioned the importance of high culture and took seriously the role of folk culture. Not surprisingly, many of his colleagues at Cambridge University viewed his ideas with suspicion and skepticism. Throughout most of his career, he labored in relative obscurity at his own university while achieving a growing reputation among left-wing intellectuals at other academic institutions and in the British media.

Toward the end of the 1960s and into the 1970s Williams (1967, 1974) turned his attention to mass media. Although media weren't the primary focus of his work, he developed an innovative, pessimistic perspective of mass media's role in modern society. His ideas inspired a generation of young British cultural studies scholars, first at the Centre for Contemporary Cultural Studies at the University of Birmingham and then at other universities across England and Europe. Williams was more broadly concerned with issues of cultural change and development, as well as elite domination of culture. Committed to certain basic humanistic values, including cultural pluralism and egalitarianism, he argued that mass media posed a threat to worthwhile cultural development. In contrast with most humanists of his time Williams rejected the literary canon as a standard, and with it traditional notions of high culture. But he was equally reluctant to embrace and celebrate folk culture—especially when it was repackaged as popular mass media content. If there were to be genuine progress, he felt, it would have to come through significant reform of social institutions.

The first important school of cultural studies theorists was formed at the University of Birmingham during the 1960s and was led initially by Richard Hoggart and then by Stuart Hall. Hall (1982) was especially influential in directing several analyses of mass media that directly challenged limited-effects notions and introduced innovative alternatives. Building on ideas developed by Frankfurt School–trained Jurgen Habermas (1971, 1989) and Williams, Hall (1981b) understood ideology to be "those images, concepts, and premises which provide frameworks through which we represent, interpret, understand, and make sense of some aspect of social existence" (p. 31). As such, he argued that mass media in liberal democracies can best be understood as a **pluralistic public forum** in which various forces struggle to shape popular notions about social existence. In this forum new concepts of social reality are negotiated and new boundary lines between various social worlds are drawn. Unlike traditional neo-Marxists, however, Hall argued that elites did not maintain complete control over this forum, nor did they need it to advance their interests. The culture expressed in this forum is not a mere superficial reflection of the superstructure but is instead a dynamic creation of opposing groups. To Hall (1981a, p. 228), popular culture "is the ground on which the transformations are worked." Elites, however, *do* retain many advantages in the struggle to define social reality. Counterelite groups must work hard to overcome them. Hall acknowledged that heavy-handed efforts by elites to promote their ideology can fail, and well-planned efforts to promote alternative perspectives can succeed even against great odds. Nevertheless, the advantages enjoyed by elites enable them to retain a long-term hold on power.

This disagreement over the immutability of ideology, "the relatively determined nature of social life and cultural forms under industrial capitalism" in the words of media theorist Klaus Bruhn Jensen (1991, p. 28), highlights the distinction between the more traditional Marxist **structuralist view** of culture and Hall's **culturalist view**. Where Hall saw culture as a site of social struggle and a place where change could occur, theorists such as Louis Althusser (1970) saw much less freedom, as elite control over the superstructure in their view was near total. When culture becomes too free, elites enforce their ideology through that part of the superstructure Althusser called *repressive state apparatuses*—for example, the police and other law-making and enforcing institutions. But that is typically unnecessary because of their hegemonic control over *ideological state apparatuses*, the media and other social institutions like schools and religion.

A key strength *and* limitation of some British cultural studies theorists is their direct involvement in various social movements. In keeping with their commitment to critical theory, they not only study movements but also enlist in and even lead them. Some cultural studies advocates argue that a person cannot be a good social theorist unless he or she is personally committed to bringing about change (O'Connor, 1989). Cultural studies theorists have been active in a broad range of British social movements, including feminism, youth movements, racial and ethnic minority movements, and British Labour Party factions. But active involvement can make objective analysis of movements and movement culture difficult. These cultural studies theorists usually don't worry about this because their axiology rejects the possibility of objectivity anyway and dismisses its utility for social research. Their intention is to do research that aids the goals of movements rather than conduct work that serves the traditional aims of scholarship or science. As Jeffrey Juris (2017) explains, the activist-researcher must "become entangled with complex relations of power, and live the emotions associated with direct action organizing and activist networking" (p. 165).

British cultural studies has addressed many questions and produced a variety of research on popular media content and the use specific social groups make of it. Does this content exploit and mislead individuals, or does it enable them to construct meaningful identities and experiences? Can people take ambiguous content and interpret it in new ways that fundamentally alter its purpose for them? Can useful social change be achieved through cultural reform rather than through social revolution?

INSTANT ACCESS

BRITISH CULTURAL STUDIES

Strengths

1. Asserts value of popular culture
2. Empowers "common" people
3. Empowers minorities and values their culture
4. Stresses cultural pluralism and egalitarianism
5. Developed audience reception research as a way of understanding media influence

Weaknesses

1. Is too political; call to action is too value-laden
2. Typically relies on qualitative research; is based on unsystematic subjective observation
3. Can overlook subtle, indirect ways that elites control media and audience reception

In the United States, British cultural studies was an early influence on scholars in many fields, particularly the work of feminists (Long, 1989) and those who study popular culture (Grossberg, 1989). They saw it as offering an innovative way of studying media audiences holding many advantages over approaches grounded in postpositivist limited-effects theory.

POLITICAL ECONOMY THEORY

Political economy theorists study elite control of economic institutions, such as banks and stock markets, and then show how this control affects many other social institutions, including the mass media (Murdock, 1989a). In certain respects political economists accept the classic Marxist assumption that the base dominates the superstructure. They investigate the means of production by looking at economic institutions, expecting to find that these institutions shape media to suit their interests and purposes. For example, Herb Schiller, "one of the most widely recognized and influential political economists of communication" (Gerbner, 2001, p. 187), wrote for decades that "corporate influence pervades nearly every aspect of society. From simple things, like our daily diet and the clothes we wear, to matters of larger scale, like the way we communicate with each other" (Schiller, 2000, p. 101).

Political economists have examined how economic constraints limit or bias the forms of mass culture produced and distributed through the media. We've already seen Frankfurt School theorists express similar concerns. Political economists are not interested in investigating how mass culture influences specific groups or subcultures. They focus on how the processes of content production and distribution are economically and industrially constrained. Why do some forms of culture dominate prime-time television schedules whereas other forms are absent? Does audience taste alone explain those differences, or can other, less obvious reasons be linked to the interests of economic institutions? Critical scholar Sut Jhally (1989) offers a near-perfect example of a political economy answer to these questions. He explains, "All commodities have two fundamental features: they have *exchange-value* (that is, they are worth something and can be exchanged in the marketplace) and they have *use-value* (that is, they do something that makes them useful to human beings). What is the use-value of a cultural commodity? Its function, and its importance, stems from the *meaning* it generates. . . . Within the United States there has never been any questioning of the domination of use-value by exchange-value. . . . [We] call government interference domination, and marketplace governance freedom. We should recognize that the marketplace does not automatically ensure diversity, but that . . . the marketplace can also act as a serious constraint to freedom" (pp. 80–81).

During the past four decades, compared to cultural studies theorists, political economy theorists have worked in relative obscurity. Although political economy theories gained respect in Europe and Canada, they were largely ignored in the United States. Later in this chapter we'll consider the work of Harold Innis, a Canadian economist who pioneered political economy research in Canada. Even though American communication theorists were intrigued by cultural studies theory, few found the views of political economists interesting or persuasive until quite recently, as we'll see later in this chapter.

POLITICAL ECONOMY THEORY

Strengths

1. Focuses on how media are structured and controlled
2. Offers empirical investigation of media finances and industry structure
3. Seeks link between media content production, media structure, and media finances

Weaknesses

1. Has little explanatory power at microscopic level
2. Is not concerned with causal explanation; is based on subjective analysis of industry structure and finances
3. Is not concerned with audience reception or media use

The Debate between Cultural Studies and Political Economy Theorists

Although the two schools of neo-Marxist theory—British cultural studies and political economy theory—appear to be complementary, there has been considerable rivalry between them (Murdock, 1989b). Some genuine theoretical differences separate the two, but they also differ in their research methods. With their macroscopic focus on economic institutions and their assumption that economic dominance leads to or perpetuates cultural dominance, political economists were slow to acknowledge that cultural changes can affect economic institutions. Nor do political economists recognize the diversity of popular culture or the variety of ways in which people make sense of cultural content. Murdock suggested that the two schools should cooperate rather than compete. For this to happen, however, researchers on both sides would have to give up some of their assumptions and recognize that the superstructure and the base—culture and the media industries—can influence each other. Both types of research are necessary to produce a complete assessment of the role of media.

Other differences as well have led to serious debates between these two major schools of cultural theory. Cultural studies theorists tend to ignore the larger social and political context in which media operate. They focus instead on how individuals and groups consume popular culture content. Their research has led them to become increasingly skeptical about the power of elites to promote hegemonic forms of culture. Instead, they have found that average people often resist interpreting media content in ways that would serve elite interests (see the discussion of oppositional decoding in Chapter 9). Some cultural studies theorists have been less interested in making or influencing social policy, and their research often doesn't provide a clear basis for criticizing the status quo. Political economy theorists accuse some cultural studies researchers of abandoning the historical mission of critical theory in favor of an uncritical celebration of popular culture. They argue that it is important for theorists to actively work for social change. You can get some idea of why they think this is important by reading the box entitled "Media Coverage of Workers and the Working Poor."

Political economy theorists have remained centrally concerned with the larger social order and elites' ownership of media. They have criticized the growing privatization of European media, the decline of public service media institutions in Europe, and the increasing privatization and centralization of media ownership around the world.

THINKING ABOUT THEORY

MEDIA COVERAGE OF WORKERS AND THE WORKING POOR

In 2008 the "Great Recession" nearly took down the world economy; eight million Americans lost their homes to foreclosure, and trillions of dollars in wealth disappeared (Schwartz, 2018). It was a time, in the words of journalist M. H. Miller (2018), of "simmering populist rage that threatened to cleave the country in two; a broken shadow banking system operating without regulatory oversight; [and] . . . young voters . . . who would be entering a bleak job market with an average debt of five figures a person and little hope of paying it off" (p. SR3). For millions of people the situation was so bad that the obvious question was "Why did no one see it coming?" How was it that "the press missed the crisis—and, in fact, continued to lionize financial executives even as it was beginning to unfold" (Gold, 2018)? Where were the media in this time of anger, out-of-control banks, and college kids sinking in debt? "Journalism," wrote business reporter Howard Gold (2018), "failed to alert its readers to the coming disaster, to appreciate the complicity of the Wall Street banks, and to understand the inability or unwillingness of regulators to grasp the problem" (para. 4). The "watchdogs failed to bark," wrote Greg Mitchell (2009), editor-in-chief of *Editor & Publisher*. "Missing stories of this enormity," he predicted, would have "consequences that will echo . . . for decades" (p. 16).

Echo, indeed. More than a decade later, the level of income inequality in the United States continues to grow at a faster rate than in most of the rest of the developed world. The top 1% of American households owns 40% of the nation's wealth, more than the bottom 90% combined (Vanden Heuvel, 2019). The net worth of the median American household is 20% lower than it was before the crash, and there are millions of working-age adults, not counted in the official unemployment statistics, who "are not working, not looking for work, not going to school, and not taking care of children. Many of them would like to work, but they can't find a decent-paying job and have given up looking," laments political writer David Leonhardt (2018, p. SR2). Of those who are working, more than 41.7 million, a third of the American work force, earn less than $12 an hour, most with no employer-provided health insurance. The federal minimum wage of $7.25 an hour nets a person working full time $15,080 a year, well under the $24,600 federal poverty level for a family of four. "'Paid labor as the antidote to poverty,'" writes Matthew Desmond (2018), "has become

a pernicious lie" (p. 37). And those college kids? Forty-four million, with an average debt of over $37,000 and a 40% default rate, start their work lives burdened with debilitating debt that, unlike almost everyone else thanks to bank-friendly federal legislation, they cannot discharge through bankruptcy (Senderowicz, 2018).

Will the media bark now? An analysis of 10,489 campaign stories from eight of the most influential news outlets in the country over a six-month period in the 2012 presidential election discovered that only 17.02% addressed the poor and poverty in any substantive way (Garces & Rendall, 2012). A study of 705 campaign stories in local newspapers during the 2016 campaign showed that only 11% were about jobs, 8% about income inequality, and 13% about the economy (Sacco, Potts, Hearit, Sonderman, & Stroud, 2017). Why the disconnect? Why, especially after their dismal performance leading up to the last global economic disaster that hit the poor and working people the hardest, do the media continue to ignore the economic situation of those very people? Is it because most national journalists are removed from the real lives of most Americans, with 25% of the country's 40,000 working journalists living in Los Angeles, New York, and Washington? Their relative comfort making it difficult for them to "fathom the deep, seething, often unspoken economic discontent that afflicts so many Americans" (Gabler, 2016)? Is it because at the country's two preeminent newspapers, the *New York Times* and the *Wall Street Journal*, just short of half of all staff writers and editors attended elite universities, so in terms of educational attainment they "resemble senators, billionaires, and World Economic Forum attendees" more than they do the people they are supposed to report on (Richardson, 2018)? "Covering the poor doesn't seem to be a beat that many or most reporters aspire to. It's not generally the beat rising stars are promoted into," explains Barbara Raab of the Ford Foundation (as cited in Savchuk, 2016).

Surely entertainment media can help fill the void, telling the interesting, often-dramatic stories of everyday people. Unfortunately the characters in television entertainment programming "compose a community far removed from our own: a town with a data-capture expert but no dishwasher, a rocket scientist but no sanitation worker, and a tech magnate but no truck driver. [Television] is full of people who run their own businesses, often inherited: an

(Continued)

THINKING ABOUT THEORY *(Continued)*

inn, a brew pub, a winery, a portrait gallery. Compared to the rest of us, they're much more likely to be wrangling with underlings or regulators rather than bosses" (Eidelson, 2011). "Who wants to become involved with characters fretting about losing their homes when there's fresh dirt on Britney?" asks *Variety's* Cynthia Littleton (2008, p. 1). Television writers and producers are "well-compensated creatures of the entertainment industry, mostly unaffected by a shrinking economy. That disconnection sanitized TV against the complexities of race and class," explains media critic Wesley Morris (2016, pp. 76–79).

Political economy theorists would acknowledge all these explanations, but they would group them under a more general argument, the overwhelming influence of money. American journalism, explains journalist Jim Naureckas (2009), "is founded on a couple of very bad ideas: It's a bad idea to have journalism mainly carried out by large corporations whose chief interest in news is how to make the maximum amount of money from it. And it's a bad idea to have as these corporations' main or sole source of revenue advertising from other large corporations" (p. 5). "You don't need to be a rocket scientist or a social scientist," argues syndicated columnist Norman

Solomon (2009), "to grasp that multibillion-dollar companies are not going to own, or advertise with, media firms that challenge the power of multibillion-dollar companies" (p. 16). "It's not to the advantage to ABC or CBS or NBC to tell stories that make Walmart look bad, or make Calvin Klein look bad," explains Roberta Reardon, vice president of the AFL-CIO (as cited in Ludwig, 2013).

Is the American media system capable of providing better coverage of workers and the working poor? Will it present workers and the working poor more frequently and realistically any time soon? Of course not, answer critical theorists; our media system is immersed in and enriched by a political economy that benefits from the devaluation of work and workers. Your turn. What do you think? Is this a realistic or pessimistic view of the American economic and media systems? Before you answer, however, consider this explanation of the ideology of one influential part of that media system, the editorial page of the *New York Times*, as expressed by its editor James Bennet: "I think we are pro-capitalism. The *New York Times* is in favor of capitalism because it has been the greatest engine of, it's been the greatest anti-poverty program and engine of progress that we've seen" (as cited in Johnson, 2018).

They take pride in staying true to the mission of critical theory by remaining politically active and seeking to shape social policy. They have formed social movements and serve as leaders in others. Above all, political economy theorists are critical—they have an explicit set of values providing a basis for their evaluation of the status quo.

CULTURAL STUDIES: TRANSMISSIONAL VERSUS RITUAL PERSPECTIVES

James Carey was a leading American proponent of cultural studies, writing and speaking prolifically. At a time when US media researchers viewed most cultural studies work with suspicion and skepticism, Carey, in a series of seminal essays (1989), drew on the work of British and Canadian scholars to defend cultural studies and contrast it with the media-effects trend. One essential difference he found is that effects theories focus on the transmission of accurate information from a dominant source to passive receivers, whereas cultural studies is concerned with the everyday rituals people rely on to structure and interpret their experiences. Carey argued that the limited-effects view is tied to the **transmissional perspective**—the idea that mass communication is the "process of transmitting messages at a distance for the purpose of control. The archetypal case . . . then is persuasion, attitude change, behavior modification, socialization through the transmission of information, influence, or conditioning" (Newcomb & Hirsch, 1983, p. 46). In the transmissional perspective car commercials attempt to persuade us to buy a certain make of automobile, and political campaign messages are simply that: messages designed to cause us to vote one way or another. They might or might not be effective in causing us to act as they intend.

The **ritual perspective**, on the other hand, links communication to "'sharing,' 'participation,' 'association,' 'fellowship,' and 'the possession of a common faith.'" It shares the same root with the words "'commonness,' 'communion,' 'community.' . . . A ritual view of communication is directed not toward the extension of messages in space but toward the maintenance of society in time; not the act of imparting information but the representation of shared beliefs" (Carey, 1989, pp. 18–19). Carey (1975) believed, in other words, that "communication is a symbolic process whereby reality is produced, maintained, repaired, and transformed" (p. 177). According to Carey, a car commercial sells more than transportation. It is, depending on its actual content, possibly reaffirming the American sense of independence ("Chevy, the American Revolution!"), reinforcing cultural notions of male and female attractiveness (we don't see many homely actors in these ads), or extolling the personal value of consumption, regardless of the product itself ("Be the first on your block to have one"). Similarly, political campaign messages often say much more about our political system and us as a people than they say about the candidates featured in them.

Carey traced the origin of the ritual view to hermeneutic literary criticism. Scholars who study great literary works have long argued that these texts have far-reaching, long-lasting, and powerful effects on society. A classic example is the impact that Shakespeare has had on Western culture. By reshaping or transforming culture, these works indirectly influence even those who have never read or even heard of them. Literary scholars argue that contemporary cultures are analyzed and defined through their arts, including those that depend on media technology. These scholars have not been interested in finding evidence of direct media effects on individuals. They are more concerned with macroscopic questions of cultural evolution—the culture defining itself for itself. Thus, ritual perspective theorists presume a grand-scale interaction between the culture, the media used to convey that culture, and the individual media-content consumers of that culture.

During the 1970s and 1980s a variety of communication theorists began to move away from more transmissionally oriented questions like "What effects do media have on society or on individuals?" and "How do people use the media?" toward broader examinations of how cultures become organized, how people negotiate common meaning and are bound by it, and how media systems interact with the culture to affect the way culture develops. This allowed cultural theories to become home for a variety of people who presumed the operation of powerful mass media—for example, advertising and market researchers, neo-Marxist media critics, and even sophisticated effects researchers. The primary focus was no longer on whether media have certain effects on individuals, but rather on the kind of people we are, we have become, or we are becoming in our mass-mediated world.

Research on Popular Culture in the United States
During the 1960s and 1970s some American literary scholars began to focus their research on popular culture. By 1967 this group had grown large enough to have its own division (Popular Literature Section) within the Modern Language Association of

America and to establish its own academic journal, *The Journal of Popular Culture*. These scholars were influenced by British cultural studies and by Canadian media scholar Marshall McLuhan. They adapted a variety of theories and research methods, including hermeneutics and historical methods, to study various forms of popular culture. Unlike British critical theorists, most are not activists and have no links to social movements. They focus much of their attention on television and, now, the Internet as the premier medium of the electronic era. Many express optimism about the future and the positive role of media, rather than subscribing to the pessimistic vision of Williams.

Some of the best examples of popular culture research have been provided by Horace Newcomb in *TV: The Most Popular Art* (1974) and in his much-respected anthology, *Television: The Critical View* (1976), which has had several updated editions (the most recent in 2007). These books summarize useful insights produced by researchers in popular culture, emphasizing that popular media content generally, and television programming specifically, are much more complex than they appear on the surface. Multiple levels of meaning are often present, and the content itself is frequently ambiguous—open to various interpretations that serve different purposes for audiences.

Sophisticated content producers recognize that if they put many different or ambiguous meanings into their content, they will have a better chance of appealing to different audiences. If these audiences are large and loyal, the programs will have high ratings. Though Newcomb wrote long before the advent of broadcast television shows like *Modern Family*, *Family Guy*, and *This Is Us*; cable television series such as *South Park*, *Game of Thrones*, and *Homeland*; and streaming service hits like *The Handmaid's Tale*, *Dear White People*, and *Stranger Things*, these programs illustrate his argument. They make an art of layering one level of meaning on top of another so that fans can watch the same episode over and over to probe its meaning.

A second insight well articulated by Newcomb is that audience interpretations of content are likely to be quite diverse. The fact that some people make interpretations at one level of meaning, whereas others make their interpretations at other levels, is referred to as **multiple points of access**. Some interpretations will be highly idiosyncratic, and some will be very conventional. Sometimes groups of fans will develop a common interpretation, and sometimes individuals are content to find their own meaning without sharing it. We'll revisit this theme in the discussion of reception studies in Chapter 9.

One researcher whose work combines the popular culture approach with neo-Marxist theory is Larry Grossberg (1983, 1989). His take on popular culture "signals [the] belief in an emerging change in the discursive formations of contemporary intellectual life, a change that cuts across the humanities and the social sciences. It suggests that the proper horizon for interpretive activity, whatever its object and whatever its disciplinary base, is the entire field of cultural practices, all of which give meaning, texture, and structure to human life" (Grossberg & Nelson, 1988, p. 1). Although his synthesis proved controversial (O'Connor, 1989), it has gained wide attention. Part of its popularity stems from his application of contemporary European theories to the study of popular culture. More recently he has moved more toward neo-Marxist theory and has coedited two large anthologies of research, *Marxism and the Interpretation of Culture* (Nelson & Grossberg, 1988) and *Cultural Studies* (Grossberg, Nelson, & Treichler, 1992).

The serious study of popular culture poses a direct challenge to mass society theory, the limited-effects perspective, and notions of high culture for several reasons. In asserting the power of audiences to make meaning, popular culture researchers grant a respect to *average* people that is absent from mass society and limited-effects thinking. In treating popular culture as culturally important and worthy of study, they challenge high culture's bedrock assumption of the inherent quality of high-culture artifacts like symphonies and opera. In suggesting that individual audience members use media content to create personally relevant meaning, they open the possibility of media effects that are consumer-generated or -allowed. In short, in arguing the crucial cultural role played by the interaction of people and media texts, researchers studying popular culture lend support to all the cultural theories.

Research on News Production in the United States

Over the past five decades there have been several important efforts to critically analyze how journalists routinely cover news (Crouse, 1973; Epstein, 1973; Fishman, 1980; Gans, 1979; Gitlin, 1980; Tuchman, 1978; Whiten, 2004). News production research continues to be regularly published in two UK-based academic journals—*Journalism* and *Journalism Studies*.

W. Lance Bennett (1988, 2005) surveyed this **news production research** literature and summarized four ways in which current news production practices distort or bias news content:

1. *Personalized news*: Most people relate better to individuals than to groups or institutions, so most news stories center around people. According to Bennett (1988), "The focus on individual actors who are easy to identify with positively or negatively invites members of the news audience to project their own private feelings and fantasies directly onto public life" (p. 27). Thus, personalization helps people relate to and find relevance in remote events. It does this, however, at a cost. "When television news reports about poverty focus on an individual's situation rather than on poverty more generally," wrote *New York Times Magazine* editor Alexander Star (2008), "viewers look for someone (the poor person or someone else) who caused the hardship. But this . . . is to avoid the whole complicated process that brought someone grief. Stories call our attention away from chance, the influence of institutions or social structures, or the incremental contributions that different factors typically make to any outcome. And they follow conventions that verge on melodrama: events are caused by individuals who act deliberately, and what those individuals do reflects their underlying character. This, to put it mildly, is not how most things happen" (p. 10).

2. *Dramatized news*: Like all media commodities, news must be attractively packaged, and a primary means of doing this involves dramatization. Edward Jay Epstein (1973) provided the following quotation from a network television policy memorandum: "Every news story should, without any sacrifice of probity or responsibility, display the attributes of fiction, of drama. It should have structure and conflict, problem and denouement, rising action and falling action, a beginning, a middle, and an end. These are not only the essentials of drama;

they are the essentials of narrative" (pp. 4–5). The all-to-frequent federal budget crises become dramatic contests between the president and the opposition party. . . . Who will blink first? Who will prevail? There is little reporting on what these conflicts mean for everyday people or for the future of representative democracy.

3. *Fragmented news*: The typical newspaper or news broadcast is made up of brief capsulized reports of events—snapshots of the social world. By constructing news in this way, journalists attempt to fulfill their norm of objectivity. They treat events in isolation with little effort to interconnect them. Connection requires putting them into a broader context, and this would require making speculative, sometimes controversial linkages. Is there a link between three isolated plane crashes, or between three separate toxic waste spills? Should journalists remind readers of a candidate's three divorces when reporting on her opposition to same-sex unions in the name of "preserving the sanctity of marriage"? By compartmentalizing events, news reports make it difficult for news consumers to make their own connections. These stories might meet the norm of being "balanced," but they don't assist people in making sense of things.

4. *Normalized news*: Stories about disasters or about social movements tend to "normalize" these potential threats to the status quo. Elite sources are allowed to explain disasters and to challenge movement members. Elites are presented as authoritative, rational, knowledgeable people who are effectively coping with threats. They can be trusted to bring things back to normal. If there is a problem with aircraft technology, it will be repaired—the FAA has the flight recorder and will pinpoint the cause of the crash. If social movements make legitimate demands, they will be satisfied—the governor has announced the formation of a blue-ribbon commission to study the problem. Threat of terrorist attack? Don't worry, the government says it's just a little bit of surveillance. Why normalization? First, availability; reporters can always easily find officials. Second is the need to maintain access to valued news sources. A third reason for normalizing the news is the political economy of the news business. The business and its practitioners are well situated inside the status quo. This is evident in a 2009 *Newsweek* cover story by journalist Evan Thomas on why liberals were upset with President Obama's handling of the economic recovery. He wrote, "If you are of the establishment persuasion (and I am), reading [liberal criticism] makes you uneasy. . . . By definition, establishments believe in propping up the existing order. Members of the ruling class have a vested interest in keeping things pretty much the way they are. Safeguarding the status quo, protecting traditional institutions, can be healthy and useful, stabilizing and reassuring" (p. 22).

Gaye Tuchman (1978) conducted a now-classic example of news production research. She studied how the values held by journalists influence news, even when they make considerable effort to guard against that influence. She observed journalists as they covered social movements and concluded that production practices were implicitly biased toward support of the status quo. She found that reporters engage in **objectivity rituals**—they have set procedures for producing unbiased news stories that actually introduce bias.

INSTANT ACCESS

NEWS PRODUCTION RESEARCH

Strengths

1. Provides recommendations for potentially useful changes in news production practices
2. Raises important questions about routine news production practices
3. Can be used to study production of many different types of news
4. Can be combined with studies of news uses and effects to provide a comprehensive understanding of news
5. Can be used to assess how journalistic practices have been altered by the Internet and social media

Weaknesses

1. Focuses on news production practices but has not empirically demonstrated their effect
2. Has pessimistic view of journalists and their social role
3. Has been ignored and rejected as impractical by practicing journalists
4. Has not been widely used by US journalism educators to reform how news production is taught

For example, when journalists interviewed leaders of a controversial movement, their statements were never allowed to stand alone. Reporters routinely attempted to "balance" movement statements by reporting the views of authorities who opposed them. They frequently selected the most unusual or controversial statements made by movement leaders and contrasted these with the more conventional views of mainstream group leaders. Reporters made little effort to understand the overall philosophy of the movement. Lacking understanding, they inevitably took statements out of context and misrepresent movement ideals. Thus, though reporters never explicitly expressed negative views about these groups, their lack of understanding, their casual methods for selecting quotes, and their use of elite sources led to stories harmful to the movements they covered. Recall Daniel Schorr's Martin Luther King anecdote from earlier in this chapter.

Critical Feminist Scholarship

Feminist popular culture researchers were instrumental in legitimizing and popularizing critical cultural theory in the United States. They adopted Carey's ritual perspective (communication is directed not toward the act of imparting information, but the representation of shared beliefs) rather than the effects trend's causal model of media influence. Some also worked in the neo-Marxist tradition of European cultural studies, making them open to a greater variety of research methods than those "approved" by traditional American postpositivist researchers. Feminist critical scholars brought literary criticism, linguistics, anthropology, history, and even quantitative methods to their study of male domination of females and its consequences.

Naturally, however, it was the culture's ongoing and systematic sexism that motivated their research, as Noreene Janus explained in her classic 1977 "Research on Sex-Roles in Mass Media: Toward a Critical Approach":

> One of the most striking developments in American social life during the past decade is the growth of a feminist movement which has energetically and persistently challenged the sexist nature of our society. As part of a comprehensive attack on sexism, US feminists have analyzed the major institutions—such as family, school, church, and mass media—to understand how sexism as an ideology is perpetuated. They have repeatedly charged that, of all these institutions, the mass media are especially potent mechanisms for the transmission of sexist ideas due to their ever-increasing role in our daily lives. (p. 19)

Although she readily acknowledged that there existed much good research on the portrayal of sex-roles in the media, Janus believed that not only was this not sufficient, it was detrimental to the cause of feminism. She argued for *critical* feminist research as a substitute for what she called the work of *liberal feminists.* For Janus (1977), the way American liberal feminists posed their research problems, selected their methodologies, framed their questions, and drew their conclusions inevitably produced an "affirmation of the very framework" that produced the inequalities they were studying. "A liberal feminist, believing that the most important social division is between men and women," she wrote, "may set up research measuring the men against the women and then conclude that the research proves that the sexual division is the most fundamental" (p. 22). But, she argued, "the most fundamental division within society is not that of men vs. women but rather that between the classes" (p. 24). Feminist cultural scholarship, therefore, would become feminist critical cultural scholarship when researchers focused their attention on larger social and economic structures. "The problem of sexism in the media must not be seen in terms of males oppressing females without at the same time demonstrating the historical development of sexism and its present relationship to capitalist relations of production. . . . A critical perspective will demonstrate not only that the women in the media are inferior to men, but also the limited and demeaning images of women are structurally related to the functioning of capitalism" (p. 29).

If Janus's neo-Marxism was a fruitful route of inquiry for critical feminist scholarship, so, too, was political economy theory. As Eileen Meehan and Ellen Riordan (2002) more recently explained, "For the United States and the emerging global economy, sex plus money equals power. Addressing this equation in media studies requires the integration of feminism and political economy. This integrative approach is not simply a matter of adding one to the other. Rather, we argue that all media structures, agents, processes, and expressions find their raison d'être in the relationships shaped by sex and money" (p. x).

Eventually this feminist critical cultural scholarship would bring "new insights and a sense of crucial urgency to longstanding questions in communication research" (Wartella & Treichler, 1986, p. 4). Those insights tended to flow from four general approaches to feminist critical scholarship (Rakow, 1986). The *images and representations approach* attempts to answer the questions: What kinds of images of women are there in the media, and what do they reveal about women's position in the culture; whose images are they, and whom do they benefit; what are the consequences of those images; and how do these images come to have meaning? The *recovery and reappraisal approach* asks: How have women managed to express themselves in a male-dominated culture; why is women's creativity overlooked, undervalued, or ignored; how do women and men's creativity differ; and what are women's myths and stories? The *reception and experience approach* focuses on female media consumers' experiences and perceptions, primarily of cultural products they find popular, as a means of granting women the means to speak for themselves about their own lives and experiences. Finally, *the cultural theory approach*, rather than examining content, as do the first three approaches, focuses on the organization and production of culture. It "stands back" from content to get a better view of the social and economic structures that produce culture in order to examine how they influence women's experiences and social positions.

Critical feminist media scholarship in the United States had another source, textual analysis of film and cinema based in **psychoanalytic theory**, which, drawn from Freudian psychology, argues that all human thought and action is driven by inner psychological and emotional factors, often outside of people's awareness. Its home in critical cultural theory is clear in Laura Mulvey's 1975 "Visual Pleasures and Narrative Cinema." Hollywood, she argued, "always restricted itself to a formal mise-en-scène reflecting the dominant ideological concept of the cinema" (Mulvey 1975/1999, p. 834). And, she admitted, although Hollywood's monolithic grip on the film industry was at the time weakening, its ideology remained (typically presenting men and women differently, with men the active drivers of the movie's action and narrative and women existing primarily as passive objects for men's desire and fetishistic gazing.) Deeply rooted in the pleasure humans find in looking at other people as objects, movies, as a capitalistic culture product, "portray a hermetically sealed world which unwinds magically, indifferent to the presence of the audience, producing for them a sense of separation and playing on their voyeuristic phantasy" (pp. 835–836). Because the world is "ordered by sexual imbalance," she writes, "the determining male gaze projects its phantasy on to the female figure which is styled accordingly" (p. 837). Why is the female figure "styled" to encourage the male gaze? Cinema, "artisanal as well as capitalist," seeks an audience (But why not also "style" male characters to attract the female gaze?) "According to the principles of the ruling ideology and the psychical structures that back it up, the male figure cannot bear the burden of sexual objectification" (p. 838). As a result, women are left with two options, identify with the onscreen males or identify with the objectified females. Either way, their film viewing reinforces the very ideology that denigrates them. For Mulvey, women's image has "continually been stolen and used" to further traditional narrative film's "voyeuristic active/passive mechanisms" (p. 844). Her solutions? One is to make film less interesting: "It is said that analyzing pleasure, or beauty, destroys it. That is the intention of this article." The second, more reasonable and in line with the goals of critical theory, is emancipatory kn⟨ ⟩ alternative is the thrill that comes from leaving the past behind witho⟨ ⟩ transcending outworn or oppressive forms, or daring to break with norm⟨ ⟩ expectations in order to conceive a new language of desire" (p. 835).

Much recent critical feminist scholarship has therefore centered o⟨ ⟩ common cultural assumptions that reinforce **rape culture**, "sets of beli⟨ ⟩ that provide an environment conductive to rape" (Boswell & Spade, 199⟨ ⟩ cultures, write Manuela Thomae and G. Tendayi Viki (2013), are "bas⟨ ⟩ attitudes toward women as well as traditional gender scripts. Assumptic⟨ ⟩ gression and dominance and female acquiescence and passivity as well a⟨ ⟩

female qualities, rape myths, and ambiguities about what constitutes rape and how to define consent sustain rape cultures" (p. 250). Assumption-dependent (and assumption-reinforcing) sexist humor and rape jokes are just one example of this line of inquiry. Work by Raúl Pérez and Viveca Greene (2016) determined that "the dominant framing/interpretation of rape jokes reinforces patriarchal and free-market ideologies, and deny real-world implications of misogynistic humor, particularly when comedians/audiences defend such jokes as harmless fun" (p. 265). They were particularly interested in the acceptance of rape humor by women, especially in the presence of men, particularly because of the demonstrated link between exposure to sexist humor and tolerance of discrimination against women (Ford, 2000) and correlations between misogynistic humor, sexual harassment, tolerance for sexual violence, and rape proclivity (e.g., Ford, Boxer, Armstrong, & Edel, 2008; Romero-Sánchez, Durán, Carretero-Dios, Megías, & Moya, 2010). Viveca Greene and Amber Day (2020), accepting that "rape jokes are constitutive of rape culture," examined feminist comedians' use of satire to challenge rape culture. While recognizing the value of this critique, they noted the exclusion of women of color from traditional feminism, leaving Black women, as explained by Alexis Okeowo (2017), "to pick between being politically black or politically female" (par. 3). They make the case for **intersectionality**, the intersections in people's lives of the different positions they hold in relation to gender, race, class, and other social categories when confronting rape culture, arguing that any meaningful critique of rape culture must recognize that while it impacts everyone, its ugliness is visited differently on, and sometimes compounded for, different people. Kimberlé Crenshaw, who initially coined the term (Crenshaw, 1989), described intersectionality in a 2017 interview as "a lens through which you can see where power comes and collides, where it interlocks and intersects. It's not simply that there's a race problem here, a gender problem here, and a class or LBGTQ problem there. Many times that framework erases what happens to people who are subject to all of these things" ("Kimberlé Crenshaw," 2017). In 1974, 15 years before Crenshaw coined the term, self-proclaimed radical feminist Andrea Dworkin explained its operation. "The 'closely interwoven fabric of oppression' in America," she wrote in *Woman Hating*, meant that "wherever one stood, it was with at least one foot heavy on the belly of another human being" (as cited in Goldberg, 2019, p. 4).

Feminist communication researchers are also addressing the hostility that feminist scholars and activists face online, where they are regularly harassed by a "loose online network known as the manosphere" (Marwick & Caplan, 2018, p. 543). "Harassment is often used to police women's online behavior," they observe, "and may have a chilling effect on women's participation in the public sphere both on and offline" (p. 545). A variety of misogynistic groups are active on the Internet and have precipitated a number of high-profile attacks on women, including Gamergate, an ongoing effort to harass and marginalize female video game players (Waterlow, 2016).

MARSHALL MCLUHAN: THE MEDIUM IS THE MESSAGE AND THE MASSAGE

During the 1960s a Canadian literary scholar, Marshall McLuhan, gained worldwide prominence as someone who had a profound understanding of electronic media and their impact on both culture and society. McLuhan was highly trained in literary criticism but also read widely in communication theory and history. Although his writings contain few citations to Marx (McLuhan actually castigated Marx for ignoring communication), he based much of his understanding of media's historical role on the work of Harold Innis, a Canadian political economist. Still, in his theory, McLuhan synthesized many other diverse ideas. We place him at the end of this chapter because he did his most influential writing in the 1960s, when cultural studies emerged as a serious challenge to limited-effects perspectives on media. His ideas, which later became known as **media ecology theory** because of their attention to the macro-level relationships between technology, mass media, and communication and how they influence or shape human environments (Postman, 2000), anticipate the development of the culture-centered theories that are the focus of Chapter 13's discussion of meaning-making theories and can therefore be read as a preface to much of what is covered there.

With James Carey, whom many consider the founder of American cultural studies and who shared McLuhan's respect for Innis, McLuhan did much to inspire and legitimize macroscopic theories of media, culture, and society in North America. He wrote at a time when the limited-effects perspective had reached the peak of its popularity among academics in the United States, a time when most American communication researchers regarded macroscopic theory with suspicion, if not outright hostility. In the humanities it was a time when the high-culture canon still consisted largely of "classic" work (European novels, symphonies, serious theater) produced by white, Anglo-Saxon males, now dead. McLuhan's focus on the cultural role of popular media quickly posed a challenge both to limited-effects notions and to the canon.

McLuhan and his ideas are again in vogue. It is no small irony that McLuhan, hailed (or denigrated) in the 1960s as the "High Priest of Popcult," the "Metaphysician of Media," and the "Oracle of the Electronic Age," to this day is listed as "Patron Saint" on the masthead of *Wired* magazine, the "Bible of Cyberspace." "McLuhan came up with a theory of media generation and consumption so plastic and fungible that it describes the current age without breaking a sweat," writes technologist David Carr (2011, p. 10).

McLuhan's "theory" is actually a collection of many intriguing ideas bound together by some common assumptions. The most central of these, "All media, from the phonetic alphabet to the computer, are extensions of man that cause deep and lasting changes in him and transforms his environment" (McLuhan, 1962, p. 13), argued that changes in communication technology inevitably produce profound changes in both culture and social order.

Even though McLuhan drew on critical cultural theories such as political economy theory to develop his perspective, his work was rejected by political economists because it failed to provide a basis on which to produce positive social change. McLuhan had no links to any political or social movements. He seemed ready to accept whatever changes were dictated by and inherent in communication technology. Because he argued that technology inevitably causes specific changes in how people think, in how society is structured, and in the forms of culture that are created, McLuhan was often labeled a **technological determinist**.

Harold Innis: The Bias of Communication

Harold Innis was one of the first scholars to systematically speculate at length about the possible linkages between communication media and the various forms of social structure found at certain points in history. In *Empire and Communication* (1950) and

The Bias of Communication (1951), he argued that the early empires of Egypt, Greece, and Rome were based on elite control of the written word. He contrasted these empires with earlier social orders dependent on the spoken word. Innis maintained that before elite discovery of writing, dialogue was the dominant mode of public discourse and political authority was much more diffuse. Gradually, the written word became the dominant mode of elite communication, and its power was magnified enormously by the invention of new writing materials (specifically paper) that made writing portable yet enduring. With paper and pen, small, centrally located elites were able to gain control over and govern vast regions. Thus, new communication media made it possible to create empires.

Innis argued that written word–based empires expanded to the limits imposed by communication technology. Expansion, therefore, depended not as much on the skills of military generals as it did on the communication media used to disseminate orders from the capital city. Similarly, the structure of later social orders also depended on the media technology available at certain points in time. For example, the telephone and telegraph permitted even more effective control over larger geographic areas. Everett Rogers (2000) paraphrased Innis, noting, "The changing technology of communication acted to reduce the cost and increase the speed and distance of communication, and thus to extend the geographic size of empires" (p. 126). As such, the introduction of new forms of media technology gave centralized elites increased power over space and time.

Innis traced the way Canadian elites used various technologies, including the railroad and telegraph, to extend their control across the continent. As a political economist he harbored a deep suspicion of centralized power and believed that newer forms of communication technology would make even greater centralization inevitable. He referred to this as the inherent **bias of communication**. Because of this bias the people and the resources of outlying regions that he called *the periphery* are inevitably exploited to serve the interests of elites at *the center*.

INSTANT ACCESS

MCLUHANISM

Strengths

1. Is comprehensive
2. Is macroscopic
3. Resonated with the general public in the 1960s and 1970s
4. Elevates cultural value of popular media content
5. Anticipates a future in which media play a central role in fostering community
6. Enjoys longevity as a result of introduction of Internet-based media

Weaknesses

1. Can't be verified by effects research
2. Is overly optimistic about technology's influence
3. Ignores important effects issues
4. Calls for nonlinear thinking, the value of which is questioned
5. Is overly apologetic of electronic media
6. Questions the value of literacy, and argues for its inevitable decline

McLuhan: Understanding Media

Although he borrowed freely from Innis, McLuhan didn't dwell on issues of exploitation or centralized control. His views on the cultural consequences of capitalist-dominated media were much more optimistic than those of the Frankfurt School. He was fascinated by the implications of Innis's arguments concerning the transformative power of media technology. He didn't fear the ways elites might exercise this power. If the technology itself determines its use, then there is nothing to fear from elites.

So McLuhan began asking different questions. Was it possible, for example, that media could transform our sensory experiences as well as our social order? After all, the acts of reading a book and viewing a movie or television program employ different sensory organs. During the 1960s we were clearly moving from a mass communication era grounded in print technology to one based on electronic media. If communication technology plays such a critical role in the emergence of new social orders and new forms of culture, McLuhan wanted to know, what are the implications of abandoning print in favor of electronic media?

McLuhan explained his vision of the implications of the spread of electronic media with catchy, and what proved to be lasting, phrases. He proclaimed that **the medium is the message** *(and the massage)*. In other words, new forms of media transform (massage) our experience of ourselves and our society, and this influence is ultimately more important than the content that is transmitted in its specific messages—technology determines experience. He used the term **global village** to refer to the new form of social organization that would inevitably emerge as satellite-based instantaneous electronic media tied the entire world into one great social, political, and cultural system. Unlike Innis, McLuhan didn't bother to concern himself with questions about control over this village or whether village members would be exploited. To McLuhan these questions didn't matter. He was more concerned with microscopic issues, with the impact of media on our senses and where this influence might lead. McLuhan also proclaimed, as we've seen, media to be **the extensions of man** [*sic*] and argued that they literally extend sight, hearing, and touch through time and space. Electronic media would open up new vistas for average people and enable them to be everywhere instantaneously. But was this an egalitarian and democratic vision? What would ordinary people do when their senses were extended in this way? Would they succumb to information overload? Would they be stimulated to greater participation in politics? Would they flee into the virtual worlds opened to them by their extended senses? In his writing and interviews McLuhan tossed out cryptic and frequently contradictory ideas that addressed such questions. Occasionally his ideas were profound and prophetic. Sometimes they were arcane, mundane, or just confusing.

Though he was often a cryptic prophet, McLuhan's observations concerning the global village and the role of electronic media in it are seen by many as anticipating the most recent developments in Internet-based electronic media—this is precisely why the editors of *Wired* made McLuhan their patron saint. At a time when satellite communication was just being developed, he foretold the rise of 24-hour cable news networks and their ability to seemingly make us eyewitnesses to history as it's made on the battlefield or at the barricade. When mainframe computers filled entire floors of office buildings, he envisioned a time when personal computers would be everywhere and connected; they would give everyone instant access to immense stores of information. But as one media critic (Meyrowitz, 1985) noted, to be everywhere is to be nowhere—to have no sense of place. To have access to information is not the same thing as being able to effectively select and use information. The global village isn't situated in space or time. Is it possible to adjust to living in such an amorphous, ambiguous social structure? Or will the global village merely be a façade used by cynical elites to exploit people? These questions go far beyond the paeans to electronic media found throughout McLuhan's *Understanding Media* (1964).

McLuhan's ideas achieved enormous public popularity. He became one of the first pop culture gurus of the 1960s. His pronouncements on the Nixon/Kennedy presidential race propelled him to national prominence. (Nixon was too "hot" for the "cool" medium of television; Kennedy was appropriately "cool.") McLuhan's ideas received serious attention but then fell into disfavor. Why the rise and sudden fall?

Initially, McLuhan's work fit the spirit of the early 1960s—"The Age of Camelot." In sharp contrast with political economists like Innis or neo-Marxist thinkers like those of the Frankfurt School, he was unabashedly optimistic about the profound but ultimately positive changes in our personal experience, social structure, and culture that new media technology would make possible. Unlike limited-effects theorists he didn't dismiss media as unimportant. McLuhan was the darling of the media industries—their prophet with honor. For a brief period he commanded huge fees as a consultant and seminar leader for large companies. His ideas were used to rationalize rapid expansion of electronic media with little concern for their negative consequences, and they were corrupted to become broadcast industry gospel: So what if children spend most of their free time in front of television sets and become functionally illiterate? Reading is doomed anyway—why prolong its demise? Eventually we will all live in a global village where literacy is as unnecessary as it was in preliterate tribal villages. Why worry about the negative consequences of television when it is obviously so much better than the old media it is replacing? Just think of the limitations that print media impose. Linear, logical thinking is far too restrictive. If the triumph of electronic media is inevitable, why not get on with it? No need for government regulation of media. The ideal form of media can be expected to evolve naturally, no matter what we try to do. No need to worry about media conglomerates. No need to complain about television violence. No need to resist racist or sexist media content. Adopt McLuhan's long-term global perspective. Think big. Think nonlinearly. Just wait for the future to happen.

But even as McLuhan's work became more accepted within the media industries, it aroused increasing criticism within academia. Perhaps the most devastating criticism was offered by other literary critics, who found his ideas too diverse and inconsistent. They were astounded by his notion that literacy was obsolete and found his praise of nonlinear thinking nonsensical, even dangerous. These critics thought nonlinear thinking was just an excuse for logically inconsistent, random thoughts. They called McLuhan's books brainstorms masquerading as scholarship. McLuhan answered by charging that his critics were too pedantic, too concerned with logic and linear thinking. They were too dependent on literacy and print media to be objective about them. They were the elitist defenders of the high-culture canon. Their jobs depended on the survival of literacy. He recommended that they work hard to free their minds from arbitrary limitations. Not surprisingly, few were willing to do so.

Effects-trend media researchers were also uniformly critical of McLuhan, but for different reasons. Although a few tried to design research to study some of his notions, most found his assumptions about the power of media to be absurd. They were indoctrinated in effects theories and skeptical about the possibility that media could transform people's experience. Even if this was possible, how could research be designed to systematically study things as amorphous as "people's experience of the social world" or the "global village"? When early small-scale empirical studies failed to support McLuhan's assertions, their suspicions were confirmed. McLuhan was just another grand theorist whose ideas were overly speculative and empirically unverifiable.

McLuhan fared equally poorly with most critical cultural theorists. Although many respected Innis, they found McLuhan's thinking to be a perversion of his basic ideas. Rather than attempt reform of the superstructure or lead a revolution to take control of the base, McLuhan seemed to be content to wait for technology to lead us forward into the global village. Our fate is in the hands of media technology, and we are constrained to go wherever it leads, he implied. Political economists saw this as a self-fulfilling prophecy, encouraging and sanctioning the development of potentially dangerous new forms of electronic media. These might well lead us to a painful future—a nightmare global village in which we are constantly watched and coerced by remote elites. As long as existing elites remained in power, political economists saw little hope for positive change. They condemned McLuhan for diverting attention from more important work and perverting the radical notions found in Innis's writing. Some political economists even saw McLuhan's ideas as a form of disinformation, deliberately designed to confuse the public so they would ignore or misinterpret neo-Marxist work. Despite these criticisms, much of McLuhan's work merits attention. Everett Rogers (2000) has argued that McLuhan's perspective deserves more attention by mass communication scholars, especially those interested in studying new media. Some young scholars found it an exciting starting point for their own thinking (Wolf, 1996). This is possible because McLuhan's work is so eclectic and open-ended.

REVIEW OF LEARNING OBJECTIVES

- Describe the critical cultural media trend, contrast it with the media-effects trend, and differentiate the types of research questions that can be answered by each.

Over the past four decades the critical cultural theory trend has provided important alternative perspectives on the role of media in society. It includes theories that have their intellectual roots in Marxist theory, but they have incorporated and been influenced by other perspectives, including literary criticism. Theorists argue that mass media often support the status quo and interfere with the efforts of social movements to bring about useful social change. But they also argue that ordinary people can resist media influence and that media might provide a pluralistic public forum in which the power of dominant elites can be effectively challenged.

- Draw distinctions between macroscopic and microscopic mass communication theory, between critical and cultural theories and those based on empirical research, and between the transmissional and ritual perspectives on mass communication.

Macroscopic theories focus on societal or cultural influences of mass communication (for example, how media institutions are structured within capitalist economies). Microscopic theories deemphasize larger issues about the social order in favor of questions involving the everyday life of groups of average people. In contrast with the quantitative empirical research methods, the techniques used by many critical or cultural researchers are often qualitative methods; that is, they highlight essential differences (distinctive qualities) in phenomena. The ritual perspective of mass communication sees the media as central to the representation of shared beliefs. This contrasts with the transmissional perspective that views media as mere senders of information, usually for the purpose of control. As dissatisfaction with media-effects trend theories grew in the 1970s and 1980s, more and more communication theorists, even some with a postpositivist orientation, began to move toward this ritual perspective.

- Identify the roots of critical and cultural theory in Marxism, neo-Marxism, the Frankfurt School, textual analysis and literary criticism, political economy theory, and critical feminist scholarship.

Some cultural theory is critical theory, more or less explicitly based on a set of specific social values such as egalitarianism. Critical theorists use these values to critique existing social institutions and social practices. They also criticize institutions and practices that undermine or marginalize important values, offering alternatives and developing theory to guide useful social change. Recent neo-Marxist cultural theorists reject the view that mass media are totally under the control of well-organized dominant elites who cynically manipulate media content in their own interest. Instead they view media as a pluralistic public forum in which many people and groups can participate. However, they do recognize that elites enjoy many advantages in the forum because most media content, they believe, implicitly or explicitly supports the status quo. Also, critical theorists reject simplistic notions of powerful and negative audience effects like those found in mass society theory. Even when media content explicitly supports the status quo, audiences can reinterpret or reject this content. Cultural theorists make bold assertions and explicitly incorporate values into their work. They provide a useful challenge to mainstream media theory, as do popular culture researchers who grant much power to audiences and cultural value to such popular texts as television series and popular music. Critical feminist scholars, too, have raised important questions not only about media and women, but about the way the discipline has traditionally examined that relationship.

- Identify differences and similarities in political economy theory and cultural studies.

Theoretical and methodological differences separate the two. Political economists have a macroscopic focus on economic institutions and assume that economic dominance perpetuates cultural dominance; cultural studies assumes that cultural changes can affect economic institutions. Political economists do not recognize the diversity of popular culture or the variety of ways in which people make sense of cultural content. Cultural studies theorists ignore the larger social and political context in which media operate. They focus instead on how individuals and groups consume popular culture content. Some cultural studies theorists have been less interested in making or influencing social policy, and their research often doesn't provide a clear basis for criticizing the status quo. As such, political economy theorists accuse them of abandoning the historical mission of critical theory in favor of an uncritical celebration of popular culture. Theorists, they say, should actively work for social change.

CRITICAL THINKING QUESTIONS

1. Critical theory, by definition, questions and challenges the status quo in hopes of changing it. But is this a proper role for any social scientific theory? After all, the status quo seems to be working for most of us; it certainly is for those who engage in critical theory. They probably have well-paid jobs at universities or think tanks. Can you reconcile fundamental assumptions about the value of your social system with efforts to change it?

2. Does your hometown or state capital have a sponsored symphony, theater, or dance troupe—for example, the Boston Opera House, the New York Philharmonic, or the Houston Ballet? Why do municipal or state governments offer financial support to elite arts organizations such as these? Shouldn't the market decide? If these operations cannot survive on their own, why should taxpayers underwrite them? After all, does your city or state underwrite hip-hop or jazz clubs, rock 'n' roll or R&B venues? What would someone from the Frankfort School say about this state of affairs? What would a political economy theorist say?

3. What kind of car do you want, ideally, once you leave school (if any)? Why? What realities do you attribute to what is, in effect, little more than a sophisticated piece of steel, plastic, and glass? Where did these realities originate? How free are you to develop your own personally meaningful reality of the car you drive? And does it matter that you might not be as independent or idiosyncratic as you think? If you think cars are important primarily to men, why would this be the case? Does it suggest that the "reality" of cars is indeed constructed? If not, wouldn't men and women share the same reality? If the question asked you to consider style and fashion instead of cars, would your answers be the same?

KEY TERMS

culture

cultural studies

hegemonic culture

political economy theory

critical theories

qualitative methods

grand social theories

Marxist theory

base (or substructure) of society

superstructure

ideology

high culture

Frankfurt School

culture industries

pluralistic public forum

structuralist view

culturalist view

transmissional perspective

ritual perspective

multiple points of access

news production research

objectivity rituals

psychoanalytic theory

rape culture

intersectionality
media ecology theory
technological determinist
bias of communication

the medium is the message
global village
the extensions of man

GLOSSARY

culture: The learned behavior of members of a given social group

cultural studies: Focus on use of media to create forms of culture that structure everyday life

hegemonic culture: Culture imposed from above or outside that serves the interests of those in dominant social positions

political economy theory: Focus on social elites' use of economic power to exploit media institutions

critical theories: Theories openly espousing certain values and using these values to evaluate and criticize the status quo, providing alternate ways of interpreting the social role of mass media

qualitative methods: Research methods that highlight essential differences (distinctive qualities) in phenomena

grand social theories: Highly ambitious, macroscopic, speculative theories that attempt to understand and predict important trends in culture and society

Marxist theory: Theory arguing that the hierarchical class system is at the root of all social problems and must be ended by a revolution of the proletariat

base (or substructure) of society: In Marxist theory, the means of production

superstructure: In Marxist theory, a society's culture

ideology: In Marxist theory, ideas present in a culture that mislead average people and encourage them to act against their own interests

high culture: Set of cultural artifacts including music, art, literature, and poetry that humanists judge to have the highest value

Frankfurt School: Group of neo-Marxist scholars who worked together in the 1930s at the University of Frankfurt

culture industries: Mass media that turn high culture and folk culture into commodities sold for profit

pluralistic public forum: In critical theory, the idea that media may provide a place where the power of dominant elites can be challenged

structuralist view: Elite control over the superstructure through repressive and ideological state apparatuses

culturalist view: View that culture is the site of social struggle and a place where change occurs

transmissional perspective: View of mass communication as merely the process of transmitting messages from a distance for the purpose of control

ritual perspective: View of mass communication as the representation of shared belief where reality is produced, maintained, repaired, and transformed

multiple points of access: Idea that some people make interpretations at one level of meaning, whereas others make their interpretations at others

news production research: The study of how the institutional routines of news production inevitably produce distorted or biased content

objectivity rituals: In news production research, the term for professional practices designed to ensure objectivity that are implicitly biased toward support of the status quo

psychoanalytic theory: All human thought and action is driven by inner psychological and emotional factors, often outside of people's awareness

rape culture: Sets of beliefs and values that provide an environment conductive to rape

intersectionality: Intersection in people's lives of the different positions they hold in relation to gender, race, class, and other social categories

media ecology theory: Name given to McLuhan's ideas because of their attention to relationships between technology, mass media, and communication and how they shape human environments

technological determinist: A person who believes that all social, political, economic, and cultural change is inevitably based on the development and diffusion of technology

bias of communication: Innis's idea that communication technology makes centralization of power inevitable

the medium is the message: McLuhan's idea that new forms of media transform our experience of ourselves and our society, and this influence is ultimately more important than the content of specific messages

global village: McLuhan's conception of a new form of social organization emerging as instantaneous electronic media tie the entire world into one great social, political, and cultural system

the extensions of man: McLuhan's idea that media literally extend sight, hearing, and touch through time and space

CHAPTER 7

Theories of Media and Social Learning

American children begin attentively watching television by the age of three. Kids age 8 and under spend an average of 2 hours and 19 minutes a day in front of a media screen; just under half "often" or "sometimes" watch TV or videos or play video games in the hour right before bedtime; and for four in 10 the TV is on "always" or "most of the time" in their home, whether anyone is watching or not. Children who have yet to reach their second birthday spend three quarters of an hour a day in front of screens (Rideout, 2017). A typical American kid spends 900 hours in school each year and 1,200 hours watching television. Seventy percent of American school-age kids have a TV in their bedrooms (Kelmon, 2018). All this despite evidence that increased screen time is associated with children's reduced sense of personal well-being, higher levels of anxiety and lower levels of curiosity, self-control, and emotional stability (e.g., Twenge & Campbell, 2018), and the development of attention problems (e.g., Swing, Gentile, Anderson, & Walsh, 2010), and despite results from a large-scale, long-term National Institute of Health study of thousands of children that discovered thinning of the cortex—the outermost layer of the brain that processes information from the five senses—in the brains of some children who are on smartphones, tablets, and video games more than seven hours a day (Cooper, 2018).

Parents, educators, politicians, and the general public have fretted over kids and screens ever since the first simple black-and-white silent movies. That concern reached its zenith in the 1960s and 1970s with the diffusion of a much more powerful and ubiquitous medium—television—and dramatically reemerged in the 1990s with the new interactive video game screens.

LEARNING OBJECTIVES
After studying this chapter you should be able to
- Explain how the social and technological changes that followed World War II paved the way for television and a theoretical reconsideration of media influence.

- Distinguish between various "violence theories" such as catharsis and social cognitive theory, as well as explain the operation of their many components such as aggressive cues, imitation and identification, observational learning, inhibitory and disinhibitory effects, priming effects, and the cognitive-neoassociationistic perspective.
- Identify the many important contextual variables that can influence the demonstration of media-influenced aggression.
- Recognize how the active theory of television viewing and the developmental approach have enriched the understanding of media effects.
- Explain how research on violent video games not only supports the television violence theories but has produced deeper understandings of media effects on aggression.

OVERVIEW

On August 6, 1945, the United States dropped an atom bomb on Hiroshima, Japan, effectively ending World War II. That four-year global conflict forced cataclysmic changes in the nation's economic, industrial, demographic, familial, and technological character, the impact of which would be felt most powerfully in the 1960s.

The mass medium that was to transform that decade—television—had an inauspicious introduction as a novelty at the 1939 World's Fair in New York. Its tiny picture, poor sound quality, and high cost led some to doubt its future as a popular medium. How could it compete with movies? Would people really want to sit at home and watch ghostly black-and-white images on a small screen when they could walk a few blocks to see powerful Technicolor images on a gigantic screen? During the next three years a small number of experimental television stations began broadcasting a limited number and variety of programs to a minuscule audience. When the United States entered the war, television's already limited diffusion to the public halted, as the technologies and materials needed to improve and produce the medium went to the war effort. Technological research, however, did not stop. Therefore, when the war ended and materials were once again available for the manufacture of consumer goods, a technologically mature new medium was immediately available. Anticipating not only this, but also dramatic changes in American society that would benefit the new medium, the national commercial radio networks were already planning to move their hit shows and big stars to television.

This technological advance occurred simultaneously with profound alterations in US society. The war changed the country from a primarily rural society boasting an agriculturally based economy into a largely urban nation dependent on an industrially based economy. After the war more people worked regularly scheduled jobs (rather than the sunrise-to-sunset workday of farmers), and they had more leisure. More people had regular incomes (rather than the seasonal, put-the-money-back-into-the-land farmer's existence), and they had more money to spend on that leisure. Because the manufacturing capabilities developed for the war were still in existence, the economy had the ability to mass produce items on which that money could be spent. Because more consumer goods were competing in the marketplace, there was a greater need to advertise, which provided the economic base for the new television medium. Because non-White Americans had fought in the war and worked in the country's factories, they began to demand their rightful share of the American dream. Because women entered the workforce while the men were off to battle, it was more common and acceptable to have both parents working outside the home. Because people had moved away from their small towns and family roots, the traditional community anchors—church and school—began to lose their dominance in the social and moral development of children who were present in the 1960s—in their teenage years—in inordinately large numbers because of the baby boom that occurred soon after war's end.

As in all periods of significant societal change, there were serious social problems. The rapid rise in the number of teenagers brought sharp increases in delinquency and crime. Critics blamed the schools for failing to educate children into responsible citizenship. Crime waves swept one city after another. Riots broke out in several urban areas. Successive social movements captured the attention of the nation, especially the civil rights, women's equality, and the anti–Vietnam War movements. Some activists, like the Black Panthers and the Weathermen, became notorious for their willingness to use violence to pursue their objectives. Political instability reached new heights with the assassinations of President John F. Kennedy, Martin Luther King, Jr., and Robert Kennedy. Young people were behaving strangely. Many were listening more to new, unfamiliar music and less to their increasingly "old-fashioned, irrelevant" parents. Social scientists discovered the existence of a "generation gap" between conservative middle-class parents and their increasingly liberal, even radical children.

Media's role in all these changes was hotly debated. Although social researchers and media practitioners continued to put forward arguments based on limited-effects research findings, a new generation of observers charged that media were harming children and disrupting their lives. Evidence mounted that families, schools, and churches had become less important to children. As Urie Bronfenbrenner (1970) said, the backyards were growing smaller and the schoolyards growing bigger. In other words, young people were increasingly being socialized away from parents' influence. Bronfenbrenner's research demonstrated that, whereas parents and church had been the primary socializing agents for prewar American adolescents, by the mid-1960s media and peers shared top billing in the performance of that crucial function.

It is no surprise, then, that the media, particularly television, became the target of increasing criticism and the object of intense scientific inquiry, especially where harmful effects were presumed. But these renewed efforts to probe the negative influence of mass media occurred when the effects trend was at the height of its influence among academics, and virtually all research findings pointed to limited effects. An intense and continuing debate erupted between social researchers who had confidence in that approach and those skeptical of its conclusions despite the consistency of its empirical findings. Strong advocates of limited-effects notions were accused of being paid lackeys of the media industries, and overzealous critics of television were labeled as unscientific and charged with oversimplifying complex problems and ignoring alternative causes.

But psychologists working outside the prevailing media-effects trend thought they could explain some of the contemporary social turmoil in microscopic—that is, individual—terms. Psychologists turned their attention to how people, especially children, learned from the mass media, especially television. What would eventually become known as **social cognitive theory** and its early attention to children moved communication theorists from their focus on the effects trend's findings of limited media influence. They came to direct much of their attention toward increases in the amount of real-world violence and the possible contribution of the new medium of television to that rise.

Social scientists developed several different perspectives on the effects of television violence, including catharsis, social learning, social cognitive theory, aggressive cues, and priming effects. Whereas the latter four perspectives see media as a possible factor in increasing the likelihood of actual violence, catharsis argues just the opposite. We will study these approaches as well as the context of mediated violence—that is, how violence and aggression are presented in the media. We will also examine differing understandings of how children interact with the media, specifically the active theory of television viewing and the developmental perspective. Additionally, we will look at recent interest in the media/violence link fueled by the explosion of realistic, interactive video games. This repurposing of the original television violence theories has produced a new model of media effects, the **general aggression model (GAM)**, which argues that "the enactment of aggression is largely based on knowledge structures (e.g., scripts, schemas) created by social learning processes" (Anderson & Dill, 2000, p. 773).

FOCUS ON CHILDREN AND VIOLENCE

The argument about the media's role in fomenting social instability and instigating violence reached a peak in the late 1960s. After disruptive race riots in the Los Angeles suburb of Watts and in the cities of Cleveland, Newark, and Detroit, President Lyndon Johnson established two national commissions, the Kerner Commission in 1967 and the National Commission on the Causes and Prevention of Violence in 1968. They offered serious criticism of media and recommended a variety of changes in both news reporting and entertainment content. Writing in the preface to the 1968 commission's staff report, *Violence and the Media*, editor Paul Briand asked, "If, as the media claim, no objective correlation exists between media portrayals of violence and violent behavior—if, in other words, the one has no impact upon the other—then how can the media claim an impact in product selection and consumption, as they obviously affect the viewers' commercial attitudes and behavior? Can they do one and not the other?" (Baker & Ball, 1969, p. vii). This question reflected growing public and elite skepticism concerning effects trend–supported assumptions of a benign mass media.

The federal government itself tried to locate new answers to this problem by establishing the Surgeon General's Scientific Advisory Committee on Television and Social Behavior in 1969. Its purpose was to commission a broad range of research on television effects that might determine whether television could be an important influence on children's behavior. What did this collection of scientists conclude after two years and a million dollars of study? The surgeon general, Jesse L. Steinfeld, reported to a US Senate subcommittee:

> While the . . . report is carefully phrased and qualified in language acceptable to social scientists, it is clear to me that the causal relationship between televised violence and antisocial behavior is sufficient to warrant appropriate and immediate remedial action. The data on social phenomena such as television and violence and/or aggressive behavior will never be clear enough for all social scientists to agree on the formulation of a succinct statement of causality. But there comes a time when the data are sufficient to justify action. That time has come. (US Congress, 1972, p. 26)

Nevertheless, this report did little to end the controversy over television's effects. Industry officials and lobbyists worked hard to block development and implementation of new FCC regulations for children's programming. They cited inconclusive research and restated limited-effects arguments. Eventually the industry agreed to a self-imposed family viewing hour in which violent content was ostensibly minimized, and at the time, the television networks tightened their programming standards and worked closely with program producers to limit gratuitous violence.

TELEVISION VIOLENCE THEORIES

The most important outcome of this television violence research was the gradual development of a set of theories that summarized findings and offered increasingly useful insight into the media's role in the lives of young people. Taken together, they now provide strong support for the link between television viewing and aggression. For example, nearly three decades ago (and 20 years after the surgeon general's call for action), after reviewing years of relevant research on the question, Aletha Huston and her colleagues wrote, "The accumulated research clearly demonstrates a correlation between viewing violence and aggressive behavior—that is, heavy viewers behave more aggressively than light viewers. . . . Both experimental and longitudinal studies support the hypothesis that viewing violence is causally associated with aggression. . . . Field [naturalistic] experiments with preschool children and adolescents found heightened aggression among viewers assigned to watch violent television or film under some conditions" (Huston et al., 1992, pp. 54–55).

Ten years after that Brad Bushman and Craig Anderson (2001) again reviewed the literature and concluded that the link between media violence and subsequent aggression has more scientific support than that of the relationship between self-examination and early detection of breast cancer, the amount of calcium intake and bone mass, and the use of condoms to prevent sexually transmitted disease. According to Brandon Centerwall in the *Journal of the American Medical Association*, "Manifestly, every violent act is the result of an array of forces coming together—poverty, crime, alcohol and drug abuse, stress—of which childhood exposure to television is just one. Nevertheless, the epidemiological evidence indicates that if, hypothetically, television technology had never been developed, there would today be 10,000 fewer homicides each year in the United States, 70,000 fewer rapes, and 700,000 fewer injurious assaults" (as cited in Vander Neut, 1999, p. 40).

Still, debate persists, or to be more precise, it persists inasmuch as a small number of scholarly skeptics (see Bushman, Rothstein, & Anderson, 2010) and many media industry spokespeople (see Tsukayama, 2013) continue to claim the science is inconclusive. Even an overwhelming majority, 77%, of American parents accept the media violence–aggression connection (Mandese, 2013).

Catharsis

The findings from the surgeon general's report on one aspect of the television violence debate, **catharsis**, were quite clear and did generate significant agreement. CBS's Joseph Klapper testified, "I myself am unaware of any, shall we say, hard evidence that seeing violence on television or any other medium acts in a cathartic or sublimated manner. There have been some studies to that effect; they are grossly, greatly outweighed by studies as to the opposite effect" (US Congress, 1972, p. 60). Yet catharsis (sometimes called sublimation)—the idea that viewing violence is sufficient to purge or at least satisfy a person's aggressive drive and therefore reduce the likelihood of aggressive behavior—has lived a long if not thoroughly respectable life in mass communication theory.

Common sense and your own media consumption offer some evidence of the weakness of the catharsis hypothesis. It assumes that aggression is an innate drive, much like the drive to reproduce or eat. But when you watch couples engaged in physical affection on the screen, does it reduce your sexual drive? Do media presentations of families devouring devilish chocolate cakes purge you of your hunger drive? If viewing mediated sexual behavior does not reduce the sex drive and viewing media presentations of people dining does not reduce our hunger, why should we assume that seeing mediated violence can satisfy an aggressive drive? Aggression, however, is not innate. It is learned; as such, given how the brain operates, catharsis is an impossibility. "Consider one common way to remember a telephone number," wrote psychologist Douglas Gentile (2013). "We read it or repeat it several times. After seeing it enough times, we no longer need to continue—we have learned it. . . . Each additional repetition of seeing something burns it deeper into the brain. If the aggression catharsis hypothesis were true, seeing the telephone number one more time should make us *less* likely to remember it—it should take it away from us. But in fact, repeating experiences is one of the most effective ways to learn something. . . . Therefore, if one plays a violent video game in which one practices aggressive thoughts, feelings, and responses, it *cannot* lead to lowered aggressive thoughts, feelings, or responses over the long term" (p. 503).

Yet it isn't difficult to see why the proposition seemed so attractive. For one thing, the philosopher Aristotle originally discussed catharsis in his *Poetics* to explain audience reaction to Greek tragedy. Even though he never wrote of the "purging" of an innate aggressive drive, but rather about audiences "purging" their own emotions of pity and fear because in a tragic play they saw misfortune befalling others (Gadamer, 1995), catharsis developed a conventional wisdom–based validity. For another, catharsis suggested that television violence had social utility—that is, it was functional, providing young people with a harmless outlet for their pent-up aggression and hostility. In television's early days, many people were anxious to rationalize their use of this attractive new medium, and the effect trend's embrace of functionalism (Chapter 5), supported that rationale.

There was even early scientific evidence suggesting that catharsis was indeed at work. Seymour Feshbach (1961) demonstrated what he said was catharsis by insulting college-age men with "a number of unwarranted and extremely critical remarks" in an experimental setting and then having them watch either filmed aggression (a brutal prize fight) or a neutral film (on the spread of rumors). The men were then asked to evaluate the experiment and the insulting experimenter. Those who had seen the prize fight were less aggressive in their attitudes as measured on a paper-and-pencil inventory than were those who had seen the other film.

Nonetheless, as F. Scott Andison wrote in 1977 after reviewing 20 years' worth of scientific evidence, "We can conclude on the basis of the present data cumulation that television, as it is shown today, probably does stimulate a higher amount of aggression in individuals within society. Therefore, it seems reasonable to tentatively accept the 'TV violence as a stimulant to aggression' theory and to reject the . . . 'cathartic' theories" (p. 323). Or as James D. Halloran (1964/1965), then director of Britain's Center for Mass Communication Research at the University of Leicester, more directly put it, catharsis is a "phony argument" (p. 62).

But Feshbach *did* demonstrate a reduction in aggression after viewing, and he obtained similar results in a subsequent study (Feshbach & Singer, 1971) conducted with funding from the NBC television network. The research was undertaken in a group home for preadolescent boys. For six weeks, half of the boys were restricted to watching television programs with little or no violence while the other half were allowed to watch violent content. A variety of behavioral measures indicated that the boys viewing the violent programs were less aggressive. These results may not have been caused by catharsis, however. The boys who were placed in the nonviolent programming group may have been frustrated because they were not allowed to watch some of their favorite shows. Heightened frustration might account for their increased aggressiveness.

What social scientists would eventually learn, however, is that certain presentations of mediated violence and aggression *can reduce* the likelihood of subsequent viewer aggression, but not because of catharsis. Rather, viewers *learn* that violence might not be appropriate in a given situation. Reconsider the first Feshbach study (1961). Maybe those who had seen the brutal boxing match, who had seen unnecessary pain inflicted on another human, simply said to themselves, "Aggression is not a good thing." Their aggressive "drive" was not purged; they simply *learned* that such treatment of another human is inappropriate. In other words, their inclination toward aggression (remember, they had been insulted) was inhibited by the information in the media presentation. This leads us to the theory that is generally accepted as most useful in understanding the influence of media violence on individuals—social cognitive theory.

Social Learning Theory

Humans learn from observation. There has been some question, however, about how much and what kinds of behaviors people learn from the media. This debate has been fueled, in part, by a definitional problem. No one questions whether people can imitate what they see in the media. **Imitation** is the direct mechanical reproduction of behavior. After watching Spike TV's *Ultimate Fighting Championship*, 23 Connecticut teens engage in a backyard slugfest/tournament that results in their arrest. A Washington-state man strangles his girlfriend and attempts to dissolve her body in a tub of acid, a technique he learned from an episode of *Breaking Bad*. Both are true stories; both demonstrate imitation. The problem for mass communication theory, however, is that these obvious examples of media influence, dramatic as they may be, are relatively rare. Moreover, such gross examples of media influence lend substance to the argument that negative effects occur only for those "predisposed" to aggression—in other words, those who are already more likely to act aggressively.

Identification, on the other hand, is "a particular form of imitation in which copying a model, generalized beyond specific acts, springs from wanting to be and trying to be like the model with respect to some broader quality" (White, 1972, p. 252). Although only one or a very few people might have *imitated* the behaviors seen in our *Ultimate Fighting Championship* and *Breaking Bad* examples, how many others *identified* with their characters? How many others might choose different forms of violence against someone they might encounter? How many others identified with the characters' mode of problem solving, although they might never express it exactly as did our mediated aggressors? Imitation from media is clearly more dramatic and observable than is identification. But identification with media models might be the more lasting and significant of the media's effects. (For a detailed discussion of this distinction and its importance to media theory, see Baran & Meyer, 1974.)

The first serious look at learning through observation was offered by psychologists Neal Miller and John Dollard (1941). They argued that imitative learning occurred when observers were motivated to learn, when the cues or elements of the behaviors to be learned were present, when observers performed the given behaviors, and when observers were positively reinforced for imitating those behaviors. In other words, people could imitate behaviors they saw; those behaviors would be reinforced and therefore learned.

Instead of presenting a means of understanding how people learn from models (including media models), however, Miller and Dollard were simply describing an efficient form of traditional stimulus-response learning. They assumed that individuals behaved in certain ways and then shaped their behavior according to the reinforcement they actually received. The researchers saw imitation as replacing random trial-and-error behaviors. Imitation simply made it easier for an individual to choose a behavior to be reinforced. That actual reinforcement, they argued, ensured learning. But this insistence on the operation of reinforcement limited their theory's application for understanding how people learn from the mass media. Its inability to account for people's apparent skill at learning new responses through observation rather than from actually receiving reinforcement limited its applicability to media theory.

Two decades later, Miller and Dollard's ideas about what they called **social learning** and imitation were sufficiently developed, however, to become valuable tools in understanding media effects. Whereas Miller and Dollard saw social learning as an efficient form of stimulus-response learning (the model provided information that helped the observer make the correct response to be reinforced), contemporary social cognitive theory (as social learning theory is now known) argues that observers can acquire symbolic representations of the behavior, and these "pictures in their heads" provide them with information on which to base their own subsequent behavior. Media characters (models) can influence behavior simply by being depicted on the screen. The audience member need not be reinforced or rewarded for exhibiting the modeled behavior.

Social Cognition from Mass Media

Operant (or traditional) learning theory as developed by the early behaviorists (see Chapter 2) asserts that people learn new behaviors when they are presented with stimuli (something in their environment), make a response to those stimuli, and have those responses reinforced either positively (rewarded) or negatively (punished). In this way, new behaviors are learned, or added to people's **behavioral repertoire**—the behaviors available to an individual in a given circumstance.

Two things are clear, however. First, this is an inefficient form of learning. We all know, for example, how to deal with fire. If each of us had to individually and personally learn our fire-related behavior, we would have overcrowded hospitals. According to operant learning theory, each of us, when presented with that stimulus (fire), would render a chance response (put our hand in it), and be burned. To ensure that we would not be scorched in the future, we would add avoidance of fire to our behavioral repertoire. Because that initial burned hand "increases the probability of a given behavior over time" (in our case, avoiding flames), the stimulus (the burned hand) is a **negative reinforcer** (Zimbardo & Weber, 1997, p. 215). This process is very inefficient. Instead we observe the operation of that stimulus-response-reinforcement chain in a variety of settings (mass-mediated and otherwise), and we in turn add avoidance to the store of behaviors that we can use when confronted in everyday life by the stimulus. In essence, then, we have substituted a representation—a picture in our head—of an experience for an actual (and, in this case, painful) experience.

A second obvious point is that we do not learn in only this operant manner. We have all experienced learning through observation, even when we have not seen the stimulus-response-reinforcement chain—that is, when there has been no reinforcement, either to us or to the person in the representation. Observation of a behavior is sufficient for people to learn that behavior. Even people who have never shot an arrow from a bow, for example, can do it. **Modeling** from the mass media, then, is an efficient way to learn a wide range of behaviors and solutions to problems that we would otherwise learn slowly or not at all or pay too high a price to learn in the actual environment.

This learning from observation of the environment, or social cognition, is the basis of social cognitive theory. According to Albert Bandura (1994), "Social cognitive theory explains psychosocial functioning in terms of triadic reciprocal causation. In this model of reciprocal determinism, behavior; cognitive, biological, and other personal factors; and environmental events all operate as interacting determinants that influence each other bidirectionally" (p. 61). In other words, things they experience in their environments (e.g., mass media) can affect people's behaviors, and that effect is influenced by various personal factors specific to those people and their situations.

This social cognition through the use of media representations operates in one or more of three ways (see Bandura, 1971, 1994, for excellent extended discussions):

1. **Observational learning**. Consumers of representations can acquire new patterns of behavior by simply watching these representations. We all know how to shoot a gun, although many of us have never actually performed or been reinforced for that act. Many of us probably even think that we can rob a convenience store. We've seen it done.

2. **Inhibitory effects**. Seeing a model in a representation punished for exhibiting a certain behavior decreases the likelihood that observers will make that behavior. It is as if viewers themselves are actually punished. We see the villain brought low for evil deeds, or in *A Christmas Story* we observe Flick, challenged by Schwartz's triple-dog-dare, with his tongue painfully stuck to the frozen flag pole as the bell rings and his friends scurry away. Our likelihood of responding to various real-world stimuli in similar ways is reduced. Experimental studies

using film and video of people being punished for various behaviors have shown that these representations can inhibit in observers such things as aggression, exploratory behavior, and antisocial interaction with peers.

3. **Disinhibitory effects**. A media representation that depicts reward for a threatening or prohibited behavior is often sufficient to increase the likelihood that the consumer of the representation will make that behavior. A young man sees Johnny Knoxville and his *Jackass* crew set themselves afire, apparently suffering no ill effects. His likelihood of responding to various real-world stimuli in similar ways is increased. Experimental studies using film and television representations of various threatening and prohibited encounters have successfully reduced fear of dentists, dogs, and snakes and increased aggression by reducing viewers' inhibitions regarding such action.

Vicarious reinforcement is central to social cognition through the mass media. Although observational learning can occur in the absence of any reinforcement, vicarious or real, whether observers *actually engage in* that learned behavior is a function of the **reinforcement contingencies** (positive or negative) they associate with it. For example, when we see a television character rewarded or punished for some action, it is as if we ourselves have actually been rewarded or punished. This vicarious reinforcement tells us where to place the observationally learned behavior in our *behavioral hierarchy*—the likelihood that we will choose a given behavior in a given situation. When presented with certain stimuli in our environment, we will be likely to choose a highly placed behavior for demonstration. One that promises punishment will be given a lower place in that hierarchy. We do not actually have to experience those rewards and sanctions; we have experienced them vicariously through the use of media representations.

Clearly there are times when we ignore possible negative consequences and perform a behavior that we associate with punishment or restraints, such as running into a burning house. In these cases, sufficient incentive is present in the actual environment (saving a child from the flames, for example) to move that behavior up the hierarchy to a point where we choose it from among a number of alternatives. Bandura (2009) calls this **social prompting** of previously learned behaviors. This effect is "distinguished from observational learning and disinhibition because no new behavior has been acquired, and disinhibitory processes are not involved because the elicited behavior is socially acceptable and not encumbered by restraints" (p. 108).

Bandura (1965) conducted what is now considered a classic experiment in modeling aggressive behavior from television, one having direct bearing on several aspects of the media-effects debate. He showed nursery school children a television program in which a character, Rocky, was either rewarded for aggression (given candy and a soft drink and called a "strong champion") or punished for those same behaviors (reprimanded, called a "bully," and spanked with a rolled-up magazine). Those who saw aggression rewarded showed more aggressive activity in a "free play" period (disinhibition), and those who saw it punished displayed less (inhibition). You can almost hear those people who believe that media have no effects on viewer aggression crowing, "See, the bad guy is punished, so media portrayals of violence actually reduce subsequent aggression."

SOCIAL COGNITIVE THEORY

Strengths

1. Demonstrates causal link between media and behavior
2. Applies across several viewer and viewing situations
3. Has strong explanatory power (e.g., rejects catharsis, stresses importance of environmental and content cues)

Weaknesses

1. Laboratory demonstration raises question of generalizability
2. Experimental demonstration might overestimate media power
3. Has difficulty explaining long-term effects of media consumption
4. Underestimates people's active use of media messages
5. Focuses too narrowly on individual rather than on cultural effects

But Bandura went one step further. He later offered those in the inhibited group "sticker-pictures" for each of Rocky's aggressive acts they could demonstrate. Boys and girls alike could produce the "forbidden" behaviors (those actions moved up the behavioral hierarchy). The environment offered them sufficient reward to demonstrate those observationally learned but previously inhibited behaviors (social prompting). The response to the "TV violence apologists," then, is simple: The bad guy is usually "out-aggressed" by the good guy, who is rewarded for his or her more proficient display of aggression, and besides, that might not matter because the behaviors are observationally learned and can appear later when the conditions in the viewer's world call them (or similar ones) forward.

Aggressive Cues

One direct outgrowth of social cognitive theory focuses on the **aggressive cues** inherent in media portrayals of violence. People who see mediated violence are believed to show higher levels of subsequent aggression. The question involves when and against whom do they aggress. The answer is that media portrayals of violence are almost always in some narrative context, and that context provides information, or *cues*, telling viewers when and against whom violence is acceptable.

Leonard Berkowitz (1965) produced a representative piece of research in which male college students were shown a film of a brutal boxing scene (the closing sequence of the movie *The Champion*). To some, it was presented in the context of a story that said the loser deserved his beating—that is, the violence against him was justified. In a second version of the narrative, the defeated boxer was victimized—that is, the violence against him was unjustified.

The students were then given an opportunity to "grade" another student's design of "an original and imaginative floor plan for a house." Unbeknownst to them, all the participants were given the same floor plan from that other student (who was actually Berkowitz's accomplice). In half the cases that accomplice introduced himself as a "college boxer," and in the other half as a "speech major." A "new form of grading" was to be used, grading by electrical shock: one shock was very good; 10 was very bad. Of course, the accomplice was not actually zapped; the shocks administered by the participants were read by a metering device as the accomplice feigned a response. Any differences in shocking the accomplice would be the result of differences in what participants had seen on the screen. To confuse matters even more, half the participants were insulted (angered) by the experimenter before they began.

What happened? The "college boxer" was shocked more than the speech major; the angered subjects gave more shocks regardless of whom they were shocking; and those who had seen the justified version of the film also gave more shocks. Berkowitz's conclusions? First, viewers' *psychological state* (how they are feeling when consuming media) can lead them to respond to cues in programs that meet the needs of that state. Second, viewers who see justified violence not only learn the behavior but also learn that it can be a good or useful problem-solving device (disinhibition). Third, cues associated with a victim, in this case a boxer, can disinhibit viewers toward aggression against similar people in the real world. Berkowitz said, "The findings show that the film context can affect the observer's inhibitions against aggression and that the people encountered soon afterwards vary in the extent to which they can evoke aggressive responses from the observer" (p. 368). In a later study (Berkowitz & Geen, 1966), Berkowitz produced similar results simply by having the real-world target of the viewers' aggression share little more than the same first name (Kirk) as the character in the film.

This idea of aggressive cues is supported by contemporary thinking on **priming effects**, which "maintains that the presentation of a certain stimulus having a particular meaning 'primes' other semantically related concepts, thus heightening the likelihood that thoughts with much the same meaning as the presentation stimulus will come to mind" (Jo & Berkowitz, 1994, p. 46). Berkowitz labeled this the **cognitive-neoassociationistic perspective**, explaining "that frequent viewing of violent media portrayals primes particular constructs (e.g., aggression, hostility) and thus makes these constructs more likely to be used in behavioral decisions as well as judgments about others" (Shrum, 2009, p. 56).

Aggressive cues, priming effects, and the cognitive-neoassociationistic perspective form the basis of some of the most interesting and controversial media violence research now being conducted. As the link between media violence and viewer aggression came to be generally accepted, attention turned to the issue of violence against a specific target—women. As Richard Frost and John Stauffer (1987) wrote, "But even though members of an audience for a violent film or television program may not be moved to actual behavioral imitation, do they not experience different levels of emotional arousal? . . . Could arousal also be influenced by the type of violence being portrayed, such as violence against women as opposed to men?" (p. 29).

In terms of aggressive cues, media portrayals cue viewers to consider women likely or appropriate targets of violence. In terms of priming effects and the cognitive-neoassociationistic perspective, media presentations of women as victims of violence heighten the likelihood that viewers, when confronted by real-life women, will have similar thoughts (constructs) about them; heavy viewing of such content primes those constructs, increasing the likelihood they will be employed.

The operation of all three concepts is evident in Michelle Kistler and Moon Lee's (2010) research on highly sexual hip-hop music videos. They demonstrated that college men who were exposed to this content "expressed greater objectification of women, sexual permissiveness, stereotypical gender attitudes, and acceptance of rape" than those who were not (p. 67). In suggesting that these videos primed particular constructs "more likely to be used in behavioral decisions," the authors wrote. "The most disturbing finding . . . is the significant effect of exposure on male participants' acceptance of rape myths. Men in the highly sexual hip-hop videos were portrayed as powerful, sexually assertive, and as having a fair degree of sexual prowess, whereas the women were portrayed as sexually available, scantily clad, and often preening over the men. This might have served as a cue to male participants that sexual coercion is more acceptable and that women exist for the entertainment and sexual fulfillment of men" (p. 83). Melinda Burgess and Sandra Burpo (2012) undertook a similar investigation, focusing not on hip-hop but on a "high sexualization/objectification" Top 40 music video from female country music artist Jessica Simpson. Their results mirrored those of Kistler and Lee's research: "For college males viewing mainstream, commercially available music videos, the highly sexualized portrayal of a female artist is associated with judging a date rapist as less guilty. For both males and females, this portrayal was associated with less empathy for the victim. For women, this portrayal was associated with greater judgment of responsibility for the victim" (p. 757).

Loss of empathy is an attitudinal or emotional effect, but closely related is **desensitization**, the mitigation or reduction of anxious physiological arousal in response to depictions of violence, both mediated and real-world, as the result of habitual consumption of mediated violence. Desensitization has been well documented, as research has consistently shown that "the more time individuals spent watching violent media depictions, the less emotionally responsive they became to violent stimuli" (Krahé et al., 2011, p. 631). For example, Barbara Krahé and her colleagues were able to identify reduced physiological reactivity to violent films in college students who admitted to a heavy diet of violent fare (Krahé et al., 2011), and Nicholas Carnagey, Craig Anderson, and Brad Bushman (2007) demonstrated that even 20 minutes of violent video game play could produce desensitization to scenes of real-world violence.

The Context of Mediated Violence

Writing in 1994, Bandura summed up the accumulated knowledge of social cognitive theory to conclude that television viewers "acquire lasting attitudes, emotional reactions, and behavioral proclivities towards persons, places, or things that have been associated with modeled emotional experiences" (p. 75). So, what is it about specific presentations of media violence that encourages this acquisition through modeling? W. James Potter (1997) identified seven important **contextual variables**:

1. **Reward/punishment**. Rewarded aggression is more frequently modeled; punished aggression is less frequently modeled. We know these to be disinhibitory and inhibitory effects, respectively.
2. **Consequences**. Mediated violence accompanied by portrayals of negative or harmful consequences produces less modeling. Again, this shows inhibitory effects at work.
3. **Motive**. Motivated media aggression produces greater levels of modeling, and unjustified media violence results in less viewer aggression. Viewers are cued to the appropriateness (or inappropriateness) of using aggression.
4. **Realism**. Especially with boys, realistic media violence tends to produce more real-world aggression. As Potter explained, "Realistic [media] perpetrators are

more likely to reduce inhibitions because their behaviors are more applicable to real life situations than are unrealistic perpetrators such as cartoon or fantasy characters" (p. 234).

5. **Humor**. Because it reduces the seriousness of the behavior, humorously presented media violence leads to the greater probability that viewers will behave aggressively in real life.

6. **Identification with media characters**. The more viewers identify with media characters (e.g., with those they consider like themselves or attractive), the more likely it is that they will model the behaviors demonstrated by those characters.

7. **Arousal**. Potter explained, "Emotional appeals can serve to increase the dramatic nature of the narrative, and this can increase attention, . . . positive dispositions toward the characters using violence, . . . and higher levels of arousal." This dramatically induced arousal and emotional attachment to violent characters, according to Potter, are "likely to result in aggressive behavior" (p. 235).

Active Theory of Television Viewing

The operation of these contextual variables underscores the idea that media consumers do indeed bring something to the viewing situation. That is, they make judgments about what it is they are seeing as they consume: for example, Is this violence justified? Or, What are the consequences of engaging in that behavior? Presenting "a theory of visual attention to television which has as its central premise the cognitively active nature of television viewing," Daniel Anderson and Elizabeth Lorch (1983, pp. 27–28), as well as several other researchers (e.g., Bryant & Anderson, 1983), challenged the idea that "television viewing is fundamentally reactive and passive."

This **active theory** of television viewing sees viewers in general—and in the violence debate, particularly children—as actively and consciously working to understand television content. This position argues that by the age of two and a half, children have sufficiently developed **viewing schema** that allow them to comprehend specific television content conventions. "Beyond two and a half years," they wrote, "visual attention to television increases throughout the preschool years . . . and may level off during the school-age years. . . . We suggest this increase reflects cognitive development, increased world knowledge, and an understanding of the cinematic codes and format structures of television" (Anderson & Lorch, 1983, p. 13).

Those who argue for this active theory of viewing claim that social cognitive theorists generally subscribe "to the proposition that the child is an active, cognitive, and social being [but] television is seen as providing such an exceptionally powerful influence that the child becomes reactive in its presence" (Anderson & Lorch, 1983, p. 5). This pessimistic view of children's viewing and cognitive abilities, they claim, inevitably leads social cognition advocates to overestimate the power of the medium and underestimate the influence that individual viewers have in determining effects. Put another way, this "reactive theory" assumes that attention causes comprehension and, therefore, effects. The active theory of television viewing assumes that comprehension causes attention and, therefore, effects (or no effects).

As we will see in later chapters, this debate over the ability of individual television viewers to resist the influence of powerful content has emerged as a central theme in contemporary mass communication theory. One of the most important sets of these media theories is referred to as **active-audience theories**, which argue that average audience members can routinely resist the influence of media content and make it serve their own purposes. They are, however, opposed by other perspectives questioning people's ability to resist the influence of messages systematically structured to convey certain meanings. Both perspectives are increasingly supported by growing bodies of empirical evidence. It's quite possible that both are valid, even if they seem to offer contradictory views of the relative power of media over audiences. There is a third view, however, relevant especially when considering the media-violence link. It is that viewers are indeed active, but they are active in using violent content in support of the *increase* in their subsequent levels of aggression. For example, in demonstrating that young male and female adults who were exposed to media portrayals of aggression in romantic relationships showed higher levels of aggression in their real-life romantic relationships, Sarah Coyne and her colleagues (2011) offered the possibility that "more aggressive individuals turn to viewing more media violence for social comparison reasons—i.e. it makes them feel less abnormal in their own aggression." They pointed to the **downward spiral model** of media influence. "This model," they wrote, "posits that individuals tend to seek out violent media that is consonant with their aggressive tendencies, and, by extension, reinforces and exacerbates such tendencies" (p. 57).

The Developmental Perspective

But obviously not all viewers, especially children, are active viewers, and not all are equally active. This understanding has led to support for the **developmental perspective**, one that assumes that children undergo "extensive and varied cognitive growth between birth and adulthood . . . that is extremely rich, complex, and multifaceted" (Flavell, 1992, p. 998). As such, this perspective also assumes that an important aspect of people's power to deal with television is their ability to comprehend it at different stages in their intellectual development. Logically, older children will "read" television differently than will younger children. As Ellen Wartella (1979) wrote, this developmental perspective "seeks to describe and explain the nature of the communicative differences between four-year-olds, six-year-olds, ten-year-olds, etc., and adults" (p. 7).

Those differences certainly exist. For example, there is significant research evidence that children under 8 are unable to understand advertising's intent, uncritically accept its claims as true, and are unable to distinguish between commercials and the television programming that houses them. But, as Esther Rozendaal, Moniek Buijzen, and Patti Valkenburg (2011) demonstrate, kids' ability to recognize a variety of advertiser goals and tactics eventually develops around age 10, with understanding progressing steadily from 8 to 12 years old, as they develop the ability to take the perspective of others and reason at an abstract level. Likewise, Leslie Shade, Nikki Porter, and Wendy Sanchez (2005) demonstrated developmental differences in children's ability to understand the Internet's true nature, with preteens unable to comprehend that Internet content does not reside "inside" the computer itself. Zheng Yan (2009) found "significant age differences . . . in technical [the physical reality of computer networks] and social [the personal consequences of Internet use] understandings of the Internet across age groups 9–17" (p. 112).

This notion of developmental stages in children's communicative abilities is drawn from developmental psychology, especially the work of Jean Piaget, who argued that children, as they move from infancy through adolescence, undergo qualitative changes in the level of cognitive and intellectual abilities available to them. Logically, then, it is easy to assume that older children's processing of television's messages is more developed and therefore somehow better at insulating them from television effects. But this is neither the conclusion of developmental research, nor is it the goal. Yes, wrote Ellen Wartella (1979), the developmental perspective asks "new questions and [deals with] different sorts of communication issues regarding children's learning from television and use of television" (pp. 8–9). But the misleading Piagetian assumption of ever-increasing cognitive *competency* has produced the **empowered child model** of television effects research, which assumes that children eventually become "competent, self-aware users of television . . . [and] tends to emphasize the positive aspects of children's engagement with television. Less emphasis in such studies is placed on questions of the consequences of media use for children's health and welfare, in particular, their cognitive, emotional, and physical development" (Wartella, 1999, pp. 84–85). In other words the developmental perspective, rather than demonstrating that children pass through ordered stages of cognitive growth and eventually develop into competent users of the media, might actually suggest that media use can interfere with that development. Recall some of the data on children's engagement with media that opened this chapter: attentively watching before 3 years old, significant daily time before glowing screens, the number of little kids with televisions and game consoles in their bedrooms. *How* do children develop in this new media environment, especially as "the years from birth to age three are seen as crucial for development to proceed?" How does this engagement with media alter children's development, given that "new work studying sociocultural influences on development suggests that the ways in which children participate in structured social activities with their families, other adults, and children influence the rate and sorts of domain-specific developmental progressions that occur" (Wartella, 1999, p. 86)? We'll return to this issue in the next chapter in our discussion of adolescents.

INSTANT ACCESS

DEVELOPMENTAL PERSPECTIVE

Strengths	Weaknesses
1. Provides an age-based perspective on media effects	1. Misused to justify argument that as kids get older, likelihood of negative effects declines
2. Respects children as competent, self-aware media consumers able to moderate media influence	2. Overestimates children's competence and self-awareness as media consumers in moderating media influence
3. Offers evidence of the eventual reduction of harmful effects and increase in positive media influence	3. Does not sufficiently appreciate role of media use in disrupting or otherwise influencing development

Video Games Reignite Interest in Media Violence

The link between television and viewer aggression is accepted by all but the most ardent media defenders. As a result, most recent media violence research has focused on video games. This work, based in social cognitive theory, demonstrates the causal link between playing violent video games and subsequent player aggression and, as such, has expanded the field's confidence in the television violence findings. This research is uniform in its assessment. "Violent video game play was positively related to aggressive behavior and delinquency" (Anderson & Dill, 2000, p. 772); "video game violence [is] positively correlated with trait hostility" (Gentile, Lynch, Linder, & Walsh, 2004, p. 18); video game exposure is "related to increases in aggressive behavior . . . aggressive affect . . . aggressive cognitions (i.e., aggressive thoughts, beliefs, and attitudes) . . . and physiological arousal" (Anderson et al., 2003, p. 92); "violent video games increase aggression and aggression-related variables and decrease prosocial outcomes. . . . These effects [are] reliable across experimental, correlational, and longitudinal studies, indicating that video game exposure causally affects social outcomes and that there are both short and long-term effects" (Greitemeyer & Mügge, 2014, p. 578).

Of particular interest to media-effects researchers in much of this inquiry is an important difference between games and television; *players* are much more involved in the on-screen activity than are television *viewers*. This interactivity renders them participants in, not merely observers of, the violence. This active involvement in the on-screen violence is problematic because, as social cognitive theory argues, "rehearsal" of observed behaviors greatly increases the amount of modeling (Bandura, 1994), and as Potter (1997) argues, identification and realism increase modeling. What could be more real than aggression in which players themselves participate? With whom could they identify more closely than themselves as they play? "It is true," wrote Craig Anderson and his colleagues, "that as a player you are 'not just moving your hand on a joystick' but are indeed interacting 'with the game psychologically and emotionally.' It is not surprising that when the game involves rehearsing aggressive and violent thoughts and actions, such deep game involvement results in antisocial effects on the player" (Anderson et al., 2010, p. 171). This line of thinking has been extended to the **weapons effect** in single-shooter games, the use of highly realistic gun controllers that capture players' motions. These devices increase game realism and immerse players more fully into the action, producing increases in player aggression (McGloin, Farrar, & Fishlock, 2015). Jessica LaCroix, Christopher Burrows, and Hart Blanton (2018) demonstrated this effect, experimentally confirming that the "increasingly immersive nature of modern video games . . . amplify their influence on players, including effects that promote hostility and aggression toward women" (p. 413).

Elly Konijn, Marije Bijvank, and Brad Bushman (2007) specifically examined the issue of games' psychological and emotional interactivity by differentiating between two types of identification. Identification, as typically understood in social cognitive theory, is **similarity identification**, in which the observer identifies with a character because they share some salient characteristic. For example, both are male or both are American. However, a more powerful form of identification also exists, one particularly pertinent to participatory video games, **wishful identification**. Here the observer "desires to emulate the character, either in general terms (as a role model for future action or identity development) or in specific terms (extending responses beyond the viewing situation or imitating a particular behavior)." Because wishful identification provides a glimpse of "what if," wrote the researchers, "it is a powerful predictor of future behavior, especially in adolescents," particularly boys, and as a result, "is closer to [Bandura's] concept of vicarious learning" (p. 1039). Their research did indeed demonstrate that wishful identification with violent characters in realistic games produced greater levels of aggression in players.

THE GENERAL AGGRESSION MODEL

Considering the issue settled science, Craig Anderson and his colleagues attempted to provide a general framework for the argument that mediated violence does indeed increase viewer aggression (Anderson, Deuser, & DeNeve, 1995). Their goal was "to integrate existing mini-theories of aggression into a unified whole" (Anderson & Bushman, 2002, p. 33). The outcome, based primarily in social cognitive theory, is the general aggression model (GAM)—a model of human aggression that argues that cognition, affect, and arousal mediate the effects of situational and individual personal variables on aggression. It "incorporates biological, personality development, social processes, basic cognitive processes (e.g., perception, priming), short-term and long-term processes, and decision processes into understanding aggression" (DeWall, Anderson, & Bushman, 2011, p. 246).

To explain how exposure to mediated violence could have short-term effects (for example, in the laboratory) and long-term effects (for example, in real life when away from violent content), GAM assumes that "social behavior depends upon the individual's construal of events in the present environment, including the person's interpretation of these events, beliefs about typical ways of responding to such events, perceived competencies for responding in different ways, and expectations regarding likely outcomes." As such, "these cognitions provide a basis for some stability of behavior across a variety of situations (because each individual tends to resolve situational ambiguities in characteristic ways), but also allow considerable situational specificity (because of reality constraints upon possible construals)." Because people's "knowledge structures develop from experience; influence all types of perception, from basic visual patterns to complex behavioral sequences; can become automatized with use; are linked to affective states, behavioral programs, and beliefs; and guide interpretations and behavioral responses to the social and physical environments," write Craig Anderson and Nicholas Carnagey (2004), "decisions that initially require considerable conscious thought can, in fact, become effortless and occur with little or no awareness" (p. 173).

GAM has two parts: the *episode*—when a person is in a social situation and can behave either with or without aggression toward another—and *developmental/personality processes*—the aggression-related knowledge structures brought to that situation. In the episode (Figure 7.2), *inputs* include *situation factors* that might increase or inhibit aggression. An insult, for example, might increase the likelihood of aggression; the presence of your parents might decrease it. *Person factors* "include all the characteristics a person brings to the situation, such as personality traits, attitudes, and genetic predispositions" (Anderson & Bushman, 2002, p. 35). *Routes* include the person's *present internal state*, its affect, cognition, or arousal (the dotted line between the three elements means they also influence one another). *Affect* refers to mood and emotion. *Cognition* refers to the accessibility of aggressive concepts or behavior scripts—that is, how easily (or not) aggressive thoughts are primed. *Arousal* refers to the level of physical and psychological excitement the person feels at the moment. *Outcomes* refer to what ultimately happens in the encounter. The person judges the situation, makes a decision, and responds either thoughtfully or impulsively. But remember, these *appraisal and decision processes* are the product of the inputs and the routes they traveled. The resulting social encounter now adds to the inputs brought to the next social encounter.

Media enter the model as part of a person's *developmental/personality processes* (Figure 7.1). The model asserts that *repeated violent game playing increases learning, rehearsal, and reinforcement of aggression-related cognitions*. These include *beliefs and attitudes* about aggression, the way aggression is *perceived*, *expectations* surrounding aggression, *scripts* or models for aggressive behavior, and *desensitization* to aggression. These five factors produce an *increase in aggressive personality* that influences *personal and situational variables*, which are, in fact, the person and situation inputs (at the top of Figure 7.2) that produce either aggressive or nonaggressive behaviors in social encounters. Note, though, that Figure 7.1's top-most box could just as easily read "Repeated exposure to violent media content" or "Environmental modifiers" (Anderson & Bushman, 2002).

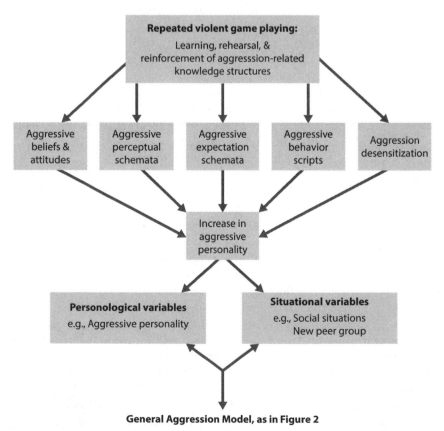

FIGURES 7.1   General Aggressive Model: Developmental/Personality Processes (in the example of violent game play)

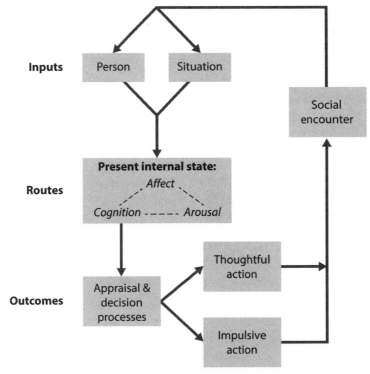

FIGURES 7.2   General Aggressive Model: The Episode

In addition, the logic of GAM has been applied to a wide array of video game effects beyond violence, especially in producing prosocial outcomes such as reductions in aggression and increases in empathy, benevolence, and self-regulation. This research relies not on the General *Aggression* Model, but on the General *Learning* Model (e.g., Coyne, Warburton, Essig, & Stockdale, 2018; Greitemeyer & Mügge, 2014).

INSTANT ACCESS

GENERAL AGGRESSION MODEL (GAM)

Strengths

1. Provides a comprehensive overview of media-human aggression link
2. Incorporates a wide variety of personal and situational variables
3. Applies across several media user and media use situations
4. Explains both short-term and long-term effects

Weaknesses

1. Number and variety of elements and linkages make empirical investigation and validation impossible
2. Declines in real-world youth violence suggest model overstates media influence on aggression
3. Does not explain research showing no link between media violence and subsequent aggression
4. Reliance primarily on laboratory research reinforces experiments' built-in bias toward strong effects

REVIEW OF LEARNING OBJECTIVES

- Explain how the social and technological changes that followed World War II paved the way for television and a theoretical reconsideration of media influence.

At war's end a technologically mature new medium was immediately available. The national commercial radio networks were poised to move their hit shows and big stars to television. The war changed the country from a primarily rural society boasting an agriculturally based economy into a largely urban nation dependent on an industrially based economy. More people worked regularly scheduled jobs, and they had more leisure. Because the manufacturing capabilities developed for the war were still in existence, the economy had the ability to mass produce items on which that money could be spent, so there was a greater need to advertise, which provided the economic base for the new television medium. Minorities began to demand their rightful share of the American dream. It was more common and acceptable to have both parents working outside the home. Traditional community anchors began to lose their dominance in the social and moral development of children. Delinquency and crime were on the rise. Media's role in all these changes was hotly debated.

- Distinguish between various "violence theories" such as catharsis and social cognitive theory, as well as explain the operation of their many components such as aggressive cues, imitation and identification, observational learning, inhibitory and disinhibitory effects, priming effects, and the cognitive-neoassociationistic perspective.

Catharsis, the idea that viewing violence can purge or at least satisfy aggressive drives and therefore reduce the likelihood of aggressive behavior, has been convincingly debunked. Social cognitive theory explains how observers imitate (directly reproduce observed behavior) and identify with (wanting to be and trying to be like an observed model relative to some broader characteristics or qualities) through observational learning (when the observation of a behavior is sufficient to learn that behavior), inhibitory effects (seeing a model punished for a behavior reduces the likelihood that the observer will engage in that behavior), and disinhibitory effects (seeing a model rewarded for a prohibited or threatening behavior increases the likelihood that the observer will engage in that behavior). These processes are often aided by a priming effect (presentations in the media heighten the likelihood that people will develop similar thoughts about those things in the real world) and cognitive-neoassociation (frequent viewing of violent media portrayals primes particular constructs, making them more likely to be used in behavioral decisions).

- Identify the many important contextual variables that can influence the demonstration of media-influenced aggression.

The context of mediated violence, how violence is presented, can influence subsequent viewer aggression. Among them are reward/punishment. Rewarded aggression is more frequently modeled; punished aggression less so. Consequences, whereby mediated violence accompanied by portrayals of negative or harmful consequences produces less modeling. Motive, whereby motivated media aggression produces greater levels of modeling; unjustified media violence results in less. Realism tends to produce more real-world aggression. Because it reduces the seriousness of the behavior, humorously presented media violence leads to the greater probability that viewers will behave aggressively. The more viewers identify with media characters, the more likely it is that they will model the behaviors demonstrated by those characters. And arousal, as emotional appeals can serve to increase the dramatic nature of the narrative.

- Recognize how the active theory of television viewing and the developmental approach have enriched the understanding of media effects.

The active theory of television viewing sees viewers as actively and consciously working to understand television content. By the age of two and a half, even children have sufficiently developed viewing schema that allow them to comprehend specific television content conventions. The developmental approach assumes that an important aspect of people's power to deal with television is their ability to comprehend it at different stages in their intellectual development.

- Explain how research on violent video games not only supports the television violence theories but has produced deeper understandings of media effects on aggression.

Research on video game violence, based in social cognitive theory, demonstrates the causal link between violent games and subsequent player aggression and, as such, has expanded the field's confidence in the television violence findings. Violent game play adds variables such as interactivity, rehearsal, identification with on-screen agents, and reward for progress through the game to the content-aggression equation.

CRITICAL THINKING QUESTIONS

1. Are you convinced of the causal link between mediated violence and subsequent viewer aggression? Why or why not? Was your view altered by the information presented in this chapter? Why or why not? Where there are seemingly contradictory effects findings, might both be correct? Under what circumstances might those contradictory results both be valid?

2. Are you a video game player? If so, what is your reaction to the research presented in this chapter? If you think it does not apply to you, why is that? What about your friends? Is it possible you are engaging in the third-person effect discussed in Chapter 1? Do you draw a distinction between different kinds of games or game play when you consider the issue of effects?

3. Of course you are an active media consumer; you think about what's on the screen and work to make sense of what you're watching. But do you ever lose yourself in an exciting television show or engrossing video game? Naturally that's what makes engaging media fun. But what happens to your meaning making when you willingly suspend disbelief and enter the world of the media narrative? Whose reality is active then? Can you speculate on what this immersion into mediated narratives has to do with producing effects?

KEY TERMS

social cognitive theory
general aggression model (GAM)
catharsis
imitation
identification
social learning
operant (or traditional) learning theory
behavioral repertoire
negative reinforcer
modeling
observational learning
inhibitory effects
disinhibitory effects
vicarious reinforcement
reinforcement contingencies

social prompting
aggressive cues
priming effects
cognitive-neoassociationistic perspective
desensitization
contextual variables
active theory
viewing schema
active-audience theories
downward spiral model
developmental perspective
empowered child model
weapons effect
similarity identification
wishful identification

GLOSSARY

social cognitive theory: Theory of learning through interaction with the environment that involves reciprocal causation of behavior, personal factors, and environmental events

general aggression model (GAM): Model of human aggression that argues that cognition, affect, and arousal mediate the effects of situational and individual personal variables on aggression

catharsis: Also called *sublimation;* the idea that viewing mediated aggression sates, or reduces, people's natural aggressive drives

imitation: The direct reproduction of observed behavior

identification: A special form of imitation that springs from wanting to be and trying to be like an observed model relative to some broader characteristics or qualities

social learning: Encompasses both imitation and identification to explain how people learn through observation of others in their environments

operant (or traditional) learning theory: Asserts that learning occurs only through the making and subsequent reinforcement of behavior

behavioral repertoire: Learned responses available to an individual in a given situation

negative reinforcer: A particular stimulus whose removal, reduction, or prevention increases the probability of a given behavior over time

modeling: The acquisition of behaviors through observation

observational learning: When the observation of a behavior is sufficient to learn that behavior

inhibitory effects: The effects of seeing a model punished for a behavior, thus reducing the likelihood that the observer will engage in that behavior

disinhibitory effects: The effects of seeing a model rewarded for a prohibited or threatening behavior, thus increasing the likelihood that the observer will engage in that behavior

vicarious reinforcement: Reinforcement that is observed rather than directly experienced

reinforcement contingencies: The value, positive or negative, associated with a given reinforcer

social prompting: Demonstration of previously learned behavior when it is observed as socially acceptable or without restraints

aggressive cues: Information contained in media portrayals of violence that suggests (or cues) the appropriateness of aggression against specific victims

priming effects: Idea that presentations in the media heighten the likelihood that people will develop similar thoughts about those things in the real world

cognitive-neoassociationistic perspective: Frequent viewing of violent media portrayals primes particular constructs, making them more likely to be used in behavioral decisions

desensitization: Idea that habitual consumption of mediated violence will mitigate or reduce anxious arousal in response to depictions of violence

contextual variables: Information (or context) surrounding the presentation of mediated violence

active theory: View of television consumption that assumes viewer comprehension causes attention and, therefore, effects or no effects

viewing schema: Interpretational skills that aid people in understanding media content conventions

active-audience theories: Theories that focus on assessing what people do with media; audience-centered theories

downward spiral model: Model of media influence suggesting that individuals tend to seek out violent media that is consonant with their aggressive tendencies

developmental perspective: View of learning from media that specifies different intellectual and communication stages in a child's life that influence the nature of media interaction and impact

empowered child model: Television effects research that assumes that children eventually become competent, self-aware users of television

weapons effect: In single-shooter video games, the use of highly realistic gun controllers that capture players' motions increases game realism and immerses players more fully into the action, producing increases in player aggression

similarity identification: Observer identifies with a character because they share some salient characteristic

wishful identification: Observer desires to emulate the character, either in general or specific terms

CHAPTER 8

Theories of Media and Human Development

Before most children start school or form close relationships with peers, they have learned the names of countless television characters and are fans of particular programs. By 5 years old they show recognition rates as high as 92% for dozens of different advertised brands in a wide variety of product categories (Andronikidis & Lambrianidou, 2010). Increasingly children and young adults live in a mediated world where face-to-face communication with others is supplemented by and interwoven with a broad range of mediated communication. "The media environment that children grow up in has changed dramatically, and the amount of time they spend consuming media has exploded," writes media researcher Victoria Rideout (2012). "Childhood and adolescence have been inundated with—and possibly transformed by—reality TV, smartphones, iPads, Facebook, Twitter, YouTube, *World of Warcraft*, *Angry Birds*, and texting, to name just a few" (p. 5). As the authors of the Kaiser Family Foundation's study of "Generation M²" (the *M* standing for *media*) argued, "As anyone who knows a teen or a tween can attest, media are among the most powerful forces in young people's lives today. Eight- to 18-year-olds spend more time with media than in any other activity besides (maybe) sleeping—an average of more than 7½ hours a day, seven days a week. The TV shows they watch, video games they play, songs they listen to, books they read, and websites they visit are an enormous part of their lives, offering a constant stream of messages about families, peers, relationships, gender roles, sex, violence, food, values, clothes, and an abundance of other topics too long to list" (Rideout, Foehr, & Roberts, 2010, p. 2). The obvious question, then, is how do children grow into young adults in this new mediated reality, one further complicated by their near-universal engagement with social media? Nearly half of all American teens are online "almost constantly," and counting those who visit social networking sites "several times a day," that proportion rises to 89% (Anderson & Jiang, 2018).

LEARNING OBJECTIVES

After studying this chapter you should be able to

- Develop answers to questions, asked by both effects and critical researchers, on the relationship between media consumption and young people's cognitive and emotional development.
- Appreciate cultural criticism of kinderculture and its redefining of childhood.
- Explain the contributions—positive and negative—to young people's personal development and well-being brought about by social media.

OVERVIEW

It was concern over media violence that first directed mass communication researchers' attention to young people, as you read in Chapter 7. But their interest very quickly moved beyond the important, but somewhat narrow, question of the relationship between on-screen mayhem and real-world aggression. If media could teach kids violence, they asked, what else could they teach them? If media provided scripts for resolving conflict situations, surely they offered scripts for dealing with the much wider array of situations that young people in a rapidly changing and complex world faced every day. And every bit as important, how good were those teachers? How beneficial were those scripts? As mass communication theorist George Gerbner (2010) explained, these were not unimportant questions. "For the first time in human history," he said, "most of the stories most of the time to most of the children are told no longer by the parents, no longer by the school, no longer by the church, no longer by the community, no longer hand-crafted, no longer community-based, no longer historically inspired, inherited, going from generation to generation, but essentially by a small group of global conglomerates that really have nothing to tell but have a lot to sell."

Postpositivist researchers, once the media-violence link was established to the satisfaction of all but the most stubborn skeptics, turned their attention to the question of how children grow up in Gerbner's new world of mediated and conglomerated storytellers. Critical cultural scholars also took an interest in issues of young people's development, specifically in the relationship between their increased media consumption and the **adultification** and commercialization of childhood. And as advances in mass communication theory and research are often driven by the introduction of new technologies and efforts to control their impact, scholars from across the discipline's traditions began asking interesting—and challenging—questions about young people's engagement with large-scale social media and how it might influence their development into competent, functioning young women and men, an especially important line of inquiry at a time of rapidly rising rates of teenage depression (Geiger & Davis, 2019; "Major Depression," 2018) and growing numbers of college students seeking mental health treatment (Wolverton, 2019).

MEDIA AND CHILDREN'S DEVELOPMENT

The issue of media's contribution to children's development—that is, their evolution from children into functioning, competent adolescents and young adults—has attracted significant theoretical attention. For example, summarizing the existing research for the American Academy of Pediatrics, a team of researchers argues that media "present youth with common 'scripts' for how to behave in unfamiliar situations such as romantic relationships . . . [and] **superpeer theory** states that the media are like powerful best friends in sometimes making risky behaviors seem like normative behavior" (Strasburger, Jordan, & Donnerstein, 2010, p. 758). The World Health Organization (2019) has gone so far as to warn parents that children under 5 should spend no more than 1 hour a day with screens, arguing that even less time than that is wiser. It recommends no screen time at all for kids under 18 months. And there is indeed quite a bit of postpositivist effects research demonstrating that media consumption, especially of television and video games, can impede children's and young people's development. Among the negative developmental effects the postpositivists have investigated are reduced reading and writing skills (Weis & Cerankosky, 2010); attentional disorders (Christakis, Zimmerman, DiGiuseppe, & McCarty, 2004); psychological distress (Page, Cooper, Griew, & Jago, 2010); limited vocabulary development (Christakis, et al., 2009); aggression in the classroom (Martins & Wilson, 2011); lower social competence, greater impulsivity, and increased levels of depression and social phobias (Gentile, et al., 2011); loss of sleep and memory (Dworak, Schierl, Burns, & Struder, 2007); and declines in creativity, productivity, and problem-solving and decision-making skills (Ward, Duke, Gneezy, & Bos 2017).

Postpositive research has also been employed in understanding the effects of media use on more overarching issues of development for both children and adolescents. Amy Nathanson and her colleagues studied preschoolers' television exposure and its effects on **theory of mind** (ToM). ToM is essential to children's development as social beings. It involves recognizing other people's beliefs, desires, and intentions in order to understand why they act a certain way or to predict how they will act. Rapidly developing during preschool years, "children achieve ToM when they understand that mental states (including thoughts, intentions, beliefs, desires, and emotions) are representational, can be private, and can change and differ across individuals. . . . Prior to ToM development, children believe that everyone perceives and participates in the same reality." In other words, what the child thinks is, of course, what everyone thinks. "ToM development reflects children's understanding that actions stem from individual beliefs and desires. . . . Without a ToM, children cannot easily understand deception, the moral distinction between mistakes and lies, or second-order mental states (e.g., what someone believes someone else thinks). As a result, these children may have less successful social lives" (Nathanson, Sharp, Aladé, Rasmussen, & Christy, 2013, p. 1089). Because ToM develops in rapid stages between 3 and 5 years old, reasoned Nathanson and her colleagues, important sources of interaction, information, and socialization—for example, parents, family structure, and media—would surely influence that development. Their research demonstrated that having a television in the bedroom and being exposed to higher levels of background television were related to reduced understanding of others' mental states, including their beliefs, desires, intentions, and emotions. Of note, though, parental discussion of what was on the screen was positively related to kids' ToM performance, an unsurprising result, as you'll read in the discussion of media literacy in Chapter 12.

Recognizing that young people use adolescence as a time to build and manage new identities and life stresses, Kristen Harrison (2006) studied television's effects on **self-complexity**, seeing oneself as having different self-concepts across different situations. Adolescents high in self-complexity can better manage the inevitable emotional and physical challenges that come with those turbulent years. "One might conceptualize high self-complexity as having one's self-concept 'eggs' in multiple 'baskets,'" she explains. "If one basket falls and its eggs break, there are still some intact because the trauma does not generalize to other baskets. Thus, an individual high in self-complexity who suffers a setback with respect to one aspect of self (e.g., a student who receives a poor grade in his [*sic*] senior honors seminar) has many other aspects of self (e.g., his loyalty, musical talent, good looks, and creativity) to fall back on to preserve his well-being and self-esteem" (p. 253). Self-complexity develops as young people encounter different situations, relationships, and social roles, and of course, they do so in large part through interaction with television. But where we might assume that the medium's wealth of (vicarious) situations, relationships, and social roles might help adolescents enrich their self-complexity, Harrison hypothesized that the opposite was more likely the case, in part because of the "narrow scope" of most television portrayals and the fact that "media use, itself an activity, may interfere with youngsters' opportunities to take part in new activities that would introduce them to real-life interests, roles, and ways of living, activities that build self-complexity through real life experience" (p. 254). Her discovery that declines in self-complexity occurred at about 20 hours of viewing per week led her to propose the **scope of self model**, which asserts that adolescents who have heavier media diets, television in particular, are exposed to "only a narrow slice of the vast diversity in real-world human existence . . . a constricted and simplified view of human attributes and endeavors" (p. 266) at the expense of more robust, real-life experiences. This effect will be strongest for those with fewer competing sources of information about themselves, such as family and community.

Gender Issues

Despite their focus on causal-effects models and their limited concern for broader social and cultural issues, by the 1970s effects researchers were starting to show interest in the developmental aspects of adolescents' gender and sexual identities. For example, Stanley Baran (1976a, 1976b) demonstrated the relationship between adolescents' and college students' satisfaction with their sexual identities and their consumption of film and television portrayals of physically romantic relationships, discovering greater dissatisfaction for those who were heavier consumers of those portrayals. In the 1980s Baran and John Courtright identified media portrayals of these relationships as a primary source of young people's acquisition of sexual information (Courtright & Baran, 1980). And in the 1990s George Comstock (1991) reviewed decades of research on young people's sex role socialization and concluded that a "modest but positive association" exists between television exposure and the holding of traditional notions of gender and sex roles (p. 175). He also acknowledged that those who consume nontraditional portrayals of gender can and do develop similarly nontraditional perceptions of sex roles. Moreover, not only can media portrayals socialize children by encouraging certain expectations of themselves, these portrayals can encourage expectations of others. Comstock noted, "Portrayals in television and other media of highly attractive persons may encourage dissatisfaction [with] or lowered evaluations of the attractiveness of those of the pertinent sex in real life" (p. 176).

This line of inquiry is not only alive and well today but is finding even stronger evidence of media influence than much of the early work. For example, Lelia Samson and Maria Grabe (2012) studied the "sexual propensities of emerging adults"— college students 17 to 25 years old—and their consumption of a wide variety of media (music videos, network and cable television, movies, and the Internet). Their results "point to media as a significant sexual socializing agent in shaping human psychosexual propensities. In fact, [their] study showed that media use has independent statistical associations with sexual excitation and inhibition mechanisms" (p. 293). Similarly, Hilary Gamble and Leslie Nelson (2016) studied college students, examining their use of television programming featuring relationships to shape expectations for sexual interaction in their real-life romantic relationships. The researchers relied on **scripting theory**, the idea that young people learn about sex through "snippets of information" they collect from a variety of sources, including peers, formal sex education, media, parents, and religion, from which they piece together memory structures called scripts that shape their attitudes, expectations, and behaviors surrounding sex (p. 149). Gamble and Nelson discovered that young women's viewing of that content was associated with the expectation of more sexual interaction, and with slight variation related to the realism of the content, they uncovered a similar pattern for men.

A related area of inquiry examines how media influence young people's perceptions of their attractiveness to others. Levina Clark and Mirika Tiggemann (2007), for example, examined young girls' satisfaction with their own appearance. Searching for the sources of 9- to 12-year-old girls' "body dissatisfaction," they demonstrated that "increased exposure to appearance media (both television and magazines) and taking part in peer appearance conversations were related to body dissatisfaction and dieting behaviors" (p. 84). Kimberly Bissell and Peiqin Zhou (2004), writing that there is "clear evidence that exposure to TDP (thinness depicting and promoting) media leads to distorted body-image perception in school-age females and college women," examined the effects specifically of entertainment and sports media exposure (p. 5). They discovered that women who were frequently exposed to "thin ideal media" were more likely to be dissatisfied with the way they looked and to take "dangerous steps to modify their body shapes" (p. 17). Similarly, Laura Vandenbosch and Steven Eggermont (2012) demonstrated "direct relationships between sexually objectifying media and the internalization of beauty ideals [in adolescent girls], and indirect relationships between sexually objectifying media and self-objectification, and body surveillance through the internalization of beauty ideals" (p. 869). And lest you think that these effects are female-specific, Laramie Taylor and Jhunehl Fortaleza (2016) demonstrated that exposure to violent narratives produced lower levels of self-perceived attractiveness, greater body anxiety, and increased endorsement of body modification practices in college-age men, as did viewing muscular-ideal images.

Critical researchers, like their effects-trend colleagues, have also examined gender issues. **Objectification theory**, drawn from feminist critical theory, is central to this work. It "posits that girls and women are typically acculturated to internalize an observer's perspective as a primary view of their physical selves" (Fredrickson & Roberts,

1997, p. 173). Taking that perspective, Rachael Calogero and Tracy Tylka (2010) argue that people's "gendered experiences of the body constrain and impact body image." As a result, "human bodies are not allowed to naturally develop into a diverse range of shapes, sizes, and attributes. They are shaped by societal stressors and pressures that render the majority of people's natural bodies deficient in some capacity, and thus in need of chronic bodily evaluation and modification in order to produce bodies that meet prescriptive social roles, enhance social value, and secure social power. In other words, gender is critical not only for determining what people's bodies are capable of, but also for constructing how bodies should look and be looked at to meet societal expectations for what it means to be a heterosexual woman or man" (p. 1). The result is low self-esteem, chronic body surveillance, and eating pathology.

Advertising to Children

Advertising's impact on children's development has also been studied from a variety of perspectives. Research indicates that children younger than 7 or 8 cannot distinguish between a television program and the advertising it houses. And although near 7 or 8 years old they can distinguish between commercials and other content, they do not necessarily understand the commercials' selling intent. The use of "nontraditional" advertising such as movie and in-video game product placements, product licensing, program sponsorship, and advergames makes matters even worse, as children as old as 10 "appear to have limited knowledge of [these] alternative marketing tactics and consequently lack the cognitive skills to evaluate them critically" (Owen, Lewis, Auty, & Buijzen, 2013, p. 195).

Much scholarly attention has centered on the advertising to kids of junk food and sugared snacks (Frechette, 2016; Boyland & Halford, 2012), linking it to epidemic levels of obesity in American children, who see anywhere from 4,400 to 7,600 food ads per year, the large majority of which are for unhealthy eating options (American Academy of Pediatrics, 2011). There is much research demonstrating a causal relationship between these commercials and children's preference and request for "high-calorie and low-nutrient foods and beverages" (Gottesdiener, 2012). There is even evidence that advertising alters young children's brains such that the mere presence of a brand logo activates those portions of their brains that control motivation (Bruce et al., 2014). Alcohol advertising to young children has also received research scrutiny. For example, Jerry Grenard and his colleagues demonstrated that younger adolescents are susceptible to the persuasive messages contained in televised alcohol commercials, and their positive response to those ads influences "some youth to drink more and experience drinking-related problems later in adolescence" (Grenard, Dent, & Stacy, 2013, p. e369).

Like their postpositivist colleagues, critical researchers—quite aware of the fact that the United States is the only developed nation in the world that allows unfettered and unregulated advertising to children (Sheehan, 2014)—have also taken on food advertising and other nutrition-related cultural factors and their implications for young people's physical development. "We are raising our children in a world that is vastly different than it was 40 or 50 years ago," explains obesity doctor Yoni Freedhoff. "Childhood obesity is a disease of the environment. It's a natural consequence of normal kids with normal genes being raised in unhealthy, abnormal environments" (as cited in Haelle, 2013). Freedhoff identified as problematic school schedules that deny teens sufficient sleep, the ubiquity of fast food, developments in technology, the disappearance of home-cooked meals, the flood of food advertising aimed at kids, the ready availability of low-cost processed foods, the expansion of sugared-soda serving sizes, and ready access to unhealthy snacks in vending machines in every corner of a young person's life (as cited in Haelle, 2013).

In fact, the occurrence of childhood and adolescent obesity has tripled in the United States since 1970, afflicting one in five school-age kids (Centers for Disease Control and Prevention, 2018). Data such as these have, according to researcher Charlene Elliott (2012), "prompted an increased scrutiny of the foodscape, along with the call for innovative strategies to make our social environments more supportive of healthy eating." Her approach to the issue was to examine the way supermarkets package child-targeted food to make them "fun" (p. 303). Elliot's semiotic analysis of 354 child-targeted products revealed that supermarkets employ bright colors, specialized fonts and graphics, labels on products identifying them as "fun foods," packaging for portability, and even though three out of four products she examined derived more than a fifth of their calories from sugar, nutrition claims to frame food as fun. Taking the "food is fun" critique in a somewhat different direction, Deborah Thomson (2010) examined online advergames (commercials disguised as video games). Analyzing the websites of two leading brands of sugared cereals, she argued that their "online cereal marketing disciplines the child (as) consumer/commodity through an immersive simulation of cereal marketing narratives. Both Frootloops.com and Luckycharms.com represent cereal as a valued (treasured, magical) item, and reward players not just for consuming/manipulating the desired food item, but also for mastering the marketing narratives/discourses guiding online play. Players are disciplined (through play) into a potentially unhealthy nutritional logic in which the most nutritionally bereft food items are most valuable and the consumptive possibilities are endless" (p. 438). Thomson's reading of these sites led her to argue, "It is thus imperative that cultural critics carefully unpack these emergent environments, along with their attendant discourses, narratives, and logics, not only in order to understand these new media forms, but also to expose their internal contradictions and raise important questions related to corporate ethics and public policy. This task is all the more pressing when it comes to the manipulation of childhood pleasures associated with digital game play as a persuasive agent to market food to children" (p. 441). You yourself can weigh in on an intriguing developmental argument against the advertising to children in the box entitled, "Advertising to Kids: We Protect Adults; Why Not Children?"

Loss of Childhood

Critical cultural studies researchers have also been concerned about the influence of media on childhood and adolescence beyond the issue of food advertising. They share effects-trend notions about media as young people's **early window**. That is, media allow children to see the world well before they are developmentally capable of competently interacting with it. As Joshua Meyrowitz (1985), speaking specifically of television, explained, it "escorts children across the globe even before they have permission to cross the street" (p. 238). What happens to young people's social development, he asks, when television treats them as "mini-adults"? Children's books, for example, are

ADVERTISING TO KIDS: WE PROTECT ADULTS; WHY NOT CHILDREN?

False or deceptive advertising is against the law. Section 5 of the Federal Trade Commission Act specifically states that unfair or deceptive advertising acts or practices are unlawful. And to make things clearer, Section 15 of that Act defines a false ad as one which is "misleading in a material respect." The FCC also has regulations covering deception in advertising. Section 317 of the Communications Act mandates that all broadcast advertising "be announced as paid for or furnished as the case may be." Most of the time the announcements are unnecessary. A commercial for a Chevy is a commercial, but less obvious commercials must be identified—for example, teaser ads with no identifiable sponsor (Carter, Franklin, & Wright, 2008). Of course, marketers are given wide latitude, as puffery, the little white lie, is permissible. No one really believes that Red Bull will give them wings.

So it's clear; our laws say people should be protected from false or misleading advertising. "It is a long-standing principle in communication law that for advertising to be considered fair, it must be readily identifiable as such to its intended audience," argues the American Psychological Association Task Force on Advertising and Children. "The premise underlying this legal requirement is that it is unfair and deceptive for commercials to bypass the cognitive defenses against persuasion which adults are presumed to have when they understand that a given message consists of advertising content and can identify the source of the message." This makes perfect sense, but the task force's authors continue, "If it is unfair and deceptive to seek to bypass the defenses that adults are presumed to have when they are aware that advertising is addressed to them, then it must likewise be considered unfair and deceptive to advertise to children in whom these defenses do not yet exist" (Wilcox et al., 2004, p. 40). Their argument is simple—all advertising to young children under 8 is in fact illegal. The Task Force continues, "It is clear that the age-based constraints on children's comprehension of the nature and purpose of commercials are grounded in fundamental limitations in youngsters' cognitive abilities. . . . Thus, based upon the compelling evidence . . .

that documents young children's limited ability to recognize and defend against commercial persuasion, we believe the most obvious implication of this knowledge is that advertising specifically directed to audiences of children below the age of roughly 7–8 years should be considered unfair" (p. 40).

What do you think? We learned in Chapter 2 that the First Amendment is based in part on the libertarian philosophy that people are good and rational and can discern good messages from bad. But, by definition, young children cannot. So should advertising to children who are developmentally incapable of judging the "goodness" of an ad's message—in fact, who are incapable of recognizing that an ad is an ad—be deserving of First Amendment protection as is other commercial speech?

Maybe looking at how other nations deal with the issue might help you formulate your answer. Would you be surprised to learn that of all the industrialized nations in the world, the United States is alone in relying solely on industry self-regulation to protect young people from advertising? For example, Norway, Quebec, and Sweden ban all advertising during television programming aimed at kids; more than 30 countries—for example, Australia, Malaysia, Korea, and Russia—have national laws that set various limits on television advertising to children; dozens of countries, among them the United Kingdom, Nigeria, Thailand, the Philippines, China, Denmark, and Romania, regulate the advertising of junk and sugared foods to young people. Quebec has a ban on fast food advertising to kids. It has the lowest obesity rate of all the Canadian provinces, and officials claim that the ban "decreases children's consumption by an estimated two to four billion calories" (Gottesdiener, 2012). Can you explain why the US seems out of step with other countries in shielding young children from potentially harmful commercials? How would political economy theorists answer this question? What might critical scholars Henry Giroux and Shirley Steinberg say? So now back to you. Should American children have the same protections from commercial influence as do kids in most of the rest of the world?

the only type of books that children are capable of reading, and their themes are geared to children's interests and experiences. Yet, as Meyrowitz argues, because all television is "educational television," there's no such thing as "children's television." The medium "allows the very young child to be 'present' at adult interactions," he writes. It "removes barriers that once divided people of different ages and reading abilities into different social situations." He likens parents' willingness to sit their kids in front of the set to a "decision to allow young children to be present at wars and funerals, courtships and seductions, criminal plots and cocktail parties. Young children may not fully understand the issues of sex, death, crime, and money that are presented to them on television. Or, put differently, they may understand these issues only in childlike ways. Yet television nevertheless exposes them to many topics and behaviors that adults have spent several centuries trying to keep hidden from children. Television thrusts children into a complex adult world" (p. 242).

Sociologist Neil Postman's (1994) argument for "the disappearance of childhood" rests in large part on this idea of the early window. He wrote, "Unlike infancy, childhood is a social artifact, not a biological category," one that is "difficult to sustain and, in fact, irrelevant," because ubiquitous connection to the media robs youngsters of "the charm, malleability, innocence, and curiosity" of childhood, leaving them "degraded and then transmogrified into the lesser features of pseudo-adulthood" (pp. xi–xii). And critical theory attention to young people extends well beyond the early window. Its central theme is the corporate takeover of children's and adolescents' development. They reject the view of childhood expressed by pioneering children's marketer James McNeal. "The consumer embryo begins to develop during the first year of existence," he said. "Children begin their journey in infancy, and they certainly deserve consideration as consumers at that time" (as cited in Barbaro, Earp, & Jhally, 2008).

As such, developmental researcher Shirley Steinberg (2011) argues that effects research on young people's development is of limited value in the face of **kinderculture**, the corporate construction of childhood. The writers of children's and adolescent's "cultural curriculum," she argues, "are not educational agencies but rather commercial concerns that operate not for the social good but for individual gain. Cultural pedagogy is structured by commercial dynamics, forces that impose themselves into all aspects of our own and our children's private lives" (p. 18). She continues, "The study of power and kinderculture reveals insights into North American politics that may at first glance seem only incidental to parents and child professionals—especially those of the positivist paradigm. When one begins to explore child activist avenues, he or she is immediately confronted with the concentration of power into fewer and increasingly corporate hands. . . . In light of the failure of oppositional institutions to challenge corporate hegemony, corporations to a large extent have free reign to produce almost any kinderculture that is profitable" (p. 31).

The product of this "hostile takeover of childhood," argues psychologist Susan Linn (2004), is the "adultification of children," in which their "physical, psychological, social, emotional, and spiritual development are all threatened when their value as consumers trumps their value as people" (p. 10). Young people, observes critical theorist Henry Giroux, arguably the most influential critic of the corporate takeover of youth, "now inhabit a cultural landscape in which, increasingly, they can only recognize themselves in terms preferred by the market. . . . [Y]outh are educated to become consuming subjects rather than civic-minded and critical citizens . . . [and] the culture of the market displaces civic culture" (Giroux & Pollock, 2011). Elsewhere, Giroux (2011) notes that the "'relentless expansion of a global market society' targets all children and youth, devaluing them by treating them as yet another 'market' to be commodified and exploited and conscripting them into the system through creating a new generation of consuming subjects. . . . The stark reality here is that the corporate media are being used to reshape kids' identities into that of consumers rather than citizens. . . . Kids may think they are immune to the incessant call to 'buy, buy, buy' and to think only about 'me, me, me,' but what is actually happening is a selective elimination and reordering of the possible modes of political, social, and ethical vocabularies made available to youth" (para. 15). And elsewhere as well, "As culture becomes increasingly commercialized, the only type of citizenship that adult society offers to children is that of consumerism" (Giroux, 2000, p. 19).

Finally, critical research and theory's ultimate goal is social change. As such, when considering media and young people's development, social critic Benjamin Barber (2007) calls for the creation of a truly civil society "that acknowledges the real delights of childhood and helps children be children again by preserving them from the burdens of an exploitative and violent adult world"—a society that "refuses to 'free' them from parents and other gatekeepers in order to turn them over to market-mad pied pipers who lead them over a commercial precipice down into the mall." Barber concludes, "Children should play not pay, act not watch, learn not shop. . . . Not everything needs to earn a profit, not everyone needs to be a shopper—not all the time" (p. 338).

GROWING UP CONNECTED: NEW PERSONAL TECHNOLOGIES AND DEVELOPMENT

Effects and critical cultural researchers and theorists alike have undertaken serious study of youthful use of personal technologies—smartphones, tablets, and social networking sites (SNS). We will devote parts of several upcoming chapters to the challenges these new and emerging technologies pose for mass communication theory. Here, though, we address some growing areas of interest, specifically as they relate to individuals' use of those technologies. First, as we've seen earlier in this chapter, effects research has demonstrated a wide variety of harmful effects brought about by young people's interaction with screens rather than with other humans. The new personal communication technologies carry with them the same set of concerns—for example, reduced human contact, especially with parents and peers, and a lack of stimulation from the natural environments. Consumption data suggest these concerns are warranted. Apple and Google offer tens of thousands of kid apps with names such as *BabyPlayFace* and *Elmo's Birthday*, and just under two thirds of American parents admit giving their children a smartphone or tablet to keep them busy (Richter, 2013). Ninety-five percent of American teens have a smartphone or access to one, and while 81% claim it keeps them "more connected" with their friends, nearly half say they are "overwhelmed by the drama" they experience online (Anderson & Jiang, 2018). More than half of youthful smartphone users acknowledge that they spend too much time on their devices (Jiang, 2018). And perhaps leaving the technology behind might be wise, as recent research has discovered that people's constant attention to their cellphones, with its attendant "cognitive distraction [and] reduced situation awareness," has produced physical alterations in walking, ultimately impacting "gait to such a degree that it may compromise safety" (Lamberg & Muratori, 2012, p. 688). Other medical research shows that young adults' excessive use of smartphones and tablets (with heads constantly craned downward toward the screen) is causing the unnatural development of boney protuberances—something akin to horns—sticking out from their skulls, just above the neck (Shahar & Sayers, 2016).

While much social scientific interest centers on time—every minute with a device is one minute less with a human (kids need laps, not apps)—the subject of alterations in the way young people interact and identify with these technologies also motivates much inquiry. For example, Adrian Ward and his colleagues demonstrated the operation of the **brain drain hypothesis**, noting that "the mere presence of one's own smartphone may occupy limited-capacity cognitive resources." They observed that even if users "are successful at maintaining sustained attention—as when avoiding the temptation to check their phones—the mere presence of these devices reduces available cognitive capacity" (Ward, Duke, Gneezy, & Bos 2017, p. 140). In other words, because users are forcing themselves to not think about their phones, their capacity to focus on what they are actually doing is diminished. Moreover, as users are increasingly dependent on their phones, they come to see them as extensions of themselves. As a result, according to Seunghee Han, Ki Joon Kim, and Jang Hyun Kim (2017), "They are more likely to get attached to the devices, which, in turn, leads to **nomophobia** by heightening the phone proximity-seeking tendency" (p. 419). Nomophobia, they write, is a feeling of "discomfort or anxiety caused by the nonavailability of a mobile device enabling habitual virtual communication" (p. 419). The easiest path to ameliorating this discomfort? Reconnection.

But not all analysis of these technologies is so pessimistic, with some researchers focusing on the technologies' ability to expand opportunities for interaction beyond what might otherwise be available to some users. For example, Sherri Grasmuck, Jason Martin, and Shanyang Zhao (2009) discovered that racial and ethnic minorities use Facebook to present "highly social, culturally explicit and elaborated narratives of self [to] reflect a certain resistance to the racial silencing of minorities by dominant color-blind ideologies of broader society" (p. 158). Likewise, Levi Baker and Debra Oswald (2010) demonstrated that "online social networking services may provide a comfortable environment within which shy individuals can interact with others" (p. 873). There is even evidence that online dating services, because they expand the circle of people users typically interact with, have produced an increase in the number of interracial marriages over the last two decades in the United States (Ortega & Hergovich, 2017).

Effects and critical researchers alike are also investigating other developmentally important issues such as the online building and maintenance of identity, the redefinition of friendship and community, and the interaction of technology and civic involvement. But as a prelude to that inquiry, an obvious question needs to be addressed: Why do people use social networking sites to interact with others, especially when distance isn't a factor? Given that there are more than two billion users on Facebook alone, there must be some gratification in online interactions with others. To address this question, psychologists Ashwini Nadkarni and Stefan Hofmann (2012) offered their **dual-factor model of Facebook (FB) use**, which can be applied to SNS use in general. They explain, "FB use is primarily motivated by two basic social needs: (1) *the need to belong*, and (2) *the need for self-presentation*. The *need to belong* refers to the intrinsic drive to affiliate with others and gain social acceptance, and the *need for self-presentation* to the continuous process of impression management. These two motivational factors can co-exist, but can also each be the single cause for FB use" (p. 245; italics in the original). This need to belong is important because people are highly dependent on social support from others, and exclusion can cause loss of self-esteem and reduced emotional well-being. Self-esteem, according to Nadkarni and Hofmann, serves as a *sociometer*, a monitor of acceptability by others. Because social network sites foster a sense of belonging, their use can increase self-esteem and therefore feelings of acceptability. People's need for self-presentation online is the same as offline. We know ourselves through our interaction with others, and if others who are of importance to us are online, that's where we must be to present ourselves. But this raises questions of obvious interest to researchers working in the symbolic interactionism tradition (see Chapter 13): *How* do we present ourselves on social networking sites? Can and do we work to shape the reflection we see in the responses of online significant others? Who is a significant other online?

SNS users routinely employ "screen names, profiles, and messages" as a means to "foster others' impression formation about them," and these "users may select what information they want to include in a profile to highlight their most positive qualities" (Zywica & Danowski, 2008, p. 6). But how and why do they do this? These researchers offered as their explanation the **idealized virtual identity hypothesis**, which posits the tendency for creators of social network site profiles to display idealized characteristics that do not reflect their actual personalities. Mitja Back and his colleagues tested this hypothesis and discovered it happens far less frequently than most people think. In fact, they demonstrated that, for most users, what they called online social networking (OSN) "may constitute an extended social context in which to express one's actual personality characteristics, thus fostering accurate interpersonal perceptions. OSNs integrate various sources of personal information that mirror those found in personal environments, private thoughts, facial images, and social behavior, all of which are known to contain valid information about personality." In opposition to the idealized virtual identity hypothesis, they proposed the "**extended real-life hypothesis** [which] predicts that people use OSNs to communicate their real personality" (Back et al., 2010, p. 372). But why don't social networkers routinely create less than totally accurate idealized virtual identities since it's easy enough to do? The researchers offered two answers: "Creating idealized identities should be hard to accomplish because (a) OSN profiles include information about one's reputation that is difficult to control (e.g., wall posts) and (b) friends provide accountability and subtle feedback on one's Profile" (p. 372). They note further that "Individuals cannot be separated from social processes and interactions" (p. 39). This is exactly what a symbolic interaction approach would have predicted: Identity is constructed and maintained through interaction with others; we look to others for "accountability and subtle feedback" to know who we are. Online or off, we present ourselves based on who others think we are, which itself is based on the responses from others that we have already received.

A related question is: What are the interpersonal communication advantages and disadvantages of using this particular medium for interacting with others? Petter Brandtzæg (2012) assessed the "social costs and benefits" of social networking and determined that SNS use builds "social capital and might strengthen social bonds as SNSs give free and easy communication with family, friends, and acquaintances regardless of time and place. . . . Examining the results [of his research] in light of the current media debate, they do not support the anxiety about 'antisocial networking' or low social involvement. SNS communication does not seem to replace intimacy or face-to-face interaction. In fact, SNS users are actually more likely to socially interact face-to-face and report more social capital compared to nonusers" (pp. 481–482). "Social capital" in this instance is the building of social connections and networks and the resulting norms and trust that are built, enabling people to act together more effectively.

But are we acting together more efficiently? In the "early days" of the Internet, Robert Kraut and his colleagues undertook a study of what they called "the Internet paradox." The Internet, they wrote, "could change the lives of average citizens as much as did the telephone in the early part of the 20th century and television in the 1950s and 1960s. Researchers and social critics are debating whether the Internet is improving or harming participation in community life and social relationships." They studied 169 Internet users in 73 different households during the users first 1 to 2 years online and discovered that "the Internet was used extensively for communication. Nonetheless, greater use of the Internet was associated with declines in participants' communication with family members in the household, declines in the size of their social circle, and increases in their depression and loneliness" (Kraut et al., 1998, p. 1017).

This concern, what Brandtzæg (2012) called "anxiety" over "antisocial networking," has never faded. Are the new communication technologies connecting us to the world as they disconnect us from each other another? Are we are losing our sense of community? Are we increasingly socially isolated, spending time in the real world with smaller numbers of people who are very much like ourselves? "The implications of such a trend are alarming," observe Keith Hampton and his colleagues. "They indicate a decline in the availability of broad social support within social networks in the form of companionship and instrumental and emergency aid and an increased likelihood that important matters are discussed only within small, closed groups" (Hampton, Sessions, & Her, 2010, p. 131). These researchers' analysis of more than 20 years' worth of data from the US General Social Survey (a standard core of demographic, behavioral, and attitudinal questions asked annually and overseen by the National Science Foundation) suggests that these fears about the increasing isolation of Americans, while not completely unreasonable, are exaggerated. They found that "neither Internet nor mobile phone use is associated with having fewer core discussion confidants or having less diverse ties with whom to discuss important matters" (p. 148). In fact, their analysis demonstrated that smartphone ownership and some SNS activity actually increased the number of close confidants, and Internet users were far more likely to discuss important issues with people outside their immediate families and even with those of different political stripes.

Yet there is indeed evidence justifying critics' "anxiety" over growing social isolation. John Cacioppo, known for his development of the elaboration likelihood model (see Chapter 10), has taken up this line of inquiry. He examined the connection between loneliness and the frequency of people's interactions on Facebook, chat rooms, online games, and dating sites, comparing them to the frequency of interactions conducted face-to-face. His results? "The greater the proportion of face-to-face interactions, the less lonely you are . . . The greater the proportion of online interactions, the lonelier you are." But his argument was not that Facebook makes people lonely, but that it is a "tool." "It's like a car," he said. "You can drive it to pick up your friends. Or you can drive alone" (as cited in Marche, 2012, para. 25–26).

Fenne große Deters and Matthias R. Mehl (2012) studied precisely this issue, experimentally demonstrating that social networking may not be as relationally isolating as many critics believe. They discovered that an increase in "status updating activity reduced loneliness . . . [and] that the decrease in loneliness was due to participants feeling more connected to their friends on a daily basis" (p. 579). Friends' feedback did not reduce loneliness; the simple act of updating one's status—that is, activity—reduced anxiety, mirroring the beneficial influence of active use on well-being discussed later in this chapter.

But why do so many users spend so much time on these platforms? Are the benefits worth the cost of the use? Tracii Ryan and her colleagues examined **SNS addiction**—use that is habitual, excessive, or motivated by a desire for mood alteration—as one answer. Recognizing that SNS use is intentional and for the pursuit of benefits such as relationship maintenance, passing time, entertainment, and companionship, the researchers discovered that such use (specifically of Facebook in their analysis) can indeed become excessive or habitual, especially if users primarily use social networking to escape from negative moods (Ryan, Chester, Reece, & Xenos, 2014). They reference the **social skills model of problematic SNS use**, which argues that users who *prefer* communication with others online (and are presumably less socially skilled) are at greater risk of succumbing to addiction. In fact, the American Psychiatric Association lists "Internet addiction disorder" as a recognized mental illness in its *Diagnostic and Statistical Manual of Mental Disorders*.

Social Media and Well-Being

Writing for the American Academy of Pediatrics, Gwenn O'Keefe and Kathleen Clarke-Pearson (2011) identified the existence of **Facebook depression**: "depression that develops when preteens and teens spend a great deal of time on social media sites, such as Facebook, and then begin to exhibit classic symptoms of depression. Acceptance by and contact with peers is an important element of adolescent life. The intensity of the online world is thought to be a factor that may trigger depression in some adolescents" (p. 802). Then why do users spend so much time on SNS? Christina Sagioglou and Tobias Greitmeyer (2014) argued that it is because they expect something better, a pleasurable experience. The problem, they said, resides in **affective forecasting error**—the discrepancy between the expected and actual emotions generated by Facebook activity. The researchers demonstrated that this unmet expectation produced declines in users' mood after using the social networking site. In fact, their findings led them to express surprise "that Facebook enjoys such great popularity" (p. 361).

Larry Rosen and his colleagues also examined this relationship between social networking and depression. They discovered that a greater amounts of SNS use and working harder to manage one's self-impression on those sites predicted increased clinical symptoms of major depression and dysthymia (persistent depressive disorder) (Rosen, Whaling, Rab, Carrier, & Cheever, 2013). Conversely, Melissa Hunt and her colleagues experimentally demonstrated that lowering the amount of time college students spent on SNS led to (caused) reductions in loneliness, depression, and anxiety (Hunt, Marx, Lipson, & Young, 2018).

Scholarly attention to SNS has expanded beyond depression to include the broader realm of subjective well-being—that is, how people feel about themselves. Subjective well-being involves both how people feel about themselves in the moment and how satisfied they are, in general, with their own lives, and is strongly related to a wide variety of beneficial life outcomes, such as better health and a longer life (Boehm, Peterson, & Kubzansky, 2011), career success (Diener, Nickerson, Lucas, & Sandvik, 2002), and greater marital satisfaction (Lyubomirsky, King, & Diener, 2005). Ethan Kross and his colleagues (Kross et al., 2013) examined how Facebook use influenced college students' well-being while online and away from SNS. They found that "Facebook use predicts negative shifts on both of these variables over time. . . . [T]he more [people] used Facebook over two weeks, the more their life satisfaction levels declined over time" (p. 1). Holly Shakya and Nicholas Christakis (2017) also discovered that Facebook use was negatively associated with well-being. Their research showed that the more times users clicked "like" on someone else's content, clicked a link to another site or article, or updated their own Facebook status, the more likely they would be to self-report mental health decline, leading Shakya and Christakis to conclude, "The negative associations of Facebook use were comparable to or greater in magnitude than the positive impact of offline interactions" (p. 203).

Philippe Verduyn and his colleagues demonstrated, however, that it is not SNS use itself but how active people are in that use that is significant. Specifically, *passive* use leads to lower subjective well-being and *active* use boosts it. They wrote, "Passively using social network sites [monitoring other people's lives without engaging in direct exchanges with others] provokes social comparisons and envy, which have negative downstream consequences for subjective well-being. In contrast, when active usage of social network sites [activities that facilitate direct exchanges with others] predicts subjective well-being, it seems to do so by creating social capital and stimulating feelings of social connectedness" (Verduyn, Ybarra, Résibois, Jonides, & Kross, 2017, p. 274). This research, like much of the wealth of related inquiry making similar findings, is based in **social comparison theory**, the idea that people, in order to satisfy their need to evaluate their own opinions and abilities and to reduce uncertainties they may have about themselves, make "comparative judgments of social stimuli on particular content dimensions" (Kruglanski & Mayseless, 1990, p. 196). That comparison can be either upward, where people see others as superior in some aspect, or downward, where the comparison leads them to think themselves superior. If you've spent any time at all on SNS, you know that the vast majority of what users post about themselves and their lives is quite positive (few people post their failures), so most comparisons are made "up" against the best and brightest (Krasnova, Wenninger, Widjaja, & Buxmann, 2013). The same holds true for the viewing of "selfies," photo self-portraits posted to SNS (Wang, Yang, & Haigh, 2017). Finally, Hunt Allcott and his research team tracked nearly 3,000 Facebook users who were paid to "deactivate" Facebook for four weeks. They discovered that a month away from this particular SNS and its "diverse" benefits (for example, "entertainment, a means to organize a charity or an activist group, or a vital social lifeline for those who are otherwise isolated") produced more face-to-face time with friends and family, less political knowledge but also less political partisanship, an extra hour a day of "downtime," and a slight improvement in well-being (Allcott, Braghieri, Eichmeyer, & Gentzkow, 2019, p. 35).

REVIEW OF LEARNING OBJECTIVES

- Develop answers to questions, asked by both effects and critical researchers, on the relationship between media consumption and young people's cognitive and emotional development.

Television is children's early window on a world they might not yet be equipped to engage. As such, researchers took up questions of the development of young people's gender and sexual identity, the influence of advertising on their physical development, and how the corporate takeover of childhood has redefined the concept of childhood altogether. They have identified effects such as media serving as superpeers and impeding the development of theory of mind and scope of self.

- Appreciate cultural criticism of kinderculture and its redefining of childhood.

Cultural critics contend that kinderculture, the corporate construction of childhood, is a product of media's commercial self-interest. Children learn a "cultural curriculum" that benefits the market, not their development, ultimately rendering them adultified.

- Explain the contributions—positive and negative—to young people's personal development and well-being brought about by social media.

Effects research has demonstrated a wide variety of harmful effects brought about by young people's interaction with screens rather than with other humans. The new personal communication technologies carry with them the same set of concerns—for example, reduced human contact, especially with parents and peers, and lack of stimulation from the natural environments. Nonetheless, people use SNS for self-presentation and because of their need to belong. They tend to present a realistic version of themselves when on social media. That use, however, comes with some drawbacks, as explained, for example, by the brain drain hypothesis, which holds that the mere presence of one's smartphone may occupy limited-capacity cognitive resources. Users may also experience nomophobia, a feeling of discomfort or anxiety caused by the nonavailability of their smartphone. Some users may suffer from Facebook depression or Facebook envy, raising questions of the relationship between SNSs and subjective well-being, and social media use can lead to social isolation or it may not; the outcome is dependent on how users choose to participate in social media. Positive findings surrounding SNS focus on their ability to give voice to shy people and groups typically silenced by the larger culture.

CRITICAL THINKING QUESTIONS

1. Do you think the concept of childhood has been redefined in contemporary times? Talk about this with your parents. Ask them if they think their childhoods were similar to the one you lived. If they see differences, ask them why they think those differences exist. How much attention do they pay to mass media issues? How much attention do you?

2. How important are brands to you? How important were they—designer jeans, expensive sneakers, and the like—when you were a teenager? How much of your identity, your sense of who you were, was tied up in what you wore, drove, and consumed? Did you ever reflect on why those products held such value for you? If so, what conclusions about them—and you—did you come to?

3. Are you on SNS? Based on their findings, the Hunt research team identified 30 minutes a day as the point at which well-being begins to suffer. Do you usually exceed that amount of time? If so, how do you usually feel while online and after ending a session? How active is your use? The Verduyn team seems to have thrown users a lifeline with their argument about active use. Can you legitimately accept it? Do you tend to make upward or downward comparisons? How do they make you feel about yourself?

KEY TERMS

adultification
superpeer theory
theory of mind
self-complexity
scope of self model
scripting theory
objectification theory
early window
kinderculture
brain drain hypothesis

nomophobia
dual-factor model of Facebook (FB) use
idealized virtual identity hypothesis
extended real-life hypothesis
SNS addiction
social skills model of problematic
   SNS use
Facebook depression
affective forecasting error
social comparison theory

GLOSSARY

adultification: When children's value as consumers trumps their value as people, threatening their physical, psychological, social, emotional, and spiritual development

superpeer theory: Media serve as powerful best friends in sometimes making risky behaviors seem like normative behavior

theory of mind: Children's recognition of others' beliefs, desires, and intentions in order to understand why they act a certain way or to predict how they will act

self-complexity: Seeing oneself as having different self-concepts across different situations

scope of self model: Adolescents who have heavier media diets are exposed to a constricted and simplified view of human attributes and endeavors at the expense of more robust, real-life experiences, reducing their sense of self-complexity

scripting theory: Young people learn about sex through snippets of information they collect from a variety of sources from which they piece together scripts that shape their attitudes, expectations, and behaviors surrounding sex

objectification theory: Theory arguing that females internalize others' perspective as a primary view of their physical selves

early window: Idea that media allow children to see the world before they have the skill to successfully act in it

kinderculture: The corporate construction of childhood

brain drain hypothesis: Idea that the mere presence of one's own smartphone occupies limited-capacity cognitive resources that might be better used on the task at hand

nomophobia: Feelings of discomfort or anxiety caused by the nonavailability of a mobile device enabling habitual virtual communication

dual-factor model of Facebook (FB) use: Social networking use is primarily motivated by the need to belong and the need for self-presentation

idealized virtual identity hypothesis: Tendency for creators of social network site profiles to display idealized characteristics that do not reflect their actual personalities

extended real-life hypothesis: Idea that people use social networking sites to communicate their real personality

SNS addiction: Use of SNS that is habitual, excessive, or motivated by a desire for mood alteration

social skills model of problematic SNS use: Idea that SNS users who prefer communication with others online are at greater risk of succumbing to addiction

Facebook depression: Depression that develops when preteens and teens spend a great deal of time on social media sites and then begin to exhibit classic symptoms of depression

affective forecasting error: Discrepancy between the expected and actual emotions generated by SNS activity

social comparison theory: Theory that people evaluate their own opinions and abilities and reduce uncertainties by making comparative judgments of social stimuli on particular content dimensions

CHAPTER 9

Audience Theories: Uses and Reception

Consider the ways we use media during a typical day. For most of us that use is a routine activity that takes up a considerable amount of our free time and requires little planning. With the development of large-scale social media and smartphones to access and use legacy media, we can surround ourselves with powerful forms of entertainment and information wherever we go. In the past we could carry print media or portable audio devices with us, but now we can enjoy rich audiovisual media wherever and whenever we choose. If there are empty spaces in our daily routines, we can easily fill them with media content. How often do you use your smartphone while you are in the middle of situations involving family and friends? You may be checking Instagram, sending a text message, watching the latest K-pop video on YouTube, or defending your empire from invasion. But why do we use media the way we do? What are we seeking from media, and are we getting what we want? Do media easily satisfy us, or do we constantly change our uses in search of something more? How often do we stop to think about what we are doing with media? Has the increasing availability of social media enabled us to form stronger ties with friends or our community? Or are we merely getting more of the same things we got from legacy media but delivered in more convenient and attractive audiovisual packages?

During the past 20 years the sharing of digital media content on the Internet has risen exponentially. This growth was initially driven by Internet music services (legal and otherwise) such as Napster, Rhapsody, iTunes, RealPlayer, Kazaa, and Morpheus. Today more than 1.2 billion songs are downloaded *daily* from Internet file-sharing sites (Bundy, 2017). In addition, literally hundreds of millions of people use the Internet to share movies, television programs, photos, and e-books; anything that can be digitized can be shared. Some of this sharing is legal, but much of it involves violation of copyright laws.

This sharing is revolutionizing how we use media. We can access content anytime we want using an ever-increasing array of devices. More than 77% of Americans have Internet-capable smartphones. Fifty-three percent have tablet computers that, like the desktop and laptop computers owned by 73% of Americans (Pew Research Center, 2018), can access not only the vast treasures of the Internet but, because of

cloud computing (the storage of digital content, including personal information and system-operating software, on distant, third-party servers offering on-demand access), their own personally collected content. Sales of devices for storing, accessing, and playing digital files have risen exponentially over the past two decades. What is going on? Does it mean that Americans are becoming so active and involved in their use of media that they are willing to routinely buy expensive technology upgrades and learn the latest media-use skills needed to operate their devices? If we are collecting, organizing, and using digital files, how satisfied are we with what we are doing? Do we compete with friends to build a longer Snapchat string of images or download more movies? Now that we have easy access to unusual, highly specialized music we can't get from the local music store (if there still is one), has music become more meaningful or important in our lives? Do we appreciate the ability to create highly personalized collections of movies or television shows, or are we simply hoarding content that we rarely access?

The digital file-sharing phenomenon provides a dramatic example of how the availability of a new technology can bring about widespread changes in what people do with media. In turn, these changes can have a powerful impact on the media industries, on technology manufacturers, and on ourselves and the people around us. Even if we don't change our uses of media, we can be affected if others change theirs.

It's important to remember that our personal uses of media are never unique to ourselves. Millions of other people engage in the same activities—often at the same time. As we have seen in previous chapters, this widespread simultaneous use of media has long been of interest to media researchers. However, early researchers focused mostly on describing audiences and on determining whether media had direct effects on people. But by the 1960s effects research was not producing many new insights. As a result, over the last 50 years researchers have turned their attention to different questions and developed new theories of media that have produced insight into why people use specific media and the meaning that use has for them.

This simple idea—that people put specific media and specific media content to specific use in the hopes of having some specific need or set of needs gratified—forms the basis of the theories discussed in this chapter. Unlike many of the perspectives we've examined already, these **active-audience theories** do not attempt to understand what the *media do to people*; instead they focus on assessing what *people do with media*. For this reason they are referred to as audience-centered rather than source-dominated theories. Initially most were micro-level theories rather than macro-level perspectives. They were concerned with understanding how and why individuals use media, and they have been developed by both empirical and critical or cultural studies researchers.

Much of the postpositivist research we reviewed in previous chapters was effects-trend research, which assumed that media do things to people, often without their consent or desire. This inquiry typically focused on negative effects—the bad things that happen to people because they are exposed to problematic media content. Effects were caused by a variety of content, from political propaganda to dramatized presentations of sex and violence. In this chapter we consider a very different type of media effect—effects we consciously or routinely seek every time we turn to media for some particular purpose.

Study of these effects was slow to develop. Mass society theory and fear of propaganda focused researchers' attention on the macroscopic, source-dominated, negative consequences of media. Audience members were assumed to be passively responding to whatever content media companies made available to them. There were some early critics of this viewpoint. For example, political philosopher John Dewey (1927) argued that people could make good use of media. To him, propaganda was a problem that should be solved through public education rather than censorship; if people could be taught to make better use of media content, they wouldn't need to be sheltered from it (Chapter 2). Despite these arguments empirical research remained focused on locating evidence of how average people were manipulated by media. Similarly, early political economy and cultural studies research assumed that mass audiences were easily manipulated by elites. Media content served to promote a false consciousness that led people to act against their interests. Elites used media to control society (Chapter 5).

Eventually the early effects research discovered that people weren't as vulnerable to propaganda as mass society theory had predicted. The evidence suggested that people were protected from manipulation by opinion leaders and their own well-formed, intensely held attitudes. They were selective in choosing, interpreting, and remembering media content. But even these seemingly optimistic conclusions were associated with a pessimistic view of the average person. Most people were irrational and incapable of critically evaluating and resisting propaganda messages. Researchers concluded that if the barriers protecting people were broken down, individuals could be easily manipulated. Scholars were slow to develop the perspective that average people can be responsible media consumers who use media for their own worthwhile purposes—an active audience.

The theories covered in this chapter tend to be microscopic and have limited concern for the larger social order in which media operate. They concentrate on understanding how audiences routinely use media and are affected by this use. They ask, "Why do people seek entertainment and information from media, and what purposes does this content serve for them? How do they cope with the flow of content from those media?" They don't ask, "*Should* people be seeking information or entertainment from media, or what are the *consequences for society* when people routinely choose to use media in certain ways each day?" This doesn't mean the findings generated by the theories covered in this chapter don't have larger implications or can't be used to answer questions about the consequences of media use for the social order. Active-audience theories can be quite compatible with macroscopic theories that attempt to answer such questions, as you'll soon see.

LEARNING OBJECTIVES

After studying this chapter you should be able to

- Explain why postpositivist and cultural studies researchers became increasingly focused on media audiences rather than media effects and how the resulting active-audience theories differ from the effects theories dominant in earlier mass communication theory.
- Recognize the ways audiences can be active and how that activity can be measured.
- Identify and assess the propositions of uses-and-gratification theory.

- Differentiate media functions and media uses.
- Judge the contributions of entertainment theory to our understanding of people's use of entertainment content.
- Understand why reception studies posed a challenge to both effects-trend notions and older forms of neo-Marxist theory.
- Recognize feminist contributions to the development of reception studies.

OVERVIEW

During the 1970s and 1980s postpositivist and cultural studies researchers became increasingly focused on media audiences. Their goal was to gain a more useful understanding of what people were doing with media in their daily lives. Television viewing was exploding during the 1960s and 1970s, but very little research was undertaken to examine what people were doing when they watched. Television ratings data showed that millions of viewers were routinely drawn to TV programs and that many people watched for more than six hours every day. Were viewers primarily passive consumers of entertainment, or was television viewing serving more important purposes? Were most people couch potatoes or thoughtful, reflective viewers? As this research developed, new and less pessimistic conceptualizations of audiences were formed. Some postpositivist researchers reexamined limited-effects findings about audiences and concluded that people were not as passive as these effects theories implied. At the same time, some cultural studies researchers were conducting their own audience research and discovering that the power of elites to manipulate audiences was not as great as had been assumed by neo-Marxist theorists.

Of course, the possibility of responsible audience activity was never totally ignored in early media research, but much of it gave audiences insufficient credit for selection, interpretation, and use of media content. We will see that early development of audience-centered theories was hampered by confusion about the concepts of "functions" and "functionalism" and by methodological and theoretical disputes. We will consider what it means to be an active audience member and examine in detail several audience-centered approaches.

The theories introduced in the early part of this chapter are important because they were among the first to make a priority of studying audience activity, viewing it in a more or less positive way. As we shall see, this doesn't mean they ignored the possibility of long-term negative consequences. Active audiences can be misled by poorly constructed or inaccurate media presentations (for example, Gerbner, 2010). Audience members need to be aware of what they are doing with media and to take responsibility for their actions. We will explain how the development of audience-centered theories challenged limited-effects notions. In doing so we revisit functional analysis and discuss how it formed the basis of much audience-centered theory. We describe the **uses-and-gratifications** approach, both as initially conceived and as it matured and developed. We explore some of its central notions—for example, the meaning of an active audience, how activity is measured, and the use of this approach to understand effects.

Then we look at **entertainment theory**. It seeks to understand what our use of entertaining media content does to and for us. Sometimes, maybe even often, these effects occur without our awareness; however, other times we may have quite specific goals in mind and actively match our media use to a desired outcome—for example, as explained by James Potter (2012): "Over time, people have developed strategies to use the media to manage their moods. They learn how to do this by trial and error, so that when they are in a mood they do not like they know what media and which messages to search out" (pp. 208–209).

We will also consider another audience-centered perspective, reception studies, originally developed by cultural studies researchers in Britain. It also assumes that audiences are active, but it uses a different strategy for studying media consumers and reaches different but often complementary conclusions. Even though reception studies was consciously developed as a challenge to effects-trend notions, its conclusions aren't contradictory. In most cases the findings provide an alternate set of insights that add to rather than refute postpositivist findings.

AUDIENCE THEORIES: FROM SOURCE-DOMINATED TO ACTIVE-AUDIENCE PERSPECTIVES

Propaganda theories are concerned with audiences. As we saw in Chapter 2, the power of propaganda resides in its ability to quickly reach vast audiences and expose them to the same simple but subversive messages. In these theories the propagandist dominates the audience and controls the messages that reach it. Research focuses on how propagandists are able to manipulate audiences using messages that affect them as the propagandist intends. They are source-dominated theories, centering their attention primarily on message sources and content, not on the interests or needs of the audiences those sources want to influence. They discount or ignore audience members' ability to resist messages. As media theory developed, this focus gradually shifted. As early as the 1940s, the work of people like Herta Herzog, Robert Merton, Paul Lazarsfeld, and Frank Stanton reflected at least the implicit concern for studying an active, gratifications-seeking audience. Lazarsfeld and Stanton (1942) produced a series of books and studies throughout the 1940s that paid significant attention to how audiences used media to organize their lives and experiences. For example, they examined the value of early-morning radio reports to farmers. They developed a device to measure audience reactions to radio program content as people were listening to it. As part of that series, Bernard Berelson (1949) published a classic media-use study of the disruption experienced by readers during a newspaper strike. He reported convincing evidence that newspapers formed an important part of many people's daily routine.

Herta Herzog is often credited with being the originator of the uses-and-gratifications approach, although she most likely did not give it its name. Interested in how and why people listened to the radio, she studied fans of a popular quiz show (1940) and soap opera listeners (1944). This latter work, entitled "Motivations and Gratifications of Daily Serial Listeners," provides an in-depth examination of media gratifications. She interviewed 100 radio soap opera fans and identified "three major types of gratification." First, listening was "merely a means of emotional release"; "a second and commonly recognized form of enjoyment concerns the opportunities for wishful thinking"; and the "third and commonly unsuspected form of gratification concerns the advice obtained from listening to daytime serials" (pp. 51–55). Herzog wanted to understand why so many housewives were attracted to radio soap operas. In contrast with the typical effects research conducted in Lazarsfeld's shop, her work didn't try to measure the influence that soap operas had on women. She was satisfied with assessing their reasons and experiences—their uses and gratifications.

One of the first college mass communication textbooks, *The Process and Effects of Mass Communication*, also offered an early active-audience conceptualization. Author Wilbur Schramm (1954) asked the question, "What determines which offerings of mass communication will be selected by a given individual?" (p. 19). His answer was the **fraction of selection**:

$$\frac{\text{Expectation of Reward}}{\text{Effort Required}}$$

His point was that people weigh the level of reward (gratification) they expect from a given medium or message against how much effort they must make to secure that reward. Review your own news consumption, for example. If you are a regular television viewer, you likely think that it's easier to watch the network news or flip on CNN than it is to get news online. Television news is presented attractively and dramatically. The images are usually arresting, and the narration and anchorperson's report are typically crisp and to the point. You never have to leave your chair to watch; once you settle on a specific news broadcast, you don't have to touch the remote again, and when the show you're watching ends, you're already in place for *The Walking Dead*. This concerns only the denominator (effort required), and there is little effort required to consume a televised news program.

But if you routinely use a smartphone to access social media, you might instead choose to get your news online because the reward you expect from your online news activity (news recommended by friends, news filtered according to your past interests, news anytime you want it, ability to select just the stories you are interested in, more detail, greater depth, more variety of approach, more sophisticated reports, alternative perspectives, useful links, opportunity to comment) makes the additional effort (waiting for your social media app to retrieve relevant news, browsing through the news you receive, selecting specific news items, reading them, searching for alternative stories, accessing related links) worthwhile. You can develop your own fractions for your own media use of all kinds, but the essence of Schramm's argument remains: We all make decisions about which content we choose based on our expectations of having some need met, even if that decision is to not make a choice—say between two early evening situation comedies, for example, because we can't find the remote control and it's too much trouble to get up and change the channel—because all we really want is some background noise while we sit and daydream.

Limitations of Early Audience-Centered Research

If this is all so seemingly logical and straightforward, why didn't early mass communication researchers create theories focused on active audiences? Why didn't such theories emerge as strong alternatives to limited-effects theories? Why were source-dominated theories so powerful, and why did their influence persist so long? There are many possible answers. We have seen how mass society theory exaggerated the influence of media and centered widespread public concern on negative effects. We looked at the Payne Fund studies of the effects of movies on children and teens. During WWII media research was used to meet the threat posed by totalitarianism. Since the 1930s government agencies, private foundations, and the media industry all have been willing to provide funding to study a broad range of positive and negative effects, but they provided little money to study audience activity. Researchers also thought that it was possible to study effects more objectively and parsimoniously than was possible in the investigation of media gratifications. For example, behavioral or attitudinal effects might be observed in a laboratory following exposure to media content. Experiments could identify and measure specific effects. On the other hand, studying gratifications meant asking people to report on their subjective experiences of content. People might report hundreds of different gratifications, which then needed to be sorted out and categorized. How could this be done objectively? Herzog (1940) recommended using qualitative research to study media gratifications. But during the 1940s and 1950s postpositivist researchers were determined to avoid approaches that were unparsimonious and didn't meet what they regarded as scientific standards. They chose to focus their efforts on developing what they thought would be definitive, powerful explanations for the consequences of media use. Why bother to describe and catalog people's subjective reasons for using media?

Early postpositivist researchers thought studying people's subjective explanations would serve little purpose other than satisfying curiosity about why so many people wasted so much time using mass media. As far as they were concerned, the only things they needed to know about an audience was its size and **demographics** (the social attributes of audience members like age, gender, income, and education). Early media researchers devoted considerable effort and expense to developing scientific methods for measuring audience size and composition. These were the things that advertisers wanted to know so they could better target ads and gauge their effectiveness. But most advertisers thought there was no practical reason to know why people sought out certain radio programs or read specific newspapers.

Early media researchers were concerned that the study of media gratifications would be difficult using available scientific methods. Most attitude researchers had strong behaviorist biases that led them to be suspicious of taking people's thoughts and experiences at face value. Did people really have any useful insight into why they use media? As we saw in Chapter 2, behaviorists believed that conscious thought only serves to provide rationalizations for actions people have been conditioned to perform. They held that, to understand what really motivates people to act as they do, social scientists must observe how they have been conditioned through exposure to stimuli in past situations. But this would be very difficult and costly. Researchers worked hard to develop survey questionnaire items to measure specific attitudes using questions that only indirectly hinted at the underlying attitude being measured.

Postpositivist researchers criticized the early active-audience research as too descriptive—it did little more than take people's reasons for using media and group them into sets of arbitrarily chosen categories. Why one set of categories rather than another? Moreover, they dismissed the categorization process itself as arbitrary and subjective. For example, Herzog placed her listeners' reasons into three categories— why not five? Where did her categories come from, and how could we be certain she wasn't arbitrarily putting respondents' stated reasons into these categories? In contrast, experimental attitude-change research used what most researchers regarded as a scientifically sound set of procedures to develop attitude scales (Chapter 1). They believed that this type of research produced causal explanations rather than simple descriptions of subjective perceptions. As long as empirical effects research offered the hope of producing significant new insight into the causal power of media, researchers had little motivation to test alternate approaches. They were anxious to prove the usefulness of their empirical methods and assert their standing as social scientists rather than humanists.

Confusion of Media Functions and Media Uses

In Chapter 5, we described functional analysis and its use by early media researchers. By the 1960s notions of an active and gratification-seeking audience had been absorbed into and confused with functional analysis. Failure to adequately differentiate media *uses* from media *functions* impeded the design and interpretation of audience-centered research. Charles Wright explicitly linked the active audience to functionalism in a 1959 book. This linkage to functions had a detrimental influence on the development of active-audience theories. Although Wright cautioned his readers to distinguish "between the consequences (functions) of a social activity and the aims or purposes behind the activity" (p. 16), functions were assumed by most communication theorists to be equivalent to (synonymous with) the aims or goals of the media industries themselves. To some extent this confusion over audience uses and societal functions also involves confusion about **levels of analysis** (the focus of research attention, ranging from individuals to social systems). As an individual audience member you may have certain personal purposes for reading a newspaper, and this activity should gratify some of those needs or you will stop reading. But you are only one of many people who will read that newspaper on a given day. Other people have other purposes that may be very different from your own. They will experience different gratifications. Functionalism is not concerned with individuals; it's concerned with overall functions for society that are served by mass media.

As explained in Chapter 5, functionalism often serves to legitimize the status quo. It tends to assume that if the social order is stable, things are in balance—bad functions are offset by good functions—otherwise the social order would fall apart. To the extent that active-audience notions were conceptually confused with functionalism, critics judged them as merely another way to rationalize the way things are. Let's use the classic four functions from Chapter 5's discussion of functionalism as an example. *Surveillance of the environment* refers to the media's collection and distribution of information. We know who was elected governor of Illinois because it was in the newspaper, and we know whether to wear a sweater to class because the radio weather forecaster said that it would be chilly today. *Correlation of parts of society* refers to the media's interpretive or analytical activities. We know that the failure of the highway bond proposition means that gasoline taxes will rise to cover necessary road repair because we read online reports and editorials explaining the connection. *Transmission of the social heritage* relates to the media's ability to communicate values, norms, and styles across time and between groups. How do you and your friends decide what clothes are fashionable or form expectations of what people normally do when they go out on dates? Media provide lots of information and advice about these topics. Finally, *entertainment* means media's ability to entertain or amuse.

These seem like perfectly reasonable aims of the media, but there is a problem. These might be goals of given media organizations, but (a) they might not necessarily be the purposes they serve for the people who consume those media, and (b) these functions can be different from the audience members' intended uses. For example, you might intentionally watch a horror movie to escape boredom, and you might even learn (unintentionally) a bit about how people deal with dangerous situations. In the course of watching you might also inadvertently learn how to use a knife as a weapon. The filmmaker's goal was to entertain, but the uses (the purpose) to which you ultimately put the content—escape boredom and unintentionally learn how to deal with danger and wield a knife—were much different. In other words, the source's aim is not always the ultimate function. If we confine our research to an investigation of functions intended by media practitioners (their goals), we are likely to ignore many negative effects. Because much early functional analysis was restricted to intended functions (again, goals), critics have charged that it is too apologetic to the media industries.

Wright (1974), realizing how his conceptualization of media functions was misinterpreted, later wrote, "Our working quartet of communications—surveillance, correlation, cultural transmission, and entertainment—was intended to refer to common kinds of activities that might or might not be carried out as mass communications or as private, personal communications. These activities were not synonymous for functions, which refer to the consequences of routinely carrying out such communication activities through the institutionalized processes of mass communications" (p. 205).

The surveillance activity, its functions in our society, and the effects of those functions offer a good example of how Wright intended functionalism to be applied to media studies. Newspapers, magazines, television, and Internet news sites devote significant energy and effort to covering political campaigns and delivering the product of that effort to their audiences. If readers and viewers ignore (i.e., fail to use) the reports, no communication happens, and the intended functions fail to occur. But if readers and viewers do consume the reports, the intended function we've been calling surveillance of the environment should take place. If so, there should be certain effects—readers and viewers should learn specific information from the news. They should use this information in ways that serve the larger society. Thus, media cannot serve their intended function unless people make certain uses of their content. For surveillance to occur, routine transmission of news information about key events must be accompanied by active audience use that results in widespread learning about those events and a willingness to act on this information. Thus, news media can achieve this societal-level function only if enough individual audience members are willing and able to make certain uses of content and do so frequently and routinely.

As was implied in Chapter 3's discussion of libertarianism, one historically important and widely intended function of public communication is the creation and maintenance of an enlightened and knowledgeable electorate, one capable of governing itself wisely based on information gained from media and other people. But many of us might argue that most current-day news media transmit "infotainment" or fake news that actually serves a negative function (a **dysfunction**) in that it produces ill-educated citizens or citizens who actually become less involved in the political process because they substitute pseudo-involvement in overdramatized media depictions of campaign spectacles for actual involvement in real campaign activities (Edelman, 1988).

The intended function of the reporting of those events and our intended use of the reports might be consistent with a normative theory (libertarianism) underlying our political and media system. The overall consequences of that activity, however, might well be something completely different. As political campaigns are disrupted by intentionally fake news and cater more and more to the time, economic, and aesthetic demands of the electronic media or social media (less complexity, more staging of campaign spectacles, less information about complex issues, more attention to politically extreme assertions, more reliance on negative ads, and so on), voters might become cynical about politics, which might undermine support for government and inadvertently increase the influence of well-organized special interest groups (Gans, 1978). Voters' use of media might gradually change, so instead of seeking information that isn't there, they turn to media for the mesmerizing spectacles that are available, or they might actively seek out intentionally misleading news that reinforces their political prejudices. In this example the intended function of media hasn't changed, but its practical consequences have. These gaps between intended functions and observed societal consequences have impressed media critics, leading them to be suspicious of both functional analysis and theories that presume an active audience.

REVIVAL OF THE USES-AND-GRATIFICATIONS APPROACH

Interest in studying the audience's uses of the media and the gratifications it receives from the media had two revivals. The first occurred during the 1970s, partly as a response to the inconsequential and overqualified findings of run-of-the-mill effects research. As we discussed earlier, by the 1960s most of the important findings of effects research had been catalogued and demonstrated in study after study. In all this research, media's role was found to be marginal in comparison with other social factors. But how could this be true when media audiences were so vast and so many people spent so much of their time-consuming media? Why were advertisers spending billions to purchase advertising time if their messages had no effect? Why were network television audiences continuing to grow? Didn't any of this media use have important consequences for the people who were engaging in it? If so, why didn't effects research document this influence? Was it overlooking something—and if so, what?

The media-effects trend had become so dominant in the United States that it was hard to ask questions about media that weren't stated in terms of measurable effects. There just didn't seem to be anything else worth studying, and no other approach to media research was considered useful. But if researchers restricted their inquiry to the study of effects, all they could obtain would be predictable, modest, highly qualified results. Though they were frustrated by this situation, few could see any practical alternative.

This first revival of interest in the uses-and-gratifications approach can be traced to three developments—one methodological and two theoretical:

1. **New survey research methods and data analysis techniques allowed the development of important new strategies for studying and interpreting audience uses and gratifications.** Researchers developed innovative questionnaires that allowed people's reasons for using media to be measured more systematically and objectively. At the same time new data analysis techniques provided

more objective procedures for developing categories and for assigning reasons to them. Also, a large new generation of media researchers entered the academy in the 1970s. They were trained in the use of survey methods. As the decade advanced, the computer resources necessary to apply these methods were increasingly available—even to researchers working at smaller universities or colleges. These developments overcame some of the most serious methodological barriers to active-audience research.

2. **During the 1970s some media researchers reached the conclusion that people's active use of media might be an important mediating factor making effects more or less likely.** They argued that members of an active audience can decide whether certain media effects are desirable and set out to achieve those effects. For example, you might have decided to read this book to learn about media theories. You intend the book to have this effect on you, and you work to induce the effect. If you lack this intent and read the book for entertainment, use of the book is less likely to result in learning. Does the book cause you to learn? Or do you make it serve this purpose for you? If you hold the latter view, then you share the perspective of active-audience theorists. Your conscious decision to actively use the book is a necessary (mediating) factor that must occur so that the intended effect can take place.

3. **Some researchers began expressing growing concern that effects research was focusing too much on unintended negative effects of media while intended positive uses of media were being ignored.** By 1975 scholars knew a lot about the influence of television violence on small segments of the audience (most notably preadolescent boys) but much less about how most people were seeking to make media do things that they wanted.

The second and more recent revival of interest in uses and gratifications, as you might have guessed from this chapter's opening, is the product of the ongoing development and diffusion of the Internet and social media, most specifically because of the interactivity they encourage. Arguing that "uses-and-gratifications has always provided a cutting-edge theoretical approach in the initial stages of each new mass communications medium," Thomas Ruggiero (2000, p. 3) identified three characteristics of computer-mediated mass communication that "offer a vast continuum of communication behaviors" for uses-and-gratifications researchers to examine:

- *Interactivity* "significantly strengthens the core [uses-and-gratifications] notion of active user" (Ruggiero, 2000, p. 15) because interactivity in mass communication has long been considered "the degree to which participants in the communication process have control over and can change roles in their mutual discourse" (Williams, Rice, & Rogers, 1988, p. 10).
- *Demassification* is "the ability of the media user to select from a wide menu. . . . Unlike traditional mass media, new media like the Internet provide selectivity characteristics that allow individuals to tailor messages to their needs" (Ruggiero, 2000, p. 16).
- *Asynchroneity* means that mediated messages "may be staggered in time. Senders and receivers of electronic messages can read mail at different times and still interact at their convenience. It also means the ability of an individual to send,

receive, save, or retrieve messages at her or his convenience. In the case of television, asynchroneity meant the ability of VCR users to record a program for later viewing. With electronic mail [e-mail] and the Internet, an individual has the potential to store, duplicate, or print graphics and text, or transfer them to an online Web page or the e-mail of another individual. Once messages are digitized, manipulation of media becomes infinite, allowing the individual much more control than traditional means" (Ruggiero, 2000, p. 16).

In fact, people examining new technology have found uses-and-gratifications research to be quite helpful in studying a wide range of Internet-based media, especially e-mail and social networking sites. For example, Bonka Boneva, Robert Kraut, and David Frohlich (2001) report that women find e-mail more useful than do men in maintaining social relationships. They demonstrated increasing use of e-mail by women to keep in touch with family and friends. Anabel Quan-Haase and Alyson Young (2010) found that different goals drive people's choice to use either Facebook or instant messaging, writing, "Facebook is about having fun and knowing about the social activities occurring in one's social network, whereas instant messaging is geared more toward relationship maintenance and development" (p. 350). Another uses-and-gratifications analysis of Facebook demonstrated that females and males use the site differently, women for maintaining relationships, passing time, and being entertained, and men for meeting new people and developing new relationships (Sheldon, 2008).

Uses-and-gratifications theory may also prove to be essential in assessing how and why various Internet-based communication services are used to supplement and, in some cases, replace legacy media. For example, young adults, the demographic least likely to read a printed newspaper, actually consume more news and information content than do their parents, but they do so on their smartphones (Ellis, 2012), and telecommunications industry research indicates that smartphones have become much more than telephones as their users continue to abandon traditional media to play games, listen to music, watch television and movies, read books, and take photographs using their phones (Edmonds, 2018).

The Active Audience Revisited

Whether they are engaged in Internet-based or legacy media use, the question remains: How active are media audiences, and what forms does this activity take? Critics of uses-and-gratifications research have long charged that the theory exaggerates the amount of active use. They contend that most media use is so passive and habitual that it makes no sense to ask people about it. Mark Levy and Sven Windahl (1985) attempted to put the issue in perspective:

> As commonly understood by gratifications researchers, the term "audience activity" postulates a voluntaristic and selective orientation by audiences toward the communication process. In brief, it suggests that media use is motivated by needs and goals that are defined by audience members themselves, and that active participation in the communication process may facilitate, limit, or otherwise influence the gratifications and effects associated with exposure. Current thinking also suggests that audience activity is best conceptualized as a variable construct, with audiences exhibiting varying kinds and degrees of activity. (p. 110)

Jay Blumler (1979) claimed that one problem in the development of a strong uses-and-gratifications tradition is the "extraordinary range of meanings" given to the concept of *activity*. He identified several meanings for the term, including the following:

- **Utility:** Media have many uses for people, and people can put media to those uses.
- **Intentionality:** Consumption of media content can be directed by people's prior motivations.
- **Selectivity:** People's use of media might reflect their existing interests and preferences.
- **Imperviousness to influence:** Audience members are often obstinate; they might not want to be controlled by anyone or anything, even mass media. Audience members actively avoid certain types of media influence.

Blumler's list summarized the forms of audience activity that the early uses-and-gratifications researchers studied, all relating to overall choices of content and media-use patterns. These types of activity did not, however, consider what people actually did with media content once they had chosen it. Recent research has begun to focus on this type of audience activity—the manner in which people actively impose meaning on content and construct new meaning that serves their purposes better than any meaning that might have been intended by the message producer or distributor.

A good example is the many meanings fans and critics made from the Oscar-nominated 2018 movie *Black Panther*, a film based on the Marvel comic book about the battle for the crown of the mythical African nation of Wakanda. Some conservatives charged that it was made to "piss off Whitey"; that its message was "The United States . . . is an awful place for black people" and "The U.S. military is terrible"; and that it represented "Cinematic Trump derangement: Less than 100% support for 'Black Panther' is racism." Other conservatives read the film as a laudatory metaphor for the presidency of Donald Trump, arguing, "The movie's hero is Trump; the villain is Black Lives Matter. . . . If T'Challa is Trump, Killmonger is Black Lives Matter"; and "By the end of the movie, T'Challa is even more like Trump inasmuch as he sees that his country of Wakanda cannot completely isolate itself from the world because he has a moral responsibility to help others." Still others praised the film for its fundamentally conservative message, stating, "*Black Panther* takes the side of sober, wise elites patiently enacting incremental change rather than of charismatic mob leaders fanning the flames of rage and revolution" (all quotes cited in Edroso, 2018). And what did liberals make of the movie? Many "found its ending political message far more conservative than the revolutionary possibilities teased by anything with 'Black' and 'Panther' in the title" (Thrasher, 2018). And as *Black Panther* was 2018's top Hollywood money maker and the ninth-highest worldwide earner in movie history, quite a few filmgoers read the movie as something else: a special-effects laden, explosion-rich, holiday blockbuster designed to amass billions of dollars for its creators and investors while providing a pleasurable few hours of diversion for those willing to pay the price of a ticket.

Two ways to clarify the issue are to distinguish between "activity" and "activeness" and to see the "active audience" as a relative concept. "Activity" and "activeness" are related, but the former refers more to what the audience does (e.g., chooses to read online news rather than watch television news), and the latter is more what the uses-and-gratifications people had in mind—that is, the audience's freedom and autonomy in the mass communication situation, as illustrated in the *Black Panther* example. This activeness, no doubt, varies from one person to the next. Some audience members are more active, and some are more passive. This is obvious; we all know too many couch potatoes, people who live their lives through the movies, or people addicted to their smartphones, suffering from phantom-vibration syndrome, feeling their phones vibrating when in fact they are not (Dokoupil, 2012). But we also know many people who fit none of these descriptions. And an inactive user can become active. Our level of activity might vary by time of day and by type of content. We might be active users of the Web by day and passive consumers of late-night movies. What the uses-and-gratifications approach really does, then, is provide a framework for understanding when and how different media consumers become more or less active and what the consequences of that increased or decreased involvement might be for themselves and possibly for society at large.

The classic articulation of this framework is the one offered by Elihu Katz, Jay Blumler, and Michael Gurevitch (1974). They described five elements, or basic assumptions, of the uses-and-gratifications model:

1. **The audience is active, and its media use is goal-oriented.** We've seen some confusion about exactly what is meant by *active*, but clearly various audience members bring various levels of activity to their consumption (if nothing else, at least in choice of preferred medium in given situations or preferred content within a given medium). You choose a printed magazine over its website because you like its portability and the feel of its glossy pages, and when reading that magazine, you like biographies more than you do articles about finance.

2. **The initiative in linking need gratification to a specific media choice rests with the audience member.** Scarlett Johansen, even teamed with the three Chrises—Evans, Pratt, and Hemsworth—cannot make you see *Avengers: Infinity War*. Rachel Maddow and Anderson Cooper cannot compel you to be a news junkie.

3. **The media compete with other sources of need satisfaction.** This is what Joseph Klapper meant when he said that media function "through a nexus of mediating factors and influences" (Chapter 4). Simply put, the media and their audiences do not exist in a vacuum. They are part of the larger society, and the relationship between media and audiences is influenced by events in that environment. If all your needs for information and entertainment are being satisfied by conversations with your friends, then you are much less likely to turn on a television set or go online for news. When students enter college, some forms of media use tend to sharply decline because these media don't compete as well for students' time and attention. In the current media environment, legacy media (television, radio, newspapers) increasingly compete for our attention with a growing range of Internet-based media that serve similar needs more cheaply, easily, or efficiently (Sundar & Limperos, 2013).

4. **People are aware enough of their own media use, interests, and motives to be able to provide researchers with an accurate picture of that use.** This, as we've seen earlier, is a much-debated methodological issue, explained succinctly here by James Potter (2012): "Think about the experience of filling out a questionnaire that asks you how much time you spend on each type of [media] message,

then asks you how much enjoyment you got from each type of message. Are you likely to say you spent a huge amount of time with a particular kind of media message yet received no enjoyment from it? Even if this were the case, you would not be likely to admit it to a researcher that you are such a loser" (p. 134).

But as research methods are continually refined, social scientists are increasingly able to offer better evidence of people's awareness of media use. In fact, research suggests that as media choices grow, people are being forced to become more conscious of their media use (La Ferle, Edwards, & Lee, 2000). For example, you can blunder into watching television shows by flipping to a channel and leaving the set tuned there all night. You can fall into certain viewing habits if everyone around you is regularly watching certain shows. But if you pay to access a movie on your smartphone, you are more likely to make an active choice. You don't pick the first title in the streaming menu. You scan the options, weigh their merits, read the provided descriptions, maybe watch the offered trailers, and then settle on a movie. Your choice is much more likely to reflect your interests than when you "zone out" viewing one channel or watch whatever was already on the screen in the student center lounge.

5. **Value judgments regarding the audience's linking of its needs to specific media or content should be suspended.** For example, the "harmful effects" of consumer product advertising on our culture's values might only be harmful in the researcher's eyes. If audience members want those ads to help them decide what's "cool," that's their decision. This is perhaps the most problematic of Katz, Blumler, and Gurevitch's assertions. Their point is that people can use the same content in very different ways, and therefore the same content could have very different consequences, not that researchers should not care about their findings. Viewing *Black Panther* might reinforce political attitudes for some people. Viewing movies that show violent treatment of minorities could reinforce some people's negative attitudes and yet lead others to be more supportive of minority rights. We each construct our own meaning of content, and that meaning ultimately influences what we think and do. Defenders of new media advocate the merits of using social networking websites, e-mail, and text messaging to maintain contact with a wide range of distant friends. But what if people never develop new friendships because they are satisfied maintaining superficial online contact with old friends? When you started college, did you stay in touch with high school friends using SNS or exchanging texts? Did this affect your desire to make new friends or the time you had to do so? Or did you use social media to seek out and establish new relationships in college? Your decisions about how to use social media determined the purposes that these media served for you.

This synopsis of the uses-and-gratifications perspective's basic assumptions raises several questions. What factors affect audience members' level of activeness or their awareness of media use? What other things in the environment influence the creation or maintenance of the audience members' needs and their judgments of which media use will best meet those needs? Katz, Blumler, and Gurevitch (1974, p. 27) addressed these issues, arguing that the "social situations" that people find themselves in can be "involved in the generation of media-related needs" in any of the following ways:

1. **Social situations can produce tensions and conflicts, leading to pressure for their easement through media consumption.** You're worried about your body image and think you have a weight problem, so you read magazines or search the Internet for advice about dieting. Or you seek out movies or sitcoms in which characters struggle with similar problems. Or you decide to watch some of YouTube's anorexia-themed videos.

2. **Social situations can create an awareness of problems that demand attention, information about which might be sought in the media.** You're out with friends and you notice that the most popular people in that circle are those who are the most socially outgoing; you also see that they get invitations that you do not. You increase your consumption of style and fashion magazines to better understand the social scene, or you go online, knowing that Google can help you find in-depth information about most social problems.

3. **Social situations can impoverish real-life opportunities to satisfy certain needs, and the media can serve as substitutes or supplements.** Your student budget does not allow you to buy the "in" clothes or to pay the cover charge at the dance club, so the Style Network's *How Do I Look?* keeps you company. When you come to college, you might use SNS to stay in contact with old friends as a substitute until you make new ones. Talk shows on radio and television provide an endless stream of chatter to fill up spaces in our lives and create a sense of being involved with other people.

4. **Social situations often elicit specific values, and their affirmation and reinforcement can be facilitated by the consumption of related media materials.** The fact that you are a young adult in college often means that you are part of a group that values going to parties. To check this out, do some research on Facebook and see the attention people your age give to their social lives. This media content not only promotes the party scene, it reinforces your attitudes toward it.

5. **Social situations can provide realms of expectations of familiarity with media, which must be met to sustain membership in specific social groups.** What? You don't watch *The Walking Dead*? You don't know how Justin Timberlake became famous? You didn't know that Aubrey Graham was Jimmy on *Degrassi: The Next Generation* before he became the rap artist known as Drake? You haven't seen the latest dating flick? Or what about sports? Who won the World Series? Can LeBron replace Michael? Can Mahomes replace Brady? How about those Patriots, those Chiefs, those Rams?

Of course, if you see media as important sources of effects, you might ask whether the mass media themselves might have been instrumental in creating certain social situations (such as those in our examples), and for making the satisfaction of those situations' attendant needs so crucial, and for making themselves, the media, the most convenient and effective means of gratifying those needs. Would we worry so much about body image if the media didn't present us with an endless parade of slender, fit, attractive people? Would we care as much about sports if they weren't constantly being promoted by media? But that is typically not of concern in traditional uses-and-gratifications thinking because the members of the audience personally and actively determine what gratifications of what needs will and will not occur from their own exposure to media messages.

INSTANT ACCESS

USES-AND-GRATIFICATIONS THEORY

Strengths

1. Focuses attention on individuals in the mass communication process
2. Respects intellect and ability of media consumers
3. Provides insightful analyses of how people experience media content
4. Differentiates active uses of media from more passive uses
5. Studies the use of media as a part of everyday social interaction
6. Provides useful insight into adoption of new media

Weaknesses

1. Too often mistakenly associated with functionalism, which can create a bias toward the status quo
2. Cannot easily address the presence or absence of effects
3. Many of its key concepts are criticized as unmeasurable
4. Is too oriented toward the micro-level
5. Media gratifications are often not associated with effects

ENTERTAINMENT THEORY

As we saw in Chapter 5, Harold Mendelsohn pioneered an attempt to apply psychological theories to assess what entertainment media do for us and to us. The discipline now regards his functional analysis approach to entertainment as too heavily biased toward a status quo that was not literally in disarray. But his view of the need to understand how audiences actually do use entertainment resonates today in some important post-positivist research.

Dolf Zillmann is credited with leading the way in the development of contemporary entertainment theory (Bryant, Roskos-Ewoldsen, & Cantor, 2003). Its proponents place it within the larger context of a psychology of entertainment. It seeks to conceptualize and explicate key psychological mechanisms underlying entertainment and to differentiate entertainment processes from those that underlie media's role in information, education, or persuasion (Bryant & Vorderer, 2006, p. ix). What separates current entertainment theory from earlier notions is that it doesn't see entertainment as simply an affective consequence of exposure to certain forms of media content. According to James Bryant and Peter Vorderer (2006), it envisions an overall process in which entertainment activity is "influenced, triggered, and maybe even shaped by the media product that is selected" (p. 4). Although audience members do voluntarily control their selection of entertainment content, there are often underlying psychological processes they don't consciously control. It is these conscious and unconscious processes that provide a comprehensive explanation of how and why we use entertainment media, and they help explain the consequences of this use.

Entertainment theory integrates findings from research examining the effects of many different types of entertainment content. Dolph Zillman and Peter Vorderer (2000) summarize research on horror, comedy, conflict, suspense, sex, affect-talk, sports, music, and video games. They assess gender and age differences and identify a range of effects resulting from exposure to these forms of content. Some effects are intended by users, but many are not. For example, research finds that there may be a health benefit when we laugh, so viewing situation comedies could make us healthier.

INSTANT ACCESS

ENTERTAINMENT THEORY

Strengths

1. Stresses media's prosocial influence
2. Assesses cognitive, affective, and behavioral effects
3. Provides cogent multivariate explanations for why people seek entertainment from media
4. Is grounded in an expanding body of empirical media-effects research
5. Provides a useful basis for conducting experiments

Weaknesses

1. Tends to accept status quo uses of entertainment media as a starting point for research
2. Has so far found effects that are mostly limited and minimal
3. Tends to ignore and doesn't provide a good basis for assessing cumulative effects
4. Tends to consider entertainment effects in isolation from other types of effects

Regular viewing of television programs featuring sexual content is linked to phenomena such as ambivalence toward marriage, perceived frequency of sexual activity by others, and attitudes toward homosexuality. It's not likely that most viewers would have intended these effects or been aware of them. On the other hand, as Mary Beth Oliver (2008) notes—and as your own experience no doubt confirms—it is clear that people often have **hedonistic motivations** for their media choices, intentionally selecting "content that serves to maintain and maximize pleasure and to diminish and minimize pain both in terms of intensity and duration" (p. 40). That must be the reason moviegoers flocked to *Crazy Rich Asians* and *Mama Mia! Here We Go Again*. But they also turned out for "difficult" movies like *If Beale Street Could Talk*, *Three Billboards Outside Ebbing Missouri*, *Roma*, and *The Hurt Locker*. This is because people also have **eudaimonic motivations**, choosing content that provides opportunities for personal insight, self-reflection, and contemplation of "the poignancies of human life" (p. 40).

The Bryant and Vorderer (2006) edited collection of work on entertainment theory has chapters devoted to a large number of psychological processes thought to be involved in or associated with entertainment, including selective exposure, motivation, attention, comprehension, information processing, attribution, disposition, empathy, identification with characters, involvement, mood management, social identity, and **parasocial interaction** ("interaction" between audience members and characters in media content; for example, talking to the television characters or dressing up for a soap opera wedding). Each can be studied individually, or several can be combined and used to study one or more forms of entertainment content. Some processes are more likely to be involved with certain forms of content. One way research can advance in the future is to assess which processes are most centrally involved with which forms of entertainment.

For example, thinking on parasocial interaction has been extended to audience involvement with lesbian and gay characters. Bradley Bond (2018), looking specifically at "relationally vulnerable" LGBTQ adolescents, demonstrated that parasocial interaction, traditionally thought of as supplemental to people's real-life social relationships, serves a more "compensatory" role for LGBTQ youth "attempting to fill a relational void left by the absence of real-life [LGBTQ] peers" (p. 457). And using the developing same-sex relationship between 13-year-olds Jude and Connor, characters on the television program *The Fosters*, Traci Gillig and Sheila Murphy (2016) experimentally demonstrated that sexual orientation and gender identity did indeed influence viewers' emotional connection to the characters and involvement with the show's narrative. "For LGBTQ youth," they wrote, "the story evoked hope and fostered positive attitudes; however, it tended to produce a boomerang effect among heterosexual/cisgender youth, eliciting the emotion of disgust and leading to significantly more negative attitudes toward LGBTQ people and issues" (p. 3828).

As entertainment theory evolved, "subtheories" were created that focused on the various psychological processes listed here. One of the most interesting is **mood management theory**. We'll take a closer look at this idea because you might find it useful in analyzing your own media use. It argues that a predominant motivation for using entertainment media is to moderate or control our moods. It articulates some of our commonsense notions about what we are doing when we seek out entertainment. If we're in a "bad mood," we connect to a streaming service like Spotify and listen to music. When we're "stressing out" from studying, we can take a break and surf the Net or turn on a televised comedy. Silvia Knobloch-Westerwick (2006) provides a description of this theory: "The core prediction of mood management theory claims that individuals seek out media content that they expect to improve their mood. Mood optimization in this sense relates to levels of arousal—plausibly, individuals are likely to avoid unpleasant degrees of arousal, namely boredom and stress. By selecting media content, media users can regulate their own mood with regard to arousal levels" (p. 240).

According to Knobloch-Westerwick, there are four types of media content attributes relevant to mood management: excitatory potential, absorption potential, semantic affinity, and hedonic valence. *Excitatory potential* involves the ability of content to arouse or calm emotion—to get us excited or to reduce stress. *Absorption potential* involves the ability of content to direct our thoughts away from things that induce a negative mood and toward other things that induce positive feelings. *Semantic affinity* concerns the degree to which entertaining content involves things that are similar to (mean the same as) the things that are inducing a bad mood. *Hedonic valence* refers specifically to the potential that content has to induce positive feelings.

It should be possible for you to think about your recent use of entertainment content and assess the extent to which mood management theory can explain what you did and what happened to you. First, did your use of the content change your mood in the way you desired? If your mood did change, why do you think this happened? Did the content get you excited? Did it divert your thoughts from things that were bothering you? Was the content unrelated to your personal problems and therefore able to direct your thoughts toward something that made you feel better? Was the content capable of inducing positive feelings—of making you feel good? Can you remember an instance when you went to a movie and expected to be entertained but the opposite happened? What went wrong? Was the movie boring? Did it fail to distract you from your problems, or worse, did it actually remind you of the problems? Did it fail to arouse positive feelings?

Mood management theory can help to explain why our efforts to manage our moods can fail or why media content can be entertaining even when it concerns seemingly unpleasant things—like chainsaw massacres or devastating earthquakes.

We might assume that situation comedies should always make us feel better, but they could remind us of our problems or they might just be boring. Conversely, we might expect that a horror movie or a thriller will arouse bad feelings, but it could be quite diverting and exciting—it could have high excitation and absorption potential.

Mood management theorists argue that we don't have to be consciously aware of these content attributes. We don't need to use them to consciously select content. Instead we can be guided by our feelings about content—our vague expectations about what will make us feel better as opposed to having a well-thought-out, rational strategy guiding our selection. We don't ponder the hedonic valance or the semantic affinity of the television shows we select. According to Knobloch-Westerwick (2006), "Awareness of mood optimization needs does not have to be assumed [by the researcher] . . . mood management processes may go by-and-large unnoticed by those who act on them—at least very little cognitive elaboration usually takes place" (p. 241).

This view of audience members can be contrasted with that of uses-and-gratifications theorists, who rely on audience members to report both uses and gratifications. Mood management theorists don't necessarily expect audience members to be able to report how they use content to manage moods. They don't ask people to fill out questionnaires rating the expected hedonic valence or the excitation potential of various types of entertainment content. They know people don't always consciously make these types of assessments about content.

Since they can't conduct surveys to study mood moderation, they base their conclusions primarily on findings produced by experiments in which audience members are exposed to media content that the theory predicts should influence them in certain ways. Subjects are exposed to content with high or low excitation potential or semantic affinity, for example. But these experiments can be difficult to design. Researchers need to develop stimulus materials containing the proper amount of the attributes they are manipulating. But how do you take people's moods into account? Research ethics would make it difficult to deliberately induce bad moods prior to exposure to content.

Some audience members (maybe you) would reject the mood management explanation of what audience members are doing when they seek out entertainment content. You might argue that you're choosing content that is aesthetically pleasing or just mindless entertainment. Altering your mood may be the furthest thing from your mind. But is it? Might you be more concerned about managing your mood than your conscious mind is willing to acknowledge? Could you have been "conditioned" by past experiences with media content to know which forms of content will induce feelings that you unconsciously want to experience? Maybe you should take another look at what you're doing when you choose to zone out in front of your television for an evening or surf the Net until four in the morning. Could your fascination with zombie apocalypse movies involve more than mere relief from boredom?

Knobloch-Westerwick (2006) reminds us that it's also important to differentiate between moods that tend to endure over time and temporarily induced changes in feelings. Moods could often be due to long-term, enduring personal or situational factors. They may be altered only temporarily by media content. For example, if you recently broke up with a close friend, this could induce a long-term negative mood. Watching a situation comedy might make you feel better temporarily, but the negative mood will return. You'd be managing your mood, but it would be only a short-term fix. In seeking out media content you would need to avoid material that shows good friends because it might have too much semantic affinity. Maybe horror movies or thrillers would be preferable. They would be exciting and diverting but wouldn't dwell much on human relationships.

Like most ideas related to entertainment theory, mood management theory accepts media as benign. What could be wrong with providing people with solace for everyday troubles? These contemporary theories for the most part suggest that the status quo is acceptable—much as Mendelsohn did many years ago. Mood management theory implies that media can help us cope with problems in our lives—problems that regularly induce bad moods. We don't have to develop a complex strategy to make media be helpful to us; we can rely on what we've learned from past experience with media, from what media have taught us to expect, and from the way we've been conditioned by exposure to a lifetime of entertainment programming.

Two recent expansions of entertainment theory, both at home in uses-and-gratifications thinking, suggest its value in understanding why we choose certain content and what we hope to derive from that exposure. The first is the **selective exposure self and affect management model (SESAM)**, originally developed by Silvia Knobloch-Westerwick (2015). It argues that "media users select messages to manage and regulate their self-concept along with affective and cognitive states and behaviors" (p. 965). When you select a piece of content, your purpose in influencing how you perceive yourself in that moment will play an important role. *You* are seeking media effects for *yourself*, and SESAM emphasizes social comparison in that process. Knobloch-Westerwick explains, "The SESAM model suggests that media users often engage in social comparisons with people featured in mediated communication—either for self-consistency when looking at others with the same views, or for self-improvement to inspire themselves to work towards certain goals, or for self-enhancement to feel better about themselves after looking at others who are worse off" (Knobloch-Westerwick & Westerwick, 2020). So, favoring posts that align with your point of view, you cruise your favorite political blogs to see what they have to say about the recent failures of Congress (fostering a sense of self-consistency); you browse the images in a fitness magazine during a grueling treadmill exercise session, inspired by the healthy, fit bodies you see there (working toward self-improvement); you watch old episodes of *Jersey Shore*, engaging in comparisons with its characters that lead you to thank your lucky stars that you are not them (boosting self-enhancement). You can see the SESAM graphically represented in Figure 9.1.

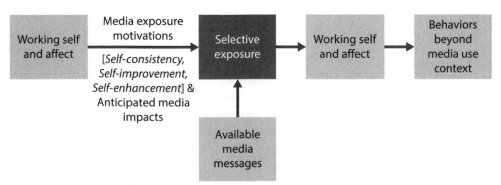

FIGURE 9.1   The Selective Exposure Self- and Affect Management Model (Knobloch-Westerwick & Westerwick, 2020)

Michael Slater and his colleagues wanted to understand why we engage with media stories not so much to regulate our self-concepts but to expand the real-world, everyday constraints on those concepts. Their **temporarily expanding the boundaries of the self perspective** argues that reality inevitably constrains us—that even if we are successful in achieving most or all of our personal goals and realizing the social roles we deem important, those achievements come at the cost of other goals and roles that were not or could not be pursued simultaneously. In other words, we can never achieve total agency, total autonomy, and total social affiliation because we're busy achieving what we can as we negotiate everyday life. So, they ask, why not dive into media narratives to temporarily expand the boundaries of that everyday life that limit us in those ways (Slater, Johnson, Cohen, Comello, & Ewoldsen, 2014)? Slater and colleagues explain, "In the course of such experience, the accustomed boundaries of personal and social self are expanded to accommodate the realities, characters, and assumptions in the narrative. Identification with story characters and transportation into a story world provide, imaginatively and transiently, expanded agency" (p. 443). It is precisely our need for autonomy, agency, and affiliation "that cannot be entirely satisfied within the confines of the personal and social self" that motivates engagement in media narratives (p. 446). In other words, when we choose to be transported or absorbed into media narratives, we can experience being faster than a speeding bullet, know what it's like to be more powerful than a locomotive, and feel the sensation of leaping tall buildings in a single bound (á la Superman). When consuming media narratives, the boundaries of our true personal and social selves are expanded to accommodate the story's realities, assumptions, situations, and characters. We can safely and efficiently expand the boundaries, or limits, of everyday life, gaining transient enjoyment and quite possibly more lasting self-knowledge through easily accessible and relatively low-cost media consumption.

USES-AND-GRATIFICATIONS AND SOCIAL NETWORKING

As you read earlier in this chapter, the Internet—with users rather than audiences—was an important factor in the revival of uses-and-gratifications theory. For example, Shyam Sundar and Anthony Limperos (2013) argued for a broadening of uses-and-gratifications theory so that it provides a better basis for studying Internet-based media, labeling their approach "Uses and Grats 2.0." They believe that Internet-based media require users to be more active in seeking and consuming content, and that users therefore will derive unique gratifications from both the content and the process of engaging with these media. Use of legacy media involved flipping switches or pushing buttons—activities that required little to no involvement. But Internet-based media require skill to locate, post, comment on, forward, or in other ways engage with media content and the other people involved with it. But what of the resulting gratifications? Chamil Rathnayake and Jenifer Winter (2018) summarized some of the most important new gratification measures that have been developed over the past several years, including socializing, virtual community, socialization-seeking, interpersonal utility, reciprocity, expressive information sharing, companionship, social interaction, meeting new people, and spiritual support. Jacqueline Incollingo (2018) conducted a survey of 632 digital news subscribers who routinely used mobile devices to access news. She found that in addition to the classic surveillance gratification, these users derived strong gratification from the convenience and easy accessibility of mobile news use. Eun Hwa Jung and Shyam Sundar (2018) concluded that the older Facebook users they studied derived important gratification from specific online activities such as status updating and posting personal stories. Participating in conversations on comment threads provided interaction gratification.

DEVELOPMENT OF RECEPTION STUDIES: DECODING AND SENSE MAKING

At the same time that audience-centered theory was attracting the attention of American empirical social scientists, British cultural studies researchers were developing a different but compatible perspective on audience activity. As we've seen, uses-and-gratifications researchers challenged the effects trend, at the time the dominant approach in US mass communication research. In Britain innovative cultural studies researchers were challenging both Marxist film critics (Moores, 1993) and British proponents of the postpositivist effects trend (Proctor, 2004; Rojek, 2009).

Chapter 6 introduced the Birmingham University Centre for Contemporary Cultural Studies and the work of Stuart Hall, its most prominent scholar. Initially, Hall (1973) produced a mimeographed report that proved important in developing and focusing the work of his center. It was later published as a book chapter (Hall, 1980) that argued that researchers should direct their attention toward (1) analysis of the social and political context in which content is produced (encoding), and (2) the consumption of media content (decoding). Researchers shouldn't make unwarranted assumptions about either encoding or decoding, he argued, but instead should conduct research permitting them to carefully assess the social and political context in which media content is produced and the everyday-life context in which it is consumed.

In laying out his views on decoding, Hall proposed an approach to audience research that became known as **reception studies**, or reception analysis. One of its central features is its focus on how various types of audience members make sense of specific forms of content. Hall drew on French semiotic theory to argue that any media content can be regarded as a *text* made up of *signs*. These signs are structured; that is, they are related to one another in specific ways. To make sense of a text—to *read* a text—you must be able to interpret the signs and their structure. For example, when you read a sentence, you must not only decode the individual words but also interpret its overall structure to make sense of it as a whole. Some texts are fundamentally ambiguous and can be legitimately interpreted in several different ways; they are **polysemic**. To return to an earlier example, consider the differences in readings of *Black Panther* not only between conservatives and liberals, but among conservatives as well.

Hall argued that although most texts are polysemic, the producers of a message generally intend a **preferred, or dominant, reading** when they create a message. As a critical theorist, Hall assumed that most popular media content had a preferred reading reinforcing the status quo. But in addition to this dominant reading, it is possible for audience members to make alternate interpretations. They might disagree with or misinterpret some aspects of a message and come up with an alternative or **negotiated meaning** differing from the preferred reading in important ways. In some

INSTANT ACCESS

RECEPTION STUDIES

Strengths

1. Focuses attention on individuals in the mass communication process
2. Respects intellect and ability of media consumers
3. Acknowledges range of meaning in media texts and the likelihood of many different interpretations
4. Seeks an in-depth understanding of how people interpret media content
5. Can provide an insightful analysis of the way media content is interpreted in everyday social contexts

Weaknesses

1. Is usually based on subjective interpretation of audience reports
2. Doesn't address presence or absence of effects
3. Uses qualitative research methods, which preclude causal explanations
4. Has been too oriented toward the micro-level (but is attempting to become more macroscopic)

cases audiences might develop interpretations in direct opposition to a dominant reading. In that case they are said to engage in **oppositional decoding**. As explained by Jesus Martin-Barbero (1993), although people are susceptible to domination by communication technologies, "they are able to exploit contradictions that enable them to resist, recycle, and redesign those technologies, . . . and people are capable of decoding and appropriating received messages and are not necessarily duped by them" (p. 225).

A student and colleague of Hall, David Morley, published one of the first detailed studies applying Hall's insights, one that served as a model for subsequent reception studies. Morley (1980) brought together 29 groups of people drawn from various levels of British society. They ranged from business managers to trade unionists and apprentices. These groups were asked to view an episode from *Nationwide*, a British television news magazine show, assessing the economic consequences on three families of the government's annual budget. Once the program ended, the groups discussed what they had watched and offered their interpretations. Morley chose *Nationwide* because an earlier analysis had identified it as a program that routinely offered status quo explanations for social issues (Brunsdon & Morley, 1981). Moreover, it was produced in a way designed to appeal to lower- and middle-class audiences. Thus, the researchers expected that the program would be able to communicate status quo perspectives to those audiences.

Morley tape-recorded the group discussions and analyzed them, placing them into one of three categories: (1) dominant, (2) negotiated, or (3) oppositional decoding. He found that although an upper-class group of business managers dismissed the program as mere entertainment, they had no complaints about the views it offered. Morley labeled their decoding as a dominant reading. At the other extreme, a group of union shop stewards liked the format of the program but objected to its message. They saw it as too sympathetic to middle management and failing to address fundamental economic issues. Morley labeled their decoding as oppositional. In the negotiated decoding category were groups of teacher trainees and liberal arts students. Very few groups articulated only a dominant reading of the program. Aside from managers, only a group of apprentices was found to merely repeat the views offered by the program. Most offered a negotiated reading, and several provided oppositional readings.

Because the reception studies approach has developed in cultural studies, researchers have been careful to differentiate their empirical audience research from that conducted by postpositive researchers. They stress their effort to combine macroscopic encoding research with microscopic decoding studies. They also point to their reliance on qualitative rather than quantitative research methods. Reception studies are often conducted with focus groups. For example, people who frequently use certain types of content (fans) are sometimes brought together to discuss how they make sense of the content. In other cases groups of people who belong to certain racial or ethnic groups are chosen so that the researcher can assess how these groups are routinely interpreting media content. In some cases researchers undertake in-depth interviews to probe how individuals engage in "meaning making." In others the researcher tries to assess how a focus group reaches a consensus concerning the meaning of content.

THINKING ABOUT THEORY

SEMIOTIC DISOBEDIENCE

British cultural theorist John Fiske (1987) coined the phrase *semiotic democracy* to refer to audience members' ability to make their own meaning from television content. In his words viewers possessed the skill—and the right—to produce personal "meanings and pleasures" when interacting with media texts (p. 236). In "meanings" you can see evidence of reception studies, and in "pleasures" you can see hints of uses-and-gratifications theory. But a new generation of active-audience writers and thinkers takes a more critical theory approach to the concept of an active audience. They argue that semiotic democracy, quite naturally, is evolving into **semiotic disobedience**, individuals' ability to reinvent or subvert media content, not to impose a personally meaningful reading, but to oppositionally redefine that content for themselves and others.

Examples abound. In San Francisco the Billboard Liberation Front "improves" billboard advertising so the new "preferred" reading is in direct opposition to the one intended by the original advertiser. For example, a billboard for the American Red Cross is altered to explain the necessity for charity "cuz the government ain't doing squat." The Media Foundation, best known for its Buy Nothing Day, Digital Detox Week, and the magazine *Adbusters*, produces a series of magazine and online ads featuring a smoking, cancerous Joe Chemo bearing a remarkable likeness to the cigarette icon Joe Camel. Its American flag, with 50 brand logos rather than 50 stars, has filled a full page of the *New York Times*. Hamburger giant McDonald's has also had its name and logo oppositionally subverted and redefined in online games. In *McDonald's Video Game* players decide how much rain forest to clear in order to raise more cows for slaughter.

These forms of protest have arisen, according to semiotic disobedience advocates such as technologist David Bollier (2005), because in our contemporary hyper-commercialized, corporate-dominated media "we are being told that culture is a creature of the market, not a democratic birthright. It is privately owned and controlled, and our role is to be obedient consumers. Only prescribed forms of interactivity are permitted. Our role, essentially, is to be paying visitors at a cultural estate owned by major 'content providers'" (p. 3). Legal Scholar Sonia Katyal (2006) expanded on this argument, identifying three "contemporary cultural moments in the world" (p. 491) giving rise to semiotic disobedience. The first was the dominance by corporate speech over public discourse; the second was abuse of copyright law—the "intellectual propertization of artistic creativity" (p. 492) stifling people's First Amendment freedoms; the third was creative artists' willingness to engage in "illegal" expression in order to liberate themselves from that domination, becoming what the Reverend Martin Luther King called, in his *Letter from a Birmingham Jail*, "creative extremists."

What do you think? Do you find value in the subversion of a content provider's intended reading? Do you think these activities serve any meaningful function? Do you see semiotic disobedience as the next logical cultural step for people in the Internet Age? After all, we are able to impose our own oppositional readings on various texts; now we have a ready technology permitting us to create our own preferred readings in opposition to some elite's idea of what is "preferred." But because we can, should we? After all, illegal use of someone else's content is still illegal.

Sociologist Pertti Alasuutari (1999) has argued that reception research has entered its third stage. The first stage was centered on Hall's encoding-and-decoding approach. The second was dominated by Morley's pioneering audience ethnography work. The third stage, Alasuutari wrote, "Entails a broadened frame within which one conceives of the media and media use. . . . [T]he objective is to get a grasp of our contemporary 'media culture,' particularly as it can be seen in the role of the media in everyday life, both as a topic and as an activity structured by and structuring the discourses within which it is discussed." The overall goal, he continues, is understanding "the cultural place of the media in the contemporary world. It may entail questions about the meaning and use of particular programmes to particular groups of people, but it also includes questions about the frames within which we conceive of the media and their contents as reality and as representations—or distortions—of reality" (pp. 6–7).

Thus, this third generation of reception studies attempts to return to some of the more macroscopic concerns that initially motivated critical theorists. It represents an effort to integrate these critical theory issues with reception analysis to establish a challenging research agenda. You can read about what some critical theorists are calling reception studies' latest incarnation in the box entitled "Semiotic Disobedience."

Feminist Reception Studies

Janice Radway (1984/1991) was one of the first American cultural studies researchers to exemplify the shift away from an exclusive focus on textual analysis and toward an increased reliance on reception studies. Her work provided an influential model for American scholars and is frequently cited as one of the best examples of feminist cultural studies research. Radway initially analyzed the content of popular romance novels. She argued that romance characters and plots are derived from patriarchal myths in which a male-dominated social order is assumed to be both natural and just. These books routinely presented men as strong, aggressive, and heroic, whereas women are weak, passive, and dependent. Women in their pages must gain their identity through their association with a male character.

After completing her content analysis of those books, Radway (1984/1991, 1986) interviewed women who read them and met regularly in groups to discuss them. She was surprised to find that many readers used these books as part of a silent rebellion against male domination, which they were able to express in an "eloquence about their own lives" (1984/1991, p. 6). They read them as an escape from housework or child rearing. Many romance readers rejected key assumptions of the patriarchal myths, expressing strong preferences for male characters who combined traditionally masculine and feminine traits—for example, physical strength combined with gentleness. Similarly, readers preferred strong female characters who controlled their own lives but retained traditional feminine attributes. Thus, romance reading could be interpreted as a form of passive resistance against male-dominated culture. Romance readers rejected the preferred reading and instead engaged in negotiated or oppositional decoding. Their personal meaning making, Radway wrote, was their "declaration of independence" (1984/1991, p. 11). Her work, she said, "was less an account of the way romances as texts were interpreted than of the way romance reading as a form of behavior operated as a complex intervention in the ongoing social life of actual social subjects, women who saw themselves first as wives and mothers" (1984/1991, p. 7). Research on female viewers of soap operas offered similar interpretations of their decoding of content. Dorothy Hobson (1982) discovered that, as with most media texts, "there is no overall intrinsic message or meaning in the work. . . . [I]t comes alive and communicates when the viewers add their own interpretation and understanding to the programme" (p. 170).

Another feminist cultural studies researcher offers evidence that women routinely engage in oppositional decoding of popular media content. Linda Steiner (1988) examined 10 years of the "No Comment" feature of *Ms.* magazine, in which readers submit examples of subtle and not-so-subtle male domination. She argued that *Ms.* readers routinely engage in oppositional decoding and form a community acting together to construct these readings. Magazine examples can teach women how to identify these texts and help them develop interpretations serving their own interests rather than those of a patriarchal elite. Angela McRobbie (1982), committed to "research *on* or *with* living human subjects, namely women or girls" (p. 46), came to a similar conclusion in her study of teenage girls' negotiated readings of the movies *Flashdance* and *Fame.* She concluded that young girls' "passion" for these films "had far more to do with their own desire for physical autonomy than with any simple notion of acculturation to a patriarchal definition of feminine desirability" (McRobbie, 1984, p. 47). Feminist reception theory remains quite useful in the contemporary media environment—for example, in examining rape jokes (Pérez & Greene, 2016) and screen portrayals of lesbians (Scanlon, 2016).

REVIEW OF LEARNING OBJECTIVES

• Explain why postpositivist and cultural studies researchers became increasingly focused on media audiences rather than media effects and how the resulting active-audience theories differ from the effects theories dominant in earlier mass communication theory.

Effects theories tend to be source-dominated, centering their attention on message sources and content, not on the interests or needs of the audiences those sources want to influence. They discount or ignore people's ability to resist messages. Eventually postpositivist researchers began to reexamine limited-effects findings about audiences, concluding that people were not as passive as these effects theories implied. And cultural studies researchers began to discover that the power of elites to manipulate audiences was not as great as had been assumed by neo-Marxist theorists.

• Recognize the ways audiences can be active and how that activity can be measured.

Audience activity can mean utility (media have many uses, and people can put media to those uses), intentionality (consumption of content can be directed by people's prior motivations), selectivity (people's use of media can reflect their existing interests and preferences), imperviousness to influence (audience members are often obstinate; they actively avoid certain types of media influence), and meaning construction (people can make personally meaningful, idiosyncratic readings of media content). Activity is a relative concept; some people are more active media consumers than are others.

- Identify and assess the propositions of uses-and-gratifications theory.

The uses-and-gratifications approach assumes that the audience is active and its media use is goal-oriented; the initiative in linking need gratification to a specific media choice rests with the audience member; the media compete with other sources of need satisfaction; people are aware enough of their own media use, interests, and motives to be able to provide researchers with an accurate picture of that use; and value judgments regarding the audience's linking its needs to specific media or content should be suspended. Media use is influenced by social situations, which can produce tensions and conflicts, leading to pressure for their easement through media consumption; can create an awareness of problems that demand attention, information about which might be sought in the media; can impoverish real-life opportunities to satisfy certain needs, and can serve as substitutes or supplements; can elicit specific values, and their affirmation and reinforcement can be facilitated by the consumption of related media materials; and can provide realms of expectations of familiarity with media, which must be met to sustain membership in specific social groups.

- Differentiate media functions and media uses.

The functions of the media are not synonymous with the aims or goals of the media industries. People's use of media and their content ultimately determines the functions that media serve for individuals and the larger society.

- Judge the contributions of entertainment theory to our understanding of people's use of entertainment content.

Entertainment theory seeks to understand what entertaining media content does to and for people. Sometimes these effects occur without awareness; other times people may have specific goals in mind and actively match media use to a desired outcome. That use can be hedonic, serving to maintain and maximize pleasure and to diminish and minimize pain, or it can be eudaimonic, providing opportunities for personal insight and self-reflection. Audience members can use entertainment media for mood management, to manage and regulate their self-concept as well as their affective and cognitive states and behaviors, and to temporarily expand the boundaries of their understandings of themselves.

- Understand why reception studies posed a challenge to both effects-trend notions and older forms of neo-Marxist theory.

Reception studies focuses on how various types of audience members make sense of specific forms of content. Texts are fundamentally ambiguous—polysemic—and can be legitimately interpreted in different ways. Audience members can make the preferred or dominant meaning (the one intended by the source), or a negotiated meaning (an alternative understanding differing from the preferred reading in important ways), or they may engage in oppositional decoding, developing interpretations in direct opposition to a dominant reading. As such, reception studies challenged source-dominated effects thinking as well as the assumption of elite power granted to media by neo-Marxists.

- Recognize feminist contributions to the development of reception studies.

In its belief that meaning made from media content could be influenced by a gendered view of the content itself and the lived experience of the audience member, feminist reception studies helped move cultural studies research away from its textual analysis roots to include readings made by individual audience members.

CRITICAL THINKING QUESTIONS

1. Where does the greater amount of power reside in the media/audience relationship? That is, do media do things to people, or do people do things with media? Are there circumstances when the "balance of power" might shift? That is, are there circumstances when audience members have greater control over their reading than others? Have the new digital media shifted the balance, giving individual audience members more power? How much control do you exercise over your meaning making when using digital media like video games and SNS? Do you ever make meaning with your friends using these media's interactivity? Why or why not?

2. Choose a media consumption choice that you may often have to make, such as selecting a movie streamed to your laptop versus one at the multiplex, choosing an episode of your favorite situation comedy downloaded to your smartphone versus one on your big-screen television set, or scanning online headlines versus spending 30 minutes with a print newspaper. Subject that decision to Schramm's fraction of selection. Which "wins"? Which elements in the numerator and denominator might you change to produce a different outcome? What does this tell you about your media uses and gratifications?

3. Why would you ever impose an oppositional reading of a piece of media content? After all, the producers went to great lengths to create a text that would bring you some satisfaction. Why not just enjoy it? There are always other texts that can provide you with the reading you prefer. Some feminist researchers argue that most mainstream media content reflects an implicit patriarchal culture and that audiences should impose oppositional readings. Do you agree or disagree?

KEY TERMS

cloud computing
active-audience theories
uses-and-gratifications approach
entertainment theory
fraction of selection
demographics
levels of analysis
dysfunction
hedonistic motivations
eudaimonic motivations
parasocial interaction

mood management theory
selective exposure self and affect
   management model (SESAM)
temporarily expanding the boundaries
   of the self perspective
reception studies
polysemic
preferred, or dominant, reading
negotiated meaning
oppositional decoding
semiotic disobedience

GLOSSARY

cloud computing: Storage of digital content on distant, third-party servers

active-audience theories: Theories that focus on assessing what people do with media; audience-centered theories

uses-and-gratifications approach: Approach to media study focusing on the uses to which people put media and the gratifications they seek from those uses

entertainment theory: Examines key psychological mechanisms underlying audience use and enjoyment of entertainment-oriented media content

fraction of selection: Graphic description of how individuals make media and content choices based on expectation of reward and effort required

demographics: Social attributes of audience—i.e., age, gender, income, education

levels of analysis: The focus of research attention, ranging from individuals to social systems

dysfunction: A negative function

hedonistic motivations: Choosing content to maintain and maximize pleasure and diminish and minimize pain

eudaimonic motivations: Choosing content that provides opportunities for personal insight, self-reflection, and contemplation

parasocial interaction: "Interaction" between audience members and characters in media content

mood management theory: A predominant motivation for using entertainment media is to moderate or control moods

selective exposure self and affect management model (SESAM): Idea that media users select messages to manage and regulate their self-concept along with affective and cognitive states and behaviors

temporarily expanding the boundaries of the self perspective: Idea that, inevitably constrained by everyday life, people turn to media narratives to expand their personal sense of agency, autonomy, and social affiliation

reception studies: Audience-centered theory that focuses on how various types of audience members make sense of specific forms of content

polysemic: The characteristic of media texts as fundamentally ambiguous and legitimately interpretable in different ways

preferred, or dominant, reading: In reception studies, the producer-intended meaning of a piece of content; assumed to reinforce the status quo

negotiated meaning: In reception studies, the result when an audience member creates a personally meaningful interpretation of content that differs from the preferred reading in important ways

oppositional decoding: In reception studies, the process of an audience member developing interpretations of content that are in direct opposition to a dominant reading

semiotic disobedience: Individuals' ability to reinvent or subvert media content to oppositionally redefine that content for themselves and others.

CHAPTER 10

Theories of Media Cognition and Information Processing

The outcome of the 2018 mid-term Congressional elections was historic. The Democrats wrested control of the House of Representatives from the Republicans, a reversal of their 2011 loss. The voting also sent a record number of women, Muslims, and self-described socialists to that chamber, and not unrelated to this, three of the dominant campaign issues for candidates from both parties were immigration, the treatment of women, and the economy (Somin, 2018). Yet only one in three voters could pass the citizenship test that immigrants must pass in order to become Americans (Riccards, 2018); only 52% could name a single Supreme Court justice, although several Court cases on reproductive rights and the brutal confirmation hearing of Brett Kavanaugh—credibly accused of teenaged sexual assault—had dominated the news that summer (Kilgore, 2018); and surveys indicated that "most Americans" had very little knowledge of how federal spending actually operates, vastly underestimating "the percentage of federal spending that goes to big entitlement programs, and greatly overestimat[ing] the amount that goes to foreign aid and some other small programs, such as public broadcasting." For example, although foreign aid accounts for only 1% of the federal budget, nearly half of Americans think it contributes "a great deal" (Somin, 2017, para. 2).

These data are not anomalies, as "a substantial amount of scholarship . . . has sought to determine whether citizens can participate meaningfully in politics. Recent work has shown that most citizens appear to lack factual knowledge about political matters . . . and that this deficit affects the issue opinions that they express" (Nyhan & Reifler, 2010, p. 303).

But how can this be? Are Americans simply not very bright? Given the country's impressive social, cultural, and technological achievements, this seems unlikely. Is it that there is insufficient access to information and analysis? This is improbable in the age of constant media connection and the Internet. Political writer Lee Harris (2012) suggested another possibility in his essay "Are Americans Too Dumb for Democracy?" "The difficulty we human beings face in making the right decision is not owing to our lack of smarts," he wrote. "The challenge we face is one we all face together—it stems from the maddening complexity and relentless perversity of the world we live in. It is cognitive hubris to think that any degree of intelligence or expertise can do away with this most stubborn of all stubborn facts" (para. 31).

LEARNING OBJECTIVES

After studying this chapter you should be able to

- Explain the major ideas encompassed by information-processing theory, including the concept of limited cognitive resources.
- Apply information-processing theory to making sense of television news.
- Better appreciate how schema theory has enriched the study of mass communication, especially in the realm of processing political communication.
- Recognize the influence of the hostile media effect on processing information.
- Find value in the elaboration likelihood model's explanation of how people come to process information systematically and heuristically.
- Judge the value of newer theories of information processing, such as narrative persuasion theory and the extended elaboration likelihood model, especially to health-oriented media messages.
- Evaluate those information-processing theories that suggest people may not be completely rational when making meaning from media messages, ideas such as affective intelligence, motivated reasoning, and the backfire effect.
- Assess the value to mass communication theory of incorporating various neuroscience perspectives into our understanding of information processing.

OVERVIEW

These questions—What do Americans know (and not know)? How do they know it? Where do they get their information? How well do they remember information? How do they use that information? How well do they differentiate good ideas from bad?— have been at the heart of mass communication theory and research from the field's earliest days. You read in earlier chapters that the rise of propaganda and powerful new forms of mass media led many to argue that democracy was obsolete. Average people couldn't be trusted to govern themselves. Walter Lippmann (1922) claimed that the social world had become too complex for people to understand. These concerns motivated the first systematic investigation of the power of media messages to move people to action. Lazarsfeld's voting research and Hovland's research on attitude change just before and after World War II allayed some of the most serious concerns about the power of propaganda. They found that propaganda wasn't as powerful as many feared. Most people were protected from its influence by their social relationships and preexisting attitudes. But researchers also found that people did not have the ability to independently assess and reject problematic messages. Even better-educated people were vulnerable to certain types of propaganda messages. The postpositivist tradition of media effects research begun by Lazarsfeld and Hovland continues to today, with important work on information processing and cognition that raises new questions as it attempts to answer some that are decades old. America seems to be dividing into two nations served by different sets of media outlets. Increasingly people seek out media that confirm and reinforce what they already believe, and media outlets are evolving to serve this desire. Widespread ignorance persists in many important areas of science, health, safety, and technology. Entertainment media continue to dominate our attention while information media are marginalized. Fanciful myths about the nature of the social world abound while scientifically based accounts are greeted with widespread skepticism. To what extent are media responsible for these problems? Is there something interfering with how people learn about and make sense of the social world? Could media do a better job of informing and educating the public concerning the social world?

In this chapter we'll look at a wide variety of microscopic-level theories of how individuals gather, process, and evaluate the flow of information, much of it from the media, that they continuously encounter. Most of the early research in this area came from cognitive psychologists, social scientists interested in how an individual, employing mental structures and processes, "observes and makes sense out of a complex environment" (Axelrod, 1973, p. 1249). These cognitive psychologists rejected behaviorist assertions that people simply react to stimuli in their environments and later use their cognitions to justify those responses (see Chapter 2). Clearly much more was going on as people lived their lives. As Robert Axelrod (1973) explained, "The world is complex, and yet people are able to make some sense out of it. A national or international political arena, for example, is so huge and so complex that to make any sense out of it seems to be a superhuman task. And yet national leaders and even the man [sic] in the street do make more or less intelligent interpretations about political events and relationships. How do they do this?" (p. 1248). Among the tools researchers have to answer that question is **information-processing theory**, a means of understanding how people deal with sensory information. But despite what we might like to believe, much of our information processing is out of our conscious control. And that may indeed be a good thing . . . sometimes.

Mass communication theory, as you've read, had its roots in the study of propaganda and persuasion, so it came to embrace the idea that people processed information—well or poorly, correctly or incorrectly—based on identifiable and measurable variables. But as the discipline matured, and as newer and newer media appeared, and as media content became increasingly visual and sophisticated, those early understandings had to be enriched. Mass communication scholars' appreciation of people's cognitive abilities and respect for their use of personal experience to make meaning began to grow. New theories came to the field from political science and psychology, themselves soon enriched and improved by the introduction of mass communication questions and variables. If people were indeed cognitive misers (naturally avoiding strenuous mental processing of information when they could), maybe theory could be used to guide the construction of media content that could take advantage of that seeming limitation to do some societal good. And at the same time, perhaps theory could help explain why some people, in the eyes of others, "just don't get it."

INFORMATION-PROCESSING THEORY

Cognitive psychologists have developed a perspective on the way individuals routinely cope with sensory information: information-processing theory. It is actually a large set of diverse and disparate ideas about cognitive processes and provides yet another avenue for studying media audience activity (Chapter 9). Researchers work to understand how people take in, process, store, and then use various forms of information provided by media.

Drawing on the same metaphors as systems theory (see Chapter 5), information-processing theory often uses mechanistic analogies to describe and interpret how each of us takes in and makes sense of the flood of information our senses encounter every moment of each day. It assumes that individuals operate like complex biocomputers, with certain built-in information-handling capacities and strategies. Each day we are exposed to vast quantities of sensory information, but we filter this information so only a small portion of it ever reaches our conscious mind. We single out for attention and processing only a tiny fraction of this information, and we eventually store only a tiny amount of that in long-term memory. We are not so much information *handlers* as information *avoiders*—we have developed sophisticated mechanisms for screening out irrelevant or useless information. When our capacity to cope with sensory information is overwhelmed, we make mistakes by failing to take in and process critical information.

Cognitive psychologists make an important distinction between cognitive processes and consciousness. Much of what takes place in our brain never reaches our consciousness. Although this activity often affects our conscious thoughts, it does so only very indirectly through its influence on other cognitive processes. Our consciousness acts as a supreme overseer of this cognitive activity but has very limited and typically quite indirect control over it. This perspective on cognition is contrary to what most of us would like to assume about our ability to control what goes on in our minds. It contradicts our personal experience, which is largely based on what conscious reflection is able to reveal to us. When we watch a televised news report, we have the sense that we are getting every bit of useful information that it contains. But recent research finds that only a fraction of the original information reaches us, even when we pay close attention. We get distracted by compelling pictures and waste precious cognitive resources processing them while we miss important auditory information.

How can we have so little control over these important processes supplying us with such critical information? If we are making mistakes and missing important information, maybe all we need to do is concentrate harder, but are you always successful when you've tried to force yourself to remember something for an exam? Did it work? If cognitive theorists are right, we need to be much more distrustful of the experiences our consciousness weaves together for us based on the very limited and attenuated flow of information that eventually reaches it. Research is beginning to reveal just how easily and often consciousness fails to provide accurate or even useful representations of the social world.

Some cognitive psychologists argue that many of the processing mechanisms we use to screen in and screen out information developed when early human beings were struggling to adapt to and survive in a hostile physical environment (Wood & McBride, 1997). In that environment it was critical that potential predators and prey be quickly identified so swift action could be taken. There was no time for conscious processing of such information and no need for conscious reflection before action. If you sensed a predator nearby, you ran away. If you sensed nearby prey, you attacked. Those who didn't either died at the hands of predators or died of starvation. Humans who developed the requisite cognitive skills survived.

These cognitive processing mechanisms became critical to adapting to and surviving in close social relationships with other human beings. For example, much of the cognitive processing capacity of the human brain is effectively devoted to taking in and unconsciously interpreting subtle body and facial movements, enabling us to sense what others are feeling and anticipate how they are likely to act. We don't think about the information these cognitive processes produce. We experience this information as an intuition—we have a sense that others feel certain ways or will act certain ways. These processing mechanisms might have become more important to survival than processing information about prey and predators precisely because human beings are relatively weak and defenseless compared with many predators. Humans quickly die when food supplies fluctuate or temperatures vary. Human children require nurturing for much longer periods than do the young of other mammals. As a result, it is essential that humans form communities in which they can band together to survive. But living in communities requires cognitive skills far more sophisticated than those needed to sense predators and prey.

How relevant are these ideas for understanding how we deal with sensory information? Think about it for a moment. As you sit reading this book, consider your surroundings. Unless you are seated in a white, soundproof room with no other people present, there are many sensory stimuli around you. If you have been sitting for some time, your muscles might be getting stiff and your back might have a slight ache. Those around you might be laughing. A radio might be playing. All this sensory information is potentially available, but if you are good at focusing your attention on reading, you are routinely screening out most of these external and internal stimuli in favor of the words on this printed page or e-book screen.

Now consider what you do when you watch a television program. Unless you have a DVR player and can review scenes in slow motion, you can't pay attention to all the images and sounds. If you do watch them in slow motion, the experience is totally different from viewing them at normal speed. Viewing television is actually a rather complex task using very different information-processing skills than reading a textbook. You are exposed to rapidly changing images and sounds. You must sort these out and pay attention to those that will be most useful to you in achieving whatever purpose you have for your viewing. But if this task is so complex, why does television seem to be such an easy medium to use? Because the task of routinely making sense of television appears to be so similar to that of routinely making sense of everyday experience. And making sense of that experience is easy, isn't it?

Information-processing theory offers fresh insight into our routine handling of information. It challenges some basic assumptions about the way we take in and use sensory data. For example, we assume that we would be better off if we could take in more information and remember it better. But more isn't always better. Consider what happens when you fill the hard drive of your computer with more and more content. It becomes increasingly difficult to find things quickly. Some important documents may be lost among thousands of useless or trivial items. Everything just slows down.

It's not surprising, then, that some people experience severe problems because they have trouble routinely screening out irrelevant environmental stimuli. They are overly sensitive to meaningless cues such as background noise or light shifts. Others remember too much information. You might envy someone with a photographic memory—especially when it comes to taking an exam. But total recall of this type can pose problems as well. Recall of old information can intrude on the ability to experience and make sense of new information. A few cues from the present can trigger vivid recall of many different past experiences. If you've watched reruns of the same television show several times—*Family Guy* or *The Simpsons*, for example—you probably have found that as you watch one episode it triggers recall of bits and pieces of previous episodes. If you were asked to reconstruct a particular episode of either program, you would likely weave together pieces from several different shows. Everyday life is like that—if we remember too much, the past will constantly intrude into the present. Forgetting has advantages.

Another useful insight from information-processing theory is its recognition of the limitations of conscious awareness. Our culture places high value on conscious thought processes, and we tend to be skeptical or suspicious of the utility of mental processes only indirectly or not at all subject to conscious control. We associate consciousness with rationality—the ability to make wise decisions based on careful evaluation of all available relevant information. We associate unconscious mental processes with things like uncontrolled emotions, wild intuition, or even mental illness. We sometimes devalue the achievements of athletes because their greatest acts are typically performed without conscious thought—"She's in the zone"; "He's a natural." No wonder we are reluctant to acknowledge our great dependency on unconscious mental processes.

The overall task of coping with the everyday flow of information is much too complex for conscious control to be either efficient or effective. We have to depend on routinized processing of information and must normally limit conscious efforts to instances when intervention is crucial. For example, when there are signs of a breakdown of some kind, when routine processing fails to serve our needs properly, then conscious effort might be required.

One advantage of the information-processing perspective is that it provides an objective perspective on learning. Most of us view learning subjectively. We blame ourselves if we fail to learn something we think we should have learned or that appears to be easy to learn. We assume that with a little more conscious effort, we could have avoided failure. How often have you chided yourself by saying, "If only I'd paid closer attention or studied harder"; "I should have given it more thought"; "I made simple mistakes that I could have avoided if only I'd been more careful"? But would a little more attention or study really have helped all that much? Information-processing theory recognizes that we have **limited cognitive resources**. If more resources are directed toward one task, another task will be performed badly. As a result, more attention to one aspect of information processing often leads to breakdown in some other aspect of processing. We typically deal with information in environments where it is coming at us from several different media at the same time. We're watching television, monitoring nearby people, surfing the Net, keeping track of instant messages, and posting images to Snapchat—all at the same time. The current college generation is rightly labeled the "M" generation—both for its ubiquitous use of *media* and for its constant *multitasking.* No wonder our cognitive resources are pushed to the limit. No wonder we make mistakes and fail to learn what we intend.

For example, when we do something as simple as watching television, we are taking in visual and verbal information. Information-processing research has demonstrated that we will place priority on processing visual information; as a result, complex, powerful visual images compel us to devote more cognitive resources to making sense of them. But if we do that, we miss the verbal information. Of course, sometimes additional conscious effort can do wonders. We can choose to ignore the compelling pictures and pay close attention to the verbal information. But what we might need is some overall revamping of our routine information-handling skills and strategies—a transformation of our information-processing system. This can take considerable time and effort—not just trying harder in one specific instance. Thus, information-processing theory provides a means of developing a more objective assessment of the mistakes we make when processing information. These mistakes are routine outcomes from a particular cognitive process or set of processes—not personal errors caused by personal failings.

Information-processing theory doesn't blame audience members for making mistakes when they use media content. Instead it attempts to predict these mistakes based on challenges posed by the content and normal limitations in people's information-processing capacity. In some cases it links routine or common errors to breakdowns in information processing and suggests ways to avoid them. For example, research has repeatedly demonstrated that poorly structured news stories will routinely be misinterpreted even if journalists who write them are well intentioned and news consumers try hard to understand them (Gunter, 1987). Rather than retraining people to cope with badly structured stories, it may be more efficient to change the structure of the stories so more people can use them without making mistakes. But that would require changes in journalistic practices—news production routines that journalists resist changing.

Processing Television News

Information-processing theory has been used extensively in mass communication research to guide and interpret research on how people decode and learn from television news broadcasts. Numerous studies have been conducted, and useful reviews of this literature are now available (Davis, 1990; Davis & Robinson, 1989; Graber, 1988; Gunter, 1987; Robinson & Davis, 1990; Robinson, Levy, & Davis, 1986). Different types of research, including mass audience surveys and small-scale laboratory experiments, have produced remarkably similar findings. A rather clear picture of what people do with television news is emerging.

Though most of us view television as an easy medium to understand and one that can make us eyewitnesses to important events, it is actually a difficult medium to use. Information is frequently presented in ways that inhibit rather than facilitate learning. Part of the problem rests with audience members. Most of us view television primarily as an entertainment medium. We have developed many information-processing skills and strategies for watching that serve us well in making sense of entertainment content but that interfere with effective interpretation and recall of news. We approach televised news passively and typically are engaging in several different activities while viewing. Our attention is only rarely focused on the screen. We depend on visual and auditory cues to draw our attention to particular stories. In fact, content producers are

INSTANT ACCESS

INFORMATION-PROCESSING THEORY

Strengths

1. Provides specificity for what is generally considered routine, unimportant behavior
2. Provides objective perspective on learning; mistakes are routine and natural
3. Permits exploration of a wide variety of media content
4. Produces consistent results across a wide range of communication situations and settings

Weaknesses

1. Is too oriented toward the micro-level
2. Overemphasizes routine media consumption
3. Focuses too much on cognition, ignoring such factors as emotion

aware of the power of our **orienting response**, humans' instinctive reaction to sudden or novel stimulus. So they use the medium's technical conventions—edits, quick cuts, zooms, pans, sudden noises and movements—to trigger involuntary responses—that is, to attract our attention (Reeves & Thorson, 1986).

We rarely engage in deep, reflective processing of news content that might allow us to assume more conscious control over this meaning making (Kubey & Csikszentmihalyi, 2002). So most news story content is never adequately processed and is quickly forgotten. Even when we do make a more conscious effort to learn from news, we often lack the information necessary to make in-depth interpretations of content or to store these interpretations in long-term memory.

But although we have many failings as an audience, news broadcasters also bear part of the blame. The average newscast is often so difficult to make sense of that it might fairly be called "biased against understanding." The typical broadcast contains too many stories, each of which tries to condense too much information into too little time. Stories are individually packaged segments typically composed of complex combinations of visual and verbal content (to better activate our orienting response). All too often, the visual information is so powerful that it overwhelms the verbal. Viewers are left with striking mental images but little contextual information. Often pictures are used that are irrelevant to stories—they distract and don't inform. Findings presented by Dennis Davis and John Robinson (1989) are typical of this body of research. They interviewed more than 400 viewers to assess what they learned or failed to learn from three major network news broadcasts. They identified numerous story attributes that enhanced or inhibited learning. Viewers poorly understood stories with complex structure and terminology or powerful but irrelevant visual images. Human-interest stories with simple but dramatic storylines were well understood. Viewers frequently confused elements of stories and wove together information drawn from similar reports. But how much blame is fairly aimed at news professionals? "The task that democratic theory prescribes for American general-purpose mass media is extremely difficult at best, and, in most instances, impossible," writes public opinion researcher Doris Graber (1984). "To gain the attention of mass audiences, the media must tell political stories simply and interestingly. But most political stories are neither simple nor appealing to general audiences. Most cannot be condensed to fit the brief attention span of the public. The attempt to be both simple and interesting leads to oversimplification and an emphasis on sensational human-interest features of events" (pp. 214–215).

None of this, however, is to say that viewers cannot learn from television news. There is indeed evidence that the more conscious attention people give to the news, the more accurate information they learn. As Steve Chaffee and Joan Schleuder (1986) demonstrated, "Attention to news media appears to be a consistent individual difference that accounts for substantial variation in learning beyond the effects of simple exposure. There is some evidence of fluctuation in attention from one medium to another, one kind of news to another, and one time to another, but these dimensions of variation are overshadowed by the general trait that we might call attentiveness to news media" (p. 102). Researcher Mira Sotirovic (2003) explains, "The way people process information also has been found to have important implications for the effects of news media. . . . Information-processing strategies help individuals to cope with the vast amount of incoming news items and allow them to achieve meaning and understanding appropriate to their needs. . . . Basically, the strategies can be more effortful, elaborate, and analytic, or less demanding, simple, and heuristic. More elaborated active processing is related to greater recall of news and greater exclusion of irrelevant information" (p. 125).

Information-processing theory has great potential to permit exploration of a wide variety of media content beyond news. Researchers apply it to such diverse topics as advertising (Lang, 1990), televised political content, and children's programming (Young, 1990). This research is rapidly revealing how we tailor our innate cognitive skills to make sense of and use media content. Our ability to do this is most strikingly demonstrated by children as they learn to watch television. Within a few years, they move from being dazzled by shifting colors and sound on the screen to making complex differentiations (good/bad, strong/weak, male/female) about program characters and making accurate predictions about the way storylines will unfold. For example, children come to recognize that Disney stories will have happy endings despite the efforts of evil characters. But underlying these seemingly simple and routine acts of meaning making are complex cognitive processes that have been adapted to the task of watching television.

SCHEMA THEORY

Doris Graber (1984), in *Processing the News*, her landmark effort to understand how people "tame the information tide," brought **schema theory** to the discipline. Schema theory can be traced back to 1932 and cognitive psychologist Sir Frederic Bartlett's initially ill-received *Remembering*. His contemporaries rejected his assertion that remembering is not reproductive, but reconstructive. That is, people do not hold memories in their minds as details of things past, to be called forth when required; instead memories are new constructions cobbled together from bits and pieces of connected experiences and applied as situations demand. What make this construction possible are **schemas**, cognitive structures people build up that are abstracted from prior experience and used for processing new information and organizing experiences. Bartlett (1932) himself defined a schema as "an active organization of past reactions, or of past experiences" (p. 201). These complex, unconscious knowledge structures "are active, without any awareness at all" (p. 200). Moreover, schemas are "generic"; that is, after a person has encountered a phenomenon first once, then many times, he or she builds—and continues to build—an abstract, general cognitive representation (a schema) and all new incoming information related to that phenomenon is processed in terms of that schema. Schemas are also "generative"—that is, they can handle an indefinite number of new instances because individuals are constantly building and revising their schemas in response to new information (Brewer & Nakamura, 1984).

Consider your schema for something simple—for example, *boat*. Even if you have never been on a boat, your boat schemas no doubt contain knowledge about boats in general (float, move, hulls, decks), and quite likely information about specific types of boats, such as motor boats (sleek, fast, powerful) and sailboats (sails, wind, ropes, masts, lean over). You might also think of boats in the larger context of water-bound transportation devices—for example, tankers, navy ships, container ships, and barges are large, functional boats propelled by motors; yachts are large pleasure boats; and submarines are a special class of boat that sometimes travels under water. You may have personal experience with boats, so those experiences are part of your boat schema—musty smell, seasickness, vacationing at the ocean or lake, water skiing, swimming with friends, romance. Each new boat experience builds more information into your boat schema. So, when you hear a 45-second radio news report about a sailboat race through Capitol City's industrial harbor, you can quite easily and efficiently make sense of the story and more than likely produce a fair account for a friend who later asks you about it.

But you also have schemas for much more complex phenomena. What is your Republican schema? Your Democrat schema? Your war-on-terror schema? Your socialism or authoritarianism schemas? How broad and deep are they? How were they built? That is, what experiences—real-world and mass-mediated—contributed to their construction and the connections they call up when something in your experience activates them?

Some schemas are for events rather than things or concepts. When these schemas are constructed episodically—if this . . . then that . . . then this . . . then that—they are called **scripts**, or "standardized generalized episode[s]" (Schank & Abelson, 1977, p. 19). People "understand what they see and hear" by matching those inputs to scripts, "pre-stored groupings of actions they have already experienced" (p. 67). You don't rely on scripts? What about your last trip to a restaurant? Did you have some clear expectations about the way in which actions would take place—greeted by a host, seated at a table, presented with a menu, and so on? What if the waiter never delivered a bill? What would you do?

Now recall from earlier in this chapter Graber's (1984) "defense" of American news media and their impossible task of trying to report on complex and unappealing events for an audience with a short attention span. In this situation, she argues, schemas serve four important functions for news consumers who, by nature, are cognitive misers:

1. They determine what information will be noticed, processed, and stored so that it becomes available for later retrieval from memory.
2. They help people organize and evaluate new information, fitting it into their already-established perceptions. People do not have to construct new concepts when familiar information is presented in the news.

3. They make it possible for people to go beyond the immediate information presented in a news report, helping them fill in missing information.

4. They help people solve problems because they contain information about likely scenarios and ways to cope with them; that is, they serve as scripts. This makes them important tools in helping people decide how to act. (p. 24)

Graber's (1984) study of a panel of 21 registered voters/news consumers to see how people make sense of the news confirmed her assessment of the value of schema. "People tame the information tide quite well," she wrote. "They have workable, if intellectually vulnerable, ways of paring down the flood of news to manageable proportions" (p. 201). "People from all walks of life, endowed with varying capabilities, can manage to extract substantial amounts of political knowledge from this flood of information," she continued, "All panelists had mastered the art of paying selective attention to news and engaging in the various forms of relatedness searches. All had acquired schemas into which they were able to fit incoming political information. All were able to work with an adequate array of schema dimensions, and all frequently used multiple themes in their various schemas" (p. 204).

In fact, Graber (1988) discovered voters bring several well-formed schemas to their interpretation of political news (p. 193):

- *Simple Situation Sequences*—people do not process news stories to remember precise details; instead they condense the account to their bare essentials to understand what they mean in specific contexts.
- *Cause-and-Effect Sequences*—people link reported situations to their likely causes.
- *Person Judgments*—people easily process news about individuals in terms of their demographic groups because they have built schemas about human nature, goals, and behaviors.
- *Institution Judgments*—just as people have schemas for the behavior of individuals, they have schemas for the way institutions are supposed to operate.
- *Cultural Norms and American Interests*—people have a general "the American way" schema that includes the construction that democracy is the best form of government for the United States and for the world as a whole.
- *Human Interest and Empathy*—people interpret reports in terms of self-perception: "Is the situation depicted in the news story similar to what I have experienced directly or vicariously or similar to what I would do under the circumstances?" (p. 212).

You can read more about what happens when news frames bump up against people's schemas in the box "Battle of the Competing Schemas."

Schema theory has also been applied to advertising content, typically in assessing the impact of **schema-inconsistent advertising**—that is, advertising that intentionally violates people's expectations of that form of content. For example, arguing that advertisers' immediate goal is to attract consumers' attention and have them engage their commercial messages, Hazel Warlaumont (1997) reasoned that "[o]ne aspect of schema theory is that if a text conforms to a person's expectations, or schema, then perception will be smooth and logical; if not, it will seem incongruous, or 'schema-inconsistent.' If

BATTLE OF THE COMPETING SCHEMAS

One of the drawbacks of schema theory is that people from different disciplines, and sometimes from the same fields, often use the term a bit casually. For example, in his very fine work on news frames and consumers' schemas, Fuyuan Shen (2004) writes, "It is theorized here that, in response to news discourses, individuals will engage in active thinking and bring *their own mental frames or schemas* [emphasis added] to the interpretative process" (p. 401). Sometimes, as in this example, *frames* and *schemas* are used interchangeably; sometimes they represent different phenomena. Sometimes *scripts* and *schemas* are interchangeable; sometimes a *script* is a specific type of schema. Sometimes scholars try to refine the term *schema*—for example, employing constructs such as *propositions* or *frame keepers* (Brewer & Nakamura, 1984, p. 31). We'll revisit the many different definitions of frames and framing in Chapter 13.

In his classic work on media coverage of presidential elections, *Out of Order*, Thomas Patterson (1993) defines *schema* as this text does: "a cognitive structure that a person uses when processing new information and retrieving old information. It is a mental framework the individual constructs from past experiences that helps make sense of a new situation" (p. 56). He also talks about *frames*, using that term as Shen did—that is, to refer to how news reports are constructed around a specific theme.

Patterson argues that reporters and voters have differing schemas for elections, and that this clash of mental frameworks produces such a disconnect between journalism and voters that "the United States cannot have a sensible campaign as long as it is built around the news media" (p. 25).

Regarding elections, he notes, voters have a "governing schema" that values "policy problems, leadership traits, policy debates, and the like." Patterson quotes another political scientist, Samuel Popkin, to say that this schema produces "voters [who] actually do reason about parties, candidates, and issues. They have premises, and they use those premises to make inferences from their observations of the world around them" (p. 59). But reporters, according to Patterson, frame politics as a "game." "When journalists encounter new information during an election, they tend to interpret it within a schematic framework according to which candidates compete for advantage. . . . [C]andidates are strategic actors whose every move is significant. . . . [P]olitics is essentially a game played by individual politicians for personal advancement, gain, or power" (pp. 57–58).

What meanings of the electoral process do reporters construct using the game frame? When candidates speak about issues, the press hears ulterior motives. When candidates make promises, reporters hear pie-in-the-sky proposals that can't possibly be kept. For campaign reporters, elections are about the horse race: Who's ahead; how far; what do the polls say? "In the game schema [or frame], the focus is on a few individuals—the candidates—rather than on the larger interests they represent and the broader political forces that shape their campaign," writes Patterson. "To the press, strategy and maneuvers are not merely a component of the campaign; they are a decisive element" (p. 63).

What kind of reporting results from these constructions? In other words, how are news stories about elections framed? When Patterson wrote *Out of Order* in 1993, the horse-race frame (a news account's organizing structure) made up 35% of network television news coverage, and reporting on polls accounted for another 33%. Policy issues made up less than one third of all reporting. Things did not improve much in the next 15 years. In the 2008 election, 71% of all political stories in all the major media were horse-race reports; only 13% dealt with policy. These data led William Hudson (2013) to write, "This journalistic 'schema' or 'frame' of an election as a strategic game between opposing campaign teams not only diminishes discussion of issues but also distorts such discussion at the rare times when issues are raised. Rather than portraying the candidates' issue statements as serious proposals for addressing the country's problems, the strategic game frame treats such statements merely as positions taken to attract the support of particular constituencies" (p. 196). The press's framing of campaign news stories damages democracy because, as Patterson (2013) argued, "[V]oters are intensely interested in learning about candidates' issue positions as a way of evaluating their capacity to address real problems, even though the journalists' strategic frame lets little of that information get through to them" (p. 196). And there is evidence that this is not good for democracy. Nicholas Valentino and his colleagues demonstrated that framing

(Continued)

affects turnout, trust in government, civic duty, and the perceived value of elections. Nonpartisans and people with less than a college degree are most impacted by strategy-based framing, becoming more alienated and less motivated to vote, more so than partisans (Valentino, Beckmann, & Buhr, 2001).

Do you agree with researchers Patterson and Hudson? Do you think journalists and voters actually have these dramatically different schemas/frames for elections? Is it possible that these scholars are overly generous in their view of American voters and maybe a little too negative about the press? Here are some data on news coverage, trust in news media, and voter turnout to help you with your answers. In the 2016 presidential primaries, when voters were still deciding who would represent their political party in the general election, 56% of all news reports were horse-race coverage; 35% were about campaign process, such as which states to campaign in,

fundraising, and so on; and 11% of coverage was on policy issues (Patterson, 2016b). Once the candidates, Donald Trump and Hillary Clinton, were selected, general election coverage did not get much better. Forty-two percent of news coverage was horse-race; 17% covered controversies; only 10% was about policy. And when news reports did deal with the candidates' "fitness for office," 82% were negative for both contenders (Patterson, 2016a). In the wake of that election, nearly 7 in 10 Americans, 69%, said they had lost trust in the news media ("Indicators of News Media," 2018). Finally, despite a very close and contentious presidential election, major issues at stake, and $6.5 billion spent in the presidential and congressional races, voter turnout was its lowest in two decades, with fewer than 60% of voting-age Americans making their way to the polls, or, expressed differently, more than 4 in 10 citizens in the "world's greatest democracy" did not vote (Wallace, 2016).

SCHEMA THEORY

Strengths

1. Focuses attention on individual cognitive processing in the mass communication process
2. Respects the information-processing ability of media consumers
3. Provides specificity in describing the role of experience in information processing
4. Provides exploration of a wide variety of media information
5. Provides consistent results across a wide range of communication situations and settings

Weaknesses

1. Too oriented toward micro-level
2. Suffers from label confusion (e.g., schema, frame, script)
3. Insufficiently accounts for neurological influences
4. More research is needed to understand the processes involved in schema formation and change

the stimuli are not what was expected, it may arouse a mild 'perturbation' or a feeling of surprise that may motivate the viewer to attempt to make sense out of the discrepancy through involvement with the stimuli" (p. 41). Her research demonstrated that this was indeed the case.

HOSTILE MEDIA EFFECT

What happens to information processing when individuals believe the media "favor or are hostile toward specific topics or groups? . . . [These] attitudes toward media have been shown to be important because they affect a host of social and political behaviors" (Tsfati & Cohen, 2013, p. 1). Research into the **hostile media effect (HME)** has consistently demonstrated that partisans—those who feel strongly about an issue—see media coverage of their topic of interest as less sympathetic to their side, more sympathetic to the opposing side, and generally hostile to their point of view. Specifically:

- Partisans, viewing the very same piece of media content, interpret it as biased against their position (Vallone, Ross, & Lepper, 1985).
- When asked to recall the contents of an account, partisans remember more negative references to their position that positive ones (Vallone, Ross, & Lepper, 1985).
- Partisans believe that neutral audiences will be persuaded against their point-of-view by hostile media coverage, although the evidence suggests that this is not necessarily the case (Perloff, 1989).

Albert Gunther and Cathleen Schmitt (2004) demonstrated that partisans did indeed place the perceived hostility to their positions at the feet of the media. They presented people with the same neutral write-up on genetically modified foods drawn from actual newspaper stories. In one condition the account was presented as a newspaper article; in the other, as a student essay. They discovered that "partisans saw the information as disagreeably biased in a news story format. In student-essay format, however, the hostile media perception disappeared" (p. 55). But why attribute hostility specifically to the media? Gunther and Janice Liebhart (2006) demonstrated that it may be the media's *reach to a potentially larger audience* (a story on genetically modified food would or would not be published) that fueled partisans' perception of an account's hostility. They wrote, "Partisans in both groups were virtually identical in their perceptions of content when the author was a student; the same uniform perception appeared when the context was a composition unlikely to reach any audience beyond the classroom. However, when either the author was a journalist or the context was a nationally circulated news article, partisan perceptions diverged conspicuously. Under those circumstances, participants on opposing sides saw identical information as significantly biased in opposite directions—a direction counter to their own point of view" (p. 462).

But what happens when these partisans encounter media reports that are actually and clearly supportive of their positions? When it becomes impossible for these people to see the reporting as hostile, they tend to judge it as less supportive than do their opponents and even nonpartisans (Gunther & Chia, 2001). This is the *relative HME*, "to denote that while clearly favorable coverage is not seen as objectively hostile, the bias does not completely disappear but rather just becomes relative" (Tsfati & Cohen, 2013, p. 6).

Robert Vallone, Lee Ross, and Mark Lepper (1985) explain that the HME is a product of people's routine cognitive processing—selective perception and systematic information processing. "Partisans who have consistently processed facts and arguments in light of their preconceptions and prejudices (accepting information at face value or subjecting it to harsh scrutiny, as a function of its congruence with these preconceptions and prejudices) are bound to believe that the preponderance of reliable, pertinent evidence favors their viewpoint." As such, "to the extent that the small sample of evidence and argument featured in a media presentation seems unrepresentative of this larger 'population' of information, perceivers will charge bias in the presentation and will be likely to infer hostility and bias on the part of those responsible for it" (p. 579).

This "investment" in their position leads to the *different standards mechanism*, in which partisans' conviction that opposing arguments—by definition—are inferior renders their mere inclusion in a media account proof of biased or hostile reporting (Giner-Sorolla & Chaiken, 1994). This also suggests, and Glenn Hansen and Hyunjung Kim (2011) have documented, that the HME is more pronounced as people become more involved in the reported topic.

ELABORATION LIKELIHOOD MODEL

Not all information-processing theory involves learning from news and advertising. Much of this work is devoted to how people interpret and react to persuasive messages. Psychologists Richard Petty and John Cacioppo (1986) developed a model of persuasion, the **elaboration likelihood model (ELM)**, which, while accepting the cognitive psychology view that people are "cognitive misers" (Taylor, 1981), acknowledges that when presented with a persuasive message, people will sometimes put a lot of effort into their cognition; sometimes, though, they rely on less demanding, simple analysis. As *social* psychologists, Petty and Cacioppo (1986) argued that there must be something more than the efficient use of cognitive capacity that motivates these different information-processing strategies. Their ELM (Figure 10.1), then, is based on the assumption that for social reasons, people are motivated to hold "correct" attitudes. Why? Because "incorrect attitudes are generally maladaptive and can have deleterious behavioral, affective, and cognitive consequences. If a person believes that certain objects, people, or issues are 'good' when they are in fact 'bad,' a number of incorrect behavioral decisions and subsequent disappointments may follow" (p. 127). But although "people want to hold correct attitudes, the amount and nature of issue-relevant elaboration in which they are willing or able to engage to evaluate a message vary with individual and situational factors" (p. 128). In other words, not everyone is willing or able to process information in a way that will get them to that correct attitude, at least not all the time. Sometimes they take an easier, more automatic route to their opinion. You can hear echoes of dissonance theory and social categories from our earlier discussion of attitude change (Chapter 4). This is because this **peripheral route** of information processing (the right side of Figure 10.1) does not rely on elaboration (scrutiny) of the message as much as it does on cues unrelated to the information—for example, attractive sources, catchy jingles, or political party labels—exactly as dissonance theory and social categories suggest. These cues serve as **heuristics**, simple decision rules that substitute for more careful analysis of persuasive messages. This happens for a very good reason. As Richard Miller and his colleagues explained, it would be "irrational to scrutinize the plethora of counterattitudinal messages revived daily. To the extent that one possesses only a limited amount of information-processing time and capacity, such scrutiny would disengage the thought processes from the exigencies of daily life" (Miller, Brickman, & Bolen, 1975, p. 623).

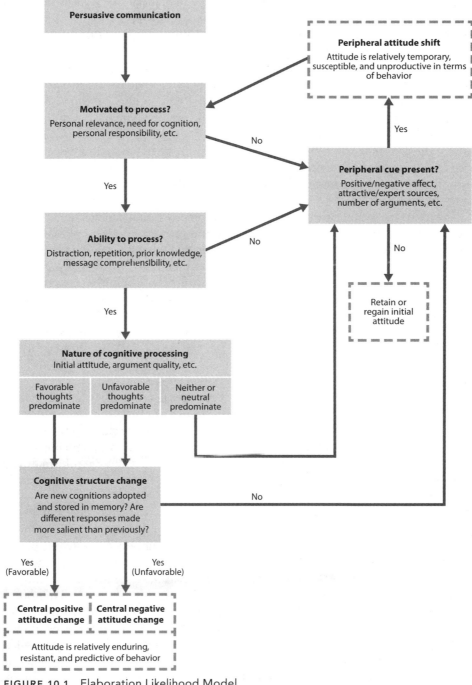

FIGURE 10.1   Elaboration Likelihood Model

But obviously there often are circumstances when people actively, willingly work through an argument or issue. When motivated by the relevance of the information, a need for cognition, or a sense of responsibility, people will use the **central route** of information processing (the left side of Figure 10.1), in which they bring as much scrutiny to the information as possible. They engage in "issue-relevant thinking," and the "elaboration likelihood" is high. ELM sees the likelihood of elaboration as running along a continuum from no thought about the information at hand to "complete elaboration of every argument, and complete integration of the elaborations into the person's attitude schemas" (Petty & Cacioppo, 1986, p. 8). Attitudes that are the product of this more stringent elaboration tend to be more deeply held, more enduring, and more predictive of subsequent behavior. Attitudes developed through the peripheral route tend to be less deeply held, less enduring, and less predictive of behavior.

The **heuristic-systematic model** of information processing, much like ELM, argues that people process information systematically and heuristically, but it sees these two processes as working together. It is a *dual-process model* in that it recognizes concurrent, parallel modes of information processing that are qualitatively different (Chaiken & Trope, 1999). Also like ELM, it assumes that people are cognitive misers. As economy-minded information processors, we want to minimize effort while satisfying whatever motivations led us to that processing. The heuristic-systematic model, therefore, says we accomplish this by holding to the **sufficiency principle**—we will exercise only as much systematic processing as is necessary (sufficient) to meet that need. If a little bit of hard mental work does the job, so be it; time for heuristics to carry the processing load. If more work is necessary to reach the *sufficiency threshold*, that point when need for cognition is satisfied, great; time for heuristics to take over (Chen & Chaiken, 1999). As a result, if the two processes produce a judgment that is congruent—that is, similar—the outcome is *additive*. It produces more stable attitude change that is a better predictor of later behavior. If they are incongruent or in opposition, systematic processing *attenuates*, or diminishes, the strength of the heuristics. When the information or arguments under consideration are ambiguous, heuristics tend to *bias* the information processing, even biasing people's systematic processing.

ELM has been tested in scores of research trials in scores of settings and has enjoyed widespread acceptance. So it is no surprise that mass communication researchers find it useful, especially because much media consumption, even of obvious persuasive messages such as marketing and political messages, occurs routinely (without much elaboration) and, as we've already seen, theorists have identified difficulties in information processing even when audience members do attempt to pay attention to (elaborate) messages. ELM's most common application to mass communication, then, is in the realm of information campaigns. Petty, Pablo Briñol, and Joseph Priester (2009) explain, "If the goal of a mass media influence attempt is to produce long-lasting changes in attitudes with behavioral consequences, the central route to persuasion appears to be the preferred persuasion strategy. If the goal is immediate formation of a new attitude, even if it is relatively ephemeral (e.g., attitudes toward the charity sponsoring a telethon), the peripheral route could prove acceptable. . . . We now know that media influence, like other forms of influence, is a complex, though explicable process" (pp. 153–154).

INSTANT ACCESS

ELABORATION LIKELIHOOD MODEL

Strengths

1. Focuses attention on individuals in the mass communication process
2. Respects intellect and ability of media consumers
3. Provides specificity in describing process of information processing
4. Provides exploration of a wide variety of media information
5. Provides consistent results across a wide range of communication situations and settings

Weaknesses

1. Too oriented toward micro-level
2. Dismisses possibility of simultaneous, parallel information processing
3. Sacrifices testable causal relationships in favor of multiple cues present in messages
4. Less useful in explaining persuasive effects of entertainment media

Lance Holbert, Kelly Garrett, and Laurel Gleason (2010) attempt to reduce that complexity by arguing that the Internet-based media make clear ELM's value to mass communication theory and research. Legacy media, they argue, are *push media;* they push information toward audience members, who either accept it or don't accept it. But Internet-based media are *pull media;* audience members pull from media the information they seek. For example, when you make a Google inquiry, you are pulling information from Google's servers. "When you have the user in control, pulling down political media content, what do you have from the standpoint of ELM?" they write. "You have *motivation*—audience members who want to consume politically persuasive media messages. In addition, audience members in a pull media environment are more likely to consume their chosen political media messages at desirable times, in preferred places/contexts, and utilizing formats that best match their particular learning styles. Each of these characteristics of the media-use experience facilitates greater *ability* to process political information" (p. 27). Consider the last time you encountered political information. Was it pushed at you by a television program, or did you pull it from the Facebook News Feed? How motivated were you to make sense of this information? What do you remember from it?

NARRATIVE PERSUASION THEORY AND THE EXTENDED ELABORATION LIKELIHOOD MODEL

Narrative persuasion theory argues that being "absorbed" into a media narrative "is a key mechanism whereby the story can influence one's real-world beliefs and behaviors. . . . Once individuals become immersed in the story, perceive it as realistic, and identify with story characters, there is a greater probability that narrative-based belief change will occur" (Kim, Bigman, Leader, Lerman, & Cappella, 2012, p. 473). Engagement with a media narrative consists of transportation, perceived similarity to characters in the story, and empathetic feeling toward those characters. **Transportation** is "a convergent process, where all the person's mental systems and capacities become focused on the events in the narrative" (Green & Brock, 2000, p. 701).

Transportation theory's developers, Melanie Green and Timothy Brock (2000), explained how transportation differs from ELM but can ultimately produce the same degree of attitude change. They wrote, "Rather than amount of thought per se, transportation theory posits processing that is qualitatively different from the traditional systematic or heuristic modes described in dual-process models of persuasion. . . . Elaboration implies critical attention to major points of an argument whereas transportation is an immersion into a text. Elaboration leads to attitude change via logical consideration and evaluation of arguments, whereas transportation may lead to persuasion through other mechanisms." What are those mechanisms? First, transportation into a narrative can reduce "negative cognitive responding" because content consumers may "be less likely to disbelieve or counterargue story claims, and thus their beliefs may be influenced." Second, immersion into a storyline can render the narrative more real, and "direct experience can be a powerful means of forming attitudes . . . and to the extent that narratives enable mimicry of experience, they may have greater impact than nonnarrative modes." And third, "transportation is likely to create strong feelings toward story characters," imbuing those characters' experiences or beliefs with greater influence (p. 702).

Perceived similarity and empathy, while clearly involved in transportation, are more closely connected to identification. You may remember identification from social cognitive theory (Chapter 7), and it carries much the same meaning in narrative persuasion theory: "An imaginative process through which an audience member assumes the identity, goals, and perspective of a character" (Cohen, 2001, p. 261). Identification, then, involves a cognitive response (perceived similarity) and an emotional response (empathy). Moreover, transportation and identification, because they rely on the individual content consumer's imagination, operate similarly for fiction and nonfiction narratives alike. Sheila Murphy and her colleagues delineated the cognitive processes thought to occur during transportation: "First, the audience member loses awareness of his or her surroundings and all cognitive facilities are focused entirely on the mediated world. Second, transported viewers feel heightened 'emotions and motivations.' . . . A transported viewer is so completely immersed in the media world that his or her responses to narrative events are strong, as though they were actually experiencing those events. Third, when viewers emerge from the transported state, they are often changed as a result of being so deeply engrossed in the narrative" (Murphy, Frank, Moran, & Patnoe-Woodley, 2011, pp. 410–411).

Murphy and another group of researchers compared the effectiveness of a specifically prepared dramatic narrative video (*The Tamale Lesson*) and a nonfiction narrative featuring doctors, health experts, and charts (*It's Time*) in imparting information about cervical cancer and the need for Pap tests. Although both were successful in raising awareness of cervical cancer and creating positive attitudes toward testing, the fictional narrative was more effective, especially as viewers' level of transportation increased (Murphy, Frank, Chatterjee, & Baezconde-Garbanati, 2013). A different, much more dramatically constructed and presented media narrative, a six-episode-long storyline in the network television show *Desperate Housewives* that focused on non-Hodgkin's lymphoma (cancer), proved effective in linking involvement with a specific character and the narrative itself with increased knowledge and even behavioral intention in the form of further information seeking and talking to friends and family about cancer (Murphy et al., 2011).

The value of narrative persuasion theory can be seen in another piece of research on the persuasive power of media narratives about health, but one that makes no reference to narrative persuasion theory. Susan Morgan and her colleagues studied the effect of entertainment television narratives on intention to become an organ donor. Employing actual episodes of prime-time network programs *CSI:NY*, *Numb3rs*, *House*, and *Grey's Anatomy*, each of which had organ donation as a plot line, they argued that "the influence of the media on modeling behaviors is likely to be dependent on how emotionally involving and absorbing people find a particular episode" (Morgan, Movius, & Cody, 2009, p. 137). As you might recognize from these words, these researchers pinned the power of television narratives to social cognitive theory (modeling), but their logic suggests that they just as easily might have made a narrative entertainment theory argument, especially as they demonstrated that emotional involvement in these programs (transportation and identification) significantly affected intention to talk to someone about organ donation, urging others to become organ donors, and deciding to become an organ donor.

Michael Slater and Donna Rouner (2002) made that very argument in their development of the **extended elaboration likelihood model (E-ELM)**. They wrote, "The impact of entertainment-education messages on beliefs, attitudes, and behavior is typically explained in terms of social cognitive theory principles. However, important additional insights regarding reasons why entertainment-education messages have effects can be derived from the processing of persuasive content in narrative messages. Elaboration likelihood approaches suggest that absorption in a narrative, and response to characters in a narrative, should enhance persuasive effects and suppress counterarguing if the implicit persuasive content is counterattitudinal" (p. 173). Traditional ELM, they argue, is "robustly" suited to obvious persuasive efforts, but "of limited use in understanding entertainment-education" (p. 174). **Entertainment-education (EE)** occurs when prosocial messages are imbedded in popular media content, either with the specific intent of influencing attitudes or behavior or simply as a dramatic device, but one that serves incidentally to promote a prosocial end.

INSTANT ACCESS

NARRATIVE PERSUASION THEORY

Strengths

1. Focuses attention on individuals in the mass communication process
2. Can enrich the elaboration likelihood model
3. Respects people's cognitive processing of entertainment content
4. Provides exploration of a wide variety of media information
5. Provides a model for the construction of prosocial content
6. Accounts for the operation of affect and cognition

Weaknesses

1. Too oriented toward micro-level
2. Has not demonstrated that effects of entertainment content are enduring and significant
3. More needs to be known about the factors that enhance or prevent narrative persuasion effects

Emily Moyer-Gusé (2008) went one step further, joining the extended elaboration liklihood model and social cognitive theory to create the **entertainment overcoming resistance model**. Note on Figure 10.2 where she identifies the contribution of each to her model. The basic premise of the entertainment overcoming resistance model is that there are "features of entertainment media that facilitate involvement with characters and/or narrative involvement [that] should lead to story-consistent attitudes and behaviors by overcoming various forms of resistance" (p. 420). Involvement with entertainment-education narratives refers to viewers' interest in following the story as it plays out. In this sense it is the same as transportation and represents individuals as "primarily engaged in the storyline, rather than in one's immediate environment, and experiencing vicarious cognitive and emotional responses to the narrative as it unfolds" (p. 409).

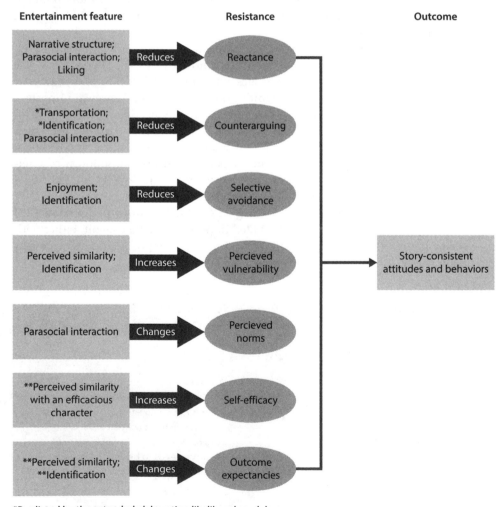

*Predicted by the extended elaboration likelihood model
**Predicted by social cognitive theory

FIGURE 10.2 Entertainment Overcoming Resistance Model

Involvement with characters is a bit more complicated, as it integrates identification, wishful identification, similarity, parasocial interaction, and liking. In the entertainment overcoming resistance model:

- *Identification* is an emotional and cognitive process in which individuals take on the role of a narrative's character, forgetting their own reality and for the time becoming the character and adopting the character's perspective. Identification has four dimensions—empathic (sharing feelings with the character), cognitive (sharing the character's perspective), motivational (internalizing the character's goals), and absorption (losing self-awareness during consumption of the narrative).
- *Wishful identification* occurs when individuals want to be like, desire to emulate, and look up to the character (Chapter 7).
- *Similarity*, sometimes called homophily, is the degree to which individuals think that they are similar to a character. It can occur as similarity of physical attributes, demographic variables, beliefs, personality, or values.
- *Parasocial interaction* is individuals' interaction with a narrative's characters, forming a "pseudo relationship" (Chapter 9). Parasocial interactions seem like face-to-face relationships but, of course, are not reciprocated by media characters.
- *Liking* is individuals' positive evaluations of a narrative's characters; it is sometimes called affinity or social attraction.

Not all narrative persuasion research examines normative messages—those designed to generate positive health attitudes and behaviors. Juan-José Igartua and Isabel Barrios (2012) wanted to expand narrative persuasion theory and the extended elaboration likelihood model to explanations of attitude change when narratives deal with controversial or polemical topics or stories that otherwise deal with values that people hold important. No one, they argued, could be opposed to the health messages embedded in the stories typically used in narrative persuasion and E-ELM research. So they asked, what about "research into the impact of public narratives that sow controversy or agitate public opinion" (p. 515)? Using the film *Camino*, a Spanish movie about the death of a 14-year-old girl that presented the controversial Catholic religious group Opus Dei and religion in general in a negative light, they demonstrated that exposure to the film "induced a greater degree of agreement with the beliefs 'Opus Dei is an organization harmful for society' and 'religion is an obstacle to living a full life'" (p. 526). These judgments grew stronger with greater identification with the film's main character. The persuasive power of narratives, they argued, should be studied across a wider range of media, issues, and contexts than had been the case.

Health Communication
Internet-based media researchers and scholars interested in **health communication** increasingly work together to assess use of both media and face-to-face communication to inform and influence people's decisions about their health. Among the most promising venues of inquiry are the use of the Internet as a substitute for a traditional visit to a health professional and the use of Internet-based media in the service of public health campaigns.

Eighty percent of American Internet users search online for health information, and search engines are the starting point for 80% of those searches (Weaver, 2018). And because three quarters of the health articles they do find are either misleading or include some false information (lack of context, exaggerating harm of a potential threat, or overstating research findings; Raphael, 2019), only about half of the self-diagnoses they produce are accurate (Park, 2018), and fully one third of young adults, 18- to 24-year-olds, lack even basic health literacy (Schwartz, 2017), there has been increasing interest in **health literacy**, the ability to obtain, process, and understand basic health information and services needed to make appropriate health decisions. As you've read, entertainment education in its various forms can play a role here.

Social networking is another site of research interest, especially the use of information shared among social networking friends to improve health outcomes. For example, medical professionals have developed an app that searches for keywords in users' newsfeeds to alert them to their increased risk of catching the flu. If, for example, four of your SNS friends post that they missed class and three others post that they're kind of achy, you're likely to receive the message, "You have a chance of getting the flu *today*." Other researchers have applied a similar approach to sexually transmitted infections (STI). Tracy Clark-Flory (2012) notes that "[r]eal-world social networks—in other words, a person's circle of friends and sexual partners—have already proved to be strong predictors of STI risk. . . . It follows that sites like Facebook, which convene all of those real-world connections in one virtual setting, have huge potential in this arena" (para. 2). The logic is that if keywords in SNS posts suggest sexually risky behavior or social contact with an infected individual, users will get a message to exercise extra care. Alternatively, in states where sexual partner notification is the law, people diagnosed with an STI can be asked for a list of sexual partners and friends whom they think might benefit from testing. Those people can be contacted using Facebook with an alert that someone they know has been diagnosed with an STI, they might be at risk, and they should be tested. Facebook is also being used to promote safe sex among high school and college students. Sheana Bull and her colleagues conducted an experiment in which they sent different messages to different recipients. Those who received News Feed messages about sexual health—items about "condom negotiation," HIV testing, and healthy sexual relationships in a weekly feature called Just/Us—showed better rates of condom use. The researchers chose to use News Feed rather than information from more formal SNS safe-sex advocates because "there is little evidence to suggest a majority of youth actively seek out and engage with organizations on Facebook. Thus, approaches like that of Just/Us to 'push' messages out through RSS feed offer one way to get messages in front of a large number of youth" (Bull, Levine, Black, Schmiege, & Santelli, 2012, pp. 472–473). Likewise, Wasim Ahmed and his colleagues demonstrated the value of a large-scale Twitter campaign in increasing awareness of autism and the generation of positive affect toward sufferers (Ahmed, Bath, Sbaffi, & Demartini, 2018).

THE DELAY HYPOTHESIS

The persuasive power of narratives, as we've just seen, has been quite convincingly demonstrated, so much so that it has become the foundation of both the extended elaboration likelihood and the entertainment overcoming resistance models. But some scholars logically wonder if these narratives, so effective in influencing correct (that is, prosocial and healthful) attitudes and behaviors, may be just as effective in influencing incorrect ideas or judgments. In proposing the **delay hypothesis**, Jakob Jensen and his colleagues wrote, "People are bombarded by mass media every day all over the world, and a sizeable (and growing) body of mass communication research has demonstrated that much of this content is distorted in a multitude of ways. Media narratives provide misrepresentations or inaccurate information about gender, race, class, sexual orientation, and a variety of social behaviors. . . . Thus, the opportunity for delayed message effects in narrative situations—small or sizeable—is considerable" (Jensen, Bernat, Wilson, & Goonewardene, 2011, p. 523).

The delay hypothesis contends that media effects can occur over time as people engage in information processing and recall. "Fictional media narratives," they wrote, "may produce small or no immediate effects on receiver beliefs that then increase or manifest over time as components of the message decay, become dissociated in memory, and/or are reappropriated in alternative ways by cognitive networks" (p. 509). The subsequent effect might be a *delayed drip*—a delayed cumulative effect— or a *delayed drench*—a delayed large effect. Nonetheless, "many effects will occur well after initial exposure to fictional narratives, especially those with vivid content and imagery" (p. 510).

The logic of the delay hypothesis is similar to that of the **sleeper effect**, the idea that attitude change, while not immediately measurable after reception of a persuasive message, might occur over time as recipients forget factors that typically influence persuasion, such as source, evidence, and so on (Hovland, Lumsdaine, & Sheffield, 1949). The sleeper effect was originally a product of the World War II persuasion research accompanying the *Why We Fight* film series (Chapter 4) and has since had mixed research support. The delay hypothesis, however, in much the same way as narrative persuasion theory, contends that there is a fundamental difference between attitude change based on a persuasive message (where attention is on the argument being made) and that produced by narratives, where attention is on plot, characters, and action and where message consumers are transported into the narrative itself, especially as dramatized narrative fictions are typically more vivid and exciting than real life and therefore likely to distort people's memories (Shrum, 2009).

To test the delay hypothesis, Jensen and his colleagues showed college students an episode of the ABC television network program *Boston Legal*. And like the narrative persuasion research we've already discussed, it dealt with health and medicine, but unlike that work, it did so incorrectly (ABC eventually issued a public apology and explanation). The specific episode, entitled "Nuts," incorrectly presented allergy auto-injectors (shots for the emergency treatment of life-threatening allergic reactions) as ineffective in treating severe peanut allergies. In this particular narrative, a teacher who had administered the treatment a few seconds after a child was stricken was being sued because of the death of that child. The researchers demonstrated that when participants were queried 2 weeks after viewing, they reported more false knowledge than they did immediately after seeing the program, confirming the delay hypothesis. The researchers also discovered that the perceived reality of the narrative influenced the delayed effect.

AFFECTIVE INTELLIGENCE, MOTIVATED REASONERS, AND THE BACKFIRE EFFECT

Over the last few decades a different perspective on information processing has begun to take hold. Political scientists James Kuklinski and Paul Quirk (2000) describe the trend this way: "The [cognitive] psychologist starts with the layperson's commonsense perception that people are generally rational. . . . Heuristic judgments disappoint such expectations, often profoundly. In describing their effects, therefore, psychologists highlight the error. Political scientists, on the other hand, start with the research showing that people are politically ignorant. They find evidence that political heuristics can save them from being strictly clueless. So unlike psychologists, they are inclined to stress the positive side" (p. 166). In other words, many of the information-processing shortcuts to which humans are prone may be functional rather than dysfunctional. "Judging from anthropological research," they explain, "ancestral humans fought frequent wars and faced a high likelihood of death by homicide. . . . The hazardous conditions presumably rewarded stereotyping, ethnocentrism, and quick-trigger responses to fear and anger, major traits that frequently create conflict in modern politics. . . . [A]ncestral humans also lived in an information environment radically different from ours—with no writing or formal arithmetic, few concerns about remote consequences, and little or no specialized knowledge. This environment may account for the relative ineffectiveness of abstract and systematic information in persuasion. . . . [T]o the extent that we possess evolved processes for responding to persuasion, they are not adapted for this new-fangled information" (p. 165).

The theory of **affective intelligence** flows directly from this view of humans as "survivalist information processors." It sees affect (emotion) and reason, not in opposition when processing information, but as working in concert. The concept's originators, George Marcus, Russell Newman, and Michael MacKuen (2000), explain theirs "is a theory about how emotion and reason interact to produce a thoughtful and attentive citizenry." It focuses "on the dynamics between feeling and thinking through which busy individuals come to pay some attention to the hubbub of the political world that swirls around them." Because most people are not deeply involved in the details of public policy, they rely on "political habits. Reliance on habit is deeply ingrained in our evolution to humanity. So when do we think about politics? When our emotions tell us to." As a result, people "monitor political affairs by responding habitually, and for the most part unthinkingly, to familiar and expected political symbols; that is, by relying on past thought, calculation, and evaluation." The central claim of affective intelligence theory, then, "is that when citizens encounter a novel or threatening actor, event, or issue on the political horizon, a process of fresh evaluation and political judgment is activated" (p. 1). As a result, negative (or counterattitudinal) information encourages individuals to learn more by heightening their attention to the new information and increasing the effort they take to process it. Negative affect (emotion), then, motivates people to learn more about the stimulus and the environment, producing better decisions.

The theory of **motivated reasoning** assumes a relationship between emotion and reason similar to that described in affective intelligence, but argues that the outcome is not necessarily better decision-making because individuals are psychologically motivated to maintain and find support for existing evaluations. David Redlawsk and his colleagues wrote, "Motivated reasoners make an immediate evaluation of new information and use it to update an online tally that summarizes their evaluative affect. Newly encountered information carries with it an affective value. Given an existing evaluation (represented by the online tally), these affective components interact so that the online tally directly influences how the new information is evaluated *before* it is used to update the tally. . . . Even anxious voters presumably motivated to learn more and make more accurate assessments may well be subject to the processing biases of motivated reasoning as they affectively evaluate *before* they begin to cognitively process new information." So motivated reasoning, like affective intelligence, accepts an "interaction between existing affective evaluations and new information, but . . . the effect of affect may lead to *less* accurate updating, rather than more" (Redlawsk, Civettini, & Emmerson, 2010, p. 567). You may hear echoes of dissonance theory in this explanation, and that is no surprise as the theory of motivated reasoning is based, in part, on that classic conception of information processing (Chapter 4).

Brendan Nyhan and Jason Reifler (2010) produced evidence for motivated reasoning in their study of the **backfire effect**—when people who receive unwelcome, correcting information not only resist that challenge to their views, they actually come to hold their original, erroneous position even more strongly. Individuals may simply selectively perceive the new information as consistent with their existing beliefs, but the backfire effect suggests something else is operating: As people cognitively counterargue the challenging information, especially if they do so vigorously, they construct even more firmly held supporting opinions, leading them to positions that are more extreme than those originally held. In a series of experiments testing misconceptions about politically loaded topics such as the Iraq War and weapons of mass destruction, stem cell research, and tax cuts, Nyhan and Reifler demonstrated that corrections failed to reduce misconceptions for the most committed partisans and that "direct factual contradictions can actually *strengthen* ideologically grounded factual beliefs" (p. 323). There is recent research, however, that argues that backfire effects, when applied to the reporting of fact-checking organizations, tended to be found only for "particularly contentious topics, or where the factual claim being asked about was ambiguous" (Owen, 2019, para. 2).

THE NEUROSCIENCE PERSPECTIVE

In 2004 mass communication researcher John Sherry wrote, "The field of mass communication and its most influential scholars emerged from [social scientific] traditions that were intellectually antagonistic to the idea that biology may play a role in determining behavior. As time went by, researchers moved toward even more environmentally based social interactional theories found in the human action perspective . . . sociocultural theories . . . or even theories that may share more with humanities than the sciences, such as semiotics and the critical/cultural studies schools" (p. 91). But, he argued, developmental psychologists, cognitive scientists, neuroscientists, and biologists have all demonstrated that nature *and* nurture interact to determine human behavior. Mass communication research and theory, then, were in danger of becoming "outmoded" (p. 102).

Sherry offered five areas long of interest to mass communication researchers that have suffered from the discipline's inattention to the **neuroscience perspective**—the view of human agency, in the words of Rolf Muuss (1988), as a "complex system of interlinked and interdependent relationships of our biological and social environment" (p. 300):

- *Attention*—Why is our attention drawn to media; how do we differently attend to different media and genres; why are there individual differences in attention?
- *Emotion*—How does emotion enhance media experiences; how do media and mood interact; where do medium and genre preferences originate; how and why do people become habituated or addicted to media and media content?
- *Learning and memory*—What is the connection between individual differences in learning ability and memory and media effects?
- *Motivation*—How does media use interact with basic human drives?
- *Perception*—How might differing perceptual abilities influence media experiences and preferences?

Here's an example. If the elaboration likelihood model's central-route processing is in part dependent on the individual's motivation and ability to process an argument, how can a researcher ignore the quite real possibility that different people are differently disposed, often by nature, to do so? But it isn't as if the field of mass communication has completely ignored the nature aspect of the **nature/nurture divide** (genetics and brain physiology vs. learning and culture). Sherry himself acknowledged several evolutionary and trait-based media effects studies from the 1990s—for example, research on biological and cultural evolution and attraction to negative news (Shoemaker, 1996), work on evolutionary differences in the appeal of erotic content to men and women (Malamuth, 1996), and the investigation of young people's exposure to violent content and the trait of sensation seeking (Krcmar & Greene, 1999). You also saw in Chapter 7 that even earlier, in 1979, Ellen Wartella proposed a developmental perspective of children's television use that could be employed to describe and explain the communicative differences between children of different ages and differences between children and adults. Twenty years later, in 1999, she made the same argument, expressly linking this developmental perspective to the "neuropsychological effects of format characteristics and viewing styles of children" (Wartella, 1999, p. 81). And for decades advertisers and marketers have been employing **neuromarketing research**—biometric measures like brainwaves, facial expressions, eye-tracking, sweating, and heart rate monitoring—to find the "magic keys" to by-passing consumers' reason and logic in order to directly reach their subconscious.

The neuroscience perspective recognizes that the brain has several parts, each serving important functions. The part of the brain that governs survival is the *limbic system*. Sometimes people refer to it as the old brain, sometimes as the lizard or reptilian brain, because it has been with all animal species since they first evolved onto land. The new brain (about 100 million years old), the conscious, reasoning part, is the *cerebral cortex*. It serves learning and memory. James Potter (2012) suggests we think of our brains as 'hard wired' to perform certain functions, but they also include a lot of software that gives us the capability to think for ourselves" (pp. 89–90). Nobel Prize–winning economist Daniel Kahneman (2011) adopts a similar metaphor in his book *Thinking, Fast and*

Slow. He says the brain operates through two systems, System 1 and System 2. System 1 is the old brain, or Potter's hard drive. It runs automatically, can never be turned off, and makes very quick, usually correct decisions based on very little information. System 1 loves heuristics, mental short-cuts. Why? Primitive people could not survive if they paused to ponder whether that rustle in the bushes was a lion or not, and if it was, might it be a nice lion, or maybe one in need. By the time they answered these questions, they'd be lion food. System 1 works so naturally, so smoothly and quickly, that it usually overrules people's rational selves, System 2. System 2 is slow and inefficient. It requires attention, energy, and time. Kahneman doesn't say that people are cognitive misers, but his view of System 2 as deferring, even justifying, System 1 (we would call it dissonance reduction) suggests he believes we are. System 1, however, does have limitations. It has "biases," Kahneman explains, "systematic errors that it is prone to make in specified circumstances. . . . It sometimes answers easier questions than the one it was asked, and it has little understanding of logic and statistics" (p. 25). And while the fact that it can never be turned off might seem to be a good thing (for survival, at least), it may be a problem as well, as when the task at hand demands System 2's particular strengths.

But as Sherry (2004) explained, mass communication's disciplinary attention to learning and memory, those aspects of our rational selves, has caused the field to discount the questions raised by the operation of the old brain/System 1. To remedy this, he argues, mass communication theory and research must "account for the contribution of biology (e.g., sex, temperament, hormones, physical appearance, etc.) and of the social environment (e.g., parents, peers, culture, etc.). The neuroscience paradigm," he continues, "assumes that (a) all human behavior is rooted in neurophysiological processing, (b) one's neurophysiological makeup is genetically determined, but (c) is plastic across the life span (including in utero) and is therefore susceptible to environmental influence" (pp. 92–93). Peter Hatemi, Enda Byrne, and Rose McDermott (2012), a team of social scientists and geneticists, explain the interaction and plasticity of genetic makeup and environment. "In a neurobiological view, the environment represents much more than simply the stimuli that the entire organism faces," they write. "Rather the environment refers to both internal cellular processes *and* the external forces operating on an individual." They explain that "the environment refers to many factors, including the cellular environment, in utero hormones and maternal stress during gestation, and all processes that manifest across the lifespan, including the environment one's parents were in when a person was conceived, the environment a person faces as both a child and an adult, diet, parenting, family environment, social and economic issues, emotional bonding, and random life events." In other words, "the environment can refer to everything both inside and outside the body before and after an individual was born" (p. 309).

The relationship between genetics and attitudes has been amply demonstrated in studies of twins. Identical twins (monozygotic—siblings with the same genetic makeup, having been conceived from a single egg) are consistently more alike ideologically and attitudinally than fraternal twins (dizygotic—siblings conceived from two different eggs and thus genetically different) on issues such as the death penalty, ethnocentrism, morality, unions, unemployment, and abortion (Eaves & Eysenck, 1974). This distinction persists even when identical twins are raised apart from one another (Tesser, 1993). Twin studies have also demonstrated that fraternal twins tend to be ideologically and attitudinally similar while they are being raised in the same home

INSTANT ACCESS

NEUROSCIENCE PERSPECTIVE

Strengths
1. Focuses attention on individuals in the mass communication process
2. Brings clarity to the nature/nurture debate
3. Enriches traditional notions of communicative activity
4. Shows the value of automatic, unconscious information processing
5. Accounts for the operation of affect and cognition

Weaknesses
1. Too oriented toward micro-level
2. Can lack specificity, especially "if the environment can refer to everything"
3. Can appear overly deterministic
4. Usefulness for understanding important aspects of media influence needs to be demonstrated

(nurture is indeed powerful), but once they move away (and apart), they develop markedly different attitudes. This is as we would expect, as they are then free to choose their own friends, environments, and experiences, and their genetic dispositions can take them where they will in these interactions (nature is freer to express itself). But this does not happen for identical twins. Even when apart, even when free to choose their own friends, environments, and experiences, they remain attitudinally similar because they possess similar genetic dispositions (Hatemi et al., 2009).

We've seen how the evolution of the brain may influence how we react to the world, but as you have just read, the neuroscience perspective also includes consideration of genes and genetics. But keep in mind, genetics do not *determine* attitudes and behaviors. There is no "gene for xxxxxx"—for example, a "liberal gene," "conservative gene," or "media-use gene." The effects of genetics in general on the propensity to demonstrate complex social traits and behaviors is indirect and the result of the interaction of literally thousands of genes in interaction with what is already going on in the body and in the surrounding environment. Hatemi, Byrne, and McDermott (2012) explain:

> It can be overwhelming to consider how every single emotional or physical thought or action that we experience, even those we cannot see, such as the way our immune system reacts to the incursion of bacteria, the influence of a person's touch, a smile, or the feeling of warm sunlight on our face, is initiated by the combination of some stimulus and the concomitant expression of genes within our cells. This leads to the reciprocal action of other cells, which result[s] in signals that govern the expression of other genetic and neurobiological systems, which eventually inspire feeling, thought, and behavior. Once we combine this fascinating interaction with the human ability to transcend our biology, to reason, to feel, to perceive, to question, to talk, to love, to empathize, and all other self-reflective dynamics that make us human, only then can we appreciate both the wonder and complexity of the human genome. (p. 308)

Less poetically, genes regulate the environment of our bodies' cells; they provide the information that tells those cells which proteins to make, which then open or close other neurobiological pathways that encourage or discourage our states and traits. These states and traits "operate through a complex cognitive and emotive architecture." These processes "then become operationalized through a psychological architecture in a human organism that walks around, moves, and experiences the world, resulting in outcomes we observe at the macro level as behaviors, preferences, attitudes, and other recognizable measures" (Hatemi, Byrne, & McDermott, 2012, p. 309).

Mass communication researchers have begun to heed Professor Sherry's call. For example, Ashley Kirzinger, Christopher Weber, and Martin Johnson (2012) employed a twin study to demonstrate that "a nontrivial portion of variation [in media consumption and communication behavior] is explained by genetic factors" (p. 159). Theresa Correa, Amber Hinsley, and Homero de Zúñiga (2010) connected three elements of the "Big Five" model of personality traits—extraversion, neuroticism, and openness to experiences—to an individual's use of social networking. They discovered positive relationships between use of social networking and extraversion and openness to new experiences, and a negative relationship between social networking and neuroticism, or emotional stability. They also demonstrated gender and age differences.

Arguably, however, it is in the realm of political communication that scholars have been most active in linking genetics and internal dispositions to attitudes. Indicative is the work of Peter Hatemi and his colleagues on political attitudes and fear, a "genetically informed, stable, but malleable trait-based disposition, as well as a transitory state-based response that can be elicited or manipulated by environmental conditions" (Hatemi, McDermott, Eaves, Kendler, & Neale, 2013, p. 280). They demonstrated a "latent genetic factor" that is part of a social phobic disposition that generates mistrust of unfamiliarity, the idea that social contexts can be dangerous, fear of social exposure and of being awkward, and feeling humiliated in social contexts, resulting in negative attitudes toward out-groups (people unlike themselves). They concluded that "political preferences represent a manifestation of a genetic disposition expressed within the context of modern circumstances" (p. 12). And although they found that "common genetic disposition mutually influences social fear and out-group attitudes," they cautioned that "the relationship between any specific gene, fear disposition, and a particular social or political attitude is not likely to be hard-wired. Indeed, people may have divergent dispositions to be fearful of unfamiliar others, but long-term exposure to the unfamiliar makes it unfamiliar no more" (p. 13). Brad Verhulst and his colleagues applied the **top-down/bottom-up theory of political attitude formation** to demonstrating that "ideological preferences within the American electorate are contingent on both the environmental conditions that provide the context of the contemporary political debate and the internal predispositions that motivate people to hold liberal or conservative policy preferences" (Verhulst, Hatemi, & Eaves, 2012, p. 375). Political attitudes, they argued, are a combination of social experiences (top-down) and genetic pathways (bottom-up). The former are those things that we usually associate with political attitudes, such as life experience and exposure to news and political information. The latter exert stable influence on attitudes and behavior over time and across different situations.

REVIEW OF LEARNING OBJECTIVES

- Explain the major ideas encompassed by information-processing theory, including the concept of limited cognitive resources.

Information-processing theory challenges assumptions about the way people take in and use sensory data. More information and deeper processing do not necessarily lead to improved cognition. People are cognitive misers and have limited conscious awareness of the environment around them. They have finite cognitive resources: If more resources are directed toward one task, another task will be performed badly.

- Apply information-processing theory to making sense of television news.

Information on television is frequently presented in ways that inhibit rather than facilitate learning. People view TV primarily as an entertainment medium and develop information-processing skills and strategies that are well suited to enjoying entertainment content but interfere with effective interpretation and recall of news. They rarely engage in deep, reflective processing of news content that might allow more conscious control over meaning making. Further, producers depend on visual and auditory cues to draw attention to stories that rely on viewers' orienting response, their instinctive reaction to sudden or novel stimulus. TV news programs often consist of numerous short stories that are structured so that interpretation and recall are difficult.

- Better appreciate how schema theory has enriched the study of mass communication, especially in the realm of processing political communication.

Schemas are cognitive structures people build up that are abstracted from prior experience and used for processing new information and organizing experiences. For news consumers, they serve important functions: They determine what information will be noticed, processed, and stored so that it becomes available for later retrieval from memory; they help organize and evaluate new information, fitting it into already-established perceptions; they make it possible for people to go beyond the immediate information presented in a news report, helping fill in missing information; and they help people solve problems because they contain information about likely scenarios and ways to cope with them. People bring several well-formed schemas to their interpretation of political news: simple situation sequences, cause-and-effect sequences, person judgments, cultural norms and American interests, and human interest and empathy.

- Recognize the influence of the hostile media effect on processing information.

Research into the hostile media effect has consistently demonstrated that partisans—those who feel strongly about an issue—see media coverage of their topic of interest as less sympathetic to their side, more sympathetic to the opposing side, and generally hostile to their point of view.

- Find value in the elaboration likelihood model's explanation of how people come to process information systematically and heuristically.

The elaboration likelihood model is based on two assumptions: People are "cognitive misers," and for social reasons, they are motivated to hold "correct" attitudes. As such, when presented with a persuasive message, they will sometimes put a lot of effort into their cognition, but sometimes they rely on less demanding, simple analysis. Its value is that in addition to offering insight into the many variables that influence persuasion and cognition, it explains when the central processing route (high elaboration) is utilized and when less elaboration (use of heuristics) calls the peripheral route of information processing into use.

- Judge the value of newer theories of information processing, such as narrative persuasion theory and the extended elaboration likelihood model, especially to health-oriented media messages.

Narrative persuasion theory, which identifies an imaginative process through which audience members assume the identity, goals, and perspective of a character, extends understanding of information processing through its introduction of engagement and transportation into the meaning-making process. In narratives, people's mental systems and capacities become focused on the events in the story. The extended elaboration likelihood model advances this idea by suggesting that absorption in a narrative and response to its characters enhance persuasive effects and suppress counterarguing if the implicit persuasive content is counterattitudinal as it avoids more stringent central processing. Both have been extensively applied to persuasive health campaigns, especially in entertainment-education and the entertainment overcoming resistance model.

- Evaluate those information-processing theories that suggest people may not be completely rational when making meaning from media messages, ideas such as affective intelligence, motivated reasoning, and the backfire effect.

Contemporary thinking holds that many of the information-processing shortcuts to which humans are prone may be functional rather than dysfunctional. The theory of affective intelligence sees people as "survivalist information processors" who use affect (emotion) in concert with reason when processing information. The theory of motivated reasoning also makes this argument, but counters that the outcome is not necessarily better decision-making because individuals are psychologically motivated to maintain and find support for existing evaluations. The backfire effect supports this notion, as people who receive unwelcome, correcting information often not only resist that challenge to their views, they actually come to hold their original, erroneous position even more strongly.

- Assess the value to mass communication theory of incorporating various neuroscience perspectives into our understanding of information processing.

The neuroscience perspective views human behavior as a complex system of interlinked and interdependent relationships of our biological and social environments. In recognizing at least some influence of people's genetic makeup, it offers insight into important information-processing factors such as attention, emotion, learning and memory, motivation, and memory.

CRITICAL THINKING QUESTIONS

1. Earlier in the chapter you were asked, "What is your war-on-terror schema?" Information-processing theory predicts that you did not spend much cognitive energy on that question at the time because you applied the example-posed-as-a-question heuristic. But now take a moment to answer the question. Much of this country's internal politics have been driven by the war on terror, and much American foreign policy is based on those politics. Billions of dollars have been spent and continue to be spent on this war. The more than four billion passengers who board the world's

airlines every year invest considerable time and energy complying with regulations deemed necessary to fight this war. In other words, the war on terror warrants your systematic cognitive effort. So again, what is your war-on-terror schema, and from what experiences has it been constructed?

2. A large proportion of the American public has little or no trust at all in the media to report the news fully, fairly, and accurately. How much of this negative opinion do you think is a product of the hostile media effect? In other words, will people who hold strong political opinions inevitably and always find legacy, more or less objective media as hostile? Do you?

3. How open are you to divergent media voices? Do you limit yourself to a few attitudinally comfortable media outlets? Are you aware of how social media filter news for you so you don't encounter divergent views? Are you concerned about this? Why or why not? Do you think that our democracy would be better served if more people exposed themselves to differing points of view? Explain your response in terms of the information-processing theories you studied in this chapter.

KEY TERMS

information-processing theory
limited cognitive resources
orienting response
schema theory
schemas
scripts
schema-inconsistent advertising
hostile media effect (HME)
elaboration likelihood model (ELM)
peripheral route
heuristics
central route
heuristic-systematic model
sufficiency principle
narrative persuasion theory
transportation

extended elaboration likelihood model (E-ELM)
entertainment-education (EE)
entertainment overcoming resistance model
health communication
health literacy
delay hypothesis
sleeper effect
affective intelligence
motivated reasoning
backfire effect
neuroscience perspective
nature/nurture divide
neuromarketing research
top-down/bottom-up theory of political attitude formation

GLOSSARY

information-processing theory: Theory for understanding how people deal with sensory information

limited cognitive resources: In information-processing theory, idea that as more resources are directed toward one task, another will suffer

orienting response: Humans' instinctive reaction to sudden or novel stimulus

schema theory: Information-processing theory arguing that memories are new constructions constructed from bits and pieces of connected experiences and applied to meaning making as situations demand

schemas: Cognitive structures built up as people interact with the environment in order to organize their experience

scripts: Form of schema; standardized generalized episodes

schema-inconsistent advertising: Advertising that intentionally violates people's expectations of that form of content

hostile media effect (HLM): Idea that partisans see media as less sympathetic to their side, more sympathetic to the opposing side, and generally hostile to their point of view

elaboration likelihood model (ELM): Model of information processing that seeks to explain the level of elaboration, or effort, brought to evaluating messages

peripheral route: In ELM, information processing that relies on cues unrelated to the issue at hand

heuristics: Simple decision rules that substitute for more careful analysis of persuasive messages

central route: In ELM, information processing characterized by heightened scrutiny of information related to the issue at hand

heuristic-systematic model: Dual-process model of information processing that argues for the parallel operation of systematic and heuristic processing

sufficiency principle: Idea that when processing information, people exercise only as much systematic effort as is necessary (sufficient) to meet their need for cognition

narrative persuasion theory: Idea that absorption into a media narrative is a key mechanism in the story's power to influence real-world beliefs and behaviors

transportation: When a person's mental systems and capacities become focused on the events in a media narrative

extended elaboration likelihood model (E-ELM): Idea that absorption in a narrative and response to its characters enhance persuasive effects and suppress counterarguing if the story's implicit persuasive content is counterattitudinal

entertainment-education (EE): Occurs when prosocial messages are imbedded in popular media content

entertainment overcoming resistance model: Idea that entertainment media features can facilitate involvement with characters and/or narrative involvement leading to story-consistent attitudes and behaviors by overcoming various forms of resistance

health communication: The use of various forms of communication to inform and influence people's decisions that enhance health

health literacy: The ability to obtain, process, and understand basic health information and services needed to make appropriate health decisions

delay hypothesis: Idea that media effects can occur over time as people engage in information processing and recall, often leading to incorrect cognitions

sleeper effect: Idea that attitude change not immediately measurable after reception of a persuasive message might occur over time as recipients forget factors typically influencing persuasion

affective intelligence: Idea that affect (emotion) and reason beneficially work in concert in information processing

motivated reasoning: Idea that affect (emotion) and reason work in concert in information processing, but not necessarily beneficially as individuals are psychologically motivated to maintain and find support for existing evaluations

backfire effect: Idea that people who receive unwelcome, correcting information not only resist that challenge to their views but come to hold their original, erroneous position even more strongly

neuroscience perspective: View of information processing as a complex system of interlinked and interdependent relationships of people's biological and social environments

nature/nurture divide: Question of the source of human attitudes and behavior—genetics and brain physiology vs. learning and culture

neuromarketing research: Marketers' use of biometric measures to find the "magic keys" to consumer behavior

top-down/bottom-up theory of political attitude formation: Theory that ideological preferences are products of environmental conditions (top-down) and internal predispositions (bottom-up) that motivate people to hold liberal or conservative policy preferences

Theories of the Effect of Media on Knowledge, Information, and Perception of Social Issues

Viewers tuning into the February 2019 Super Bowl football game were treated to a moving ad from the *Washington Post*, voiced by Tom Hanks. Over a "soaring score," the beloved actor proclaimed, "Knowing empowers us, knowing helps us decide, knowing keeps us free." Inspiring words, but for former US attorney for the Southern District of New York Preet Bharara (2019), it was "an astonishing thing to witness—an iconic news organization feeling the need to hawk not the quality of its writing and reporting, but the most fundamental virtues of its entire industry's mission. Like truth. And knowledge. Values thought to be long settled. Merely having your business model enshrined in the First Amendment to the Constitution is no longer sufficient; now you need airtime during the Big Game—alongside Bud Light, Hyundai and Doritos" to remind Americans of the value of a free press (p. 9). Perhaps at a time when half the public says it has "hardly any confidence at all in the press" ("Poll," 2019, p. 68) and when, for the first time in the 17 years it has been gauging the state of journalism around the globe, Reporters without Borders designated press freedom in the United States "problematic" and rated the American media system only the 48th freest in the world ("United States," 2019), it was indeed necessary to buy 60 seconds of the world's most expensive commercial time to remind people of the inseparability of democracy and a free media. And that necessity is only one of many troubling issues related to media.

For example, since the 2016 presidential election, there has been a rising storm of criticism of social media. In earlier chapters we traced the rise of large-scale social media corporations. Today the most successful and aggressive SNSs span the globe and link billions of people. Control over the most popular SNSs has become highly concentrated in the hands of a few corporations. Dominant sites like Facebook, YouTube, and Twitter operate much like the big television networks in their golden age of the 1950s, 1960s, and 1970s. Like those networks, large-scale social media routinely earn hundreds of millions of dollars in advertising and find ways to block or subvert potential rivals. Like their more traditional elders, they rarely produce media content themselves, yet they serve as important gatekeepers for a broad range of different types of information and entertainment content. Until recently SNSs operated with very little public awareness. They employed expensive public relations firms and spent millions to lobby government (Romm, 2019) to maintain positive perceptions of their activities and prevent enactment of laws that would affect their profits. But over the past few years Facebook has faced criticism for its use and marketing of user data, sale of political advertising to Russian agents bent on subverting American democracy, crass attempts to crush rivals, political lobbying to limit government oversight of its operation, and fueling of genocide in Myanmar and killings in several other countries (Alterman, 2019; Mozur, 2018). Added to these troubles is what one analyst has termed the "Facebook Armageddon"—the site's domination of the flow of news from most major news sources to its hundreds of millions of American users (Ingram, 2018). This allows Facebook to earn advertising revenue from news content and pay original sources a fraction of what it costs them to produce it. Even more troubling, Facebook routinely uses algorithms that select the news items that are prominently displayed to users. These algorithms overrule the editorial decisions made by news sources and bias news presentation so that it highlights reports that are most likely to increase the time users spend on the site and thus increase the company's advertising income at the expense of news that serves user interests, news producer interests, or the public interest (Bell & Owen, 2017).

In Chapter 3 we reviewed normative theories that examine the ways media provide essential support to democracy and identify key public services essential to citizens' self-governance. It is becoming increasingly clear that our current media system is failing to provide adequate support for democracy and necessary public services. Public attention is being diverted away from useful information and drawn to media content that does little more than earn profits. This is not the first time in American history that the US media system has shown signs of stress. The current failings mirror those that occurred in the late 1930s, when radio and movies were powerful new media and most urban newspapers were owned and operated by partisan Republicans. As politically extreme totalitarian regimes came to dominate polities in Europe and demonstrated the power of control over media and the effective use of propaganda, American leaders debated the need for government control over media and the necessity for censorship (Chapter 2). While today's leaders aren't likely to censor social media, they have begun to consider laws that would force them to be more transparent about the way they earn their income and how they use algorithms to structure the delivery of services to users (Stacey, 2019).

What do you do when your media system seems to be failing, when it seems vulnerable to powerful new forms of communication that subvert the public interest? One thing you can do is conduct research on media and develop theories to help understand what they are doing. In Chapters 2 and 4 we argued that the rise of empirical media research in the 1940s and 1950s was due in large part to the desire for clear and indisputable evidence of media's power. Such evidence could serve as a basis for regulating media so that necessary control could be exercised while at the same time allowing them to operate as freely as possible without endangering the public interest. The outcome of this research was the limited-effects perspective, a view that media rarely have important direct effects but do reinforce trends attributable other factors. Since the 1970s there has been rising criticism of the limited-effects perspective and the research on which it is grounded. Recent media theory and research are producing a more nuanced perspective on the role of media—one that identifies key ways media have important influence.

Most of the theories that we discuss in this chapter were created after 1960 in an effort to better understand what media might be doing to or for society. They helped assess the rise of television and studied problems associated with this at-the-time new medium. Research based on these theories seemed at home in the limited-effects tradition but hinted that that existing way of thinking might need some updating. By the 1990s these theories allowed us to develop a fairly good understanding of a legacy media system dominated by television. To some extent this understanding was possible because in the 1980s and the 1990s American media entered a period of unusual stability and profitability. Television networks and major newspapers earned unprecedented profits year after year. It was possible for scholars to conduct research on a media system whose stability simplified their research and ensured that findings from one year tended to mirror those from others. As such, those findings could be easily added up and summarized.

This golden age of legacy media and the scholarship that probed it began a slow decline with the rise of the Internet. Initially the Internet seemed unlikely to do much to alter a very powerful and well-established media system. Academics exchanging e-mail and folks posting messages on bulletin boards or joining chat rooms seemed unlikely to disrupt the big corporations that controlled television, newspapers, magazines, radio, and film. Now, with the passage of more than three decades, the damage to legacy media is clear. Most notably, newspapers are struggling to survive in their present form; broadcast television networks face ever-growing competition for audiences and advertising dollars; and Internet-based media have risen to dominate Americans' attention and compete for advertising dollars—in 2019 the Internet for the first time generated more advertising revenue than all legacy media combined (Wagner, 2019). For media theorists and researchers the challenges posed by this transformation are daunting. How do you conduct useful research in an era of constant change? Which of the hundreds of SNSs do you study, and how do you study them? Can you adapt theories developed to understand legacy media when you want to understand a medium like Facebook, Instagram, or YouTube? We'll provide some contemporary answers to these questions in this chapter, but media scholars will be pursuing more definitive understandings for decades to come.

LEARNING OBJECTIVES

After studying this chapter you should be able to

- Assess the changing role played by media in society now that large-scale social media have become an important part of the mass media system.
- Discuss how mass media's attention to specific events and issues influences the importance we assign to those events and issues, how we interpret them, how those interpretations come to shape the political agenda, and how some people are moved to speak less openly about them.

- Find value in a number of contemporary mass communication theories that offer evidence of media's ability to produce macro-level effects, such as the knowledge gap hypothesis, innovation diffusion theory, and social marketing theory.

OVERVIEW

Early in this century the relevance of most of the theories in this chapter came under challenge. Some critics argued that new media need new theories; we shouldn't simply assume that we can explain these powerful and innovative media using old notions. But now the outlines of a new American media system have begun to clearly emerge, and the new system looks a lot like the old. It has a handful of large-scale social media and legacy media companies at its center, surrounded by a myriad of large and small media content sources. These sources include each of us, the people formerly known as the audience, as potential content contributors (Gilmor, 2004). Though SNSs give us the ability to be creative and interact with media, most of us rarely do more than post occasional comments and send links to friends (Davis, 2015). Internet technology is vital to this system, as are the growing array of mobile devices that can be used to access Internet content. The big SNSs increasingly serve as gatekeepers for the flow of content in this system. We look to them to highlight and make appealing content available to us, just as we did with legacy media. Since this new media system has many similarities to the old, it should be possible to adapt existing theories so they provide useful insights. Throughout this chapter we explain how researchers are doing this.

The contemporary media theories presented in the last four chapters were microscopic theories, concerned with explaining what happens to individuals when they use or are exposed to media content. They have implications for society if large numbers of individuals are affected in similar ways over long periods of time, but they are generally not concerned with describing or explaining such macroscopic societal level effects. Their focus is on individuals, not on aggregates or social groups. The authors of these theories are usually hesitant to generalize about large-scale consequences of the effects they describe and study. Their research studies media effects by observing individuals. Speculation about macroscopic effects is possible, but the researchers have no data that allow them to reach such conclusions.

The theories in this and the next three chapters are different. They are macroscopic level theories; they are concerned with how mass communication can bring about major changes in the social world. As James Potter (2012) explains, macroscopic theory and effects are "concerned with aggregates rather than individuals. An aggregate is a combined whole that is formed by the gathering together of all the particular elements. The public is an aggregate because it is the collection of all individuals" (p. 237). In other words, you may have a very specific, well-constructed, and stable terrorism schema (to borrow an example from the last chapter), but so do the millions of other people with whom you must share your world. When millions of people develop sharply different but strongly held schemas about terrorism, there is likely to be conflict. For example, the vitriolic 2019 debate over the need for a wall between the United States and Mexico can be traced to the different schemas held by different groups of Americans. Disagreements are the result of macroscopic—or aggregate—effects of people holding opinions and making judgments based on the micro-level schemas they have learned from and had reinforced by exposure to different media content.

The theories in these latter chapters provide differing but compatible explanations of how various media effects occur at the aggregate level. They describe how certain forms of media activity can bring about long-term, widespread, significant changes. All are concerned with how various forms of media content and their flow to aggregates of individuals can produce important effects on society. Some argue that, as the structure of media institutions changes, there will be important changes in the type and flow of different forms of media content. Over time these changes will have subtle, or occasionally dramatic, effects on the way large numbers of people think and act. As thoughts and actions change, the social institutions that shape our realities and thereby shape our everyday lives can change.

Macroscopic theories about media offer varying perspectives. Some are cautiously optimistic about the role of media in society, while others are strongly pessimistic. They seek to explain how different forms of media content can shape our understanding of the social world. We don't often think of news or entertainment as something that can—or should—alter the social world. Entertainment is just a diversion; it's not important. News is supposed to be a report about things that are happening; it's not supposed to *influence* what is happening. Journalists continue to tell us that they only provide objective news coverage. The theories in this chapter reject these simple assertions and challenge us to look differently at news and entertainment. News is not simply a mirror that reflects the social world, and entertainment is not simply trivial amusement that distracts us from that world; both can be forces capable of shaping it.

Even if we personally don't pay attention to politics, we will live in a world shaped by the way news reports politics. Even if we personally dislike celebrity culture and sports, for example, our lives are affected by them because so many others around us are influenced by them. Many of us may not know the name Umar Farouk Abdulmutallab; we might not even have paid attention to the news of his Christmas Day 2009 attempt to bring down an airliner by exploding a bomb in his underwear; but whether we did or didn't follow this story, we still have to deal with long lines, full body scans, heightened security at airports, and election campaigns that turn on which political party makes the best promises about keeping us safe from terrorism.

The contemporary media theories we consider might seem familiar to you based on your reading of previous chapters. Most of them draw on older theories to offer cogent and insightful analyses of the role of media in society. For the most part they are grounded in empirical social research. Although this work is quite diverse, the theories it supports have many similarities. As you will see, the assessment some theories provide of contemporary media and their social role is mostly negative. Several argue that media routinely foster problematic conceptions of the social world. Others argue that the hours we spend every day using media have many consequences that we don't expect or desire.

It is important to keep in mind that, despite their negative tone, none of these contemporary media theories should be confused with mass society theory. None argues that media will inevitably destroy high culture, bring an end to democracy, and plunge us into a dark age of totalitarianism. Their view of the social order is far more sophisticated than the mass society thinking central to many earlier theories, and their understanding of individuals is similar to the perspectives presented in Chapter 10. It's generally positive but mixed, based in part on active audience assumptions but tempered by the recognition that much human behavior is habitual and not consciously controlled. People don't always do what's reasonable or most useful when it comes to media. On the other hand, media don't easily manipulate passive individuals. Instead their power rests on their ability to provide communication services that we routinely use and that are central to the maintenance of our personal identities and our social world.

KNOWLEDGE GAPS, DIGITAL DIVIDES, AND DIGITAL INEQUALITIES

A team of researchers at the University of Minnesota (Donohue, Tichenor, & Olien, 1986; Tichenor, Donohue, & Olien, 1970, 1980) conducted surveys to better understand how newspapers were serving citizens in their state. Their research showed that news media systematically informed some segments of the population better than others, and these differences increased with increases in the flow of news. Why? Increased news reporting should help everyone become more informed, shouldn't it? No. The research found that people in higher socioeconomic groups became better informed but those in lower groups did not. The result was an enlarged **knowledge gap** between people in higher and lower socioeconomic groups. They concluded that "as the infusion of mass media information into a social system increases, segments of the population with higher socioeconomic status tend to acquire this information at a faster rate than the lower segments, so that the gap in knowledge between these segments tends to increase rather than decrease" (Tichenor, Donohue, & Olien, 1970, pp. 159–160). The knowledge gap hypothesis asserts that there is a preexisting gap between these segments of the population, one that can be exacerbated by audience and media factors. Subsequent research on knowledge gaps has shown that they increase because of differences in each group's ability and motivation to process and interpret information. Those of higher status tend to be more motivated to seek out and pay attention to serious forms of information such as political or science news. These types of stories tend to be written and demographically targeted by media at those more affluent groups. Of greatest concern is the finding that when the amount of serious news coverage increases, knowledge gaps tend to increase. The only situation that reduces gaps is when social conflict occurs. The researchers concluded that conflict increases the degree to which people talk about serious news topics, and this could level knowledge about such topics. Information is being transmitted by word of mouth, and conflict increases people's motivation to seek out news. However, they also found that conflicts can result in learning that polarizes groups, and this can escalate rather than defuse conflicts (Tichenor, Donohue, & Olien, 1980).

Other research has assessed whether the quality of media information could influence knowledge gaps. In a comparative study of knowledge gaps in four nations—the United States, Britain, Denmark, and Finland—James Curran, Shanto Iyengar, Brink Lund, and Inka Salovaara-Moring (2009) discovered a significant knowledge gap between American television news viewers and those in the other countries. They attributed the gap to the public service orientation of television news in those latter three countries, which "devotes more attention to public affairs and international news . . .

gives greater prominence to news [broadcasting news several times an evening in what Americans would call prime time] . . . and encourages higher levels of news consumption" (p. 5). These factors were strong enough to minimize the knowledge gap in those countries between the well educated and less educated and between those who were financially well off and those who weren't.

Yoori Hwang and Se-Hoon Jeong (2009) conducted a meta-analysis of 46 "primary" investigations of the knowledge gap conducted from 1970 to 2004, demonstrating support for its central assertion that there are indeed knowledge disparities between different social strata. They also discovered that the gap was greatest for "sociopolitical" and international topics, but less so for health-related and local information. Their analysis did challenge the knowledge gap's original contention that the gap widens over time, instead finding support for the *constant gap*—that is, a preexisting gap that is not increased but also is not reduced when news flow is increased. The researchers acknowledged that the presence of a constant gap is "disappointing particularly when it exists despite planned media campaigns that attempt to provide useful health or political information. This constant gap among high and low SES individuals can be problematic as a health knowledge gap can lead to health disparities and a political knowledge gap can result in differences in participatory behaviors" (p. 533).

Thomas Holbrook (2002) examined the knowledge gap on a national level, finding that the gaps actually narrowed during the course of presidential campaigns. He analyzed data from the National Election Studies from 1976 to 1996 and found that specific events such as political debates were linked to decreases in knowledge gaps. Holbrook's findings are consistent with earlier findings linking reduction of gaps to increases in social conflict that spark widespread public discussion and information seeking. Televised debates could stimulate discussion across socioeconomic groups, and this would reduce knowledge gaps.

The rise of Internet-based media has reignited interest in knowledge gap theory. Could social media spark and support public debates over issues that might close knowledge gaps? Would social media provide better access to information that low socioeconomic groups might find easier to understand? Heinz Bonfadelli (2002) conducted research that reached pessimistic conclusions about the role of Internet-based media in reducing knowledge gaps. In Switzerland he found a **digital divide** between affluent, better-educated young adults who regularly used the Internet for information and their less-affluent, less-educated peers who either didn't have access to the Internet or used it mostly for entertainment. Not surprisingly this divide was linked to gaps in knowledge.

In the United States research on knowledge gaps is increasingly accompanied by concern about this digital divide. Research has documented the chronic lack of access to new communication technologies by specific groups of people, especially lower-income (Anderson & Kumar, 2019) and more rural individuals (Feldman, 2019). Because only a small proportion (11%) of Americans do not regularly access the Internet, contemporary concern about the digital divide centers on access to high-speed Internet—35% do not have broadband or other high-speed Internet at home and 15% can access the Net neither from home nor a smartphone (Smith & Olmstead, 2018). But even when people are wired, a social participation gap remains. A Pew Internet & American Life Project national study discovered that "contrary to the hopes of some advocates, the Internet is not changing the socio-economic character of civic engagement in America. Just as in offline civic life, the well-to-do and well-educated are more likely than those less well-off to participate in online political activities such as emailing a government official, signing an online petition, or making a political contribution" (Smith, Schlozman, Verba, & Brady, 2009).

Additionally, as access to smartphones has put the Internet into the hands of most American adults, there has been a focus on what these adults do with this access (Huffman, 2018). As was the case with legacy media, lower socioeconomic groups tend to use smartphones mostly for entertainment and diversion. Critics charge that the most popular smartphone apps, those provided by the big SNSs, aggravate this problem by steering lower socioeconomic users toward entertainment or diversion since these hold a greater potential for generating advertising revenue. Indeed, Lu Wei and Douglas Hindman (2011) demonstrated that the digital divide (not in the availability of technology but in the nature of its use) produces gaps greater than those discovered in research based on legacy media. They wrote, "The digital divide, which can be better defined as inequalities in the meaningful use of information and communication technologies, matters more than its traditional counterpart" (p. 217). Stephanie Huffman (2018) documented the ways in which lower socioeconomic and minority groups are unable to make effective use of Internet access, and she called for a global effort to educate and train people to better use Internet-based media, especially mobile media. But this itself is not without problems, as Internet researcher Mary Madden (2017) has demonstrated that lower-income people, for whom "smartphones have become an indispensable source of internet access" because they "may lack other technology resources in their homes and communities" (para. 7), tend to suffer inequalities in personal privacy and information security as mobile technologies are more easily tracked and less secure.

Recent research by Michael Beam, Jay Hmielowski, and Myiah Hutchens (2018) focused attention on **digital inequalities** with regard to politics. The researchers studied online political engagement during the 2016 election campaign using the **OMA (opportunities-motivation-ability) model**, which predicts that differences in opportunities, motivations, and abilities to access information will predict knowledge and political action. People with less opportunity, lower motivation, and less cognitive ability will learn less and be less likely to engage in political activity. They cite several earlier studies using this model that found that lower education, lower Internet skill, and lower political interest were all key predictors of online political communication effects such as lower knowledge and less online or offline political action. They concluded that greater Internet skill and increased political interest, but not higher education, were related to greater online news reading and sharing, arguing that Internet skill may compensate for educational differences, especially if it is combined with political interest. If this is correct, efforts to overcome digital inequities might focus on improving Internet skills and encouraging political interest among lower socioeconomic groups. They warn, however, that if partisan political interests are encouraged, greater political polarization would be likely. They are especially concerned that SNS algorithms can increase user access to partisan news consistent with existing political interests. Although this might reduce digital inequities, the long-term consequences for politics (and democracy) could be problematic.

INSTANT ACCESS

THE KNOWLEDGE GAP

Strengths

1. Identifies potentially troublesome gaps between groups
2. Provides ideas for overcoming gaps
3. Presumes reciprocity and audience activity in communication
4. Is grounded in systems theory

Weaknesses

1. Assumes gaps are always dysfunctional; not all researchers agree
2. Older research focused on gaps involving news and social conflicts
3. Doesn't address fundamental reasons for gaps (e.g., poor schools, differences in cognitive skills, or limited access to information sources)

The dilemma here is similar to the one identified by the original knowledge gap research team—you can reduce knowledge gaps if you increase conflict, but the knowledge gained can fuel more conflict.

In sum, the introduction of and growing access to Internet-based media via smartphones is not closing knowledge gaps. Instead other inequities are being identified—access, motivation, cognitive ability—that are associated with differences in knowledge but also differences in political communication and personally or socially beneficial action. Even with the increasing availability of Internet-based media, lower socioeconomic groups are less likely to use these media for serious purposes. Differences in knowledge and action are likely to remain. Critical researchers see these divides and inequalities persisting for the immediate future given the massive financial and lobbying clout wielded by the cable and telecommunications industries against many cities' efforts to bring fast, affordable broadband Internet service to all citizens in the form of **municipal broadband**, providing broadband Internet access to a given locale as a low-cost utility, a practice that has demonstrably reduced digital divides and information gaps where implemented (Snyder & Witteman, 2019).

INFORMATION (INNOVATION) DIFFUSION THEORY

In 1962 Everett Rogers combined information-flow research findings with studies about the flow of information and personal influence in several fields, including anthropology, sociology, and rural agricultural extension work. He developed what he called diffusion theory. Rogers's effort at integrating information-flow research with diffusion theory was so successful that information-flow theory became known as **information diffusion theory** (and when it is applied to the diffusion of something other than information—that is, technologies—it is called *innovation diffusion theory*). Rogers used both labels to title subsequent editions of his book.

Rogers's work also illustrates the power of **meta-analysis** when it comes to developing a more useful middle-range theory. A meta-analysis identifies important consistencies in previous research findings on a specific topic and systematically integrates them into a fuller understanding. If previous research has been grounded in several different but related middle-range theories, these can be combined to create new, more macroscopic theories. Rogers had access to a large archive of data from research conducted over several decades by agricultural extension agents and university scholars. It documented how hundreds of agricultural innovations—new varieties of grain, new machinery, new crop rotation practices—were adopted or rejected by farmers. Rogers wanted to know if there was a consistent pattern to the way adoption took place. He concluded that when new technological innovations are introduced, they pass through a series of stages before wide adoption. First, most farmers become aware of them, often through information from mass media. Second, the innovations will be adopted by a very small group of innovators, or **early adopters**. These tend to be farmers who like to experiment with new things. Third, opinion leaders observe and learn first-hand from the early adopters. Then they try the innovation themselves. Fourth, if opinion leaders find the innovation useful, they encourage their friends—the opinion followers. Finally, after most people have adopted the innovation, a group of laggards, or late adopters, makes the change. Farmers who adopt a useful innovation early are rewarded by higher crop production and greater income while laggards are punished. Laggards adopt when overall crop production is up and prices for crops are falling. They must pay for the new innovation but don't earn a higher income. There are clear winners and losers when it comes to agricultural innovation diffusion.

Information/innovation diffusion theory is an excellent example of the strength and the limitations of a middle-range theory (Chapter 4). It successfully integrates a vast amount of empirical research. Rogers reviewed hundreds of studies. Information/innovation diffusion theory allowed him to identify a consistent pattern in the data. Nevertheless, it has some serious limitations. Like information-flow theory and social marketing theory (discussed later in this chapter), information/innovation diffusion theory is a source-dominated theory that sees the communication process from the point of view of an elite who has decided to diffuse specific information or an innovation. Diffusion theory "improves" on information-flow theory by providing more and better strategies for overcoming barriers to diffusion. It offers a better understanding of how face-to-face communication can efficiently and effectively be combined with media messages to produce desired effects. However, the driving force behind agricultural innovation is not strategic communication—it is the rewards provided to early innovators and the punishment incurred by late adopters. When Rogers tried to use his theory to guide innovation diffusion in other parts of the world, it often failed to be useful if rewards of some kind weren't provided.

Information/innovation diffusion theory assigns a limited role to mass media: They mainly create awareness of new innovations. But it does assign a very central role to different types of people critical to the diffusion process. Media *do* directly influence early adopters, but these people are generally well informed and careful media users. Early adopters try out innovations and then tell others about them. They directly influence opinion leaders, who in turn influence everyone else. **Change agents** are also key people involved with diffusion. Agricultural extension agents serve as change agents for farming innovations. Their job is to be highly informed about such innovations and assist anyone who wants to make changes. Rogers recommended that change agents lead diffusion efforts; for example, they could go into rural communities and directly influence early adopters and opinion leaders about new agricultural practices.

In addition to drawing attention to innovations, media can also be used to provide a basis for group discussions led by change agents.

Information/innovation diffusion theory represented an important advance over earlier effects-trend theories. Like other classic work of the early 1960s, it drew from existing empirical generalizations and synthesized them into a coherent, insightful perspective. It was consistent with most findings from effects surveys and persuasion experiments; above all it was very practical, as it laid the foundation for numerous promotional communication and marketing theories and the campaigns they support even today. But the limitations of information/innovation diffusion theory were also serious. It had some unique drawbacks stemming from its application. For example, it facilitated the adoption of innovations that were sometimes not well understood or even desired by adopters. To illustrate, a campaign to get Georgia farm wives to preserve vegetables was initially judged a great success until researchers found that very few women were using the vegetables. They mounted the glass jars on the walls of their living rooms as status symbols. Most didn't know any recipes for cooking preserved vegetables, and those who tried using canned vegetables found that family members didn't like the taste. This sort of experience was duplicated around the world: Corn was grown in Mexico and rice was grown in Southeast Asia that no one wanted to eat; farmers in India destroyed their crops by using too much fertilizer; farmers adopted complex new machinery only to have it break down and stand idle after change agents left. Mere top-down diffusion of innovations didn't guarantee long-term success.

Much of the recent research using diffusion theory has focused on diffusion of new media technology, finding it useful in explaining the way new media technologies have been adopted during the past two decades (Vishwanath & Barnett, 2011). Other work has confirmed the applicability of diffusion theory in our new media environment (Atkin, Hunt, & Lin, 2015). Often diffusion theory was combined with uses and gratifications theory to produce useful insights into technology adoption. Carolyn Lin (2003) proposed an integrated technology adoption model that combines micro- and macro-level theory notions drawn from several perspectives. David Atkin and his colleagues argue that research findings based on such integrated models can provide a useful basis for formulating media policies designed to avoid or minimize problems in technology access (Atkin, Hunt, & Lin, 2015).

INSTANT ACCESS

INFORMATION/INNOVATION DIFFUSION THEORY

Strengths

1. Integrates large number of empirical findings into useful theory
2. Provides practical guide for information campaigns in the United States and abroad
3. Has guided the successful adoption of useful innovations in the US and abroad

Weaknesses

1. Is linear and elite source-dominated
2. Underestimates power of media, especially contemporary media
3. Can stimulate adoption by groups that don't understand or want an innovation

Social Marketing Theory

In the early 1970s a macroscopic theory of media and society began to take shape that shared important similarities with diffusion theory—**social marketing theory**. Over time, social marketing theory has been useful in areas such as health and political communication. It is not a unified body of thought, but rather a more-or-less integrated collection of middle-range notions dealing with the process of "creating, communicating, and delivering benefits that a target audience(s) wants in exchange for audience behavior that benefits society without financial profit to the marketer" (Kotler & Lee, 2008, p. 7). Public health practitioners have been especially drawn to this theory, with many using it to promote or discourage various health-related behaviors, and as you might imagine, elaboration likelihood and narrative persuasion theory (Chapter 10) figure quite prominently in contemporary social marketing theory. But rather than describing each of the theories that make up social marketing theory, we will look at the overarching theoretical framework and then discuss some of its important features. Readers interested in a more extended discussion of these theories and their application might consult other sources (Kotler & Lee, 2008; Grier & Bryant, 2004; Friedman, Kachur, Noar, & McFarlane, 2016).

Like diffusion theory, social marketing theory is practically oriented and essentially source-dominated. It assumes the existence of benign information providers seeking to bring about useful, beneficial social change. It gives them a framework for designing, carrying out, and evaluating information campaigns. In its most recent forms it pays increased attention to audience activity and the need to reach active audiences with information they are seeking. As such, it is sometimes combined with uses-and-gratifications theory (Chapter 9).

In addition to sharing many assumptions and concerns with diffusion theory, social marketing theory is also a logical extension of the persuasion theories outlined in Chapter 10. It represents an effort to increase the effectiveness of mass media–based information campaigns through greater understanding and manipulation of societal and psychological factors. Social marketing theory does this by identifying a variety of social system–level and psychological barriers to the flow of information and influence. It anticipates them and includes strategies for overcoming them. Some strategies are ingenious; others involve the brute force of saturation advertising or in-home advocacy. Social marketing theory has several key features:

1. **Methods for inducing audience awareness of campaign topics.** A key first step in promoting ideas is to make people aware of their existence. The easiest but most costly way to do this is with a saturation television advertising campaign. As social marketing theories have gained sophistication, other methods have been developed that are almost as effective but much less costly. These include using news coverage, embedding messages in entertainment narratives, and new media channels to induce awareness.

2. **Methods for targeting messages at specific audience segments most receptive or susceptible to those messages.** Limited-effects research demonstrated how to identify audience segments most vulnerable to specific types of messages. Once identified, messages can be targeted at them. **Targeting** is one of several concepts borrowed from product marketing and converted to the marketing of

beneficial ideas or behaviors. By identifying the most vulnerable segments and then reaching them with the most efficient channel available, targeting strategies reduce promotional costs while increasing efficiency. Targeting has become easier with the availability of social media data that facilitate person-specific targeting.

3. **Methods for reinforcing messages within targeted segments and for encouraging these people to influence others through face-to-face communication.** Even vulnerable audience members are likely to forget or fail to act on messages unless they are reinforced by similar information coming from several channels. Various strategies have been developed to make certain that multiple messages are received from several channels, including visits by change agents, group discussions, messages placed simultaneously in several media, and SNS reinforcement of messages delivered by traditional media.

4. **Methods for cultivating images and impressions of people, products, or services.** These methods are most often used when it is difficult to arouse audience interest. If people aren't interested in a topic, it is unlikely they will seek and learn information about it. Lack of interest forms a barrier to the flow of information. One prominent method used to cultivate images is image advertising that presents easily recognizable, visually compelling images designed to imply a relationship between these attractive images and the attitude or behavior being promoted. Current social marketing thinking naturally accepts that these relationships can be easily, and more successfully, made through entertainment narratives.

5. **Methods for stimulating interest and inducing information seeking by audience members.** Information seeking occurs when a sufficient level of interest in ideas can be generated. Social marketers have developed numerous techniques to do just this. Using popular prime-time television programs is one example, but so, too, are 5K races, bus tours, colored-ribbon and wrist-band campaigns, and celebrity involvement.

6. **Methods for inducing desired decision-making or positioning.** Once people are aware and informed, or at least have formed strong images or impressions, they can be moved toward either a conscious decision or an unconscious prioritization or positioning. Media messages can be transmitted through a variety of channels and used to highlight the value of choosing a specific option or prioritizing one service or behavior relative to others. Change agents and opinion leaders can also be used, though these are more expensive. This is a critical stage in any communication campaign because it prepares people to take an action desired by social marketers.

7. **Methods for activating audience segments, especially those who have been targeted by the campaign.** Ideally these audiences will include people who are properly positioned but have not yet found an opportunity to act. In other cases people will have prioritized an attitude, service, or behavior but must be confronted with a situation in which they are compelled to act. These are *contemplators*; they are *awake* but not yet *in action* (Kotler & Lee, 2008, p. 273). Many communication campaigns fail because they lack a mechanism for stimulating action. People seem to be influenced by campaigns, but that influence isn't

INSTANT ACCESS

SOCIAL MARKETING THEORY

Strengths

1. Provides practical guide for information campaigns in the United States and abroad
2. Can be applied to serve socially desirable ends
3. Builds on attitude change and diffusion theories
4. Is accepted and used by media campaign planners, especially for health campaigns

Weaknesses

1. Is elite source–dominated
2. Often doesn't adequately consider all of the consequences of campaigns—just those that serve elite-source interests
3. Underestimates intellect or motivation of average people
4. Ignores constraints to reciprocal flow of information
5. Can be costly to implement

effectively translated into action. Social marketers employ a variety of techniques to activate people—for example, change agents, free merchandise, free and convenient transportation, free services, moderate fear appeals, and broadcast or telephone appeals from high-status sources.

Critics of social marketing point to limitations very similar to those raised in our discussion of diffusion theory. Though social marketing theory squeezes some benefit out of the older source-dominated linear-effects models, it also suffers many of their limitations. In social marketing models sources use feedback from target audiences to adjust their campaigns. This use is generally limited to changes in messages; however, long-term persuasion or information goals typically don't change. Thus, the social marketing model is tailored to situations in which elite sources are able to dominate elements of the larger social system. These powerful sources can prevent counter-elites from distributing information or marshaling organized opposition. This problem is well illustrated by the growing movement against certain vaccines that critics argue have serious or even fatal side-effects. As social conflict has escalated over "forced" vaccinations, social marketing theory offers no advice on how to convince people to risk doing something they are convinced will be harmful. The theory can't be applied to situations in which conflict has escalated to even moderate levels. It applies best to diffusion of routine forms of beneficial information, technology, and action. It's not surprising, then, that the area in which it is most often applied is health communication. Allison Friedman and her colleagues examined findings from 26 articles that reported on 16 different social marketing campaigns designed to prevent and control sexually transmitted disease. They argue that these campaigns are essential given the culture of silence that surrounds sexual health in the United States. Overall the campaigns were modestly successful, with increased exposure to campaign content being associated with greater behavioral change in areas such as condom use, discussion of sexually transmitted diseases with sex partners, and HIV testing. The researchers argue that even the relatively small effects of such campaigns do save lives (Friedman, Kachur, Noar, & McFarlane, 2016).

AGENDA-SETTING, PRIMING, AND AGENDA-BUILDING

What were the crucial issues facing voters in the 2016 presidential election? It was a very unusual campaign. Important problems confronted the nation, including thousands of people dying from opioid addiction, high unemployment in America's Rust Belt, military involvement in seemingly endless and costly Middle Eastern conflicts, rapid and unprecedented global climate change, the overburdening of a generation of college graduates by school loans, and growing inequity between the haves and have-nots. Would these important issues feature prominently in the campaign? Many voters were intrigued by a businessman-turned-politician, Donald Trump, who focused attention on undocumented migrants, castigating them as mostly criminals and promising to keep them out of America by building a wall along the border with Mexico, which that country would pay for. He also promised to repeal the Affordable Care Act, known informally as "Obamacare" (a federal program intended to bring low-cost health insurance to the uninsured), and replace it with an even better method of funding health care. He ran against Hillary Clinton, a former first lady, US senator, and secretary of state who wanted to preserve Obamacare and was generally supportive of immigrants. Though there was some news coverage of substantive issues in this campaign, reporting focused mainly on the personalities, histories, and the candidates' staged events. The criticisms of election news offered by Tom Patterson (1993) in Chapter 10 apply here. Much of the coverage fit game and horse-race schema. Again and again Trump was shown leading boisterous rallies where attendees were encouraged to vilify Clinton and shout "Lock her up!" because he claimed suspicious e-mails had gone missing from her computer server. Clinton was shown giving speeches in which she argued that Trump had many obvious character flaws and business failures that demonstrated his inability to govern effectively. News coverage contrasted her reasonable and sensible demeanor with Trump's often caustic and vituperative language. Analyses of news coverage after the campaign showed that Trump had received unusually high levels of campaign coverage, but that it had failed to adequately address many of the spectacular but false claims he made throughout the campaign (Watts & Rothschild, 2017).

What do you remember from the mass media as the important issues and images of that campaign? Journalists penned up and demeaned during Trump rallies? Trump's salacious discussion of women on the *Access Hollywood* tape? Wikileaks' ongoing publication of e-mails pirated from Democrats? Of all the substantive issues that were listed above—drug deaths, lost manufacturing jobs, war in the Middle East, climate change, student loan debt, income inequality—only a few became dominant in the minds of most American voters; only a few were viewed as the most important issues facing the country. This is **agenda-setting**—a process in which only a few issues become prioritized by the public while equally or even more important issues are ignored.

Although he did not specifically use the term, Bernard Cohen (1963) is generally credited with identifying the process that would come to be called agenda-setting. "The press is significantly more than a purveyor of information and opinion," he wrote. "It may not be successful much of the time in telling people what to think, but it is stunningly successful in telling its readers what to think about. And it follows from this that the world looks different to different people, depending not only on their personal interests, but also on the map that is drawn for them by the writers, editors, and publishers of the papers they read" (p. 13). Cohen's perspective might have lingered in obscurity had it not been empirically confirmed by the research of Maxwell E. McCombs and Donald Shaw (1972). They explained their interpretation of agenda-setting: "In choosing and displaying news, editors, newsroom staff, and broadcasters play an important part in shaping political reality. Readers learn not only about a given issue, but how much importance to attach to that issue from the amount of information in a news story and its position. . . . The mass media may well determine the important issues—that is, the media may set the 'agenda' of the campaign" (p. 176).

During September and October of the 1968 presidential election, McCombs and Shaw (1972) interviewed 100 registered voters who had yet to commit to either candidate (presumably these people would be more open to media messages). By asking each respondent "to outline the key issues as she or he saw them, regardless of what the candidates might be saying at the moment," they were able to identify and rank by importance just what these people thought were the crucial issues facing them. They then compared these results with a ranking of the time and space accorded to various issues produced by a content analysis of the television news, newspapers, newsmagazines, and editorial pages available to voters in the area where the study was conducted. The results? "The media appear to have exerted a considerable impact on voters' judgments of what they considered the major issues of the campaign. . . . The correlation between the major item emphasis on the main campaign issues carried by the media and voters' independent judgments of what were the important issues was +.967," they wrote. "In short, the data suggest a very strong relationship between the emphasis placed on different campaign issues by the media . . . and the judgments of voters as to the salience and importance of various campaign topics" (pp. 180–181).

This important and straightforward study highlights both the strengths and limitations of agenda-setting as a theory of media effects. It establishes that there is an important relationship between the number of media reports and people's ranking of public issues. On the negative side we can see that the logic of agenda-setting seems well suited for the question of news and campaigns, but what about other kinds of content and other kinds of effects? More important, though, is the question of the actual nature of the relationship between news and its audience. Maybe the public sets the media's agenda and then the media reinforce it. The McCombs and Shaw analysis, like most early agenda-setting research, suggests a direction of influence from media to audience—that is, it implies causality. But the argument that the media are simply responding to their audiences can be easily made. Few journalists have not uttered at least once in their careers, "We only give the people what they want." McCombs (1981) himself acknowledged these limitations. Subsequent agenda-setting research has tried to address the question of causality in different ways.

It is important not to judge the utility of the agenda-setting approach based on the earliest studies. For example, Shanto Iyengar and Donald Kinder (1987) attempted to overcome some of the problems of earlier work in a series of experiments designed to test the "agenda-setting hypothesis: Those problems that receive prominent attention on the national news become the problems the viewing public regards as the nation's most important" (p. 16). Their series of experiments examined agenda-setting, the vividness of news reports, the positioning of stories, and what they called **priming**. Experiments allowed them to assess causality since people were exposed first to media content and then their views on issues were measured.

- *Agenda-setting*: Iyengar and Kinder (1987) demonstrated causality. They wrote:

  Americans' view of their society and nation are powerfully shaped by the stories that appear on the evening news. We found that people who were shown network broadcasts edited to draw attention to a particular problem assigned greater importance to that problem—greater importance than they themselves did before the experiment began, and greater importance than did people assigned to control conditions that emphasized different problems. Our subjects regarded the target problem as more important for the country, cared more about it, believed that government should do more about it, reported stronger feelings about it, and were much more likely to identify it as one of the country's most important problems. (p. 112)

- *Vividness of presentation*: The researchers found that dramatic news accounts undermined rather than increased television's agenda-setting power. Powerfully presented personal accounts (a staple of contemporary television news) might focus too much attention on the specific situation or individual rather than on the issue at hand, much like a dramatic advertisement that fails to make a useful link to a product.
- *Position of a story*: Lead stories had a greater agenda-setting effect. They offered two possible reasons for this result. First, people paid more attention to the stories at the beginning of the news, and these were less likely to fall victim to the inevitable interruptions experienced when viewing at home. Second, people accepted the news program's implicit designation of a lead story as most newsworthy.
- *Priming*: This is the idea that even the most motivated citizens cannot consider all that they know when evaluating complex political issues. Instead people consider the things that come easily to mind, or as the researchers said, "those bits and pieces of political memory that are accessible." You can hear echoes of schema theory here. Iyengar and Kinder's research (1987) strongly demonstrated that "through priming [drawing attention to some aspects of political life at the expense of others] television news [helps] to set the terms by which political judgments are reached and political choices made" (p. 114). Writing in a later study, Iyengar (1991) offered this distinction: "While agenda-setting reflects the impact of news coverage on the perceived importance of national issues, priming refers to the impact of news coverage on the weight assigned to specific issues in making political judgments" (p. 133). We'll return to a consideration of priming in Chapter 13 when we discuss it as part of framing theory.

Agenda-setting is complemented by an equally important macro-level process known as **agenda-building**, "the often-complicated process by which some issues become important in policy making arenas" (Protess et al., 1991, p. 6). Kurt Lang and Gladys Lang (1983) defined *agenda-building* as "a collective process in which media, government, and the citizenry reciprocally influence one another" (pp. 58–59). Agenda-building presumes cognitive effects, a political elite that works strategically to highlight certain issues, an active audience, and societal-level effects. Its basic premise—that media can profoundly affect how a society (or nation or culture) determines what are its important concerns and therefore can mobilize its various institutions toward meeting them—has allowed this line of inquiry, in the words of David Protess and his colleagues, to "flourish" (Protess et al., 1991) Pamela Shoemaker and Stephen Reese (2014) have offered an updated view of agenda-building that pays particular attention to factors that influence newsroom agendas. As with agenda-setting, journalists are reluctant to see themselves as playing an active role in building agendas; they are there to simply report the efforts of elites to draw public attention to specific issues. But like agenda-setting, agenda-building is influenced by the schemas typically used by journalists. The Langs studied agenda-building during Watergate and concluded that the horse race and conflict frames used by journalists during the 1972 election campaign prevented the scandal from becoming an important campaign issue despite the ongoing efforts of Democrats to call attention to it.

Russell Neuman and his colleagues proposed a strategy for using "big data" to assess agenda-building at a time when social media have become prominent sources of information about issues. They argued that a much more dynamic process is emerging in which agenda-building and agenda-setting are closely interlinked. Examining traditional print/broadcast media and social media content (i.e., SNSs, blogs, discussion boards) for 29 issues during the calendar year 2012, they looked at daily differences in the coverage of the issues and found that every day there were more than 17,000 references to each issue across all the media they looked at. Examining correlations between the issue coverage of traditional media and that of social media to determine whether one type of media influenced coverage in the other, they found evidence of mutual influence. Social media coverage of issues of natural disasters, gun control, LGBTQ issues, and the Arab Spring preceded mainstream media coverage, and mainstream media coverage of economic policy and foreign affairs preceded social media coverage (Neuman, Guggenheim, Jang, & Bae, 2014). Mike Gruszczynski and Michael Wagner (2017) presented findings consistent with this discovery. By combining measures of mainstream and more narrowly targeted media coverage (i.e., Free Republic, Daily Kos, Fox News) with data on public Internet searches provided by Google Trends, they concluded that social media and mainstream media may be important in promoting different types of issues.

Agenda-building and -setting research has come a long way from the relatively simple surveys and content analyses conducted by early scholars. Now vast archives of digitized news and social media content are analyzed to assess which content is more influential in raising and promoting specific types of issues. Researchers are finding that certain types of issues are more likely to be promoted by social media while others are more likely to be promoted by legacy media. The fact that these outlets can, and often do, influence one another has led to the recognition of **intermedia agenda-building**, when online news sites and legacy media shape one another's news coverage (Vonbun, Kleinen-von Königslöw, & Schönbach, 2016). This interaction between old and new media is hardly without journalism-distorting consequences, as all news outlets, in their quest for audience, delegate their editorial judgment not to editors and journalists but to data on social media sharing and Internet searches—in a process Zsolt Katona and his colleagues call **agenda-chasing**. "In this new environment dominated by social media, where consumers' sharing behavior can quickly propel a news item to the top," they write, "competition among news providers is best described as a permanent contest where firms have to 'bet' on a (few) topics and the

INSTANT ACCESS

AGENDA-SETTING

Strengths

1. Explains how news media can have important effects without changing opinions on issues
2. Empirically demonstrates links between media exposure, audience motivation to seek orientation, and audience perception of the importance of public issues
3. Integrates a number of similar ideas, including priming, story positioning, and story vividness
4. Explains how Internet-based media can set or build the public agenda

Weaknesses

1. Difficult to demonstrate that news media cause agenda-setting effects
2. Is most applicable to (and often limited to) studies of news and political campaigns
3. Direction of agenda-setting effect is increasingly questioned due to social media

'winners' divide the advertising revenues generated from pageviews (the 'prize' of the contest). As such, rather than 'setting the agenda,' as they did in the past, today's news providers are 'chasing the agenda' mostly set by consumers' sharing behavior on the Internet" (Katona, Knee, & Sarvary, 2017, p. 784). But there is another aspect of social media agenda-chasing that these scholars don't consider. It's not only social media-user sharing behavior that determines news content—it's social media algorithms that determine how news gets provided to most users. We need research to assess the degree to which these algorithms are coming to play an important role in setting or building agendas. There is also a growing focus on the way issues are presented or framed across these different media. We'll take a close look at framing research in Chapter 13. We'll also examine a form of agenda-setting that McCombs and Ghanem (2001) have labeled *attribute agenda-setting* or *second-order agenda-setting*.

THE SPIRAL OF SILENCE

A somewhat more controversial theory of media and public opinion is the concept of the **spiral of silence**. It can be regarded as a form of agenda-setting, but one clearly focused on societal-level consequences. In the words of its originator, Elisabeth Noelle-Neumann (1984), "Observations made in one context [the mass media] spread to another and encourage people either to proclaim their views or to swallow them and keep quiet until, in a spiraling process, the one view dominated the public scene and the other disappeared from public awareness as its adherents became mute. This is the process that can be called a 'spiral of silence'" (p. 5).

Spiral of silence theory argues that people's fear of isolation or separation from those around them leads them to keep their attitudes to themselves when they think they are in the minority. The media, because of a variety of factors, tend to present one (or at most two) sides of an issue to the exclusion of others, which further encourages those people to keep quiet and makes it even tougher for the media to uncover and register opposing viewpoints. Spiral of silence provides an excellent example of a theory that argues for cumulative effects of media. Once a spiral of silence is initiated, the magnitude of media influence will increase to higher and higher levels over time. If various viewpoints about agenda items are ignored, marginalized, or trivialized by media reports, people will be reluctant to talk about them. As time passes, those viewpoints will cease to be heard in public and therefore cannot affect political decision making.

The way news is collected and disseminated, Noelle-Neumann (1973) argued, effectively restricts the breadth and depth of selection available to citizens. She identified three characteristics of the news media that produce this scarcity of perspective:

1. *Ubiquity*: The media are virtually everywhere as sources of information.
2. *Cumulation*: The various news media tend to repeat stories and perspectives across their different individual programs or editions, across the different media themselves, and across time.
3. *Consonance*: The congruence, or similarity, of values held by journalists influences the content they produce.

This view of media effects suggests that two different social processes, one microscopic and one macroscopic, simultaneously operate to produce effects. Audience members, because of their desire to be accepted, choose to remain silent when confronted with what they perceive to be prevailing opinions that differ from their own views. Journalists, because of the dynamics of their news-gathering function, present a restricted selection of news, further forcing into silence those in the audience who wish to avoid isolation.

Spiral of silence theory has been the recipient of praise and criticism. It has been lauded as heralding a return to the view that media can have important effects. But critics like Elihu Katz (1983) see it as little more than an updating of mass society theory: "Even in the democracies, media—like interpersonal communication—can impose acquiescence and silence in defiance of the free flow of information" (p. 91). Charles Salmon and F. Gerald Kline (1985) wrote that the effects explained by the spiral of silence could just as easily be understood as the product of the bandwagon effect (everybody wants to join a winner) or projection (people's natural tendency to use their own opinions to form perceptions of the general climate of opinion around them). In addition these critics argued that individual factors, such as a person's degree of ego-involvement in an issue, should be considered (regardless of the climate of opinion surrounding you, if you feel very strongly about the issue, you might not want to remain silent, even if isolation is a threat). Drawing on the notion that pluralistic groups can mediate media effects, Carroll Glynn and Jack McLeod (1985) faulted spiral of silence theory for underestimating the power of people's communities, organizations, and reference groups in mitigating media influence on the larger society. They also questioned the generalizability of Noelle-Neumann's research (initially conducted almost exclusively in what was then West Germany) to the American situation, and they raised the possibility of situations in which media can actually move people to speak up rather than remain silent. Noelle-Neumann (1985) responded that the media, especially television, adopt a prevailing attitude in any controversy as a matter of course, and as a result, they present a "dominant tendency." Holders of the minority viewpoint are willing to speak out if they feel that they are supported by the media's dominant tendency (as during the civil rights movement).

Despite these disagreements, spiral of silence continues to hold research interest and enjoy empirical support. For example, Andrew Hayes and his colleagues tested Noelle-Neumann's idea of media activating the "quasi-statistical organ," something of a sixth sense allowing individuals, in her words, to assess the "distribution of opinions for and against his ideas, but above all by evaluating the strength (commitment), the urgency, and the chances of success of certain proposals and viewpoints" (1974, p. 44). In a cross-cultural study of eight nations, they demonstrated that "those who reported relatively greater FSI [fear of social isolation] reported relatively more attention to public opinion polls [suggesting] that such fear does serve to stimulate the quasi-statistical organ to tune into the signal of public opinion transmitted through the mass media in the form of public opinion poll results" (Hayes, Matthes, & Eveland, 2011, p. 18). Social scientists have also demonstrated the operation of the spiral of silence in online environments. Michael Chan (2018) found that FSI was associated with reluctance to talk about politics face-to-face or on Facebook during an election campaign in Hong Kong, and Jesse Fox and Lanier Holt (2018) reported that Facebook users who have concerns about the persistence of posts or a concern about upsetting other people were less likely to express opinions on Facebook about police discrimination.

Spiral of silence research is undergoing important changes as the theory is applied to Internet-based media. Researchers are identifying and measuring new factors that can affect people's willingness to become involved in online communication about controversial topics. They are looking at new ways that people can assess the climate of opinion. They have moved beyond a focus on fear of social isolation and are looking at users' fears about online privacy and the persistence of content on the Internet. Users are also worried about how their comments might impact friends who are linked to them via SNSs. Some fear that trolls will attack their views. With all of these concerns it's not surprising that many people are silent when they use the Internet, even when they encounter issues online in which they are intensely interested or which arouse their concerns.

INSTANT ACCESS

THE SPIRAL OF SILENCE

Strengths

1. Has macro- and micro-level explanatory power
2. Is dynamic
3. Accounts for shifts in public opinion, especially during campaigns
4. Raises important questions concerning the role and responsibility of news media

Weaknesses

1. Has overly pessimistic view of news media influence and of journalists
2. Ignores other, simpler explanations of silencing
3. Ignores possible demographic and cultural differences in the silencing effect
4. Discounts power of community to counteract silencing
5. The effect varies widely from one nation to another due to cultural and political differences

REVIEW OF LEARNING OBJECTIVES

- Assess the changing role played by media in society now that large-scale social media have become an important part of the mass media system.

When social media were developed they held great potential for involving people in the production and distribution of content. Journalism could be transformed by citizen journalists writing blogs and joining news teams organized by local newspapers. Hollywood entertainment could be replaced by people posting locally produced content on YouTube. But the greatest hope was their potential for the development of virtual communities—places where people could create and share meaningful ideas and interests with like-minded friends. This potential was lost as a small number of companies gained control over the social media apps that most people use. These companies focused on turning social media into a means of earning profits from advertisers. As a result, large-scale social media haven't changed the role of mass media, but they have altered the way media influence is exercised. Like all forms of mass media, social media distribute content designed to attract and monopolize the attention of users. They deliver user attention to advertisers seeking to target and influence certain types of users. It is clear that social media are not creating virtual communities and that ordinary users produce only a small fraction of the content they distribute. The most important immediate consequence of social media is their impact on other media. Social media are forcing a restructuring of the media system much like the restructuring brought about by the introduction of television. And as they derive much of their content from other mass media they become important gatekeepers, filtering and featuring content tailored to user interests in ways designed to attract and hold attention.

- Discuss how mass media's attention to specific events and issues influences the importance we assign to those events and issues, how we interpret them, how those interpretations come to shape the political agenda, and how some people are moved to speak less openly about them.

At any point in time, our nation faces many important societal problems warranting public attention and concern. Agenda-setting research shows that mass media typically draw our attention and interest to only a small number of these problems. Media feature only one or two ways they might be resolved. As time passes we come to see these issues as more important than others not featured in media content. We tend to interpret them as they are presented to us by media, and we focus on solutions featured in media. Media can prime us to remember certain issues and certain interpretations of these issues. This priming can affect how we think about, talk about, and act on issues. Spiral-of-silence research indicates some people routinely assess the social acceptability of certain issue positions or political candidates. People who have a fear of social isolation are likely to avoid talking about or posting online comments about less acceptable issue positions or candidates.

- Find value in a number of contemporary mass communication theories that offer evidence of media's ability to produce macro-level effects, such as the knowledge gap hypothesis, innovation diffusion theory, and social marketing theory.

Research on knowledge gaps shows that for many important topics there are large differences in what people with higher income and education levels know compared to others. If the flow of information from media is increased, these differences remain, even when the overall level of knowledge increases. People with higher income and education tend to have greater interest in important topics and more ability to learn about these topics. The introduction of social media has not closed knowledge gaps. Research has identified digital inequities that prevent the closing of gaps. For example, people in lower economic groups are more likely to use apps that provide diversion and entertainment rather than locate useful information. Innovation diffusion theory and social marketing theory seek to understand the barriers preventing people from learning about and using innovations or engaging in use activities. These include lack of knowledge and interest, dislike or fear of change, and acceptance of the status quo. Both theories have shown how media can bring about useful effects if there are resources available to overcome barriers. Both tend to focus on top-down campaigns to promote changes in action or technology adoption. Elite sources use media to overcome barriers so that source-identified public interests are served. Social media provide an additional tool to be used by elite sources to overcome barriers, but people need to be trained to access and use them effectively.

CRITICAL THINKING QUESTIONS

1. Have your opinions about a controversial issue in the news ever been spiraled into silence? If so, what was the situation? Might you have hesitated to defend your position on an issue or a favored political candidate? If not, have you ever had to resist the temptation to remain silent in the face of opposing opinion? If so, what were the circumstances? Do you pay attention to opinion polls so you can avoid talking about things that are becoming unpopular? Has social media, with its promises of anonymity and ease of use, altered your willingness to speak out or remain silent on controversial issues? Do you think it matters much if you express your views online? Have you or your friends encountered online criticism of views posted online? Have you recently become more or less hesitant to express your views online? Why?

2. Do you vote? Why or why not? How important do you think your participation in the democratic process really is? That is, can one citizen make a difference? If you answer yes, do you find the theories presented in this chapter troubling? Why or why not? If you answer no, can you find an explanation for that response in the theories discussed here? Are there forms of political participation that do not involve traditional activities like voting or political party activities that you do engage in? What are they? Why do you choose these over more traditional forms of activity?

3. When it comes to social media apps, are you a change agent, an early adopter, an opinion leader, or an opinion follower? What is it about you that determines where you stand in the process of the diffusion of social media? Do you know any social media early adopters? What makes them similar to or different from you? Do you think there are gender differences—that is, are there some social media apps in which one gender of user rather than the other might be more likely to take the lead? Why or why not?

KEY TERMS

knowledge gap
digital divide
digital inequities
OMA (opportunities-motivation-ability)
    model
municipal broadband
information diffusion theory
meta-analysis
early adopters

change agents
social marketing theory
targeting
agenda-setting
priming
agenda-building
intermedia agenda-building
agenda-chasing
spiral of silence

GLOSSARY

knowledge gap: Systematic differences in knowledge between better informed and less-informed segments of a population

digital divide: Lack of access to communication technology among people of color, the poor, the disabled, and those in rural communities

digital inequities: Differences in abilities to make use of access to digital media for serious purposes among people of lower education and income

OMA (opportunities-motivation-ability) model: Idea that differences in opportunities, motivations, and abilities to access information will predict knowledge and political action

municipal broadband: Providing broadband Internet access to a given locale as a low-cost utility

information/innovation diffusion theory: Theory that explains how innovations are introduced and adopted by various communities

meta-analysis: Identifies important consistencies in previous research findings on a specific issue and systematically integrates them into a fuller understanding

early adopters: In information/innovation diffusion theory, people who adopt an innovation early, even before receiving significant amounts of information

change agents: In information/innovation diffusion theory, those who directly influence early adopters and opinion leaders

social marketing theory: Collection of middle-range theories concerning the promotion of socially valuable information

targeting: Identifying specific audience segments and reaching them through the most efficient available channel

agenda-setting: Idea that media don't tell people what to think, but what to think about

priming: In agenda-setting, the idea that media draw attention to some aspects of political life at the expense of others

agenda-building: Collective process in which media, government, and the citizenry reciprocally influence one another in areas of public policy

intermedia agenda-building: The process of online news sites and legacy media shaping one another's news coverage

agenda-chasing: News outlets' use of consumers' Internet behavior to determine their coverage

spiral of silence: Idea that people holding views contrary to those dominant in the media are moved to keep those views to themselves for fear of rejection

CHAPTER 12

Theories of the Effect of Media on Community and Everyday Culture

The 2019 World Happiness Report, issued by the United Nations Sustainable Development Solutions group, ranks the level of happiness in 156 countries, based on a number of variables. Every year it takes a somewhat different focus, and that year's report looked specifically at happiness and community. So, where do you think the United States ranked? The good old USA killed it, right? Maybe not. "The years since 2010 have not been good ones for happiness and well-being among Americans," offered the report. "Even as the United States economy improved after the end of the Great Recession in 2009, happiness among adults did not rebound to the higher levels of the 1990s, continuing a slow decline ongoing since at least 2000" (Helliwell, Layard, & Sachs, 2019, p. 88). In fact, at 19th place, the US dropped one spot from the previous ranking and five spots since 2017. America's nearest neighbors? Belgium at number 18 and the Czech Republic at 20. And how did the US rank on the individual measures? Sixty-first for freedom; 42nd for corruption; 39th for healthy life expectancy; 37th for social support; 12th for generosity; and on a more positive note, 10th for income.

But maybe this is no surprise to you, as January 2019 saw 63% of Americans saying they thought the country was "on the wrong track," and when offered an opportunity to identify a short word or phrase that they would use to describe how they felt about the state of the country, 68% gave negative answers like "disaster," "divided," and "downhill." Only 17% could provide a positive word or phrase (Murray, 2019).

LEARNING OBJECTIVES

After studying this chapter you should be able to

- Explain how media affect communities in both useful and problematic ways.
- Detail the nature of cultivation analysis and its contributions to our understanding of media influence.
- Assess the potential for media literacy and media literacy interventions to enhance positive media effects and limit those that may be harmful.

OVERVIEW

The disheartening data that opened this chapter are at the core of much important contemporary mass communication theory and research. How can this state of affairs exist in the "greatest democracy on earth," where all people are created equal, where life, liberty, and the pursuit of happiness are enshrined in the nation's foundational document, the Declaration of Independence? And what might media's contribution be not only to the perception that the country is adrift but to the actual state of affairs that leads to such pessimism?

The macro-level theories in this chapter suggest some answers. More time spent with screens means less time with the real people in our communities and those of our neighbors. As we disengage from our fellow citizens, we come to know them increasingly from their media portrayals . . . and those aren't always accurate. As we disengage from our neighbors, we become more insular and less trusting—only 31% of Americans know "all or most" of their neighbors (Parker et al., 2018), and only about half of those trust "most or all" of them (Gao, 2016). But maybe people are just being smart; you can never be too careful these days. In reality violent crime and property crime are at their lowest levels in 30 years, yet six in 10 Americans believe crime is going up from year to year (Gramlich, 2019). Is it that the world we see at a distance—on screens—is scarier than the one we might actually enjoy away from their glow? And perhaps there is an antidote, a way to determine what's real and useful among the hours and hours we spend with media. Social capital theory—originally developed when television was beginning to reshape American culture—and cultivation analysis—born of the country's fear of crime and violence—can help us identify the roots of much of our distress. And media literacy, long of interest to those concerned with media influence, may help us make better use of media to do exactly that.

MEDIA AND SOCIAL CAPITAL/COMMUNITY RESEARCH

A growing body of research on media relies on **social capital theory** (Dubos, 2001). A loosely connected set of assumptions underlying a broad range of empirical research in sociology, political science, and communication rather than a clearly articulated set of ideas, this theory argues that there are important benefits, such as trust, cooperation, and reciprocity, that flow from involvement in various social networks. Social capital theory, versions of which have been articulated by James Coleman (1988) and Robert Putnam (2000), shares some assumptions with mass society theory in that it looks back to past eras when the social "fabric" was strong, when myriad social groups bound everyone, whether rich or poor, together in pluralistic groups or shared activities. In those "ideal" times members of differing cultural, racial, and economic groups were linked together by overarching social organizations such as political parties, churches, and fraternal and recreational groups. Ideally these pluralistic organizations allowed or even compelled people from all levels of society to meet and work or play together. The mutual understanding and trust that arose when these organizations were effective is the essence of **social capital**. Once social capital is created it becomes a resource that prevents future social misunderstanding from arising, and it can be drawn upon to bring about understanding when social conflict does occur. For example, racial conflict should be less likely to occur if social capital has been created because most people regularly meet or work with members of different races. Sociologists and political scientists have speculated about the conditions in society that give rise to increasing levels of social capital and have also raised concerns about the conditions that lead to its reduction. Mass media are among the factors thought to undermine social capital. For example, Putnam (2000) points out that the rise of television coincided with the decline of many important social groups such as recreational and fraternal organizations. People stay home to be entertained by TV rather than participate in groups. His catchphrase to describe this phenomenon, "bowling alone," quickly entered the public's everyday conversations.

Political scientists who favor pluralistic theories of democracy tend to view political parties as playing an essential role in generating and preserving social capital. Ideally they can operate as coalitions of smaller, more geographically or economically isolated groups. Parties can bring leaders of culturally, racially, and economically diverse groups together to create a political elite that spans these divisions. To be effective this elite needs to maintain a grassroots base in local, regional, and national social organizations—from local parent–teacher groups to the national Red Cross. If this base is maintained, political parties can serve as umbrella organizations in which leaders of various groups broker power. Most members of this elite don't hold political office but work behind the scenes serving the interests of their constituencies. Political scientists are concerned because there is growing evidence that this pluralistic political system is breaking down and that mass media are playing a role in this process (Patterson, 1993). These theorists see the decline in social capital as having many detrimental consequences. When politicians can no longer rely on local groups to which they had or have a connection to rally grassroots support, they are forced to turn to political consultants who advise them on how to use media to appeal to voters. But the televised political advertising and dramatic news coverage required to rally apathetic supporters come with a high price. Elites must devote precious time to raising money from wealthy donors and then spend it on questionable forms of campaign communication. The rise of Internet-based media hasn't changed this situation. While there are instances where SNSs may have helped low-budget campaigns, use of social media by politicians has required even more fundraising and employment of social media experts, and the more outrageous the SNS post, the greater the number of clicks. Some political scientists argue that as social capital has eroded, grassroots political party activity has also declined. This falloff has been well documented, as has been the drop in political affiliation and voting (Entman, 1989). Again, these changes in political parties occurred at the same time that television became a dominant medium. The rise of large-scale SNSs has not altered these trends.

Social capital theorists frequently cite the findings of the news production researchers to support their positions. They claim that political reports are too personalized, too dramatized, and too fragmented. Politics is often reported as a game between opposing teams, with the major politicians viewed as star players. Stories focus on media-hyped spectacles—big plays, life-and-death struggles—to score points. These reports don't help news consumers—in other words, citizens—develop a useful understanding of politics. They don't systematically inform people about issues and how candidates deal with issues. Rather, they encourage consumers to become political spectators, content to sit on the sidelines while the big guns play the game.

Robert Entman (1989) argues that a solution can be reached only if politicians, journalists, and the public change their behavior. Politicians must stop relying on manipulative and expensive strategies; journalists must cover issues rather than spectacles; and the public must give serious attention to issues, not campaign spectacles and personalities. But how likely is it that these solutions can actually be implemented? Politicians and journalists are reluctant to change patterns of behavior that serve their immediate purposes—getting elected to office and attracting audiences to campaign coverage. And after every recent election campaign, private foundations have sponsored major conferences at which politicians and journalists have pledged to improve the quality of campaign communication. But the same mistakes are repeated in campaign after campaign. For example, total campaign spending in the 2016 national, state, and local elections was $6.5 billion. Television stations were happy to reap windfall profits from campaign advertising, journalists expressed frustration about the way politicians, particularly Donald Trump, manipulated news coverage . . . and little changes. Soon after the 2012 election, political scientist Norman Ornstein had this prophetic advice to those who head news organizations: "I understand your concerns about advertisers. I understand your concerns about being labeled as biased. But what are you there for? What's the whole notion of a free press for if you're not going to report without fear or favor and you're not going to report what your reporters, after doing their due diligence, see as the truth? . . . And if you don't do that, then you can expect I think a growing drumbeat of criticism that you're failing in your fundamental responsibility. Your job is to report the truth" (as cited in Froomkin, 2012).

Despite the fears of sociologists and political scientists that media use threatens social capital, there is a long-standing tradition of media scholarship looking at the ability of media to strengthen communities and create social capital (Jeffres, Lee, Neuendorf, & Atkin, 2007). Researchers have found strong ties between use of media for information and involvement in social groups and volunteer work. Reading local newspapers correlates with involvement in neighborhoods and participation in neighborhood projects and is associated with registering to vote and voting. Indeed, frequency of newspaper reading has been found to be correlated with a long list of important values, including participation in the political system, tolerance of other people, being involved in the community, and attachment to community (Jeffres et al., 2007). Kristy Hess (2015) provides a strong argument for the power of small-town newspapers to strengthen their communities by promoting the development of different forms of social capital, and Joshua Darr, Matthew Hitt, and Johanna Dunaway (2018) demonstrated that in the absence of such newspapers, not only did citizens become less engaged in the life of their communities but, forced to rely more on polarizing national news media, community members became more polarized. When there is no local newspaper, fewer people run for office, reducing the number of options from which voters can choose (Rubado & Jennings, 2019). And recent research on **news deserts**—communities unserved by local media—further demonstrates the damaging impact of such an information deficit on social capital. There are more than 1,300 American communities unserved by a local newspaper; 900 have lost all local news coverage (i.e., in all forms of media) since 2004 (Stites, 2018). News desert communities suffer from high school and college graduate rates below, and poverty rates above, the national average (Darrach, McCormick, & Sultan, 2019). Half of America's

INSTANT ACCESS

SOCIAL CAPITAL THEORY

Strengths

1. Explains how media may be disrupting important social groups
2. Provides a critical analysis of the way media influence communities and threaten social capital
3. Explains how newspapers could play a useful role in communities

Weaknesses

1. Focuses on disruption by media, but research has not conclusively demonstrated that media cause social capital to decline
2. Has overly pessimistic view of media and their social role
3. Assumes that social groups usually build social capital in communities and that media are a threat to this

suburban citizens and four in 10 of those in rural communities say that local media do not serve their interests, and large majorities, 60% and 69% respectively, say that when they do, they do not have much influence (Grieco, 2019). This "impoverishment of local political news in recent years is driving down citizen engagement," resulting in voters who are less politically active, less knowledgeable about political candidates, and less likely to vote (Stearns, 2018). Civic engagement is also depressed in **orphan counties**, counties where people receive no news coverage and political advertising for their own statewide elections, irrelevant information about candidates in a neighboring state, or both, estimated to represent 10% of the US electorate. Citizens in orphan counties, naturally, show lower rates of interest in politics and lower voter turnout (Hutchins, 2019).

So, what can we conclude from the research on social capital? On the one hand, entertainment media can distract people from community involvement; on the other hand, reading newspapers encourages involvement, but the prospect of a robust future for local newspapers is dismal. News media coverage of politics seems to do little to further well-informed, meaningful public political discourse, and the addition of social media seems likely to exacerbate rather than ameliorate this problem. Once again the problems caused by media seem to center on their misuses, and those misuses are encouraged rather than discouraged by media.

CULTIVATION ANALYSIS

Cultivation analysis, a theory developed by George Gerbner during the 1970s and 1980s, addresses macro-level questions about the media's role in society, although it represents a hybrid combining aspects of both macroscopic and microscopic cultural theories. Some researchers regarded it as a likely prototype for future research, whereas others considered it a poor example of how to do social science. This controversy was pivotal in the development of mass communication theory. It came at a time when the limited-effects perspective was strong but beginning to show signs of waning and cultural theories were receiving more serious attention from media scholars. The controversy reveals a great deal about various opposing perspectives, some of which are still widely held. As you'll see from our review, this theory has undergone and continues to undergo important changes. The cultivation theory employed by most researchers today is very different from that originally formulated by Gerbner. As it has evolved it has attracted growing interest from postpositivist researchers. Somewhat ironically, a theory that was rejected by many postpositivists three decades ago is now widely accepted as a useful way to understand and study media effects using postpositivist research methods.

You can begin your own evaluation of cultivation analysis by answering three questions:

1. In any given week, what are the chances that you will be involved in some kind of violence: about 1 in 10 or about 1 in 100? In the actual world, about 0.41 violent crimes occur per 100 Americans, or less than 1 in 200. In the world of prime-time television, though, more than 64% of all characters are involved in violence. Was your answer closer to the actual or to the television world?

2. What percentage of all working males in the United States toil in law enforcement and crime detection: 1% or 5%? The US Census says 1%; television says 12%. What did you say?

3. Of all the crimes that occur in the United States in any year, what proportion is violent crime, like murder, rape, robbery, and assault? Would you guess 15% or 25%? If you hold the television view, you chose the higher number. On television, 77% of all major characters who commit crimes commit the violent kind. The *Statistical Abstract of the United States* reports that in actuality only 10% of all crime in the country is violent crime.

These questions come from Gerbner and his colleagues (Gerbner, Gross, Morgan, & Signorielli, 1980), but their point was much more complex than simply stating that those who watch more television give answers more similar to the "TV answer" than to those provided by official data. Their central argument is that television is a "message system" that "cultivates" or creates a worldview that, although possibly inaccurate, becomes the reality simply because we, as a people, believe it to be the reality and base our judgments about our own everyday worlds on that "reality."

You'll remember from Chapter 7 that during the 1960s and early 1970s interest in television as a social force, especially the medium's relationship to increasing individual and societal violence, reached its zenith. Two very important national examinations of the media, again especially television, were undertaken. The first was the National Commission on the Causes and Prevention of Violence, held in 1967 and 1968, and the second was the 1972 Surgeon General's Scientific Advisory Committee on Television and Social Behavior. One scientist involved in both efforts was Gerbner. His initial task was simple enough: produce an annual content analysis of a sample week of network television prime-time fare—the **Violence Index**—that would demonstrate, from season to season, how much violence was actually present in that programming. The index, however, was not without its critics, and serious controversy developed around it. *TV Guide* magazine called it the "million-dollar mistake."

Debate raged about the definition of *violence*. How was "television violence" defined? Was verbal aggression really violence? Were two teenagers playfully scuffling violence? Was cartoon violence a problem? Critics raised other issues. Why examine only network prime-time? After school, early evening, and weekends are particularly heavy viewing times for most children. Why count only violence? Why not racism and sexism? Nonetheless, Gerbner and his associates attempted to meet the demands of their critics and each year refined their definitional and reporting schemes.

Regardless of the attacks on the researchers' work, one thing did not change: Year in, year out, violence still appeared on prime-time television to a degree unmatched in the "real world," and it was violence of a nature unlike that found in that "real world." If television was truly a mirror of society, or if that medium did simply reinforce the status quo, this video mirror, the Violence Index seemed to say, was more like one found in a fun house than in a home. In their 1982 analysis of television violence, for example, Gerbner and his colleagues discovered that "crime in prime time is at least ten times as rampant as in the real world [and] an average of five to six acts of overt physical violence per hour involves over half of all major characters" (Gerbner, Gross, Morgan, & Signorielli, 1982, p. 106).

Although the Violence Index identified similar disparities between real-world and televised violence from its very start, the single most important criticism of that annual measure—"So what?"—was finally addressed in 1973. To demonstrate a causal link between the fluctuating levels of annual televised mayhem and viewers' perceptions of their world, the Gerbner team moved beyond the Violence Index, redefining its work as the **Cultural Indicators Project**. In it the researchers conducted regular periodic examinations of television programming and the "conceptions of social reality that viewing cultivates in child and adult audiences" (Gerbner & Gross, 1976, p. 174). And now that they were addressing the "So what?" question, they extended their research to issues well beyond violence.

The cultural indicators research made five assumptions. First, *television is essentially and fundamentally different from other forms of mass media.* Television is in more than 98% of all American homes. It does not require literacy, as do newspapers, magazines, and books. Unlike the movies, it's free (if you don't count the cost of advertising added to the products we buy). Unlike radio, it combines pictures and sound. It requires no mobility, as do places of worship, movies, theaters, and bowling alleys. Television is the only medium in history with which people can interact at the earliest and latest years of life, not to mention all those years in between.

Because of television's accessibility and availability to everyone, the second assumption of the Cultural Indicators Project is *the medium is the "central cultural arm" of American society*; it is, as Gerbner and his colleagues argued, "the chief creator of synthetic cultural patterns (entertainment and information) for the most heterogeneous mass publics in history, including large groups that have never shared in any common public message systems" (Gerbner, Gross, Jackson-Beeck, Jeffries-Fox, & Signorielli, 1978, p. 178).

The third assumption flows logically from this shared reality: *"The substance of the consciousness cultivated by TV is not so much specific attitudes and opinions as more basic assumptions about the 'facts' of life and standards of judgment on which conclusions are based"* (Gerbner & Gross, 1976, p. 175).

Because most television stations, cable and broadcast networks, and even video streaming services must generate profit (and therefore are entrenched in the status quo), they target more or less the same audiences, and because they depend on relatively generic, formulaic, cyclical, repetitive, recognizable forms of programs and stories, the fourth cultural indicators assumption is the idea that *television's major cultural function is to stabilize social patterns, to cultivate resistance to change*. It is a medium of socialization and enculturation. Again, Gerbner and his cohorts said it well: "The repetitive pattern of television's mass-produced messages and images forms the mainstream of the common symbolic environment that cultivates the most widely shared conceptions of reality. We live in terms of the stories we tell—stories about what things exist, stories about how things work, and stories about what to do—and television tells them all through news, drama, and advertising to almost everybody most of the time" (Gerbner et al., 1978, p. 178).

If you're reading closely, you can hear echoes of Carey's call to understand television as a ritual rather than transmissional medium (Chapter 6). In adopting this more ritualistic view, however, the cultural indicators researchers' fifth assumption—*the observable, measurable, independent contributions of television to the culture are relatively small*—caused additional controversy. In explaining this position, Gerbner used his **ice-age analogy**: "But just as an average temperature shift of a few degrees can lead to an ice age or the outcomes of elections can be determined by slight margins, so too can a relatively small but pervasive influence make a crucial difference. The 'size' of an 'effect' is far less critical than the direction of its steady contribution" (Gerbner, Gross, Morgan, & Signorielli, 1980, p. 14). The argument was not that television's impact was inconsequential, but rather that although television's measurable, observable, independent effect on the culture at any point in time might be small, that impact was, nonetheless, present and significant. Put somewhat differently, television's impact on our collective sense of reality is real and important, even though that effect might be beyond clear-cut scientific measurement, might defy easy observation, and might be inextricably bound to other factors in the culture.

The Products of Cultivation Analysis

To scientifically demonstrate their view of television as a culturally influential medium, cultivation researchers developed a four-step process. The first they called **message system analysis**—detailed content analyses of television programming to assess its most recurring and consistent presentations of images, themes, values, and portrayals. The second step is the formulation of questions about viewers' social realities. Remember the earlier questions about crime? Those were drawn from a cultivation study. The third step is to survey the audience, posing the questions from step two and asking them about their amount of television consumption. Finally, step four entails comparing the social realities of light and heavy viewers. The product, as described by Nancy Signorielli (1990), should not be surprising: "The questions posed to respondents do not mention television, and the respondents' awareness of the source of their information is seen as irrelevant. The resulting relationships . . . between amount of viewing and the tendency to respond to these questions in the terms of the dominant and repetitive facts, values, and ideologies of the world of television . . . illuminate television's contribution to viewers' conceptions of social reality" (p. 99).

What is television's contribution? Cultivation theorists argue that its major contribution is **cultivation**, a cultural process relating "to coherent frameworks or knowledge and to underlying general concepts . . . cultivated by exposure to the total and organically related world of television rather than exposure to individual programs and selections" (Gerbner, 1990, p. 255). This cultivation occurs in two ways. The first is **mainstreaming**, where, especially for heavier viewers, television's symbols monopolize and dominate

---

THINKING ABOUT THEORY

HOW DO I SEE THE WORLD: MY REALITY VS. THE DATA

Central to cultivation analysis is the idea that media cultivate, or grow, a generally held, mainstreamed picture of reality. One way it examines this effect is by comparing media consumers' judgments about the world against official data, demonstrating that heavier consumers typically offer probability judgments of real-world phenomena that are closer to the media's representations of those things than are actually the case. So, take this quiz and let's see how good your judgments about the world are. Then we can speculate about why you are so accurate . . . or not.

1. Which of these states has the lowest divorce rate?
   a) Arkansas
   b) Oklahoma
   c) New York
2. Which group of Americans has the highest rate of drug overdose death?
   a) Whites
   b) Hispanics
   c) African Americans
3. Which of these American cities ranks in the top 20 of *Economist* magazine's index of the safest cities in the world?
   a) Indianapolis
   b) Omaha
   c) Chicago
4. What is the median income (half earn less, half earn more) for an American worker?
   a) $32,000
   b) $45,000
   c) $60,000
5. Of these three states, which has the *lowest* rate of teenage pregnancy?
   a) Mississippi
   b) Texas
   c) Massachusetts

Answers:

1. C. Liberal northeastern New York's divorce rate of 2.2 out of every 1,000 marriages is far lower than heartland states Arkansas's (3.7) and Oklahoma's (4.1; Krisch, 2018).
2. A. The rate of death by overdose for Whites is 50% higher than it is for African Americans and 167% higher than for Hispanics (Berezow, 2018).
3. C. Using a variety of data, including personal safety, the *Economist*'s Intelligence Unit determined that Tokyo is the world's safest city. Chicago came in at number 19 (Lakritz, 2018).
4. A. The median income for workers in this country is $31,786 (Amadeo, 2019).
5. C. Of these states, Massachusetts has the lowest rate of teen pregnancy (12 per 1,000 15- to 19-year-olds, compared to 42/1,000 for Mississippi and 41/1,000 for Texas; Lowen, 2018).

How did you do? While this, of course, is not a true cultivation study (we did not ascertain your levels of media consumption, nor did we compute the "media answer"), it is clear that you made your judgments based on a set of assumptions. Where did they come from? Finally, think about the way media represent the phenomena covered by this little exercise. How many people with low-wage jobs do you see in the media? How do entertainment media typically portray drug abuse? How do they present the "Heartland" cities and states compared to those on the East and West Coasts? Of course, they tell us crime is a big-city problem, especially in places with large populations of people of color. Do you think you might have offered different answers if you were a lighter consumer of the mass media? Why or why not?

other sources of information and ideas about the world. People's internalized social realities eventually move toward the mainstream, not a mainstream in any political sense, but a culturally dominant reality more closely aligned with television's reality than with any objective reality. Is the country crime ridden? Is the criminal justice system failing us? If we think that's what's happening, that's what's happening. The second way cultivation manifests itself is through **resonance**, when viewers see things on television that are most congruent with their own everyday realities. In essence, these people get a "double dose" of cultivation because what they see on the screen resonates with their actual lives. Some city dwellers, for example, might see the violent world of television resonated in their deteriorating neighborhoods. Both effects manifest themselves in two ways. **First-order cultivation effects** are viewers' estimates of the occurrence of some phenomenon (for example, violence or political corruption) typical of early cultivation research. These are probability judgments about the world. **Second-order cultivation effects** are the attitudes and beliefs that are formed as a result of those judgments (for example, reluctance to go out at night or increased disdain for politicians; Intravia, Wolff, Paez, & Gibbs, 2017; Shrum, 2004). You can test your own probability judgments about the world in the box "How Do I See the World: My Reality vs. the Data."

Researchers have employed cultivation analysis to investigate the impact of television content on issues beyond violence and crime. It has been used in examinations of people's perceptions of affluence, divorce, and working women (Potter, 1991); acceptance of sexual stereotypes (Ward & Friedman, 2006); materialism (Reimer & Rosengren, 1990); mental health (Diefenbach & West, 2007); alcohol use (Coenen & Van Den Bulck, 2018); feelings of alienation (Signorielli, 1990); environmental concern (Shanahan, Morgan, & Stenbjerre, 1997); work (Signorielli & Kahlenberg, 2001); female body image (Van Vonderen & Kinnally, 2012); welfare (Sotirovic, 2003); and marital expectations (Segrin & Nabi, 2002). The assumptions of cultivation are supported throughout, although the strength of findings and the quality of the research vary greatly. These consistent results led Professor Gerbner (1987) to identify what he called the **3 Bs of television**:

1. Television *blurs* traditional distinctions of people's views of their world.
2. Television *blends* their realities into television's cultural mainstream.
3. Television *bends* that mainstream to the institutional interests of television and its sponsors.

Gerbner's (1990) assessment of the way television dominates our social world is reminiscent of arguments about popular culture made by Max Horkheimer and Theodor Adorno more than half a century ago (see Chapter 6):

> The historical circumstances in which we find ourselves have taken the magic of human life—living in a universe erected by culture—out of the hands of families and small communities. What has been a richly diverse hand-crafted process has become—for better or worse, or both—a complex manufacturing and mass-distribution enterprise. This has abolished much of the provincialism and parochialism, as well as some of the elitism, of the pretelevision era. It has enriched parochial cultural horizons. It also gave increasingly massive industrial conglomerates the right to conjure up much of what we think about, know, and do in common. (p. 261)

CULTIVATION ANALYSIS

Strengths

1. Combines macro- and micro-level theories
2. Provides detailed explanation of television's unique role as a story-telling system
3. Enables empirical study of widely held humanistic assumptions
4. Redefines effect as more than observable behavior change
5. Links media effects to genre-specific content
6. Sees media as important for story-telling, and links story-telling to important effects

Weaknesses

1. Early research had methodological limitations
2. Assumes homogeneity of television content and the worldview embedded in it
3. Initially focused on heavy users of television
4. Is difficult to apply to media used less heavily than television

Clearly, Gerbner does not seem to think that this is a particularly fair trade-off, and as such, he places cultivation analysis in the realm of critical theory. Others do the same. James Shanahan and Vicki Jones (1999), for example, argue, "Cultivation is sometimes taken as a return to a strong 'powerful effects' view of mass media. This view isn't completely incorrect, but it misses the point that cultivation was originally conceived as a critical theory, which happens to address media issues precisely and only because the mass media (especially television) serve the function of storytelling. . . . Television is the dominant medium for distributing messages from cultural, social, and economic elites. . . . Cultivation is more than just an analysis of effects from a specific medium; it is an analysis of the institution of television and its social role" (p. 32).

Since its early days cultivation research has steadily moved away from attributing effects to amounts of television exposure to studying the influence of specific forms of media content, in what has become known as **genre-specific cultivation theory**. Chris Segrin and Robin Nabi (2002), for example, applied cultivation analysis to romance-oriented genres such as soap operas, romantic comedies, and relationship-based reality television. Erica Scharrer and Greg Blackburn (2018) examined reality TV, testing its power to cultivate viewers' realities surrounding normative beliefs about aggression. And Jae Eun Chung (2014) demonstrated that heavy watchers of medical dramas like *ER*, *Grey's Anatomy*, and *Chicago Hope* were more likely than light viewers to underestimate the severity of serious illnesses like cancer and cardiovascular disease. This specific content can be delivered by a variety of different platforms, including Internet-based media. One way of looking at Internet-based media is that to some extent they give each of us the power to shape the message system that cultivates our understanding of the social world. We're no longer at the mercy of the big TV networks, but that doesn't mean that media have ceased to cultivate our understanding of ourselves and the people around us. "There is little evidence," observe Michael Morgan, James Shanahan, and Nancy Signorielli (2015), "that proliferation of channels has led to any substantially greater diversity of content. Indeed, the mere availability of more channels does not fundamentally change the socio-economic dynamics that drive the production and distribution of programs. On the contrary, that dynamic is intensi-fied by increased concentration of ownership and control. . . . Even when new digital delivery systems threaten dominant interests, they are quickly swallowed up within the existing institutional structure. The much-ballyhooed rise of user-generated video services such as YouTube have [*sic*] been absorbed by dominant players (Google) and are already being exploited for their benefits to advertisers" (pp. 45–46). "As long as there are popular storytelling systems and purveyors of widely shared messages," note Michael Morgan and James Shanahan (2009), "Gerbner's main ideas are likely to persist" (p. 350). "Spoiler alert," write these authors along with Nancy Signorielli. "There's nothing particularly 'new' about new communication technologies" (Morgan, Shanahan, & Signorelli, 2015, p. 675). They add:

> But we need to know if today's (and tomorrow's) new media are offering more mean-ingfully different and diverse messages than did yesterday's new media in terms of their underlying lessons about life and society. If not, then the primary question for cultivation will still be whether massive, long-term, common exposure is occurring, and what consequences that has for viewers' beliefs about social reality. If the mes-sages they provide have not changed fundamentally, then cultivation, as an explana-tory model, will be as relevant today—and tomorrow—as it was 50 years ago. (p. 687)

Take some time to consider your personal use of Internet-based and legacy media. Have you created a personal "story-telling system?" Are you taking advantage of Internet-based media to tell or seek out diverse stories that are radically different from mainstream storytelling? If you did start telling a new kind of story, how do you think your SNS-linked friends would react? Would they share equally unusual stories, or would they decide they made a mistake friending you? Could you use social media to locate new friends who also like "out-of-the-box" stories? Are you surprised that seem-ingly open-ended SNSs cultivate many of the same beliefs and values as the legacy media system?

MEDIA LITERACY

Implicitly or explicitly, communication scholars are responding to the many theories and research findings discussed throughout this text. There is a growing sense that the role of media for individuals and for society is problematic—but not beyond people's control. Many scholars feel that our current understanding of the role of media for individuals and society is sufficiently developed that action can and should be taken. This view is no longer restricted to critical theorists—it is generally expressed by lead-ing postpositivist as well as critical cultural researchers. One way scholars are taking action is that they are leading the drive to improve **media literacy**.

The media literacy movement is based on insights derived from many different sources. We list some of the most important here:

- Audience members are indeed active, but they are not necessarily very aware of what they do with media (uses and gratifications).
- The audience's needs, opportunities, and choices are constrained by access to media and media content (critical cultural studies).

- Media content can implicitly and explicitly provide a guide for action (social cognitive theory, schema theory, cultivation, and as you'll see in the next chapter, social construction of reality, symbolic interaction, and framing).
- People must realistically assess how their interaction with media texts can determine the purposes that interaction can serve for them in their environments (cultural theory).
- People have differing levels of cognitive processing ability, and this can radically affect how they use media and what they are able to get from media (information-processing theory and knowledge gap).

From a postpositivist perspective, the best way to ensure functional (rather than dysfunctional) use of media is to improve individuals' media-use skills. From a cultural studies perspective, we all need to develop our ability to critically reflect on the purposes media and media content serve for us. We need to be able to decide which media to avoid and which to use in ways that best serve our purposes. From the perspective of normative theory, we as citizens of a democracy must make good and effective use of our free press. This is media literacy.

Anthropologists, sociologists, linguists, historians, communication scientists—researchers from virtually all disciplines that study how people and groups communicate to survive and prosper—have long understood that as humans moved from preliterate, or oral, culture to literate culture, they assumed greater control over their environments and lives. With writing came the ability to communicate across time and space. People no longer had to be in the presence of those with whom they wished to communicate (Eisenstein, 1979; Innis, 1950).

The invention of the movable-type printing press in the mid-1400s infinitely expanded the importance and reach of the written word, and power began to shift from those who were born into it to those who could make the best use of communication. If literacy—traditionally understood to mean the ability to read and write—increases people's control over their environments and lives, it logically follows that an expanded literacy—one necessitated by a world in which so much "reading" and "writing" occurs in the mass media—should do the same. Critical theorist Stuart Ewen (2000) explains, "Historically, links between literacy and democracy are inseparable from the notion of an informed populace, conversant with the issues that touch upon their lives, enabled with tools that allow them to participate actively in public deliberation and social change" (p. 448). As such, he argues elsewhere, "In a society where instrumental images are employed to petition our affections at every turn—often without a word—educational curricula must . . . encourage the development of tools for critically analyzing images. For democracy to prevail, image making as a communicative activity must be undertaken by ordinary citizens as well" (Ewen, 1996, p. 413).

Alan Rubin (1998) offered three definitions of media literacy: (1) from the National Leadership Conference on Media Literacy—the ability to access, analyze, evaluate, and communicate messages; (2) from media scholar Paul Messaris—knowledge about how media function in society; and (3) from mass communication researchers Justin Lewis and Sut Jhally—understanding cultural, economic, political, and technological constraints on the creation, production, and transmission of messages. Rubin added, "All definitions emphasize specific knowledge, awareness, and rationality, that is, cognitive processing of information. Most focus on critical evaluations of messages, whereas some include the communication of messages. Media literacy, then, is about understanding the sources and technologies of communication, the codes that are used, the messages that are produced, and the selection, interpretation, and impact of those messages" (p. 3).

Communication scholars William Christ and W. James Potter (1998) offer an additional overview of media literacy: "Most conceptualizations [of media literacy] include the following elements: Media are constructed and construct reality; media have commercial implications; media have ideological and political implications; form and content are related in each medium, each of which has a unique aesthetic, codes, and conventions; and receivers negotiate meaning in media" (pp. 7–8). A careful reader can easily find in these two summations evidence of all the audience- and culture-centered theories we've discussed in this book.

Elements and Assumptions of Media Literacy

Mass communication scholar Art Silverblatt (1995) provided one of the first systematic efforts to place media literacy in audience- and culture-centered theory and frame it as a skill that must and can be improved. His core argument parallels a point made earlier: "The traditional definition of literacy applies only to print: 'having a knowledge of letters; instructed; learned.' However, the principal channels of media now include print, photography, film, radio, and television. In light of the emergence of these other channels of mass communications, this definition of literacy must be expanded" (pp. 1–2). As such, he identified five elements of media literacy (pp. 2–3):

1. An awareness of the impact of the media on the individual and society
2. An understanding of the process of mass communication
3. The development of strategies with which to analyze and discuss media messages
4. An awareness of media content as a "text" that provides insight into our contemporary culture and ourselves
5. The cultivation of an enhanced enjoyment, understanding, and appreciation of media content

W. James Potter (1998) takes a slightly different approach, describing several foundational or bedrock ideas supporting media literacy:

1. *Media literacy is a continuum, not a category.* "Media literacy is not a categorical condition like being a high school graduate or being an American. . . . Media literacy is best regarded as a continuum in which there are degrees. . . . There is always room for improvement" (p. 6).
2. *Media literacy needs to be developed.* "As we reach higher levels of maturation intellectually, emotionally, and morally we are able to perceive more in media messages. . . . Maturation raises our potential, but we must actively develop our skills and knowledge structures in order to deliver on that potential" (pp. 6–7).
3. *Media literacy is multidimensional.* Potter identifies four dimensions of media literacy. Each operates on a continuum. In other words, we interact with

media messages in four ways, and we do so with varying levels of awareness and skill:

    a. The cognitive domain refers to mental processes and thinking.

    b. The emotional domain is the dimension of feeling.

    c. The aesthetic domain refers to the ability to enjoy, understand, and appreciate media content from an artistic point of view.

    d. The moral domain refers to the ability to infer the values underlying the messages. (p. 8)

4. *The purpose of media literacy is to give us more control over interpretations.* "All media messages are interpretations. . . . A key to media literacy is not to engage in the impossible quest for truthful or objective messages. They don't exist" (p. 9).

Media Literacy Interventions

Research on media literacy typically takes the form of evaluating the effectiveness of **media literacy interventions**—efforts "to reduce harmful effects of the media by informing the audience about one or more aspects of the media, thereby influencing media-related beliefs and attitudes, and ultimately preventing risky behaviors" (Jeong, Cho, & Hwang, 2012, p. 454). The content subjected to these intervention efforts runs the entire range of that offered by the media—for example, food advertising (Livingstone & Helsper, 2006), alcohol advertising (Austin, et al., 2002), racist portrayals (Ramasubramanian & Oliver, 2007), health narratives (Bergsma & Carney, 2008), portrayals of tobacco use (Gonzales, Glik, Davoudi, & Ang, 2004), violence (Nikkelen, Vossen, Piotrowski, & Valkenburg, 2016), altruism (Farsides, Pettman, & Tourle, 2013), and bullying (Johnson, August, & Agiro, 2012). Se-Hoon Jeong, Hyunyi Cho, and Yoori Hwang (2012) applied meta-analysis to empirically evaluate 51 interventions. They demonstrated that "media literacy interventions may be an effective approach for reducing potentially harmful effects of media messages. Intervention effects were found across divergent topics for diverse audiences and for a broad range of media-related (e.g., knowledge) and behavior-related (e.g., attitudes and behaviors) outcomes. The results—showing that intervention effects did not vary according to target age, the setting, audience involvement, and the topic—suggest that interventions can be equally effective across a spectrum of settings (e.g., school, community, or lab), age groups, levels of audience involvement, and topics (e.g., alcohol, violence, and sex)" (p. 464). Smita Banerjee and Robert Kubey's (2013) review of the short-term and long-term effects of media literacy interventions came to a similar conclusion. Although observing that not all interventions are successful, they noted, "Some media literacy interventions do seem to help participants to become better 'critical thinkers' about media content, processes, and effects. . . . Media literacy instruction also appears to trigger some thought about media content and its comparison to 'the real world'" (p. 14).

Parental interventions have become of particular interest to media literacy scholars, especially with the coming of the Internet and SNS. Lynn Clark (2011) detailed **parental mediation theory**, originally developed as a means of conceptualizing an active parental role in regulating and managing children's experiences with television. But as with so many other mass communication theories, Clark notes, it has had to evolve in the digital era to become "a hybrid communication theory that, although rooted primarily in social/psychological media effects and information processing theories, also implicitly foregrounds the importance of interpersonal communication between parents and their children" (p. 323–324). Clark argues that the parental mediation strategies that were effective with children's television viewing—**active mediation** (talking with children about television content), **restrictive mediation** (setting rules and limits on their viewing), and **co-viewing** (watching television with them)—need to be augmented in the digital age with a fourth strategy, **participatory learning**, designed "to recognize that although children might encounter risks in the digital and mobile media environment, they might also engage with parents in activities that foster strengthened interpersonal relationships, individual and collaborative creativity, and even cognitive development" (p. 335). Hee Jhee Jiow, Sun Sun Lim, and Julian Lin (2017) also recognized that parental mediation theory "must be refined to accommodate the fast-changing media landscape that is populated by complex and intensively used media forms such as video games, social media, and mobile apps" (p. 309). Their research led them to conclude, "Rather than viewing parental mediation as broad monolithic categories . . . we propose that it is more productive to view mediation as a variable composite of activities that are undertaken in fluid combinations" (p. 315). In other words parents, of necessity, switch and mingle mediation strategies as circumstances require. These researchers identified **gatekeeping activities**—various actions parents take to regulate children's exposure to technology—for example, rules and restrictions on access to specific content and on duration of use. **Discursive activities** are those conversations or discussions between parents and children about the technologies, their content, and dangers and benefits. **Investigative activities** refer to "information-seeking and skill acquisition activities" (p. 319) that parents undertake to better mediate their children's media activities. These can include personally examining the content in advance and even planned and unplanned checks on children's time of use and mis-use of technology—for example, using the Internet for gaming when it is supposed to be for homework. Investigations can lead to restrictions. Finally, **diversionary activities** are parents' intentional efforts to direct their children away from the technologies themselves, perhaps by encouraging them to go outside, play sports, join clubs, or other healthier or beneficial activities.

As you might imagine in a time of growing concern about kids' use of a sometimes-dangerous Internet, there have been a number of digital technology–specific parental mediation interventions designed to help parents boost their children's digital literacy. For example, Sonia Livingston and her colleagues identified **enabling mediation**—combining safety efforts for more Internet-skilled kids and restrictive mediation for those less so in order to "maximize their children's online opportunities while also minimizing online risks" (Livingstone et al., 2017, p. 82). The work of Isabel Rodríguez-de-Dios and colleagues was similar, but it favored more active parental mediation rather than restriction (Rodríguez-de-Dios, van Oosten, & Igartua, 2018). And as you might also imagine given the widespread awareness of and anger at digitally spread fake news, several interventions are designed to boost **news media literacy**, empowering news consumers to seek useful and accurate information in order to make informed decisions related to the political, social, and cultural structures of society (Ashley, Maksl, & Craft, 2013). You can read more in the box "News Media Literacy as the Antidote to Fake News."

Faced with a different problem, Kiran Vinod Bhatia and Manisha Pathak-Shelat (2019) employed yet another form of media literacy intervention, **critical media education**, to combat not the influence of fake news, but of otherwise legitimate media content in India that served to highlight differences and exacerbate frictions between Hindu and Muslim people in the Indian state of Gugarat. The emphasis in critical media education is on the *critical* (see Chapter 6), as its goal is to "upend societal hierarchies." Critical media education, therefore, is "a set of pedagogic strategies to encourage adolescents to challenge power relations by identifying resources for resistance within themselves and their immediate media environments" (2019). Using traditional media literacy tactics—for example, encouraging deeper or more personal reading of media texts, and having participants collaboratively create and evaluate their own content—the researchers were able to improve understanding and quality of interaction between school-age Muslim and Hindu youth.

THINKING ABOUT THEORY

NEWS MEDIA LITERACY AS THE ANTIDOTE TO FAKE NEWS?

We've read at several junctures of this text about the insidious effects of fake news not only on the practice of journalism, but on American democracy and the country's ability to self-govern. Historian David Bell (2019) explains, "Social media, by turning every individual user into an author and publisher of sorts, drastically lowers the perceived difference between *The New York Times*, scientific journals, or the federal government, on the one hand, and a dyspeptic relative expostulating at his keyboard. In short, the ability of democratic societies to maintain common, authoritative sources of truth in the face of reactionary demagogues and media provocateurs has drastically withered, producing vastly destabilizing consequences" (p. 31). The problem, however, extends beyond those dispensers of fake news, in large part because of people's **confirmation bias**, their tendency to accept information that confirms their beliefs and dismiss information that does not, and their willingness to pass it on with little evaluation.

Might improved news media literacy help limit that bias, reduce the likelihood that false reports will be shared, and as such, mitigate, at least somewhat, the spread and impact of fake news? Stephanie Craft, Seth Ashley, and Adam Maksl (2017) discovered that those most likely to spread online fake news were those who had comparatively little understanding of how the news media operate. The converse held as well: "The greater one's knowledge about the news media—from the kinds

of news covered, to the commercial context in which news is produced, to the effects on public opinion news can have—the less likely one will fall prey to conspiracy theories" (p. 396). The researchers combined their results with existing media literacy literature to argue for news media literacy interventions that would cultivate improved norms of accuracy and produce greater levels of news skepticism and current events knowledge. Those interventions exist, because as Monica Bulger and Patrick Davison (2018) explained, "Media literacy has become a center of gravity for countering fake news, and a diverse array of stakeholders—from educators to legislators, philanthropists to technologists—have pushed significant resources toward media literacy programs" (p. 1).

For example, the American Society of Newspaper Editors (2019) maintains a news literacy committee to help member outlets better explain to their readers how they do journalism. The Stanford History Education Group (2016) has produced a detailed set of curricula individually designed for middle school, high school, and college students designed to improve home page analysis, evidence evaluation, and judgment of social media claims. Faculty at Harvard University developed a four-rule regime for combatting fake news: *Vet the publisher's credibility*; *Pay attention to quality and timeliness*; *Check sources and citations*; *Ask a pro*—that is, access reputable fact-checking sites such as FactCheck.org, International Fact-Checking Network, PolitiFact, and Snopes (Nagler, 2018).

(Continued)

THINKING ABOUT THEORY *(Continued)*

These researchers and institutions believe that news media literacy is the antidote to fake news. But what about you? S. Mo Jang and Joon Kim (2018) found that there is public support for news media literacy . . . for others. People holding greater levels of third-person perceptions—"Media influence others, not me" (see Chapter 1)—were more likely to favor those interventions. Does this describe you? Do you think you're a good fake-news detector but that other people need help? One problem is that the magnitude of the task calls into question even the most earnest news literacy intervention, as a fake-news story is 70% more likely to be passed on precisely because it is false. According to researchers at the Massachusetts Institute of Technology who followed more than 126,000 rumors spread among three million people from 2006 to 2017, fake news tends to be more novel than true news, and people like to share what's new. The researchers discovered that "false news reached more people than the truth; the top 1% of false news cascades diffused to between 1,000 and 100,000 people,

whereas the truth rarely diffused to more than 1,000 people. Falsehood also diffused faster than the truth. The degree of novelty and the emotional reactions of recipients may be responsible for the differences observed." It must be bots spreading that much fake news, right? "Contrary to conventional wisdom," wrote Soroush Vosoughi, Deb Roy, and Sinan Aral (2018), "robots accelerated the spread of true and false news at the same rate, implying that false news spreads more than the truth because humans, not robots, are more likely to spread it" (p. 1146). Additionally, research conducted after the 2016 presidential election discovered that about a quarter of Americans passed on fake news, and half of those did it with full knowledge that it was false (Mullin, 2016). For those people, maybe the problem has nothing to do with low news media literacy. Can you offer any optimism for a turnaround, given what you've read in this chapter and in Chapter 10's discussion of humans as sometimes (often?) uncritical and unsystematic cognitive processors?

REVIEW OF LEARNING OBJECTIVES

- Explain how media affect communities in both useful and problematic ways.

Social capital theory and research have focused on the ways that that media can intrude into and disrupt communities. Entertainment media can distract attention away from important social activities and undermine the ability of groups to be effective. Social capital theory sees groups as essential in developing and maintaining social order in communities. To the extent that groups are ineffective, there will be many problematic consequences—rising juvenile delinquency, drug use, depression, even suicide. Media tend to cover politics in ways that focus on conflict and polarize how people perceive and participate in politics. But media can have positive consequences for communities. If individuals regularly read newspapers to follow events in their communities and learn about other community members, they will be more likely to participate in their communities. But spreading news deserts threaten papers' unifying potential.

- Detail the nature of cultivation analysis and its contributions to our understanding of media influence.

Cultivation analysis addresses macro-level questions about the media's role in society. Its central argument is that television is a "message system" that "cultivates" or creates a worldview that, although possibly inaccurate, becomes the reality simply because we, as a people, believe it to be the reality and base our judgments about our own everyday worlds on that "reality." Its five basic assumptions are: Television is essentially and fundamentally different from other forms of mass media; television is the "central cultural arm" of American society; the substance of the consciousness cultivated by TV is not so much specific attitudes and opinions as more basic assumptions about the "facts" of life and standards of judgment on which conclusions are based; television's major cultural function is to stabilize social patterns, to cultivate resistance to change; and the observable, measurable, independent contributions of television to the culture are relatively small. Cultivation analysis has been successfully applied to media beyond television as well as to new digital technologies and specific TV genres. Thus far, research on social media cultivation effects has not found major differences from TV effects.

- Assess the potential for media literacy and media literacy interventions to enhance positive media effects and limit those that may be harmful.

Most understandings of media literacy assume that media both construct and are constructed by reality, that they have commercial implications, and that they have ideological and political implications. Such understandings also acknowledge that form and content are related in all media, each of which has its unique aesthetic, codes, and conventions. Another central idea is that receivers negotiate meaning. The five elements of media literacy are an awareness of the impact of the media on the individual and society; an understanding of the process of mass communication; the development of strategies with which to analyze and discuss media messages; an awareness of media content as a "text" that provides insight into our contemporary culture and ourselves; and the cultivation of an enhanced enjoyment, understanding, and appreciation of media content. The bedrock assumptions of the media literacy movement are that media literacy is a continuum, not a category; it must developed; it is multidimensional; and its purpose is to give us more control over interpretations. People's media literacy can be improved through interventions—efforts to reduce harmful effects and increase beneficial outcomes of media use. Interventions have proven successful across a wide array of media, different forms of content, and a host of knowledge and behavioral outcomes, with much recent attention directed at news media literacy as a way to combat the flood of fake news made possible by SNS and other Internet-based media. Many interventions involve the interaction of parents and their children, leading to the development of parental mediation theory—different perspectives on active parent involvement in the full array of children's media experiences.

CRITICAL THINKING QUESTIONS

1. Return to the World Happiness Report discussed at the chapter's start. How do you feel about the United States' relatively poor showing? Tenth in income might be pretty good, but what about the 61st for freedom and 39th for healthy life expectancy? How might a critical scholar reconcile the high income ranking with those two more desultory scores? How might they see media contributing to that state of affairs? How do you?

2. How media literate are you? What about your friends? Do you suffer from a media-literacy third-person effect? You're good, but those other people need help? What are your weaknesses as a media-literate person? Your strengths?

3. How trusting are you of your neighbors? Of strangers? Were you surprised at the data indicating that violent crime is down in the United States? If so, why? If not, to what would you attribute your more realistic impression of the prevalence of crime?

KEY TERMS

social capital theory
social capital
news deserts
orphan counties
cultivation analysis
Violence Index
Cultural Indicators Project
ice-age analogy
message system analysis
cultivation
mainstreaming
resonance
first-order cultivation effects
second-order cultivation effects
3 Bs of television
genre-specific cultivation theory

media literacy
media literacy intervention
parental mediation theory
active mediation
restrictive mediation
co-viewing
participatory learning
gatekeeping activities
discursive activities
investigative activities
diversionary activities
enabling mediation
news media literacy
critical media education
confirmation bias

GLOSSARY

social capital theory: Argues that there are important benefits, such as trust, cooperation, and reciprocity, that flow from involvement in various social networks

social capital: The influence potential leaders develop as a result of membership and participation in social groups

news deserts: Communities unserved by local media

orphan counties: Counties where people receive no news coverage and political advertising for their own statewide elections, irrelevant information about candidates in a neighboring state, or both

cultivation analysis: Theory that television "cultivates" or creates a worldview that, although possibly inaccurate, becomes the reality because people believe it to be so

Violence Index: Annual content analysis of a sample week of network television prime-time fare demonstrating how much violence is present

Cultural Indicators Project: In cultivation analysis, periodic examinations of television programming and the conceptions of social reality cultivated by viewing

ice-age analogy: In cultivation analysis, idea that the degree of television's influence is

less critical than the direction of its steady contribution

message system analysis: In cultivation analysis, detailed content analyses of television programming to assess recurring and consistent presentations of images, themes, values, and portrayals

cultivation: In cultivation analysis, television's contribution to the creation of a culture's frameworks or knowledge and underlying general concepts

mainstreaming: In cultivation analysis, the process, especially for heavier viewers, by which television's symbols monopolize and dominate other sources of information and ideas about the world

resonance: In cultivation analysis, when viewers see things on television that are congruent with their own everyday realities

first-order cultivation effects: Viewers' estimates of the occurrence of some phenomenon; probability judgments

second-order cultivation effects: Attitudes and beliefs that are formed as a result of viewers' probability judgments

3 Bs of television: In cultivation analysis, the idea that television blurs, blends, and bends reality

genre-specific cultivation theory: Extension of cultivation theory's logic—message consumption "cultivates" or creates a worldview that, although possibly inaccurate, becomes the reality because people believe it to be so—to specific content genres

media literacy: The ability to access, analyze, evaluate, and communicate messages

media literacy intervention: An effort to reduce harmful effects of the media by informing the audience about one or more aspects of those media

parental mediation theory: Theory of active parent involvement in the full array of children's media experiences

active mediation: Talking with children about television content as a parental mediation strategy

restrictive mediation: Setting rules and limits on children's television consumption as a parental mediation strategy

co-viewing: Watching television with children as a parental mediation strategy

participatory learning: Children and parents together engaging in new media activities as a parental mediation strategy

gatekeeping activities: Various actions parents take to regulate children's exposure to technology as a parental mediation strategy

discursive activities: Conversations between parents and children about the technologies, their content, and dangers and benefits as a parental mediation strategy

investigative activities: Information-seeking and skill acquisition activities that parents undertake to better mediate their children's media activities as a parental mediation strategy

diversionary activities: Parents' intentional efforts to divert their children from media technologies as a parental mediation strategy

enabling mediation: Parental mediation strategy based on children's level of Internet-use skill designed to maximize opportunities and minimize risks

news media literacy: Empowering news consumers to seek useful and accurate information in order to make informed decisions related to the political, social, and cultural structures of society

critical media education: Pedagogic strategies help media consumers identify resources for resistance within themselves and their immediate media environments

confirmation bias: Tendency to accept information that confirms one's beliefs and dismiss information that does not

CHAPTER 13

Media and Culture Theories: Meaning Making in the Social World

How would you describe your experience the last time you went shopping or spent a night out with friends? Were you fearful because there were lots of strangers in the stores or clubs? When you're out in public, do you often feel like events might spin out of control, or are you confident that nothing unusual or threatening will happen to you? If you're a college student attending classes on a large campus, you are constantly encountering people you don't know in places you haven't been. Do you worry about that? Do you frequently find yourself in bizarre situations that are impossible to understand? These may seem like odd questions since most of us rarely have difficulty adjusting to everyday situations, even in new places where there are crowds of strangers. We routinely move through a wide range of everyday-life situations without serious difficulties. But think about it. Why is it so easy for you to anticipate and plan for situations even when they involve strangers? It's easy because you share an everyday culture with others that enables you to anticipate and make sense of most situations and the people in them.

You're constantly learning about everyday culture, one that is constantly changing in subtle but important ways. For most of human history, everyday culture was learned through face-to-face communication with a handful of other people in repetitious, quite similar situations. Life was relatively static but varied so greatly from one place to another that even people living fairly close to one another found it hard to understand each other. Even when people in a region shared a common language, the dialects differed so dramatically from village to village that it limited communication and discouraged travel.

There are a number of reasons this has changed, but one of the most important is that media have become central to how we—and almost everyone else around the world—learn about everyday culture. It's likely that before you ever went to a hospital or a bar, television and movies showed you how people acted in these places. These media constantly offer you many different types of people in a wide range of situations. Your consumption of media content has helped you form useful expectations about other people (and, unfortunately, has also reinforced problematic stereotypes). And now the Internet and social media have increased the ways you can learn about quite complex forms of everyday culture. It's not your great grandparents' social world anymore.

If you have grown up with large-scale social media and YouTube on mobile devices, these seem like very natural and normal ways to learn about and relate to other people. Facebook, Twitter, Snapchat, and Instagram provide a constant flow of information about friends, family, celebrities, and even politicians. But as we have pointed out frequently in previous chapters, not everyone is convinced that these new media are all that benign. How can we begin to understand what they are doing to transform our experience of the social world? Can theories developed to understand television be adapted for social media when the way Internet-based media are used and the content they deliver seem so different? Remember from Chapter 3 that Dan Gilmor (2004) labeled you "the people formerly known as the audience." Media writer Steve Smith (2013) adds to the recasting of today's media users, explaining that the people formerly known as the audience have also become programming executives: "I now think about where certain kinds of content fit into my routines and life, just as I push podcasts of different kinds and lengths to car, gym, walking, or other use cases where I want to experience them" (para. 4). In previous chapters we've looked at how media researchers are addressing these changes. Some approaches, like uses-and-gratifications theory and cultivation analysis, have been adapted to help explain large-scale social media. Most of the findings so far are similar to those found for legacy media. In this chapter we'll look at theories that are increasingly being used to understand how both Internet-based and legacy media affect our understanding of everyday culture. If you want to understand how media are changing the way people understand and experience the social world, these theories provide an excellent starting point.

LEARNING OBJECTIVES
After studying this chapter you should be able to
- Describe symbolic interactionism and pragmatism, and explain how they differ from behaviorist or stimulus-response theory. Be able to explain how they differ from social constructionism.
- Describe the notions of self-identity and social identity and how they are formed through communication.
- Describe framing theory, and discuss its increasing popularity for studying news media and their effects.
- List key findings from framing research, and discuss the insight they provide into the way news shapes our views of the social world.

OVERVIEW

In Chapter 6 we traced the rise of cultural theories of media, giving particular attention to early schools of critical theory and cultural studies. This chapter and Chapter 14 look at more contemporary theories that focus on culture. Cultural theories have a long and, as we've seen, controversial history in the field of mass communication. They predate the rise of postpositivist theories examining media effects on individuals. For example, during the 1920s and 1930s scholars at the University of Chicago advanced theories of community with a central focus on the role of communication in shaping everyday culture. From the 1950s to the 1980s cultural theories were marginalized by American mass communication scholars in favor of media-effects theories. The media-effects trend in theory development pushed aside competing approaches. Media theory textbooks written in the United States during this era often omitted any mention of cultural theories or gave them little attention. They tended to be categorized with mass society theory, and their usefulness was questioned.

In the 1980s, when the discipline began to take cultural theories more seriously, a furious debate broke out between adherents and their postpositivist opponents. The field was declared to be in "ferment" ("Ferment in the Field," 1983). Advocates of media-effects perspectives claimed their theories were more scientific because they were based on highly structured empirical observations and they were falsifiable—new findings could lead to their rejection. They attacked cultural theories as too speculative, too complex, and based on loosely structured qualitative research methods. There was no way to test their causal assertions. But since that time, cultural theories have gained acceptance, as have qualitative methods. Although there is growing respect between postpositivists and advocates for cultural theories, they still mostly work independently, especially in the United States. Some textbooks, like this one, consider the strengths and limitations of both theories and the research methods on which they are based. But most remain focused on either postpositivist or critical cultural theory. The feuding between the two approaches may have ended, but they remain divided in different books and journals and by different methodology toolboxes.

In this chapter we will focus on micro-level cultural theories, though some of these theories do have macro-level implications. These theories examine the everyday use of media by individuals and local communities. In Chapter 14 we will move to theories that deal with macro-level concerns and look at media's role in the larger social order. We use two terms to refer to the theories in this chapter and the next. We refer to them as *culture-centered* because they study culture as a primary means of understanding the social world and the role media play in it. They provide different perspectives on how media influence culture and what the consequences of that influence are for individuals and society. We also refer to them as *meaning-making* theories because they are focused on understanding the way media influence how we make sense of the social world and our place in it—how we make meaning. Despite their common focus on culture and meaning making, these theories are diverse. Some were developed by American scholars; others originated in Europe. Some are critical—they assess how media frustrate our efforts to pursue valued objectives. Others are satisfied to provide in-depth assessments of what we do with media and how our experiences of and actions in the social world are affected by our involvement with them.

SYMBOLIC INTERACTIONISM

Symbolic interactionism was one of the first social science theories to address questions of how communication is involved with the way we learn culture and how culture structures our everyday experience. Symbolic interaction theory developed during the

1920s and 1930s as a reaction to and criticism of behaviorism (see Chapter 2), and it had a variety of labels until Herbert Blumer (1969) gave it its current name. One early name was **social behaviorism**. Unlike traditional behaviorists, social behaviorists rejected simplistic conceptualizations of stimulus-response conditioning. They were convinced that attention must be given to cognitive processes mediating learning. They also believed that the social environment in which learning takes place must be considered. Early behaviorists tended to conduct laboratory experiments in which they exposed animals to certain stimuli to condition them to behave in specific ways. Social behaviorists judged these experiments too simplistic. They argued that human existence was far too complex to be understood through conditioning of animal behavior.

George Herbert Mead (1934), a University of Chicago philosopher and social activist, provided a way of understanding social life that differed profoundly from behaviorist notions. Rather than observe rats running through mazes, he proposed a more useful way to understand how people learn to make sense of everyday life and structure their actions. He suggested we look at how people learn to play baseball (or any team sport). How do we learn to play these games? Surely not by reading a textbook titled *The Theory of Playing Second Base*. Not simply through stimulus-response conditioning as we get rewarded or punished for specific actions. Mead argued that what occurs on a playing field is a sophisticated form of mutual conditioning: The players teach each other how to play the game *while* they are playing it. Players must learn to structure their actions in very complex ways to cover their positions effectively. But each position must be played differently, so teammates can't rely on simple mimicry of one another. According to Mead, each player learns a social role—the pitcher role, the catcher role, or the left fielder role. Each role is learned by observing and modeling good players and by interacting with other team members. As they play, team members receive encouragement and friendly criticism from teammates and fans. If they play well, they have the satisfaction of being accepted by others as a productive member of a social unit—a community.

Mead saw a baseball team as a microcosm of society. Each of us learns many different social roles through interaction with others. We are members of many different communities. Our actions are constantly being subtly "conditioned" by others, while at the same time we are affecting their actions. The goal is not to manipulate or dominate one another but to create and sustain a productive social unit—a community providing its members with certain rewards in return for their willingness to take on specific roles. As we grow up we try out various roles, and then ideally we are able to select those that best fit our interests and personal abilities. Social roles and many other aspects of culture are learned through interaction—through experiences in daily life situations. Over time we internalize the rules inherent in various situations and structure our actions accordingly.

Only in rare cases do we consciously reflect on and analyze our actions. If asked to explain what we are doing and why we are doing it, we are puzzled—the question seems strange, much like those that opened this chapter. Why don't you call your mother by her first name? Why do you ride an elevator silently facing forward and not backward or chatting with others? Why do you text rather than phone? Why post a status update on Facebook rather than send an e-mail? We do things because they are common sense; it's the way everybody does them; they are the normal, the logical, the right way to do things. Once internalized, these roles provide us with a powerful means of controlling our actions. In time our identity becomes bound up with them: We understand ourselves, both emotionally and consciously, in terms of the roles we play and the personal identities that are associated with these roles. We value ourselves to the extent that these roles are respected by others. And sometimes, like athletes whose physical skills inevitably fail, we experience identity crises because we can't play a role as we or others expect us to or because we aspire to a role that proves to be beyond our ability or resources.

Mead's analogy is insightful and powerful, but it has some important limitations common to microscopic theories. Mead assumes that baseball teams operate as a sort of mini-democracy. Perhaps that's a useful way to look at amateur teams who play for fun. But what about professional teams? Who organizes them and pays the players? Who defines the rules of the game? Who sells the tickets, pays expenses, and profits from the entire enterprise? Yes, team members mutually influence each other, but often coaches and a few older or more experienced players will dominate professional teams. Teams have owners and general managers who make decisions about hiring and firing team members and who plays which positions.

The baseball team analogy also isn't very helpful for understanding how mass media might affect socialization. Ball players directly interact with one another. What happens when communication occurs through media—when people use Facebook or Snapchat to relate to dozens or even hundreds of others? Unlike baseball players who physically confront each other on the field, social media users meet each other in cyberspace. They use tablets or tap away at their smartphones to exchange messages. They post information about themselves (express their personal identity), but often this information provides a very fragmentary or even fictional description of who they are. They get constant updates of the activities of friends, and they post details of what they are doing. How is everyday culture being created and shared? Certainly not the way teammates do it.

Mead offered another important insight into the socialization process. Unlike animals conditioned to respond to stimuli in a predetermined manner, humans are socialized in ways that permit more or less conscious interpretation of stimuli and planned responses. What is the secret that enables us to do what animals cannot? Symbols. **Symbols**, in general, are arbitrary, often quite abstract, representations of unseen phenomena. Think of the words you use—all are arbitrary vocalizations that are essentially meaningless except to others who know how to decode them. When we write, we cover pages with complicated markings. To read them, someone must be literate in our language. According to Mead, the use of symbols transforms the socialization process—freeing it from the bonds of both space and time. Using symbols, we can create vivid representations of the past and we can anticipate the future. We can be transported anywhere on the globe or even into the far reaches of space.

In *Mind, Self, and Society*, Mead (1934) argues that we use symbols to create our experience of consciousness (mind), our understanding of ourselves (self), and our knowledge of the larger social order (society). In other words, symbols mediate and structure all our experience because they structure our ability to perceive and interpret what goes on around us. This argument is similar to the one made by information-processing theorists (see Chapter 10). In information-processing theory, *schemas* (sets of symbols) that we have learned in the past enable us to routinely make sense of the new sensory information we take in. Likewise, Mead believed that mind, self, and society are internalized as complex sets of symbols. They serve as filtering mechanisms for our experiences.

This might seem to be an extreme argument. Most of us take for granted our ability to look at the world around us and see the things that are obviously there. We might assume that we were born with this ability. But think about it. Why do we notice certain things and not others? As we move through daily life, we're constantly encountering ambiguous, complex situations. Unless we are unusually fastidious, for example, we will not notice small amounts of dust and dirt when we enter a room. We'll ignore most of the background sounds. According to Mead, human perceptual processes are extremely malleable and can be shaped by the sets of symbols we learn so that we will see only what our culture has determined is worth seeing. Has your perception of Middle Eastern cultures changed since the United States' involvement in Iraq and Afghanistan? Are you more likely now to notice a woman wearing a head scarf? What mental images spring to mind when you hear the word *terrorist*? Twenty years ago the image might have been of an Irish Republican Army bomber or a Latin American drug criminal; now it's most likely a Middle Eastern male. Mead's arguments anticipated cognitive psychology research, which, as you saw in Chapter 10, is beginning to empirically demonstrate much of what he hypothesized.

Thus, symbolic interactionism posits that our actions in response to symbols are mediated (or controlled) largely by those same symbols. Therefore, our understanding of and relation to physical or objective reality is mediated by the symbolic environment—the mind, self, and society we have internalized. Put another way, the meanings we give to symbols define us and the realities we experience. As we are socialized, culturally agreed-upon meanings assume control over our interactions with our environments. Consider the meaning that you attach to the stitched red, white, and blue cloth that constitutes an American flag. A flag is, in reality (objectively), little more than a piece of colored cloth. That is, it is little more than a piece of cloth until someone attaches symbolic meaning to it. We have decided that a particular array and formulation of colors and shapes should become our flag. Each of us experiences the flag differently, yet there is shared meaning as well. But that shared meaning can be contested when there is conflict over what the flag stands for. Over the past few years, for example, some professional football players have refused to stand for the national anthem and the presentation of the American flag. Colin Kaepernick, one of the first to do so, argued that he couldn't acknowledge the flag as long as Black citizens were discriminated against and denied rights accorded to White citizens. Regardless of the meaning we *individually* attach to the flag, however, none of us is free from its symbolic power. When a color guard passes before us at a sporting event, how free are we to remain sitting—especially now that refusing to stand would imply sympathy for Kaepernick's protest? The one-time star quarterback, only 5 years removed from taking his team to the Super Bowl championship game, cannot find a team to hire him, even as other players with far inferior records have secured million-dollar contracts to play his position (Belson & Draper, 2019). Your situation might not be as dramatic, but at a school function, how free do you feel to continue chatting with your friends during the Pledge of Allegiance to that tricolored piece of fabric?

Pragmatism and the Chicago School

Mead developed symbolic interactionism by drawing on ideas from **pragmatism**, a philosophical school of theory emphasizing the practical function of knowledge as an instrument for adapting to reality and controlling it. Pragmatism developed in America as a reaction against ideas gaining popularity at home and in Europe at the end of the 19th century—simplistic forms of materialism such as behaviorism and German idealism. Both behaviorism and idealism rejected the possibility of human *agency*, the idea that individuals could consciously control their thoughts and actions in some meaningful and useful way. Idealism argued that people are dominated by culture, and behaviorism argued that all human action is a conditioned response to external stimuli. From the preceding description of Mead's ideas, you can see how he tried to find a middle ground between these two perspectives—a place that would allow for some degree of human agency. If we consider Mead's arguments carefully, they suggest that while individuals do have some control over what they do, that agency lies with the community (or in the baseball example, with the team). Communities rather than individuals create and propagate culture, those complex sets of symbols that guide and shape our experiences. When we act in communities, we are mutually conditioned so we learn culture and use it to structure experience. These pragmatist notions about culture and human agency are at the heart of many of the cultural theories developed in the United States. As a school of thought, pragmatism continues to attract interest in a number of disciplines. In philosophy Richard Rorty (1991; Rorty, Schneewind, & Skinner, 1982) has popularized neo-pragmatism. In political science a number of scholars have advocated John Dewey's pragmatism as a way of moving that field in a useful direction (Farr, 1999). Chris Russill (2006, 2008, 2012) and Robert Craig (2007) discuss the ongoing relevance of pragmatism for contemporary communication theory.

For pragmatists the basic test of the power of culture is the extent to which it effectively structures experience within a community. When some aspect of culture loses its effectiveness, it ceases to structure experience and becomes a set of words and symbols having essentially no meaning. For example, we can still find certain words in a dictionary and we could use them to decode old media content, but they would have no force in our lives—no connection to our experience. What does "twenty-three skidoo" mean? Do you have "the skinny"? You might understand these as "let's dip" and "the tea," respectively. Or maybe not, depending on your experience. Culture is constantly changing—new elements are developed, and old elements are abandoned. This change doesn't typically happen because it's planned by elites who manipulate culture to serve their interests. Rather, culture changes as situations in which communities act change. Culture can also change when people use media to relate to each other in new ways. Consider how quickly *hashtag, sexting, swipe right,* and *to poke someone* entered our consciousness and how they now prove useful in structuring everyday action.

Many of the most productive symbolic interactionists were, like Mead, located at the University of Chicago. They became known as the Chicago School. We discussed the Chicago School in Chapter 3 when we considered the arguments they made concerning social responsibility of the press. These ideas, pragmatism and social interactionism, were at the heart of that normative theory. Chicago School theorists in the 1920s saw the city that housed their campus as a gigantic social experiment—a place where many folk cultures were suddenly thrown together in situations where people were forced to understand and relate to others whose cultures were very different from their own. As you may recall, they used the term *Great Community* to refer to Chicago. It's useful to contrast this term with another used quite a bit in this textbook, *mass society*. The distinction highlights some key differences between pragmatism and mass society theory—between a theory that's cautiously optimistic about the future of large-scale social orders and one that's quite pessimistic. Mass society theorists worried that individuals would become "atomized" in large-scale social orders. The networks of social relationships holding people together would necessarily break down as people moved from rural communities to urban ghettos. High culture would give way to mass culture, leaving people's existence degraded and dehumanized. Media make things worse by providing a more efficient mechanism for transmitting mass culture.

If mass societies are places where human existence is degraded, great communities are places where the potential for human existence is explored and new opportunities for developing culture are found. One of the most creative members of the Chicago School was Robert E. Park, a man who worked as a journalist, studied philosophy with John Dewey in Michigan and sociology with Georg Simmel in Germany, exposed colonialism in the Belgian Congo, and served as an aide to educator, author, and early African American civil rights leader Booker T. Washington (Goist, 1971). With his colleagues, Park developed a perspective on urban life that was essentially optimistic while at the same time acknowledging that there were many problems. Cities were places where new forms of culture could be created—where many new and dynamic communities could be formed. Cities were made up of thousands of more or less interconnected local communities. It is this interconnection that allows or compels the creation of more innovative forms of culture.

Not surprisingly Park saw newspapers as playing an essential role in interconnecting the communities making up great communities. The most important thing about the newspaper, he thought, was that it served as a means of transmitting "news." It held "the larger society together. . . . Public opinion rests on news, on people talking about present events, and that is what newspapers make possible. While news is primarily local in character, the real power of the press, and other means of mass communication as well, is in providing the basis for public opinion and political action" (Goist, 1971, p. 57).

Park's argument concerning the function of the press in cities was abstract, and the Chicago School was not able develop a theory clearly explaining how and why newspapers performed their role. Systematic research was never conducted to validate these ideas. In Chapter 12 we considered research that assessed the way media can create or destroy social capital. It has validated some of Park's notions but also identified problematic media effects. As we saw in Chapter 3, members of the Hutchins Commission on Freedom of the Press argued for extensive local coverage that would permit people living in different communities to learn more about other communities. Unfortunately the large Chicago newspaper publishers didn't see much reader interest in this type of news. They ignored or rejected the Hutchins Commission's advice as impractical. In the 1950s and 1960s big urban papers earned increasing amounts of money from sales in the growing and more affluent suburbs. Other than to report bad news about crime and social unrest, they ignored inner-city ethnic neighborhoods, often neglecting to distribute newspapers there as their residents depressed the papers' suburb-enriched, advertiser-attractive, up-scale demographics (Kirkhorn, 2000). It's doubtful that these newspapers played the role Park envisioned for them. But they undoubtedly contributed to (and disrupted) urban culture in other ways.

There are important similarities between the views of Chicago newspaper publishers in the 1950s and today's large-scale social media executives. People like Mark Zuckerberg are making decisions about providing news so that corporate profits are maximized with little concern for community or public interest (Ingram, 2018). If you rely on the Facebook News Feed as your primary means of staying informed about the larger social world, are you likely to be connected to a Great Community or sheltered in a silo of like-minded folks?

Current Applications of Symbolic Interactionism

Although Mead first articulated his ideas in the 1930s, it was not until the 1970s and 1980s that mass communication researchers began paying serious attention to symbolic interaction. Given the great emphasis that Mead placed on interpersonal interaction and his disregard for media, it is not surprising that media theorists were slow to see its relevance. Michael Solomon (1983), a consumer researcher, provided a summary of Mead's work that is especially relevant for media research:

1. Cultural symbols are learned through interaction and then mediate that interaction.
2. The "overlap of shared meaning" by people in a culture means that individuals who learn a culture should be able to predict the behaviors of others in that culture.
3. Self-definition is social in nature; the self is defined largely through interaction with the environment.
4. The extent to which a person is committed to a social identity will determine the power of that identity to influence his or her behavior.

Among the earliest efforts by communication scholars to apply this symbolic interactionist thinking to our use of mass media was the book *Communication and Social Behavior: A Symbolic Interaction Perspective,* by Don F. Faules and Dennis C. Alexander in 1978. Basing their analysis on their definition of communication as "symbolic behavior that results in various degrees of shared meaning and values between participants," they offered three fundamental propositions on symbolic interaction and communication:

1. **People's interpretation and perception of the environment depend on communication.** In other words, what we know of our world is largely a function of our prior communication experiences in that world. This conforms to Solomon's idea of interaction with cultural symbols. As Faules and Alexander wrote, "Communication allows for the reduction of uncertainty without direct sensory experience. The media are a prime source of indirect experience, and for that reason have impact on the construction of social reality" (p. 23).
2. **Communication is guided by and guides the concepts of self, role, and situations, and these concepts generate expectations in and of the environment.** Our use of communication in different settings is related to our understanding

of ourselves and others in those situations. This is analogous to Solomon's point about learning a culture and predicting the behavior of others.

3. **Communication consists of complex interactions "involving action, interdependence, mutual influence, meaning, relationship, and situational factors"** (p. 23). Here we can see not only a communication-oriented restatement of Solomon's precepts three and four but also a rearticulation of James Carey's ritual perspective (see Chapter 6). Faules and Alexander are clearly reminding us that our understanding of our world and our place in it are created by us in interaction and involvement with media symbols.

Before we get any further into symbolic interactionism, however, we must mention some definitional differences between this perspective and its close relative, social construction of reality, discussed in the next section of this chapter. In symbolic interaction theory, a **sign** is any element in the environment used to represent another element in the environment. Signs can be classified in two ways. **Natural signs**, are those things in nature (the changing color of leaves) that represent something else in nature (the coming of autumn). **Artificial signs** have been constructed (a handshake) to represent something else in the social world (a friendly greeting). These artificial signs work only if the people using them agree on their meaning—that is, if they are "interactive"; two or more people must agree on their meaning and must further agree to respond to that sign in a relatively consistent fashion. Social construction of reality uses the concept of signs somewhat differently, as you'll soon see.

Another difference between symbolic interactionism and social constructionism is the distinction between signals and symbols. In symbolic interactionism, **signals** are artificial signs that produce highly predictable responses, like traffic lights. **Symbols**, on the other hand, are artificial signs for which there is less certainty and more ambiguity of response, like the flag. As Faules and Alexander (1978) explained, "Signals are used to regulate normative behavior in a society, and symbols are used to facilitate communicative behavior in a society" (p. 36).

INSTANT ACCESS

SYMBOLIC INTERACTIONISM

Strengths

1. Rejects simple stimulus-response conceptualizations of human behavior
2. Considers the social environment in which learning takes place
3. Recognizes the complexity of human existence and the importance of mental processes
4. Foregrounds individuals' and the community's role in agency
5. Provides basis for many methodologies and approaches to inquiry

Weaknesses

1. Gives too little recognition to power of social institutions
2. In some contemporary articulations, grants too much power to media content
3. Overestimates the control that individuals have over everyday life actions

SOCIAL CONSTRUCTIONISM

What almost all theories classified as culture-centered have in common is an under-lying assumption that our experience of reality is an ongoing social construction in which we have some responsibility, not something that is sent, delivered, or other-wise transmitted by some authority or elite. But although there is general agreement that human communities construct the social world, there is disagreement concern-ing the level of agency individual humans have in the processes by which this world is constructed and maintained. We've seen that symbolic interactionists are strong believers in the power of individuals to have a significant level of control over culture and their social world. If culture is forged on a daily basis in the millions of situations in which we all participate, there should be great potential for cultural innovation and change. If nothing else, people make mistakes, and that alone should lead to innovation.

Another school of social theory, **social constructionism**, questions the amount of control individuals have over culture. Social constructionism argues that once social institutions such as schools, churches, businesses, military, and media organizations are constructed, individuals' power to oppose or reconstruct these institutions is lim-ited. Its proponents see these institutions dominating the practice of culture on a day-to-day basis.

According to social constructionists, social institutions wield enormous power over culture because they view the culture they propagate as having a reality beyond people's control. Here's an example. Students are often told that when they graduate they will get jobs in the *real* world. Implicit in this assertion is the assumption that college life is somehow *unreal* whereas the world of work is *real*. But what does *reality* mean in this context? Your daily life at college is not a fantasy world. There are classes to attend and exams to take. But you do have quite a bit of control over how you play your role as a student. You have the autonomy to decide what you will do and when you will do it. You can skip classes without risk of being expelled. Your grades must be consistently very low before you will be denied permission to re-enroll. On the other hand, a primary reason the world of work is *real* is that individuals have much less control over their actions and any consequences they might produce. Although the rules governing work are becoming more flexible, most jobs still require people to work certain hours of the day. Between those hours employees are required to do whatever tasks are assigned. Many workplaces are still hierarchically structured, with a few people at the top dictating what everyone else does. Unlike the university, even occasional violations of the rules of the workplace can get you fired. *Real*, in this ex-ample, then, means that work is externally structured with little or no input from you and therefore beyond your personal control. Think about the social institutions that structure your social world. To what extent are you able to ignore or violate their rules? What are the consequences of rule violations in places structured by your church, the military, or your family?

Social constructionism's view of the role of media contrasts sharply with both mass society theory and the limited-effects notions. Mass society theory envisioned vast populations living in nightmare realities dominated by demagogues. Limited-effects research found that personal influence was much stronger than media in the transmission of ideas, attitudes, and information from dominant sources to passive receivers. When social constructionism is applied to mass communication, it makes assumptions similar to those of symbolic interactionism; it assumes that audiences are active. Audience members don't simply passively take in and store bits of information in mental filing cabinets; they actively process this information, reshape it, and store only what serves culturally defined needs. They are active even when this activity largely serves to reinforce what they already know—to make them more willing to trust and act on views of the social world communicated to them by media. Thus, media can serve as an important way for social institutions to transmit culture to us; they let us know what social roles and personal identities are appropriate.

Audience members use the media's symbols to make sense of their environments and the things in it, but those definitions have little value unless others share them—that is, unless the symbols also define things for other people in the same way. A Lexus, for example, can be as expensive an automobile as a Porsche, and both are functionally the same thing: automobiles that transport people from here to there. Yet the "realities" that surround both cars (and the people who drive them) are quite different. Moreover, how these different drivers are treated by other people may also vary, not because of any true difference in them as humans but because the "reality" attached to each car is used to define their drivers (Baran & Blasko, 1984). We'll discuss this more later. For now it's worth noting that your power as an individual to control the "realities" surrounding these cars is limited. But if you can afford to buy one or the other, you can choose to participate in the "reality" that surrounds it.

Alfred Schutz (1967, 1970), a banker whose avocation was sociology, provided some early systematic discussions of ideas that have become central to social constructionism. Like many meaning-making theorists, he was fascinated by what he regarded as the mysteries of everyday existence. For example, as a banker he was conscious of how dependent our economic system was on people's willingness to routinely accept that money—identically printed on standardized pieces of paper, differing only slightly, primarily on the numbers printed on their face and back—could have radically different value. But money is just one everyday mystery. Schutz sought a broader understanding of how we make sense of the world around us in order to structure and coordinate our daily actions. He asked, "How are we able to do this with such ease that we don't even realize we are doing it?"

For answers to riddles about the origin and maintenance of social order, Schutz turned to a body of social theory developed in Europe, **phenomenology**. Relying on phenomenological notions, he asks that we bracket, or set aside, our commonsense, taken-for-granted explanations for what we do and recognize that everyday life is actually much more complicated than we assume. Schutz argues that we conduct our lives with little effort or thought because we have developed stocks of social knowledge that we use to quickly make sense of what goes on around us and then structure our actions using this knowledge. Our knowledge of how to use money, as well as our attitudes toward and feelings about money, are just one example of a small part of these stocks of social knowledge. It's important to note that we usually don't have much conscious awareness of this knowledge. When we are questioned about how or why we are engaging in a wide range of everyday actions, we find the questions puzzling or absurd. There are no obvious answers to these questions, but why would anyone even bother to ask them?

Schutz labeled one of the most important forms of knowledge we possess **typifications**. Typifications enable us to quickly classify objects and actions we observe and then quickly and routinely structure our own actions in response. But typifications operate to some extent like stereotypes—though they make it easy to interpret even ambiguous situations, they also distort and bias our experience of these situations. Typifications we've learned before can be applied over and over again as long as we have the sense that they enable us to see things as they "really" are. We're likely to go on applying them even when problems arise and our interpretations cause trouble.

The concept of typifications is similar to Mead's idea of symbols and the notion of schemas in information-processing theory. It differs in emphasizing that these elements of culture can be beyond our conscious control even when they are quite crucial in making sense of things and guiding our actions. Mead thought of symbols as created in face-to-face interaction. But are the roles on his hypothetical baseball team really that flexible? Maybe they might better be conceived of as made up of Schutz's typifications. A Little League team might tolerate a lot of innovation, but on a "real" team, when the game is being played "for real," players' actions are expected to closely adhere to certain norms, including such seemingly minor things as how to warm up or what's allowable chatter from the bench. Batters who have an odd stance at the plate or who swing the bat in unusual ways are closely scrutinized and told they should change their behavior.

Typifications may get communicated in face-to-face interactions, but they are propagated by social institutions and serve to preserve the power and authority of those institutions. What would happen to our banks if lots of people suddenly had doubts about the value of paper money? Consider what happens to people who, finding it hard to take the security procedures seriously, joke about bombs or weapons while going through airport security checks. They are lucky if all that happens is that they miss their flights. If we don't apply typifications correctly, our actions may be punished. We could be kicked off the team or wind up being grilled as potential terrorists.

Schutz's ideas were elaborated in *The Social Construction of Reality* by sociologists Peter Berger and Thomas Luckmann. Published in 1966, the book made virtually no mention of mass communication, but with the explosion of interest in the media accompanying the dramatic social and cultural changes of that turbulent decade, mass communication theorists (not to mention scholars from numerous other disciplines) quickly found Berger and Luckmann's **social construction of reality** and identified its value for developing media theory, an influence that continues to this day, as you'll read later in the next chapter's discussion of mediatization.

In explaining how reality is socially constructed, the two sociologists assumed first that "there is an ongoing correspondence between my meanings and their meanings in the world [and] that we share a common sense about [their] reality" (Berger &

Luckmann, 1966, p. 23). Let's use a common household article as our example. Here are three symbols for that object:

1. Knife

2.

3.

In social construction of reality, a **symbol** is an object (in these instances, a collection of letters or drawings on a page) representing some other object—what we commonly refer to as a knife. Here are three other symbols for that same object:

1. Messer
2. Cuchillo
3.

But unless you speak German or Spanish, respectively, or understand the third symbol to be a drawing of a butter knife, these symbols have no meaning for you; there is no correspondence between our meaning and yours. We share no common sense about the reality of the object being symbolized.

But who says that *knife* means what we all know it to mean? And what's wrong with those people in Germany and Mexico? Don't they know that it's *knife,* not *messer* or *cuchillo*? In English-speaking countries, the cultural consensus has been formed that *knife* means that sharp thing we use to cut our food, among other things, just as the folks in German- and Spanish-speaking lands have agreed on something else. There is no inherent truth, value, or meaning in the ordered collection of the letters k-n-i-f-e giving it the reality that we all know it has. *We* have given it meaning, and because we share that meaning, we can function as a people (at least when the issue is household implements).

But Berger and Luckmann (1966, p. 35) recognized that there is another kind of meaning we attach to the things in our environments, one that is subjective rather than objective. They call these **signs**, objects explicitly designed "to serve as an index of subjective meaning"; this is analogous to symbolic interaction's concept of symbols. If you were to wake up tomorrow morning, head on your pillow, to find a knife stuck into the headboard inches above your nose, you'd be fairly certain that this was some sort of sign. In other words, people can produce representations of objects that have very specific, very subjective agreed-upon meanings. What does the knife in the headboard signify? Says who? What does a Lexus signify? Says who? What do several pieces of cloth—some red, some white, some blue—sewn together in a rectangle in such a way to produce 13 alternating red and white stripes and a number of stars against a blue field in the upper-left-hand corner signify? Freedom? Democracy? Empire? The largest car dealer on the strip? A place to buy breakfast? Says who?

Remember that symbolic interaction defines signs and symbols in precisely the opposite way as does social construction of reality theory. This small problem aside, how do people use these signs and symbols to construct a reality that allows social order to be preserved? Berger and Luckmann (1966) developed Schutz's notion of typifications into what they refer to as **typification schemes**, collections of meanings we assign to some phenomenon that come from our stock of social knowledge to pattern our interaction with our environments and the things and people in it. A bit more simply, we as a people, through interaction with our environment, construct a "natural backdrop" for the development of "typification schemes required for the major routines of everyday life, not only the typification of others . . . but typifications of all sorts of events and experiences, both social and natural" (p. 43).

Of course media theorists and practitioners, especially advertisers and marketing professionals, understand that whoever has the greatest influence over a culture's definitions of its symbols and signs has the greatest influence over the construction of the typification schemes individuals use to pattern their interactions with their various social worlds. In other words, social institutions have the most influence in or control over the social world because they often are able to dominate how typification schemes get created and used. Why, for example, is one beer more "sophisticated" than another? Are we more likely to serve an expensive local micro-brew beer to our party guests than we are to serve whatever brand was on sale that week? Why? What makes brand-name products or clothes with designer labels better than generic alternatives?

Alternately, return to the example of airport security checks. We as individuals don't have much control over what we're able to do during these inspections. If we travel frequently, we've probably worked out strategies to enable ourselves to move efficiently through the checks. We go to the airport early, expecting that there could be a long wait. As we wait, we move all metal objects from our pockets to our luggage. We wear shoes that slip off easily. We place our photo ID and ticket where we can easily access them. We know not to joke about guns and bombs. But even after all this preparation, an alarm may go off as we pass through the metal detector. We know to stop immediately and allow ourselves to be scanned with an intrusive hand wand. If we happen to travel on a day when security is especially tight, agents may open and search our carry-on luggage. They may ask us to turn on our electronic equipment to make certain it is operational. In many other situations we would consider this kind of treatment demeaning, frustrating, or humiliating. But now it's just a routine part of flying. We have learned and accepted a typification scheme enabling us to cope.

So, who's right about the amount of agency exercised by individuals in the social world? Are symbolic interactionists correct when they argue that important ways of interpreting things (symbols) get created through everyday interaction? Or are social constructionists correct when they argue that typifications are handed down to us and enforced primarily by institutions that dominate the social world? Could both of these perspectives provide useful insights into different aspects of the social world? What about the role of media? Is advertising a powerful tool in the hands of social elites because it enables them to communicate and reinforce typifications so they are widely accepted and applied? Could social media give us greater control over meaning making by allowing us to easily and routinely share the meanings *we* attach to things with others? If social media did give us greater control, might that subvert elite power and undermine social stability in the larger society? Could it enable us to form

SOCIAL CONSTRUCTIONISM

Strengths

1. Rejects simple stimulus-response conceptualizations of human behavior
2. Considers the social environment in which learning takes place
3. Recognizes the complexity of human existence
4. Foregrounds social institutions' role in agency
5. Provides basis for many methodologies and approaches to inquiry

Weaknesses

1. Gives too little recognition to power of individuals and communities
2. In some contemporary articulations, grants too much power to elites who control media content

new communities with others, as has been asserted by Mark Zuckerberg, the creator of Facebook? "For the past decade," he wrote, "Facebook has focused on connecting friends and families. With that foundation, our next focus will be developing the social infrastructure for community—for supporting us, for keeping us safe, for informing us, for civic engagement, and for inclusion of all" (Zuckerberg, 2017, para. 6).

FRAMING AND FRAME ANALYSIS

While critical cultural researchers were developing reception analysis during the 1980s, a new approach to audience research was taking shape in the United States. It had roots in symbolic interaction and social constructionism. As we've seen, both of these approaches argue that the expectations we form about ourselves, other people, and our social world are central to social life. You have probably encountered many terms in this and other textbooks that refer to such expectations—stereotypes, attitudes, typification schemes, and biases. All assume that our expectations are socially constructed. They share the following assumptions concerning expectations:

1. Expectations are based on previous experience of some kind, whether derived from a media message or direct personal experience (in other words, we aren't born with them).
2. Expectations can be quite resistant to change, even when they are contradicted by readily available factual information.
3. Expectations are often associated with and can arouse strong emotions such as hate, fear, or love.
4. We typically are not consciously aware of our expectations and therefore can't make useful predictions about how we will feel or act in future situations based on these expectations.
5. Expectations guide our actions without our conscious awareness, especially when strong emotions are aroused or there are distractions that interfere with our ability to focus our attention and consciously interpret new information available in the situation.

Are you skeptical about these assumptions? Do you think you have more awareness and conscious control over your expectations? Try paying close attention to your
actions over the next few hours. Try predicting what you will do and how others will
act before you enter a new situation. How useful were your predictions? Did you act
precisely as you thought you would? Did others act as you predicted? If your predictions weren't very good, did this mean you had difficulty making sense of the situation
and taking action in it? Did the actions of others seem unusual or abnormal? Even
when we can't consciously make useful predictions about situations, we usually have
no difficulty making sense of them and acting in them in ways that seem ordinary.

Developing and using expectations is a normal and routine part of everyday life.
As human beings, we have cognitive skills allowing us to continually scan our environment, make sense of it, and then act on these interpretations. Our actions are
routinized and habitual. Our inability to adequately understand these skills in no way
prevents them from operating, but it does impede our ability to make sense of or even
gain an awareness of our own meaning making. We constantly make interpretations of
the world around us. Sometimes we will understand what we are doing, but more often
we won't because, typically, it doesn't matter whether we do or not. But if we would
like to or want to assume more responsibility for our actions, we should be concerned.

Based in part on Ludwig Wittgenstein's linguistic philosophy—particularly his
notion of language games—sociologist Erving Goffman (1974) developed **frame analysis** to provide a systematic account of how we develop and use expectations to make
sense of everyday life situations and the people in them (the theory is graphically represented in the box entitled "The Framing Process"). Goffman was a keen observer
of everyday life interactions. He wondered how we manage to cope so easily with the
complicated situations we constantly encounter. He decided that the best way to gain
insight into everyday situations was to focus on the mistakes we make as we go through
daily life—including the mistakes we never notice, such as when one person mistakes
another's courtesy for flirting, or when someone's effort to move quickly through an
airport is seen as suspicious. Goffman was especially intrigued by the way magicians
and con artists are able to trick people. All magicians have to do is distract our attention so they can perform a trick without detection. Why are people often so gullible?
Why have Internet scammers been able trick people out of millions of dollars using
what appear to most folks to be outrageous e-mail scams (e.g., Whitman, 2019)? Like
Alfred Schutz, Goffman was convinced that daily life is much more complicated than
it appears and that we have ways of dealing with these complications (Ytreberg, 2002).

Although Goffman agreed with social constructionist arguments concerning typification schemes, he found them too simple. He argued that we constantly and often
radically change the way we define or typify situations, actions, and other people as we
move through time and space. We are able to adjust the schemes to fit specific circumstances and other individuals. We don't have only one typification scheme—we have
whole sets of similar schemes ranging along various dimensions. But we usually won't
have any conscious awareness of when we are shifting from one scheme to another.
In other words, our experience of the world can be constantly shifting, sometimes
in major ways, yet we usually won't notice these shifts. We can step from one realm
of experience to another without recognizing that a boundary has been crossed. We
don't operate with a limited or fixed set of expectations about social roles, objects, or

situations. Thus, we don't have a simple stock of institutionally controlled knowledge as most social constructionists contend. Rather, we have enormous flexibility in creating and using expectations. Goffman argued that our experience of reality is bound up with our ability to move effortlessly through daily life making sense of situations and the people in them. If we do encounter problems, we have strategies for resolving them so routinely that we can proceed as though nothing unusual has happened.

Goffman used the term **frame** to refer to a specific set of expectations used to make sense of a social situation at a given point in time. Frames are like Berger and Luckmann's typification schemes, but they differ in certain important respects. According to Goffman, individual frames are like notes on a musical scale—they spread along a continuum from those structuring our most serious and socially significant actions to those structuring playful, trivial actions. Like notes on a musical scale, each is different, even though there is underlying structural continuity. For social action the continuity is such that we can learn how to frame serious actions by first learning frames for playful actions. Using the musical scale analogy, we first learn to play simple tunes using a narrow range of the musical scale in preparation for playing more complex scores. Likewise many of our games and sports provide useful preparation for more serious forms of action. We can learn from playing Little League baseball and then apply it when we play a more serious game—a real game of life in which there's more at stake. If we can perform well under the pressures of a big game, we may handle the demands of other life situations better. We can learn to be "team players" who recognize how best to work with others and apply the frames for action that allow us to do that. Goffman argued that we are like animal cubs that first play at stalking frogs and butterflies and then are able to transfer these skills to related but more serious situations.

When we move from one set of frames to another, we **downshift or upshift**. We reframe situations so we experience them as more or less serious. Remember when you pretended to fight with a friend as a child, but someone got hurt and the fight turned serious? Suddenly you no longer pulled punches but tried to make them inflict as much pain as possible; you downshifted. You used many of the fighting skills learned during play but with a different frame—now you were trying to hurt your friend. Perhaps, as you both got tired, one of you told a joke and cued the other that you wanted to upshift and go back to a more playful frame. In our airport security example, an alarm going off is likely to bring about a quick downshift in our framing.

Let's consider that example again. We may be traveling with a group of friends. It's a nice day, and we've been having fun. We find it hard to take the security check seriously, or it slips our mind that we need to be careful. We forget some of the things we normally do when we're taking a security check seriously. But then the alarm goes off. Suddenly things get serious. We have to make fast readjustments, but we do it fairly easily. Our smile vanishes. We stand up straight and pay close attention to the security agents. It's likely that we blame ourselves for making stupid mistakes; we forgot to take off our shoes or to remove our keys from our pockets. According to Goffman, we've gone from framing the situation playfully to imposing a serious frame.

If the symbolic interactionists are right and our meaning-making ability is so great, so innovative, and so flexible, why is there any pattern or order to daily existence? How are we able to coordinate our actions with others and experience daily existence as having order and meaning—how can we routinely adjust ourselves to life within the boundaries set by social institutions, as social constructionists believe we do? Life, Goffman argued, operates much like a staged dramatic performance. We step from one social realm or sphere to another in much the same way that actors move between scenes. Scenes shift, and as they shift we are able to radically alter how we make sense of them and the way we act in them. As scenes shift we locate and apply new sets of expectations. Sometimes, as in the example of the problematic security check, we don't make the proper shift and then we're forced to do so by the people around us.

Framing involves shifting expectations. But just how do we and the people around us know when to make shifts? How do we know when one scene is ending and another beginning and act jointly so a shift can be made so seamlessly that we don't even notice that it has happened? According to Goffman, we are always monitoring the social environment for **social cues** that signal when we are to make a change, and we are often quite skilled at using these cues. For example, when we view a play in a theater, we rely on many conventional cues to determine when a shift in scenes takes place. One of the oldest and most obvious cues involves the curtain—it rises when a scene begins and falls when a scene ends. Other cues are subtler—shifts in lighting and music tempo often signal changes. As lights dim and music becomes ominous, we know danger threatens. Movies employ many similar conventions. Goffman believed we use the same cognitive skills to make sense of daily life that we do to make sense of plays or movies. His theory implies that we can learn social cues through everyday interaction and from observing how these cues are used in media content.

Back to the airport. What if security agents dressed in street clothes or in beachwear? What if they casually stood around, ignored scanner alarms, and told people just to keep walking? What if they were playing games on a smartphone instead of carefully monitoring the equipment scanning your luggage? Would we take them seriously, or would we frame the situation playfully? Social cues can make a big difference in how we structure our actions—especially when we are acting routinely and not paying attention to what we are doing.

So how do media come into this theory? Goffman made several heuristic explorations of the way media might influence our development and use of frames, including an essay entitled "Radio Talk" appearing in his book *Forms of Talk* (1981) and in another book, *Gender Advertisements* (1979). In the latter he presented an insightful argument concerning the influence advertising could have on our perception of women. According to Goffman, ads are **hyperritualized representations** of social action (Ytreberg, 2002). They are edited to highlight very specific representations. Advertising using the sex appeal of women to attract the attention of men could inadvertently teach or reinforce social cues that might have inadvertent but serious consequences. Goffman showed how women in many ads are presented as less serious and more playful than men. They smile, place their bodies in nonserious positions, wear playful clothing, and in various ways signal deference and a willingness to take direction from men. Not only are they vulnerable to sexual advances, they signal their desire for them. No wonder these ads attract the attention of men. No wonder they are useful in positioning products. But could these representations of women be teaching or reinforcing social cues that have difficult consequences? Feminist theorists have long made similar arguments (Walters, 1995). A recent content analysis of popular magazines targeted at girls and women (Speno & Aubrey, 2018) found that they were systematically

THINKING ABOUT THEORY

THE FRAMING PROCESS

In a different book (Davis & Baran, 1981), we developed this version of Goffman's theory of framing. Can you explain how it allows for upshifting and downshifting? Can you speculate on how errors in framing can occur?

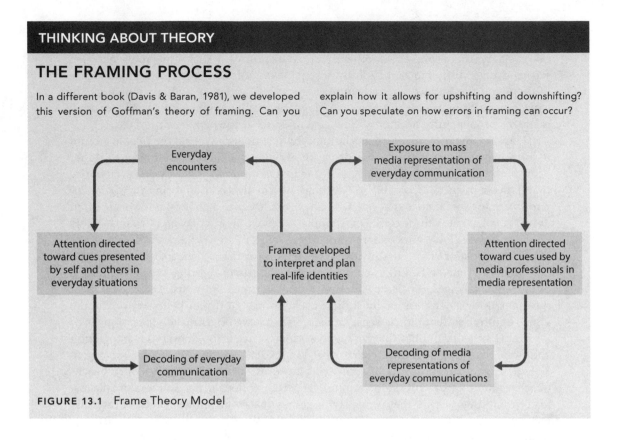

FIGURE 13.1 Frame Theory Model

misrepresented using social cues that "adultified" girls and "youthified" women. You might ask yourself, "To what end?"

We might be learning more than product definitions from these ads. We could be learning a vast array of social cues, some blatant but others quite subtle. Once learned, these cues could be used in daily life to make sense of members of the same or opposite sex and to impose frames on them, their actions, and the situations in which we encounter them. Or it's possible that these ads simply reinforce the cues we've already learned in daily life. But the constant repetition of these cues leads us to give them greater importance or priority—they prime us to apply certain cues rather than others. For example, exposure to advertising could prime men to be overly sensitive to playful cues from women and increase the likelihood that they will upshift in ways that women don't expect or intend. Men learn such a vast repertoire of these cues that it might be hard for women to avoid displaying them. Men could routinely misinterpret inadvertent actions by women. Advertising might make it hard for women to maintain a serious frame for their actions. If they smile, bend their elbows in a particular way, or bow their heads even briefly, men might perceive a cue when none was intended. The more physically attractive the woman, the more likely this problem will arise, because most advertising features such women.

Goffman's theory provides an intriguing way of assessing how media can elaborate and reinforce a dominant public culture. Advertisers didn't create sex-role stereotypes, but, Goffman argued, they have homogenized how women are publicly depicted. This is the danger of hyperritualization. Goffman contrasted the wide, idiosyncratic variety of ways women are represented in private photos with their standardized (hyperritualized) depiction in advertising. Marketers routinely use powerful visual imagery to associate products with women who explicitly and implicitly signal their willingness to be playful sexual partners. There are many subtle and not-so-subtle messages in these ads. "Consume the product and get the girl" is one dominant message. Another is that physically attractive women are sexually active and fun-loving. Ads both teach and reinforce cues. They regularly prime us to frame situations one way rather than another. The specific messages each of us gets from the ads may be different, but their long-term consequences may be similar—dominant myths about women are retold and reinforced.

Compared with the other theories we examine in this chapter, Goffman's is the most open-ended and flexible. He was convinced that social life is a constantly evolving and changing phenomenon, and yet we experience it as having great continuity. Though we have the capacity to constantly reframe our experience from moment to moment, most of us can maintain the impression that our experiences are quite consistent and routine. According to Goffman, we do this by firmly committing ourselves to live in what we experience as the **primary, or dominant, reality**—a real world in which people and events obey certain conventional and widely accepted rules. We find this world so compelling and desirable that we are constantly reworking our experience and patching up its flaws, and we don't notice when rule violations occur. Compare this view of reality to the conception offered by social constructionists. How do you experience reality? Is it something you embrace as providing useful order, or is it a rigid set of rules established and enforced by social institutions?

Goffman argued that we work so hard maintaining our sense of continuity in our experience that we inevitably make many framing mistakes. We literally see and hear

INSTANT ACCESS

FRAME ANALYSIS

Strengths	Weaknesses
1. Focuses attention on individuals in the mass communication process	1. Is overly flexible and open-ended (lacks specificity)
2. Micro-level theory but is easily applicable to macro-level issues	2. Postpositivists and critical cultural researchers have different versions of this theory
3. Is highly flexible and open-ended	3. Causal explanations are only possible when there is a narrow focus on framing effects
4. Is consistent with recent findings in cognitive psychology	4. Can be hard for researchers to develop and apply useful definitions of frames
5. Identifies important limitations of everyday life sense-making	
6. Can predict framing errors people make when using problematic frames	

things that aren't—but should—be there according to the rules we have internalized. For example, most college campuses in America today face the problem of date rape. And ultimately, what is the basic issue in most of these occurrences? Goffman might answer that the issue involves upshifting and downshifting problems between men and women as they attempt to frame the situations (dating) they find themselves in. Alcohol consumption is often associated with date rape, increasing the likelihood that social cues will be misread or ignored. Or consider the even more common problem on campuses of binge drinking. Most students have a hard time taking drinking seriously. They've learned to frame drinking as an essentially playful, youthful activity. Advertising continually reinforces this frame along with its related social cues. The unwanted consequences of excess drinking don't appear in advertising. When they are portrayed in the anti-binge-drinking public service advertising, students have a hard time taking them seriously.

From Goffman's viewpoint, primary reality is the touchstone of our existence—the real world in every sense of that term. We do permit ourselves constant and socially acceptable escapes into clearly demarcated alternative realities we experience as recreational or fantasy worlds (recall entertainment theory and its variants in Chapter 9). These are places where we can escape the pressures of being center stage in an unfolding drama we know can have long-term consequences. Not many students would expect to earn a high grade on an important essay exam by writing jokes about the instructor, but as the date rape example suggests, when we make framing mistakes in a playful reality, the results can be just as devastating to our real world. News media frequently report framing mistakes involving social media. We forget that the seeming playful space offered by Facebook can be quite public if we fail to take steps to guard our privacy.

THE DEVELOPMENT OF THEORIES OF FRAMES AND FRAMING

Frame analysis theory as developed by Goffman is a micro-level theory focusing on how individuals learn to routinely make sense of their social world. After Goffman's work in the 1960s and 1970s, framing theory continued to gain interest and acceptance. One of its most important applications looks at how news events are initially framed by journalists and then framed by news users. Scholars took Goffman's ideas and extended them to create a conceptual framework that considers (1) the social and political context in which news-event framing takes place, (2) how journalists develop and impose frames on ambiguous events to create news stories, (3) how news readers learn and apply frames to make sense of news, and (4) the long-term social and political consequences of news media frames. Framing theory can be applied to any form of media content, including both legacy media entertainment and user-produced SNS content, but most framing research is focused on news.

The increasing popularity of framing theory has resulted in the development of differing versions of the theory (Borah, 2011). Critical cultural researchers have developed forms that differ radically from those of postpositivist scholars. The latter group has focused on identifying and measuring specific effects of certain types of frames on audiences or readers. They have identified "generic" frames that are frequently found in news stories that fundamentally alter how audiences view events. These include conflict or contest frames, horse-race frames, strategic frames, economic frames, moral frames, thematic frames, and episodic frames. Critical cultural researchers have focused on elite control over framing, how social movements use frames to advance their goals, and how people's understanding of the social world is shaped by frames learned from media. We will describe both types of framing theory, and we will consider the strengths and limitations of each. In general, postpositivists and critical cultural scholars have produced compatible findings even though their approaches differ. Research projects are being developed that use both approaches to produce more comprehensive findings (de Vreese, 2012).

Early examples of framing research applied to journalism can be found in the scholarship of two sociologists whom you met in the Chapter 6, Todd Gitlin (1980) and Gaye Tuchman (1978). Their work is frequently referenced and has played an important early role in extending Goffman's ideas. Tuchman and Gitlin are critical cultural studies scholars interested in elite control over framing that is evidenced when journalists frame ambiguous news events. Gitlin focused on news coverage of politically radical social movements during the late 1960s. He argued that media framing of these movements demeaned their members, criticized their activities, and ignored their ideas. These representations made it difficult for movements to achieve their objectives. Tuchman focused on routine news production work and the serious limitations inherent in specific strategies for coverage of events. Although the intent of these practices is to provide objective news coverage, the result is news stories in which events are routinely framed in ways that eliminate much of their ambiguity and instead reinforce socially accepted and expected ways of seeing the social world. Both Gitlin and Tuchman concluded that news mainly serves to perpetuate the status quo and to undermine the ability of social movements to bring about important changes.

One of the most productive and creative framing researchers is William Gamson (1989; Gamson, Croteau, Hoynes, & Sasson, 1992). He authored and coauthored a series of books, book chapters, and articles that have helped shape current perspectives on framing theory and its explanation of how news has influence in the social world. Gamson argues that framing of many societal issues and events is highly contested. Increasingly, frames used in public discourse are developed and promoted by individuals and groups having an interest in advancing certain ways of seeing the social world rather than others. He has traced the success and failure of social movements in promoting frames consistent with their ideological interests, specifically in the realm of nuclear power and global warming (Gamson & Modigliani, 1989). A more contemporary example resides in the frame contest at the heart of the debate over health care in the United States. Activists promoting a universal, public insurance system similar to that used in virtually all other developed nations advance plans for "publicly financed health care." The for-profit insurance industry opposes this as a "government-run" system, a framing adopted by most media outlets. How might the debate shift if the issue is framed as "publicly financed health care" versus "corporate-run health care?" "By drawing a contrast between 'government' and 'private' insurance [rather than the more linguistically symmetrical *government-run* and *corporate-run* insurance that names the actors]," answer framing researchers at the National Economic and Social Rights Initiative (2019), the media and polling organizations explicitly invoke government control of public insurance while rendering private insurance companies invisible" (par. 4).

Gamson's interest is in the ability of activist movements to bring about social change. He shares the social constructionist view that social institutions and the elites who lead them are able to dominate the social world by propagating frames serving their interests. Lone individuals have little ability to resist this framing. But, he argues, social movements can generate and promote alternate frames that can bring about important change. For this to happen they need to develop cogent frames expressing their views, and they need to persuade journalists to produce news stories that effectively and sympathetically present these frames. Only then will these frames be disseminated to a larger audience so more people begin to view the social world the way movement members do. If enough people change their views, public pressure may build so that leaders of social institutions make changes. Still, Gamson (1992) concedes, cultural and political elites maintain the advantage because "some frames have a natural advantage because their ideas and language resonate with a broader political culture. Resonances increase the appeal of a frame by making it appear natural and familiar. Those who respond to the larger cultural theme will find it easier to respond to a frame with the same sonorities" (p. 135). Charles Rowling and his colleagues elaborate, "As a result, culturally resonant messages possess high potential to cascade through the framing hierarchy. . . . [F]rames that tap into and resonate with cultural values—by celebrating or reinforcing them—will be more difficult to challenge; meanwhile, frames that do not engage with, or go so far as to overtly challenge, prevailing cultural values will be more likely to elicit contestation by other political actors, journalists, and the public" (Rowling, Jones, & Sheets 2011, p. 1046). They base their argument on Robert Entman's (2004) **cascading activation model** of framing, which posits that there is a "framing hierarchy in public discourse, with executive branch officials at the highest level, Congress followed by policy experts and ex-government officials at the middle level, and the press at the lowest level" (p. 1045). Using this model, Rowling and his colleagues demonstrated how elite frames dominated journalists' framing and therefore public perception of the debate surrounding torture by American military forces at Abu Ghraib prison in Iraq, rendering the complaints of anti-war and human rights activist groups ineffective. Robert Benford and David Snow (2000) have provided a useful summary of social movement research grounded in framing theory, as have Hank Johnston and John Noakes (2005). You can see how frames surrounding one recent movement competed in the box entitled "Framing Occupy Wall Street."

Effects of Frames on News Audiences

Over the past 30 years postpositivist researchers have used effects research to document the influence frames can have on news audiences. The most common finding is that exposure to news coverage results in learning that is consistent with the frames that structure the coverage. If the coverage is dominated by a single frame, especially one originating from an elite source, learning will tend to be guided by this frame (Ryan, Carragee, & Meinhofer, 2001; Valkenburg & Semetko, 1999). This research has

FRAMING OCCUPY WALL STREET

In mid-2011, as pro-democracy protests were erupting across the Middle East, ushering in what was to become known as "The Arab Spring," activists at the anti-consumer organization Adbusters sent an e-mail to their subscribers suggesting similar action on New York's Wall Street, the real and symbolic heart of the American financial industry. Fueled by Twitter, Facebook, and Tumblr, the idea took off, and soon there were Occupy Wall Street (OWS) protests in more than 900 cities around the world (Garofoli, 2012). The movement's physical and philosophical Wall Street home was in Zuccotti Park, where thousands of protesters set up a community, complete with a kitchen, library, and professionally staffed medical facility. Their goal was to raise public awareness of the country's growing level of income disparity—the gap between the richest Americans and those in the shrinking middle class and the swelling ranks of the poor. OWS's slogan, "We are the 99%," was designed to highlight the fact that the income and opportunity gap between the richest Americans (the 1%) and everyone else was rapidly growing and becoming a permanent part of American life (Panousi, Vidangos, Ramnath, DeBacker, & Heim, 2013). Making New York's financial district the site of its main activities was intended to signify that it was the practices of the nation's financial elites that were responsible for people's increasing economic insecurity. OWS had no leader; all decisions were made by consensus. It made no demands; its aim was to raise awareness and through its actions make the moral argument for economic fairness. It espoused non-violence.

Then the framing began. Conservative political consultant Frank Lutz advised anti-OWS politicians, when asked about the movement and its issues, to avoid expressions like *capitalism* (use *economic freedom* and *free market*), *tax the rich* (use *take from the rich*), *middle class* (use *hardworking taxpayers*), and *government spending* (use *government waste*). Never disagree with OWS's goals; instead say, "'I get it.' . . . 'I get that you're angry. I get that you've seen inequality. I get that you want to fix the system.'" Opponents' goal was to frame OWS as well-intentioned but occupying the wrong place—occupy the White House (the home of Democrat Barack Obama), not Wall Street, because that's who's actually responsible for the country's financial woes (as cited in Moody, 2011).

Liberal linguist George Lakoff (2011), warning OWS to "frame yourself before others frame you," suggested the movement frame itself as "a moral and patriotic movement. It sees Democracy as flowing from citizens caring about one another as well as themselves and acting with both personal and social responsibility. Democratic governance is about The Public, and the liberty that The Public provides for a thriving Private Sphere. From such a democracy flows fairness, which is incompatible with a hugely disproportionate distribution of wealth. And from the sense of care implicit in such a democracy flows a commitment to the preservation of nature" (para. 21). OWS's own framing would stress its love for America and desire to fix it.

How did the media frame OWS? "The media's initial portrayal of the Occupy protests was . . . airily dismissive," writes anthropologist and OWS activist David Graeber (2013). The protestors, he notes, were framed as "a collection of confused kids with no clear conception of what they were fighting for. The *New York Times*, the self-proclaimed paper of historical record, wrote absolutely nothing about the occupation [which was occurring only a few blocks from its offices] for the first five days. On the sixth, they published an editorial disguised as a news story in the Metropolitan section, titled "Gunning for Wall Street, with Faulty Aim," mocking the movement as "a mere pantomime of progressivism with no discernible purpose" (para. 9). Margaret Cissel's (2012) content analysis comparing mainstream and alternative news coverage of the movement's first three weeks confirms Graeber's view. "While the mainstream media used confusion over the event as their dominant frames, alternative media focused on what the demonstrators were actually trying to accomplish," she discovered. And "while both news sources highlighted various conflicts surrounding the events of Occupy, they did so differently. The mainstream media placed the protesters at fault for the violence, and conversely, the alternative media sources focused on the brutality of the police and their violent acts on the peaceful protestors. . . . Occupy Wall Street highlights the differences between these two media sources. On the one hand, the mainstream media portrayed Occupy as a directionless and confused gathering of 'hippies'; on the other, alternative media focused on how the police, corporations, government, and mass media are preventing them from having a voice by prohibiting their free speech through legalities and logistics" (pp. 74–75).

(Continued)

THINKING ABOUT THEORY (Continued)

But did OWS's "general refusal to identify clear leaders . . . or even express focused demands" (Greenberg, 2011) doom its own framing efforts? Did the absence of identifiable spokespeople leave reporters with no one to interview but city and police officials, denying journalists the convenience of personalizing OWS and facilitating their tendency to seek out normalizing, elite voices, as news production (Chapter 6) and framing researchers might have predicted? Did the lack of movement demands mean that reporters had to find other ways to represent OWS—for example, with constant video of drum circles? Or, as Todd Gitlin—because of the media's natural elite bias—and Gaye Tuchman—because of journalism's routine, status quo–oriented news gathering practices—might have argued, would nothing have helped OWS control the way it was framed by the traditional media?

Despite the framing wars and media neglect, the movement quickly earned the support of a majority of the public. One month after it began, 54% of likely voters held a positive view of OWS, and 80% agreed with its declaration that the country's wealth disparity was too large (Greenberg, 2011). And what about those 900 other worldwide OWS protests? And what explains the fact that the movement endures today as a national and state-based movement, with issue-specific offshoots such as Occupy Our Homes (to help foreclosed and other home owners deal with their banks)? Is it possible that opposition and traditional media framing failed to shape the public's meaning making of the movement? Is it possible that social media limited the traditional media's ability to impose a status-quo frame on OWS, or even forced them to reconsider that reflexive framing of movements? While acknowledging the power of the movement's message with a nation grown weary of an out-of-control and unaccountable financial industry, activist David Graeber (2013), with two years of hindsight, argues that that elite framing of OWS failed because "by 2011 the omnipresence of phone cameras, Twitter accounts, Facebook, and YouTube ensured such images [of movement activities] could spread instantly to millions. . . . [I]nstead of a couple thousand people coming to Zuccotti to rally or assemble for marches during the day, the crowds swelled to the tens of thousands. Thousands across America began trying to figure out how to send in contributions and started calling in an almost unimaginable wave of free pizzas. . . . In other words, for the first time in most of our living memories, a genuine grassroots movement for economic justice had emerged in America. What's more, the dream of contaminationism, of democratic contagion, was, shockingly, starting to work" (para. 6).

Despite the inability of elites to negatively frame the movement and its successfully staged event in New York, OWS ultimately failed. Its effort to organize more protest events in the United States and Canada was unsuccessful. One of the co-organizers of OWS, Micah White, in *The End of Protest* (2016), attributes the OWS failure to US and Canadian government suppression that prevented the organization of those protests. He documents how officials wielded anti-terrorism laws and agencies to thwart OWS. White argues that movements need to develop new strategies that anticipate suppression. They shouldn't depend on organizing large, long protests as a way of calling attention to their causes. Protests are too easily ignored or dismissed by elites and mainstream media. They need to be used creatively and unpredictably. White asserts that while OWS may have failed, it has ignited an anti-elite movement that continues. For example, using "passed down knowledge from Occupy Wall Street," Occupy ICE set up encampments across the US to generate resistance to Immigration and Customs Enforcement and what it saw as that agency's harsh anti-immigrant activities (Gabbatt, 2018). And other successful movements—for example, Black Lives Matter protesting police brutality against African Americans; #MeToo challenging American culture's pervasive sexism and misogyny; and the anti-gun violence movement, #Enough, started by teen survivors of the 2018 Parkland, Florida, high school mass shooting—have all benefited from OWS's experiences.

also shown that news coverage can strongly influence the way news consumers make sense of events and their major actors. This is especially true of news involving an ongoing series of highly publicized and relevant events, such as social movements (McLeod & Detenber, 1999; Nelson & Clawson, 1997; Terkildsen & Schnell, 1997). Typically news coverage is framed to support the status quo, resulting in unfavorable views of movements. The credibility and motives of movement leaders are frequently undermined by frames that depict them as overly emotional, disorganized, or childish. Their demonstrations are depicted as potentially violent so that police action is justifiable. Revisit Martin Luther King's lament over the coverage of his peaceful civil rights activities in Chapter 6. Max McCombs & Salma Ghanem (2001) have presented another postpositivist view of framing, one linked to agenda-setting theory (Chapter 11). They argue that frames can be viewed as attribute agendas. When news media routinely use specific frames for people or events, they make it more likely that we will associate certain attributes with these people or events—our attribute agenda will be set.

Both postpositivist and critical cultural framing research provide a pessimistic assessment of news and the role journalism plays in society. Frames used to structure news about major events are chosen based on journalistic traditions and newsroom norms with little consideration of how information structured by these frames will be interpreted and used by news audiences (Bennett, Lawrence, & Livingston, 2007; Patterson, 1993). Journalists widely continue to use routinized frames even though research has shown that they are misleading or problematic. They continue to frame election campaigns as horse races with a focus on who is winning or losing (Aalberg, Strömbäck, & de Vreese, 2012; Gulati, Just, & Crigler, 2004). Reporters focus attention on the strategies used by candidates to gain advantages over their opponents. They frame elections primarily as contests in which conflict is central, giving limited attention to public issues and offering considerable effort to framing the tactics, personalities, and personal lives of candidates (Van Aelst, Sheafer, & Stanyer, 2012). When journalists do cover issues, they are often portrayed as mere tools used by politicians to gain advantages in the contest. This coverage fosters political apathy and cynicism, in part because it portrays politicians as egotists willing to do anything to garner votes, defeat opponents, and gain power (Bennett, 2005; Cappella & Jamieson, 1997). Findings such as these led press critic Brian Beutler (2019) to pose what he called the "big unanswered question about political journalism." "Why, against what they claim as their own better judgment," he asked, do "journalists keep returning to a mode of reporting that is quite plainly harming the profession's credibility?" (para. 10). Such is the power of routine journalistic practices (Chapter 6) and their resulting frames.

Similarly, news reporting of health crises or threats to individual safety or national security tends to rely on frames that exaggerate threats but provide little practical advice on how to take actions that can minimize danger (Mazzarella, 2010; Berger, 2001). In fact, science news often leads to widespread public misunderstanding of science (Hargreaves & Ferguson, 2000). Overall, reporting of many issues tends to arouse undue public concerns while providing people with no way to alleviate these concerns aside from putting trust in public officials and official agencies. On the one hand, news fosters cynicism about politicians; on the other, it tells us there is no alternative but to trust these officials.

Postpositivist vs. Critical Cultural Approaches to Framing

The increasing popularity of framing research has been accompanied by arguments about ambiguity, limited scope, and inconsistency in framing theory (Cacciatore, Scheufele, & Iyengar, 2016). Some scholars argue that there are actually several different framing theories that should be carefully differentiated (Entman, 1993). Others want to integrate differing notions into a single theory (Scheufele, 1999, 2000).

Critical cultural scholars complain that elite domination of framing is often neglected by postpositivist researchers (Carragee & Roefs, 2004). Postpositivists complain that the frames used in critical cultural research are too abstract and can't be studied objectively or systematically. In part these differences in framing theory and the disagreements they generate stem from the fundamentally different views of framing held by the two camps. Postpositivists are primarily interested in framing theory as a useful way to understand and predict media effects (Scheufele, 1999, 2000). They see framing research as closely related to the theories of media cognition and information processing (Scheufele & Tewksbury, 2007; Scheufele & Iyengar, 2012) that we considered in Chapter 10. They want to know if certain types of frames can affect how event information is processed and whether exposure to framed content will have specific effects. Postpositivists are not particularly interested in the origin of frames or why journalists choose certain frames to present events. Nor are they concerned about elite control over framing or the way frames get contested and negotiated. They focus on the effects of specific frames. They conduct quantitative research using experiments and surveys to demonstrate the existence of effects (Brugman & Burgers, 2018).

Critical cultural researchers reject this narrow focus. They have developed more macroscopic conceptualizations that take into account elite efforts to control framing, how and why journalists frame events, and the way framing shapes public understanding of the social world (Quinsaat, 2014). Conducting qualitative research using field studies, content analysis, in-depth interviews, and focus-group research, they have found evidence of elite domination of framing and documented the problematic ways that news reports frame issues, politicians, and events. Some of their research focuses on framing contests pitting elites against social movements in their efforts to shape public understanding of certain aspects of the social world (Quinsaat, 2014; Entman, Livingston, & Kim, 2009; Bennett, Lawrence, & Livingston, 2007). All detail the advantages that elites have over movements.

REVIEW OF LEARNING OBJECTIVES

- Describe symbolic interactionism and pragmatism, and explain how they differ from behaviorist or stimulus-response theory. Be able to explain how they differ from social constructionism.

Pragmatism is a school of philosophy that views knowledge as something we develop in order to adapt to and control the external world. We are constantly developing new forms of practical knowledge as we move through that world. Symbolic interactionism shares this notion of practical knowledge and provides an explanation of how it is developed and used. It asserts that our knowledge of reality is a social construction—as we interact with others we share and learn to apply symbols. Once learned, symbols serve as a stock of knowledge we use to understand our experience and guide our actions. Behaviorists argue that all behavior is a result of conditioning by environmental stimuli. They dismiss our experiences as misleading and unimportant. Social constructionism argues that social institutions typically are able to dictate what people will think or do. The social norms and routines promoted by institutions shape most behavior. Although humans construct social institutions, once they are built they dominate how the social world is perceived and what action is experienced as rational and appropriate. Symbolic interactionism argues that the power of institutions is limited because it depends on how people learn symbols in everyday-life situations. Changes that affect learning of symbols will bring about changes in institutions.

- Describe the notions of self-identity and social identity and how they are formed through communication.

Symbolic interactionists argue that we come to understand ourselves and our social identity through interaction with others. We learn symbols that we can use to define who we are and how others see us. These symbols can also be used to define our place in the social world.

- Describe framing theory, and discuss its increasing popularity for studying news media and their effects.

Framing theory argues that our perceptions and experiences are guided and shaped by frames learned through interaction with others and from media content. Once frames are learned, they guide our sense-making, actions, situations, and events. They enable us to routinely and easily move through everyday life situations—even those that are quite different from past situations. We often make framing mistakes but don't correct them unless there is something that challenges the meaning we are making concerning people, actions, situations, or events. News media report events in the social world in ways that are interpretable by audience members. To do this, those events need to be framed in ways that allow them to be routinely interpreted using frames that are already known. Badly framed reports of events will be misinterpreted. Researchers believe that frames are a powerful tool in the hands of journalists. They permit journalists to guide audience sense making and interpret events in intended ways. Subtle changes in frames could lead to important shifts in the way audiences interpret events. Over time, these changes could have persuasive and pervasive effects.

- List key findings from framing research and discuss the insight they provide into the way news shapes our views of the social world.

Overall, research indicates that news consistently supports the status quo. Forces for change such as social movements are framed in problematic ways. Movement leaders are denigrated; movement actions are portrayed as irrational; and their ideologies are ignored or misrepresented. Research based on the cascading activation model has shown how elites influence the frames used by journalists so they serve elite interests.

CRITICAL THINKING QUESTIONS

1. Politicians were among the first professionals to understand the power of framing. What routinized or habitual meanings come to mind when you encounter terms like *pro-life, pro-choice, tax relief, tax and spend, socialized medicine, Medicare for all,*

gun control, gun rights, politically correct, free markets, socialism, or *bloated bureaucracy?* All are terms specifically designed to frame the meaning of the discussion that surrounds each. What meaning does each frame imply? What fuller or deeper meaning might be obscured? What is the intent of those who would employ these expressions? Is it consistent with honest democratic discourse? Why or why not?

2. Advertisers, through product positioning, make extensive use of symbolic interaction. Can you look around your life and find products (symbols) that you have intentionally acquired specifically to "position" yourself in others' meaning making of you? For example, what car (if any) do you drive and why? Do you favor a specific body scent or brand of clothes? What about tattoos—how can they guide how people perceive you? What reality are you trying to create with your product choices?

3. Researchers have found that people become cynical about politics when the news they read frames politics in terms of conflict and strategy. How do you view politics and politicians? How do you react when you read about government gridlock, government shutdowns, or politicians voting in certain ways to gain reelection? Would you consider a career in politics? Could a politician who puts the public interest first ever be successful? Have you read or heard about this type of politician in the media recently?

KEY TERMS

symbolic interactionism

social behaviorism

symbols

pragmatism

sign (in symbolic interaction)

natural signs

artificial signs

signals

symbols (in symbolic interaction)

social constructionism

phenomenology

typifications

social construction of reality

symbol (in social construction of reality)

signs (in social construction of reality)

typification schemes

frame analysis

frame

downshift or upshift

social cues

hyperritualized representations

primary, or dominant, reality

cascading activation model (of framing)

GLOSSARY

symbolic interactionism: Theory that people give meaning to symbols and that those meanings come to control those people

social behaviorism: View of learning that focuses on the mental processes and the social environment in which learning takes place

symbols: In general, arbitrary, often abstract representations of unseen phenomena

pragmatism: US philosophical school of theory emphasizing the practical function of knowledge as an instrument for adapting

to and controlling reality. It opposed a European school of idealism.

sign: (in symbolic interaction) Any element in the environment used to represent another element in the environment

natural signs: In symbolic interaction, things occurring in nature that represent something else in nature

artificial signs: In symbolic interaction, elements that have been constructed to represent something else in the social world

signals: In symbolic interaction, artificial signs that produce highly predictable responses

symbols: (in symbolic interaction) Artificial signs for which there is less certainty of response

social constructionism: School of social theory that argues that individuals' power to oppose or reconstruct important social institutions is limited

phenomenology: Theory developed by European philosophers focusing on individual experience of the physical and social world

typifications: "Mental images" that enable people to quickly classify objects and actions and then structure their own actions in response

social construction of reality: Theory that assumes an ongoing correspondence of meaning because people share a common sense about its reality

symbol: (in social construction of reality) An object that represents some other object

signs: (in social construction of reality) Objects explicitly designed to serve as an index of subjective meaning

typification schemes: In social construction of reality, collections of meanings assigned to some phenomenon, which come from a social stock of knowledge to pattern interaction with the environment and things and people in it

frame analysis: Goffman's idea about how people use expectations to make sense of everyday life

frame: In frame analysis, a specific set of expectations used to make sense of a social situation at a given point in time

downshift and upshift: In frame analysis, to move back and forth between serious and less serious frames

social cues: In frame analysis, information in the environment that signals a shift or change of action

hyperritualized representations: Media content constructed to highlight only the most meaningful actions

primary, or dominant, reality: In frame analysis, the real world in which people and events obey certain conventional and widely accepted rules

cascading activation model: Perspective on framing that posits a framing hierarchy in public discourse, with powerful public officials at the top and the press at the lowest level

CHAPTER 14

Media and Culture Theories: Commodification of Culture and Mediatization

Unless you are a member of a racial or cultural minority group or have lived in a culturally diverse neighborhood, you likely formed many of your early impressions of minority groups based on media content. Unless your family traveled frequently and widely, most of your early views of places in the world were formed based on media content. To what extent do these early impressions and views still dominate your understanding of the larger social world? In previous chapters we've looked at theories like cultivation theory or feminist theories tha t identify important biases in the way media represent the social world. Some of this bias is due to the desire of media companies to maximize profits, and some of it reflects inherent biases in how most people in our culture tend to look at the social world. Feminist media scholars have been aggressive and insightful in assessing how patriarchal notions are embedded in everyday culture and reflected in the way that everyday culture is represented in media. These notions have ongoing consequences even though some of them have been effectively challenged and marginalized.

In Chapter 12 we considered theories that look at the role that media can or should play in communities. These theories argue that media are both a positive and a negative force. Media can help unite communities, or they can foster cultural or political divisions. Media can undermine community organizations by distracting people from participation and providing attractive diversions during group activities. But media also provide an important tool for promoting groups and soliciting support. Are functionalist theorists right—do the positive functions outweigh the negative? Or could communities be in greater danger than these theories imply?

The rise of large-scale social media has renewed concerns about the power of mass media and their ability to globally foster misrepresentations and undermine communities in new and dangerous ways. But are such concerns justified? Every time mass media technology has changed, fears about media have risen, as you read in Chapter 2. Even the lowly quill raised Greek philosopher Plato's suspicion some 2,400 years ago. Writing was "a passive, impersonal product that serves as a poor substitute for speech," he argued in *Phaedrus*. Unlike speech, he asserted, "writing is inhuman, a thing, a technological product; it weakens the memory of those who rely on it; it cannot respond to new questions; and it cannot defend itself" (as cited in Ong, 2002, pp. 274–277). More recently fears about media resurfaced in the early 1900s, in the 1930s, and in the 1960s. But over time individuals and communities adjusted to the technological changes. People became more media literate and learned how to avoid problematic uses of media. Threats to social order and democracy were effectively countered, and irresponsible actions by media were reined in by regulations. It's tempting to view our current media system as just a variation of the old system. How harmful could it be? Does the global reach and scale of the new system make it fundamentally different?

Should we be worried about the consequences of the misrepresentations of the social world that are routinely promoted by our current media system? In general the media theories we have considered thus far raise only modest concerns about the role of media in the social world. They do identify ways that media can have a negative influence on society, but they don't argue that mass media have the power to corrupt everyday culture or undermine the social order. Postpositivist theories tend to conceptualize media as relatively benign agents—at worst blundering giants that inadvertently cause problems when profits are given priority over public service. Problematic notions are cultivated, minority political views are silenced, and bad social agendas are fostered, but these happen without malicious intent, and they are balanced by good things done by media. Critical theorists are more skeptical about the motives of media owners and more concerned about the damage they do, but they usually don't argue that there will be catastrophic consequences. The theories presented in this chapter are different. They do foresee the possibility that our media system could profoundly damage both our everyday culture and our social order.

LEARNING OBJECTIVES
After studying this chapter you should be able to
- Explain commodification-of-culture notions, and discuss the way commodification systematically alters how the social world is presented in media content.
- Describe common ways that advertising commodifies culture and systematically misrepresents everyday life.
- Describe mediatization theory, and explain how it compares to framing theory. Be able to explain how deep mediatization could alter important social institutions as well as change how we experience the social world.

OVERVIEW

The theories presented in this chapter argue that when media foster misrepresentations of the larger social world there are serious, mostly negative consequences. Misrepresentations undermine the basis for social order, creating problems for individuals, for social groups, and for social institutions. Social scientists have long recognized some of the problems such as racial or sexual discrimination that stem, and are perpetuated at least in part, from misrepresentations. In previous chapters we looked at theories that address these misrepresentations. In Chapter 3 we explained how Chicago School theorists concluded that journalists needed to take a proactive role in addressing such problems so that Great Communities could flourish rather than collapse into warring factions. In Chapter 13 we looked at framing theories that explain how and why misrepresentations arise and persist.

So what makes the theories in this chapter different? How do they go beyond the theories that we have already looked at? Some postpositivist scholars would argue that the theories in this chapter are simply a return to mass society theory because one of its basic arguments was that media are a corrupting agent within the social order (see Chapter 2). The theory held that media corrupt that order by undermining traditional culture and replacing it with superficial but highly attractive mass culture. Mass society theorists saw capitalism, with its focus on urbanization and mechanization, as the driving force behind this effort to corrupt culture. The theories in this chapter do see media as a corrupting agent, but their reasons for this are very different from those found in mass society theory.

The first theory presented in this chapter is commodification-of-culture theory. Its development traces back to mass society theory since it has a focus on forms of culture fostered by media. But unlike mass society theory it doesn't see these forms of culture as primarily the tool of greedy capitalists. As you'll see, commodification of culture is about more than creating attractive media content that will be consumed by millions. The second theory we will examine is mediatization theory. This has been primarily a European theory—initially developed in Germany and then across the European Union. It asserts that the constraints and structure of media are altering all other social institutions, from the family to politics, from the military to business. Mediatization theorists argue that media are transforming the social order much like climate change is altering the physical world we live in.

MEDIA AS CULTURE INDUSTRIES: THE COMMODIFICATION OF CULTURE

One of the most intriguing and challenging perspectives to emerge from critical cultural studies is the **commodification of culture**, the study of what happens when culture is mass produced and distributed in direct competition with locally based cultures (Enzensberger, 1974; Hay, 1989; Jhally, 1987; Gunster, 2004). According to this viewpoint, media are industries specializing in the production and distribution of cultural commodities. As with other modern industries, they have grown at the expense of small local producers, and the consequences of this displacement have been and continue to be disruptive to people's lives.

In earlier social orders, such as medieval kingdoms, the culture of everyday life was created and controlled by geographically and socially isolated communities. Though kings and lords might dominate an overall social order and have their own culture, it was often totally separate from and had relatively little influence over the folk cultures structuring the everyday experience of average people. Only in modern social orders have elites begun to develop subversive forms of mass culture capable of intruding into and disrupting the culture of everyday life, argue commodification-of-culture theorists. These new forms function as subtle but effective ways of thinking, leading people to misinterpret their experiences and act against their own self-interests.

Elites are able to disrupt everyday cultures by using a rather insidious yet ingenious strategy. They take bits and pieces of folk culture, weave them together to create attractive mass culture content, and then market the result as a substitute for everyday forms of folk culture (Tunstall, 1977). Thus, elites not only subvert legitimate local cultures but earn profits doing so. People actually subsidize the subversion of their everyday culture. If you've ever debated hip-hop and rap artists "selling out," you've been part of a discussion of the commodification of culture. How did rap evolve from its roots in urban verbal warfare to become a billion-dollar recording genre and vehicle for paid product placements (Hinz, 2018)?

Commodification-of-culture theorists argue that this strategy has been especially successful in the United States, where media entrepreneurs have remained relatively independent from political institutions. Mass culture gained steadily in popularity, spawning huge industries that successfully competed for the attention and interest of most Americans. As a result, compared to what occurred in Europe, criticism of mass culture in the United States was muted. Most Americans accepted the cultural commodities emerging from New York and Hollywood as somehow their own. But these same commodities aroused considerable controversy when US media entrepreneurs exported them to other nations (Gunster, 2004). The power of these commodities to reshape daily life was more obvious in most developing nations, and even more disruptive.

In *The Media Are American* (1977), Jeremy Tunstall provided a cogent description of how American media entrepreneurs developed their strategy for creating universally attractive cultural commodities. He also traced how they succeeded internationally against strong competition from formerly dominant world powers France and Britain. In the late 19th and early 20th centuries, American entrepreneurs had access to powerful new communications technology but no clear notion of how it could be used to make profits. Most big industrialists regarded radio and movies as no more than minor and highly speculative enterprises. Few were willing to invest the money necessary to create viable industries. How could messages broadcast through the air or crude black-and-white moving images on a screen be used to earn profits? Would people really pay to see or hear these things? How should industries be organized to manufacture and market cultural products? Most early attempts to answer these questions failed, but through trial and effort, wily entrepreneurs eventually developed a successful strategy.

According to Tunstall, the Tin Pan Alley "tune factory" in New York City provided a model later emulated by other US media industries. The authors of popular music specialized in taking melodies from folk music and transforming them into short, attractive songs. These were easily marketed to mass audiences who didn't have the time or the aesthetic training to appreciate longer, more complex forms of music. In its early days, Tin Pan Alley was a music sweatshop in which songwriters were poorly paid and overworked, while sheet music and recording company entrepreneurs reaped huge profits. By keeping production and distribution costs low, rapid expansion was possible and profits grew accordingly. Inevitably expansion carried the entrepreneurs beyond the United States. Because many were first-generation European immigrants, they knew how to return to and gain a foothold in across the Atlantic. The Second World War provided an ideal opportunity to further subvert European culture. The American military demanded and received permission to import massive quantities of US-style popular culture into Europe, where it proved popular. American Armed Forces Radio was especially influential in its broadcasts of popular music and entertainment shows.

What are the consequences of lifting bits of the culture of everyday life out of their context, repackaging them, and then marketing them back to people?

Commodification-of-culture theorists provide many intriguing answers to this question:

1. **When elements of everyday culture are selected for repackaging, only a very limited range is chosen, and important elements are overlooked or consciously ignored.** For example, elements of culture important for structuring the experience of small minority groups are likely to be ignored, whereas culture practiced by large segments of the population will be emphasized. For a good illustration of this, watch situation comedies from the 1960s like *Father Knows Best* and *Leave It to Beaver*. During this era these programs provided a very homogeneous and idealized picture of American family life. They might make you wonder whether there were any poor people, working women, or ethnic groups living in the United States in the 1960s.

2. **The repackaging process involves dramatization of those elements of culture that have been selected.** Certain forms of action are highlighted, their importance is exaggerated, and others are ignored. Such dramatization makes the final commodity attractive to as large an audience as possible. Potentially boring, controversial, or offensive elements are removed. Features are added that are known to appeal to large audience segments. Thus, attention-getting and emotion-arousing actions—for example, sex and violence—are routinely featured. This is a major reason that car chases, gunfights, and verbal conflict dominate both prime-time and streaming television and Hollywood movies, but casual conversations between friends are rare (unless they include a joke every 15 seconds—then we have comedy).

3. **The marketing of cultural commodities is undertaken in a way that maximizes the likelihood that they will intrude into and ultimately disrupt everyday life.** The success of the media industries depends on marketing as much content as possible to as many people as possible with no consideration for how this content will actually be used or what its long-term consequences will be. An analogy can be made to pollution of the physical environment caused by food packaging. The packaging adds nothing to the nutritional value of the food; it is merely a marketing device—it moves the product off the shelf. Pollution results when we carelessly dispose of this packaging or when there is so much of it that there is no place to put it. Unlike trash, media commodities are less tangible and their packaging is completely integrated into the cultural content. There are no recycling bins for cultural packaging. When we consume the product, we consume the packaging. It intrudes and disrupts.

4. **The elites who operate the cultural industries generally are ignorant of the consequences of their work.** This ignorance is based partly on their alienation from the people who consume their products. They live in Hollywood or New York City, not in typical neighborhoods. They maintain ignorance partly

through strategic avoidance of or denial of evidence about consequences in much the same way the tobacco industry long concealed and lied about research documenting the negative effects of smoking. Media industries have developed formal mechanisms for rationalizing their impact and explaining away consequences. Big public relations firms specialize in assisting them when they encounter criticism. Media also have supported empirical social research and the limited-effects findings it produces. They also support professionalization. Although this can have positive effects (see Chapter 3), media practitioners can also use it to justify routine production practices that produce profitable content while they reject potentially useful innovations.

5. **Disruption of everyday life takes many forms—some disruptions are obviously linked to consumption of especially deleterious content, but other forms are very subtle and occur over long periods.** Disruption ranges from propagation of misconceptions about the social world—like those identified by cultivation analysis (Chapter 12)—to disruption of social institutions. Consequences can be both microscopic and macroscopic and may take many different forms. For example, Joshua Meyrowitz (1985) argued that media deprive us of a sense of place. Henry Giroux (2000) writes that media erase children's childhoods. Neil Postman (1985) believes that media focus too much on entertainment, with serious long-term consequences. He has also examined media disruption in books entitled *The Disappearance of Childhood* (1994) and *The End of Education* (1996). Disruption of childhood, as you saw in Chapter 7, is also the focus of Susan Linn's *Consuming Kids* (2004), Benjamin Barber's *Consumed: How Markets Corrupt Children, Infantilize Adults, and Swallow Citizens Whole* (2007), and Shirley Steinberg's *Kinderculture: The Corporate Construction of Childhood* (2011). Kathleen Jamieson (1988) lamented the decline of political speech making brought about by electronic media and, with Karlyn Campbell, media's corruption of the meaning of citizen action (Jamieson & Campbell, 1997).

Feminist researchers have used commodification-of-culture arguments to explain how male domination of the media industries has disrupted the lives of women. Victoria Collins and Dawn Rothe (2017) provide an extensive literature review to support their assessment of how patriarchal power is exercised through commodification of culture. They believe that consumption of this culture by women legitimizes a status quo dominated by men and "makes them active participants in the continuation of inequality and power structures inherent within this patriarchal society" (p. 161). They cite many examples of problematic media content and argue that media promote a rape culture that promotes and normalizes the abuse and subordination of women. It includes routine presentation of violence against women, including the normalization and romanticizing of dating violence.

In a time of branded stadiums with their corporate luxury skyboxes and jumbo video screens, product logos on uniforms, multi-billion dollar TV deals, multi-million dollar player contracts, a $15 billion-a-year merchandising industry ("Sports Merchandising," 2019), and skyrocketing ticket prices that shut out average fans (Dosh, 2018), it's no surprise that commodification-of-culture theory has also found a welcome home in sports studies. For example, fan Simon Lee lamented the "corporate rebranding" of his favorite sport, soccer. He documented the disappearance of "the traditional collective intensity, passion, and camaraderie experienced by English football supporters standing on the terrace," replaced by "an all-seated, passive, and individualized experience where the possession of an extensive (and expensive) collection of replica shirts, club merchandise, and a satellite dish have become the benchmarks by which an increasingly middle-class audience has expressed its transient enthusiasm for football" (as quoted in Robertson, 2009, p. 301). Andy Ruddock and his colleagues studied the website MyFootballClub, through which fans could buy a controlling stake in a nonleague English football club. This attempt at "football democracy," they wrote, is an effort to use media to reclaim that which has been disrupted by media, that is, the traditional team/fan relationship, allowing members to "recreate football-as-folk-culture fantasies through the processes of mediation and commodification that are otherwise blamed for killing 'the people's game'" (Ruddock, Hutchins, & Rowe, 2010, p. 323). And Ian Culpan and Caroline Meier (2016) detailed how the commodification of sport "by global market forces" has hollowed out its "moral and ethical base," challenging its "value in enhancing the human condition." As such, they recommended regulation as a way to "protect sport's social, educative and moral underpinnings" (p. 143).

Commodification of Culture in the Age of Social Media

When social media were initially developed, they offered the potential to break elite control over content production and commodification of culture. Instead, as we have explained in earlier chapters, large-scale social media companies, much like their more traditional predecessors, have in fact come to exercise considerable control over content production and distribution. They have created computer algorithms to filter content posted to their platforms, but they are designed to filter selectively in ways that serve their specific interests. One important consequence of this is the prioritization of controversial content that attracts and holds user attention. For example, after the 2018 mass shooting at Stoneman Douglas High School, YouTube staff suggested changing algorithms to curb conspiracies and limit their presence among the videos the site recommended to users. Higher-ups at the company rejected the suggestion, preferring the maximization of "engagement" (Bergen, 2019).

As such, users seeking to earn money from social media or to promote extreme views produce content that commodifies culture using successful formulas developed for older forms of mass media—those that promise the greatest audience, not the greatest good. But unlike more traditional media, they aren't bound by the legal and ethical restraints that have gradually been placed on producers of content for those older forms. As a result, highly objectionable content that promotes extreme views has become widespread. Jessica Megarry (2018), for example, cites evidence that male-dominated social media companies are choosing to ignore feminist complaints and allow extreme views on topics like date rape or female subordination to circulate freely. The companies argue that some of this content is only controversial humor rather than hate speech. True or not, allowing these views in fact works to the companies' advantage, as extreme content sparks user debates and these debates attract and hold even more attention.

Feminist scholars argue that social media companies are allowing extreme anti-feminist views to be promoted on their platforms (Megarry, 2018) and that feminist challenges to this content result in systematic harassment and intimidation of the critics. Social media companies deny responsibility for these problems. They argue they are simply providing a platform for users to exercise their free speech rights, and that naturally some of that speech may be objectionable to some. Nonetheless, critics point out that social media have increased the degree to which a number of problematic views are routinely and widely promoted, including female inferiority, date rape myths, female desire for subordination, violence against minorities, and White supremacy. Elite control over commodification of culture may be diminished by social media, but at a high cost. In fact, a number of other online incidents involving objectionable content have attracted widespread notice and comment. These include the "Fappening" in August 2014, involving "the hack, theft, and digital dissemination of hundreds of nude celebrity photos" (Lawson, 2018, p. 825); Gamergate, involving social shaming and intimidation of feminist critics of video game culture (Marwick & Caplan, 2018); and #mencallmethings—a Twitter campaign begun by women reporting harassment experiences that encountered serious criticism (Megarry, 2014).

Megarry (2018) believes that male control over social media has resulted in problematic surveillance of feminist activism on social media. She argues that feminists are being disadvantaged in the online struggle between feminism and misogyny. Although feminists have been successful in utilizing social media as a platform for their views, online opposition is escalating, and social media companies do little to moderate these attacks. She points out that online feminist discussions occur in public, mixed-sex, proprietary environments that are quite different from the single-sex, consciousness-raising feminist groups common in the 1970s and 1980s. Megarry believes that the presence of men in online feminist forums has compromised their usefulness for developing ideas and planning activities. You can read more about one well-known online attack on female users in the box entitled "Gamergate: Feminist Challenges and Manosphere Responses."

Why have social media become a very powerful but problematic agent for the commodification of culture? Unlike older forms of mass media, they are not restrained by laws and regulations developed to bring these media under control. Most social media companies embrace free speech values in favor of public service norms. They argue that they are serving the public interest by allowing whatever content the public wants to circulate. Their views mirror those of early libertarian theorists (see Chapter 3). They seem to assume that in the new marketplace of ideas created by social media, good ideas will eventually win out over bad ideas. But how likely is a positive outcome in this struggle? Social media platforms have become hosts for a growing number of proponents for controversial views that are widely reviled, and at the same time they encourage savage attacks on otherwise well-established and widely held views.

GAMERGATE: FEMINIST CHALLENGES AND MANOSPHERE RESPONSES

Since the late 1990s feminists have raised concerns about video games and the gaming industry for its sexist representation of women in the games themselves and the mistreatment of female players (Jenson & de Castell, 2008). The issue exploded into public awareness in 2014 when feminist criticism touched off an abusive online anti-feminist campaign. In late summer of that year video-game developer Zoe Quinn was accused in a long online article by an ex-partner, Eron Gjoni, of using sexual favors to gain status in the industry (Salter, 2018). Quinn was harassed online, and her Tumblr account was hacked. On August 27 the actor Adam Baldwin first used the hashtag #GamerGate with the intent of mobilizing his 190K followers against Quinn. The movement soon "discovered" a feminist conspiracy to undermine the gaming industry and to promote feminist values using games.

Anita Sarkeesian was one of the first feminist scholars to be targeted by the movement. Since 2012 she had been developing a series of YouTube videos that questioned the dominance of men in game production and promotion. Her videos provided many illustrations of the problematic ways that men and women are routinely represented in games (Sarkeesian, 2014). Megarry (2018) reports that Sarkeesian "was sent rape and death threats, her personal social media pages were hacked, her private information was distributed, her Wikipedia page was amended to include sexual images, and an interactive game was created in which players could click on her face to beat her up" (p. 1078). In 2017 Sarkeesian's appearance on a panel at VidCon (an annual assembly of game industry and fans) was met by anti-feminist YouTubers who filled the first three rows of the audience (Marwick & Caplan, 2018). Their goal? Sarkeesian explains, "There's a toxicity within gaming culture . . . that drives this misogynist hatred, this reactionary backlash against women who have anything to say, especially those who have critiques or who are feminists. There's this huge drive to silence us, and if they can't silence us, they try to discredit us in an effort to push us out." Gamergate, she adds, is "trying to hold on to this status quo, this illusion that gaming is for men" (as cited in Collins, 2014).

Shira Chess and Adrienne Shaw (2015) discussed how they were caught up in Gamergate. As feminist gaming scholars they have been active in publishing articles and making academic conference presentations that criticize gaming culture and the gaming industry. Their work drew the attention of Gamergate anti-feminists who saw their work as evidence of a conspiracy to destroy video games and the video game industry. Chess and Shaw are concerned that their work and that of other feminist scholars is being taken out of context and reframed as a sinister effort to take control of gaming. They argue that anti-feminists either don't understand how and why academic scholarship is conducted or they are deliberately distorting its interpretation.

In the wake of Gamergate, Alice Marwick and Robyn Caplan (2018) argued that a loose online network known as the **manosphere** has emerged that manages a set of blogs, podcasts, and forums. They documented how the manosphere targets and harasses feminist media critics and activists using **misandry**—an extreme framing of feminist views as anti-male. They cite evidence that harassment techniques developed by the manosphere in early online confrontations are now widely used by anti-feminists, including governments, to suppress feminist views.

How do you view Gamergate and the rise of the manosphere? Was there a conspiracy against video gaming that threatened to undermine the industry? Were feminist criticisms likely to bring about the major changes feared by anti-feminists? Could there have been a more responsible and reasoned challenge to feminist concerns? Does the manosphere pose a serious threat to feminist online activity? If so, how should this threat be addressed? Could or should social media corporations intervene in contentious online disputes? When does free speech degenerate into hate speech?

Advertising: The Ultimate Cultural Commodity

Not surprisingly, critical cultural studies researchers direct some of their most devastating criticism toward advertising. They view it as the ultimate cultural commodity (Hay, 1989; Hoffman, 2015; Jhally, 1987). Advertising packages promotional messages so they will be attended to and acted on by people who often have little interest in and no real need for most of the advertised products or services. Marketers routinely portray consumption of specific products as the best way to construct a worthwhile personal identity, have fun, make friends and influence people, or solve problems (often ones that consumers never knew they had). "You deserve a break today." "Just do it." "Be the most interesting man in the world."

Compared to other forms of media content, advertising comes closest to fitting older Marxist notions of ideology. It is intended to encourage consumption that serves the interest of product manufacturers but may not be in the interest of individual consumers. Advertising is clearly designed to intrude into and disrupt routine buying habits and purchasing decisions. It attempts to stimulate and reinforce consumption, even if consumption might be detrimental to individuals' long-term health or their budget. For some products, such as cigarettes, alcohol, and even fast food, successful advertising campaigns move people to engage in self-destructive actions. In other cases we are simply encouraged to consume things serving little real purpose for us or serving only the purposes that advertising itself creates. One obvious example is when we buy specific brands of clothing because their advertising has promoted them as status symbols. Clothing does indeed provide basic protection for our bodies, but used clothing from a thrift store provides the same protection as do the most well-known brands. Former ad agency executive turned anti-commercialism activist Jelly Helm (2002) believes advertising's intrusion into American culture has created a country that is "sick. . . . We work too hard so that we can buy things we don't need, made by factory workers who are paid too little, and produced in ways that threaten the very survival of the earth." The United States "will be remembered as the greatest wealth-producer ever. It will be a culture remembered for its promise and might and its tremendous achievements in technology and health. It also will be remembered as a culture of hedonism to rival any culture that has ever existed, a culture of materialism and workaholism and individualism, a culture of superficiality and disposability, of poverty and pollution, and vanity and violence, a culture denuded of its spiritual wisdom" (n.p.).

MEDIATIZATION THEORY

Over the past two decades a new macroscopic theory of media has emerged. Pioneered by German media theorists, **mediatization theory** has become a dominant theory for cultural studies researchers in Europe (Lunt & Livingstone, 2016). It shares many conceptions with American mass communication theories, but unlike its US counterparts it is grand and all-encompassing. Even fairly ambitious US theories such as information-processing theory, cultivation analysis, or framing theory make no claims about the ability of media to transform the social order in an ever more profound way. Mediatization theory asserts that media have become so central and essential for all modern social orders that those social orders are continually changing in quite important ways to accommodate ever-changing media. Mediatization theorists believe that all modern societies are now locked into a process of change centered around media. The social institutions that make up modern social orders, such as politics, religion, business, education, and the military, have been "mediatized"—their structures and their routine social practices have been altered and continue to be altered to accommodate media. For example, American intelligence and Pentagon agencies work hand in hand with media producers to ensure favorable representation. They rewrite scripts, lend equipment, censor storylines, and on occasion even stop production (Secker & Alford, 2017). The US Army uses video games to train soldiers on shooting and ammunition discipline (Evans-Thirlwell, 2017), and the British military actively recruits "binge gamers and phone zombies" (Molina, 2019).

These institutions don't just use media—they are used by media and made to fit within constraints set by media. Their everyday functioning is dependent on media. At the microscopic level of modern society, the everyday life of individuals has come to center around the use of media—especially Internet-based, mobile media. Media provide the dominant way that most people come to understand themselves and their place in the social world. Media guide people through daily life, entertain them, comfort them, and give a structure to everyday action. Without media, people would be unable to construct their identity or make sense of an increasingly complex social world. These arguments about the central role of media should sound familiar since we have described other theories, such as framing theory and cultivation analysis, that make similar assertions about the role of media. What makes mediatization theory different is its argument that *all* social institutions are being mediatized and that this mediatization process is ongoing with profound, difficult-to-anticipate consequences.

Some mediatization theorists argue that we have entered a new phase of mediatization, **deep mediatization** (Couldry & Hepp, 2017). In this stage the changes in social institutions already caused by media are beginning to create ever more profound changes—a cascading process of change that is potentially out of control. Comparisons can be made to climate change, globalization, and urbanization—other macroscopic processes that are ongoing and mostly uncontrollable, and that have deep consequences for life and social order on our planet.

Mediatization theory has only recently begun to be seriously considered by American scholars. One event that triggered this attention was the International Communication Association presidential address delivered by Sonia Livingstone in 2008. Livingstone (2009) argued for a perspective that she labeled *mediation theory* rather than mediatization theory. She later provided a much more elaborate discussion of mediation and mediatization in a book chapter coauthored with Peter Lunt. Livingstone and Lunt (2014) question whether mediatization is something that has a long history or whether it is a phenomenon that has emerged recently with the rise of large-scale media corporations, along with their use of a variety of Internet-based platform media to appeal to worldwide audiences. Rather than embrace mediatization theory as an established perspective, Livingstone and Lunt argue there is a need for a comprehensive, multidisciplinary research effort to probe its usefulness. Mediatization research, they argue, should be focused on understanding how social institutions are changing in response to media and on the long-term consequences of these changes. This will require researchers from different social science disciplines to focus on examining the role of media within the specific social institutions that are central to their disciplines. Political scientists will need to look at government, elections, and political parties; economists should look at business and banking; education scholars should look at schools and universities; and religious studies scholars should look at denominations and churches. But will other social scientists, especially those in the United States, take media seriously and conduct the research necessary to develop and validate mediatization theory? Will task forces of social scientists be assembled? Imagine the scientific resources currently devoted to understanding climate change or globalization. Could such significant resources be marshalled to study mediatization? Until recently most American social scientists, other than media scholars, ignored media because they believed that limited-effects research had already proven that media were not important. The rise of social media does seem to have drawn interest from younger scholars across academia, and we have reviewed their research in earlier chapters. But it is unlikely that a multidisciplinary task force will be assembled in the United States to investigate mediatization theory.

Nick Couldry and Andreas Hepp have provided one of the most elaborate and comprehensive presentations of mediatization theory in *The Mediated Construction of Reality* (2017). They position their social constructionist perspective on media in relation to a book discussed earlier in this text, *The Social Construction of Reality* (Berger & Luckmann, 1966). Berger and Luckmann presented a social constructionist perspective on society with very little consideration of the role of media. Couldry and Hepp (2017) argue that since Berger and Luckmann's book was published, the role of media has become central to most social institutions and to daily life. In particular, with the rise of large-scale social media, they believe we have entered a deep mediatization phase of societal development. Media no longer serve simply as an efficient means of message transmission, but rather have become an organizing force that determines how all other social institutions will develop and dictates the conditions of everyday life for everyone. They explain, "What does it mean when the social world, as we know it, is constructed in and through mediated communication? A way of capturing this deep, consistent, and self-reinforcing role of media in the construction of the social world is to say that the social world is not just mediated but mediatized: that is, changed in its dynamics and structure by the role that media continuously (indeed recursively) play in its construction." As a result, they argue, "the social world has significantly more complexity when its forms and patterns are, in part, sustained in and through media and their infrastructures. Even if we do things without directly using media, the horizon of our practices is a social world for which media are fundamental reference-points and resources" (p. 15). Take a few simple examples: When you talk about politics, from where did you learn your facts and figures? Where did you "meet" any of the people you reference? Where did the building blocks for your opinions originate? No interest in politics? What do you and your friends talk about when hanging out away from media? No doubt much of your conversation revolves around media content ("Did you see *Black Panther 3*?" "Did you catch the game?" "That was a strange post by Alex? What's up with her?") or your use of media ("Too bad your car doesn't have WiFi." "Did you update your resume on LinkedIn?" "I gotta get me that new iPhone!"). And would gender-reveal stunts even exist if it were not for social media turning the identification of a soon-to-be-newborn into a reality TV-show "big reveal"? Would there be such things as destination bachelorette parties if not for Instagram and TikTok? And why must marriage proposals and their resulting weddings be video spectacles lest their legitimacy be suspect?

Another useful description of mediatization theory is provided by a team of Scandinavian researchers, Mats Ekström and his colleagues, who are part of a Nordic effort to assess mediatization theory and decide whether to mobilize a task force to study it:

> Mediatization is indeed a recurrent diagnosis today—in public debate, in social and cultural life, as well as within the humanities and social sciences (Kaun, 2011; Kaun & Fast, 2014). It serves as a synthesizing formula to cover interrelated processes such as the growth in number, diversity, and reach of communication media; their multiplying efficiency in terms of speed, storage, and penetrating capacity; the increasing portion of people's daily lifetime spent on media uses; the growing influence of media institutions and industries, and the allegedly growing general significance of media texts and technologies in widening spheres and fields of life, society, and culture. (Ekström, Fornäs, Jansson, & Jerslev, 2016, p. 1091)

The products of this mediatization? "In all cultural sub-fields," they write, "heightened media presence seems to change the conditions for the making, dissemination, and use of sounds, images, and texts, with ambiguous implications for aesthetics, industries, education, policy, and publicness. Ordinary everyday life, too, is affected, not least by online networks of social media" (p. 1091).

Criticism of mediatization theory comes from researchers who question what they regard as vague assertions concerning the causal power of media. David Deacon and James Stanyer (2014) outline their reservations based on a review of 13 studies conducted using mediatization theory. They argue, first, that mediatization scholars fail to specify the causal processes that underlie media power. There are many societal agencies that restrict media power. For example, government policies regulate the actions of media, and this means that media can't exercise independent causal power. Second, the agents of media power are not clearly specified by mediatization researchers. Who are the individuals or groups who exercise the power provided by media? Third, mediatization research doesn't clearly indicate how media influence communicative practices within the social institutions affected by media. Mediatization scholars speculate about a variety of practices that might be altered by media, but they don't explain how specific changes take place. Finally, mediatization scholars are unclear about the time period when mediatization happened. Some vaguely refer to long time spans but focus attention only on recent time periods. Deacon and Stanyer could only find two published studies that looked at mediatization over time, and these didn't report much evidence that the influence of media had increased.

If you look back to earlier chapters in this book, you will find that these criticisms echo the concerns that postpositivist researchers have always made about critical cultural theory. Postpositivists want to pin down the specific causes of media effects so they can be observed and measured. But the effort to specify and measure even simple forms of causation has been difficult. The first generation of postpositivists concluded that media had limited effects because they couldn't measure any consistently important media influence. The current generation of postpositivists is having more success at identifying and measuring media effects. As you've seen in previous chapters, recent postpositivist research is finding consistent evidence of media impact on cognition and action. They are using methods for data collection and analysis that are far more sophisticated than those available in the 1950s. In particular, so-called "big data" is yielding intriguing results in areas like agenda-setting and cultivation analysis. Even with the growing evidence of media effects, it is likely that contemporary postpositivists will continue to regard mediatization theory as merely a useful guide for their research rather than a bedrock assumption, or paradigm, for the discipline. They believe media may be having some important effects but that they are an unlikely source of major changes in most or all social institutions.

Still, mediatization theory offers an important challenge to the social sciences, not just to media scholars. It argues that we need to work quickly to understand the role of media in society or we risk losing control over the social institutions that underlie our social order. We can choose to ignore this challenge. We can conclude that mediatization theory is simply yet another version of mass society theory—that after more than a century of thinking about and studying media, we are right back where we started at the turn of the last century. Or we can accept the challenge posed by mediatization theory and find a way of fitting many of the theoretical perspectives and research findings considered in this book into mediatization's overarching framework. Should we explore whether mediatization could serve as a paradigm for media theory and research? Mediatization involves the microscopic and macroscopic processes that are explained by theories such as uses-and-gratifications, agenda-setting, spiral of silence, cultivation analysis, framing, and so on. To the extent that each of these theories has been empirically tested, any or all of them could provide support for development of an over-arching theory of mediatization. Europeans have not tried to integrate American theories into the mediatization perspective. How about you—could you use the theories covered in this book as building blocks that develop and validate a theory of mediatization? Or do you think mediatization theory is making speculative and unwarranted claims about the role of media? If so, which claims do you think are most problematic?

MEDIATIZATION

Strengths

1. Focuses attention on the role of media, especially social media, in social institutions
2. Macro-level theory, but has clear implications for micro-level issues
3. Identifies problematic changes in social institutions linked to media
4. Can be evaluated using "big data"
5. Existing media theories could be integrated into this theory
6. Could guide development of useful media regulation policies

Weaknesses

1. Doesn't clearly specify how media cause changes in social institutions
2. Doesn't provide a clear agenda for research
3. Early efforts to apply the theory have found weak, inconsistent changes in social institutions
4. Gives little recognition to power of individuals
5. Comprehensive research would require a taskforce made up of social researchers from many disciplines
6. Is overly pessimistic about the role of media and the power of media

REVIEW OF LEARNING OBJECTIVES

- Explain commodification-of-culture notions, and discuss the way commodification systematically alters how the social world is presented in media content.

Commodification of culture works by decontextualizing cultural items from the culture in which they are embedded and then simplifying them so that ambiguous attributes are removed and a few attractive attributes are highlighted. The items selected can be as simple as songs or as complex as myths. Early forms of the theory viewed the sole purpose of commodification agents as creating commodities that could be sold for a profit, even if they might undermine elite control. More recent forms have focused on the power of commodities to promote specific ideologies such as those underlying male dominance. Commodification of culture results in media representations of the social world that are highly simplified and attractive, compelling, or dramatic. These representations tend to perpetuate inaccurate commonsense assumptions and expectations.

- Describe common ways that advertising commodifies culture and systematically misrepresents everyday life.

To create effective advertising, commodification of culture needs to be especially effective at selecting and packaging cultural items so they can serve as a vehicle for promoting specific products or services. Commodification of culture misrepresents products or services and the social context in which they are used. In doing so it often perpetuates inaccurate or problematic commonsense notions about the social world. Advertising may imply that consumption of a product will enhance social status or attract desirable attention. In doing so it suggests that certain forms of social status or certain types of attention from others are more important than others and should be sought.

- Describe mediatization theory, and explain how it compares to framing theory. Be able to explain how deep mediatization could alter important social institutions as well as change how we experience the social world.

Mediatization theory argues that media have become an important or even dominant force in the social world. All social institutions that underlie modern social orders must rely on media to function effectively. The structure of social institutions is being changed to accommodate media. As media undergo changes, such as the rise of Internet-based media, they force institutions to make even more changes, which result in what theorists label *deep mediatization*. For example, there is concern across the West that democratic elections are being threatened by large-scale social media. These media are thought to circulate fake news that polarizes electorates and undermines democratic decision-making processes. Mediatization theory is a macroscopic social constructionist theory that sees social institutions as socially constructed and as necessary for social order. The theory tends to view media as a destabilizing force—one that can rapidly undermine institutions and make it difficult for them to function effectively. Framing theory is a microscopic social constructionist theory (that has some clear macroscopic implications). It is concerned about the way that frames structure how individuals make sense of their social world. It is concerned about the social institutions that develop and promote frames and the short-term and long-term consequences of that frame development and promotion. Framing research has tended to demonstrate how social institutions use frames to maintain power in the social world and prevent opposing frames from being developed and used. But it has also offered evidence that oppositional frames can be developed and promoted. Thus, framing theory and mediatization theory tend to reach opposing conclusions about the role of media in maintaining or undermining the power of social institutions. Framing theory tends to be optimistic about the liberating potential of new frames that oppose social institution frames, while mediatization theory tends to be pessimistic because changes in media could undermine the structure of social institutions and destabilize the social order.

CRITICAL THINKING QUESTIONS

1. Has commodification of culture resulted in misrepresentations that have been problematic for you? Commodification theory has focused on problematic racial and gender misrepresentations. Do you agree or disagree with the arguments that have been made? If you agree, how should these misrepresentations be challenged or corrected?

2. Are you aware of or involved in an organization that increasingly relies on media for its day-to-day operation? Has proliferation of screens intruded into group activities? Does reliance on media fundamentally alter the way the group operates? Has there been a change in group objectives or achievements? Have relationships between group members changed? Are you becoming more interested and involved in the group? Why or why not?

3. Do you see evidence that particular social institutions are being altered in fundamental ways by their use of media? Politics is the social institution most often

identified as having been transformed by media. Political polarization and political alienation have been linked to mediatization. Do you agree or disagree? Has this transformation been useful or problematic?

KEY TERMS

commodification of culture
manosphere
misandry

mediatization theory
deep mediatization

GLOSSARY

commodification of culture: The study of what happens when culture is mass produced and distributed in direct competition with locally based cultures

manosphere: Collection of blogs, podcasts, and forums targeting and harassing feminist media critics and activists

misandry: Extreme framing of feminist views as anti-male

mediatization theory: A European theory that explains how media force social institutions and individuals to make useful and problematic changes

deep mediatization: Latest stage in mediatization—media influence on social institutions and everyday life is becoming ever more widespread and recursive, with problematic long-term consequences

REFERENCES

PREFACE

Chaffee, S. H., & Metzger, M. J. (2001). The end of mass communication? *Mass Communication & Society, 4*, 365–379.

Delli Carpini, M. X. (2013). Breaking boundaries: Can we bridge the quantitative versus qualitative divide through the study of entertainment and politics? *International Journal of Communication, 7*, 531–551.

Jensen, K. B., & Neuman, W. R. (2013). Evolving paradigms of communication research. *International Journal of Communication, 7*, 230–238.

Potter, W. J. (2009). *Arguing for a general framework for mass media scholarship.* Thousand Oaks, CA: Sage.

Silverman, J. (2019, January 20). Big tech is watching. *New York Times Book Review*, p. 10.

Wu, T. (2019, April 14). The way capitalism betrayed the right to be left alone. *New York Times*, p. SR3.

Zuboff, S. (2019). *The age of surveillance capitalism.* New York: Public Affairs.

CHAPTER 1

Alasuutari, P. (1999). Introduction: Three phases of reception studies. In P. Alasuutari (Ed.), *Rethinking the media audience* (pp. 1–21). Thousand Oaks, CA: Sage.

Andrews, R., Biggs, R. M., & Seidel, M. (1996). *The Columbia world of quotations.* New York: Columbia University Press.

Average number of Facebook friends of users in the United States in 2016. (2018). *Statista.* Retrieved from https://www.statista.com/statistics/398532/us--user-network-size/

Bailey, K. D. (1982). *Methods of social research.* New York: Free Press.

Bandura, A. (2008). The reconstrual of "free will" from the agentic perspective of social cognitive theory. In J. Baer, J. C. Kaufman, & R. F. Baumeister (Eds.), *Are we free? Psychology and free will* (pp. 86–27). Oxford: Oxford University Press.

Bauer, R. A., & Bauer, A. H. (1960). America, mass society, and mass media. *Journal of Social Issues, 10*, 3–66.

Benoit, L. W., & Holbert, R. (2008). Empirical intersections in communication research: Replication, multiple quantitative methods, and bridging the quantitative–qualitative divide. *Journal of Communication, 58*, 615–628.

Berelson, B. (1959). The state of communication research. *Public Opinion Quarterly, 23*, 1–2.

Berger, C. R. (2005). Interpersonal communication: Theoretical perspectives, future prospects. *Journal of Communication, 55*, 415–447.

Blackford, L. B. (2012, August 14). GOP lawmakers question standards for teaching evolution in Kentucky. *Kentucky.com.* Retrieved from https://www.kentucky.com/news/politics-government/article44372157.html

Bowers, J. W., & Courtright, J. A. (1984). *Communication research methods.* Glenview, IL: Scott Foresman.

Brantlinger, P. (1983). *Bread and circuses: Theories of mass culture as social decay.* Ithaca, NY: Cornell University Press.

Buffardi, L. E., & Campbell, W. K. (2008). Narcissism and social networking websites. *Personality and Social Psychology Bulletin, 34*, 1303–1314.

Burrell, G., & Morgan, G. (1979). *Sociological paradigms and organization analysis.* London: Heinemann.

Campbell, A., Converse, P. W., Miller, W. E., & Stokes, D. E. (1960). *The American voter*. New York: Wiley.

Carey, J. (1977). Mass communication research and cultural studies: An American view. In J. Curran, M. Gurevitch, J. Woollacott, J. Marriott, & C. Roberts (Eds.), *Mass communication and society* (pp. 409–425). London: Open University Press.

Delo, C. (2012, October 4). Facebook hits billionth user, reveals first major ad from global agency of record. *Advertising Age*. Retrieved from http://adage.com/article/digital/facebook-serves-1-billion-makes-a-video-ad-celebrate/237571/

Deutschmann, P. J., & Danielson, W. A. (1960). Diffusion of knowledge of the major news story. *Journalism Quarterly, 37*, 345–355.

Feldman, S. (2018, December 14). Facebook loses the public's trust. *Statista*. Retrieved from https://www.statista.com/chart/16431/tech-company-trust/

Gosling, S. D., Augustine, A. A., Vazire, S., Holtzman, N., & Gaddis, S. (2011). Manifestations of personality in online social networks: Self-reported Facebook-related behaviors and observable profile information. *Cyberpsychology, Behavior, and Social Networking, 14*, 483–488.

Grier, S., & Brumbaugh, A. (2007). Compared to whom? The impact of status on third person effects in advertising in a South African context. *Journal of Consumer Behaviour, 6*, 5–18.

Griffin, E. A. (1994). *A first look at communication theory*. New York: McGraw-Hill.

Gurevitch, M., Coleman, S., & Blumler, J. G. (2010). Political communication—Old and new media relationships. *Annals of the American Academy of Social Sciences, 625*, 164–181.

Hall, S. (1982). The rediscovery of "ideology": Return of the repressed in media studies. In M. Gurevitch, T. Bennett, J. Curran, & J. Woollacott (Eds.), *Culture, Society, and the Media* (pp. 52–86). New York: Methuen.

Holbert, R. L., Garrett, R. K., & Gleason, L. S. (2010). A new era of minimal effects? A response to Bennett and Iyengar. *Journal of Communication, 60*, 15–34.

Ingram, M. (2018, Winter). The Facebook armageddon: The social network's increasing threat to journalism. *Columbia Journalism Review*. Retrieved from https://www.cjr.org/special_report/facebook-media-buzzfeed.php/

Kearse, S. (2018, December 23). Foggy notion. *New York Times Magazine*, pp. 9–11.

Kerlinger, F. N. (1986). *Foundations of behavioral research*. New York: Holt, Rinehart, & Winston.

Klapper, J. T. (1960). *The effects of mass communication*. New York: Free Press.

Knobloch-Westerwick, S. (2015). The selective exposure self- and affect-management (SESAM) model: Applications in the realms of race, politics, and health. *Communication Research, 42*, 959–985.

Lazarsfeld, P. F. (1941). Remarks on administrative and critical communication research. *Studies in Philosophy and Social Science, 9*, 2–16.

Lazarsfeld, P. F. (1969). An episode in the history of social research: A memoir. In D. Fleming & B. Bailyn (Eds.), *The intellectual migration: Europe and America, 1930–1960* (pp. 270–337). Cambridge, MA: Belknap Press of Harvard University.

Lazarsfeld, P. F., Berelson, B., & Gaudet, H. (1944). *The people's choice: How the voter makes up his mind in a presidential campaign*. New York: Duell, Sloan & Pearce.

Leedy, P. D. (1997). *Practical research: Planning and design*. New York: Macmillan.

Littlejohn, S. W., & Foss, K. A. (2011). *Theories of human communication*. Long Grove, IL: Waveland Press.

Matsa, K. E., & Shearer, E. (2018, September 10). News use across social media platforms 2018. *Pew Research Center*. Retrieved from http://www.journalism.org/2018/09/10/news-use-across-social-media-platforms-2018/

McCarthy, N. (2019, March 11). Is Facebook becoming social media's retirement home? *Statista*. Retrieved from https://www.statista.com/chart/17306/share-of-the-us-population-using-facebook-by-age-group/

Meyrowitz, J. (2008). Power, pleasure, patterns: Intersecting narratives of media influence. *Journal of Communication, 58*, 641–663.

Miller, K. (2005). *Communication theories: Perspectives, processes, and contexts*. New York: McGraw-Hill.

Moerman, M. (1992). Life after C. A.: An ethnographer's autobiography. In G. Watson & R. M. Seller (Eds.), *Text in context: Contributions to ethnomethodology* (pp. 30–34). Newbury Park, CA: Sage.

Mosco, V., & Herman, A. (1981). Critical theory and electronic media. *Theory and Society, 10*, 869–896.

Nadkarni, S., & Hofmann, S. G. (2012). Why do people use Facebook? *Personality and Individual Differences, 52*, 243–249.

Neuman, W. R., & Guggenheim, L. (2011). The evolution of media effects theory: A six-stage model of cumulative research. *Communication Theory, 21*, 169–196.

Neuman, W.R., Guggenheim, L., Mo Jang, S., & Bae, S. Y. (2014). The dynamics of public attention:

Agenda-setting theory meets Big Data. *Journal of Communication, 64*, 193–214.

Newcomb, H. (1974). *TV: The most popular art.* New York: Oxford University Press.

Otto, S. L. (2011). *Fool me twice: Fighting the assault on science in America.* New York: Rodale.

Pierce, C. (1955). Essentials of pragmatism. In J. Buchler (Ed.), *Philosophical writings of Pierce* (pp. 251–268). New York: Dover.

Pollitt, K. (2012, June 4). What's the matter with creationism? *The Nation.* Retrieved from http://www.thenation.com/article/168385/whats-matter-creationism#

Popper, K. (1934), *The logic of scientific discovery.* Tubingen, Germany: Mohr Siebeck Verlag. (German edition).

Potter, W. J. (2013) Synthesizing a working definition of "mass" media. *Review of Communication Research, 1*, 1–30.

Scheufele, D. A. (2000). Agenda setting, priming, and framing revisited: Another look at cognitive effects of political communication. *Mass Communication and Society, 3*, 297–316.

Schutt, R. K. (2009). *Investigating the social world*, 6th ed. Thousand Oaks, CA: Sage.

Sloane, G. (2018, December 10). Snapchat creators say the platform is losing its appeal. *Advertising Age.* Retrieved from https://adage.com/article/digital/snapchat-creators-app-losing-cool/315911/

Spangler, T. (2018, June 14). Facebook bets $1 billion on content, but will it pay off? *Variety.* Retrieved from https://variety.com/2018/digital/news/facebook-content-1202844037/

Stevens, J. (2012, June 24). Political scientists are lousy forecasters. *New York Times*, p. SR6.

Turner, J. H. (1998). *The structure of sociological theory*, 6th ed. Belmont, CA: Wadsworth.

US Election Project. (2018a, December). 2018 November general election turnout rates. Retrieved from http://www.electproject.org/2018g

US Election Project. (2018b, September). 2016 November general election turnout rates. Retrieved from http://www.electproject.org/2016g

Webster, J. G. (2017). Three myths of digital media. *Convergence, 23*, 352–361.

Wise, J. (2018, July 11). Poll: Record number of Americans believe in man-made climate change. *The Hill.* Retrieved from https://thehill.com/policy/energy-environment/396487-poll-record-of-americans-believe-in-man-made-climate-change

CHAPTER 2

Adbusters. (2002, January/February). The Rev. Jerry Falwell. *Adbusters*, n.p.

Alterman, E. (2008, February 24). The news from Quinn-Broderville. *Nation*, pp. 11–14.

Alterman, E. (2017, March 31). The perception of liberal bias in the newsroom has nothing whatsoever to do with reality. *Nation.* Retrieved from https://www.thenation.com/article/the-perception-of-liberal-bias-in-the-newsroom-has-nothing-whatsoever-to-do-with-reality/

Altschull, J. H. (1990). *From Milton to McLuhan: The ideas behind American journalism.* New York: Longman.

Apuzzo, M., & LaFraniere, S. (2018, February 17). Indictment bares Russian network to twist 2016 vote. *New York Times*, p. A1.

Arendt, H. (1951). *The origins of totalitarianism.* Berlin: Schocken Books.

Bagdikian, B. H. (1992). *The media monopoly*, 4th ed. Boston: Beacon.

Bagdikian, B. H. (2004, March 20). Print will survive. *Editor & Publisher*, p. 70.

Bajomi-Lázár, P., & Horváth, D. (2013). The continued relevance of the concept of propaganda: Propaganda as ritual in contemporary Hungary. *Global Media and Communication, 9*, 219–237.

Bauerlein, M. (2017, December 14). The firehose of falsehood. *Nieman Lab.* Retrieved from http://www.niemanlab.org/2017/12/the-firehose-of-falsehood/

Becker, H. (1949). The nature and consequences of black propaganda. *American Sociological Review, 14*, 221–235.

Beniger, J. R. (1987). Toward and old new paradigm: The half-century flirtation with mass society. *Public Opinion Quarterly, 51*, S46–S66.

Blatchford, T. (2018, June 27). Journalists could actually help audiences identify misinformation. *Poynter Institute.* Retrieved from https://www.poynter.org/fact-checking/2018/reliability-ratings-from-journalists-could-actually-help-audiences-identify-misinformation/

Boboltz, S. (2018, May 22). "60 Minutes" reporter reveals Trump's chilling reason for slamming the press. *Huffington Post.* Retrieved from https://www.huffingtonpost.com/entry/60-minutes-reporter-trump-chilling-reason-for-slamming-press_us_5b048109e4b07c4ea102c8ca

Brantlinger, P. (1983). *Bread and circuses: Theories of mass culture as social decay.* Ithaca, NY: Cornell University Press.

Bridge, J. A., Greenhouse, J. B., Ruch, D., Stevens, J., Ackerman, J., Sheftall, H. A., ... Campo, J. V. (2019). Association between the release of Netflix's 13 Reasons Why and suicide rates in the United States: An interrupted times series analysis. *Journal of the American Academy of Child & Adolescent Psychiatry, 64*, in press.

Bryner, J. (2009, June). TV causes learning lag in infants. *Live Science*. Retrieved from https://www.livescience.com/5480-tv-learning-lag-infants.html

Buckman, A. (2018, February 9). HGTV and the barn door-ization of America. *Media Post*. Retrieved from https://www.mediapost.com/publications/article/313968/hgtv-and-the-barn-door-ization-of-america.html

Bunch, W. (2019, January 3). Many papers (like this one) urged Bill Clinton to resign. Trump? Meh. Is that a problem? *Philadelphia Inquirer*. Retrieved from http://www.philly.com/opinion/commentary/newspaper-editorial-resignation-impeachment-donald-trump-bill-clinton-20190103.html

Carey, B. (2018, July 3). Hold the brain scans and antidepressants. *New York Times*, p. B5.

Carey, J. W. (1989). *Communication as culture: Essays on media and society*. Winchester, MA: Unwin Hyman.

Carey, J. W. (1996). The Chigaco School and mass communication research. In E. E. Dennis & E. Wartella (Eds.), *American communication research: The remembered history* (pp. 21–38). New York: Routledge.

Chandra, A., Martino, S. C., Collins, R. L., Elliott, M. N., Berry, S. H., Kanouse, D. E., & Miu, A. (2008). Does watching sex on television predict teen pregnancy? Findings from a national longitudinal survey of youth. *Pediatrics, 122*, 1047–1054.

Chomsky, N. (1969). *American power and the new mandarins*. New York: Pantheon.

Chomsky, N. (1991). *Deterring democracy*. New York: Verso.

Corcoran, M. (2016, February 11). Democracy in peril: Twenty years of media consolidation under Telecommunications Act. *Truthout*. Retrieved from http://www.truth-out.org/news/item/34789-democracy-in-peril-twenty-years-of-media-consolidation-under-the-telecommunications-act

Coulter, A. (2006). *Godless: The church of liberalism*. New York: Crown.

Curnalia, R. M. L. (2005). A retrospective on early studies of propaganda and suggestions for reviving the paradigm. *The Review of Communication, 5*, 237–257.

Davies, D. R. (1997). An industry in transition: Major trends in American daily newspapers, 1945–1965 (doctoral dissertation). Retrieved from http://ocean.otr.usm.edu/~w304644/ch4.html

Davis, R. E. (1976). *Response to innovation: A study of popular argument about new mass media*. New York: Arno.

Dewey, J. (1927). *The public and its problems*. New York: Holt.

Drutman, L., Diamond, L., & Goldman, J. (2018, March). Follow the leader: Exploring American support for democracy and authoritarianism. *Voter Study Group*. Retrieved from https://www.voterstudygroup.org/publications/2017-voter-survey/follow-the-leader

Dunstan, D. W., Barr, E. L. M., Healy, G. N., Salmon, J., Shaw, J. E., Balkau, B., Magliano, D. J., Cameron, A. J., Zimmet, P. Z., & Owen, N. (2010). Television viewing time and mortality. The Australian diabetes, obesity and lifestyle study. *Circulation, 121*, 384–391.

Dwoskin, E., & Gowen, A. (2018, July 24). On WhatsApp, fake news is fast—and can be fatal. *Washington Post*. Retrieved from https://www.washingtonpost.com/business/economy/on-whatsapp-fake-news-is-fast—and-can-be-fatal/2018/07/23/a2dd7112-8ebf-11e8-bcd5-9d911c784c38_story.html?noredirect=on&utm_term=.740897432987

Fazio, L. K., Brashier, N. M., Payne, B. K., & Marsh, E. J. (2015). Knowledge does not protect against illusory truth. *Journal of Experimental Psychology: General, 144*, 993–1002.

FOX's file. (2018). *Politifact*. Retrieved from https://www.politifact.com/punditfact/tv/fox/

Frenkel, S., Conger, K., & Roose, K. (2019, February 1). After Russia, false posts on Twitter going global. *New York Times*, p. B1.

Friedman, U. (2018, January 21). Trust is collapsing in America. *Atlantic*. Retrieved from https://www.theatlantic.com/international/archive/2018/01/trust-trump-america-world/550964/

Fukuyama, F. (1999, May). The great disruption: Human nature and the reconstruction of social order. *Atlantic Monthly*, pp. 55–80.

Galbraith, J. K. (2019, January 2). Piketty's World Inequality Review: A critical analysis. *Institute for New Economic Thinking*. Retrieved from https://www.ineteconomics.org/perspectives/blog/pikettys-world-inequality-review-a-critical-analysis

Gelles, D. (2018, January 9). Prodding Apple on addiction. *New York Times*, p. B1.

Gitlin, T. (1991). Bites and blips: Chunk news, savvy talk, and the bifurcation of American politics. In P. Dahlgren & C. Sparks (Eds.), *Communication and citizenship: Journalism and the public sphere in the new media age* (pp. 119–136). London: Routledge.

Gold, H. (2014, May 6). Survey: 7 percent of reporters identify as Republican. *Politico*. Retrieved from https://www.politico.com/blogs/media/2014/05/survey-7-percent-of-reporters-identify-as-republican-188053

Goldberg, B. (2003). *Arrogance: Rescuing America from the media elite*. New York: Warner Books.

Goldberg, B. (2009). *A slobbering love affair: The true (and pathetic) story of the torrid romance between Barack Obama and the mainstream media*. Washington, DC: Regnery.

Gomez, P. (2018, August 19). Giuliani says "Truth isn't truth" in defense of Trump's legal strategy. *New York Times*. Retrieved from https://www.nytimes.com/2018/08/19/us/giuliani-meet-the-press-truth-is-not-truth.html?hp&action=click&pgtype=Homepage&clickSource=story-heading&module=first-column-region&region=top-news&WT.nav=top-news

Greitemeyer, T. (2013). Exposure to media with pro-social content reduces the propensity for reckless and risky driving. *Journal of Risk Research, 16*, 583–594.

Guilford, G. (2018, May 3). The epic mistake about manufacturing that's cost Americans millions of jobs. *Quartz*. Retrieved from https://qz.com/1269172/the-epic-mistake-about-manufacturing-thats-cost-americans-millions-of-jobs/

Herman, E. S., & Chomsky, N. (1988). *Manufacturing consent*. New York: Pantheon.

Hobbs, R., & McGee, S. (2014). Teaching about propaganda: An examination of the historical roots of media literacy. *Journal of Media Literacy Education, 6*, 56–67.

Howard, R. (2016, June 20). Ultra-right ministers call Pulse shooting God's wrath. *Gayly*. Retrieved from http://www.gayly.com/ultra-right-ministers-call-pulse-shooting-god%E2%80%99s-wrath

Ifeanyi, K. C. (2018, April 16). Women who watched "The X-Files" pursued more careers in STEM. *Fast Company*. Retrieved from https://www.fastcompany.com/40558899/women-who-watched-the-x-files-pursued-more-careers-in-stem

Institute of Politics & David Axelrod. (2018, August 18). Ep. 264—Dean Baquet & Marty Baron. *Axe Files*. CNN. Retrieved from https://www.cnn.com/specials/politics/axe-files

Jamieson, K. H. (2018). *Cyberwar: How Russian hackers and trolls helped elect a president*. New York: Oxford University Press.

Jamieson, K. H., & Waldman, P. (2003). *The press effect*. New York: Oxford University Press.

Jones, B. (2019, February 5). Republicans and Democrats have grown further apart on what the nation's top priorities should be. *Pew Research Center*. Retrieved from http://www.pewresearch.org/fact-tank/2019/02/05/republicans-and-democrats-have-grown-further-apart-on-what-the-nations-top-priorities-should-be/

Jowett, G. S., & O'Donnell, V. (1999). *Propaganda and persuasion*. Thousand Oaks, CA: Sage.

KBOI Web Staff. (2013, March 14). No premarital sex on television please, lawmakers urge. *KBOI2.com*. Retrieved from https://idahonews.com/news/local/no-premarital-sex-on-television-please-lawmakers-urge

Kircher, M. M. (2017, November 9). Sean Parker: We built Facebook to exploit you. *New York Magazine*. Retrieved from http://nymag.com/selectall/2017/11/facebook-sean-parker-talks-about-psychology-of-hooking-users.html

Krause, E., & Sawhill, I. V. (2018, June 5). Seven reasons to worry about the American middle class. *Brookings Institute*. Retrieved from https://www.brookings.edu/blog/social-mobility-memos/2018/06/05/seven-reasons-to-worry-about-the-american-middle-class/

Laitinen, R. E., & Rakos, R. F. (1997). Corporate control of media and propaganda: A behavior analysis. In P. A. Lamal (Ed.), *Cultural contingencies: behavior analytic perspectives on cultural practices* (pp. 237–267). Westport, CT: Praeger.

Lang, K., & Lang, G. E. (2009). Mass society, mass culture, and mass communication: The meaning of mass. *International Journal of Communication, 3*, 998–1024.

Lasswell, H. D. (1927a). *Propaganda technique in the World War*. New York: Knopf.

Lasswell, H. D. (1927b). The theory of political propaganda. *American Political Science Review, 21*, 627–631.

Lasswell, H. D. (1934). *World politics and personal insecurity*. Chicago: University of Chicago Press.

Lind, D. (2018, April 13). The US has all but slammed the door on Syrian refugees. *Vox.com*. Retrieved from https://www.vox.com/2018/4/13/17233856/syria-attack-refugees-war-assad-trump

Lippmann, W. (1922). *Public opinion.* New York: Macmillan.

Macdonald, D. (1953). A theory of mass culture. *Diogenes, 1,* 1–17.

Maldonado, A. (2017, August 20). Can Disney fix its broken "Princess Culture"? *Salon.* Retrieved from https://www.salon.com/2017/08/20/disney-princesses-dream-big-girl-up/

Mandese, J. (2018, August 28). Global marketing approaches $1.3 trillion, U.S. = two-fifths of it. *MediaPost.* Retrieved from https://www.mediapost.com/publications/article/324030/global-marketing-approaches-13-trillion-us.html?utm_source=newsletter&utm_medium=email&utm_content=headline&utm_cam paign=110624&has hid=t7UjdKvzy7DLtjNFSFu0JxMrZIo

Marcuse, H. (1941). Some social implications of modern technology. In A. Arato & E. Gebhardt (Eds.), (1978). *The essential Frankfurt School reader* (pp. 138–162). New York: Urizen.

Marshall, A. G. (2013, April 12). The propaganda system that has helped create a permanent overclass is over a century in the making. *Alternet.* Retrieved from http://www.alternet.org/media/propaganda-system-has-helped-create-permanent-overclass-over-century-making?page=0%2C0

Martindale, D. (1960). *The nature and types of sociological theory.* Boston: Houghton-Mifflin.

Mathis-Lilley, B. (2018, January 30). In what is probably not a good sign, the Pentagon is censoring data about whether we're winning in Afghanistan. *Slate.* Retrieved from https://slate.com/news-and-politics/2018/01/pentagon-censors-afghanistan-data.html

Matson, F. M. (1964). *The broken image: Man, science, and society.* New York: Braziller.

McChesney, R. W. (1997). *Corporate media and the threat to democracy.* New York: Seven Stories.

McChesney, R. W. (2004). *The problem of the media: U.S. communication politics in the 21st Century.* New York: Monthly Review Press.

McChesney, R. W. (2013). *Dollarocracy: How the money-and-media-election complex is destroying America.* New York: Nation Books.

Meet the Press. (2017, January 22). *NBC News.* Retrieved from https://www.nbcnews.com/meet-the-press/meet-press-01-22-17-n710491

Menand, L. (2017, August 28). The stone guest. *The New Yorker,* pp. 75–82.

Mitchell, G. (2009, April 16). *Watchdogs failed to bark on economy. Editor & Publisher,* p. 16.

Moffitt, B. (2016). *The global rise of populism: performance, political style, and representation.* Stanford, CA: Stanford University Press.

Molla, R., & Kafka, P. (2018, June 18). Here's who owns everything in Big Media today. *Recode.* Retrieved from https://www.recode.net/2018/1/23/16905844/media-landscape-verizon-amazon-comcast-disney-fox-relationships-chart

Morris, D., & McGann, E. (2008). *Fleeced.* New York: Harper.

Mudde, C., & Kaltwaser, C. R. (2017). *Populism: A very short introduction.* New York: Oxford University Press.

Murphy, S. T., Frank, L. B., Chatterjee, J. S., & Baezconde-Garbanati, L. (2013). Narrative versus nonnarrative: The role of identification, transportation, and emotion in reducing health disparities. *Journal of Communication, 63,* 116–137.

Nordland, R., Ngu, A., & Abed, F. (2018, September 9). How the US government misleads the public on Afghanistan. *New York Times,* p. 12.

Nyhan, B. (2019, February 4). Why fears of fake news are overhyped. *Medium.* Retrieved from https://medium.com/s/reasonable-doubt/why-fears-of-fake-news-are-overhyped-2ed9ca0a52c9

Parker-Pope, T. (2011, February 22). Cellphone use tied to changes in brain activity. *New York Times.* Retrieved from https://well.blogs.nytimes.com/2011/02/22/cellphone-use-tied-to-changes-in-brain-activity/

Pratkanis, A. R., & Aronson, E. (1992). *Age of propaganda: the everyday use and abuse of persuasion.* New York: W. H. Freeman.

The right overshadows the left. (2017, March 20). *The Nation,* p. 17.

Risen, J. (2018, August 18). Donald Trump is a dangerous demagogue. It's time for a crusading press to fight back. *Intercept.* Retrieved from https://theintercept.com/2018/08/16/donald-trump-media-enemy-of-the-people/

Rosenberg, E. (2018, April 3). Trump said Sinclair "is far superior to CNN." What we know about the conservative media giant. *Washington Post.* Retrieved from https://www.washingtonpost.com/news/style/wp/2018/04/02/get-to-know-sinclair-broadcast-group-the-conservative-local-news-giant-with-a-growing-reach/?utm_term=.1354610ed595

Rosenstiel, T., & Elizabeth, J. (2018, May 9). Journalists can change the way they build stories to create organic news fluency. *American Press Institute*. Retrieved from https://www.americanpressinstitute.org/publications/reports/white-papers/organic-news-fluency/

Schiappa, E., Gregg, P. B., & Hewes, D. E. (2005). The parasocial contact hypothesis. *Communication Monographs, 72*, 92–115.

Schiller, H. I. (1989). *Culture, Inc.: The corporate takeover of public expression*. New York: Oxford University Press.

Scruton, R. (2000). *An intelligent person's guide to modern culture*. South Bend, IN: St. Augustine's Press.

Shapiro, B. (2011). *Primetime propaganda: The true Hollywood story of how the left took over your TV*. New York: Harper Collins.

Shils, E. (1962). The theory of mass society: Prefatory remarks. *Diogenes, 10*, 45–66.

Smith, B. L. (1941). Propaganda analysis and the science of democracy. *Public Opinion Quarterly, 5*, 250–259.

Snowball, D. (1999). Propaganda and its discontents. *Journal of Communication, 49*, 165–172.

Snyder, T. (2017). *On tyranny: Twenty lessons from the Twentieth Century*. New York: Tim Duggan Biiks.

Sproule, J. M. (1987). Propaganda studies in American social science: The rise and fall of the critical paradigm. *Quarterly Journal of Speech, 73*, 60–78.

Sproule, J. M. (1994). *Channels of propaganda*. Bloomington, IN: EDINFO.

Sproule, J. M. (1997). *Propaganda and democracy: The American experience of media and mass persuasion*. New York: Cambridge University Press.

Stanley, J. (2015). *How propaganda works*. Princeton, NJ: Princeton University Press.

Stein, S. (2018, August 7). New poll: 43% of Republicans want to give Trump power to shut down media. *Daily Beast*. Retrieved from https://www.thedailybeast.com/new-poll-43-of-republicans-want-to-give-trump-the-power-to-shut-down-media

Sullivan, A. (2018, March 18). Can Donald Trump be impeached? *New York Times Book Review*, p. 1.

Suskind, R. (2004). *The price of loyalty: George W. Bush, the White House, and the education of Paul O'Neill*. New York: Simon & Schuster.

Thomson, O. (1977). *Mass persuasion in history*. Edinburgh, UK: Paul Harris.

Tillinghast, C. H. (2000). *American broadcast regulation and the First Amendment: Another look*. Ames: Iowa State University Press.

Tönnies, F. ([1887/ 1922). *Gemeinschaft und gesellschaft: grundbegriffe der reinen soziologie* (4th ed.). Berlin: Curtius.

Vaglanos, A. (2019, August 5). Ohio GOP lawmaker blames mass shootings on trans people, gay marriage and more. *Huffington Post*. Retrieved from https://www.huffpost.com/entry/ohio-gop-mass-shootings-trans-people-gay-marriage_n_5d481fbfe4b0acb57fcfe3e1

Williams, J. (2017, October 30). Juan Williams: Trump's war on media is truly dangerous. *The Hill*. Retrieved from http://thehill.com/opinion/white-house/357748-juan-williams-trumps-war-on-media-is-truly-dangerous

Wineburg, S., McGrew, S., Breakstone, J., & Ortega, T. (2016, November 22). Evaluating information: The cornerstone of civic online reasoning. *Stanford Digital Repository*. Retrieved from http://purl.stanford.edu/fv751yt5934

Wise, J. (2018, July 24). Trump: What you're seeing in the news "is not what's happening." *The Hill*. Retrieved from http://thehill.com/homenews/administration/398606-trump-what-youre-seeing-in-the-news-is-not-whats-happening-inbox-x

"World War II: The Propaganda Battle." *A Walk through the 20th Century with Bill Moyers*. (1984). New York: PBS Video.

Ybarra, M. L., Diener-West, M., Markow, D., Leaf, P. J., Hamburger, M., & Boxer, P. (2008). Linkages between Internet and other media violence with seriously violent behavior by youth. *Pediatrics, 122*, 929–937.

CHAPTER 3

Adams-Bloom, T., & Cleary, J. (2009). Staking a claim for social responsibility: An argument for the dual responsibility model. *International Journal on Media Management, 11*, 1–8.

Alster, N. (2015). Captured agency: How the Federal Communications Commission is dominated by the industries it presumably regulates. *Edmond J. Safra Center for Ethics*. Cambridge, MA: Harvard University.

Alterman, E. (2017, July 3/10). A climate of denial. *The Nation*, pp. 6–7.

Alterman, E. (2018, January 31). The news is breaking. *Nation*. Retrieved from https://www.thenation.com/article/the-news-is-breaking/

Altschull, J. H. (1990). *From Milton to McLuhan: The ideas behind American journalism*. New York: Longman.

Altschull, J. H. (1995). *Agents of power: The media and public policy*. White Plains, NY: Longman.

Anderson, M., & Jiang, J. (2018, May 31). Teens, social media & technology 2018. *Pew Research Center*. Retrieved from http://www.pewinternet.org/2018/05/31/teens-social-media-technology-2018/

Apuzzo, M., & LaFraniere, S. (2018, February 17). Indictment bares Russian network to twist 2016 vote. *New York Times*, p. A1.

Barnouw, E. (1966). *A history of broadcasting in the United States: A tower in Babel, vol. 1*. New York: Oxford University Press.

Barthel, M. (2018, August 21). 5 Facts about the state of the news media in 2017. *Pew Research Center*. Retrieved from http://www.pewresearch.org/fact-tank/2018/08/21/5-facts-about-the-state-of-the-news-media-in-2017/

Bates, S. (1995). *Realigning journalism with democracy: The Hutchins Commission, its times, and ours*. Washington, DC: The Annenberg Washington Program in Communications Policy Studies of Northwestern University.

Bennett, W. L. (1988). *News: The politics of illusion*, 2nd ed. New York: Longman.

Benton, J. (2016, November 9). The forces that drove this election's media failure are likely to get worse. *Nieman Lab*. Retrieved from http://www.niemanlab.org/2016/11/the-forces-that-drove-this-elections-media-failure-are-likely-to-get-worse/

Bollinger, L. C. (2018, May 30). Remarks by Columbia University president Lee C. Bollinger. *Columbia University*. Retrieved from https://president.columbia.edu/content/2018-pulitzer

Brisbane, A. S. (2012, January 12). Should *The Times* be a truth vigilante? *New York Times*. Retrieved from http://publiceditor.blogs.nytimes.com/2012/01/12/should-the-times-be-a-truth-vigilante/

Bromwich, J. E. (2018, April 22). Pulp fiction: Podcasts go mass-market. *New York Times*, p. ST4.

Chait, J. (2016, July 25). The case against the media, by the media. *New York Magazine*. Retrieved from http://nymag.com/daily/intelligencer/2016/07/case-against-media.html

Christians, C. G., Ferre, J. P., & Fackler, P. M. (1993). *Good news: Social ethics and the press*. New York: Oxford University Press.

Coleman, S., & Blumler, J. G. (2009). *The internet and democratic citizenship: Theory, practice, and policy*. New York: Cambridge University Press.

Colistra, R. (2018). Power pressures and pocketbook concerns: Perceptions of organizational influences on news content in the television industry. *International Journal of Communication, 12,* 1790–1810.

Commission on Freedom of the Press. (1947). *A free and responsible press*. Chicago: University of Chicago Press.

Concha, J. (2019, March 12). Dem lawmakers unveil Journalist Protection Act amid Trump attacks on media. *The Hill*. Retrieved from https://thehill.com/homenews/media/433709-dem-lawmakers-unveil-journalist-protection-act-amid-trump-attacks-on-media

Cooper, A. (2008, September/October). The bigger tent. *Columbia Journalism Review*, pp. 45–47.

Coppins, M. (2017, Fall). What if the right-wing media wins? *Columbia Journalism Review*, pp. 52–59.

Curran, J. (1991). Mass media and democracy: A reappraisal. In J. Curran & M. Gurevitch (Eds.), *Mass media and society* (pp. 82–117). London: Edward Arnold.

Davis, D. K. (1990). News and politics. In D. L. Swanson & D. Nimmo (Eds.), *New directions in political communication: A resource book* (pp. 147–184). Newbury Park, CA: Sage.

Davis, D. K., & Robinson, J. P. (1989). Newsflow and democratic society in an age of electronic media." In G. Comstock (Ed.), *Public communication and behavior, vol. 3* (pp. 59–102). New York: Academic.

Durkin, E. (2018, August 15). Almost 350 news outlets to publish editorials denouncing Trump's "dirty war" on press. *Guardian*. Retrieved from https://www.theguardian.com/us-news/2018/aug/15/trump-press-editorials-defence-fake-news-media-attacks-us

Epstein, E. J. (1973). *News from nowhere: Television and the news*. New York: Random House.

Fishburne, C. (2019, April 2). Wason poll: "Enemy of the people attacks" like "kerosene" for GOP. *NPR Community Idea Stations*. Retrieved from https://ideastations.org/node/324395

Fishman, M. (1980). *Manufacturing the news*. Austin: University of Texas Press.

Frei, W. (2018, August 17). Senate unanimously passes resolution asserting that the press isn't the enemy. *Huffington Post*. Retrieved from https://www.huffingtonpost.com/entry/senate-resolution-press-not-enemy_us_5b769c22e4b018b93e92c999

Friedman, W. (2018, August 24). Trump squawks, but consumer trust in media rises. *MediaPost*.

Retrieved from https://www.mediapost.com/publications/article/324050/trump-squawks-but-consumer-trust-in-media-rises.html

Galbraith, J. K. (2019, January 2). Piketty's World Inequality Review: A critical analysis. *Institute for New Economic Thinking*. Retrieved from https://www.ineteconomics.org/perspectives/blog/pikettys-world-inequality-review-a-critical-analysis

Gans, H. (1979). *Deciding what's news: A study of CBS Evening News, NBC Nightly News, Newsweek and Time*. New York: Pantheon Books.

Gillmor, D. M., & Barron, J. A. (1974). *Mass communication law. Cases and comments*. St. Paul, MN: West.

Gilmor, D. (2004). *We the media—Grassroots journalism by the people, for the people*. Sebastopol, CA: O'Reilly.

Glasgow University Media Group, eds. (1976). *Bad news*. London: Routledge and Kegan Paul.

Glasgow University Media Group, eds. (1980). *More bad news*. London: Routledge and Kegan Paul.

Goode, L. (2009). Social news, citizen journalism and democracy. *New Media & Society, 11*, 1287–1305.

Goodman, M. (2001). The Radio Act of 1927 as a product of progressivism. *Media History Monographs*. Retrieved from https://www.scripps.ohiou.edu/mediahistory/mhmjour2-2.htm

Gottfried, J., & Shearer, E. (2017, September 7). Americans' online news use is closing in on TV news use. *Pew Research Center*. Retrieved from http://www.pewresearch.org/fact-tank/2017/09/07/americans-online-news-use-vs-tv-news-use/

Graber, D. A. (1987). *Processing the news*, 2nd ed. New York: Longman.

Greenwald, G. (2009, January 6). Jay Rosen on the media's control of political debates. *Salon*. Retrieved from https://www.salon.com/2009/01/16/rosen/

Grieco, E. (2019, July 9). US newsroom employment has dropped by a quarter since 2008, with greatest decline at newspapers. *Pew Research Center*. Retrieved from https://www.pewresearch.org/fact-tank/2019/07/09/u-s-newsroom-employment-has-dropped-by-a-quarter-since-2008/

Grothaus, M. (2018a, September 7). Get ready for the "splinternet": The web might not be worldwide much longer. *Fast Company*. Retrieved from https://www.fastcompany.com/90229453/get-ready-for-the-splinternet-the-web-might-not-be-worldwide-much-longer

Grothaus, M. (2018b, September 7). Twitter finally permanently bans Alex Jones and Infowars. *Fast Company*. Retrieved from https://www.fastcompany.com/90233481/twitter-finally-permanently-bans-alex-jones-and-infowars

Hachten, W. A. (1992). *The world news prism*. Ames, IA: Iowa State University Press.

Hallin, D. C. (1986). *The uncensored war: The media & Vietnam*. New York: Oxford University Press.

Heim, J. (2018, February 21). Hate groups in the U.S. remain on the rise, according to new study. *Washington Post*. Retrieved from https://www.washingtonpost.com/local/hate-groups-in-the-us-remain-on-the-rise-according-to-new-study/2018/02/21/6d28cbe0-1695-11e8-8b08-027a6ccb38eb_story.html?utm_term=.5462877db54d

House of Commons Digital, Culture, Media, and Sport Committee. (2019). *Disinformation and "fake news": Final report*. London, UK: House of Commons.

Howard, P. N., Duffy, A., Freelon, D., Hussain, M., Mari, W., & Mazaid, M. (2011, September 1). Opening closed regimes. *Project on Information Technology & Political Islam*. Retrieved from http://philhoward.org/opening-closed-regimes-what-was-the-role-of-social-media-during-the-arab-spring/

Huang, C. (2003). Transitional media vs. normative theories: Schramm, Altschull, and China. *Journal of Communication, 53*, 444–459.

Internet users in the world by regions—March, 2019. (2019). *Internet Society*. Retrieved from https://www.internetworldstats.com/stats.htm

Jensen, R. (2010, May 20). The collapse of journalism, and the journalism of collapse. *Truthout*. Retrieved from https://truthout.org/articles/the-collapse-of-journalism-and-the-journalism-of-collapse/

Johnson, K. (2018, January 7). For voices of low-power radio, a collective shout. *New York Times*, p. A16.

Jones, S. (2018). The great remove. *Columbia Journalism Review*, pp. 74–80.

Katsingris, P. (2018). The Nielsen total audience report, Q1, 2018. *The Nielsen Company*. Retrieved from http://www.nielsen.com/us/en/insights/reports/2018/q1-2018-total-audience-report.html

Keane, J. (1991). *The media and democracy*. Cambridge: Polity Press.

Landler, M. (2018, July 30). *Times* publisher and Trump clash over President's threats against press image. *New York Times*, p. A12.

Lavey, W. G. (1993). Inconsistencies in applications of economics at the Federal Communications Commission. *Federal Communications Law Journal, 45*, 437–490.

Lepore, J. (2019, January 28). Hard news. *New York Times Magazine*, pp. 18–24.

Lind, R. A., & Rockier, N. (2001). Competing ethos: Reliance on profit versus social responsibility by laypeople planning a television newscast. *Journal of Broadcasting and Electronic Media*, 45, 118–134.

MacDonald, T., & Hymas, L. (2019, March 11). How broadcast TV networks covered climate change in 2018. *Media Matters*. Retrieved from https://www.mediamatters.org/research/2019/03/11/How-broadcast-TV-networks-covered-climate-change-in-2018/223076

Magra, I. (2019, February 12). BBC cameraman is attacked at Trump rally. *New York Times*. Retrieved from https://www.nytimes.com/2019/02/12/us/politics/bbc-cameraman-attacked.html

Marantz, A. (2018, March 19). Antisocial media. *The New Yorker*, pp. 58–67.

Marsh, D. (2012, October 16). Digital age rewrites the role of journalism. *Guardian*. Retrieved from https://www.theguardian.com/sustainability/sustainability-report-2012-people-nuj

McIntyre, J. S. (1987). Repositioning a landmark: The Hutchins Commission and freedom of the press. *Critical Studies in Mass Communication*, 4, 95–135.

McQuail, D. (2010). *Mass communication theory: An introduction*, 6th ed. London: Sage.

McQuail, D. (2005). *Mass communication theory: An introduction*, 5th ed. Thousand Oaks, CA: Sage.

Meiklejohn, A. (1960). *Political freedom*. New York: Harper.

Misra, T. (2019, February 14). Why the rural opioid crisis is different from the urban one. *City Lab*. Retrieved from https://www.citylab.com/equity/2019/02/opioid-epidemic-data-drug-addiction-deaths-urban-rural/582502/

Moyers, B. (2001, May 7). Journalism and democracy: On the importance of being a "public nuisance." *The Nation*, pp. 11–17.

Moynihan, M. (2012, October 14). Nicholas Lemann: Journalism is doing just fine. *Daily Beast*. Retrieved from http://www.thedailybeast.com/articles/2012/10/14/nicholas-lemann-journalism-is-doing-just-fine.html

Napoli, P. M. (1999). The marketplace of ideas metaphor in communications regulation. *Journal of Communication*, 49, 151–169.

Neidig, H. (2017, December 12). Poll: 83 percent of voters support keeping FCC's net neutrality rules. *The Hill*. Retrieved from http://thehill.com/policy/technology/364528-poll-83-percent-of-voters-support-keeping-fccs-net-neutrality-rules

New York Times Co. v. United States, 403 U.S. 713 (1971).

Newman, R. (2019). Journalism, media and technology trends and predictions 2019. *Reuters Institute for the Study of Journalism*. Retrieved from http://www.digitalnewsreport.org/publications/2019/journalism-media-technology-trends-predictions-2019/

Noack, R., & Beck, L. (2018, December 20) When the news really is fake: German reporter admits fabricating coverage at leading news magazine. *Washington Post*. Retrieved from https://www.washingtonpost.com/world/2018/12/20/when-news-really-is-fake-german-reporter-admits-fabricating-coverage-leading-news-magazine/?utm_term=.5424b8b67847

Nordenson, B. (2008, November/December). Overload! *Columbia Journalism Review*, pp. 30–40.

Number of blogs in the United States from 2014 to 2020 (in millions). (2019). *Statista*. Retrieved from https://www.statista.com/statistics/187267/number-of-bloggers-in-usa/

Orso, A. (2019, April 1). In the age of "enemy of the people" rhetoric, do young people still want to be journalists? *Philadelphia Enquirer*. Retrieved from https://www.philly.com/news/journalism-young-people-donald-trump-fake-news-temple-penn-state-enemy-of-the-people-central-conestoga-20190401.html

Packer, G. (2006, October 16). Keep out. *The New Yorker*, pp. 59–60.

Papacharissi, Z. (2002). The virtual sphere: The Internet as a public sphere. *New Media & Society*, 4, 9–27.

Perez, C. (2017, August 13). White nationalists are being outed on Twitter—and one lost his job. *New York Post*. Retrieved from https://nypost.com/2017/08/13/white-nationalists-are-being-ousted-on-twitter-and-one-lost-his-job/

Perrin, A., & Jiang, J. (2018, March 14). About a quarter of US adults say they are "almost constantly" online. *Pew Research Center*. Retrieved from http://www.pewresearch.org/fact-tank/2018/03/14/about-a-quarter-of-americans-report-going-online-almost-constantly/

Pickard, V. (2010). Whether the giants should be slain or persuaded to be good: Revisiting the Hutchins Commission and the role of media in a democratic society. *Critical Studies in Media Communication*, 27, 391–411.

Quah, N. (2018, June 12). Grow the pie: Podcast revenue seems to be growing fast enough for everyone to get a slice. *Nieman Lab*. Retrieved from http://www.niemanlab.org/2018/06/grow-the-pie-podcast-revenue-seems-to-be-growing-fast-enough-for-everyone-to-get-a-slice/

The Radio Television Digital News Association's Code of Ethics and Professional Conduct. (2015). *Radio Television Digital News Association*. Retrieved from https://www.rtdna.org/content/rtdna_code_of_ethics

Raymond, A. K. (2018, August 30). "You're the enemy of the people": Man arrested for threatening to kill reporters. *New York Magazine*. Retrieved from http://nymag.com/daily/intelligencer/2018/08/man-who-quoted-trump-arrested-for-reporter-death-threats.html

Rosen, J. (2009, January 12). Audience atomization overcome: Why the internet weakens the authority of the press. *Pressthink*. Retrieved from http://archive.pressthink.org/2009/01/12/atomization.html

Rosen, J. (2012, January 12). So whaddaya think: Should we put truthtelling back up there at number one? *Pressthink*. Retrieved from http://pressthink.org/2012/01/so-whaddaya-think-should-we-put-truthtelling-back-up-there-at-number-one/

Selk, A. (2017, September 18). Chelsea Manning denies betraying the US, feels as if she lives in a "dystopian novel." *Washington Post*. Retrieved from https://www.washingtonpost.com/news/checkpoint/wp/2017/09/18/chelsea-manning-denies-betraying-the-u-s-feels-like-she-lives-in-a-dystopian-novel/?utm_term=.208662041ac8

Shearer, E., & Matsa, K. E. (2018, September 10). News use across social media platforms 2018. *Pew Research Center*. Retrieved from http://www.journalism.org/2018/09/10/news-use-across-social-media-platforms-2018/

Siebert, F. S., Peterson, T., & Schramm, W. (1956). *Four theories of the press*. Urbana, IL: University of Illinois Press.

Simon, T., Atwater, T., & Alexander, R. (1988, August). FCC broadcast content regulation: Policymaking in a vacuum. Paper presented at the annual meeting of the Association for Education in Journalism and Mass Communication, Portland, OR.

"Sizing up the damage to local newspapers." (2019, August 4). *New York Times*, p. F4.

Starr, P. (2012). An unexpected crisis: The news media in post-industrial democracies. *The International Journal of Press/Politics, 17*, 234–242

Stepp, C. S. (2006, February/March). The blog revolution. *American Journalism Review*, p. 62.

Stevenson, R. L. (1994). *Global communication in the twenty-first century*. New York: Longman.

Stoll, M., & McManus, J. (2005, April 1). Downward spiral: Many journalists say media's duties, ethics sliding in order to conform to the company's bottom line. *Quill*. Retrieved from http://www.gradethenews.org/2005/downwardspiral.htm

Timberg, C., & Dwoskin, W. (2018, July 6). Twitter is sweeping out fake accounts like never before, putting user growth at risk. *Washington Post*. Retrieved from https://www.washingtonpost.com/technology/2018/07/06/twitter-is-sweeping-out-fake-accounts-like-never-before-putting-user-growth-risk/

Trench, M. (1990). *Cyberpunk. Mystic fire videos*. New York: Intercon.

Tuchman, G. (1978). *Making news: A study in the construction of reality*. New York: Free Press.

Vosoughi, V., Roy, D., & Aral, S. (2018). The spread of true and false news online. *Science, 359*, 1146–1151.

Watson, A. (2019, May 28). Frequency of using selected news sources among millennials in the United States as of April 2019. *Statista*. Retrieved from https://www.statista.com/statistics/1010456/united-states-millennials-news-consumption/

Watts, D. J., & Rothschild, D. M. (2017, December 5). Don't blame the election on fake news. Blame it on the media. *Columbia Journalism Review*. Retrieved from https://www.cjr.org/analysis/fake-news-media-election-trump.php

Wojcik, S., Messing, S., Smith, A., Rainie, L., & Hitlin, P. (2018, April 9). Bots in the Twittersphere. *Pew Research Center*. Retrieved from http://www.pewinternet.org/2018/04/09/bots-in-the-twittersphere/

Wu, T. (2017, September). Is the First Amendment obsolete? *Knight First Amendment Institute*. Retrieved from https://knightcolumbia.org/content/tim-wu-first-amendment-obsolete

Yilek, C. (2015, December 21). Trump on journalists: I hate them, but wouldn't kill them. *The Hill*. Retrieved from http://thehill.com/blogs/ballot-box/presidential-races/263969-trump-on-journalists-i-hate-them-but-wouldnt-kill-them

Zuckerberg, M. (2017, February 16). Building Global Community. *Facebook*. Retrieved from https://www.facebook.com/notes/mark-zuckerberg/building-global-community/10154544292806634/

CHAPTER 4

Allport, G. W., & Postman, L. J. (1945). The basic psychology of rumor. *Transactions of the New York Academy of Sciences, 8*, 61–81.

Bakshy, E., Messing, S., & Adamic, L. A. (2015). Exposure to ideologically diverse news and opinion on Facebook. *Science, 348*, 1130–1132.

Charters, W. W. (1933). *Motion pictures and youth.* New York: MacMillan.

Crockett, Z. (2016, September 13). "Gang member" and "thug" roles in film are disproportionately played by black actors. *Vox.* Retrieved from https://www.vox.com/2016/9/13/12889478/black-actors-typecasting

DeFleur, M. L. (1970). *Theories of mass communication.* New York: David McKay.

Faris, R. M., Roberts, H., Etling, B., Bourassa, N., Zuckerman, E., & Benkler, Y. (2017). *Partisanship, propaganda, and disinformation: Online media and the 2016 U.S. presidential election.* Berkman Klein Center for Internet & Society Research Paper. Retrieved from https://dash.harvard.edu/handle/1/33759251

Festinger, L. (1957). *A theory of cognitive dissonance.* Stanford, CA: Stanford University Press.

Festinger, L. (1962). Cognitive dissonance. *Scientific American, 207*, 93.

Fletcher, M. A. (2018, April). For Black motorists, a never-ending fear of being stopped. *National Geographic.* Retrieved from https://www.nationalgeographic.com/magazine/2018/04/the-stop-race-police-traffic/

Garrett, R. K. (2009). Echo chambers online?: Politically motivated selective exposure among Internet news users. *Journal of Computer-mediated Communication, 14*, 265–285.

Gerbner, G. (1990). Epilogue: Advancing on the path of righteousness (maybe). In N. Signorielli & M. Morgan (Eds.), *Cultivation Analysis: New Directions in Media Effects Research* (pp. 249–262). Newbury Park, CA: Sage.

Gitlin, T. (1978). Media sociology. *Theory and Society, 6*, 205–253.

Gramlich, J. (2018, January 12). The gap between the number of blacks and whites in prison is shrinking. *Pew Research Center.* Retrieved form http://www.pewresearch.org/fact-tank/2018/01/12/shrinking-gap-between-number-of-blacks-and-whites-in-prison/

Hovland, C. I., Lumsdaine, A. A., & Sheffield, F. D. (1949). *Experiments on mass communication.* Princeton, NJ: Princeton University Press.

Iyengar, S., & Hahn, K. S. (2009). Red media, blue media: Evidence of ideological selectivity in media use. *Journal of Communication, 59*, 19–39.

Jowett, G. S., Jarvie, I., & Fuller, K. (1996) *Children and the movies: Media influence and the Payne Fund controversy.* New York: Cambridge University Press.

Kristof, N. (2009). The daily me. *New York Times,* p. A31.

Lazarsfeld, P. F., Berelson, B., & Gaudet, H. (1944). *The people's choice: How the voter makes up his mind in a presidential campaign.* New York: Duell, Sloan & Pearce.

Lazarsfeld, P. F., & Franzen, R. H. (1945). Prediction of political behavior in America. *American Sociological Review, 10*, 261–273.

Merton, R. K. (1967). *On theoretical sociology.* New York: Free Press.

Messing, S., & Westwood, S. J. (2014). Selective exposure in the age of social media: Endorsements trump partisan source affiliation when selecting news online. *Communication Research, 41*, 1042–1063.

Negroponte, N. (1995). *Being digital.* New York: Knopf.

Pooley, J. (2008). The new history of mass communication research. In D. W. Park & J. Pooley (Eds.), *The History of Media and Communication Research: Contested Memories* (pp. 43–69) New York: Peter Lang.

Posner, L. (2018, February 5). The Philadelphia Super Bowl riots expose a racist double standard. *Alternet.* Retrieved from https://www.alternet.org/news-amp-politics/philadelphia-super-bowl-riots-expose-racist-double-standard

Rosnow, R. L., & Robinson, E. J. (1967). *Experiments in persuasion.* New York: Academic.

Smiley, C. J., & Fakunle, D. (2016). From "brute" to "thug:" the demonization and criminalization of unarmed Black male victims in America. *Journal of Human Behavior in the Social Environment, 26*, 350–366.

Sobieraj, S., Berry, J. M., & Connors, A. (2013). Outrageous political opinion and political anxiety in the US. *Poetics, 41*, 407–432.

Tuchman, G., & Farberman, H. A. (1980). Facts of the moment: The study of news. *Symbolic Interaction, 3*, 9–20.

CHAPTER 5

Bauer, R. A., & Bauer, A. H. (1960). America, mass society, and mass media. *Journal of Social Issues, 10*, 3–66.

Berman, E. (2015, July 13). How the G.I. Bill changed the face of higher education in America. *Time.* Retrieved from http://time.com/3915231/student-veterans/

Bryant, J., & Miron, D. (2004). Theory and research in mass communication. *Journal of Communication, 54*, 662–704.

Campbell, A., Converse, P. W., Miller, W. E., & Stokes, D. E. (1960). *The American voter.* New York: Wiley.

Castro, D., & McQuinn, A. (2018, August 22). Most Americans are not that concerned about online privacy. *Information Technology and Innovation Foundation.* Retrieved from https://itif.org/publications/2018/08/22/most-americans-are-not-concerned-about-online-privacy

Davis, D. K. (1990). News and politics. In D. L. Swanson & D. Nimmo (Eds.), *New Directions in Political Communication* (pp. 147–184). Newbury Park, CA: Sage.

DeFleur, M. L., & Larsen, O. N. (1958). *The flow of information.* New York: Harper.

Funkhouser, G., & McCombs, M. (1971). The rise and fall of news diffusion. *Public Opinion Quarterly, 50*, 107–113.

Greenberg, B., & Parker, E. (Eds.) (1965). *The Kennedy assassination and the American public.* Stanford, CA: Stanford University Press.

Holbert, R. L., Garrett, R. K., & Gleason, L. S. (2010). A new era of minimal effects? A response to Bennett and Iyengar. *Journal of Communication, 60*, 15–34.

Katz, E., & Lazarsfeld, P. F. (1955). *Personal influence: The part played by people in the flow of communications.* New York: Free Press.

Kenny, C. (2009, November/December). Revolution in a box. *Foreign Policy*, pp. 68–74.

Klapper, J. T. (1960). *The effects of mass communication.* New York: Free Press.

Kornhauser, A., & Lazarsfeld, P. F. (1935). The technique of market research from the standpoint of a psychologist. *Institute of Management, 16*, 3–15, 19–21.

Kunkel, D., Wilcox, B.L., Cantor, J., Palmer, E., Linn, S., & Dowrick, R (2004). *Report of the APA task force on advertising and children.* Washington, DC: American Psychological Association.

Kuralt, C. (1977). *When television was young (videotape).* New York: CBS News.

Lasswell, H. D. (1949). The structure and function of communication in society. In W. S. Schramm (Ed.), *Mass communication* (pp. 216–228). Urbana, IL: University of Illinois Press.

Lazarsfeld, P. F., & Merton, R. K. (1948). Mass communication, popular taste and organized social action. In L. Bryson (Ed.), *The communication of ideas: A series of addresses* (pp. 95–118). New York: Institute for Religious and Social Studies.

Mendelsohn, H. (1966). *Mass entertainment.* New Haven, CT: College and University Press.

Merton, R. K. (1949). *Social theory and social structure.* Glencoe, IL: Free Press.

Merton, R. K. (1967). *On theoretical sociology.* New York: Free Press.

Mills, C. W. (1951). *White collar: The American middle classes.* New York: Oxford University Press.

Mills, C. W. (1956). *The power elite.* New York: Oxford University Press.

Mills, C. W. (1959). *The sociological imagination.* New York: Oxford University Press.

Potter, W. J. (2009). *Arguing for a general framework for mass media scholarship.* Thousand Oaks, CA: Sage.

Pooley, J. (2006). Fifteen pages that shook the field: Personal influence, Edward Shils, and the remembered history of mass communication research. *The ANNALS of the American Academy of Political and Social Science, 608*, 130–156.

Schramm, W., Lyle, J., & Parker, E. (Eds.), (1961). *Television in the lives of our children.* Stanford, CA: Stanford University Press.

Summers, J. H. (2006, May 14). The deciders. *New York Times Book Review*, p. 39.

Wiener, N. (1954). *The Human use of human beings: Cybernetics and society.* Garden City, NY: Doubleday Anchor.

Wiener, N. (1961). *Cybernetics* (2nd ed.). Cambridge, MA: MIT Press.

Wright, C. R. (1959). *Mass communication: A sociological perspective.* New York: Random House.

CHAPTER 6

Adorno, T., & Horkheimer, M. (1972). *Dialectic of enlightenment.* New York: Herder and Herder.

Althusser, L. (1970). *For Marx. Translation by Ben Brewster.* New York: Vintage.

Arato, A., & Gebhardt, E. (Eds.). (1978). *The essential Frankfurt School reader.* New York: Urizen.

Bennett, W. L. (1988). *News: The politics of illusion*, 2nd ed. New York: Longman.

Bennett, W. L. (2005). *News: The politics of illusion*, 6th ed. New York: Longman.

Bloom, A. D. (1987). *The closing of the American mind: How higher education has failed democracy and impoverished the souls of today's students.* New York: Simon & Schuster.

Boswell, A. A., & Spade, J. Z. (1996). Fraternities and collegiate rape culture: Why are some fraternities more dangerous places for women? *Gender and Society, 2,* 133-147.

Campbell, W. J. (2011, June 8). Bra-burning, a myth "that will never die?" *Media Myth Alert.* Retrieved from http://mediamythalert.wordpress.com/2011/06/08/bra-burning-a-media-myth-that-will-never-die/

Caplan, S. E. (2005). A social skill account of problematic internet use. *Journal of Communication, 55,* 721–736.

Carey, J. (1975). Culture and communication. *Communication Research, 2,* 173–191.

Carey, J. (1989). *Communication as culture: Essays on media and society.* Winchester, MA: Unwin Hyman.

Carr, D. (2011, January 9). Media savant. *New York Times Book Review,* pp. 1, 10–11.

Cissel, M. (2012). Media framing: A comparative content analysis on mainstream and alternative news coverage of Occupy Wall Street. *The Elon Journal of Undergraduate Research in Communications, 3,* 67–77.

Crenshaw, K. (1989). Demarginalizing the intersection of race and sex: A Black feminist critique of antidiscrimination doctrine, feminist theory and antiracist policy. *University of Chicago Legal Forum, 1,* 139–167.

Crouse, T. (1973). *The boys on the bus.* New York: Random House.

Desmond, M. (2018, September 16). Why work doesn't work anymore. *New York Times Magazine,* pp. 36–41, 36–49.

Duncan-Shippy, E. M., Murphy, S. C., & Purdy, M. A. (2017). An examination of mainstream media as an educating institution: The Black Lives Matter Movement and contemporary social protest. In R. M. Elmesky, C. C. Yeakey, & O. Marcucci (Eds.) *The power of resistance (Advances in education in diverse communities: Research, policy and praxis, vol. 12),* pp. 99–142. Sommerville, MA: Emerald Publishing Limited.

Eidelson, J. (2011, July 13). Welcome to TV-ville, population: People richer than you. *Dissent.* Retrieved from https://www.dissentmagazine.org/blog/welcome-to-tv-ville-population-people-richer-than-you

Epstein, E. J. (1973). *News from nowhere: Television and the news.* New York: Random House.

Fishman, M. (1980). *Manufacturing the news.* Austin: University of Texas Press.

Ford, T. E. (2000). Effects of sexist humor on tolerance of sexist events. *Personality and Social Psychology Bulletin, 26,* 1094–1107.

Ford, T. E., Boxer, C. F., Armstrong, J., & Edel, J. R. (2008). More than "just a joke": The prejudice-releasing function of sexist humor. *Personality and Social Psychology Bulletin, 34,* 159–170.

Gabler, N. (2016, April 24). The mainstream media's big disconnect: Why they don't get Middle America. *Alternet.* Retrieved from http://www.alternet.org/media/mainstream-medias-big-disconnect-why-they-dont-get-middle-america

Gans, H. (1972). *The politics of culture in America: A sociological analysis.* In D. McQuail (Ed.), *Sociology of Mass Communication* (pp. 372–385). Harmondsworth, England: Penguin.

Gans, H. (1979). *Deciding what's news: A study of CBS Evening News, NBC Nightly News, Newsweek and Time.* New York: Pantheon Books.

Garces, M., & Rendall, S. (2012, September). Media not concerned about the very poor. *Fair.* Retrieved from https://fair.org/extra/media-not-concerned-about-the-very-poor/

Garnham, N. (1995). Political economy and cultural studies: Reconciliation or divorce? *Critical Studies in Mass Communication, 12,* 95–100.

Gerbner, G. (2001). The cultural arm of the corporate establishment: Reflections on the work of Herb Schiller. *Journal of Broadcasting and Electronic Media, 45,* 186–190.

Giroux, H. (2011). The crisis of public values in the age of new media. *Critical Studies in Media Communication, 28,* 8–29.

Gitlin, T. (1980). *The whole world is watching: Mass media in the making and unmaking of the New Left.* Berkeley: University of California Press.

Gold, H. R. (2018, September 17). Ten years after the financial crisis, business journalism awaits its reckoning. *Columbia Journalism Review.* Retrieved from https://www.cjr.org/business_of_news/ten-years-financial-crisis-business-journalism.php

Goldberg, M. (2019, February 24). Not the fun kind of feminist. *New York Times,* p. 4.

Goodman, A. (2004). *The exception to the rulers: Exposing oily politicians, war profiteers, and the media that love them.* New York: Hyperion.

Greene, V., & Day, A. (2020). Asking for it: Rape myths, satire, and feminist lacunae. *Signs: Journal of Women in Culture and Society, 5,* in press.

Grossberg, L. (1983). Cultural studies revisited and revised. In M. S. Mander (Ed.), *Communications in Transition* (pp. 39–70). New York: Praeger.

Grossberg, L. (1989). The circulation of cultural studies. *Critical Studies in Mass Communication, 6,* 413–421.

Grossberg, L., & Nelson, C. (1988). Introduction: The territory of Marxism. In C. Nelson & L. Grossberg (Eds.), *Marxism and the interpretation of culture* (pp. 1–16). Urbana, IL: University of Illinois Press.

Grossberg, L., Nelson, C., & Treichler, P. (Eds.). (1992). *Cultural studies*. London: Routledge.

Habermas, J. (1971). *Knowledge and human interest*. Boston: Beacon.

Habermas, J. (1989). *The structural transformation of the public sphere*. Cambridge, MA: MIT Press.

Hall, S. (1980). Encoding and decoding in the television discourse. In S. Hall (Ed.), *Culture, media, language* (pp. 117–127). London: Hutchinson.

Hall, S. (1981a). Notes on deconstructing "the popular." In R. Samuel (Ed.), *People's history and socialist theory* (pp. 227–240). London: Routledge.

Hall, S. (1981b). The whites of their eyes: Racist ideologies and the media. In G. Bridges, & R. Brundt (Eds.), *Silver linings* (pp. 28-52). London: Lawrence and Wishart.

Hall, S. (1982). The rediscovery of "ideology": Return of the repressed in media studies. In M. Gurevitch, T. Bennett, J. Curran, & J. Woollacott (Eds.), *Culture, Society, and the Media* (pp. 52–86). New York: Methuen.

Huyssen, A. (1975). Introduction to Adorno. *New German Critique, 6,* 3–11.

Innis, H. A. (1950). *Empire and communication*. Toronto: University of Toronto Press.

Innis, H. A. (1951). *The bias of communication*. Toronto: University of Toronto Press.

Janus, N. V. (1977). Research on sex-roles in the mass media: Toward a critical approach. *Critical Sociology, 7,* 19–31.

Jensen, K. B. (1991). *A handbook of qualitative methodology for mass communication research*. New York: Taylor & Francis.

Jhally, S. (1989). The political economy of culture. In I. Angus & S. Jhally (Eds.), *Cultural politics in contemporary America* (pp. 65–81). New York: Routledge.

Johnson, A. (2018, March 1). Top NYT editor: "We are pro-capitalism, the Times is in favor of capitalism." *Fair*. Retrieved from https://fair.org/home/top-nyt-editor-we-are-pro-capitalism-the-times-is-in-favor-of-capitalism/

Juris, J. S. (2007). Practicing militant ethnography with the movement for global resistance in Barcelona. In S. Shukaitis, D. Graeber, & E. Biddle (Eds.), *Constituent imagination* (pp. 164–176). Oakland, CA: AK Press.

Kelman, J. (2018, June 18). Is there a TV in your child's room? *Great Schools*. Retrieved from https://www.greatschools.org/gk/articles/effects-of-tv-in-children-bedroom/

Kimberlé Crenshaw on intersectionality, more than two decades later. (2017, June 8). *Columbia Law School*. Retrieved from http://www.law.columbia.edu/pt-br/news/2017/06/kimberle-crenshaw-intersectionality

Lalami, L. (2017, October 30). The color of terrorism. *The Nation*, pp. 12–13.

Lazarsfeld, P. F. (1941). Remarks on administrative and critical communication research. *Studies in Philosophy and Social Science, 9,* 2–16.

Leonhardt, D. (2018, September 16). We're measuring the economy all wrong. *New York Times*, pp. SR1–SR2.

Lewis, J. (2008). *Cultural studies: The basics*. Thousand Oaks, CA: Sage.

Littleton, C. (2008, September 22–28). TV's class struggle. *Variety*, pp. 1, 81.

Long, E. (1989). Feminism and cultural studies. *Critical Studies in Mass Communication, 6,* 427–435.

Ludwig, M. (2013, April 10). Labor report: Four major TV news networks ignore unions. *Truthout*. Retrieved from http://truth-out.org/news/item/15655-labor-report-four-major-tv-news-networks-ignore-unions#_methods=onPlusOne%2C_ready%2C_close%2C_open%2C_resizeMe%2C_renderstart%2Concircled&id=I0_1365631425422&parent=http%3A%2F%2Ftruth-out.org&rpctoken=71088189

Mandese, J. (2018, May 29). Get woke: Time spent with media approaching total awake time. *MediaPost*. Retrieved from https://www.mediapost.com/publications/article/319872/get-woke-time-spent-with-media-approaching-total.html

Marwick, A. E., & Caplan, R. (2018). Drinking male tears: Language, the manosphere, and networked harassment. *Feminist Media Studies, 18,* 543–559.

McChesney, R. W. (2004). *The problem of the media: U.S. communication politics in the 21st century*. New York: Monthly Review Press.

McLuhan, M. (1964). *Understanding media: The extensions of Man*. New York: McGraw-Hill.

McLuhan, M. (1962). *The Gutenberg galaxy: The making of typographic man*. Toronto: University of Toronto Press.

Meehan, E. R., & Riordan, E. (2002). *Sex & money: Feminism and political economy in the media*. Minneapolis: University of Minnesota Press.

Meyrowitz, J. (1985). *No sense of place: The impact of electronic media on social behavior*. New York: Oxford University Press.

Meyrowitz, J. (2008). Power, pleasure, patterns: Intersecting narratives of media influence. *Journal of Communication, 58*, 641–663.

Miller, M. H. (2018, September 16). I came of age in the Recession. I'm still angry. *New York Times*, p. SR3.

Mitchell, G. (2009, April). Watchdogs failed to bark on economy. *Editor & Publisher*, p. 16.

Morris, W. (2016, May 1). What happened to all the working-class TV characters? *New York Times Magazine*, pp. 76–79.

Mulvey, L. (1975/1999). Visual pleasure and narrative cinema. In L. Braudy and M. Cohen (Eds.), *Film Theory and Criticism: Introductory Readings*, (pp. 833–844). New York: Oxford University Press.

Mumbry, D. K. (1997). The problem of hegemony: Rereading Gramsci for organizational communication studies. *Western Journal of Communication, 61*, 343–375.

Murdock, G. (1989a). Critical activity and audience activity. In B. Dervin, L. Grossberg, B. J. O'Keefe, & E. Wartella (Eds.), *Rethinking communication, vol. 2: Paradigm exemplars* (pp. 226–249). Newbury Park, CA: Sage.

Murdock, G. (1989b). Critical studies: Missing links. *Critical Studies in Mass Communication, 6*, 436–440.

Naureckas, J. (2009, July). Before we "save" journalism. *Extra!*, p. 5.

Negt, O. (1978). Mass media: Tools of domination or instruments of liberation? Aspects of the Frankfurt School's communications analysis. *New German Critique, 14*, 61–80.

Nelson, C, & Grossberg, L. (1988). *Marxism and the interpretation of culture*. Urbana, IL: University of Illinois Press.

Newcomb, H. (1974). *TV: The most popular art*. New York: Oxford University Press.

Newcomb, H. (2007). *Television: The critical view*, 7th ed. New York: Oxford University Press.

Newcomb, H., & Hirsch, P. M. (1983). Television as a cultural forum: Implications for research. *Quarterly Review of Film, 8*, 45–55.

O'Brien, S., & Szeman, I. (2004). *Popular culture*. Scarborough, Ontario: Nelson.

O'Connor, A. (1989). The problem of American cultural studies. *Critical Studies in Mass Communication, 6*, 405–413.

O'Keeffe, G. S., & Clarke-Pearson, K. (2011). Clinical report—The impact of social media on children, adolescents, and families. *Pediatrics, 127*, 800–804.

Okeowo, A. (2017, March 6). The provocateur Behind Beyoncé, Rihanna, and Issa Rae. *The New Yorker*. Retrieved from https://www.newyorker.com/magazine/2017/03/06/the-provocateur-behind-beyonce-rihanna-and-issa-rae

Pérez, R., & Greene, V. S. (2016). Debating rape jokes vs. rape culture: Framing and counter-framing misogynistic comedy. *Social Semiotics, 26*, 265–282.

Pleat, Z. (2019, February 20). CNN anchors misleadingly portray popular Democratic proposals such as "Medicare-for-all" and taxing the wealthy as far to the left. *Media Matters*. Retrieved from https://www.mediamatters.org/blog/2019/02/20/cnn-anchors-misleadingly-portray-popular-democratic-proposals-such-medicare-all-and-taxing-wealthy/222923

Polo, S. (2012, May 17). Jarrah Hodge drops some feminist history on us: Bra-burning is a myth. *The Mary Sue*. Retrieved from http://www.themarysue.com/jarrah-hodge-drops-some-feminist-history-on-us-bra-burning-is-a-myth/

Pooley, J. (2007). Daniel Czitrom, James W. Carey, and the Chicago School. *Critical Studies in Media Communication, 24*, 469–472.

Posner, L. (2018, February 5). The Philadelphia Super Bowl riots expose a racist double standard. *Alternet*. Retrieved from https://www.alternet.org/news-amp-politics/philadelphia-super-bowl-riots-expose-racist-double-standard

Postman, N. (2000, June 16). The humanism of media ecology. Keynote Address Delivered at the Inaugural Media Ecology Association Convention. Retrieved from http://media-ecology.org/publications/MEA_proceedings/v1/humanism_of_media_ecology.html

Rakow, L. (1986). Feminist approaches to popular culture: Giving patriarchy its due. *Communication, 9*, 19–41.

Richardson, R. (2018, March 23). Journalism of, by and for the elite. *Fair*. Retrieved from https://fair.org/home/journalism-of-by-and-for-the-elite/

Rogers, E. M. (2000). The extensions of men: The correspondence of Marshall McLuhan and Edward T. Hall. *Mass Communication and Society, 3*, 117–135.

Romero-Sánchez, M., Durán, M., Carretero-Dios, H., Megías, J. L., & Moya, M. (2010). Exposure to sexist humor and rape proclivity: The moderator effect of aversiveness ratings. *Journal of Interpersonal Violence, 25,* 2339–2350.

Ross, A. (2014, September 15). The naysayers. *The New Yorker,* pp. 88–94.

Sacco, J. M., Potts, L., Hearit, L., Sonderman, J., & Stroud, N. J. (2017, April 6). General election news coverage: What engages audiences down the ballot. *American Press Institute.* Retrieved from https://www.americanpressinstitute.org/publications/reports/white-papers/general-election-coverage/

Savchuck, K. (2016, April 6). Poor journalism: Is media coverage of the poor getting better or worse? *Cal Alumni Association.* Retrieved from https://alumni.berkeley.edu/california-magazine/just-in/2016-04-06/poor-journalism-media-coverage-poor-getting-better-or-worse

Schiller, H. I. (2000). *Living in the number one country: Reflections from a critic of American Empire.* New York: Seven Stories Press.

Schorr, D. (1992, May 17). True confessions of a lifetime TV journalist. *San Jose Mercury News,* pp. 1C, 5C.

Schwartz, N. D. (2018, September 16). The recovery was a disaster all over again. *New York Times,* p. BU3.

Senderowicz, D. (2018, September 15). Ending the secrecy of the student debt crisis. *Alternet.* Retrieved from https://www.alternet.org/ending-secrecy-student-debt-crisis?src=newsletter1096274

Smith, C. (2017, February 7). Vizio admits to spying on you through your smart TV. *BRG.* Retrieved from http://bgr.com/2017/02/07/vizio-smart-tv-spying-case/

Solomon, N. (2009, October 15). Media absence of class war. *Progressive Populist,* p. 16.

Stanley, J. (2015). *How propaganda works.* Princeton, NJ: Princeton University Press.

Star, A. (2008, August 17). Judgment call. *New York Times Book Review,* pp. 10–11.

Thomae, M., & Viki, G. T. (2013). Why did the woman cross the road? The effect of sexist humor on men's rape proclivity. *Journal of Social, Evolutionary, and Cultural Psychology, 7,* 250–269.

Thomas, E. (2009, April 6). Obama's Nobel headache. *Newsweek,* pp. 20–25.

Tuchman, G. (1978). *Making news: A study in the construction of reality.* New York: Free Press.

Vanden Heuvel, K. (2019, February 25/March 4). Time for a wealth tax! *The Nation,* pp. 3–4.

Wartella, E., & Treichler, P. A. (1986). Interventions: Feminist theory and communication studies. *Communication, 9,* 1–18.

Waterlow, L. (2016, February 13). "Rape and death threats are common": Women gamers reveal the vile online abuse they receive EVERY DAY from men who say they should "get back in the kitchen." *Daily Mail.* Retrieved from http://www.dailymail.co.uk/femail/article-3454588/Women-gamers-reveal-vile-online-abuse-receive-DAY-men-say-kitchen.html

Whiten, J. (2004, February). Bad news from Iraq? Blame the source—US officials. *Extra! Update,* p. 13.

Williams, R. (1967). *Communications.* New York: Barnes and Noble.

Williams, R. (1974). *Television: Technology and cultural form.* London: Fontana.

Wolf, G. (1996, January). The wisdom of Saint Marshall, the holy fool. *Wired,* pp. 122–125, 182–187.

CHAPTER 7

Anderson, C. A., Berkowitz, L., Donnerstein, E., Huesmann, L. R., Johnson, J. D., Linz, D., Malamuth, N. M., & Wartella, E. (2003). The influence of media violence on youth. *Psychological Science in the Public Interest, 4,* 81–110.

Anderson, C. A., & Bushman, B. J. (2002). Human aggression. *Annual Review of Psychology, 53,* 27–51.

Anderson, C. A., & Carnagey, N. L. (2004). Violent evil and the general aggression model. In A. G. Miller (Ed.), *The social psychology of good and evil* (pp. 169–192). New York: The Guilford Press.

Anderson, C. A., Deuser, W. E., & DeNeve, K. (1995). Hot temperatures, hostile affect, hostile cognition, and arousal: Tests of a general model of affective aggression. *Personality and Social Psychology Bulletin, 21,* 434–448.

Anderson, C. A., & Dill, K. E. (2000). Video games and aggressive thoughts, feelings, and behavior in the laboratory and in life. *Journal of Personality and Social Psychology, 78,* 772–790.

Anderson, C. A., Shibuya, A., Ihori, N., Swing, E. L., Bushman, B. J., Sakamoto, A., Rothstein, H. R., & Saleem, M. (2010). Violent video game effects on aggression, empathy, and prosocial behavior in eastern and western countries: A meta-analytic review. *Psychological Review, 136,* 151–173.

Anderson, D. R., & Lorch, E. P. (1983). Looking at television: Action or reaction? In J. Bryant & D. R. Anderson (Eds.), *Children's understanding of television: Research on attention and comprehension* (pp. 1–31). New York: Academic.

Andison, F. S. (1977). TV violence and viewer aggression: A culmination of study results, 1956–1976. *Public Opinion Quarterly, 41,* 314–331.

Baker, R. K., & Ball, S. J. (1969). *Violence and the media: A staff report to the National Commission on the Causes and Prevention of Violence, vol. 9A.* Washington, DC: U.S. Government.

Bandura, A. (1965). Influence of models' reinforcement contingencies on the acquisition of imitative responses. *Journal of Personality and Social Psychology, 1,* 589–595.

Bandura, A. (1971). *Psychological modeling: Conflicting theories.* Chicago: Aldine Atherton.

Bandura, A. (1994). Social cognitive theory of mass communication. In J. Bryant & D. Zillman (Eds.), *Media effects: Advances in theory and research* (pp. 61–90). Hillsdale, NJ: Erlbaum.

Bandura, A. (2009). Social cognitive theory of mass communication. In J. Bryant & M. B. Oliver (Eds.), *Media effects: Advances in theory and research* (pp. 94–124). New York: Routledge.

Baran, S. J., & Meyer, T. P. (1974). Imitation and identification: Two compatible approaches to social learning from the electronic media. *AV Communication Review, 22,* 167–179.

Berkowitz, L. (1965). Some aspects of observed aggression. *Journal of Personality and Social Psychology, 2,* 359–369.

Berkowitz, L., & Geen, R. G. (1966). Film violence and the cue properties of available targets. *Journal of Personality and Social Psychology, 3,* 525–530.

Bronfenbrenner, U. (1970). *Two worlds of childhood: US and USSR.* New York: Sage.

Bryant, J., & Anderson, D. R. (1983). *Children's understanding of television: Research on attention and comprehension.* New York: Academic.

Burgess, M. C. R., & Burpo, S. (2012). The effect of music videos on college students' perceptions of rape. *College Student Journal, 46,* 748–763.

Bushman, B. J., & Anderson, C. A. (2001). Media violence and the American public: Scientific facts versus media misinformation. *American Psychologist, 56,* 477–489.

Bushman, B. J., Rothstein, H. R., & Anderson, C. A. (2010). Much ado about something: Violent video game effects and a school of red herring: Reply to Ferguson and Kilburn. *Psychological Bulletin, 136,* 182–187.

Carnagey, N. L., Anderson, C. A., & Bushman, B. J. (2007). The effect of video game violence on physiological desensitization to real-life violence. *Journal of Experimental Social Psychology, 43,* 489–496.

Cooper, A. (2018, December 9). Groundbreaking study examines effects of screen time on kids. *CBS News.* Retrieved from https://www.cbsnews.com/news/groundbreaking-study-examines-effects-of-screen-time-on-kids-60-minutes/

Coyne, S. M., Nelson, D. A., Graham-Kevan, N., Tew, E., Meng, K. N., & Olsen, J. A. (2011). Media depictions of physical and relational aggression: Connections with aggression in young adults' romantic relationships. *Aggressive Behavior, 37,* 56–62.

Coyne, S. M., Warburton, W. A., Essig, L. W., & Stockdale, L. A. (2018). Violent video games, externalizing behavior, and prosocial behavior: A five-year longitudinal study during adolescence. *Developmental Psychology, 54,* 1868–1880.

DeWall, C. N., Anderson, C. A., & Bushman, B. J. (2011). The general aggression model: Theoretical extensions to violence. *Psychology of Violence, 1,* 245–258.

Feshbach, S. (1961). The stimulating versus cathartic effects of a vicarious aggressive activity. *Journal of Abnormal and Social Psychology, 63,* 381–385.

Feshbach, S., & Singer, R. D. (1971). *Television and aggression: An experimental field study.* San Francisco: Jossey-Bass.

Flavell, J. H. (1992). Cognitive development: Past, present, and future. *Developmental Psychology, 28,* 998–1005.

Frost, R., & Stauffer, J. (1987). The effects of social class, gender, and personality on psychological responses to filmed violence. *Journal of Communication, 37,* 29–45.

Gadamer, H. (1995). *Truth and method.* (J. Weinsheimer & D. G. Marshall, Trans.). New York: Continuum.

Gentile, D. A. (2013). Catharsis and media violence: A conceptual analysis. *Societies, 3,* 491–510.

Gentile, D. A., Lynch, P. J., Linder, J. R., & Walsh, D. A. (2004). The effects of violent video games habits on adolescent hostility, aggressive behavior, and school performance. *Journal of Adolescence, 27,* 5–22.

Greitemeyer, T., & Mügge, D. O. (2014). Video games do affect social outcomes: A meta-analytic review of the effects of violent and prosocial video game play. *Personality and Social Psychology Bulletin, 40,* 578–589.

Halloran, J. D. (1964/1965). Television and violence. *The Twentieth Century,* Winter, 61–72.

Huston, A. C., Donnerstein, E., Fairchild, H., Feshbach, N. D., Katz, P. A., Murray, J., Rubenstein, A. E., Wilcox, B. L., & Zuckerman, D. (1992). *Big world, small screen.* Lincoln: University of Nebraska Press.

Jo, E., & Berkowitz, L. (1994). A priming effect analysis of media influence: An update. In J. Bryant & D. Zillman (Eds.), *Media effects: Advances in theory and research* (pp. 43–60). Hillsdale, NJ: Erlbaum.

Kelmon, J. (2018, June 18). Is there a TV in your child's room? *Great Schools*. Retrieved from https://www.greatschools.org/gk/articles/effects-of-tv-in-children-bedroom/

Kistler, M. E., & Lee, M. J. (2010). Does exposure to sexual hip-hop music videos influence the sexual attitudes of college students? *Mass Communication and Society, 13*, 67–86.

Konijn, E. A., Bijvank, M. N., & Bushman, B. J. (2007). I wish I were a warrior: The role of wishful identification in the effects of violent video games on aggression in adolescent boys. *Developmental Psychology, 43*, 1038–1044.

Krahé, B., Möller, I., Huesmann, L. R., Kirwill, L., Felber, J., & Berger, A. (2011). Desensitization to media violence: Links with habitual media violence exposure, aggressive cognitions, and aggressive behavior. *Journal of Personality and Social Psychology, 100*, 630–646.

LaCroix, J. M., Burrows, C. N., & Blanton, H. (2018). Effects of immersive, sexually objectifying, and violent video games on hostile sexism in males. *Communication Research Reports, 35*, 413–423.

Mandese, J. (2013, January 10). Study finds more parents concerned about media than guns. *MediaPost*. Retrieved from http://www.mediapost.com/publications/article/190762/study-finds-more-parents-concerned-about-media-tha.html#axzz2I5R6LyhW

McGloin, R., Farrar, K. M., & Fishlock, J. (2015). Triple whammy! Violent games and violent controllers: Investigating the use of realistic gun controllers on perceptions of realism, immersion, and outcome aggression. *Journal of Communication, 65*, 280–299.

Miller, N. E., & Dollard, J. (1941). *Social learning and imitation*. New Haven, CT: Yale University Press.

Potter, W. J. (1997). The problem of indexing risk of viewing television aggression. *Critical Studies in Mass Communication, 14*, 228–248.

Rideout, V. (2017, October 19). The Common Sense census: Media use by kids age zero to eight. *Common Sense Media*. Retrieved from https://www.commonsensemedia.org/research/the-common-sense-census-media-use-by-kids-age-zero-to-eight-2017

Rozendaal, R., Buijzen, M., & Valkenburg, P. (2011). Children's understanding of advertisers' persuasive tactics. *International Journal of Advertising, 30*, 329–350.

Shade, L. R., Porter, N., & Sanchez, W. (2005). You can see everything on the internet, you can do anything on the internet! Young Canadians talk about the internet. *Canadian Journal of Communication, 30*, 503–526.

Shrum, L. J., (2009). Media consumption and perceptions of social reality. In J. Bryant & M. B. Oliver (Eds.), *Media effects: Advances in theory and research* (pp. 50–73). New York: Routledge.

Swing, E. L., Gentile, D. A., Anderson, C. A., & Walsh, D. A. (2010). Television and video game exposures and the development of attention problems. *Pediatrics, 126*, 214–221.

Tsukayama, H. (2013, January 11). Why the video game industry has to talk about gun violence. *Washington Post*. Retrieved from http://articles.washingtonpost.com/2013-01-11/business/36313414_1_violent-video-games-games-and-real-world-violence-game-industry

Twenge, J. M., & Campbell, W. K. (2018). Associations between screen time and lower psychological well-being among children and adolescents: Evidence from a population-based study. *Preventive Medicine Reports, 12*, 271–283.

US Congress Senate Subcommittee on Communications. (1972). *Surgeon General's Report by the Scientific Advisory Committee on Television and Social Behavior*. 92nd Congress, 2nd Session, March 21–24.

Vander Neut, T. (1999, November). Do violent images cause violent behavior? *Risk and Insurance*, pp. 38–40.

Wartella, E. (1979). The developmental perspective. In E. Wartella (Ed.), *Children communicating: Media and development of thought, speech, and understanding* (pp. 7–19). Beverly Hills, CA: Sage.

Wartella, E. (1999). Children and media: On growth and gaps. *Mass Communication and Society, 2*, 81–88.

White, R. W. (1972). *The enterprise of living: Growth and organization in personality*. New York: Holt, Rinehart & Winston.

Yan, Z. (2009). Limited knowledge and limited resources: Children's and adolescents' understanding of the internet. *Journal of Applied Developmental Psychology, 30*, 103–115.

Zimbardo, P. G., & Weber, A. L. (1997). *Psychology*. New York: Longman.

CHAPTER 8

Allcott, H., Braghieri, L., Eichmeyer, S., & Gentzkow, M. (2019, January). The welfare effects of social media.

SSRN Electronic Journal. Retrieved from http://web.stanford.edu/~gentzkow/research/facebook.pdf

American Academy of Pediatrics. (2011). Policy statement—Children, adolescents, obesity, and the media. *Pediatrics, 128*, 201–208.

Anderson, M., & Jiang, J. (2018, May 31). Teens, social media & technology 2018. *Pew Research Center*. Retrieved from http://www.pewinternet.org/2018/05/31/teens-social-media-technology-2018/

Andronikidis, A. I., & Lambrianidou, M. (2010). Children's understanding of television advertising: A grounded theory approach. *Psychology and Marketing, 27*, 299–332.

Back, M. D., Stopfer, J. M., Vazire, S., Gaddis, S., Schmukle, S. C., Egloff, B., & Gosling, S. D. (2010). Facebook profiles reflect actual personality, not self-idealization. *Psychological Science, 21*, 372–374.

Baker, L. R., & Oswald, D. L. (2010). Shyness and online social networking services. *Journal of Social and Personal Relationships, 27*, 883–889.

Baran, S. J. (1976a). How television and film portrayals affect sexual satisfaction in college students. *Journalism Quarterly, 53*, 468–473.

Baran, S. J. (1976b). Sex on television and adolescent sexual self-image. *Journal of Broadcasting, 20*, 61–68.

Barbaro, A., Earp, J., & Jhally, S. (2008). *Consuming kids: The commercialization of childhood*. Northampton, MA: Media Education Foundation.

Barber, B. R. (2007). *Consumed: How markets corrupt children, infantilize adults, and swallow citizens whole*. New York: W. W. Norton.

Bissell, K. L., & Zhou, P. (2004). Must-see TV or ESPN: Entertainment and sports media exposure and body-image distortion in college women. *Journal of Communication, 54*, 5–21.

Boehm, J. K., Peterson, C., & Kubzansky, L. (2011). A prospective study of positive psychological well-being and coronary heart disease. *Health Psychology, 30*, 259–267.

Boyland, E. J., & Halford, J. C. G. (2012). Television advertising and branding. Effects on eating behaviour and food preferences in children. *Appetite, 62*, 236–241.

Brandtzæg, P. B. (2012). Social networking sites: Their users and social implications—A longitudinal study. *Journal of Computer-Mediated Communication, 17*, 467–488.

Bruce, A. E., Bruce, J. M., Black, W. R., Lepping, R. J., Henry, J. M., J. Cherry, B. C., … Savage, C. R. (2014). Branding and a child's brain: An fMRI study of neural responses to logos. *Social Cognitive & Affective Neuroscience, 9*, 118–122.

Calogero, R. M., & Tylka, T. L. (2010). Fiction, fashion, & function: An introduction to the special issue on gendered body image, part I. *Sex Roles, 63*, 1–5.

Carter, T. B., Franklin, M. A., & Wright, J. B. (2008). *The First Amendment and the fifth estate*. St. Paul, MN: West.

Centers for Disease Control and Prevention. (2018). Childhood obesity facts. Retrieved from https://www.cdc.gov/healthyschools/obesity/facts.htm

Christakis, D. A., Gilkerson, J., Richards, J. A., Zimmerman, F. J., Garrison, M. M., Xu, D., Gray, S., & Yapanel, U. (2009). Audible television and decreased adult words, infant vocalizations, and conversational turns: A population-based study. *Archives of Pediatrics & Adolescent Medicine, 163*, 554–558.

Christakis, D. A., Zimmerman, F. J., DiGiuseppe, D. L., & McCarty, C. A. (2004). Early television exposure and subsequent attentional problems in children. *Pediatrics, 113*, 708–713.

Clark, L., & Tiggemann, M. (2007). Sociocultural influences and body image in 9- to 12-year-old girls: The role of appearance schemas. *Journal of Clinical Child and Adolescent Psychology, 36*, 76–86.

Comstock, G. (1991). *Television and the American child*. San Diego: Academic.

Courtright, J. A., & Baran, S. J. (1980). The acquisition of sexual information by young people. *Journalism Quarterly, 57*, 107–114.

Deters, F. G., & Mehl, M. R. (2012). Does posting Facebook status updates increase or decrease loneliness? An online social networking experiment. *Social Psychological and Personality Science, 4*, 579–586.

Diener, E. D., Nickerson, C., Lucas, R. E., & Sandvik, E. D. (2002). Dispositional affect and job outcomes. *Social Indicators Research, 40*, 229–259.

Dworak, M., Schierl, T., Burns, T., & Struder, H. K. (2007). Impact of singular excessive computer game and television exposure on sleep patterns and memory performance of school-aged children. *Pediatrics, 120*, 978–985.

Elliott, C. D. (2012). Packaging fun: Analyzing supermarket food messages targeted at children. *Canadian Journal of Communication, 37*, 303–318.

Frechette, S. (2016). The effect of television food advertising on children's preferences, demands, and intake of high-fat and low-nutrient products. *Annals of Spiru Haret University, 17*, 30–40.

Fredrickson, B. L., & Roberts, T. (1997). Toward understanding women's lived experiences and mental health risks. *Psychology of Women Quarterly, 21,* 173–206.

Gamble, H., & Nelson, L. R. (2016). Sex in college relationships: The role television plays in emerging adults' sexual expectations in relationships. *Communication Monographs, 83,* 145–161.

Geiger, A. W., & Davis, L. (2019, July 12). A growing number of American teenagers—particularly girls—are facing depression. *Pew Research Center.* Retrieved from https://www.pewresearch.org/fact-tank/2019/07/12/a-growing-number-of-american-teenagers-particularly-girls-are-facing-depression/

Gentile, D. A., Choo, H., Liau, A., Sim, T., Li, D., Fung, D., & Khoo, A. (2011). Pathological video game use among youths: A two-year longitudinal study. *Pediatrics, 127,* e319–e329.

Gerbner, G. (2010, February 18). The mean world syndrome—Media as storytellers (extra feature). *Media Education Foundation.* Retrieved from http://www.youtube.com/watch?v=ylhqasb1chI

Giroux, H. (2000). *Stealing innocence: Corporate culture's war on children.* New York: Palgrave.

Giroux, H. A. (2011, May 5). Youth in a suspect society: Coming of age in an era of disposability. *Truthout.* Retrieved from http://truth-out.org/news/item/923:youth-in-a-suspect-society-coming-of-age-in-an-era-of-disposability

Giroux, H. A., & Pollock, G. (2011, August 21). How Disney magic and the corporate media shape youth identity in the digital age. *Truthout.* Retrieved from http://truth-out.org/opinion/item/2808:how-disney-magic-and-the-corporate-media-shape-youth-identity-in-the-digital-age

Gottesdiener, L. (2012, November 29). 7 highly disturbing trends in junk food advertising to children. *AlterNet.* Retrieved from http://www.alternet.org/food/7-highly-disturbing-trends-junk-food-advertising-children

Grasmuck, S., Martin, J., & Zhao, S. (2009). Ethnoracial identity displays on Facebook. *Journal of Computer-Mediated Communication, 15,*158–188.

Grenard, J. L., Dent, C. W., & Stacy, A. W. (2013). Exposure to alcohol advertisements and teenage alcohol-related problems. *Pediatrics, 131,* e369–e379.

Haelle, T. (2013, April 9). Consumption junction: Childhood obesity determined largely by environmental factors, not genes or sloth. *Scientific American.* Retrieved from http://www.scientificamerican.com/article.cfm?id=childhood-obesity-determined-largely-by-environmental-factors&page=3

Hampton, K. N., Sessions, L. F., & Her, E. J. (2010). Core networks, social isolation, and new media: How internet and mobile phone use is related to network size and diversity. *Information, Communication & Society, 14,* 130–155.

Han, S., Kim, K. J., & Kim, J. H. (2017). Understanding nomophobia: Structural equation modeling and semantic network analysis of smartphone separation anxiety. *Cyberpsychology, Behavior, and Social Networking, 20,* 419–427.

Harrison, K. (2006). Scope of self: Toward a model of television's effects on self-complexity in adolescence. *Communication Theory, 16,* 251–279.

Hunt, M. G., Marx, R., Lipson, C., & Young, J. (2018). No more FOMO: Limiting social media decreases loneliness and depression. *Journal of Social and Clinical Psychology, 37,* 751–768.

Jiang, J. (2018, August 22). How teens and parents navigate screen time and device distractions. *Pew Research Center.* Retrieved from http://www.pewinternet.org/2018/08/22/how-teens-and-parents-navigate-screen-time-and-device-distractions/

Krasnova, H., Wenninger, H., Widjaja, T., & Buxmann, P. (2013). Envy on Facebook: A hidden threat to users' life satisfaction? Paper presented to the 11th International Conference on Wirtschaftsinformatik, Leipzig, Germany, March.

Kraut, R., Patterson, M., Lundmark, V., Kiesler, S., Mukopadhyay, T., & Scherlis. W. (1998). Internet paradox. A social technology that reduces social involvement and psychological well-being? *American Psychologist, 53,* 1017–1031.

Kross, E., Verduyn, P., Demiralp, E., Park, J., Lee, D. S., Lin, N., … Ybarra, O. (2013). Facebook use predicts declines in subjective well-being in young adults. *PLoS ONE, 8,* e69841.

Kruglanski, A. W., & Mayseless, O. (1990). Classic and current social comparison research: Expanding the perspective. *Psychological Bulletin, 108,* 195–208.

Linn, S. (2004). *Consuming kids.* New York: The New Press.

Lyubomirsky, S., King, L., & Diener, E. (2005). The benefits of frequent positive affect: Does happiness lead to success? *Psychological Bulletin, 131,* 803–855.

Major depression: The impact on overall health. (2018, May 10). *Blue Cross Blue Shield*. Retrieved from https://www.bcbs.com/the-health-of-america/reports/major-depression-the-impact-overall-health

Marche, S. (2012, May). Is Facebook making us lonely? *Atlantic*. Retrieved from https://www.theatlantic.com/magazine/archive/2012/05/is-facebook-making-us-lonely/308930/

Martins, N., & Wilson, B. J. (2011). Social aggression on television and its relationship to children's aggression in the classroom. *Human Communication Research, 38*, 48–71.

Meyrowitz, J. (1985). *No sense of place: The impact of electronic media on social behavior*. New York: Oxford University Press.

Nadkarni, S., & Hofmann, S. G. (2012). Why do people use Facebook? *Personality and Individual Differences, 52*, 243–249.

Nathanson, A. I., Sharp, M. L., Aladé, F., Rasmussen, E. E., & Christy, K. (2013). The relation between television exposure and theory of mind among preschoolers. *Journal of Communication, 63*, 1088–1108.

O'Keeffe, G. S., & Clarke-Pearson, K. (2011). Clinical report—The impact of social media on children, adolescents, and families. *Pediatrics, 127*, 800–804.

Ortega, J., & Hergovich, J. (2017). The strength of absent ties: Social integration via online dating. *Physics and Society*. Retrieved from https://arxiv.org/pdf/1709.10478.pdf

Owen, L., Lewis, C., Auty, S., & Buijzen, M. (2013). Is children's understanding of nontraditional advertising comparable to their understanding of television advertising? *Journal of Public Policy & Marketing, 32*, 195–206.

Page, A. S., Cooper, A. R., Griew, P., & Jago, R. (2010). Children's screen viewing is related to psychological difficulties irrespective of physical activity. *Pediatrics, 126*, e1011–e1017.

Postman, N. (1994). *The disappearance of childhood*. New York: Vintage.

Richter, F. (2013, September 26). Mobile devices: The 21st century nanny. *Statista*. Retrieved from https://www.statista.com/chart/1499/mobile-device-use-of-american-parents/

Rideout, V. (2012, Fall). Children, teens, and entertainment media: The view from the classroom. *Common Sense Media*. Retrieved from http://www.commonsensemedia.org/sites/default/files/research/view-from-the-classroom-final-report.pdf

Rideout, V. J., Foehr, U. G., & Roberts, D. F. (2010). *Generation M2: Media in the lives of 8- to 18-year-olds*. Menlo Park, CA: Kaiser Family Foundation.

Rosen, L. D., Whaling, K., Rab, S., Carrier, L. M., & Cheever, N. A. (2013). Is Facebook creating "idisorders"? The link between clinical symptoms of psychiatric disorders and technology use, attitudes and anxiety." *Computers in Human Behavior, 29*, 1243–1254.

Ryan, T., Chester, A., Reece, J., & Xenos, S. (2014). The uses and abuses of Facebook: A review of Facebook addiction. *Journal of Behavioral Addictions, 3*, 133–148.

Sagioglou, C., & Greitmeyer, T. (2014). Facebook's emotional consequences: Why Facebook causes a decrease in mood and why people still use it. *Computers in Human Behavior, 35*, 359–363.

Samson, L., & Grabe, M. E. (2012). Media use and the sexual propensities of emerging adults. *Journal of Broadcasting & Electronic Media, 56*, 280–298.

Shahar, D., & Sayers, M. G. L. (2016). A morphological adaptation? The prevalence of enlarged external occipital protuberance in young adults. *Journal of Anatomy, 229*, 286–291.

Shakya, H. B., & Christakis, N. A. (2017). Association of Facebook use with compromised well-being: A longitudinal study. *American Journal of Epidemiology, 185*, 203–211.

Sheehan, K. B. (2014). *Contemporary controversies in advertising*. Los Angeles: Sage.

Steinberg, S. R. (2011). Kinderculture: Mediating, simulacralizing, and pathologizing the new childhood. In S. R. Steinberg (Ed.), *Kinderculture: The corporate construction of childhood* (pp. 1–53). Boulder, CO: Westview Press.

Strasburger, V. C., Jordan, A. B., & Donnerstein, E. (2010). Health effects of media on children and adolescents. *Pediatrics, 125*, 756–767.

Taylor, L. D., & Fortaleza, J. (2016). Media violence and male body image. *Psychology of Men & Masculinity, 17*, 380–384.

Thomson, D. M. (2010). Marshmallow power and frooty treasures: Disciplining the child consumer through online cereal advergaming. *Critical Studies in Media Communication, 27*, 438–454.

Vandenbosch, L., & Eggermont, S. (2012). Understanding sexual objectification: A comprehensive approach toward media exposure and girls' internalization of beauty ideals, self-objectification, and body surveillance. *Journal of Communication, 62*, 869–887.

Verduyn, P., Ybarra, O., Résibois, M., Jonides, J., & Kross, E. (2017). Do social network sites enhance or undermine subjective well-being? A critical review. *Social Issues and Policy Review, 11,* 274–302.

Wang, R., Yang, F., & Haigh, M. M. (2017). Let me take a selfie: Exploring the psychological effects of posting and viewing selfies and groupies on social media. *Telematics and Informatics, 34,* 274–283.

Ward, A. F., Duke, K., Gneezy, A., & Bos, M. W. (2017). Brain drain: The mere presence of one's own smartphone reduces available cognitive capacity. *Journal of the Association for Consumer Research, 2,* 140–154.

Weis, R., & Cerankosky, B. C. (2010). Effects of video-game ownership on young boys' academic and behavioral functioning: A randomized, controlled study. *Psychological Sciences, 21,* 1–8.

Wilcox, B. L., Kunkel, D., Cantor, J., Dowrick, P., Linn, S., & Palmer, E. (2004). *Report of the APA task force on advertising and children.* Washington, DC: American Psychological Association.

Wolverton, B. (2019, February 24). The campus as counselor. *New York Times,* p. F4.

World Health Organization. (2019). Guidelines on physical activity, sedentary behaviour and sleep for children under 5 years of age. *World Health Organization.* Retrieved from https://apps.who .int/iris/handle/10665/311664

Zywica, J., & Danowski, J. (2008). The faces of Face-bookers: Investigating social enhancement and social compensation hypotheses; predicting Facebook and offline popularity from sociability, self-esteem, and extroversion/introversion; and mapping the meanings of popularity with semantic networks. *Journal of Computer Mediated Communication, 14,* 1–34.

CHAPTER 9

Alasuutari, P. (1999). Introduction: Three phases of reception studies. In P. Alasuutari (Ed.), *Rethinking the media audience* (pp. 1–21). Thousand Oaks, CA: Sage.

Berelson, B. (1949). What "missing the newspaper" means. In P. F. Lazarsfeld & F. N. Stanton (Eds.), *Communications research, 1948–1949* (pp. 111–129). New York: Harper.

Blumler, J. G. (1979). The role of theory in uses and gratifications studies. *Communication Research, 6,* 9–36.

Bollier, D. (2005). *Brand name bullies.* New York: Wiley.

Bond, B. J. (2018). Parasocial relationships with media personae: Why they matter and how they differ among heterosexual, lesbian, gay, and bisexual adolescents. *Media Psychology, 21,* 457–485.

Boneva, B., Kraut, R., & Frohlich, D. (2001). Using e-mail for personal relationships: The difference gender makes. *American Behavioral Scientist, 45,* 530–549.

Brunsdon, C., & Morley, D. (1981). "Crossroads": Notes on soap opera. *Screen, 22,* 327.

Bryant, J., Roskos-Ewoldsen, D. R., & Cantor, J. (Eds.) (2003). *Communication and emotion: Essays in honor of Dolf Zillmann.* Mahwah, NJ: Erlbaum.

Bryant, J., & Vorderer, P. (Eds.)(2006). *Psychology of entertainment.* Mahwah, NJ: Erlbaum.

Bundy, W. (2017, January 3). People streamed more music per day in 2016 than they downloaded all year. *Fader.* Retrieved from http://www .thefader.com/2017/01/03/streaming-report -buzz-angle-spotify-drake

Dewey, J. (1927). *The public and its problems.* New York: Holt.

Dokoupil, T. (2012, July 9). Is the Internet making us crazy? What the new research says. *Newsweek.* Retrieved from https://www.newsweek.com/ internet-making-us-crazy-what-new-research -says-65593

Edelman, M. (1988). *Constructing the political spectacle,* 3rd ed. Chicago: University of Chicago Press.

Edmonds, S. (2018, February 26). What are consumers doing on their smartphones, anyway? *Salesforce.* Retrieved from https://www.salesforce.com/blog/ 2018/02/consumer-smartphone-use

Edroso, R. (2018, February 20). Conservatives attack "Black Panther"—But, when it hits, declare it conservative. *Village Voice.* Retrieved from https://www.villagevoice.com/2018/02/20/ conservatives-attack-black-panther-but-when-it -hits-declare-it-conservative/

Ellis, J. (2012, December 11). Young-adult readers may have abandoned print, but they'll take news in their pockets. *Nieman Journalism Lab.* Retrieved from http://www.niemanlab.org/2012/12/young -adult-readers-may-have-abandoned-print-but -theyll-take-news-in-their-pockets/

Fiske, J. (1987). *Television culture.* London: Routledge.

Gans, C. B. (1978). The empty ballot box: Reflections on nonvoters in America. *Public Opinion, 1,* 54–57.

Gerbner, G. (2010, February 18). The mean world syndrome—media as storytellers (extra feature).

Media Education Foundation. Retrieved from http://www.youtube.com/watch?v=ylhqasb1chI

Gillig, T. K., & Murphy, S. T. (2016). Fostering support for LGBTQ youth?: The effects of a gay adolescent media portrayal on young viewers. *International Journal of Communication, 10*, 3828–3850

Hall, S. (1973). Encoding and decoding in the television discourse. *CCCS Stenciled Paper 7*, University of Birmingham.

Hall, S. (1980). Encoding and decoding. In Centre for Contemporary Culture Studies (Ed.), *Culture, media, language: Working papers in cultural studies, 1972–79* (pp. 128–138). London: Hutchinson.

Herzog, H. (1940). Professor Quiz: A gratification study. In P. F. Lazarsfeld (Ed.), *Radio and the printed page* (pp. 64–93). New York: Duell, Sloan, and Pearce.

Herzog, H. (1944). What do we really know about daytime serial listeners? In P. F. Lazarsfeld & F. N. Stanton (Eds.), *Radio research 1942–1943* (pp. 3–33). New York: Duell, Sloan, and Pearce.

Hobson, D. (1982). *Crossroads: The drama of a soap opera*. London: Methuen.

Incollingo, J. S. (2018). I'm a news junkie … I like being informed: Mobile news use by a newspaper's digital subscribers. *Newspaper Research Journal, 39*, 134–144.

Jung, E. H., & Sundar, S. S. (2018). Status update: Gratifications derived from Facebook affordances by older adults. *New Media & Society, 20*, 4135–4154.

Katyal, S. K. (2006). Semiotic disobedience. *Washington University Law Review 84*. Retrieved from http://openscholarship.wustl.edu/law_lawreview/vol84/iss3/1

Katz, E., Blumler, J. G., & Gurevitch, M. (1974). Utilization of mass communication by the individual. In J. G. Blumler & E. Katz (Eds.), *The uses of mass communication: Current perspectives on gratifications research* (pp. 19–34). Beverly Hills, CA: Sage.

Knobloch-Westerwick, S. (2006). Mood management: Theory, evidence, and advancements. In D. Zillmann & P. Vorderer (Eds.), *Media entertainment: The psychology of its appeal* (pp. 239–254). Mahwah, NJ: Erlbaum.

Knobloch-Westerwick, S. (2015). The selective exposure self and affect-management (SESAM) model. *Communication Research, 42*, 959–985.

Knobloch-Westerwick, S., & Westerwick, A. (2020). *Mediated communication dynamics: Shaping you and your society*. New York: Oxford University Press.

La Ferle, C., Edwards, S. M., & Lee, W. N. (2000). Teens' use of traditional media and the internet. *Journal of Advertising Research, 40*, 55–65.

Lazarsfeld, P., & Stanton, F. N. (Eds.) (1942). *Radio research, 1941*. New York: Duell, Sloan & Pearce.

Levy, M., & Windahl, S. (1985). The concept of audience activity. In K. E. Rosengren, L. A. Wenner, & P. Palmgreen (Eds.), *Media gratifications research: Current perspectives* (pp. 109–122). Beverly Hills, CA: Sage.

Martin-Barbero, J. (1993). *Communication, culture, and hegemony: From the media to mediations*. Translation by E. Fox & R. A. White. Newbury Park, CA: Sage.

McRobbie, A. (1982). The politics of feminist research: Between talk, text and action. *Feminist Review, 12*, 46–57.

McRobbie, A. (1984). Settling accounts with subcultures: A feminist critique. *Screen Education, 34*, 37–49.

Moores, S. (1993). *Interpreting audiences: The ethnography of media consumption*. Thousand Oaks, CA: Sage.

Morley, D. (1980). *The "nationwide" audience: Structure and decoding*. London: British Film Institute.

Oliver, M. B. (2008). Tender affective states as predictors of entertainment preference. *Journal of Communication, 58*, 40–61.

Pérez, R., & Greene, V. S. (2016). Debating rape jokes vs. rape culture: Framing and counter-framing misogynistic comedy. *Social Semiotics, 26*, 265–282.

Pew Research Center, (2018, February 5). Mobile fact sheet. Retrieved from http://www.pewinternet.org/fact-sheet/mobile/

Potter, W. J. (2012). *Media effects*. Los Angeles: Sage.

Proctor, J. (2004). *Stuart Hall*. New York: Routledge.

Quan-Haase, A., & Young, A. L. (2010). Uses and gratifications of social media: A comparison of Facebook and instant messaging. *Bulletin of Science Technology Society, 30*, 350–361.

Radway, J. (1984/1991). *Reading the romance: Women, patriarchy, and popular literature*. Chapel Hill, NC: University of North Carolina Press.

Radway, J. (1986). Identifying ideological seams: Mass culture, analytical method, and political practice. *Communication, 9*, 93–123.

Rathnayake, C., & Winter, J. S. (2018) Carrying forward the uses and grats 2.0 agenda: An affordance-driven measure of social media uses and gratifications. *Journal of Broadcasting & Electronic Media, 62*, 371–389.

Rojek, C. (2009). Stuart Hall on representation and ideology. In R. Hammer & D. Kellner (Eds.), *Media/cultural studies: Critical approaches* (pp. 49–62). New York: Peter Lang.

Ruggiero, T. E. (2000). Uses and gratifications theory in the 21st century. *Mass Communication and Society, 3*, 3–37.

Scanlon, J. (2016). Whose sexuality is it anyway? Women's experiences of viewing lesbians on screen. *Feminist Media Studies, 17*, 1005–1021.

Schramm, W. (1954). *The process and effects of mass communication.* Urbana, IL: University of Illinois Press.

Sheldon, P. (2008). Student favorite: Facebook and motives for its use. *Southwestern Mass Communication Journal, 23*, 39–55.

Slater, M. D., Johnson, B. K., Cohen, J., Comello, M. L. G., & Ewoldsen, D. R. (2014). Temporarily expanding the boundaries of the self: Motivations for entering the story world and implications for narrative effects. *Journal of Communication, 64*, 439–455.

Steiner, L. (1988). Oppositional decoding as an act of resistance. *Critical Studies in Mass Communication, 5*, 1–15.

Sundar, S.S., & Limperos, A.M. (2013) Uses and grats 2.0: New gratifications for new media. *Journal of Broadcasting & Electronic Media, 57*, 504–525.

Thrasher, S. (2018, February 20). *There is much to celebrate—and much to question—about Marvel's Black Panther. Esquire.* Retrieved from https://www.esquire.com/entertainment/movies/a18241993/black-panther-review-politics-killmonger/

Williams, F., Rice, R. E., & Rogers E. M. (1988). *Research methods and the new media.* New York: Free Press.

Wright, C. R. (1959). *Mass communication: A sociological perspective.* New York: Random House.

Wright, C. R. (1974). Functional analysis and mass communication revisited. In J. G. Blumler & E. Katz (Eds.), *The uses of mass communication: Current perspectives on gratifications research* (pp. 197–212). Beverly Hills, CA: Sage.

Zillmann, D., & Vorderer, P. (2000). *Media Entertainment: The psychology of its appeal.* Mahwah, NJ: Erlbaum.

CHAPTER 10

Ahmed, W., Bath, P. A., Sbaffi, L., & Demartini, G. (2018). Measuring the effect of public health campaigns on Twitter: The case of World Autism Awareness Day. *Proceedings of the International Conference on Information, Transforming Digital Worlds,* pp. 10–16.

Axelrod, R. (1973). Schema theory: An information processing model of perception and cognition. *American Political Science Review, 67*, 1248–1266.

Bartlett, F. C. (1932). *Remembering: A study in experimental and social psychology.* Cambridge, UK: Cambridge University Press.

Brewer, W. F., & Nakamura, G. V. (1984). The nature and functions of schema. *Center for the Study of Reading, Technical Report No. 325.* Retrieved from https://www.ideals.illinois.edu/bitstream/handle/2142/17542/ctrstreadtechrepv01984i00325_opt.pdf?s

Bull, S. S., Levine, D. K., Black, S. R., Schmiege, S. J., & Santelli, J. (2012). Social media-delivered sexual health intervention. *American Journal of Preventative Medicine, 43*, 467–474.

Chaffee, S. H., & Schleuder, J. (1986). Measurement and effects of attention to media news. *Human Communication Research, 13*, 76–107.

Chen, S., & Chaiken, S. (1999). The heuristic-systematic model in its broader context. In S. Chaiken & Y. Trope (Eds.), *Dual-process theories in social psychology* (pp. 73–96). New York: Guilford Press.

Chaiken, S., & Trope, Y. (1999). *Dual-process theories in social psychology.* New York: Guilford.

Clark-Flory, T. (2012, April 1). Facebook: The next tool in fighting STDs. *Salon.* Retrieved from http://www.salon.com/2012/04/01/facebook_the_next_tool_in_fighting_stds/

Cohen, J. (2001). Defining identification: A theoretical look at the identification of audiences with media characters. *Mass Communication & Society, 4*, 245–264.

Correa, T., Hinsley, A. W., & de Zúñiga, H. G. (2010). Who interacts on the web? The intersection of users' personality and social media use. *Computers in Human Behavior, 26*, 247–253.

Davis, D. K. (1990). News and politics. In D. L. Swanson & D. Nimmo (Eds.) *New directions in political communication* (pp. 147–184). Newbury Park, CA: Sage.

Davis, D. K., & Robinson, J. P. (1989). Newsflow and democratic society in an age of electronic media. In G. Comstock (Ed.), *Public communication and behavior, vol. 3* (pp. 89–102). New York: Academic.

Eaves, L. J., & Eysenck, H. J. (1974). Genetics and the development of social attitudes. *Nature, 249*, 288–289.

Giner-Sorolla, R., & Chaiken, S. (1994). The causes of hostile media judgment. *Journal of Experimental Social Psychology, 30*, 165–180.

Graber, D. A. (1984). *Processing the news*, 1st ed. New York: Longman.

Graber, D. A. (1988). *Processing the news*, 2nd ed. New York: Longman.

Green, M. C., & Brock, T. C. (2000). The role of transportation in the persuasiveness of public narratives. *Journal of Personality and Social Psychology, 79*, 701–721.

Gunter, B. (1987). *Poor reception: Misunderstanding and forgetting broadcast news*. Hillsdale, NJ: Erlbaum.

Gunther, A. C., & Chia, S. C. (2001). Predicting pluralistic ignorance: The hostile media perception and its consequences. *Journalism & Mass Communication Quarterly, 78*, 688–701.

Gunther, A. C., & Liebhart, J. L. (2006). Broad reach or biased source? Decomposing the hostile media effect. *Journal of Communication, 56*, 449–466.

Gunther, A. C., & Schmitt, K. (2004). Mapping boundaries of the hostile media effect. *Journal of Communication, 54*, 55–70.

Hansen, G. J., & Kim, H. (2011). Is the media biased against me? A meta-analysis of the hostile media effect research. *Communication Research Reports, 28*, 169–179.

Harris, L. (2012, June 9). Are Americans too dumb for democracy? *The American*. Retrieved from http://www.aei.org/publication/are-americans-too-dumb-for-democracy/

Hatemi, P. K., Byrne, E., & McDermott, R. (2012). Introduction: What is a "gene" and why does it matter for political science? *Journal of Theoretical Politics, 24*, 305–327.

Hatemi, P. K., Funk, C. L., Medland, S. E., Maes, H. M., Silberg, J. L., Martin, N. G., & Eaves, L. J. (2009). Genetic and environmental transmission of political attitudes over a life time. *The Journal of Politics, 71*, 1141–1156.

Hatemi, P. K., McDermott, R., Eaves, L. J., Kendler, K. S., & Neale, M. C. (2013). Fear as a disposition and an emotional state: A genetic and environmental approach to out-group political preferences. *American Journal of Political Science, 57*, 279–293.

Holbert, R. L., Garrett, R. K., & Gleason, L. S. (2010). A new era of minimal effects: A response to Bennett and Iyengar. *Journal of Communication, 60*, 15–34.

Hovland, C. I., Lumsdaine, A. A., & Sheffield, F. D. (1949). *Experiments on mass communication*. Princeton, NJ: Princeton University Press.

Hudson, W. E. (2013). *American democracy in peril*. Los Angeles: Sage.

Igartua, J. J., & Barrios, I. (2012). Changing real-world beliefs with controversial movies: Processes and mechanisms of narrative persuasion. *Journal of Communication, 62*, 514–531.

Indicators of news media trust. (2018, September 11). *Knight Foundation*. Retrieved from https://www.knightfoundation.org/reports/indicators-of-news-media-trust

Jensen, J. D., Bernat, J. K., Wilson, K. M., & Goonewardene, J. (2011). The delay hypothesis: The manifestation of media effects over time. *Human Communication Research, 37*, 509–528.

Kahneman, D. (2011). *Thinking, fast and slow*. New York: Farrar, Straus, and Giroux.

Kilgore, E. (2018, September 5). Most Americans can't name a Supreme Court justice. *New York Magazine*. Retrieved from http://nymag.com/intelligencer/2018/09/most-americans-cant-name-a-supreme-court-justice.html

Kim, H. S., Bigman, C. A., Leader, A. E., Lerman, C., & Cappella, J. N. (2012). Narrative health communication and behavior change: The influence of exemplars in the news on intention to quit smoking. *Journal of Communication, 62*, 473–492.

Kirzinger, A. E., Weber, C., Johnson, M. (2012). Genetic and environmental influences on media use and communication behaviors. *Human Communication Research, 38*, 144–171.

Krcmar, M., & Greene, K. (1999). Predicting exposure to and uses of television violence. *Journal of Communication, 49*, 24–45.

Kubey, R., & Csikszentmihalyi, M. (2002, February). Television addiction is no mere metaphor. *Scientific American*, pp. 74–80.

Kuklinski, J. H., & Quirk, P. J. (2002). Reconsidering the rational public: Cognition, heuristics, and mass opinion. In A. Lupia, M. McCubbins, & S. Popkin (Eds.), *Elements of political reason* (pp. 153–182). New York: Cambridge University Press.

Lang, A. (1990). Involuntary attention and physiological arousal evoked by structural features and mild emotion in TV commercials. *Communication Research, 17*, 275–299.

Lippmann, W. (1922). *Public opinion*. New York: Macmillan.

Malamuth, N. (1996). Sexually explicit media, gender differences, and evolutionary thought. *Journal of Communication, 46*, 8–31.

Marcus, G. E., Newman, W. R., & MacKuen, M. (2000). *Affective intelligence and political judgment*. Chicago: University of Chicago Press.

Miller, R. L., Brickman, P., & Bolen, D. (1975). Attribution versus persuasion as a means for modifying behavior. *Journal of Personality and Social Psychology*, *3*, 430–441.

Morgan, S. E., Movius, L., & Cody, M. J. (2009). The power of narratives: The effect of entertainment television organ donation storylines on the attitudes, knowledge, and behaviors of donors and nondonors. *Journal of Communication*, *59*, 135–151.

Moyer-Gusé, E. (2008). Toward a theory of entertainment persuasion: Explaining the persuasive effects of entertainment-education messages. *Communication Theory*, *18*, 407–425.

Murphy, S. T., Frank, L. B., Chatterjee, J. S., & Baezconde-Garbanati, L. (2013). Narrative versus nonnarrative: The role of identification, transportation, and emotion in reducing health disparities. *Journal of Communication*, *63*, 116–137.

Murphy, S. T., Frank, L. B., Moran, M. B., & Patnoe-Woodley, P. (2011). Involved, transported, or emotional? Exploring the determinants of change in knowledge, attitudes, and behavior in entertainment-education. *Journal of Communication*, *61*, 407–431.

Muuss, R. E. (1988). *Theories of adolescence*. New York: Random House.

Nyhan, B., & Reifler, J. (2010). When corrections fail: The persistence of political misperceptions. *Political Behavior*, *32*, 303–330.

Owen, L. H. (2019, March 22). The "backfire effect" is mostly a myth, a broad look at the research suggests. *Nieman Lab*. Retrieved from https://www.niemanlab.org/2019/03/the-backfire-effect-is-mostly-a-myth-a-broad-look-at-the-research-suggests/

Park, A. (2018, April 10). Should you diagnose yourself online? Here's what doctors think. *Time*. Retrieved from http://time.com/5230797/online-symptom-checkers-is-it-safe/

Patterson, T. E. (1993). *Out of order*. New York: Knopf.

Patterson, T. E. (2016a, December 7). News coverage of the 2016 general election: How the press failed the voters. *Shorenstein Center on Media, Politics, and Public Policy*. Retrieved from https://shorensteincenter.org/news-coverage-2016-general-election/

Patterson, T. E. (2016b, July 11). News coverage of the 2016 presidential primaries: horse race reporting has consequences. *Shorenstein Center on Media, Politics, and Public Policy*. Retrieved from https://shorensteincenter.org/news-coverage-2016-presidential-primaries/

Perloff, R. M. (1989). Ego-involvement and the third person effect of televised news coverage. *Communication Research*, *16*, 236–262.

Petty, R. E., Briñol, P., & Priester, J. R. (2009). Mass media attitude change: Applications of the elaboration likelihood model of persuasion. In J. Bryant & M. B. Oliver (Eds.), *Media effects: Advances in theory and research* (pp. 125–164). New York: Routledge.

Petty, R. E., & Cacioppo, J. T. (1986). The elaboration likelihood model of persuasion. In L. Berkowitz (Ed.), *Advances in experimental social psychology, vol. 19* (pp. 123–205). New York: Academic Press.

Potter, W. J. (2012). *Media effects*. Los Angeles: Sage.

Raphael, R. (2019, February 4). A shockingly large majority of health news shared on Facebook is false. *Fast Company*. Retrieved from https://www.fastcompany.com/90301427/a-shockingly-large-majority-of-health-news-shared-on-facebook-is-fake

Redlawsk, D. P., Civettini, A. J. W., & Emmerson, K. M. (2010). The affective tipping point: Do motivated reasoners ever "get it"? *Political Psychology*, *31*, 563–593.

Reeves, B., & Thorson, E. (1986). Watching television: Experiments on the viewing process. *Communication Research*, *13*, 343–361.

Riccards, P. (2018, October 3). National survey finds just 1 in 3 Americans would pass citizenship test. *Woodrow Wilson National Fellowship Program*. Retrieved from https://woodrow.org/news/national-survey-finds-just-1-in-3-americans-would-pass-citizenship-test/

Robinson, J. P., & Davis, D. K. (1990). Television news and the informed public: Not the main source. *Journal of Communication*, *40*, 106–119.

Robinson, J. P., & Levy, M., with Davis, D. K. (Eds). (1986). *The main source: Learning from television news*. Newbury Park, CA: Sage.

Schank, R., & Abelson, R. (1977). *Scripts, plans, goals, and understanding: An inquiry into human knowledge structure*. Hillsdale, NJ: Lawrence Erlbaum Associates.

Schwartz, L. (2017, March 17). America's health illiteracy: How easy it is to buy into health myths. *Alternet*. Retrieved from https://www.alternet.org/2017/03/americas-health-illiteracy-how-easy-it-buy-health-myths/

Shen, F. (2004). Effects of news frames and schemas on individuals' issue interpretations and attitudes. *Journalism & Mass Communication Quarterly, 81*, 400–416.

Sherry, J. L. (2004). Media effects theory and the nature/nurture debate: A historical overview and directions for future research. *Media Psychology, 6*, 83–109.

Shoemaker, P. (1996). Hardwired for news: Using biological and cultural evolution to explain the surveillance function. *Journal of Communication, 46*, 32–47.

Shrum, L. J., (2009). Media consumption and perceptions of social reality. In J. Bryant & M. B. Oliver (Eds.), *Media effects: Advances in theory and research* (pp. 50–73). New York: Routledge.

Slater, M. D., & Rouner, D. (2006). Entertainment—Education and elaboration likelihood: Understanding the processing of narrative persuasion. *Communication Theory, 12*, 173–191.

Somin, I. (2017, March 1). The perils of public ignorance about federal spending. *Washington Post.* Retrieved from https://www.washingtonpost.com/news/volokh-conspiracy/wp/2017/03/01/the-perils-of-public-ignorance-about-federal-spending/?utm_term=.e2128c6f0572

Somin, I. (2018, November 5). Political ignorance and the midterm elections. *Reason.* Retrieved from https://reason.com/volokh/2018/11/05/political-ignorance-and-the-midterm-elec

Sotirovic, M. (2003). How individuals explain social problems: The influences of media use. *Journal of Communication, 53*, 122–137.

Taylor, S. E. (1981). The interface of cognitive and social psychology. In J. H. Harvey (Ed.), *Cognition, social behavior, and the environment* (pp. 189–211). Hillsdale, NJ: Erlbaum.

Tesser, A. (1993). The importance of heritability in psychological research: The case of attitudes. *Psychological Review, 100*, 129–142.

Tsfati, Y., & Cohen, J. (2013). The third-person effect, trust in media, and hostile media perceptions. *International Encyclopedia of Media Studies: Media Effects/Media Psychology, 1*, 1–19.

Valentino, N. A., Beckman, M. N., & Buhr, T. A. (2001). When the frame is the game: Revisiting the impact of "strategic" campaign coverage on citizens' information retention. *Journalism & Mass Communication Quarterly, 78*, 93-112.

Vallone, R. P., Ross, L., & Lepper, M. R. (1985). The hostile media phenomenon: Biased perception and perceptions of media bias in coverage of the Beirut massacre. *Journal of Personality and Social Psychology, 49*, 577–585.

Verhulst, B., Hatemi, P. K., & Eaves, L. J. (2012). Disentangling the importance of psychological predispositions and social constructions in the organization of American political ideology. *Political Psychology, 33*, 375–393.

Wallace, G. (2016, November 30). Voter turnout at 20-year low in 2016. *CNN.* Retrieved from https://www.cnn.com/2016/11/11/politics/popular-vote-turnout-2016/index.html

Warlaumont, H. G. (1997). Appropriating reality: Consumers' perceptions of schema-inconsistent advertising. *Journalism & Mass Communication Quarterly, 74*, 39–54.

Wartella, E. (1999). Children and media: On growth and gaps. *Mass Communication and Society, 2*, 81–88.

Wartella, E. (1979). The developmental perspective. In E. Wartella (Ed.), *Children communicating: Media and development of thought, speech, and understanding* (pp. 7–19). Beverly Hills, CA: Sage.

Weaver, J. (2018, July 6). More people search for health online. *NBC News.* Retrieved from http://www.nbcnews.com/id/3077086/t/more-people-search-health-online/#.XFxSLLhOlPY

Wood, G., & McBride, T. (1997). Origins of orienting and defensive responses: An evolutionary perspective. In P. J. Lang, R. F. Simons, & M. Balaban (Eds.), *Attention and orienting: Sensory and motivational processes* (pp. 41–67). Hillsdale, NJ: Erlbaum.

Young, B. (1990). *Television advertising to children.* Oxford, UK: Clarendon Press.

CHAPTER 11

Alterman, E. (2019, January 10). Facebook is a social menace. *Nation.* Retrieved from https://www.thenation.com/article/facebook-spies-alterman/

Anderson, M., & Kumar, M. (2019, May 7). Digital divide persists even as lower-income Americans make gains in tech adoption. *Pew Research Center.* Retrieved from https://www.pewresearch.org/fact-tank/2019/05/07/digital-divide-persists-even-as-lower-income-americans-make-gains-in-tech-adoption/

Atkin, D. J., Hunt, D. S., & Lin, C. A. (2015). Diffusion theory in the new media environment: Toward an integrated technology adoption model. *Mass Communication & Society, 18*, 623–650.

Beam, M. A., Hmielowski, J. D., & Hutchens, M. J. (2018). Democratic digital inequalities: Threat and opportunity in online citizenship from motivation and ability. *American Behavioral Scientist, 62,* 1079–1096.

Bell, E., & Owen T. (2017) *The platform press: How Silicon Valley reengineered journalism.* New York: Tow Center for Digital Journalism. Retrieved from https://academiccommons.columbia.edu/doi/10.7916/D8R216ZZ

Bharara, P. (2019, Winter). Journalism's advocate. *New York Times Book Review,* p. 9.

Bonfadelli, H. (2002). The Internet and knowledge gaps: A theoretical and empirical investigation. *European Journal of Communication, 17:* 65–85.

Chan, M. (2018). Reluctance to talk about politics in face-to-face and Facebook settings: Examining the impact of fear of isolation, willingness to self-censor, and peer network characteristics. *Mass Communication & Society, 21,* 1–23.

Cohen, B. C. (1963). *The press and foreign policy.* Princeton, NJ: Princeton University Press.

Curran, J., S. Iyengar, B. Lund, & Salovaara-Moring, I. (2009). Media system, public knowledge and democracy: A comparative study. *European Journal of Communication, 25,* 5–26.

Davis, D. K. (2015). Afterword: What is so new about new media? In R.A. Lind (Ed.), *Producing theory in a digital world 2.0* (pp. 267–277). New York: Peter Lang.

Donohue, G. A., Tichenor, P. J., & Olien, C. N. (1986). Metro daily pullback and knowledge gaps, within and between communities. *Communication Research, 13,* 453–471.

Feldman, S. (2019, June 5). Where does the digital divide persist? *Statista.* Retrieved from https://www.statista.com/chart/18266/digital-divide-in-rural-america/

Friedman, L. A., Kachur, E. R., Noar, M. S., & McFarlane, M. (2016). Health communication and social marketing campaigns for sexually transmitted disease prevention and control. *Sexually Transmitted Diseases, 43,* S83–S101.

Fox, J., & Holt, L. F. (2018). Fear of isolation and perceived affordances: the spiral of silence on social networking sites regarding police discrimination. *Mass Communication & Society, 21,* 533–554.

Gilmor, D. (2004). *We the media—Grassroots journalism by the people, for the people.* Sebastopol, CA: O'Reilly.

Glynn, C. J., & McLeod, J. M. (1985). Implications of the spiral of silence theory for communication and public opinion research. In K. Sanders, L. L. Kaid, & D. Nimmo (Eds.), *Political communication yearbook 1984* (pp. 43–65). Carbondale, IL: Southern Illinois University Press.

Grier, S., & Bryant, C. A. (2004). Social marketing in public health. *Annual Review of Public Health, 26,* 319–339.

Gruszczynski, M., & Wagner, M. W. (2017). Information flow in the 21st century: The dynamics of agenda-uptake. *Mass Communication & Society, 20,* 378–402.

Hayes, A. F., Matthes, J., & Eveland, W. P. (2011). Stimulating the quasi-statistical organ: Fear of social isolation motivates the quest for knowledge of the opinion climate. *Communication Research, 38,* 1–24.

Holbrook, T. M. (2002). Presidential campaigns and the knowledge gap. *Political Communication, 19,* 437–465.

Huffman, S. (2018). The digital divide revisited: What is next? *Education, 138,* 239–246.

Hwang, Y., & Jeong, S. H. (2009). Revisiting the knowledge gap hypothesis: A meta-analysis of thirty-five years of research. *Journalism & Mass Communication Quarterly, 86,* 513–532.

Ingram, M. (2018, Winter) The Facebook Armageddon: The social network's increasing threat to journalism. *Columbia Journalism Review,* Retrieved from https://www.cjr.org/special_report/facebook-media-buzzfeed.php

Iyengar, S. (1991). *Is anyone responsible? How television frames political issues.* Chicago, IL: University of Chicago Press.

Iyengar, S., & Kinder, D. R. (1987). *News that matters: Television and American opinion.* Chicago, IL: University of Chicago Press.

Katona, Z., Knee, J. A., & Sarvary, M. (2017). Agenda chasing and contests among news providers. *The RAND Journal of Economics, 48,* 783–809.

Katz, E. (1983). Publicity and pluralistic ignorance: Notes on "The spiral of silence." In E. Wartella & D. C. Whitney (Eds.), *Mass communication review yearbook 4* (pp. 89–99). Beverly Hills, CA: Sage.

Kotler, P., & Lee, N. R. (2008). *Social marketing: Influencing behaviors for good.* Los Angeles, CA: Sage.

Lang, K., & Lang, G. E. (1983). *The battle for public opinion: The President, the press, and the polls during Watergate.* New York: Columbia University Press.

Lin, C. (2003). An interactive communication technology adoption model. *Communication Theory, 13,* 345–365.

Madden, M. (2017, September 27). Privacy, security, and digital inequality. *Data & Society.* Retrieved from https://datasociety.net/output/privacy-security-and-digital-inequality/

McCombs, M., & Ghanem, S. I. (2001). The convergence of agenda setting and framing. In S. D. Reese, O. H. Gandy, & A. E. Grant (Eds.), *Framing public life: Perspectives on media and our understanding of the social world* (pp. 67–82). Mahwah, NJ: Erlbaum.

McCombs, M. E. (1981). The agenda-setting approach. In D. D. Nimmo & K. R. Sanders (Eds.), *Handbook of political communication* (pp. 121–140). Beverly Hills, CA: Sage.

McCombs, M. E., & Shaw, D. L. (1972). The agenda-setting function of mass media *Public Opinion Quarterly, 36,* 176–187.

Mozur, P. (2018, October 16). Genocide across Myanmar, incited on Facebook. *New York Times,* p. A1.

Neuman, W. R., Guggenheim, L., Mo Jang, S., & Bae, S. Y. (2014). The dynamics of public attention: agenda-setting theory meets Big Data. *Journal of Communication, 64,* 193–214.

Noelle-Neumann, E. (1973). Return to the concept of the powerful mass media. *Studies of Broadcasting, 9,* 68–105.

Noelle-Neumann, E. (1984). *The spiral of silence: Our social skin.* Chicago, IL: University of Chicago Press.

Noelle-Neumann, E. (1985). The spiral of silence: A response. In K. R. Sanders, L. L. Kaid, & D. D. Nimmo (Eds.), *Political Communication Yearbook, 1984* (pp. 66–94). Carbondale, IL: Southern Illinois University Press.

Patterson, T. E. (1993). *Out of order.* New York: Knopf.

Poll: How does the public think journalism happens? (2019, March 1). *Columbia Journalism Review,* pp. 68–73.

Potter, W. J. (2012). *Media effects.* Los Angeles, CA: Sage.

Protess, D. L., Cook, F. L., Doppelt, J. C., Ettema, J. S., Gordon, M. T., Leff, D. R., & Miller, P. (1991). *The journalism of outrage.* New York: Guilford.

Rogers, E. M. (1962). *Diffusion of innovations.* New York: Free Press.

Romm, T. (2019, January 23). Google led a multimillion-dollar tech industry lobbying blitz in 2018, records show. *Washington Post.* Retrieved from https://www.washingtonpost.com/technology/2019/01/23/google-led-multimillion-dollar-tech-industry-lobbying-blitz-records-show/?noredirect=on&utm_term=.9d39cb3c1e1c

Salmon, C. T., & Kline, F. G. (1985). The spiral of silence ten years later: An examination and evaluation. In K. R. Sanders, L. L. Kaid, & D. D. Nimmo (Eds.), *Political communication yearbook, 1984* (pp. 3–30). Carbondale, IL: Southern Illinois University Press.

Shoemaker, P. J., & Reese, S. D. (2014). *Mediating the message in the 21st century: A media sociology perspective.* New York, NY: Allyn and Bacon.

Smith, A., & Olmstead, K. (2018, April 30). Declining majority of online adults say the Internet has been good for society. *Pew Research Center.* Retrieved from http://www.pewinternet.org/2018/04/30/declining-majority-of-online-adults-say-the-internet-has-been-good-for-society/

Smith, A., Schlozman, K. L., Verba, S., & Brady, H. (2009, September). The Internet and civic engagement. *Pew Internet & American Life Project.* Retrieved from https://www.pewinternet.org/2009/09/01/the-internet-and-civic-engagement/

Snyder, B., & Witteman, C. (2019, March 29). The anti-competitive forces that foil speedy, affordable broadband. *Fast Company.* Retrieved from https://www.fastcompany.com/90319916/the-anti-competitive-forces-that-foil-speedy-affordable-broadband

Stacey, K. (2019, January 6). How Washington plans to regulate Big Tech. *Financial Times.* Retrieved from https://www.ft.com/content/8aa6680e-f4e2-11e8-ae55-df4bf40f9d0d

Tichenor, P. J., Donohue, G. A., & Olien, C. N. (1970). Mass media flow and differential growth of knowledge. *Public Opinion Quarterly, 34,* 159–170.

Tichenor, P. J., Donohue, G. A., & Olien, C. N. (1980). *Community conflict and the press.* Beverly Hills, CA: Sage.

"United States." (2019). *Reporters without borders.* Retrieved from https://rsf.org/en/united-states

Vishwanath, A., & Barnett, G. A. (Eds.). (2011). *The diffusion of innovations: A communication sciences perspective.* New York: Peter Lang.

Vonbun, R., Kleinen-von Königslöw, K., & Schönbach, K. (2016). Intermedia agenda-setting in a multimedia news environment. *Journalism, 17,* 1054–1073.

Wagner, K. (2019, February 20). Digital advertising in the US is finally bigger than print and television. *Recode.* Retrieved from https://www.recode.net/2019/2/20/18232433/digital-advertising-facebook-google-growth-tv-print-emarketer-2019

Watts, D. J., & Rothschild, D. M. (2017, December 5). Don't blame the election on fake news. Blame it on the media. *Columbia Journalism Review.*

Retrieved from https://www.cjr.org/analysis/fake -news-media-election-trump.php

Wei, L., & Hindman, D. B. (2011). Does the digital divide matter more? Comparing the effects of new media and old media use on the education-based knowledge gap. *Mass Communication and Society, 14*, 216–235.

CHAPTER 12

Amadeo, K. (2019, January 22). Average income in the USA by family and household. *The Balance*. Retrieved from https://www.thebalance.com/what -is-average-income-in-usa-family-household -history-3306189

American Society of Newspaper Editors. (2019). News literacy. Retrieved from https://www.asne.org/ resources-literacy

Ashley, S., Maksl, A., & Craft, S. (2013). Developing a news media literacy scale. *Journalism & Mass Communication Educator, 68*, 7–21.

Austin, E. W., Miller, A. C., Silva, J., Guerra, P., Geisle, N., Gamboa, L., … Kuechle, B. (2002). The effects of increased cognitive involvement on college students' interpretations of magazine advertisements for alcohol. *Communication Research, 29*, 155–179.

Banerjee, S. C., & Kubey, R. (2013). Boom or boomerang: A critical review of evidence documenting media literacy efficacy. In A. N. Valdivia & E. Scharrer (Eds.), *The international encyclopedia of media studies: Media effects/media psychology* (pp. 1–24). Hoboken, NJ: Blackwell.

Bell, D. (2019, January 24). An equal say. *The Nation*, pp. 27–31.

Berezow, A. (2018, April 5). White overdose deaths 50% higher than Blacks, 167% higher than Hispanics. *American Council on Science and Health*. Retrieved from https://www.acsh. org/news/2018/04/05/white-overdose-deaths -50-higher-blacks-167-higher-hispanics-12804

Bergsma, L. J., & Carney, M. E. (2008). Effectiveness of health-promoting media literacy literature education: A systematic review. *Health Education Research, 23*, 522–542.

Bhatia, K. V., & Pathak-Shelat, M. (2019) *Challenging discriminatory practices of religious socialization among adolescents: Critical media education and pedagogies in practice*. London: Springer.

Bulger, M., & Davison, P. (2018). The promises, challenges and futures of media literacy. *Journal of Media Literacy Education, 10*, 1–21.

Christ, W. G., & Potter, W. J. (1998). Media literacy, media education, and the academy. *Journal of Communication, 48*, 5–15.

Chung, J. E. (2014). Medical dramas and viewer perception of health: Testing cultivation effects. *Human Communication Research, 40*, 333–349.

Clark, L. S. (2011). Parental mediation theory for the digital age. *Communication Theory, 21*, 323–343.

Coenen, C., & Van Den Bulck, J. (2018) Reconceptualizing cultivation: Implications for testing relationships between fiction exposure and self-reported alcohol use evaluations, *Media Psychology, 21*, 613–639.

Coleman, J. S. (1988). Social capital in the creation of human capital. *American Journal of Sociology, 94*, S95–S120.

Craft, S., Ashley, S., & Maksl, A. (2017). News media literacy and conspiracy theory endorsement. *Communication and the Public, 2*, 388–401.

Darr, J. P., Hitt, M. P., & Dunaway, J. L. (2018). Newspaper closures polarize voting behavior. *Journal of Communication, 68*, 1007–1028.

Darrach, A., McCormick, A., & Sultan, Z. (2019, Winter). Life in a news desert. *Columbia Journalism Review*, pp. 106-109.

Diefenbach, D., & West, M. (2007). Television and attitudes toward mental health issues: Cultivation analysis and third person effect. *Journal of Community Psychology, 35*, 181–195.

Dubos, R. (2001). *Social capital*. New York: Routledge.

Eisenstein, E. L. (1979). *The printing press as an agent of change: Communications and cultural transformations in early-modern Europe*. Cambridge, UK: Cambridge University Press.

Entman, R. M. (1989). *Democracy without citizens: Media and the decay of American politics*. New York: Oxford University Press.

Ewen, S. (1996). *PR! A social history of spin*. New York: Basic Books.

Ewen, S. (2000). Memoirs of a commodity fetishist. *Mass Communication and Society, 3*, 439–452.

Farsides, T., Pettman, D., & Tourle, L. (2013). Inspiring altruism: reflecting on the personal relevance of emotionally evocative prosocial media characters. *Journal of Applied Social Psychology, 43*, 2251–2258.

Froomkin, D. (2012, December 7). How the mainstream press bungled the single biggest story of the 2012 campaign. *Huffington Post*. Retrieved from http://www.huffingtonpost.com/dan-froomkin/ republican-lies-2012-election_b_2258586.html

Gao, G. (2016, April 13). Americans divided on how much they trust their neighbors. *Pew Research Center*. Retrieved from https://www.pewresearch.org/fact-tank/2016/04/13/americans-divided-on-how-much-they-trust-their-neighbors/

Gerbner, G. (1990). Epilogue: Advancing on the path of righteousness (maybe). In N. Signorielli & M. Morgan (Eds.), *Cultivation analysis: New directions in media effects research* (pp. 249–262). Newbury Park, CA: Sage.

Gerbner, G. (1987). Television's populist brew: The three B's. *Etc.*, *44*, 2-7.

Gerbner, G., & Gross, L. (1976). Living with television: The violence profile. *Journal of Communication*, *26*, 173–199.

Gerbner, G., Gross, L., Jackson-Beeck, M., Jeffries-Fox, S., & Signorielli, N. (1978). Cultural indicators: Violence profile no. 9. *Journal of Communication*, *28*, 176–206.

Gerbner, G., Gross, L, Morgan, M., & Signorielli, N. (1980). The "mainstreaming" of America: Violence profile no. 11. *Journal of Communication*, *30*, 10–29.

Gerbner, G., Gross, L, Morgan, M., & Signorielli, N. (1982). Charting the mainstream: Television's contributions to political orientations. *Journal of Communication*, *32*, 100–127.

Gonzales, R., Glik, D., Davoudi, M., & Ang, A. (2004). Media literacy and public health: Integrating theory, research, and practice for tobacco control. *American Behavioral Scientist*, *48*, 189–201.

Gramlich, J. (2019, January 3). 5 facts about crime in the US. *Pew Research Center*. Retrieved from https://www.pewresearch.org/fact-tank/2019/01/03/5-facts-about-crime-in-the-u-s/

Grieco, E. (2019, April 12). For many rural residents in US, local news media mostly don't cover the area where they live. *Pew Research Center*. Retrieved from https://www.pewresearch.org/fact-tank/2019/04/12/for-many-rural-residents-in-u-s-local-news-media-mostly-dont-cover-the-area-where-they-live/

Helliwell, J. H., Layard, R., & and Sachs, J. D. (2019). World happiness report. *United Nations Sustainable Development Solutions Network*. Retrieved from https://s3.amazonaws.com/happiness-report/2019/WHR19.pdf

Hess, K. (2015). Making connections. *Journalism Studies*, *16*, 482–496.

Hutchins, C. (2019, May 30). "Orphan counties," and a battle over what local news really means. *Columbia Journalism Review*. Retrieved from https://www.cjr.org/united_states_project/orphan-counties-fcc-colorado.php

Innis, H. A. (1950). *Empire and communication*. Toronto: University of Toronto Press.

Intravia, J., Wolff, K. T., Paez, R., & Gibbs, B. R. (2017). Investigating the relationship between social media consumption and fear of crime: A partial analysis of mostly young adults. *Computers in Human Behavior*, *77*, 158–168.

Jang, S. M., & Kim, J. K. (2018). Third person effects of fake news: Fake news regulation and media literacy interventions. *Computers in Human Behavior*, *80*, 295–302.

Jeffres, L. W., Lee, J.-W., Neuendorf, K., & Atkin, D. (2007). Newspaper reading supports community involvement. *Newspaper Research Journal*, *23*, 6–23.

Jeong, S. H., Cho, C. H., & Hwang, Y. (2012). Media literacy interventions: A meta-analytic review. *Journal of Communication*, *62*, 454–472.

Jiow, H. J., Lim, S. S., & Lin, J. (2017). Level up! Refreshing parental mediation theory for our digital media landscape. *Communication Theory*, *27*, 309–328.

Johnson, A. B., Augustus, L., & Agiro, C. P. (2012). Beyond bullying: Pairing classics and media literacy. *The English Journal*, *101*, 56–63.

Krisch, J. (2018, June 7). Mapping Americans' divorce risk by state paints an unnerving picture. *Fatherly*. Retrieved from https://www.fatherly.com/health-science/american-divorce-rate-state/

Lakritz, T. (2018, September 26). The 30 safest cities in the world. *Insider*. Retrieved from https://www.insider.com/worlds-safest-cities-2017-11

Livingstone, S., & Helsper, E. J. (2006). Does advertising literacy mediate the effects of advertising on children? A critical examination of two linked research literatures in relation to obesity and food choice. *Journal of Communication*, *56*, 560–584.

Livingstone, S., Ólafsson, K., Helsper, E. J., Lupiáñez-Villanueva, F., Veltri, G. A., & Folkvord, F. (2017). Maximizing opportunities and minimizing risks for children online: The role of digital skills in emerging strategies of parental mediation. *Journal of Communication*, *67*, 82–105.

Lowen, L. (2018, August 30). States with highest teenage pregnancy and birth rates. *ThoughtCo*. Retrieved from https://www.thoughtco.com/states-highest-teenage-pregnancy-birth-rates-3533772

Morgan, M., & Shanahan, J. (2009). The state of cultivation. *Journal of Broadcasting & Electronic Media, 54*, 337–355.

Morgan, M., Shanahan, J., & Signorielli, N. (2015). Yesterday's new cultivation, tomorrow. *Mass Communication & Society, 18*, 674–699.

Mullin, B. (2016, December 15). Nearly a quarter of Americans say they have shared fake political news. *Poynter Institute.* Retrieved from https://www.poynter.org/2016/nearly-a-quarter-of-americans-say-they-have-shared-fake-political-news/442972/

Murray, M. (2019, January 27). "Wrong track": Public sours on nation's direction after shutdown. *NBC News.* Retrieved from https://www.nbcnews.com/politics/meet-the-press/wrong-track-public-sours-nation-s-direction-after-shutdown-n963051

Nagler, C. (2018). 4 tips for spotting a fake news story. *President and Fellows of Harvard College.* Retrieved from https://www.summer.harvard.edu/inside-summer/4-tips-spotting-fake-news-story

Nikkelen, S., Vossen, H., Piotrowski, J., & Valkenburg, P. (2016). Media violence and adolescents' ADHD-related behaviors: The role of parental mediation. *Journal of Broadcasting & Electronic Media, 60*, 657–675.

Parker, K., Horowitz, J., Brown, A., Fry, R., Cohn, D., & Igielnik, R. (2018, May 22). What unites and divides urban, suburban, and rural communities. *Pew Research Center.* Retrieved from https://www.pewsocialtrends.org/2018/05/22/what-unites-and-divides-urban-suburban-and-rural-communities/

Patterson, T. E. (1993). *Out of order.* New York: Knopf.

Potter, W. J. (1991). The relationships between first and second order measures of cultivation. *Human Communication Research, 18*, 92–113.

Potter, W. J. (1998). *Media literacy.* Thousand Oaks, CA: Sage.

Putnam, R. (2000). *Bowling alone: The collapse and revival of American community.* New York: Simon & Schuster.

Ramasubramanian, S., & Oliver, M. B. (2007). Activating and suppressing hostile and benevolent racism: Evidence for comparative stereotyping. *Media Psychology, 9*, 623–646.

Reimer, B., & Rosengren, K. E. (1990). Cultivated viewers and readers: A life-style perspective. In N. Signorielli & M. Morgan (Eds.), *Cultivation Analysis: New Directions in Media Effects Research* (pp. 181–206). Newbury Park, CA: Sage.

Rodríguez-de-Dios, I., van Oosten, J. M. F., & Igartua, J. J. (2018). A study of the relationship between parental mediation and adolescents' digital skills, online risks and online opportunities. *Computers in Human Behavior, 82*, 186–198.

Rubado, M. E., & Jennings, J. T. (2019). Political consequences of the endangered local watchdog: Newspaper decline and mayoral elections in the United States. *Urban Affairs Review, 55*, in press.

Rubin, A. M. (1998). Editor's note: Media literacy. *Journal of Communication, 48*, 3–4.

Scharrer, E., & Blackburn, G. (2018). Is reality TV a bad girls club? Television use, docusoap reality television viewing, and the cultivation of the approval of aggression. *Journalism & Mass Communication Quarterly, 95*, 235–257.

Segrin, C., & Nabi, R. L. (2002). Does television viewing cultivate unrealistic expectations about marriage? *Journal of Communication, 52*, 247–263.

Shanahan, J., & Jones, V. (1999). Cultivation and social control. In D. Demers & K. Viswanath (Eds.), *Mass Media, Social Control, and Social Change* (pp. 1–50). Ames, IA: Iowa State University Press.

Shanahan, J., Morgan, M., & Stenbjerre, M. (1997). Green or brown? Television and the cultivation of environmental concern. *Journal of Broadcasting and Electronic Media, 45*, 118–134.

Shrum, L. J. (2004). The cognitive processes underlying cultivation effects are a function of whether the judgments are on-line or memory-based. *Communications: The European Journal of Communication Research, 29*, 327–344.

Signorielli, N. (1990). Television's mean and dangerous world: A continuation of the cultural indicators perspective. In N. Signorielli & M. Morgan (Eds.), *Cultivation analysis: New directions in media effects research* (pp. 85–105). Newbury Park, CA: Sage Publications.

Signorielli, N., & Kahlenberg, S. (2001). Television's world of work in the nineties. *Journal of Broadcasting and Electronic Media, 41*, 305–323.

Silverblatt, A. (1995). *Media literacy: Keys to interpreting media messages.* Westport, CT: Praeger.

Sotirovic, M. (2003). How individuals explain social problems: The influences of media use. *Journal of Communication, 53*, 122–137.

Stanford History Education Group. (2016). Evaluating information: The cornerstone of civic online reasoning. *Stanford University.* Retrieved from https://stacks.stanford.edu/file/druid:fv751yt5934/SHEG%20Evaluating%20Information%20Online.pdf

Stearns, J. (2018, June 20). How we know journalism is good for democracy. *Local News Lab*. Retrieved from https://localnewslab.org/2018/06/20/how-we-know-journalism-is-good-for-democracy/

Stites, T. (2018, October 15). About 1,300 U.S. communities have totally lost news coverage, UNC news desert study finds. *Poynter Institute*. Retrieved from https://www.poynter.org/news/about-1300-us-communities-have-totally-lost-news-coverage-unc-news-desert-study-finds

Van Vonderen, K. E., & Kinnally, W. (2012). Media effects on body image: Examining media exposure in the broader context of internal and other social factors. *American Communication Journal, 14*, 41–53.

Vosoughi, S., Roy, D., & Aral, S. (2018). The spread of true and false news online. *Science, 359*, 1146–1151.

Ward, L., & Friedman, K. (2006). Using TV as a guide: Associations between television viewing and adolescents' sexual attitudes and behavior. *Journal of Research on Adolescence, 16*, 133–156.

CHAPTER 13

Aalberg, T., Strömbäck, J., & de Vreese, C. H. (2012). The framing of politics as strategy and game: A review of concepts, operationalizations, and key findings. *Journalism, 13*, 162–178.

Baran, S. J., & Blasko, V. J. (1984). Social perceptions and the byproducts of advertising. *Journal of Communication, 34*, 12–20.

Belson, K., & Draper, K. (2019, February 17). On Kaepernick, as in concussions, NFL makes a safe call. *New York Times*, pp. SP1–SP2.

Benford, R., & Snow, D. (2000) Framing processes and social movements: An overview and assessment. *Annual Review of Sociology, 26*, 611–639.

Bennett, W. L. (2005). *News: The politics of illusion*, 6th ed. New York: Longman.

Bennett, W. L., Lawrence, R. G., & Livingston, S. (2007) *When the press fails: Political power and the news media from Iraq to Katrina*. Chicago, IL: University of Chicago Press.

Berger, C. R. (2001). Making it worse than it is: Quantitative depictions of threatening trends in the news. *Journal of Communication, 46*, 655–677.

Berger, P. L., & Luckmann, T. (1966). *The social construction of reality: A treatise in the sociology of knowledge*. Garden City, NY: Doubleday.

Beutler, B. (2019, January 11). Media can kick its horserace addiction—And it must. *Crooked Media*. Retrieved from https://crooked.com/articles/media-horserace-addiction/

Blumer, H. (1969). *Symbolic Interactionism*. Englewood Cliffs, NJ: Prentice Hall.

Borah, P. (2011). Conceptual issues in framing theory: A systematic examination of a decade's literature. *Journal of Communication, 61*, 246–263.

Brugman, B. C., & Burgers, C. (2018). Political framing across disciplines: Evidence from 21st-century experiments. *Research & Politics, 5*, 1–7.

Cacciatore, M. A., Scheufele, D. A., & Iyengar, S. (2016). The end of framing as we know it … and the future of media effects. *Mass Communication & Society, 19*, 7–23.

Cappella, J. N., & Jamieson, K. H. (1997). *Spiral of cynicism: The press and the public good*. New York: Oxford University Press.

Carragee, K. M., & Roefs, W. (2004). The neglect of power in recent framing research. *Journal of Communication, 54*, 214–233.

Cissel, M. (2012). Media framing: A comparative content analysis on mainstream and alternative news coverage of Occupy Wall Street. *The Elon Journal of Undergraduate Research in Communications, 3*, 67–77.

Craig, R. T. (2007). Pragmatism in the field of communication theory. *Communication Theory, 17*, 125–145.

Davis, D. K., & Baran, S. J. (1981). *Mass communication and everyday life: A perspective on theory and effects*. Belmont, CA: Wadsworth.

de Vreese, C. H. (2012). New avenues for framing research. *American Behavioral Scientist, 56*, 365–375.

Entman, R. M. (1993). Framing: Toward clarification of a fractured paradigm. *Journal of Communication, 43*, 51–58.

Entman, R. M. (2004). *Projections of power: Framing news, public opinion, and US foreign policy*. Chicago, IL: University of Chicago Press.

Entman, R. M., Livingston, S., & Kim, J. (2009) Doomed to repeat: Iraq news, 2002–2007. *American Behavioral Scientist, 52*, 689–708.

Farr, J. (1999). John Dewey and American political science. *American Journal of Political Science, 43*: 520–541.

Faules, D. F., & Alexander, D. C. (1978). *Communication and social behavior: A symbolic interaction perspective*. Reading, MA: Addison-Wesley.

Ferment in the field. (1983). *Journal of Communication (Special Issue), 33*.

Gabbatt, A. (2018, July 6). The growing Occupy ICE movement: "We're here for the long haul."

Guardian. Retrieved from https://www.theguardian .com/us-news/2018/jul/06/occupy-ice-movement -new-york-louisville-portland

Gamson, W. A. (1989). News as framing. *American Behavioral Scientist, 33*, 157–161.

Gamson, W. A. (1992). *Talking politics*. New York: Cambridge University Press.

Gamson, W. A., Croteau, D., Hoynes, W., & Sasson, T. (1992). Media images and the social construction of reality. *Annual Review of Sociology, 18*, 373–393.

Gamson, W. A., & Modigliani, A. (1989). Media discourse and public opinion on nuclear power: A constructionist approach. *American Journal of Sociology, 95*, 1–37.

Garofoli, J. (2012, January 26). Obama's speech echoes Occupy movement themes. *San Francisco Chronicle*, p. A1.

Gilmor, D. (2004). *We the media—Grassroots journalism by the people, for the people*. Sebastopol, CA: O'Reilly.

Gitlin, T. (1980). *The whole world is watching: Mass media in the making and unmaking of the new left*. Berkeley, CA: University of California Press.

Goffman, E. (1974). *Frame analysis: An essay on the organization of experience*. New York: Harper & Row.

Goffman, E. (1979). *Gender advertisements*. New York: Harper Colophon.

Goffman, E. (1981). *Forms of talk*. Philadelphia: University of Pennsylvania Press.

Goist, P. D. (1971). City and "community": The urban theory of Robert Park. *American Quarterly, 23*, 46–59.

Graeber, D. (2013, April 13). Occupy's legacy: The media finally covers social protest fairly. *Salon*. Retrieved from https://www.salon.com/2013/ 04/13/occupys_legacy_the_media_finally _covers_social_protest_fairly/

Greenberg, J. (2011, October 26). The Occupy movement's mobilization dilemma. *The Ideas Lab*. Retrieved from http://theideaslab.wordpress.com/2011/10/26/ the-occupy-movements-mobilization-dilemma/

Gulati, G. J., Just, M. R., & Crigler, A. N. (2004). News coverage of political campaigns. In L. L. Kaid (Ed.), *Handbook of political communication research* (pp. 237–256). Mahwah, NJ: Lawrence Erlbaum.

Hargreaves, I., & Ferguson, G. (2000). *Who's misunderstanding whom?: Science, society and the media*. Swindon, UK: Economic and Social Research Council.

Ingram, M. (2018, Winter). The Facebook armageddon: The social network's increasing threat to journalism. *Columbia Journalism Review*. Retrieved from https://www.cjr.org/special_report/facebook -media-buzzfeed.php/

Johnston, H., & Noakes, J. A. (2005). *Frames of protest: Social movements and the framing perspective*. Boston, MA: Rowman and Littlefield.

Kirkhorn, M. J. (2000, February 20). Media increasingly ignore poor. *San Jose Mercury News*, p. 3C.

Lakoff, G. (2011, October 19). How to frame yourself: A framing memo for Occupy Wall Street. *Huffington Post*. Retrieved from http://www .huffingtonpost.com/george-lakoff/occupy-wall -street_b_1019448.html

Mazzarella, S. R. (2010). Coming of age too soon: Journalistic practice in US newspaper coverage of early puberty in girls. *Communication Quarterly, 58*, 36–58.

McCombs, M., & Ghanem, S. I. (2001). The convergence of agenda setting and framing. In S. D. Reese, O. H. Gandy, & A. E. Grant (Eds.), *Framing public life: Perspectives on media and our understanding of the social world* (pp. 67–82). Mahwah, NJ: Erlbaum.

McLeod, D. M., & Detenber, B. H. (1999). Framing effects of television news coverage of social protest. *Journal of Communication, 49*, 3–23.

Mead, G. H. (1934). *Mind, self, and society*. Chicago, IL: University of Chicago Press.

Moody, C. (2011, December 1). How Republicans are being taught to talk about Occupy Wall Street. *Yahoo! News*, December 1. Retrieved from http:// news.yahoo.com/blogs/ticket/republicans-being -taught-talk-occupy-wall-street-133707949.html

National Economic and Social Rights Initiative (2019). Parroting the right: How the media, pollsters adoption of insurance industry spin warps democracy *NESRI*. Retrieved from https:// parrotingtheright.org/

Nelson, T. E., & Clawson, R. A. (1997). Media framing of a civil liberties conflict and its effect on tolerance. *American Political Science Review, 91*, 567–583.

Panousi, V., Vidangos, I., Ramnath, S., DeBacker, J., & Heim, B. (2013, March 21). Inequality rising and permanent over past two decades. *Brookings Institution*. Retrieved from https://economistsview .typepad.com/economistsview/2013/03/ inequality-rising-and-permanent-over-past-two -decades.html

Patterson, T. E. (1993). *Out of order*. New York: Knopf.

Quinsaat, S. (2014). Competing news frames and hegemonic discourses in the construction of contemporary immigration and immigrants in the United States. *Mass Communication & Society*, *17*, 573–596.

Rorty, R. (1991). *Objectivity, relativism, and truth: Political papers I*. Cambridge, UK: Cambridge University Press.

Rorty, R., Schneewind, J. B., & Skinner, Q. (1982). *Consequences of pragmatism*. Minneapolis, MN: University of Minnesota Press.

Rowling, C. M., Jones, T. M., & Sheets, P. (2011). Some dared call it torture: Cultural resonance, Abu Ghraib, and a selectively echoing press. *Journal of Communication*, *61*, 1043–1061.

Russill, C. (2006). For a pragmatist perspective on publics: Advancing Carey's cultural studies through John Dewey … and Michel Foucault?! In J. Packer & C. Robertson (Eds.), *Thinking with James Carey: Essays on communications, transportation, history* (pp. 57–78). New York: Peter Lang.

Russill, C. (2008). Through a public darkly: Reconstructing pragmatist perspectives in communication theory. *Communication Theory*, *18*, 478–504.

Russill, C. (2012). William James: Among the machines. In J. Hannan (Ed.), *Philosophical profiles in the theory of communication* (pp. 291–324). New York: Peter Lang.

Ryan, C., Carragee, K. M., & Meinhofer, W. (2001). Framing, the news media, and collective action. *Journal of Broadcasting and Electronic Media*, *45*, 175–182.

Scheufele, D. A. (1999). Framing as a theory of media effects. *Journal of Communication*, *49*, 103–122

Scheufele, D. A. (2000). Agenda setting, priming, and framing revisited: Another look at cognitive effects of political communication. *Mass Communication and Society*, *3*, 297–316.

Scheufele, D. A., & Iyengar, S. (2012) The state of framing research: A call for new directions. In K. Kenski & K. H. Jamieson (Eds.), *The Oxford handbook of political communication* (pp. 1–27). New York: Oxford University Press.

Scheufele, D. A., & Tewksbury, D. (2007). Framing, agenda setting, and priming: The evolution of three media effects models. *Journal of Communication*, *57*, 9–20.

Schutz, A. (1967). *The phenomenology of the social world*. Evanston, IL: Northwestern University Press.

Schutz, A. (1970). *On phenomenology and social relations*. Chicago, IL: University of Chicago Press.

Smith, S. (2013, April 5). We're all TV executives now: Lurching toward personal programming. *MediaPost*. Retrieved from https://www.mediapost.com/publications/article/197401/were-all-tv-executives-now-lurching-toward-perso.html

Solomon, M. R. (1983). The role of products as social stimuli: A symbolic interactionism perspective. *Journal of Consumer Research*, *10*, 319–329.

Speno, A. G., & Aubrey, J. S. (2018). Sexualization, youthification, and adultification: A content analysis of images of girls and women in popular magazines. *Journalism & Mass Communication Quarterly*, *95*, 625–646.

Terkildsen, N., & Schnell, F. (1997). How media frames move public opinion: An analysis of the women's movement. *Political Research Quarterly*, *50*, 879–900.

Tuchman, G. (1978). *Making news: A study in the construction of reality*. New York: Free Press.

Valkenburg, P. M., & Semetko, H. A. (1999). The effects of news frames on readers' thoughts and recall. *Communication Research*, *26*, 550–569.

Van Aelst, P., Sheafer, T., & Stanyer, J. (2012). The personalization of mediated political communication: A review of concepts, operationalizations, and key findings. *Journalism*, *13*, 203–220.

Walters, S. D. (1995). *Material girls: Making sense of feminist cultural theory*. Berkeley, CA: University of California Press.

White, M. (2016). *The end of protest*. Toronto: Knopf Canada.

Whitman, E. (2019, March 25). The 11 most sophisticated online scams right now that the average person falls for. *Business Insider*. Retrieved from https://www.businessinsider.com/online-scams-internet-phishing-2019-3

Ytreberg, E. (2002). Erving Goffman as a theorist of the mass media. *Critical Studies in Media Communication*, *19*, 481–498.

Zuckerberg, M. (2017, February 16). Building global community. Retrieved from https://www.facebook.com/notes/mark-zuckerberg/building-global-community/10154544292806634

CHAPTER 14

Barber, B. R. (2007). *Consumed: How markets corrupt children, infantilize adults, and swallow citizens whole*. New York: W. W. Norton.

Bergen, M. (2019, April 2). YouTube executives ignored warnings, letting toxic videos run rampant. *Bloomberg*. Retrieved from https://www.bloomberg.com/news/features/2019-04-02/youtube-executives-ignored-warnings-letting-toxic-videos-run-rampant

Berger, P. L., & Luckmann, T. (1966). *The social construction of reality: A treatise in the sociology of knowledge.* Garden City, NY: Doubleday.

Chess, S., & Shaw, A. (2015). A conspiracy of fishes, or, how we learned to stop worrying about #GamerGate and embrace hegemonic masculinity. *Journal of Broadcasting & Electronic Media, 59,* 208–220.

Collins, S. T. (2014, October 17). Anita Sarkeesian on GamerGate: "We have a problem and we're going to fix this." *Rolling Stone.* Retrieved from https://www.rollingstone.com/politics/politics-news/anita-sarkeesian-on-gamergate-we-have-a-problem-and-were-going-to-fix-this-241766/

Collins, V. E., & Rothe, D. L. (2017). The consumption of patriarchy: Commodification to facilitation and reification. *Contemporary Justice Review, 20,* 161–174.

Couldry, N., & Hepp, A. (2017) *The mediated construction of reality.* Cambridge, UK: Polity.

Culpan, I., & Meier, C. (2016). Sport and the political economy: Considerations for enhancing the human condition. *Athens Journal of Sports, 3,* 143–154.

Deacon, D., & Stanyer, J. (2014) Mediatization: Key concept or conceptual bandwagon. *Media, Culture & Society, 36,* 1032–1044.

Dosh, K. (2018, September 30). Measuring the cost of being a sports fan. *Forbes.* Retrieved from https://www.forbes.com/sites/kristidosh/2018/09/30/measuring-the-cost-of-being-a-sports-fan/#224f5c105e54

Ekström, M., Fornäs, J., Jansson, A., & Jerslev, A. (2016). Three tasks for mediatization research: Contributions to an open agenda. *Media, Culture & Society, 38,* 1090–1108.

Enzensberger, H. M. (1974). *The consciousness industry.* New York: Seabury.

Evans-Thirlwell, E. (2017, October 20). The history of the first-person shooter. *PC Gamer.* Retrieved from https://www.pcgamer.com/the-history-of-the-first-person-shooter/

Giroux, H. (2000). *Stealing innocence: Corporate culture's war on children.* New York: Palgrave.

Gunster, S. (2004). *Capitalizing on culture: Critical theory for cultural studies.* Toronto, Canada: University of Toronto Press.

Hay, J. (1989). Advertising as a cultural text (rethinking message analysis in a recombinant culture). In B. Dervin, L. Grossberg, B. J. O'Keefe, & E. Wartella (Eds.), *Rethinking communication, vol. 2: Paradigm exemplars* (pp. 129–151). Newbury Park, CA: Sage.

Helm, J. (2002). When history looks back. *Adbusters,* March/April: n.p.

Hinz, L. (2018, October 22). What does "selling out" mean in the digital age? *Hot New Hip Hop.* Retrieved from https://www.hotnewhiphop.com/what-does-selling-out-mean-in-the-digital-age-news.62471.html

Hoffman, B. (2015). *Marketers are from Mars, consumers are from New Jersey.* San Francisco: Type A Group.

Jamieson, K. H. (1988). *Eloquence in an electronic age: The transformation of political speechmaking.* New York: Oxford University Press.

Jamieson, K. H., & Campbell, K. K. (1997). *The Interplay of influence: News, advertising, politics, and the mass media.* Belmont, CA: Wadsworth.

Jenson, J., & de Castell, S. (2008). Theorizing gender and digital gameplay: Oversights, accidents and surprises. *Eludamos: Journal for Computer Game Culture, 2,* 15–25.

Jhally, S. (Ed.) (1987). *The codes of advertising: Fetishism and the political economy of meaning in the consumer society.* New York: St. Martin's.

Kaun, A. (2011) Research overview for Riksbankens Jubileumsfond—mediatisation versus mediation: Contemporary concepts under scrutiny. In J. Fornäs & A. Kaun (Eds.), *Medialisering av kultur, politik, vardag och forskning (Mediestudier vid Södertörns högskola 2011:2)* (pp. 16–38). Huddinge, Sweden.

Kaun, A., & Fast, K. (2014) *Mediatization of culture and everyday life.* Huddinge, Sweden: Södertörns högskola.

Lawson, C. E. (2018). Innocent victims, creepy boys: Discursive framings of sexuality in online news coverage of the celebrity nude photo hack. *Feminist Media Studies, 18,* 825–841.

Linn, S. (2004). *Consuming kids.* New York: The New Press.

Livingstone, S. (2009). On the mediation of everything: ICA presidential address 2008. *Journal of Communication, 59,* 1–18.

Livingstone, S., & Lunt, P. (2014) Mediatization: An emerging paradigm for media and communication research? In K. Lundby (Ed.), *Mediatization of communication: Handbooks of communication science,* vol. 21 (pp. 703–723). Berlin: De Gruyter Mouton.

Lunt, P., & Livingstone, S. (2016). Is "mediatization" the new paradigm for our field? A commentary on Deacon and Stanyer (2014, 2015) and Hepp, Hjarvard, and Lundby (2015). *Media, Culture & Society, 38,* 462–470.

Marwick, A. E., & Caplan, R. (2018). Drinking male tears: Language, the manosphere, and networked harassment. *Feminist Media Studies, 18,* 543–559.

Megarry, J. (2014). Online incivility or sexual harassment? Conceptualising women's experiences in the digital age. *Women's Studies International Forum, 47,* 46–55.

Megarry, J. (2018) Under the watchful eyes of men: Theorising the implications of male surveillance practices for feminist activism on social media. *Feminist Media Studies, 18,* 1070–1085.

Meyrowitz, J. (1985). *No sense of place: The impact of electronic media on social behavior.* New York: Oxford University Press.

Molina, B. (2019, April 1). British Army recruiting campaign targeting 'binge gamers' and 'phone zombies.' *USA Today.* Retrieved from https://www.msn.com/en-au/news/us/british-army-recruiting-campaign-targeting-binge-gamers-and-phone-zombies/ar-BBROtfj

Ong, W. J. (2002). *Orality and literacy: The technologizing of the word.* New York: Routledge.

Postman, N. (1985). *Amusing ourselves to death: Public discourse in the age of show business.* New York: Penguin.

Postman, N. (1994). *The disappearance of childhood.* New York: Vintage.

Postman, N. (1996). *The end of education.* New York: Vintage.

Robertson, C. (2009). A sporting gesture? BSkyB, Manchester United, global media, and sport. *Television & New Media, 5,* 291-314.

Robertson, C. (2009). A sporting gesture? BSkyB, Manchester United, global media, and sport. *Television & New Media, 5,* 291-314.

Ruddock, A., Hutchins, B., & Rowe, D. (2010). Contradictions in media sport culture: The reinscription of football supporter traditions through online media. *European Journal of Cultural Studies, 13,* 323–339.

Salter, M. (2018). From geek masculinity to Gamergate: The technological rationality of online abuse. *Crime Media Culture. 14,* 247–264.

Sarkeesian, A. (2014). Women as background decoration: Part 1—Tropes vs women in video games. *Tropes Vs Women in Video Games.* Retrieved from https://www.youtube.com/watch?v=4ZPSrwedvsg&list=PLn4ob_5_ttEaA_vc8F3jzE62esf9yP61index

Secker, T., & Alford, M. (2017, July 4). EXCLUSIVE: Documents expose how Hollywood promotes war on behalf of the Pentagon, CIA and NSA. *Medium.* Retrieved from https://medium.com/insurge-intelligence/exclusive-documents-expose-direct-us-military-intelligence-influence-on-1-800-movies-and-tv-shows-36433107c307

Sports merchandising market size in North America from 2009 to 2022 (in billion U.S. dollars). (2019). *Statista.* Retrieved from https://www.statista.com/statistics/194226/revenue-from-sports-merchandising-in-north-america-since-2004/

Steinberg, S. R. (2011). Kinderculture: Mediating, simulacralizing, and pathologizing the new childhood. In S. R. Steinberg (Ed.), *Kinderculture: The corporate construction of childhood* (pp. 1–53). Boulder, CO: Westview Press.

Tunstall, J. (1977). *The media are American: Anglo-American media in the world.* New York: Columbia University Press.

INDEX

A

ABC, 66, 121, 162, 275
Abdulmutallab, Umar Farouk, 290
absolutists, First Amendment, 69
absorption, 273
absorption potential, 240
abstracted empiricism, 129
Abu Ghraib prison, 354
Access Hollywood, 300
active-audience perspectives, of audience
    theories, 226–31
active-audience theories, 193–94, 223, 232
active mediation, 325
active theory of television viewing, 193–94
active use (of social networking sites), 218
activist movements, use of frames by, 354
Adams-Bloom, Terry, 84–85
Adbusters, 355
administrative research, 121, 141
Adorno, Theodor, 155–56, 319
adultification of childhood, 205
The Adventures of Ozzie and Harriet
    (television program), 118
advergames, 210
advertising, 57, 194
    to children, 209–11
    schema-inconsistent, 262, 264
    sex-role stereotypes used in, 349–51
    as ultimate cultural commodity,
        371–72
affect (general aggression model), 197
affective forecasting error, 217
affective intelligence, 276
Affordable Care Act, 300
AFL-CIO, 162
African Americans, 114, 115
agency, 16, 337
agenda-building, 302–3
agenda cutting, 83
agenda-setting, 300–304
agenda setting theory, 46
aggression
    and catharsis, 185
    and video game usage, 196
aggressive behavior, 206. *See also* general
    aggression model (GAM)
aggressive cues, 190–92
agreement, intersubjective, 14
Ahmed, Wasim, 274
Alasuutari, Pertti, 247
alcohol advertising, 209
alcohol consumption, 352

Alexander, Dennis C., 339–40
Algeria, 94
Allcott, Hunt, 218–19
Allport, Gordon, 113–15
Alterman, Eric, 54, 55, 91–92
"alternative facts," 59
Althusser, Louis, 158
American Academy of Pediatrics, 206
American Armed Forces Radio, 366
American Power and the New Mandarins
    (Chomsky), 57
American Psychiatric Association, 31
American Psychological Association Task
    for on Advertising and Children,
    211
American Red Cross, 246
American Society of Newspaper Editors
    (ASNE), 78, 88, 326
American Voter Studies, 22
Anderson, Craig, 184, 192, 197
Anderson, Daniel, 193
Andison, F. Scott, 186
Andy of Mayberry (television program), 118
anti-Semitism, 40, 50
anti-Vietnam war movement, 143
anxiety, 216–17
Apple, 213
appraisal and decision processes (general
    aggression model), 198
apps, children-oriented, 213
Arab Spring, 94, 355
Aral, Sinan, 327
Arbitron, 121
Archives of Pediatrics & Adolescent Medicine
    (journal), 32
"Are Americans Too Dumb for
    Democracy?" (Harris), 252–53
Arendt, Hannah, 47
Areopagitica (Milton), 70–71
Aristotle, 185
arousal, 193, 198
artificial signs, 340
Ashley, Seth, 326
ASNE. *See* American Society of Newspaper
    Editors
ASNE Statement of Principles, 78
asynchroneity, of computer-mediated mass
    communication, 232–33
Atkin, David, 296
AT&T, 45
attention
    marketplace of, 6

    in neuroscience perspective, 278
attentional disorders, 206
attitude-change theories, 103–14
attitudes
    correct vs. incorrect, 266
    and genetics, 279–81
attribute agendas, 357
audience-centered research, early, 227–29
audience theories-uses and reception,
    222–51
    confusion of media functions and
        media uses, 229–31
    development of reception studies,
        244–48
    early audience-centered research,
        227–29
    entertainment theory, 238–43
    overview, 225–26
    and social networking, 243–44
    uses-and-gratifications theory, 231–38
Australia, 211
authoritarian concept, 94
authoritarian theory, 70
autism, 274
automaticity, 5
awareness
    created in social situations, 237
    of mood management processes, 241
Axelrod, Robert, 254
axiology, 14, 17*b*

B

Back, Mitja, 215
backfire effect, 277
Bagdikian, 45
Bailey, Kenneth, 13, 19
Baker, Levi, 214
Bakshy, Eytan, 112
Baldwin, Alex, 370
Balkanize (term), 87
Bandura, Albert, 12, 188–90, 192
Banerjee, Smita, 324
Baran, Stanley, 207
Barber, Benjamin, 213, 367
Baron, Marty, 59
Barrios, Isabel, 273
Bartlett, Frederic, 260–61
baseball, learning to play, 334
base of society, 153
The Battle of Britain (film), 105
Bauerlein, Monika, 59
Beam, Michael, 293

beauty ideals, 208
beauty magazines, 38
behavioral hierarchy, 189
behavioral repertoire, 187
behaviorism, 50
Bell, David, 326
belong, need to, 215
Benford, Robert, 354
Beniger, James, 45–46
Bennet, James, 162
Bennett, W. Lance, 165–66
Berelson, Bernard, 23, 111, 226
Berger, Charles, 13, 373
Berger, Peter, 343–45
Berkowitz, Leonard, 190, 191
Bernays, Edward L., 48
Beutler, Brian, 357
Bharara, Preet, 286
Bhatia, Kiran Vinod, 326
bias
    of communication, 171–72
    confirmation, 326
    in news stories, 165–66
The Bias of Communication (Innis), 172
Big Brother, 147
big data, 6, 303, 375
Big Five model, 281
Bijvank, Marije, 196
Billboard Liveration Front, 246
Bill of Rights, 71
Birmingham University, 24
Birmingham University Centre for
        Contemporary Cultural Studies,
        244
Bissell, Kimberly, 208
Black, Hugo, 69
Blackburn, Greg, 320
Black Lives Matter, 356
Black Panther (film), 234
Black Panthers, 182
black propaganda, 47
Blanton, Hart, 196
blogging, 88
Blumer, Herbert, 334
Blumler, Jay G., 91, 234, 235–37
body dissatisfaction, 208
Bollier, David, 246
Bollinger, Lee, 66
Bolton, Francis, 99
Bolz, Darrell, 32
Bonanza (television program), 118
Bond, Bradley, 239–40
Boneva, Bonka, 233
Bonfadelli, Heinz, 292
Boston Globe, 65
Boston Legal (television program), 275
bots, 91
Bowers, John, 13
bra burning, 143–44
bracket, 17
brain development, 209
brain drain hypothesis, 214
Brandeis, Louis, 72
Brandzæg, Petter, 216
Brave New World (Huxley), 147
Brazil, 31
Breaking Bad (television program), 186
Briand, Paul, 183
Briñol, Pablo, 268
Brisbane, Arthur, 66
Britain, development of neo-Marxist theory
        in, 244
British Broadcasting Corporation, 38
British cultural studies, 24, 156–59
British Labour Party, 158
Brock, Timothy, 270
Bronfenbrenner, Urie, 182
Bryant, James, 238, 239

Buffardi, Laura, 1
Buijzen, Moniek, 194
Bulger, Monica, 326
Bureau for Applied Social Research
        (Columbia University), 21
Burgess, Belinda, 192
Burpo, Sandra, 192
Burrows, Christopher, 196
Bushman, Brad, 184, 192, 196
Byrne, Enda, 279, 280

C
cable television, 86–87, 125
Cacioppo, John, 216–17, 266
Calogero, Rachael, 209
Cambridge University, 157
Camino (film), 273
Campbell, Karlyn, 367
Campbell, Keith, 1
The Canons of Journalism, 78
capitalism, 16, 74, 162, 168, 169
Caplan, Robyn, 370
Caplan, Scott, 147
captured agencies, 76
car commercials, 162–63
Carey, James, 38, 55–56, 162–63, 167, 171,
        317, 340
Carnagey, Nicholas, 192, 197
Carr, David, 171
cascading activation model, 354
catharsis, 185–86
Catholic Church, 70, 71
causality, 8, 12–13, 139, 302
causal relationships, 8
cause-and-effect sequences (schema), 262
CBS, 45, 66, 121, 150, 162
CBS Evening News, 150
censorship, 70, 92
the center, 172
Centerwall, Brandon, 184
central route, of information processing,
        267, 268
Centre for Contemporary Cultural Studies
        (University of Birmingham), 157
Century, 36
cereals, sugared, 210
cerebral cortex, 278
Chaffee, Steve, 260
Chain, Robert, 65–66
Chan, Michael, 306
change agents, 295–96, 298
Channels of Propaganda (Sproule), 57
characters, identification with, 273
Charters, W. W., 99–100
Chess, Shira, 370
Chicago Hope (television program), 320
Chicago School, 79–80, 86, 337–39
childhood obesity, 209–10
children
    advertising directed at, 209–11
    diet of, 209–10
    and loss of childhood, 210, 212–13
    and media, 99, 204–5
    media and development of, 206–13
    and personal technologies, 213–19
China, 94, 211
Cho, Hyunyi, 324
Chomsky, Noam, 57
Christ, William, 323
Christakis, Nicholas, 218
A Christmas Story (film), 188
Chung, Jae Eun, 320
*Circulation: Journal of the American Heart
        Association*, 32
Cissel, Margaret, 355
civil participation, 39–40, 314
Clark, Levina, 208
Clark, Lynn, 324–25

Clarke-Pearson, Kathleen, 147
Clark-Flory, Tracy, 274
classic four functions of media, 124–25
Cleary, Johanna, 84–85
climate change, 66
climate science, 9
Clinton, Hillary, 10, 66, 264, 300
cloud computing, 222–23
cognition (general aggression model),
        197–98
cognitive consistency, 110–11
cognitive dissonance, 111
cognitive misers, 266, 279
cognitive-neoassociationistic perspective,
        191
cognitive processing, 255–56
cognitive psychology, 255
cognitive resources, limited, 257–58
Cohen, Bernard, 300–301
Cold War, 55, 120, 121, 126, 127, 147,
        152, 156
Coleman, James, 310
Coleman, Stephan, 91
Collins, Victoria, 367
Columbia University, 21, 66, 102, 120, 129,
        130, 152, 156
Comcast, 45
commodification of culture, 364–72
Commonweal, 36
communication
    bias of, 171–72
    counternorm, 106
    health, 273–74
    interpersonal, 6
    mediated, 6, 204
    systems theories and, 136–37
Communication and Persuasion (Hovland),
        105–6
Communication and Social Behavior (Faules
        and Alexander), 339–40
Communication Research Program, 105–7
Communications Act, 211
communication systems, 135
communism, 39–40, 153
communism concept, 94
comparative analysis, 16–17
computer-mediated mass communication,
        232–33
Comstock, George, 207–8
concentration (of media ownership), 45
confirmation bias, 326
consciousness, 255, 257
conscious thought, 255, 257
consent, engineering of, 48
consequences, as contextual variable, 192
conservatives, 32, 35, 42, 57–58
consonance (of news media), 305
constant gap, 292
*Consumed: How Markets Corrupt Children,
        Infantilize Adults, and Swallow
        Citizens Whole* (Barber), 367
Consuming Kids (Linn), 367
consumption, 38, 163
contextual variables, 192–93
controlled variation, 104
converts, 108
Conway, Kellyanne, 59
Cooper, Ann, 88
corporate control, of media, 246
Corporate Media and the Threat to Democracy
        (McChesney), 57
Correa, Theresa, 281
correct attitudes, 266
correlation of parts of society, 229
Coughlin, Charles, 40
Couldry, Nick, 373–74
counternorm communications, 106
co-viewing, 325

Coyne, Sarah, 194
Craft, Stephanie, 326
Craig, Robert, 337
Crazy Rich Asians (film), 239
creativity, declines in, 206
Crenshaw, Kimberlé, 170
crime, 182
critical cultural theory, 24, 357–58
critical cultural trends, 23–24, 143–79
    British neo-Marxism, 156–59
    and changes of 1960s and 1970s,
      146–47
    comparison of theories in, 151–52
    critical theory, 149–50
    feminist scholarship, 167–70
    Frankfurt School, 155–56
    literary criticism, 154–55
    macroscopic vs. microscopic theories,
      148–49
    Marxist theory, 152–54
    McLuhan's theories, 170–75
    neo-Marxism, 154, 156–59
    news production research, 165–67
    overview, 145–46
    political economy theory, 159–62
    popular culture research, 163–65
    rise of, in Europe, 152
    textual analysis, 154–55
    transmissional vs. ritual perspectives in,
      162–70
critical feminists, 168
critical media education, 326
critical theories, 15–16, 17, 18, 149–50,
    247
Crockett, Zachary, 115
Cromwell, Oliver, 71
crystallizers, 108
CSI:NY (television program), 271
Cuba, 94
cues, 266, 349–50
Culpan, Ian, 368
cultivation (cultural process), 318
cultivation analysis, 46, 314–21
cultural criticism, 24
Cultural Indicators Project, 316
culturalist view, 158
cultural norms and American interests
    (schema), 262
cultural pluralism, 157
cultural studies, 148
    British, 156–59
    and media research, 225
    political economy theory vs., 160–62
Cultural Studies (Grossberg, Nelson, and
    Treichler), 164
cultural theory, 15, 18
cultural theory approach (feminist
    scholarship), 169
culture, 146
    commodification of, 364–72
    created with social media, 335
    folk, 365
    hegemonic, 148
    high, 155
    media teaching about, 331–32
Culture, Inc.: The Corporate Takeover of Public
    Expression (Schiller), 57
culture industries, 155–56
culture theories, 331–78
    commodification of culture, 364–72
    framing and frame analysis, 346–58
    mediatization theory, 372–76
    pragmatism and Chicago school,
      337–39
    social constructionism, 341–46
    symbolic interactionism, 333–40
cumulation (of news media), 305
Curnalia, Rebecca, 58

Curran, James, 291
cybernetics, 135

D
Daily Me, 112
Daniel Boone (television program), 118
Darr, Joshua, 313
Darwin, Charles, 8
data, big, 6
data analysis techniques, 231–32
Davis, Dennis, 259
Davison, Patrick, 326
Davy Crockett (television program), 118
Day, Amber, 170
Dayton Ohio mass shooting, 42
Deacon, David, 374–75
Dear White People (television series), 164
Decatur, Illinois, 129
deceptive advertising, 211
Declaration of Independence, 71
deep mediatization, 372
DeFleur, Melvin, 109, 127
delayed drench, 275
delayed drip, 275
delay hypothesis, 274–75
demagoguery, 47
demassification, 232
democracy, 40
    informed citizenry in, 126
    Lasswell's view of, 52
    and literacy, 322
    "science" of, 53
Democratic Party, 58, 107–8, 111, 252
demographics, 228
Denmark, 211
depression, 206
    Facebook, 217–18
    and social media, 217–18
    teenage, 205
desensitization, 192
Desmond, Matthew, 161
Desperate Housewives (television show), 270
deterministic assumptions, 24
Deterring Democracy (Chomsky), 57
developmental/personality processes
    (general aggression model), 197,
    198
developmental perspective, 194–95
development concept, 93–94
Dewey, John, 50, 55–56, 224, 337, 338
Diagnostic and Statistical Manual of Mental
    Disorders, 31, 217
dialectic, in critical theory, 16
different standards mechanism, 266
digital divide, 292–93
digital inequities, 293–94
direct-effects assumption, 38
The Disappearance of Childhood (Postman),
    367
discursive activities, 325
disinformation, 46
disinhibitory effects, 189
disintermediation, 91
Disney, 45
disruptive transition (media), 67
diversionary activities, 325
Division of Labor in Society (Durkheim), 43
dizygotic twins, 279
Dollard, John, 187
Dollarocracy: How the Money-and-Media-
    Election Complex Is Destroying
    America (McChesney), 57
dominant reading, 244
dominant reality, 351
dopamine, 31
downshift or upshift, 348
downward spiral model, 194
Dragnet (television program), 118

dramatized news, 165–66
dual-factor model of Facebook (FB) use,
    215
dual responsibility model, 84–85
dual responsibility theory, 84
Dunaway, Johanna, 313
Durkheim, Émile, 43–44
Dworkin, Andrea, 170
dysfunction (negative function), 230

E
early adopters, 295
early deciders, 108
early window, 210, 212
Editor & Publisher, 161
Education, 36
education, public, 55
EE. *See* entertainment-education
E-ELM. *See* extended elaboration likelihood
    model
The Effects of Mass Communication
    (Klapper), 130–32
effects research, 223, 224, 232
Eggermont, Steven, 208
ego, 51
Egypt, 94, 172
Einstein, Albert, 8, 9
Eisenhower, Dwight D., 127
Ekström, Mats, 374
elaboration likelihood model (ELM),
    266–69
elections, framing in media coverage of,
    263–64
elections of 2018, 252. *See also* presidential
    elections
elites, 20, 49–50, 153, 154, 157, 166, 358,
    365, 366–67
elitism, 44–45
Elliott, Charlene, 210
ELM. *See* elaboration likelihood model
El Paso Texas mass shooting, 42
e-mail, and social relationships, 233
emancipatory knowledge, 16
emotion, in neuroscience perspective, 278
empathy, 270, 273
Empire and Communication (Innis), 171–72
empires, word-based, 172
empirical observations, 10
empirical research, 120–22
empiricism, abstracted, 129
empowered child model, 195
enabling mediation, 325
The End of Education (Postman), 367
The End of the Protest (White), 356
engineering of consent, 48, 58
Enlightenment, 40–41
#Enough, 356
entertainment
    defining, in functionalism, 229
    mass entertainment theory, 132–34
    news as, 290
entertainment-education (EE), 271
entertainment function, of mass media,
    125
entertainment media, portrayal of everyday
    people in, 161–62
entertainment overcoming resistance
    model, 272–74
entertainment theory, 225–26, 238–43
Entman, Robert, 313, 354
environment
    interpretation and perception of, 339
    in neuroscience perspective, 279
environmental stimuli, screening out of,
    256–57
episode (general aggression model), 17,
    197
epistemic values, 17

epistemology, 14
Epstein, Edward Jay, 165–66
ER (television program), 320
Escape from Freedom (Fromm), 34
The Eternal Jew (film), 50
eudaimonic motivations, 239
Europe
    political economy theorists in, 160,
      161
    rise of cultural theories in, 152
evolution, theory of, 9, 278
Ewen, Stuart, 322
exchange-value, 159
excitatory potential, 240
expectations, as socially constructed,
    346–47
expectations, shifting, 349
Experimental Section (of US Army), 103–5
Experiments in Mass Communication
    (Hovland, Lumsdaine, and
    Sheffield), 104
exposure, selective, 111–12
extended elaboration likelihood model
    (E-ELM), 271
extended real-life hypothesis, 215
the extensions of man, 173
extremists, 49–50

F
Facebook, 1, 86, 87, 233, 244, 286, 287,
    306, 332, 339, 346
    addictive nature of, 31
    concerns with, 7
    discourse-diminishing speech on, 92
    fake posts on, 31
    growth of, 1–2
    programming on, 7–8
Facebook depression, 217–18
Facebook News Feed, 1–2, 74
face-to-face interactions, 343
fake news, 10, 46, 65, 230–31, 325–27
Fakunle, David, 115
false advertising, 211
false consciousness, 153
Falwell, Jerry, 42
Fame (film), 248
familiarity, with media, 237
Family Guy (television program), 164
family names, 43
"Fappening," 369
Faris, Robert, 112
fascism, 39–40
Father Knows Best (television program), 118,
    366
Faules, Don F., 339–40
FCC. *See* Federal Communications
    Commission
fear of social isolation (FSI), 306
Federal Communications Commission
    (FCC), 38, 70, 76–77, 211
Federal Radio Commission (FRC), 38, 77,
    78
Federal Trade Commission, 76
Federal Trade Commission Act, 211
feedback loops, 135
feminism, 159, 208–9, 247–48, 349–50,
    367, 369, 370
feminist reception studies, 247–48
feminist scholarship, 167–70
Feshbach, Seymour, 185, 186
Festinger, Leon, 111
filter bubble, 87
First Amendment, 33, 92–93, 133, 211, 286
First Amendment absolutists, 69
first-order cultivation effects, 319
Fiske, John, 246
flags, as symbols, 336
Flashdance (film), 248
flexible social science, 19

flooding, 92
folk culture, 147, 365
"football democracy," 368
Ford, Henry, 40
Ford Foundation, 161
Forms of Talk (Goffman), 349
Fortaleza, Jhunehl, 208
Foss, Karen, 13
The Foster (television program), 240
Fourth Estate, 78
FOX, 66
Fox, Jesse, 306
Fox News, 58, 59
fraction of selection, 227
fragmented news, 166
frame(s), 348
frame analysis, 346–52
frame keepers, 263
frames, 263
framing, 46, 210, 346–58
Frankfurt School, 155–56
fraternal twins, 279
FRC. *See* Federal Radio Commission
Freedhoff, Yoni, 209–10
Freud, Sigmund, 51
Freudianism, 51, 169
Frohlich, David, 233
Fromm, Erich, 34
Frost, Richard, 191
FSI. *See* fear of social isolation
functionalism, 120
    and mass entertainment theory,
      132–34
    and systems theories, 138–39
functions, aims vs., 230

G
Gallup, 121
GAM. *See* general aggression model
Gamble, Hilary, 208
Game of Thrones (television program), 164
Gamergate, 369, 370
Gamson, William, 353–54
Gans, Herbert, 144
Garrett, Kelly, 125, 269
gatekeepers, 109
gatekeeping activities, 325
Gaudet, Hazel, 111
gay characters, 239–40
Gell-Mann, Murray, 12
gemeinschaft, 42
Gemeinschaft und Gesellschaft (Tönnies),
    41–42
gender identity, 207–9
general aggression model (GAM), 183,
    197–99
"generation gap," 182
"Generation M²," 204
genetics, and attitudes, 279–81
genre-specific cultivation theory, 320
Gentile, Douglas, 185
Gerbner, George, 205, 314–21
German Idealism, 153, 154
gesellschaft, 42
Ghanem, Salma, 304, 357
GI Bill, 118
Gibson, William, 87
Gide, André, 18
Gillig, Traci, 240
Gilmor, Dan, 332
Giroux, Henry, 147, 212–13, 367
Gitlin, Todd, 48, 144, 353, 356
Giuliani, Rudy, 59
Gjoni, Eron, 370
Gleason, Laurel, 125, 269
global media sphere, 146
global village, 173–74
Glynn, Carroll, 305
goal-oriented systems, 136

goals, human, 12
Goebbels, Joseph, 50
Goffman, Erving, 347–52
Gold, Howard, 161
Google, 87, 92, 213
Google Trends, 303
Gosling, Samuel D., 1
government regulation of media, 77–79
Grabe, Maria, 208
Graber, Doris, 259–62
Graeber, David, 355, 356
grand social theories, 152
grand theories, 3
Grasmuck, Sherri, 214
Gray, Freddie, 144
gray propaganda, 47
Great Communities, 79–80, 85, 87, 338
Great Recession of 2008, 52, 58, 85, 161–
    62, 310
Great War. *See* World War I
Greece, ancient, 172
Green, Melanie, 270
Greene, Viveca, 170
Greenwald, Glenn, 90–91
Greitmeyer, Tobias, 217
Grenard, Jerry, 209
Grey's Anatomy (television program), 271,
    320
Griffin, Emory, 13
Grossberg, Larry, 164
grosse Deters, Fenne, 217
Gruszczynski, Mike, 303
Guardian, 67
"Gunning for Wall Street, with Faulty Aim,"
    355
Gunsmoke (television program), 118
Gunther, Albert, 265
Gurevitch, Michael, 235–37

H
Habermas, Jurgen, 157
Hahn, Kyu, 112
Hall, Stuart, 157, 244, 245, 247
Hallin, Daniel, 89–90
Halloran, James D., 186
Hampton, Keith, 216
Han, Seunghee, 214
The Handmaid's Tale (television series), 164
Hanks, Tom, 286
hard news, 127
Harris, 121
Harris, Lee, 252–53
Harrison, Kristen, 207
Harvard University, 112, 326
Hatemi, Peter, 279, 280
Hays, Will, 99
health, television and, 32
health communication, 273–74
health literacy, 274
hedonic valence, 240
hedonistic motivations, 239
Hegel, Georg Wilhelm Friedrich, 153
hegemonic culture, 148
Helm, Jelly, 371
Hepp, Andreas, 373–74
Herman, Edward S., 57
hermeneutic theory, 15, 154, 155
Herzog, Herta, 226–29
Hess, Kristy, 313
heuristics, 266
heuristic-systematic model of information
    processing, 268
HGTV, 32
high culture, 155
Hindman, Douglas, 293
Hinsley, Amber, 281
Hippler, Fritz, 46, 50
Hiroshima, Japan, 181
Hirsch, Michael, 68, 91

Hitler, Adolf, 38, 49, 50, 53
Hitt, Matthew, 313
HME. *See* hostile media effect
Hmielowski, Jay, 293
Hobson, Dorothy, 248
Hofmann, Stefan, 1, 215
Hoggart, Richard, 157
Holbert, Lance, 125, 269
Holbrook, Thomas, 292
Hollywood, 99–100, 169, 365
Holt, Lanier, 306
Homeland (television program), 164
homophily, 273
homophily, ideological, 112
Hong Kong, 306
Hoover, Herbert, 77
Horkheimer, Max, 155–56, 319
hostile media effect (HME), 264–66
House (television program), 271
Hovland, Carl, 101–6, 119, 121, 126, 253–54
Howard, Philip, 94
Huang, Chengju, 94–95
Hudson, William, 263
Huffington Post (culture and political blog), 88
Huffman, Stephanie, 293
human behavior, science and, 8–13
human development, media and. *See* media and human development
human interest and empathy (schema), 262
humanism, 154–55, 157
Human Problems of an Industrial Civilization (Mayo), 34
humor, as contextual variable, 193
Hunt, Melissa, 218
The Hurt Locker (film), 239
Huston, Aletha, 184
Hutchens, Myiah, 293
Hutchins Commission, 79–80, 338
Hwang, Yoori, 292, 324
hyperritualized representations, 349–50
hypothesis, 9, 27
hysteria, 51

I
ice-age analogy, 317
id, 51
Idaho, 32
idealism, 337
idealized virtual identity hypothesis, 215
ideas, marketplace of, 73–77
identical twins, 279
identification, 270, 273
    with media characters, 193
    similarity, 196
    in social learning theory, 186–87
    wishful, 196–97
ideological homophily, 112
ideological state apparatuses, 158
ideology, as Marxist term, 153
If Beale Street Could Talk (film), 239
Igartua, Juan-José, 273
ignorance, specification of, 123
images and representations approach (feminist scholarship), 168
imitation, in social learning theory, 186–87
imitative learning, 187
imperviousness to influence, 234
impulsivity, 206
Incollingo, Jacqueline, 243–44
income disparity, 35, 161
incorrect attitudes, 266
India, 31
individual differences, 106
individual differences theory, 110
inductive approach to theory construction, 107
industrial social order, 34–35

inequalities, digital, 293–94
influence, imperviousness to, 234
information diffusion theory (innovation diffusion theory), 294–96
information-flow theory, 126–28
information-processing theory, 254–60, 335–36. *See also* media cognition and information processing theories
"infotainment," 230–31
Ingram, Mathew, 1
inhibitory effects, 188–89
Innis, Harold, 24, 159, 171–72
innovation diffusion theory. *See* information diffusion theory
inputs (general aggression model), 197
Instagram, 222, 332
instant messaging, 233
institution judgments (schema), 262
intelligence, affective, 276
intelligence agencies, 372
An Intelligent Person's Guide to Modern Culture (Scruton), 44–45
intentionality, 234
interactivity
    of computer-mediated mass communication, 232
    of signs and symbols, 340
interconnectedness, 338–39
intermedia agenda-building, 303
International Communication Association, 373
Internet
    advertising revenue generated via, 287
    censorship on, 73
    early days of, 216
    global use of, 88
    and net neutrality, 76–77
    as source of health information, 274
    See also social media
interpersonal communication, 6
interpretive theory, 15, 17
intersectionality, 170
intersubjective agreement, 14
investigative activities, 325
Iraq, invasion of, 58
iTunes, 222
Iyengar, Shanto, 112, 291, 301–2

J
Jackass (television program), 189
Jamieson, Kathleen Hall, 57, 367
Janus, Noreene, 167–68
Jefferson, Thomas, 71
Jensen, Jakob, 275
Jensen, Klaus Bruhn, 158
Jeong, Se-Hoon, 292, 324
Jersey Shore (television program), 242
Jhally, Sut, 159, 322
Jiow, Hee Jhee, 325
Johnson, Lyndon, 183
Johnson, Martin, 281
Jones, Alex, 73
Jones, Vicki, 320
journalism, 58
    corporations and, 162
    framing research applied to, 353
    Lippmann on, 54
    yellow, 20
Journalism (journal), 165
Journalism Studies, 165
Journalist Protection Act, 65
journalists, Trump's attacks on, 65–66
Journal of American Medical Association, 184
The Journal of Popular Culture, 164
Jung, Eun Hwa, 244
junk food, 209–10
Juris, Jeffrey, 158

K
Kaepernick, Colin, 336
Kahneman, Daniel, 278–79
Kaiser Family Foundation, 204
Katyal, Sonia, 246
Katz, Elihu, 129, 235–37, 305
Kazaa, 222
Keane, John, 71
Kearse, Stephen, 13
Keller, Candice, 42
Kennedy, John F., 127, 174, 182
Kennedy, Robert, 182
Kenny, Charles, 132–33
Kerner Commission, 183
Kim, Jang Hyun, 214
Kim, Joon, 327
Kim, Ki Joon, 214
Kinder, Donald, 301–2
kinderculture, 212
Kinderculture: The Corporate Construction of Childhood (Steinberg), 367
King, Martin Luther, Jr., 150, 167, 182, 246, 357
Kirzinger, Ashley, 281
Kistler, Michelle, 191–92
Klapper, Joseph, 121, 130–32, 185, 235
Klein Center for Internet & Society Research (Harvard), 112
Kline, F. Gerald, 305
Knobloch-Westerwick, Silvia, 240, 242
knowledge, emancipatory, 16
knowledge gap, 291–94
Knoxville, Johnny, 189
Konijn, Elly, 196
Krahé, Barbara, 192
Kraut, Robert, 216, 233
Kross, Ethan, 218
Kubey, Robert, 324
Kuklinski, James, 276

L
LaCroix, Jessica, 196
laissez-faire doctrine, 74
Laitinen, Richard, 57
Lakoff, George, 355
Lang, Gladys, 302–3
Lang, Kurt, 302–3
large-scale social media, 3–6, 332
Larsen, Otto, 127
Lasswell, Harold, 49, 50, 51–56, 60, 69, 102, 124, 137
latent functions, 124
laughter, health benefit from, 238
Lazarsfeld, Paul, 10, 21–23, 101–2, 107–9, 111, 119, 121, 122, 126, 128, 129, 145–46, 156, 226, 253–54
learning
    information-processing perspective on, 257–58
    in neuroscience perspective, 278
    participatory, 325
Leave It to Beaver (television program), 118, 366
Lee, Moon, 191–92
Lee, Simon, 368
legacy media, 3–4, 235
legitimate debate, 90
Leonhardt, David, 161
Lepper, Mark, 265–66
lesbian characters, 239–40
Letters from a Birmingham Jail (King), 246
levels of analysis, 229
Levy, Mark, 233
Lewis, Jeff, 146
Lewis, Justin, 322
Lexus, 342
LGBTQ youth, 239–40

liberal feminists, 168
libertarianism, 60, 69, 211
libertarian theories, 70–77
Libya, 94
Liebhart, Janice, 265
"likes," Facebook, 218
liking, 273
Lim, Sun Sun, 325
limbic system, 278
limited cognitive resources, 257–58
limited-effects perspective, 341–42
limited-effects theory, 22, 110, 165, 225
Limperos, Anthony, 243
Lin, Carolyn, 296
Lin, Julian, 325
Linn, Susan, 212, 367
Linotype, 35
Lippmann, Walter, 50, 53–55, 60, 69, 253
literacy, 37
    health, 274
    media, 321–27
literary canon, 155
literary criticism, 154–55
Littlejohn, Stephen, 13
Littleton, Cynthia, 162
Livingston, Sonia, 325
Livingstone, Sonia, 373
lobbying, 287
local origination rules, 86
The Logic of Scientific Discovery (Popper),
    10
loneliness, 217
Lorch, Elizabeth, 193
low-power FM radio (LPFM), 86
Luce, Henry, 79
Luckmann, Thomas, 343–45, 373
Lund, Brink, 291
Lunt, Peter, 373
Lutz, Frank, 355
Lyle, Jack, 134

M

Macdonald, Dwight, 39, 43
MacFadden, 129
MacKuen, Michael, 276
macroscopic structural theories, 148–49,
    290
Madden, Mary, 293
magazines, 45
mainstreaming (cultivation analysis),
    318–19
Maksl, Adam, 326
Malaysia, 211
Mama Mia! Here We Go Again (film), 239
Mandalay Bay Hotel shooting, 144
mandatory access rules, 86
manifest functions, 124
manosphere, 370
Manufacturing Consent (Herman and
    Chomsky), 57
manufacturing jobs, loss of, 35
Marcus, George, 276
Marjory Stoneman Douglas High School
    shooting, 91
marketplace of attention, 6
marketplace of ideas, 73–77
Marsh, David, 83–84
Marshall, Andrew, 48
Martin, Jason, 214
Martin-Barbero, Jesus, 245
Marwick, Alice, 370
Marx, Karl, 23, 152–54, 171
Marxism and the Interpretation of Culture
    (Nelson and Grossberg), 164
Marxist theory, 152–54, 159
Massachusetts Institute of Technology, 327
*Mass Communication: A Sociological
    Perspective* (Wright), 124–25

mass communication, defining and
    redefining, 3–8
mass communication theory(-ies), 1–26
    and axiology, 17b
    critical cultural trend in, 23–24
    critical theory, 15–16
    cultural theory, 15
    and defining mass communication,
        3–8
    and defining theory, 13–14
    evaluating, 18
    evolution of, 19
    and flexible social science, 19
    and human behavior, 10–13
    mass society and mass culture trend in,
        20–21
    meaning-making trend in, 24–25
    media-effects trend in, 21–23
    normative theory, 16–17
    postpositivist theory, 14
    and revitalized effects research, 25–26
    and science, 8–13
    trends in, 19
mass entertainment theory, 132–34
mass society, 338
mass society and mass culture theories,
    31–64
    assumptions of, 35–41
    contemporary theories, 44–46
    Durkheim's theories, 43–44
    early examples of, 41–44
    mechanical vs. organic solidarity in,
        43–44
    propaganda, 46–60
    Tönnies' theories, 41–43
mass society and mass culture trend, 20–21
mass society theory, 20, 227, 341
master symbols, 52–53
materialism, 153
Matson, Floyd, 52
Mayo, Elton, 34
McCain, John, 10
McCarthy, Joseph, 22, 130
McChesney, Robert, 57, 58, 147
McCombs, Max, 357
McCombs, Maxwell E., 301, 304
McDermott, Rose, 279, 280
McDonald's, 246
McDonald's Video Game, 246
McLeod, Jack, 305
McLuhan, Marshall, 24, 164, 170–75
McNeal, James, 212
McQuail, Denis, 81
McRobbie, Angela, 248
Mead, George Herbert, 334–37, 343
meaning-making
    and audience activity, 234
    and frames, 348–49
    and media consumption, 236
    in reception studies, 246
    and semiotic democracy, 246
    in social world, 331–32
meaning-making trend, 24–25
mechanical solidarity, 43
media
    concentration of ownership of, 45
    fearful reactions to new, 36–37
    influence of, 31–32
    push vs. pull, 269
    role of, in social constructionism,
        341–42
    role of, in societal change, 182
    sexual content in, 32
    uses of, 223–24
    violence in, 32, 205
media and human development, 204–21
    and advertising directed at children,
        209–11

and connection between social media
    and well-being, 217–19
and gender issues, 207–9
and growing up connected, 213–19
and loss of childhood, 210, 212–13
overview, 205
and personal technologies, 213–19
research on, 206–7
The Media Are American (Tunstall), 365
media characters, identification with, 193
media cognition and information
    processing theories, 252–85
    affective intelligence in, 276
    backfire effect in, 277
    delay hypothesis in, 274–75
    elaboration likelihood model, 266–69
    entertainment overcoming resistance
        model, 272–73
    extended elaboration likelihood
        model, 271
    health communication in, 273–74
    hostile media effect in, 264–66
    information-processing theory, 255–60
    motivated reasoning in, 276–77
    narrative persuasion theory, 269–71
    neuroscience perspective, 277–81
    overview, 253–54
    schema theory, 260–64
media companies, 45, 121
media ecology theory, 171
media-effects trend, 21–23, 99–142, 151
    Communication Research Program,
        105–7
    and development of postpositivist
        effects trend, 101–3
    and entertainment function of mass
        media, 132–34
    and Experimental Section of US Army,
        103–5
    and functional analysis, 124–26
    and functionalism, 138–39
    information-flow theory, 126–28
    middle range theory, 122–24
    modeling systems, 135–36
    overview, 101
    phenomenistic theory, 130–32
    and selective exposure, 111–12
    selective processes, 110–14
    strengths and limitations of, 109–10
    and systems theories of
        communication processes, 134–39
    two-step flow theory, 128–30
    and voter behavior, 107–9
The Media Foundation, 246
media functions, 229–31
media functions and media uses, confusion
    of, 229–31
media literacy, 321–27
media literacy interventions, 324–26
media narratives, 243
mediated communication, 6, 204
The Mediated Construction of Reality
    (Couldry and Hepp), 373
mediated violence
    context of, 192–93
    learning from, 186
mediation
    active vs. restrictive, 325
    enabling, 325
mediation theory, 373
mediatization theory, 372–76
media uses, 229–31
the medium is the message, 173
Meehan, Eileen, 168
Meet the Press, 59, 66
Megarry, Jessica, 368, 369, 370
Mehl, Matthias R., 217
Meier, Caroline, 368

memories, in schema theory, 260–61
memory, 278
memory loss, 206
Mendelsohn, Harold, 132, 238
Merklejohn, Alexander, 93
Merton, Robert, 122–25, 226
message system analysis, 317
Messaris, Paul, 322
Messing, Solomon, 112
meta-analysis, 294–95, 324
#MeToo, 356
Meyrowitz, Joshua, 145, 147, 210, 212, 367
"M" generation, 257–58
microscopic interpretive theories, 148–49
middle class, decline of, 35
middle-range theory, 107, 123–24
Miller, Katherine, 13, 15
Miller, M. H., 161
Miller, Neal, 187
Mills, C. Wright, 129
Milton, John, 70–71
Mind, Self, and Society, (Mead), 335
minimal-effects theory, 110
minimum wage, 161
misandry, 370
Mitchell, Greg, 161
modeling, in social cognition, 188
modeling systems, 135–36
models, 135–36
Modern Family (television program), 164
Modern Language Association of America, 163–64
Moerman, Michael, 15
Moffitt, Benjamin, 45
money, as symbol, 342
monozygotic twins, 279
mood management theory, 240–42
Moral Majority, 42
Morgan, Michael, 320–21
Morley, David, 245, 247
Morocco, 94
Morpheus, 222
Morris, Wesley, 162
Motion Picture Production Code, 100
motivated reasoning, 276–77
motivation, 209, 269, 273, 278
"Motivations and Gratifications of Daily Serial Listeners" (Herzog), 226
motive, as contextual variable, 192
Moyer-Gusé, Emily, 272
Moyers, Bill, 78–79
Ms. magazine, 248
MSNBC, 58
muckrakers, 78
multiple points of access, 164
Mulvey, Laura, 169
municipal broadband, 294
Murdock, Graham, 156–57, 160
Murphy, Sheila, 240
music sharing, via Internet, 222
mutual conditioning, 334
Muuss, Rolf, 278
MyFootballClub (website), 368

N
Nabi, Robin, 320
Nadkarni, Ashwini, 1, 215
Napoli, Philip, 76
Napster, 222
narcotizing dysfunction, 125–26
narrative persuasion theory, 269–71
Nathanson, Amy, 206
National Amusements, 45
national anthem, 53
National Commission on the Causes and Prevention of Violence, 183, 315
National Economic and Social Right Initiative, 353–54

National Institutes of Health, 32, 180
National Leadership Conference on Media Literacy, 322
National Science Foundation, 121, 216
Nationwide (British television news magazine show), 245
natural sciences, 9
natural signs, 340
nature/nurture divide, 278
Naureckas, Jim, 162
Nazi Germany (Nazism), 38, 40, 46, 47, 49, 50, 53, 102, 103, 156
NBC, 66, 121, 162
need satisfaction, 235, 237
negative function (dysfunction), 230
negative reinforcer, 188
negotiated meaning (reception studies), 244–45, 247, 248
Negroponte, Nicholas, 112
Negt, Oskar, 155
Nelson, Leslie, 208
neo-Marxism (neo-Marxist theories), 23–24, 154, 164, 167
British, 156–60
neo-pragmatism, 337
Netflix, 32
net neutrality, 76–77
Neuman, Russell, 303
Neuromancer (Gibson), 87
neuromarketing research, 278
neuroscience perspective, 277–81
Newcomb, Horace, 164
Newman, Russell, 276
New Republic, 36
news
and audience theories, 230–31
different methods of consuming, 233
effects of frames on, 354–57
as entertainment, 290
frames for, 352–53
hard vs. soft, 127
processing of, 258–60
in schema theory, 261–62
from social media, 2
newscasts, 259
New School for Social Research, 156
News Corp., 45
news deserts, 313–14
News Leaders Association, 88
news media literacy, 325–27
newspapers, 35, 45, 55, 313, 338–39
news production research, 165–67
Newsweek, 166
Newton, Isaac, 8
New York Times, 54, 66, 88, 161, 162, 246, 355
New York Times Co. v. United States, 69
New York Times Magazine, 165
nexus of mediating variables, 131
Nielsen, 121
Nigeria, 211
1984 (Orwell), 147
Nixon, Richard, 174
Noakes, John, 354
Noelle-Neumann, Elisabeth, 304–6
nomophobia, 214
nonepistemic values, 17
normalized news, 166
normative theories of mass communication, 65–98
authoritarian concept, 94
communism concept, 94
development concept, 93–94
dual responsibility model, 84–85
and government regulation of media, 77–79
libertarian theories, 70–77
and marketplace of ideas, 73–77

origin of, 69–77
and postwar compromise, 79–81
and professionalization of journalism, 78–79, 81–84
and public interest in the Internet era, 87–93
revolutionary concept, 95
social responsibility theory, 79–87
transitional media approach, 94–95
Western concept, 93
normative theory (normative media theory), 16–18
North Korea, 94
Norway, 211
Numb3rs (television program), 271
Nuts (*Boston Legal* episode), 275
Nyhan, Brendan, 277

O
Obama, Barack, 10, 77, 166
obesity, childhood, 209–10
objectification theory, 208–9
objectivity rituals, 166
observational learning, 188
Occupy ICE, 356
Occupy Our Homes, 356
Occupy Wall Street, framing, 355–56
O'Keeffe, Gwenn Schurgin, 147
Okeowo, Alexis, 170
Oliver, Mary Beth, 239
OMA (opportunities-motivation-ability) model, 293
Online News Association, 88
online social networking (OSN), 215
On Theoretical Sociology (Merton), 122, 123
ontology, 14
operant learning theory, 187–88
opinion followers, 109, 129
opinion leaders, 109, 129, 298
oppositional decoding, 245, 247, 248
The O'Reilly Factor (television program), 112
organic solidarity, 43
orienting response, 259
Orlando Florida Pulse nightclub shooting, 42
Ornstein, Norman, 313
orphan counties, 314
Ortega y Gasset, José, 34
OSN. *See* online social networking
Oswald, Debra, 214
Otto, Shawn Lawrence, 9
outcomes (general aggression model), 198
Out of Order (Patterson), 263

P
Palihapitiya, Chamath, 31
parasocial interaction, 239–40, 273
parental mediation theory, 324–25
Park, Robert E., 338
Parker, Edwin, 134
Parker, Sean, 31
participatory learning, 325
partisans, 265
passive use (of social networking sites), 218
Pasteur, Louis, 8
Pathak-Shelat, Manisha, 326
Patriot Act, 73
Patterson, Thomas, 263, 300
Payne Fund, 99–100, 102, 228
Pediatrics (journal), 32
penny press, 20
Pentagon, 372
perceived similarity, 270
perception
of environment, 339
as malleable, 336
in neuroscience perspective, 278
selective, 113

Pérez, Raúl, 170
peripheral route, of information
    processing, 266, 267
the periphery, 172
Perry Mason (television program), 118
Personal Influence (Lazarsfeld and Katz),
    129, 130
personality traits, 281
personalized news, 165
personal technologies, 213–19
person factors (general aggression model), 197
person judgments (schema), 262
Peter Gunn (television program), 118
Petty, Richard, 266, 268
Phaedrus (Plato), 362
The Phantom Public (Lippmann), 54
phenomenistic theory, 130–32
phenomenology, 342–43
Philippines, 211
Piaget, Jean, 195
Plato, 362
pluralistic groups, 79
pluralistic public forum, 157
podcasts, 88
Poetics (Aristotle), 185
political campaigns, 10, 230, 231, 357
political economy theory, 148, 159–62
Politico, 68, 88
polling services, 121
polysemic, 244
Pooley, Jefferson, 130, 145
Popkin, Samuel, 263
Popper, Karl, 10
popular culture in United States, research
    on, 163–65
populism, 34, 52
Porsche, 342
Porter, Nikki, 194
position (of story), 302
Postman, Leo, 113–15
Postman, Neil, 212, 367
postpositivism (postpositivist research),
    129, 151, 223, 225, 228–29, 322,
    357–58, 375
postpositivist theory, 14, 17, 18, 21–23
postwar compromise, 79–81
Potter, W. James, 4, 5, 192–93, 226, 235–
    36, 278, 279, 289
The Power Elite (Mills), 129
pragmatism, 55–56, 337–39
preferred reading, 244, 247
presidential elections, 292
    of 1940, 107–9
    of 1960, 174
    of 1968, 301
    of 2012, 313
    of 2016, 10, 25, 66, 91, 264, 300
The Press Effect (Jamieson and Waldman),
    57
Price, Jesse, 42
Priester, Joseph, 268
primary, or dominant, reality, 351
priming, 301–2
priming effects, 191
printing technology, 35, 322
The Problem of the Media (McChesney), 57
*The Process and Effects of Mass
    Communication* (Schramm), 227
Processing the News (Graber), 260
professionalism, 67
professionalization of journalism, 78–79,
    81–84
Project Revere, 127
propaganda, 46–60, 253–54
    and American values, 34
    and attitude-change theories, 103
    black, 47
    definition of, 46

gray, 47
Lasswell's theory of, 51–53
modern theories of, 56–60
origin of, 46–56
research on, 224
and source-dominated theories, 226
undermining, 47
white, 34, 46–47
during World War II, 102–5
*Propaganda and Democracy: The American
    Experience of Media and Mass
    Persuasion* (Sproule), 57
propositions, 263
Protess, David, 303
psychoanalytic theory, 169
psychosis, 52
public education, 55
public interest, in the Internet era, 87–93
Public Opinion (Lippmann), 54
Public Opinion Quarterly, 37
pull media, 269
Pulse nightclub shooting, 144
punishment, as contextual variable, 192
Puritans, 71
push media, 269
Putnam, Robert, 310, 311

Q
qualitative methods, 151, 228–29
Quan-Haase, Anabel, 233
Quebec, 211
Quinn, Zoe, 370
Quirk, Paul, 276

R
Raab, Barbara, 161
race riots, 183
racial stereotypes, 150
radical libertarianism, 69
radio, 36, 40, 45, 86
Radio Act of 1927, 78
"Radio Talk" (Goffman), 349
Radio Television Digital News Association
    (RTDNA), 83, 88
Radway, Janice, 247–48
Rakos, Richard, 57
rape culture, 169–70, 191–92, 352
rape humor, 170
Rathnayake, Chamil, 243
reading skills, reduced, 206
realism, as contextual variable, 192–93
reality, in social constructionism, 341
RealPlayer, 222
Reardon, Roberta, 162
reasoning, motivated, 276–77
reception and experience approach
    (feminist scholarship), 169
reception studies, 244–48
recovery and reappraisal approach
    (feminist scholarship), 168–69
Reddit, 92
Red Scare, 22
reductionism, 23
Reese, Stephen, 303
Reifler, Jason, 277
reinforcement, in social learning theory, 187
reinforcement contingencies, 189
reinforcement theory, 130–32
relative HME, 265
Relotius, Claas, 83
Remembering (Bartlett), 260
repressive state apparatuses, 158
reptilian brain, 278
Republican Party, 58, 107–8, 111, 252
"Research on Sex-Roles in Mass Media:
    Toward a Critical Approach"
    (Janus), 167–68
resonance (cultivation analysis), 319

restrictive mediation, 325
retention, selective, 113
Revere, Paul, 127
reverse censorship, 92
The Revolt of the Masses (Ortega y Gasset), 34
revolution, 153, 154
revolutionary concept, 94, 95
reward, as contextual variable, 192
Rhapsody, 222
Rideout, Victoria, 204
The Rifleman (television program), 118
Riordan, Ellen, 168
Risen, James, 59
ritual perspective, 163
robber barons, 73
Robertson, Pat, 42
Robinson, John, 259
Rockefeller Foundation, 105, 121
Rodríguez-de-Dios, Isabel, 325
Rogers, Everett, 172, 175, 294–95
Roma (film), 239
romance novels, 247
Romania, 211
Rome, ancient, 172
Roosevelt, Franklin D., 108
Roper, 121
Rorty, Richard, 337
Rosen, Jay, 66, 89–90
Ross, Lee, 265–66
Rothe, Dawn, 367
Rothschild, David, 66
Rouner, Donna, 271
routes (general aggression model), 197
Rowling, Charles, 354
Roy, Deb, 327
Rozendaal, Esther, 194
RTDNA. *See* Radio Television Digital News
    Association
Rubin, Alan, 322–23
Ruddock, Andy, 368
Ruggiero, Thomas, 232–33
Rusbridger, Alan, 67
Russia, 31, 211
Russill, Chris, 337
Ryan, Tracii, 217

S
Sagioglou, Christina, 217
Salmon, Charles, 305
Salovaara-Moring, Inka, 291
Samson, Lelia, 208
Sanchez, Wendy, 194
Sandy Hook Elementary School shooting,
    91
Sarkeesian, Anita, 370
satellite communication, 173
Saturday Review, 36–37
Scharrer, Erica, 320
schema-inconsistent advertising, 262, 264
schemas, 260–64, 335–36
schema theory, 260–64
Schiller, Herb, 57, 159
Schleuder, Joan, 260
Schmitt, Cathleen, 265
Schorr, Daniel, 150, 167
Schramm, Wilbur, 120, 134, 227
Schutz, Alfred, 342–43
science
    and human behavior, 8–13
    reliability of, 9
    reporting on, 357
"science of democracy," 53
scientific method, 8–13
scientific technocracy, 53
scope of self model, 207
screen time, 206
Scripps Howard, 78
scripting theory, 208

scripts (form of schema), 263
Scruton, Roger, 44–45
second-order cultivation effects, 319
Segrin, Chris, 320
selective exposure, 111–12
selective exposure self and affect
    management model (SESAM), 242
selective perception, 113
selective processes, 111
selective retention, 113
selectivity (in audience activity), 234
self-complexity, 207
self-consistency, 242
self-enhancement, 242
self-esteem, 215
self-improvement, 242
self-presentation, need for, 215
self-reflexivity, 12
self-regulating marketplace of ideas, 74
self-righting principle, 71
semantic affinity, 240
semiotic democracy, 246
semiotic disobedience, 246
September 11, 2001 terrorist attacks, 42, 73
SESAM. See selective exposure self and
    affect management model
Sesame Street (television program), 146
sexism, 167–68
sex role socialization, 207–8
sex-role stereotypes, 349–51
sexual content, in media, 32
sexual health, 274
sexual identity, 207–9
sexuality, of characters, 239–40
Shade, Leslie, 194
Shakespeare, William, 163
Shakya, Holly, 218
Shanahan, James, 320–21
sharing, of digital media, 222–23
Shaw, Adrienne, 370
Shaw, Donald, 301
Shen, Fuyuan, 263
Sherry, John, 277–79, 281
shibboleths, 144
Shils, Edward, 37, 43–44
Shoemaker, Pamela, 303
Short, William, 99
signals, 340
Signorielli, Nancy, 317–18, 320
signs, 340, 344
Silverblatt, Art, 323
similarity, 273
similarity, perceived, 270
similarity identification, 196
Simmel, Georg, 338
simple situation sequences (schema), 262
Simpson, Jessica, 192
Sinclair Broadcasting, 58
Sisi, Abdel Fattah el-, 94
situation factors (general aggression
    model), 197
60 Minutes, 59
Slater, Michael, 243, 271
sleeper effect, 275
sleep problems, 206
smartphones, 213–14, 293
Smiley, Calvin, 115
Smith, Adam, 74
Smith, Steve, 332
Snapchat, 7, 332
SNS addiction, 217
SNSs. See social networking sites
Snyder, Timothy, 47
soap operas, 38, 248
social behaviorism, 334
social capital, 216, 311–12
social capital theory, 311–14
social categories theory, 110

social cognition from mass media, 187–90
social cognitive theory, 183, 190
social comparisons, 242
social comparison theory, 218
social constructionism, 340, 341–46
social construction of reality, 343–45
The Social Construction of Reality (Berger and
    Luckmann), 343, 373
social creations, 15
social cues, 349–50
social hermeneutics, 15
social learning, 187
social learning theory, 186–87
social marketing theory, 297–99
social media
    and Arab Spring, 94
    children and, 205
    and culture, 332
    culture created with, 335
    developing or maintaining social
        relationships with, 236
    discourse-diminishing speech on, 92
    fake posts in, 31
    large-scale, 3–6
    news from, 2
    and phenomenistic theory, 131
    and selective exposure, 112
    and well-being, 217–19
social movements
    framing of, 356–57
    use of frames by, 354
social networking, 243–44, 274
social networking sites (SNSs), 214–19, 274
    control over, 286–87
    in social capital theory, 312
social order, media and the, 20–21
social phobias, 206
social prompting, 189
social relationships, developing/
    maintaining, with social media,
    236
social research, 121
social responsibility theory, 68, 79–87, 84
Social Responsibility Theory of the Press (Siebert,
    Peterson, and Schramm), 80
social roles, learning, 334–35
social science, flexible, 19
social scientists, 8
social selves, 236–37, 339–40
social skills model of problematic SNS use, 217
Social Theory and Social Structure (Merton),
    122, 124
sociometers, 215
soft news, 127
Solidarity (political movement), 94
solidarity, mechanical vs. organic, 43
Solomon, Michael, 339
Solomon, Norman, 162
Sotirovic, Mira, 260
source-dominated audience theories,
    226–27
source-dominated theory, 128
South Korea, 211
South Park (television program), 164
specification of ignorance, 123
sphere of consensus (democratic public
    discourse), 89–90
sphere of deviance (democratic public
    discourse), 90
sphere-of-influence model, 89–90
sphere of legitimate debate (democratic
    public discourse), 89–90
Der Spiegel, 82–83
spin control, 150
spiral of silence, 46, 304–6
Spotify, 240
Sproule, J. Michael, 46, 57
Stahl, Lesley, 59

stakeholder theory, 84
Stanford History Education Group,
    326
Stanford University, 120
Stanley, Jason, 47, 57, 153
Stanton, Frank, 121, 226
Stanyer, James, 374–75
Star, Alexander, 165
Starr, Paul, 89
Statistical Abstract of the United States, 315
Stauffer, John, 191
Steinberg, Shirley, 212, 367
Steiner, Linda, 248
Steinfeld, Jess L., 183–84
stereotypes, 150
storytelling, 147, 205, 259, 321
Stranger Things (television series), 164
structuralist view of culture, 158
structure, in critical theory, 16
student loans, 161
sublimation, 185. See also catharsis
substructure of society, 153
sufficiency principle, 268
sufficiency threshold, 268
sugared cereals, 210
sugared snacks, 209
suicide, 32
Sullivan, Andrew, 59
Sundar, Shyam, 243, 244
Super Bowl, 286
superego, 51
superpeer theory, 206
superstructure of society, 153, 158
Surgeon General's Scientific Advisory
    Committee on Television and
    Social Behavior, 183, 315
surveillance of the environment, 229, 230
survey research methods, 231–32
Sweden, 211
Switzerland, 292
symbolic interactionism, 333–40
symbols, 335, 340, 344
Syria, 94
System 1 (of brain), 279
System 2 (of brain), 279
systems, 134, 135
systems theory(-ies), 134–39
    adoption of, by mass communication
        theorists, 137
    and functionalism, 138–39
    and human communication, 136–37
    information-processing theory vs., 255
    modeling systems, 135–36
    rise of, 135

T
tablets, children and, 213–14
"talkies," 36
Talking Points Memo (political blog), 88
The Tamale Lesson (narrative video), 270
targeting, 297–98
Taylor, Laramie, 208
TDP. See thinness depicting and promoting
technocratic control, 69
technological determinists, 171
technologies, personal. See personal
    technologies
television
    cable, 86–87, 125
    concerns over influence of, 36–37
    in cultivation analysis, 315–21
    and entertainment function, 132
    evolution of, 181–83
    and heart disease, 32
    information-processing perspective on,
        256, 258–60
    in postwar era, 118
    violence on, 315–16

Television: The Critical View (Newcomb), 164
Television in the Lives of Our Children (Schramm, Lyle, and Parker), 134
television news, processing of, 258–60
television violence theories, 184–97
  active theory of television viewing, 193–94
  aggressive cues, 190–92
  catharsis, 185–86
  context of mediated violence, 192–93
  developmental perspective, 194–95
  social cognition from mass media, 187–90
  social learning theory, 186–87
  video games, 196–97
temporarily expanding the boundaries of the self perspective, 243
text, 15
textual analysis, 154–55
Thailand, 211
theory(-ies)
  defining, 3, 13–14
  evaluating, 18
  grand, 3
  interpretive, 15 *See also specific theories, e.g.:* cultural theory
A Theory of Mass Culture (Macdonald), 43
The Theory of Mass Society (Shils), 44
theory of mind (ToM), 206
thin ideal media, 208
Thinking, Fast and Slow (Kahneman), 278–79
thinness depicting and promoting (TDP), 208
third-person effect, 13
13 Reasons Why (television program), 32
This Is Us (television program), 164
Thomae, Manuela, 169–70
Thomas, Evan, 166
Thomson, Deborah, 210
Three Billboards Outside Ebbing Missouri (film), 239
3 Bs of television, 319
Tidwell, Melissa, 92
Tiggemann, Mirika, 208
Tillinghast, Charles, 58
Time Inc., 79
Tin Pan Alley, 365
ToM. *See* theory of mind
Tönnies, Ferdinand, 41–42, 43
top-down/bottom-up theory of political attitude formation, 281
totalitarianism, 39–40, 48, 70
traditional learning theory, 187. *See also* operant learning theory
transitional media approach, 94–95
transmissional perspective, 162–63
transmission of the social heritage, 229
transportation (transportation theory), 269–70
troll armies, 92
Trump, Donald, 10, 31, 59, 65–66, 234, 264, 300, 313
Tuchman, Gaye, 82, 166, 353, 356
Tumblr, 370
Tunisia, 94
Tunstall, Jeremy, 365
TV: The Most Popular Art (Newcomb), 164
twin studies, 279–80
Twitter, 7, 92, 286, 332
two-step flow theory, 128–30
Tylka, Tracy, 209
typifications, 343
typification schemes, 345

U
ubiquity (of news media), 305
Ultimate Fighting Championship (television program), 186
ultra-nationalism, 38
undermining demagoguery, 47
undermining propaganda, 47
Understanding Media (McLuhan), 174
United Nations, 66, 310
United States
  advertising to children in, 209–11
  commodification of culture in, 365
  fake social media posts in, 31
  as hedonistic culture, 371–72
  income inequality in, 161
  knowledge gaps in, 292–93
  news production research in, 165–67
  popular culture research in, 163–65
  propaganda in, 48–50
  shift in economy base of, 181–82
University of Birmingham, 157
University of Chicago, 79, 99, 337
University of Hawaii, 120
University of Illinois, 120
University of Minnesota, 291
The Untouchables (television program), 118
upshift, downshift or, 348
urbanization
  Marxist view of, 153
  and media, 34–35
US General Social Survey, 216
US Army, 372
uses-and-gratifications theory, 225, 231–38
  revival of, 231–38
  and social networking, 243–44
"Uses and Grats 2.0," 243
use-value, 159
US Supreme Court, 69, 72, 73, 88
utility
  in audience activity, 234
utopianism, 153

V
Valentino, Nicholas, 263–64
Valkenburg, Patti, 194
Vallone, Robert, 265–66
value judgments, suspending, 236
value-neutrality, 236
values, in social situations, 237
Vandenbosch, Laura, 208
Variety, 162
Viacom, 45
vicarious reinforcement, 189
VidCon, 370
video games, 31–32, 196–97, 210, 370, 372
Vietnam War, 55, 143
viewing schema, 193
Viki, G. Tendayi, 169–70
violence
  and children, 183–84
  in media, 32, 205
  on television, 315–16
  in video games, 196–97
  See also television violence theories
Violence and the Media (Baker and Ball), 183
Violence Index, 315–16
"Visual Pleasures and Narrative Cinema" (Mulvey), 169
vividness (of presentation), 302
vocabulary development, 206
Vorderer, Peter, 238, 239
Vosoughi, Soroush, 327
Voter Study Group, 59
voting behavior, 107–9, 263–64
voting patterns, 10

W
Wagner, Michael, 303
Waldman, Paul, 57
Wall Street Journal, 161
Walmart, 162
Ward, Adrian, 214
Warlaumont, Hazel, 262, 264
Wartella, Ellen, 194, 195, 278
Washington, Booker T., 338
Washington Post, 59, 78, 286
Watergate, 303
Watson, James B., 50, 51
Watts, Duncan, 66
waverers, 108
weapons effect, 196
Weathermen, 182
Weber, Christopher, 281
Webster, James, 6
Wei, Lu, 293
well-being, social media and, 217–19
Western concept, 93
Westwood, Sean, 112
WhatsApp, 31
White, Micah, 356
White Collar (Mills), 129
white propaganda, 34, 46–47
white supremacy, 38, 40
Whitney v. California, 72
Why We Fight (film series), 104, 275
Wikileaks, 66
Williams, Raymond, 157, 164
Willkie, Wendell, 107, 108
Windahl, Sven, 233
Winter, Jenifer, 243
Wired magazine, 171, 173
wishful identification, 196–97, 273
Wittgenstein, Ludwig, 347
Woman Hating (Dworkin), 170
women, in two-step flow theory, 129. *See also* feminism
word-based empires, 172
World Economic Forum, 161
World Happiness Report, 310
World Health Organization, 32, 206
World's Fair (1939), 181
World War I, 48–49, 55
World War II, 39, 55, 79, 102–5, 118, 134, 135, 181–83, 228, 275, 365–66
Wright, Charles, 124–25, 229, 230
writing skills, reduced, 206
written word, control of the, 172
Wu, Tim, 92, 94

X
xenophobia, 38
The X-Files (television show), 32

Y
Yale University, 102, 105–6, 120
Yan, Zheng, 194
yellow journalism, 20
Yemen, 94
Young, Alyson, 233
YouTube, 5, 7, 222, 286, 321, 332

Z
Zhao, Shanyang, 214
Zhou, Peiqin, 208
Zillmann, Dolf, 238
Zuccoti Park, New York, 355
Zuckerberg, Mark, 86, 339, 346
Zúñiga, Homero de, 281